SALES LAW

Donald B. King

Professor of Law
Saint Louis University

Calvin Kuenzel

L. Leroy Highbaugh, Sr. Professor of Law
Stetson University

Bradford Stone

Charles A. Dana, Sr. Professor of Law
Stetson University

W.H. Knight, Jr.

Professor of Law
University of Iowa

CASEBOOK SERIES

1997

QUESTIONS ABOUT THIS PUBLICATION?

For questions about the **Editorial Content** appearing in this volume or reprint permission, please call:

Michael A. Bruno, J.D. at .... (800) 252-9257 (ext. 2518)
Lon E. Dobbs, J.D. at .... (800) 252-9257 (ext. 2315)
Outside the United States and Canada please call .... (212) 448-2000

For assistance with shipments, billing or other customer service matters, please call:

Customer Services Department at .... (800) 533-1646
Fax number .... (518) 487-3584

This publication also appears as Chapters 1-10 and 23 of Commercial Transactions Under the Uniform Commercial Code and Other Laws (Matthew Bender, 5th ed. 1997).

ISBN 0-8205-2751-3

MATTHEW◆BENDER

MATTHEW BENDER & CO., INC.
Editorial Offices
2 Park Avenue, New York, NY 10016-5675 (212) 448-2000
201 Mission St., San Francisco, CA 94105-1831 (415) 908-3200

PREFACE

In 1968, a small group of authors edited one of the first Uniform Commercial Code casebooks. This text was also one of the first casebooks published by Matthew Bender. Subsequent editions were published in 1974, 1981, and 1987. As this current group of authors edit this fifth edition, it seemed wise also to prepare separate casebooks for Sales, Negotiable Instruments and Payment Systems, and Secured Transactions since law schools vary as to course division and content. Our goal has remained constant.

"We have designed this casebook to be the best possible teaching tool for Sales Law."

This edition, centering primarily around recent developments in caselaw and code revisions, carries forward several precepts developed over the years:

1. Ample material is given to permit each professor who uses the book to cover not only basics, but to have the option to go beyond if he or she wishes.

2. In the "to read" notations, the most recent code section cites are given that relate to each topic and each subtopic.

3. There is not only a look at individual code sections, but the "to read" cites also contain reference to sections which are related to, substantiate, or seem contrary to, the major section under discussion. The student is encouraged to integrate the code into a single fluid body of law, rather than learning random legal principles.

4. The professor is given an opportunity to concentrate teaching on either the code itself or the caselaw, or both, to whatever degree seems best. The book also furnishes a comprehensive framework of commercial law which allows the professor to incorporate his own problems and other handouts.

5. Faculty may use individualized teaching techniques concentrating in either a caselaw or a problem approach, or both.

6. Modern and up-to-date cases are stressed, but some historical landmarks are mentioned in text or notes. Almost all of the principal cases have been decided within the last decade.

7. An effort has been made to include "cutting edge" cases. Not only can one see conflicting trends which have emerged in regard to some sections of the code, but one can also explore the direction the law is taking. We have tried to select cases that have interesting fact patterns, that involve interesting personalities of our times, or that include other factors that promote easier understanding of the subject matter

8. Illustrations of some of the major commercial documents in the area of sales law are included, as well as some diagrams. These inclusions should give students a better appreciation of the documents used in practice and discussed in the cases.

9. Introductory and historical text is used throughout the text so as to form an easy bridge to learning the particular subject.

The editors recognize that many professors will use only parts of the casebook in accordance with the scope of their course and time and number of credits allotted them. Some may want to use a few of the chapters later as a basis for an advanced commercial law seminar as well. Again, our emphasis is one of material flexibility and user–friendliness.

Donald King
Calvin Kuenzel
Bradford Stone
W. H. Knight

(Matthew Bender & Co., Inc.)
(Pub.087)

DEDICATION

To our families and everyone else who has endured this effort.

Donald King

Calvin Kuenzel

Bradford Stone

W.H. Knight, Jr.

ACKNOWLEDGEMENT

The authors wish to acknowledge the many persons who have over the years or currently contributed ideas and input into this casebook, including, but not limited to Professors Gerald T. Dunne, Josef Rohlik, Dean N. W. Hines, and Research Assistants Lingling Zou, Deborah Carder, Martha Beaves, Derrick Dyer, David Hayes, Vaishali Javeri, Malik Sabree and secretarial assistance from Mary Fran Dougherty, Connie Evans, and Louise Petren.

We also appreciate the editorial and other work of Ellen Greenblatt and Michael Bruno and others associated with the production of this book.

TABLE OF CONTENTS

Chapter 1

AN INTRODUCTORY VIEW

Chapter 2

SCOPE: SUBJECT MATTER OF THE CONTRACT FOR SALE

Chapter 3

THE CONTRACT FOR SALE

Chapter 4

PROPERTY INTERESTS

Chapter 5

WARRANTY/PRODUCTS LIABILITY

Chapter 6

PERFORMANCE

 (Pub.087)

Chapter 7

REMEDIES

Chapter 8

RIGHTS OF THIRD PARTIES: GOOD FAITH PURCHASE OF GOODS

Chapter 9

LEASES OF GOODS

Chapter 10

DOCUMENTARY TRANSACTIONS

Chapter 11

LETTERS OF CREDIT

(Matthew Bender & Co., Inc.)

CHAPTER 1

AN INTRODUCTORY VIEW

§ 1.01 Historical Development

In some law schools, there are separate courses for Sales, Negotiable Instruments, Payment Systems, and Secured Transactions. In others, combinations of these are taught in a course called Commercial Transactions. Regardless, some history gives one a better perspective of the particular course, and it seems desirable to see part of that picture within the overall development of commercial law.

A broader perspective of various aspects of commercial law (Sales, Negotiable Instruments and Payment Systems, and Secured Transactions) as practiced today can be gained through a short review of its historical development. Some of the commercial law principles of today may be seen in past developments. This approach reveals how commercial law became a part of the common law, of how commercial law was placed into uniform acts, of what gave rise to the formulation of the Uniform Commercial Code (U.C.C.), the role of the U.C.C. in modern commercial law, and other statutes and laws that supplement the U.C.C., and the development of an international commercial law of sales.

The basic framework of modern commercial law is found in the U.C.C. The U.C.C. embraces the major fields of commercial law: Sales, Commercial Instruments and Payment Systems, and Secured Transactions. It also covers letters of credit, bulk sales, bills of lading, warehouse receipts, and investment securities. The basic principles are set forth in the provisions of the U.C.C. and underlying policies are explained in the U.C.C. comments. This basic framework is not static; several major parts are being revised and new subjects added.

In addition to the U.C.C., other statutes and caselaw developments govern the practice of commercial law. For example, some consumer-oriented statutes affect manufacturers, sellers, and financiers. Product liability is reflected not only in the U.C.C., but also in the Restatement of Torts and caselaw. The effect of Negotiable Instruments on cutting of consumer defenses and curtailing consumer rights in regard to default through late payments and repossession led to special consumer statutes. Government regulations also may be applicable. International conventions, customs, and rules likewise may be pertinent and are a part of the recent continuing history of commercial law.

PROBLEM 1.1

One of your senior partners is on a panel of the American Historical Society. The main speaker has proposed as his topic "Commercial Law Then and Now: Old Problems in New Containers." While the speech is not yet available, he would like your opinion on the pertinent part of this subject matter and some ideas supporting it and some opposing. He would like an opinion after you have read Chapter 1 and another after you have finished the course.

PROBLEM 1.2

Another senior partner is concerned about the various commercial laws which apply to the firm's clients. The firm represents:

(1)   businesses in states with the traditional U.C.C. (*e.g.*, Article 3 and 4 on Negotiable Instruments).

(2)   ones with the Revised U.C.C. adopted in a number of states (*e.g.*, Articles 3 & 4 Negotiable Instruments, Article 2A on Leasing and 4A Electronic Transfers).

(3)   businesses that want to be advised as to possible proposals for change that may be made in law in the next several years (*e.g.*, Revision of U.C.C. Articles and other laws).

(4)   businesses that deal with businesses in other countries (*e.g.*, Convention on the International Sale of Goods; other internationally proposed or adopted conventions, such as the Convention on International Bills of Exchange and International Promissory Notes and other international principles).

In responding to these issues, what laws and sources are you dealing with primarily? In what way can the firm be prepared to handle these matters? In some situations, its clients may have the "upper hand" in the negotiations; in others they will not. Should this make a difference? What should they be concerned about in regard to possible long range changes? Should the firm back any law reforms — and should they be on a state, federal, or international level? Your senior partner would like a preliminary opinion after you have read Chapter 1 and a final one when you have finished the course.

[A] Early Commercial Law

As tribes and early kingdoms developed, there undoubtedly was some contract and commercial law. Indeed, reference to contract law is found in the Babylonian Empire. Negotiable notes were found in Phoenician times. However, greater development of commercial law is found with the Roman Empire. Although some ideas came from the Grecian era, the Roman law established rules of contracts and of the marketplace. In terms of secured interest, the pledge of goods or property was paramount.

Another source of commercial law is found among the early merchants whose trade transcended national borders. A set of maritime laws developed concerning transportation of goods and remedies of parties, which determined duties and risks in such trade, and contributed to the overall commercial law concepts of insurance that developed from maritime trade. The merchants, dealing with others from considerable distances, also developed concepts such as negotiability of commercial paper.

In early England, the primary emphasis of the King's law was upon property and incidents of the feudal system. The commercial law, to the extent that it existed, was to be found in other forums: manor courts, fair courts, and town courts. Some cases involved matters related to negotiable paper. Customs among merchants and financiers also contributed to the emerging law of sales and negotiable paper.

With the increase of trade during the early 1300's, large commercial fairs became more frequent. These were attended by merchants from different parts of England and foreign lands and served as a convenient forum for promoting trade both between merchants and between merchants and persons able to afford the commodities offered. The importance of these fairs should not be underemphasized in relation to the commerce of the times. Much of the internal and foreign trade of England was carried on at such fairs. These fairs were established by special grant from the King and were, in effect, a grant to establish marketplaces. To handle disputes which arose there, courts were established at the fairs. These courts, picturesquely called "Piedpoudre" courts after the "dusty feet" of the merchants, quickly dispensed justice. The following excerpt from the court of St. Ives in 1319 illustrates the swift settlement of disputes:

> John of Honing was attached to answer Roger of Stanton in a plea of covenant. And whereof he complains that whereas the said John sold to the said Roger a last of red herring for nine marks of silver, to wit, on Monday after the feast of St. Gregory the Pope last past in the villa of St. Ives, and thereof showed him three kemps of good herring and assured him that all the residue of the said herring was similar to the said three kemps, and the said Roger gave him a God's penny in confirmation of the said bargain; nevertheless, after receiving the said herring, the said Roger found that the whole residue of the said herring was unlike the first three kemps, and was mixed with stickiebacks and with putrid herring. Wherefore, he says that he is injured and has damage to the value of 60s, and therefore he produces suit. And the said John comes and denies tort and force etc., and says that he broke no covenant with him, as the said Roger has alleged against him. And he craves that this be inquired, and the said Roger does likewise. Therefore, it is ordered that the bailiff cause a good inquest to come, etc. And the inquest comes and says that the said John broke the covenant with him (Roger) to his damage 40d. Therefore, it is awarded that the said Roger recover against him the said 40d. and that the said John be in mercy 6d pledge (for the fine), Thomas of Ellington.

Certain towns became commercial centers, and courts similar to the fair courts were established which handled disputes arising out of commercial transactions. In addition to the legislation by fair and town courts, a certain degree of regulation was undertaken at the same time by guilds over their own crafts. These guilds were not only concerned with members, but also the quality and sale of goods.

[B] Common Law

For centuries, the common law concerned itself primarily with property law. Even by the 12th century, a simple promise not under seal wasunenforced in the common-law courts. In the 13th and 14th centuries the emphasis of the common law courts continued to be on property law, with some developments in tort law. Despite the lack of interest in commercial law disputes during this early period of the common law, the common-law courts entered the field in the 1400's and 1500's.

In the several centuries during which the common law took jurisdiction over commercial law, the assimilation of the commercial law of the past occurred. It was not an easy transition, however, because of the common law judges' hostility toward commercial law principles. The adjustment of the common law toward the concept of negotiability, for example, was a gradual one.

In the 1500's, Dutch goldsmiths began to issue checks to those who deposited gold with them. They also collected and canceled debts on the written orders of their customers. In England, the practice took hold in the 1600's and goldsmith notes or receipts were issued promising to pay the customer or another. Also, the customers could write the goldsmith directing him to pay another — an early type of check. Goldsmiths or banks also sent these checks by messenger to other banks when asked to by their customers. When the messengers decided to meet for a drink at a mid-town cafe and simply exchange the checks there, the first bank "clearinghouse" developed.

Lord Mansfield, a Scottish lawyer who became an English judge, aided in the adjustment of common law to commercial needs from 1756 onward. In contrast to other judges of his time, he was more receptive to the needs of those engaged in commerce. During his ascendancy as Chief Justice, Lord Mansfield designed several innovations to make the legal system more compatible with commercial requirements, earning him an enduring reputation as the "father of commercial law." He established, for example, a special "jury," a set of advisors, to aid him in making decisions relating to commercial law. The commercial jury tended to increase the confidence of the commercial community in the common law. He also attempted to formulate principles of commercial law out of the chaos of mercantile custom. One of Lord Mansfield's landmark decisions utilizing merchant law did away with the doctrine of consideration in special settings. He dealt with letters of credit and negotiable instruments such as drafts. During these years, the pledge of property for a loan continued as one of the primary forms of secured transactions. But also it became recognized with the mortgaging of real property for loans or sales that there also could be personal property mortgages as well — a type of security interest.

With the steady growth of case law during the 1800's, commentators began to recognize aspects of commercial law as being distinct subject areas. In 1847, in England, one of the first books relating to sales and commercial law was published. In 1866, an English lawyer named Chalmers compiled a digest of some of the English commercial law cases. His digest of the Law of Negotiable Instruments was published in 1878. A decade later, he drafted the English Bills of Exchange Act, thus solidifying negotiable instruments law. In 1882 it was enacted in England and subsequently enacted throughout the British empire. Interestingly, Chalmers had been in India earlier, and his digest was based on some of the Indian code.

In 1868, a well-known treatise, Benjamin on Sales, was published. Judah Benjamin was an American lawyer who served as Secretary of State for the Confederacy, and then fled to England and there did his writing. By 1875, the second edition was published and contained reference to American decisions as well as to the French Civil Code. The Sale of Goods Act also was drafted by Chalmers and enacted in 1893. One of the primary new ideas which developed throughout the 1800's was that of implied warranties, and the number of cases in the field of commercial law generally continued to grow.

The continued growth of commercial enterprises, larger populations to consume more goods and technology combined with mass production made commercial law increasingly important. Not only were there more sales, but the use of credit came to be used on a large scale. Negotiable instruments and several types of secured transactions became used even more. Various state laws and caselaw developed.

[C]   Uniform Acts

In the United States, the movement for codification of the law had both successes and reversals during the latter portion of the 1800's. Codification in the area of commercial law did not occur until the very end of that century, but when it did occur, Negotiable Instruments law was put into statutory form. The Negotiable Instruments Act closely followed the English Bills of Exchange. In 1896, the Uniform Negotiable Instruments Law was drafted under the auspices of the Commissioners on Uniform State Laws. This was to be followed by the Uniform Sales Act in 1906, and a series of other uniform acts in succeeding years:

Uniform Law	Approved by Commissioners	No. of States Adopting
Negotiable Instruments Law	1896	48
Uniform Sales Act (Amended in 1922)	1906	34
Uniform Warehouse Receipts Act	1906	48
Uniform Stock Transfer Act	1909	48
Uniform Bills of Lading Act	1909	31
Uniform Conditional Sales Act	1918	10
Uniform Trust Receipts Act	1933	32

Another development took place during the same time period in both the commercial and consumer realms. The potential and desirability of using credit started to become a part of the psychological and economic milieu of the times. The enactment of the uniform laws in some states also encourages the use of credit. With these developments come the greater use of negotiable instruments and secured transactions in a variety of forms.

[D]   Diversity

Despite the efforts of the Commissioners on Uniform State Laws, uniformity was not achieved, partially due to the scattered and haphazard pattern of adoptions by states of the different uniform acts. Twenty-eight years after its approval by the Commissioners, the Negotiable Instruments Act was finally adopted in all 48 states. Uniformity also was impaired by divergent judicial decisions on various provisions. By 1948, 75 sections out of a total of 198 sections of the Uniform Negotiable Instruments Act were subject to conflicting court decisions. The Sales Act also was not being uniformly construed by the courts.

In addition, a number of courts were construing the commercial legislation in a somewhat narrow and mechanical fashion. Some of the real commercial needs and underlying policy considerations were being ignored. Further, there seemed to be a need for commercial decency, backed by sanction of law, in the performance of obligations. The diversity and uncertainty of the law, together with commercial needs, gave rise to a demand for a recodification of commercial law.

§ 1.02 The Uniform Commercial Code

It is, of course, difficult to set the precise point of origin of any major development of law. To some, the origin of the Uniform Commercial Code might be placed in the movement for codification and the early Field-Carter debates which took place in newspaper and magazine articles. David Dudley Field was a prominent New York attorney in the 1830s who argued that legal principles should be codified so everyone could understand them. Carter also was a prominent New York attorney; he believed law should be left to develop only through caselaw and was bitterly opposed to codification. Others might single out the growth of the Uniform Acts as the origin of the U.C.C. The more contemporary and perhaps more particularized point of origin, however, which has been singled out by a number of commentators is the late nineteen thirties and nineteen forties.

In 1938, a proposal had been sponsored by the Merchants Association of New York City for a federal sales act to govern all interstate sales transactions. In response to this indication of inadequacies in the Uniform Sales Act, the National Conference of Commissioners on Uniform State Laws undertook revision of the Uniform Sales Act it had originally prepared in 1906.

A revision of the Uniform Negotiable Instruments Law, originally prepared in 1896, was then also under consideration.

Growing dissatisfaction with the variety of laws and filing requirements for secured transactions made this another area ripe for reform.

In 1940, the National Conference adopted a proposal to prepare a Uniform Commercial Code, embracing a modernization and coordination of the Uniform Sales Act, the Uniform Negotiable Instruments Law, the Uniform Bills of Lading Act, the Uniform Warehouse Receipts Act, and all other Uniform Acts in the field of commercial law, with new provisions where no uniform acts existed on important and closely related commercial problems. The American Law Institute joined in the undertaking the following year, and in 1942 participated in discussions of the draft Revised Sales Act as a proposed sales chapter of the prospective Code. In 1945, work on the enlarged project was begun. (Report of Association of the Bar of the City of New York, Comm. On Uniform State Laws, May 9, 1950)

Between 1945 and 1952, a great number of drafts and redrafts of parts of the proposed Code were prepared by a reporting staff supervised by an Editorial Board. They were considered successively by advisory groups of judges, lawyers, and law teachers, and by the Council of the American Law Institute and the Commercial Acts Section and the Property Acts Section of the National Conference of Commissioners on Uniform State Laws, and then by the general membership of the two organizations. In preparing the several redrafts, the reporting and advisory groups also consulted with individuals and organizations in business and banking circles in many parts of the country who had come forward with criticisms. The first complete draft of the Code was released in May 1949. Judge Goodrich, Chairman of the U.C.C. Editorial Board described the subsequent development:

> A final text of the proposed Code was completed in September, 1951, and was also approved at that time by the House of Delegates of the American Bar Association. A final text edition was issued in November, 1951. Thereafter, a number of amendments were adopted by the sponsoring organizations in May and September, 1952. Following this action, an official edition was prepared with explanatory comments, and was published as the 1952 Official Text and Comments Edition.

> . . .[A] relatively few months after the New York Law Revision Commission's report was made public in 1956 the Editorial Board of the U.C.C. recommended the adoption of a great many amendments to meet criticisms and suggestions which had been received from the New York Revision Commission and other committees and agencies. These amendments were subsequently approved both by the National Conference of Commissioners on Uniform State Laws and the American Law Institute. The Code as thus amended was published under the title "1957 Official Edition."

> This version of the Code was enacted by Massachusetts in the fall of 1957 and by Kentucky in the spring of 1958.

(Goodrich, Forward to the Official Edition, U.C.C. (1959)).

By the mid-1960s, the Code had been enacted throughout the nation. The law of sales was primarily embodied in Article 2 of the U.C.C. Negotiable Instruments law was set forth in Articles 3 and 4. The law of Secured Transactions was in Article 9. A U.C.C. Committee reviewing Article 9 (Secured Transactions) suggested some amendments which became part of a new official 1972 edition. In 1977, some amendments were made to Article 8 on Investment Securities (uncertificated stock transfers) were added to its coverage. In the 1980's, individual states were enacting these changes into their law. Since the Code was first enacted in the mid-1960's, a number of cases relating to its provisions have been decided. Thus, there is a body of caselaw interpreting various provisions of the U.C.C. Some of the cases represent diverse interpretations. Discussions of caselaw development under the Code through court interpretations are found in some court opinions rendered in the 1980s, and are contained in this casebook.

A "Permanent Editorial Board" for the U.C.C. continues to review the Code, caselaw, and proposals for amendment of the U.C.C. This Board was established by the American Law Institute and Commissioners for Uniform State Laws, which had formulated and urged enactment of the U.C.C. Article 6 on Bulk Transfers has been revised. A new payments law for electronic transfers also was proposed by the Articles 3-4-8 Committee with a report to the Board; an American Bar Association committee also studied the matter. There were Amendments to Articles 3 and 4 and an Article 4A for Electronic Transfers. Article 2A on "leasing" was added.

In addition to the Code becoming the law of the land, other aspects of commercial law developed in the 1960's, 1970's and 1980's and 1990's. There were important developments relating to products liability, credit cards and electronic funds transfer, consumer protection, bankruptcy and letters of credit. Since these subjects are a part of modern commercial law, and fill gaps in the law not covered by the Code, this book contains some cases and materials relating to them.

The drafters of the Uniform Commercial Code were primarily concerned with a Code for the United States. Foreign representatives were excluded from the drafting process, even though at times the law of other countries was noted. Nevertheless, Article 9 (Secured Transactions) has been enacted in some Canadian provinces. In light of a new interest in comparative commercial law in recent decades, some studies have been made of Code concepts, such as unconscionability, as they exist in other countries. It is most likely that the interest in comparative commercial and consumer law will accelerate into the coming century.

The Uniform Commercial Code remains the law throughout the United States. 1999 will mark the fiftieth anniversary of its formulation. Although there will be some Amendments and even added Articles, the basic framework of the U.C.C. will remain. The student and lawyer of today with knowledge of the U.C.C. and comparable international commercial law will be well equipped to deal with commercial law into the new 21st century.

§ 1.03 The Uniform Commercial Code: Subsequent Development

The mass production and new technologies of the earlier part of the century seemed dwarfed by the later ones following World War II. Even more consumers and an even more relaxed attitude toward using credit created more production and business than ever. The last psychological barriers which some earlier generations had to the use of credit fell. New ways of doing business also brought about many changes in the Uniform Commercial Code. In addition, a vast increase in commercial activity was necessary to satisfy the needs of a growing population and new international markets. This engendered even more use of sales contracts, negotiable instruments, and security interests. Article 2A on leasing has been enacted in nearly all the states in the U.S. Consequently, a new chapter, 9A, has been added to these materials dealing with leases of goods. In addition, where similar provisions in Article 2, dealing with goods, appear in Article 2A, the parallel section citations to the lease material now appear with the Article 2 provisions.

Article 3 on commercial paper was revised along with parts of Article 4 on bank deposits and collections. Some states have adopted these provisions. A new Article 4A, entitled Funds Transfers, has been approved and enacted throughout the nation.

It was recommended by the Commissioners of Uniform State Laws and the American Law Institute that Article 6 on Bulk Transfers be repealed. However, for those states still wishing to regulate bulk sales, a revised version of the article was provided. A majority of the states considering the matter have voted for repeal.

[A]   Law Reform Oversight

PROBLEM 1.3

What position would you support if you were a member of the ALI attending this session mentioned in the following discussion?

As a member of the legal profession, what would be your view as to the handling of law reform? Should it be left to the ALI and the Commissioners for Uniform State Laws? Why or why not?

One of the purposes of the Uniform Commercial Code was to make uniform the law among the various jurisdictions (U.C.C. § 1-102(2)(c)). One can easily see how the legislative reaction of the various jurisdictions to this flurry of reform legislation can impact substantially on this purpose of uniformity. One reaction to the problem was the possible creation of a Law Reform Oversight Committee and the matter was raised at the 1990 meeting of the American Law Institute, and appears in the Record of Proceedings.

Donald Barnett King (Mo.): One thing I would like to raise at this point is the matter of this whole amendment process in the sense that what you have here, in these few years, is an amending of a number of articles of the Uniform Commercial Code. While this is desirable and while this meeting should proceed to consider the matters at hand, it seems to be that The American Law Institute must appoint a special committee on commercial law reform, a long-range committee that can deal with what is happening and what will happen as history has shown us in the past — what will happen, in regard to this whole amendment process. . ..

Through the nation, there is a lack of uniformity that is occurring. We now face the greatest lack of uniformity possible. That is, we are revising, at this point, parts of Article 3 and Article 4, and the states, as they look at these amendments, will indeed not enact them uniformly. They will be enacted over a period of varying years.

We have also Article 2, which is being revised by Dick Speidel and some others; that, too, will go through the same process of lack of uniformity. Article 2A will go through the same thing. Someone told me there may be an Article 2B proposed by a couple of lawyers who want licensing included. Article 5 is being revised; Boris Kozolchyk, among others, is working on that. Article 9 is going through further revisions; Article 8, also.

I make a motion that The American Law Institute appoint a special long-range committee on commercial law reform, because it seems to me that this is most crucial. It should be a committee with some representatives of the Permanent Editorial Board, both ALI and states, but it should be with other independent members of The American Law Institute.

I think we want to keep the same process because The American Law Institute has done a magnificent job, but we have to consider varying alternatives, including federal enactment, in part, or other alternatives for making the law reform process more efficient. Otherwise, this Institute will be proposing uniform laws amending every single article, knowing that 50 states will not enact them uniformly.

Opposition to the proposal for a special long-range committee on commercial law reform was quickly voiced.

Mr. Carlyle C. Ring, Jr. (Va.): I am from the National Conference of Commissioners on Uniform State Laws, a partner in this process of the Uniform Commercial Code. . . .

[I] think that any committee of The American Law Institute really has got to coordinate with the other bodies, and that is the point I think I am trying to make. I would hope that the Council, if this were favorably accounted upon, would take into account these inner relationships and hopefully conclude — and maybe this body should conclude — that the Permanent Editorial Board is really the right vehicle (pp. 386-387).

[B] Possible Federal Enactment

PROBLEM 1.4

As an aide to one of the U.S. Senators from your state, you have been asked to look into the possible federal enactment of the U.C.C. or portions of it. Thus, there would be a Federal Sales Act, a Federal Negotiable Instruments Act and a Federal Security Interest Act. Present the arguments *pro* and *con* and make your recommendation to the Senator. He has given you a copy of an excerpt from an article dealing with federal enactment:

Another possible way of dealing with this lack of uniformity is through federal enactment of commercial law. The U.C.C. could be enacted on the federal level so that national law could deal with commercial matters. Indeed, by trying to promote a uniform law on a state by state basis, the A.L.I. and the Commissioners indirectly acknowledge this fact. State by state enactment reaches the same goal as federal enactment. The A.L.I. should have no problem formulating an appropriate plan since it can propose legislation on either a state or federal level. The Commissioners should find it implied in their powers to promote the best commercial law for each state, whether through federal or state action. Clearly, uniformity is desirable and practical; federal enactment promotes uniformity in state law. The state can act voluntarily by appointing commissions, drafting acts, and entrusting those acts to federal enactment.

Commercial laws should not be decided on a state by state basis. Those laws do not inherently reflect a strong state interest or command state enactment. Indeed, laws that regulate the flow of goods and commercial transactions over state lines should be considered national in character. The states have little interest in the massive number of goods flowing over their boundaries or even those that are part of a national economy. Because some states might feel the need for greater consumer protection than others, those states can enact special legislation to provide such protection. In any event, the basic national framework of the commercial law should be the same.

The federal government clearly has the power to enact a federal law on commercial matters including leasing through the interstate commerce clause. That clause covers both transactions that involve crossing state boundaries and those that have an indirect economic impact. Under relevant case law, localized activity, although only remotely and indirectly affecting interstate commerce, is enough to allow federal enactment.

The case involving a farmer who raised extra wheat locally for his own local use is a good illustration of the broad federal constitutional power. Similarly, the federal government regulated a family owned restaurant, Ollie's Barbecue, although it served food only to local customers. Though not enacted for commercial purposes, the civil rights statute is constitutional since it falls within the purview of the interstate commerce clause. Undoubtedly, laws on commercial activity such as leasing fall within the interstate commerce clause power; its inclusion is constitutionally justified more easily than in the examples above. Commercial activity is national in character. More importantly, federal power was designed to promote federal regulation of commercial activity. Federal and state courts generally have concurrent jurisdiction over issues of federal law, by implication of Article III of the United States Constitution, unless Congress expressly states otherwise. Also by congressional act, federal court jurisdiction over U.C.C. issues could be negated, leaving it solely to the state courts if so desired.

King, *Major Problems With Article 2A: Unfairness, "Cutting Off" Consumer Defenses, Unfiled Interests, and Uneven Adoption*, 43 Mercer Law Rev. 869 at 873-74 (1992).

§ 1.04 International Commercial Law

[A]   Uniform International Commercial Law

PROBLEM 1.5

Your senior partner is a member of an International Academy which is discussing the matter of uniformity under the convention for the International Sale of Goods. Such discussions also may be applicable to the International Unification of Negotiable Instruments and Secured Transactions. He has looked at the educational, structural, and broad principles proposals mentioned in the next several pages and seeks your views on this matter.

There also has been work toward a uniform international commercial law, which has included efforts of UNIDROIT (International Institute for Unification of Private Law in Rome), the Hague Conference on Private International Law and UNICITRAL (United Nations Commission on International Trade Law in Vienna) over many years. American representatives involved with these efforts were experts in the U.C.C. In 1980, a diplomatic conference of sixty-two nations approved the United Nations Convention on Contracts for the International Sales of Goods. It is often referred to as the Vienna Convention or the International Sales Convention (ISC), or the Convention on the International Sale of Goods (C.I.S.G.).

This International Sales Convention applies to sales transactions between parties in different nations. It does not apply to contracts for services, consumer sales, negotiable paper, or certain miscellaneous sales involving aircraft, ships, electricity, or auctions. Parties may by contract exclude the application of the convention, terms of the contract generally prevail over provisions of the convention if they conflict. Part I (Articles 1-13) governs the scope of applications of ISC and sets forth rules of interpretation, such as good faith and trade usage.

Part II (Articles 14-24) deals with the making of the contract. This includes matters relating to offers, acceptances, and "acceptances" which deviate from the offer.

Part III (Articles 25-88) covers rights, obligations, and remedies of the parties. This includes what constitutes the seller's delivery, place and time for delivery, handing over of documents, quality or warranty of goods, and right to cure performance before or after the date of delivery.

It also includes the buyer's rights and duties of examination and giving notice and the buyer's basic obligations of payment. Risk of loss or damage to the goods, anticipatory breach, fundamental breach, and installment contracts are covered. Seller and buyer remedies and damages also are in this Part.

Part IV (Articles 89-101) deals with certain reservations permitted to nations choosing them, and with steps for bringing the Convention into force.

By early 1987, the ISC had been ratified by over ten nations, including the United States, effective January 1, 1988. As adopted by the United States the ISC is applicable to transactions between businesses that are located in different countries.

By mid-1994, thirty-seven nations had ratified the United Nations Convention on Contracts for the International Sales of Goods (CISG). We have provided in this casebook citations to CISG sections that parallel similar provisions in Article 2.

[B]   International Bills of Exchange and International Promissory Notes

In 1988, the General Assembly of the United Nations called for nations to adopt this new Convention. It pointed out that the circulation of negotiable instruments facilitates international trade and finance. This Convention would be a part of the progressive harmonization and unification of international trade law. However, there was far less success in regard to the adoption of this Convention.

[C]   Uniformity of International Commercial Law

In May of 1992, UNICITRAL celebrated its twenty-fifth anniversary with a congress to review possible further needs and possibilities regarding international commercial law. One of the major problems with the global adoption of commercial laws is the problem of diverse court interpretations. Several proposals have been made in that regard.

[1]   Informational Measures

Secretary of UNICITRAL, Gerald Hermann, suggested at the 25th Anniversary Conference that there be publication of uniform law texts and related materials, *e.g.*, Register of Texts, Official Records, Book on UNICITRAL, Yearbooks comprising regular documentation, Status of Conventions and Brochures with explanatory notes ("ten-pagers") entitled "Case Law on UNICITRAL Texts." He also suggested organization or co-sponsorship of regional or national seminars, congresses or similar programs, briefing of visiting lawyers or business representatives, training of interns, hosting of scholars, and other educative measures. The analysis of court interpretation of UNICITRAL texts and possible recommendations for uniform interpretation also was mentioned.

[2]   Structural Measures

[i]   International Uniform Law Court

Professor Louis Sohn proposed an International Uniform Laws Court at the UNICITRAL Anniversary Conference.

The rapid growth in international trade is accompanied by a constant increase in the number of international uniform laws and of international conventions establishing uniform rules for one important area after another. A parallel increase in litigation before domestic courts and commercial arbitral tribunals has resulted in inconsistent decisions and conflicting interpretations of the same uniform law or common conventional rule in different countries. This leads often to forum shopping and a conduct of litigation in an inconvenient forum with limited access to facts and witnesses. Each conflicting decision results also in diminishing the value of the uniform law or conventional rule, and the laborious effort to reach agreement on them is often wasted.

Establishment of stricter jurisdictional rules might cut down forum shopping but would not prevent discrepancy in interpretation. The only adequate remedy would be to establish an international court composed of legal experts with experience in preparation, application of interpretation of uniform laws and uniform conventional rules. It would perform in the field of private international law (in the broad sense of this phrase) the same function as is being performed by the International Court of Justice in the field of public international law. States might be willing to accept its jurisdiction for all, or at least some, international agreements establishing uniform laws or common rules to which they are parties. If some States are not willing to go that far, they might agree to least to resort to the Court when national tribunals of different countries render conflicting interpretations of a uniform text. The modalities of such a procedure might parallel the practice of the Supreme Court of the United States in case of conflicting decisions of Circuit Appeal Courts and a similar practice is developing in the European Community's judicial system. Many other problems of jurisdiction, composition and procedure would have to be solved, but the trail has been blazed by many interesting proposals and reports. The approach envisaged in this paper is preferable to the establishment of special tribunals for a variety of topics, as it would avoid the excessive cost of maintaining simultaneously a constantly increasing number of tribunals for one topic after another. Once established, a general tribunal for the interpretation of uniform laws and rules would be able to develop techniques enabling it to deal with even the most difficult or most specialized subjects. Such a tribunal is long overdue, and its establishment would constitute an important contribution to the United Nations Decade of International Law.

[ii] International Commercial Law Court

At that same Conference, Professor Donald King supported Professor Sohn's proposal, but also proposed an interim measure in the event the International Court for Uniform Treaties was not effectuated. An International Commercial Law Court could be created with jurisdiction primarily over the International Sale of Goods Act, the International Bills of Exchange and International Promissory Notes Convention and other UNICITRAL developed commercial laws. It also could handle some cases of conflicting interpretation of general international commercial principles by national arbitration bodies or courts if that seemed desirable. This would entail much less funding and effort. Because conflicting case decisions in the various countries on these international commercial provisions would be slow to arise, such a court would have to meet only a couple of months each year. The judges could be law professors, judges, governmental and UNICITRAL officials, and distinguished retired members of the legal profession. As the work of the International Commercial court grows over the years, the positions can be made full-time ones.

[iii] Development of Broad International Principles

The development of broad general principles of contract and of business ethics also would aid in the uniform interpretation of the Convention. As noted by Professor Sono of Japan at the UNICITRAL 25th Anniversary Conference:

In the field of the settlement of international commercial disputes, the success of UNICI-TRAL's activities on international commercial arbitration was fortunate as they coincided with the period of the formation and expansion of globalized economic activity in the 1970s. The flexibility of arbitration often enables arbitrators to maneuver away from those not-so-helpful national laws particularly for the settlement of disputes of complex modern contracts. And, through arbitral awards, there is a phenomenon of a resurgence of the rule of reason at a delocalized level away from the legal positivism and traditional dogma.

For complex transactions which were seldom heard of in the past, there is a tendency to resort to "the general principle of law," "lex mercatoris," or "the principle of good faith and fair dealing" particularly through arbitration clauses. During the Congress, I was told personally from a reliable source that 5 to 10 percent of the disputes which are submitted to arbitration now contain such clauses. The person who provided me with this information said "only 5 to 10 percent," but to me it is an extremely significant percentage. Yet, the contents of these principles are still far from certain. However, it is interesting to note in this context that international bodies such as UNICROIT and E.C. are presently undertaking to elaborate their contents more concretely in the form of principles of international contract law under the influence of the Vienna Sales Convention which continues to make a valuable contribution to reorient the traditional dogma-oriented jurisprudence beyond the area of sales. The International Law Association also started to elaborate global contract principles interestingly through its Committee on International Commercial Arbitration.

As Professor King also indicated, a need may soon be felt for the establishment of a global court of commerce initially for cases where resort has been made in arbitration to a national or international lex mercatoria or to general principles of contract law. At this Congress, we already heard a suggestion of Professor Sohn for the establishment of an international tribunal to interpret uniform legal texts.

[iv]   International Restatement of General Principles

In 1994, UNIDROIT issued a set of General Principles for International Sales Law. This was the work of almost 15 years by international experts. It seems quite possible that it will become recognized as an international "law merchant."

[v]   Internationalization of Security Interests

In 1994, the final draft of an International Convention on Security Interests in Mobile Equipment under the auspices of UNIDROIT was produced, with subsequent reports in 1995. This is an attempt to internationalize one aspect of secured transactions.

During this same time, studies of creating a security interest law and system for the NAFTA countries was undertaken by the National Law Center of Inter-American Free Trade.

An international-national electronic filing system with more certain identification of debtors also has been proposed (See King, Secured Transactions 4-15 (1995)). It is pointed out that the present state filing systems, which necessitate the use of writings and physical filing of financing statements, were developed before the development of new technology when such writings and filings were necessary. It urges that these systems are now obsolete, and should be scrapped, and replaced with "International-National Electronic Filing (INEF)." International electronic systems, like the Internet, make information easily accessible through a home or office computer virtually anywhere in the world. The Internet would make searches for information on security interests and filing easier and would not be constrained by state boundaries. These electronic networks make the establishment of a major national filing office unnecessary, although an overall supervisor might be in order. Combined with INEF, a system of more certain identification of debtors (CID) would eliminate more filing problems. Such an identification system should be compatible with electronic filing, possibly using Social Security numbers or tax identification numbers. Similar certain identification could be established for other countries when international expansion of the system seemed feasible.

§ 1.05 Construction and Interpretation

Read: U.C.C. § 1-102 and Comments.

Read also: CISG Art. 7.

Commercial law, as contrasted with other legal subjects, has its own unique principles of interpretation. While each of these three points could be explored at great length, some summary statements with brief excerpts from King, The New Conceptualism of the U.C.C. (1968), pp. 8-10, 99-103 (footnotes omitted) on the nature of the Code, the relationship of parties, and rejection of past concepts are sufficient to illustrate the U.C.C. methodology.

[A] Nature of the Code

PROBLEM 1.6

Some persons maintain that the "nature of the Code" is only an idealized method of interpretation and that in a common law system the courts will continue to emphasize case law development and caselaw interpretation of the Code. The Code, they say, is no different than an ordinary statute. What do you think in this regard? Consider the following excerpt along with the common law training of judges.

The U.C.C. is a Code — not an ordinary statute — and the principles of its interpretation are different.

"True" codes, systematic and comprehensive in nature, differ significantly from ordinary statutory legislation in terms of the methodology of interpretation. For one thing, a code is to be viewed by any court confronted by it as a document which is self-explanatory. The court is to look to the codified principle and its underlying purposes and policies rather than any technicalities of prior case law. Where a gap may occur, or in an unforeseen situation, the court must look to the other principles contained in the code for its answer. This may be contrasted with other statutory law where the common law or former case law is dealt with instead. Under the U.C.C., the pre-Code caselaw should not be used either for purposes of interpretation or for the solving of new problems. This same principle applies even as to case decisions interpreting provisions of the Code itself. Other courts, while recognizing such opinions as having some persuasive value, should still look to the Code itself and its qualities for the answers. As one commentator has stated, a code "remains at all times its own best evidence of what it means; cases decided under it may be interesting, persuasive, cogent, but each new case must be referred for decision to the undefiled code text." This is to be distinguished from a statute which has been interpreted over a space of time in a series of judicial opinions which have themselves "become part of the statutory complex." This view is reiterated by another authority, who emphasizes the fact that the doctrine of stare decisis should not be used in applying the Code. As he states, it may be hoped. . .that its application will be less vigorous here, that the courts will more readily return to the statutory text for their answers. . . . [C]ases construing the Code should be given the highest credit, but it should not be forgotten that the code itself is its own best evidence of what it means. Thus, the Code by its very nature dictates a return of itself and its purposes for interpretation and requires this methodology of construction.

In civil law jurisdictions, such methodology has long been used. One authority on civil law has emphasized that this new code methodology "represents a remarkable advance in the history of American law." As he points out, where the text of the Code falls short of deciding the controversy, the Code may "itself be developed or 'applied to promote its underlying reasons, purposes and policies.' "

King, *supra,* at 8-10.

[B] Relationships and Circumstances

In deciding U.C.C. cases, it has been said the courts should give consideration to the relationship of the parties affected by the transaction.

In most instances, the relationship will manifest itself in terms of the more immediate parties to a transaction, since it is primarily their relationship which will be the subject of litigation. In some instances, however, particularly those where the rights of creditors, good faith purchasers, or purchasers in the ordinary course of business have come into conflict with the rights of one of the immediate parties, other individuals may become involved. Then too, in the sales of many goods, members of the buyer's family or other persons who come into contact with the goods may become involved. Finally, where a particular class of persons is significantly affected through a number of transactions, the relationship may be more extensive and involve questions of social values.

The court also should look in U.C.C. cases to circumstances in the overall setting and at several levels:

The first is related to the particular circumstances involved in the particular transaction between the parties; this would include specific facts surrounding the transaction and such matters as course of performance and course of dealing. The second includes elements such as custom, trade usage, and any other relevant external commercial circumstances. The third includes the relationship of the particular setting to the entire social setting, comprising commercial and non-commercial factors.[1]

King, *supra*, 99-103.

Is this an ideal or can courts look to the relational factors in deciding cases? On what levels? Should courts take into account the entire social setting?

[C] Rejection of Past Concepts

The U.C.C. drafters rejected some concepts developed in pre-Code caselaw. The U.C.C. emphasizes a functional approach to commercial problems, rather than applying past sets of rules based solely on logic. Thus the U.C.C. rejects some concepts "even though these concepts have been deeply implanted within sales and contract law." In many cases, these concepts were developed during an early period of the law in which there was a distinct tendency to define

---

[1] Copyright © 1968 by Fred Rothman Co. Reprinted by permission.

legal concepts in somewhat "visible" terms. This approach, for example, permitted the "pigeon-holing" of legal actions. Even though scholars often pierced portions of the rationalizations underlying these intangible, but terminologically visible theories, the theories continued to thrive throughout the years and affected the results of numerous cases.

As Professor William D. Hawkland (author of books and articles on the U.C.C. and a member of the Permanent Editorial Board) noted, "The technical 'ribbon matching' approach of contract law is foreign to most buyers and sellers, and its rules that an acceptance can never vary an offer, that telegraphic offers must be accepted by telegraphic acceptances, and the like, often have frustrated the reasonable expectations of businessmen." Karl Llewellyn (Chief Reporter of the U.C.C., professor, and author of well known writings in commercial law and jurisprudence) dissected and exposed the artificial concept of "title" which controlled cases for years. He pointed out that it was mythical, illusive, and unsatisfactory for settling commercial disputes. Questions formerly decided by a mechanistic determination of title passage (logical analysis based on rules designed to ascertain intent) are now to be determined "in terms of step by step performance or non-performance under the contract for sales and not in terms of whether or not title to the goods has passed." King, *supra,* at 99-103.

In regard to negotiable instruments, the drafters centered on eliminating many of the controversies that centered around some of the old NIL provisions. Clarification was sought through the use of the new U.C.C. provisions and words. There were not, however, major reformulations of concepts.

In regard to secured transactions, there was a major reformulation of concept. Rather than the diverse concepts and rationale that was found among the various security devices, such as chattel mortgages, conditional sales, trust receipts, bailment leases, and field warehousing, the drafters created a new single unified concept known as the "security interest." Here too, the drafters respected the concept of "title" as having an importance in regard to the rights and obligations of the parties.

[D] Application by Analogy

PROBLEM 1.7

The Teddy Roosevelt University has contracted with several companies and is experiencing some problems with them. The University counsel has consulted you as to whether the U.C.C. or analogy could be utilized in regard to them:

(1) The contract with Bigger Foods for managing the cafeteria and providing meals has resulted in poor quality food and student protests.

(2) The contract with Flowers Landscapes to make flower beds and maintain them on campus has not been satisfactory and a campus that once had a variety of flowers all spring, summer and fall and was a joy to walk through is much more bleak with only a few blooming at a time.

(3) The law firm that drafted those two contracts did not provide for a number of things and contingencies.

University counsel is convinced that it would win on warranty of merchantability-type principles, but not on negligence. What is your advice?

In addition to understanding the unique manner in which courts should construe the U.C.C., it is also important to know that courts may sometimes apply the U.C.C. by analogy to commercial law cases outside the scope of the Code.

In applying the Code by analogy, the court may apply U.C.C. principles to a transaction not technically covered by the Code, on the basis that those principles should be more broadly applied; or it may analogize the transaction not technically covered to the transactions covered and thus bring the former within the U.C.C. coverage. In some cases, the court may be faced with applying a principle found in one U.C.C. Article to transactions covered by another U.C.C. Article.

§ 1.06 Underlying Principles

A basic principle of the Code drafters was that custom and trade usage should be looked to in solving commercial disputes. Courts should look to trade usage in interpreting contracts and a trade usage may actually be recognized as a term of the contract by the court.

Another basic principle of the Code drafters was that parties to a commercial transaction should act within ethical standards. Good faith in performance of contracts, and not making unconscionable ones, may seem to be an idealized, ethical goal. But it is much more—it is set forth expressly in the Code. Failure to exercise good faith in the performance or enforcement of a contract constitutes a breach of contract. A court may strike or modify an unconscionable term in a contract or it may hold the entire contract to be unenforceable. This has been described as the "new business ethic." If one doubts that these standards will be applied, a look at the ever increasing flow of Code cases on this matter may dispel doubt.

[A] Custom and Trade Usage

Read: U.C.C. § 1-205.

Read also: CISG Art. 9.

PROBLEM 1.8

Your client, The Black Top Company, is a seller of asphalt. As a seller, it makes bids to buyers who are in the contract and asphalt business. Your client is supplied the asphalt by one of the giant oil companies, Exaco. In the Exaco contract with Black Top, there is an express term that made the price Exaco's current posted price. There also is a trade usage that a supplier of asphalt, like Exaco, would not apply a price increase to a buyer, like Black Top, for amounts the buyer needed to satisfy bids it had already submitted to others. With the change of Exaco's management, it refused to give Black Top this price protection on some asphalt that Black Top had submitted bids on. Instead Exaco insisted on the written contract terms of the current posted price.

Should the court treat the concept of trade usage? What are the perimeters of trade usage in regard to the type of business involved? What were the geographical boundaries? What was the course of performance involved? Was this even stronger than the trade usage? Does the failure to follow trade usage or course of performance reflect a lack of good faith in the performance of the contract?

NOTES

(1) While the contract may seem to cover issues that may arise, it is sometimes custom and trade usage that becomes determinative. *Torstenson v. Melcher*, 195 Neb. 764, 241 N.W.2d 103

(1976), involved the sale of a "breeder" bull. Defendant, who was in the cattle business, sent a sale catalogue to prospective buyers, including the plaintiffs. The catalogue contained the following notice: "All animals are guaranteed to be without known defects. Animal failing to breed after trial of six months may be returned to the seller if in good condition. The seller reserves the right to try said animal for six months and if it proves a breeder to return it to the station of the buyer at his expense. If animal proves a non-breeder, a satisfactory exchange will be made or the purchase price will be refunded."

The plaintiffs purchased the bull, named H.M. Silver Domino 10. When H. M. Silver Domino 10 was turned into an 80-acre pasture with 32 of the plaintiffs' stock cows, he covered the cow herd well, but in later weeks, the plaintiff noticed the cows continued to recycle.

The bull was given a field semen test. A veterinarian, Doctor Dierks, reported that the bull was capable of breeding, and Melcher asked the plaintiffs to try him for a longer time.

Doctor Dierks suggested that the bull be rested for approximately 2 weeks before running him back in with the cow herd. Plaintiffs immediately turned the bull back in with the cows. They continued to be dissatisfied with the bull's performance, and on December 11, 1972, the bull was returned to the defendant.

Tests conducted by Doctor Stevens, another veterinarian, on January 5, 1973, indicated that 17 of the plaintiffs' 32 cows had been impregnated. About January 10, 1973, a different bull was turned in with the cows. All but one of the remaining cows were settled thereafter in one cycle.

In the trial, the defendant introduced evidence to the effect that 32 cows would be too many for a two-year-old bull to cover, and that a reduction in fertility could result from overuse. Plaintiff's evidence was that placing the bull with 32 cows would be within acceptable limits.

The issue at trial centered around the meaning to be attached to the term "breeder," contained in the catalogue warranty set out above. There was evidence that a normal bull should impregnated from 50 to 75 percent of the healthy cows he bred in each heat cycle, and that 95 percent of the cows should be settled within 3 months. There was also testimony that an animal settling 10 cows in a lifetime could technically be termed a "breeder."

After citing U.C.C. §§ 2-315 and 2-316(3)(c), the appellate court reviewed contested instruction (No. 14) of the trial court: "The jury is instructed that under the facts in this case an implied warranty of fitness for breeding purposes may be excluded by the usage of the trade in question, and that before the jury shall consider whether or not the implied warranty of fitness stated in Instruction No. 13 is breached, the jury shall consider and determine whether or not the implied warranty of fitness has been excluded by the usage of the purebred Hereford cattle trade. In the event the jury shall find the implied warranty of fitness has been excluded, then the jury shall disregard all instructions with regard to damages, for breach of the alleged and implied warranty of fitness for breeding purposes."

Plaintiffs contend that trade usage excluding the implied warranty of fitness was not properly presented by the pleadings or the evidence, so that any instruction allowing the jury to find the warranty excluded was erroneous.

The answer filed by the defendant in this case alleged: "That said written warranty is in accord with the custom and usage of the cattle trade in the community where the sale was made. That by custom (of) the trade in breeding animals there is no implied warranty of fitness for particular purpose in the case of sale of a bull." The court then cited U.C.C. § 1-205(6) and found no unfair surprise. It also found "sufficient evidence in the record to support instruction 14. The testimony of the field representative of the American Hereford Association indicated that he had observed no other warranties in his extensive experience in the trade. This evidence is sufficient to submit the issue to the jury."

It then noted plaintiff's other contention that the evidence was "insufficient to support the verdict and judgment."

Their argument is essentially that the bull could not be found to be a "breeder" since in the cattle business a bull that settles roughly half a 32-cow herd, as this one did, will not be considered acceptable. We believe the question of the bull's status as a "breeder" was properly submitted to the jury. In addition to the plaintiff's evidence that 95 percent of their herd should have been settled, there was testimony that a bull which settles 50 percent of the healthy cows he breeds may be considered a "breeder." There was also a question as to whether the bull was turned in with too many cows. One of the experts, from a semen test, said he would not expect any problem in pasture breeding with 25 females. While we may have some question on the result herein, the trial was held in a farm and ranch community. It was a question of fact for the jury. We are bound by its determination.

The verdict for the defendant was affirmed.

Consider how trade usage was used in this case. Was it for interpretation of the contract term "breeder bull"? Was it to supply a disclaimer of warranties? Or both? Do the experts agree on the trade usage? How can the jury decide what is the trade usage? Is it trade usage with the community, the state, or the cattle raising industry?

(2) See *Columbia Nitrogen Corp. v. Royster Co.,* 451 F.2d 3(4th Cir. 1971), where the court noted that extrinsic evidence may be introduced to explain or supplement a written contract despite any apparent ambiguity.

Royster manufactures and markets mixed fertilizers, the principal components of which are nitrogen, phosphate and potash. Columbia is primarily a producer of nitrogen, although it manufactures some mixed fertilizer. For several years Royster had been a major purchaser of Columbia's products, but Columbia had never been a significant customer of Royster. In the fall of 1966, Royster constructed a facility which enabled it to produce more phosphate than it needed in its own operations. After extensive negotiations, the companies executed a contract for Royster's sale of a minimum of 31,000 tons of phosphate each year for three years to Columbia, with an option to extend the term. The contract stated the price per ton, subject to an escalation clause dependent on production costs.

Columbia assigns error to the pretrial ruling of the district court excluding all evidence on usage of the trade and course of dealing between the parties. It offered the testimony of witnesses with long experience in the trade that because of uncertain crop and weather conditions, farming practices, and governmental agricultural programs, express price and quantity terms in contracts for materials in the mixed fertilizer industry are mere projections to be adjusted according to market forces.

Columbia also offered proof of its business dealings with Royster over the six-year period preceding the phosphate contract. Since Columbia had not been a significant purchaser of Royster's products, these dealings were almost exclusively nitrogen sales to Royster or exchanges of stock carried in inventory. The pattern which emerges, Columbia claimed, is one of repeated and substantial deviation from the stated amount or price, including four instances where Royster took none of the goods for which it had contracted. Columbia offered proof that the total variance amounted to more than $500,000 in reduced sales. This experience, a Columbia officer offered to testify, formed the basis of an understanding on which he depended in conducting negotiations with Royster.

The District Court held that the evidence should be excluded. It ruled that "custom and usage or course of dealing are not admissible to contradict the express, plain, unambiguous language of a valid written contract, which by virtue of its detail negates the proposition that the contract is open to variances in its terms."

The Court of Appeals reversed, admitting evidence of trade usage and course of performance. Citing U.C.C. § 1-102, the court stated that any extrinsic evidence "shall be liberally construed and applied to promote its underlying purposes and policies," which include "the continued expansion of commercial practices through custom, usage and agreement of the parties." The court in Columbia Nitrogen further stated that U.C.C. § 2-202, when read in conjunction with U.C.C. § 1-205(4), resulted in a test of admissibility which is "not whether the contract appears on its face to be complete in every detail, but whether the proffered evidence of course of dealing and trade usage reasonably can be construed as consistent with the express terms of the agreement."

PROBLEM 1.9

Suppose Honest Jake, a car dealer, sells a used car to Mrs. Buckless. In order to finance the transaction, Jake also signed an installment contract and a bank note with Mrs. Buckless. The bank required there be insurance on the car and handled the obtaining of the policy. Shortly after, Mrs. Buckless was in a car accident. The insurance company covered the accident, but then canceled the policy because Mrs. Buckless was a poor risk.

The bank did not give any notice of cancellation to Honest Jake. A short time later, Mrs. Buckless was in another accident, and this time the car was demolished. Since Mrs. Buckless is unable to make the rest of the payments on the car, the bank now sues Honest Jake for the money due on the contract and note. If there had been insurance on the car, this would have covered the total payment for it and nothing would have been owed on it by Honest Jake. Honest Jake asserts that there was a custom in the trade for the bank to give notice to him that Mrs. Buckless's insurance was canceled. The bank asserts that any custom was waived when Jake signed the contract and negotiable note that both stated that Jake expressly waives all notices and agrees his liability is absolute.

As attorney for Honest Jake, what arguments can you use that will prevail over the contract clause? What expert witnesses will you use to prove custom? Would it be easier to prove either trade usage or course of dealing? Even if one of these is established, can it prevail over the express waiver of notice clause?

NOTE

In a case similar to the Problem, *Provident Tradesman Bank Trust Co. v. Pemberton*, 24 D&C.2d 720, *aff'd*, 196 Pa. Super. 180, 173 A.2d 780 (1959), the court held that the waiver of all notices did not include those notices mandated by trade usage. Any waiver of those, said the court, must be specific. The court quoted from Comment 2 to U.C.C. § 2-202.

[B] Merchant/Non-Merchant Dichotomy

PROBLEM 1.10

One of your clients, a prosperous stockbroker, Robert Rich, made so much money that he decided to become a "gentleman" farmer. He bought a farm fifty miles outside of town which has a hundred areas for planting. Mr. Rich hires the planting and combining and trucking to a local grain company which pays for each truckload delivery. This year the company claims it has discovered that his grain, while not being useless, is of low quality. He refuses to return any of the payments and asserts that he is not a merchant of grain, knows nothing about it, spends virtually none of his time on farming, and is not responsible for the quality of the grain.

PROBLEM 1.11

Robert Rich also had thirty Beefalo (cross between cows and buffalo) which he decided he would sell. He entered into a oral contract with another farmer over a drink at the local country tavern. The farmer wrote a brief letter confirming the sale, but Mr. Rich never replied to it and now wants more money than agreed since the price of Beefalo has suddenly risen. Is Mr. Rich a merchant, and therefore under the merchant reply exception [§ 2-201(2)]?

NOTES

(1) What type of professionalism or expertise is the court looking for generally to determine if a party to a contract is a merchant? What evidence should it find relevant? What effect, if any, does the fact that someone has other businesses have upon the result? When would other farmers selling grain be merchants and in what circumstances would they not be merchants? What affect does the definition of merchant have on the legal issue(s)?

(2) Is a farmer with a lessee's interest in cattle a "merchant" within the meaning of the Code (provided that the farmer-lessee in possession of the property has the power to transfer ownership to a buyer in the ordinary course of business)? See *Bauer v. Curran*, 360 N.W.2d 88 (Iowa 1984), in which the court held that whether a farmer is a "merchant" is an issue of fact, not of law, and therefore a question for the trier of fact. The *Bauer* court outlined three basic forms of merchant status:

> Merchant status is said to take three forms: The first is transactional in nature: The seller is a dealer in the type of goods involved in the questioned transaction. The second form involves the merchant who holds himself out as having some skill or knowledge focusing on the specific transaction and goods involved. The third revolves around the principal-agent relationship. See Article, *Is He or Isn't He a Merchant? The Farmer, Part I*, 82 Com. L.J. 155, 1 56-57 (May 1977).

The Iowa court has held that a farmer, in order to be a merchant, must be:

> (1) [A] dealer who deals in goods of the kind involved, or (2) he must by his occupation hold himself out as having knowledge or skill peculiar to the practices or goods involved in the transaction, or (3) he must employ an agent, broker or other intermediary who by his occupation holds himself out as having knowledge or skill peculiar to the practices or goods involved in the transaction.

In the immediate case Carl Davidson, a farmer, leased approximately 100 head of cattle from plaintiff in the spring of 1979. Davidson did not receive title to the cattle and did not have any authority to transfer them. In the fall of 1980, Davidson sold sixteen cow-calf pairs to Curran. Curran later sold these cow-calf pairs through defendant Russell Sale Co. Mr. Curran at no time attempted to discover whether Davidson actually owned the cattle. The relevant section of the Iowa Code (section 554.2403(2)) provides:

> Any entrusting of possession of goods to a merchant who deals in goods of that kind gives him power to transfer all rights of the entrustor to a buyer in ordinary course of business.

The evidence provided a sufficient basis for a decision either way on Davidson's status. Prior to the sale in question, there was evidence that Davidson had bought, sold, and leased cattle. One year, for example, Davidson leased approximately twenty head of cattle from another individual and in addition had entered into a lease-purchase agreement with a Clearview Cattle Company. Matthew Bauer, the individual who had leased the present cattle to Davidson, testified that although he had engaged in a large number of transactions in buying and selling cattle in the area, he had never seen or met Davidson prior to 1980 when they entered into the lease agreement in question.

Most other cattle sales involving Davidson were said by him to be merely attempts to cull his herd, and, while Davidson had earlier sold part of these cattle leased from plaintiff Bauer, he had done so under Bauer's name and at his direction. Davidson appears to have only occasionally bought or sold cattle.

While other factors tended to support a finding that Davidson may have been a merchant, our question is not whether there was evidence to support a finding the jury did not make but whether reasonable minds could have drawn different inferences from the facts. We conclude they could and that the issue was therefore properly submitted to the jury.

[C]   Good Faith

Read: U.C.C. §§ 1-203, 1-201(19), 2-103(1)(b), 2-309(3).

Read also: U.C.C. § 2A-103(2); CISG Art. 7(1).

PROBLEM 1.12

Although your client had a written agreement to buy Gulfcoast Marina at a fixed price from the Standard Oil Company, the Standard now denies that there is a contract. When asked to acknowledge that there was a contract and fulfill its obligation, Standard's Sales officer laughed and said "See you in court." This denial of the contract caused serious damages for Gulfcoast Marina. Can your client successfully assert that this denial of a contract is in violation of good faith? Can you successfully argue for both compensatory and punitive damages?

PROBLEM 1.13

In a contract between the Green Company and the Red Company a price was set for the first two shipments, and a contract term that said the parties would later negotiate a price as to the third shipment. The Red Company maintains that the price for that third shipment must be the maximum price allowed by the contract and has refused to negotiate on it. As the counsel for Green, what is your strategy?

NOTE

(1) The case of *Seaman's Direct Buying Serv. v. Standard Oil,* decided by the *California Supreme Court*, 36 Cal. 3d 752, 206 Cal. Rptr. 354, 686 P.2d 1158 (Cal. 1984), involved a

situation similar to that in Problem 1.12. Standard Oil denied the existence of a contract, Seaman's sued, and the court stated the major issue:

For breach of contract the jury awarded compensatory damages of $397,050. For tortious breach of the implied covenant of good faith and fair dealing, they awarded $397,050 in compensatory damages and $11,058,810 in punitive damages.

The court went on to note:

While the proposition that the law implies a covenant of good faith and fair dealing in all contracts is well established, the proposition advanced by Seaman's — that breach of the covenant always gives rise to an action in tort — is not so clear. In holding that a tort action is available for breach of the covenant in an insurance contract, we have emphasized the "special relationship" between insurer and insured, characterized by elements of public interest, adhesion, and fiduciary responsibility. No doubt there are other relationships with similar characteristics and deserving of similar legal treatment.

When we move from such special relationships to consideration of the tort remedy in the context of the ordinary commercial contract, we move into largely uncharted and potentially dangerous waters. Here, parties of roughly equal bargaining power are free to shape the contours of their agreement and to include provisions for attorney fees and liquidated damages in the event of breach. They may not be permitted to disclaim the covenant of good faith but they are free, within reasonable limits at least, to agree upon the standards by which application of the covenant is to be measured.[2] In such contracts, it may be difficult to distinguish between breach of the covenant and breach of contract, and there is the risk that interjecting tort remedies will intrude upon the expectations of the parties. This is not to say that tort remedies have no place in such a commercial context, but that it is wise to proceed with caution in determining their scope and application.

For the purposes of this case it is unnecessary to decide the broad question which Seaman's poses. Indeed, it is not even necessary to predicate liability on a breach of the implied covenant. It is sufficient to recognize that a party to a contract may incur tort remedies when, in addition to breaching the contract, it seeks to shield itself from liability by denying in bad faith and without probable cause, that the contract exists.

It has been held that a party to a contract may be subject to tort liability, including punitive damages, if he coerces the other party to pay more than is due under the contract terms through the threat of a lawsuit, made "without probable cause and with no belief in the existence of the cause of action." There is little difference, in principle, between a contracting party obtaining excess payment in such manner, and a contracting party seeking to avoid all liability on a meritorious contract claim "justified expectations" are established, "good faith" requires the parties to act "reasonably" in light of those expectations.

In commercial contracts which lack those characteristics, the expectations and purposes of the parties necessarily differ from those of insurer and insured. Thus, the requirements of good faith in a commercial contract are different than the requirements imposed on an insurer. While those requirements are probably less stringent in a commercial context, *they definitely exist.*

___

[2] California's Commercial Code section 1102 prohibits disclaimer of the good faith obligation, as well as the obligations of diligence, reasonableness and care, but provides that "the parties may by agreement determine the standards by which the performance of such obligations is to be measured if such standards are not manifestly unreasonable."

Certain expectations derive from assumptions so basic to the very notion of a contract that they are shared by virtually all contracting parties. Foremost among these is the expectation that a breaching party will compensate the other party for losses caused by the breaching party's failure to perform. The availability of contract damages, in turn, supports the equally fundamental assumption that breach is a foreseeable and, in most situations, acceptable possibility.

Indeed, the assumption that parties may breach at will, risking only contract damages, is one of the cornerstones of contract law. "[I]t is not the policy of the law to compel adherence to contracts, but only to require each party to choose between performing in accordance with the contract and compensating the other party for injury resulting from a failure to perform. This view contains an important economic insight. In many cases it is uneconomical to induce the completion of the contract after it has been breached." (Posner, Economic Analysis of Law (1972) p. 55.) In most commercial contracts, recognition of this economic reality leads the parties to accept the possibility of breach, particularly since their right to recover contract damages provides adequate protection.

For example, one party to a contract may decide to breach if it concludes that the market will bring a higher price for its product than that set forth in the contract. In commercial contracts, the risk of such a breach is widely recognized and generally accepted. "[I]ntentional, willful, selfishly induced breach[es] of contract [are] often an anticipated, expected and encouraged reality of commercial life." (Diamond, *The Tort of Bad Faith Breach of Contract: When, If At All, Should It Be Extended Beyond Insurance Transactions?* (1981) 64 Marq. L. Rev. 425, 438).

When the breaching party acts in bad faith to shield itself entirely from liability for contract damages, however, the duty of good faith and fair dealing is violated.

This type of conduct violates the non-breaching party's justified expectation that it will be able to recover damages for its losses in the event of a breach. The expectation must be protected. Otherwise, the acceptance of the possibility of breach by the contracting parties and by society as a whole may be seriously undermined.

There is no danger that permitting tort recovery for bad faith denial of the existence of a valid commercial contract will make every breach of contract a tort. First, the vast majority of contract breaches in the commercial context do not involve this type of bad faith conduct.

Second, "it [is] well established in this state that if the cause of action arises from a breach of a promise set forth in the contract, the action is ex contractu, *but if it arises from a breach of duty growing out of the contract it is ex delicto.*" (Emphasis added.) Thus, tort "[l]iability is imposed not for a bad faith breach of the contract, but for failure to meet the duty. . .included within the implied covenant of good faith and fair dealing." There are many situations in which a defendant's actions may sound both in tort and contract. The fact that overlapping remedies may exist in some situations does not make every breach of contract a tort.

Similarly, an attempt to avoid any liability for contract damages may involve a discrete course of conduct or it may be indistinguishable from the breach of contract itself. "Breach of the covenant provides the injured party with a tort action for "bad faith," notwithstanding that the acts complained of may also constitute a breach of contract.

It is a well-established principle of law that the parties' reasonable expectations should govern the determination of what conduct constitutes a tortious breach of the implied covenant of good faith and fair dealing. Application of that principle is fully warranted here. The duty of good faith and fair dealing was violated because a party attempted to avoid all liability for a contract breach by denying, in bad faith, the very existence of the contract. Such conduct violates the nearly universal expectation that the injured party will be compensated for losses caused by the breaching party's failure to perform. This tort remedy was recognized by this court in its earlier decisions involving the implied covenant of good faith and fair dealing. Those decisions should be the basis for the holding here.

II.

A breach of contract may also constitute a tortious breach of the covenant of good faith and fair dealing in a situation where the possibility that the contract will be breached is not accepted or reasonably expected by the parties.

This could happen, for example, if at the time of contracting, the parties expressly indicate their understanding that a breach would be impermissible. Or, it could happen if it were clear from the inception of the contract that contract damages would be unavailable or would be inadequate compensation for a breach. Under these circumstances, a breach of the contract could well constitute a tortious breach of the duty of good faith and fair dealing.

These are just a few examples. If a plaintiff can show that, under the circumstances or characteristics of his contract, he was justified in expecting that the other party would not breach, then a voluntary breach by that party could well constitute a violation of the duty to deal fairly and in good faith.

On this record, there is ample evidence to support the conclusion that the parties' reasonable expectations did not include the possibility of breach. Standard was repeatedly informed that Seaman's needed a "binding commitment." Throughout the negotiations, there was an emphasis on the need for such a commitment and for a stable relationship between Seaman's and its supplier. Standard knew that Seaman's lease, and, to some extent, the entire marina development depended on these factors. Under these circumstances, it would be reasonable to conclude that the parties' justified expectations did not include the possibility of breach.

Under this cause of action, no independent showing of bad faith should be required. Where the possibility of breach was not reasonably expected at the inception of the contract, the voluntary breach of an acknowledged contract is in itself a violation of the duty to deal fairly and in good faith.

Standard's breach did not take the form of a refusal to perform under the terms of an acknowledged contract. Instead, Standard denied the existence of the contract to the federal agency and subsequently refused to stipulate to its existence. This action was tantamount to a denial. Those denials constituted anticipatory breaches of the contract.

In this setting, the simple fact that a breach occurred will not support tort recovery without a showing of bad faith. Just as a denial of the existence of a binding contract provides the basis for tort liability only upon a finding of bad faith, a contract breach predicated upon such a denial will support tort recovery on the theory of unexpected and unacceptable breach only if the denial is found to have been made in bad faith.

III.

The trial court failed to include a bad faith requirement in its instruction on the duty to refrain from denying the existence of a binding contract. This failure constituted error. Recovery will lie in tort if the denial was made in bad faith.

Standard's denial of the existence of the contract to the federal agency and the subsequent refusal to stipulate were anticipatory breaches of the contract. Neither the breach nor the underlying resistance to an assertion of contract liability is a tort if undertaken in good faith. In this case, however, Standard did not deny that a contract existed until it had been ordered by the federal government to supply fuel to Seaman's. Moreover, Standard did not make its denials forthrightly as a defense to an action for breach of contract. It used them as a trump card in its final attempt to avoid all liability for nonperformance The timing and the intended effect of both denials tend strongly to establish that they were made in bad faith.

I would affirm the judgment for Seaman's for breach of contract and breach of the duty of good faith and fair dealing.

(2) In *City Builders Supply Co. v. National Gypsum Co.*, 39 U.C.C. Rep. 826 (D. Mass. 1984), plaintiffs and defendant entered into a distributorship agreement. The agreement, entered into during September, 1979, contained no termination clause. Under the agreement, defendant would extend credit for and furnish vinyl siding and other merchandise.

On September 25, 1980, defendant advised plaintiff that it was pleased with plaintiff's performance and raised its credit limit from $125,000 to $200,000. In further praising plaintiff's performance and indicating many more profitable years for each company, defendant again raised the credit limit on December 22, 1980, to $300,000.

On January 8, 1981, defendant canceled the distributorship agreement, after secretly negotiating an agreement with a new distributor. Plaintiffs alleged that this was a breach of the duty of good faith in two respects: first, that the termination without notice was an unfair trade practice, and second, that the sale of $200,000 worth of goods to plaintiff without disclosing the impending termination was also a breach of good faith.

The district court adopted the Magistrate's Recommendation in favor of summary judgment for defendant on the first issue since plaintiff failed to prove damages. The court, however, denied defendant's motion for summary judgment on the second issue because of the defendant's "duplicitous" actions of praising plaintiff's performance and increasing its credit line while simultaneously planning to terminate the distributorship agreement.

(3) In *Goldstein v. S. & A. Restaurant Corp.*, 42 U.C.C. Rep. 81 (D.D.C. 1985), plaintiff and defendant had entered an agreement whereby plaintiff would buy meat from defendant, process it, and then distribute it to defendant's retail restaurants. Between April 1 and June 19, 1981, S. & A. paid Goldstein approximately $3.2 million for the processing and distribution of the meat. Largely due to his decision to divert funds to his real estate ventures, Goldstein fell behind between $1.15 and $ 1.5 million in his payments for the meat.

After a series of negotiations involving such things as post-dated checks and a $1 million, 30-day note, Goldstein and S & A. finally negotiated a new agreement containing a 10-day notification in the event of cancellation by either party. In October, 1981, S. & A. gave Goldstein 10 days' notice and canceled the agreement.

The district court found that the series of agreements signed by Goldstein, a sophisticated businessman, and the justifiable insecurity on the part of S. & A. occasioned by the large debt were sufficient to defeat any allegations by Goldstein of duress or bad faith by S. & A.

(4) In *First National Bank in Libby v. Twombly*, 39 U.C.C. Rep. 1192 (Mont. 1984) defendant had negotiated a secured loan with the Bank. When it became apparent that there would be difficulty in paying the note at maturity, one of the Bank officers agreed to transform the note into an installment loan. The original note came due while this officer was on vacation, whereupon the Bank withdrew $2,865 from Twombly's checking account, leaving a balance of $1.65, without first notifying Twombly.

The Montana Supreme Court held that the lower court erred by not submitting punitive damages to the jury. The court reasoned that punitive damages may be recoverable where the duty to exercise good faith is imposed by law rather than by the contract itself.

(5) Compare *Weyerhauser Co. v. Godwin Bldg. Supply,* 253 S.W.2d. 625 (1979). In *Weyerhauser* defendant asserted that Weyerhauser said it would "provide unlimited ninety percent (90%) conventional financing at locally competitive rates [up to] forty thousand dollars ($40,000) per house." However, the contractual agreement only provided that Weyerhauser would "assist dealer in arranging interim and permanent mortgage financing for Weyerhauser Registered Homes." Weyerhauser subsequently refused to provide financing as agreed and argued that "it had no duty to provide financing but only to assist in arranging financing." Without reference to the U.C.C. section on good faith which is pertinent and would have supported its decision, the court found that it is

> a basic principle of contract law that a party who enters into an enforceable contract is required to act in good faith and to make reasonable efforts to perform his obligations under the agreement. "Good faith and fair dealing" are required of all parties to a contract; and each party to a contract has the duty to do everything that the contract presupposes that he will do to accomplish its purpose.

The court went on to say that there was sufficient evidence for a jury to find that Weyerhauser had failed to make reasonable efforts to assist Godwin in obtaining financing; the jury verdict against Weyerhauser for $100,000 was upheld.

(6) In *Riveridge Associates v. Metropolitan*, 774 F. Supp. 897 (D.N.J. 1991), the issue of lack of good faith in bringing the action was raised. In that case, Riveridge had borrowed $11.5 million from its partner, Metropolitan. It alleged in an action against Metropolitan that the latter had refused to allow pre-payment of the loan and that this refusal was in violation of their agreement and a violation of fiduciary duties. The court granted a summary judgment in favor of Metropolitan, finding no law, fiduciary or otherwise, that would permit such pre-payment. Metropolitan counterclaimed that Riveridge had acted in bad faith in bringing this groundless claim and action. Riveridge's motion to dismiss, viewing the alleged facts in the most favorable light for Metropolitan, was denied by the court. It noted that while the case would have to be tried on this point, if bad faith of Riveridge's were shown, then Riveridge would be liable for all counsel fees and punitive damages. It also noted that while Riveridge's suit might not be deemed frivolous under Rule N, this was not proper standard to be used in judging its good faith or lack thereof.

[D]   Unconscionability Theory

PROBLEM 1.14

Your client needs some high speed diamond cutting equipment, to replace its current equipment which suddenly broke, in order to prepare for the New York Annual Jewelry Fair starting the next day. The salesman for the Belgium seller does not mention or point out the disclaimer clause in a printed standardized contract which is signed hastily in order to assure immediate air shipment. The cutting equipment arrives the next morning, but after two days breaks down. The Belgium company points out the disclaimer and refuses to fix the machine or return the payment. Your client wishes to argue that the disclaimer is unconscionable. What other facts do you need to know? Can your client argue unconscionability?

Read: U.C.C. §§ 2-302, 2-719(3).

Read also: U.C.C. §§ 2A-108, 2A-503(3); CISG Art. 4(a).

Section 2-302 of the U.C.C. sets forth the principle of unconscionability.

What is an "unconscionable" term? What criteria are to be used? What factors does the comment suggest be taken into account? How are these to be determined? Is the comment statement on "economic" strength clear? To what degree, if any, does this factor enter it?

The question of what constitutes unconscionability was raised in the New York Revision Commission studies. A reply was made by the late Karl Llewellyn, who had served as the Chief Reporter for the U.C.C.

Llewellyn, 1 N.Y. Law Rev. Comm. Rep., 177-178 (1954)

The same is true of the much controverted section on unconscionability. What now goes on— and this is a thing that I can't prove in any speech like this, and it would take an awful long time to bring the cases and gather them to show what now goes on—is that there is a practice among business lawyers to do a thing that no intelligent engineer would think of doing. I can't understand it. I never have understood it, but I observe that it is there.

Business lawyers tend to draft to the edge of the possible. Any engineer makes his construction within a margin of safety, and a wide margin of safety, so that he knows for sure that he is getting what he is gunning for. The practice of business lawyers has been, however—it has grown to be so in the course of time—to draft, as I said before, to the edge of the possible.

Let me rapidly state that I do not find that this is desired by the business lawyers' clients. In all the time that I have been working on this Code, and before, one of the more striking phenomena has been to me that the lawyers insist on having all kinds of things that their clients don't want at all.

This kind of thing does not make for good business, it does not make for good counseling, and it does not make for certainty. It means that you never know where you are, and it does a very bad thing to the law indeed. The bad thing that it does to the law is to lead to precedent after precedent in which language is held not to mean what it says and indeed what its plain purpose was, and that upsets everything for everybody in all future litigation.

We believe that if you take this and bring it out into the open, if you say, "When it gets too stiff to make sense, then the court may knock it out," you are going to get a body of principles of construction instead of principles of misconstruction, and the precedents are going to build up so that the language will be relied upon and will be construed to mean what it says.

We believe further that this particular section is safeguarded to a curious degree. Have you gentlemen really looked it over to see how carefully safeguarded it is to lead into principles of true construction?

The section is 2-302, and the first thing that happens is that it is taken completely out of the realm of the jury. Anything that is done under this section is going to make precedent, and the precedents can be recorded and the precedents can accumulate and guide. That is No. 1.

If the court finds the contract or any clause of the contract to be unconscionable, it may refuse to enforce the contract or may strike any unconscionable clauses and enforce the contract as if the stricken clause had never existed. That is court action, and it is reviewable. That is No. 1, and it makes precedents and guides.

Secondly, in order that we may not be left to the untutored imagination of courts that don't know the situation, in order that cases where very careful insistence, for example, upon very exact performance is reasonable because that is the way business has to be done in that trade, you have the second provision which allows all kinds of background to be presented to instruct the court. We count this, therefore, by no means as a section which threatens certainty. We regard it instead as a section which greatly advances certainty in a now most baffling, most troubling, and almost unreckonable situation.

———

Llewellyn, THE COMMON LAW TRADITION[3]

370, 371 (1960)

And the true answer to the whole problem seems, amusingly, to be one which could occur to any court or any lawyer, at any time, as readily as to a scholar who had spent a lifetime on the subject-though I doubt if it could occur to anyone without the inquiry and analysis in depth which we owe to the scholarly work.

The answer, I suggest, is this: Instead of thinking about "assent" to boiler plate clauses, we can recognize that so far as concerns the specific, there is no assent at all. What has in fact been assented to, specifically, are the few dickered terms, and the broad type of the transaction, and but one thing more. That one thing more is a blanket assent (not a specific assent) to any not unreasonable or indecent terms the seller may have on his form, which do not alter or eviscerate the reasonable meaning of the dickered terms. The fine print which has not been read has no business to cut under the reasonable meaning of those dickered terms which constitute the dominant and only real expression of agreement, but much of it commonly belongs in.

The queer thing is that where the transaction occurs without the fine print present, courts do not find this general line of approach too hard to understand: thus in the cases Prausnitz gathers, in regard to what kind of policy an oral contract for insurance contemplates; nor can I see a

---

court having trouble, where a short memo agrees in due course to sign "our standard contract," in rejecting an outrageous form as not being fairly within the reasonable meaning of the term. The clearest case to see is the handing over of a blank check: no court, judging as between the parties, would fail to reach for the circumstances, in determining whether the amount filled in had gone beyond the reasonable.

Why, then, can we not face that fact where boiler-plate is present? There has been an arm's-length deal, with dickered terms. There has been accompanying that basic deal another which, if not on any fiduciary basis, at least involves a plain expression of confidence, asked and accepted, with a corresponding limit on the powers granted: the boiler plate is assented to en bloc, "unsight, unseen," on the implicit assumption and to the full extent that (1) it does not alter or impair the fair meaning of the dickered terms when read alone, and (2) that its terms are neither in the particular nor in the net manifestly unreasonable and unfair. Such is the reality, and I see nothing in the way of a court's operating on that basis, to truly effectuate the only intention which can in reason be worked out as common to the two parties, granted good faith. And if the boiler-plate party is not playing in good faith, there is law enough to bar that fact from benefiting it. We had a hundred years of sales law in which any sales transaction with explicit words resulted in two separate contracts for the one consideration: that of sale, and the collateral one of warranty. The idea is applicable here, for better reason: any contract with boiler-plate results in two severable contracts: the dickered deal, and the collateral one of supplementary boilerplate.

Rooted in sense, history, and simplicity, it is an answer which could occur to anyone.

King, NEW CONCEPTUALISM OF THE UNIFORM COMMERCIAL CODE: ETHICS, TITLE, AND GOOD FAITH PURCHASE[4]

In contemporary society, however, an even more important factor may be that of time. One of the parties to the contract may not feel that he has the time or the energy to devote to a full reading of a lengthy form contract. Were he to devote such time to the reading and understanding of each term of every transaction into which he entered, a substantial portion of his life might be spent in the reading of form contracts rather than in the use of articles being purchased. It is not unrealistic to say that many individuals, even those with considerable education, find that they do not have the time to search through contracts for hidden disclaimers or other limitations of remedy.

King, THE TORT OF UNCONSCIONABILITY: A NEW TORT FOR NEW TIMES
23 Saint Louis U. L.J. 124 (Conclusion) (1979)[5]

The tort of unconscionability exists now and need only be recognized by the courts. Unconscionable acts or practices have been severely condemned by courts and recognized as contributing to social problems and injustice. Even though the courts have not explicitly recognized unconscionability as a tort, there is an adequate basis in statutes, dicta and reason for doing so.

---

[4] Copyright 1968 by Fred Rothman & Co. Reprinted by permission.
[5] Copyright 1979 by Saint Louis U. L.J. Reprinted by permission.

Unconscionable acts and conduct also are recognized as a legal wrong by consumer protection statutes and hence clearly satisfy the tort definition of a legal wrong. Since this legislation already deems unconscionable conduct a legal wrong, it is in effect acknowledging the tort of unconscionability although not expressly doing so. The Uniform Consumer Credit Code recognizes that unconscionable conduct is a legal wrong and may exist in several ways: in the making of unconscionable terms or provisions, in the conduct inducing debtors to enter into such transactions, or in unconscionable terms. The Model Consumer Credit Act, the Uniform Consumer Sales Act, and the New York City Consumer Protection Law, also recognize that unconscionable acts or conduct are legal wrongs.

Unconscionable conduct and practices cause considerable harm to the individual. This may encompass not only payments which he has made, but also other expenses that he has incurred. In addition, the unconscionable conduct frequently creates mental and emotional suffering for its victim. It also may create an added legal obstacle to recovery where there is a very real legal right and may require the incurring of otherwise unneeded additional legal expenses. . . .

As a matter of public policy it would seem that persons who suffer harm from the unconscionable conduct of others should be permitted to recover compensation for that harm. Indeed, they are allowed to do so in most other situations unless there is a legal reason to deprive them of compensation for the harm. Further, since unconscionability is already recognized as a legal wrong, they are being given "a right without a remedy" to the extent that their harm is not compensated.

Recognition of the tort of unconscionability has several major advantages for the consumer. One is that he is compensated for all of the harm which he has suffered, rather than simply having the contract declared unenforceable. Another is that he is placed in a more strategic position for effectuating a fair settlement. Punitive damages for this tort in some situations would further the consumer's action and have a broader impact as well. If the only detriment that the seller may suffer in a court case is that the contract will be declared unconscionable and hence unenforceable, he has nothing to lose turning down the consumer's claims and fighting the case all the way. On the other hand, if the seller is confronted with the tort of unconscionability which carries with it more compensatory damages and possible punitive damages, a settlement is more likely. Still another advantage of the tort of unconscionability is that it may serve as the basic cause of action in a class action suit or an injunction proceeding which will simultaneously benefit many consumers.

In our society some manufacturers and sellers have engaged in deliberate and outrageous unconscionable practices which have affected millions of people. Although one may invoke unconscionable concepts in regard to a particular contract clause or a particular transaction, this is insufficient. It is necessary that unconscionable acts and conduct be recognized as a tort so as to permit persons to recover for all of the harm they have suffered and to promote the courts to assess punitive damages when proper. If this is done, and the injunctive remedy also is utilized, many of the unconscionable practices of manufacturers and sellers may be restricted. The new tort of unconscionability may be a significant tool for achieving consumer justice.

PROBLEM 1.15

Your client, Green Dwarf, is a small produce company operating in Hidden Valley. It needs some machinery to process its pea crop. It purchases some farm machinery which turns out to be very inadequate, squashing all the peas. The seller's standard form printed contract contains a disclaimer of all warranties clause in bold print and a disclaimer of consequential damages in small print. The seller of the machinery points to the disclaimers and denies any legal liability. What arguments can your client make? On what basis?

PROBLEM 1.16

Your client has sold some computerized equipment to a Canadian publisher in Toronto. After four months the equipment has a serious problem requiring major repair. Your client's contract was a standard form printed one with an italicized disclaimer clause as to any defects or other problems occurring after three months. The Canadian firm refuses to make any further payments, and asserts that the disclaimer clause is unconscionable. The printed contract has no provision as to what law shall be applicable. What other facts do you need? What is your advice?

ADAMS v. AMERICAN CYANAMID CO.

Nebraska Court of Appeals
21 U.C.C. Rep Serv 2d 962, 498 N.W.2d 577 (1992)

This appeal arises from an action based on theories of strict liability and breach of warranty of merchantability under the Uniform Commercial Code. William Timothy "Tim" Adams and Carol Adams brought suit against American Cyanamid Company, and Panhandle Cooperative Association for damages sustained to a crop of edible beans which was lost after a herbicide manufactured by American Cyanamid was applied to the Adamses' field [a limitation of remedies clause in the contract was held unconscionable]. The jury awarded a judgment for the Adamses in the amount of $193,500 against American Cyanamid. American Cyanamid appeals. We affirm in part, and in part reverse and remand for a new trial.

The defendant first claims that the trial court erred by not holding a conscionability hearing on its limitation of remedy.

Guaranteed Foods v. Rison, 207 Neb. 400, 407, 229 N.W.2d 507, 512 [30 U.C.C. Rep Serv 1248] (1980), states that "the issue of unconscionability must be pleaded in order to be considered by the court." The issue of unconscionability was raised in the Adamses' reply to the defendant American Cyanamid's answer.

Limitations of remedies are governed by § 2-719(3), which states that "[c]onsequential damages may be limited or excluded unless the limitation or exclusion is unconscionable." Section 2-302 requires that the trial court make a conscionability determination for contracts in general; however, § 2-719 is silent on the issue.

We believe that the requirement that an unconscionability hearing be held under § 2-302 also applies to determinations of whether limitations of remedies are unconscionable under § 2-719(3). However, § 2-302(2) requires only that a party be afforded a reasonable opportunity to be heard. So long as sufficient evidence has been adduced concerning the commercial setting, purpose, and effect of the clause or contract, it is not necessary that a special hearing be held to determine whether a limitation of remedies is unconscionable. Rather, the issue may be raised at any time in the proceeding. In the case at bar, sufficient evidence had been adduced concerning the enforceability of the exclusion of consequential damages. The defendant had a reasonable opportunity to request a hearing on the issue of the enforcement of the provision excluding consequential damages. It never requested a hearing.

The defendant claims that it was error for the trial court not to address the unconscionability of the exclusion. Since the issue is likely to arise again on remand, we provide direction for the lower court by determining in advance whether American Cyanamid's limitation of remedies is unconscionable.

The concept of conscionability is not defined by the Code. The supreme court has quoted with approval from the comments to § 2-302: "The basic test is whether in the light of the general commercial background and the commercial needs of the particular trade or case, the clauses involved are so one-sided as to be unconscionable *under the circumstances existing at the time of the making of the contract. . .*" (Emphasis in original.) *T.V. Transmission v. City of Lincoln,* 220 Neb. 887, 896, 374 N.W.2d 49 (1985).

Although the test is stated in *T.V. Transmission,* we have not found a Nebraska case that has applied it. Accordingly, we must determine how the concept of unconscionability is to be applied. The Code's concept of unconscionability developed in the context of consumer transactions. Since our concern here is solely with a commercial contract, we must determine how the concept applies in a commercial setting.

Generally, the issue of unconscionability is divided into substantive unconscionability and procedural unconscionability. "Substantive unconscionability involves those cases where a clause or term in the contract is alleged to be one-sided or overly harsh, while procedural unconscionability relates to impropriety during the process of forming a contract." *Schroeder v. Fageol Motors,* 86 Wash.2d 256, 260, 544 P.2d 20, 23 [18 U.C.C. Rep. Serv. 584] (1975). Generally, a contract is not substantively unconscionable unless the terms are grossly unfair under the circumstances as they existed at the time the contract was formed. See *Guthmann v. La Vida Llena,* 103 N.M. 506, 709 P.2d 675 (1985). An often-quoted formulation of substantive unconscionability is the following:

"In determining reasonableness or fairness, the primary concern must be with the terms of the contract considered in light of the circumstances existing when the contract was made. The test is not simple, nor can it be mechanically applied. The terms are to be considered 'in the light of the general commercial background and the commercial needs of the particular trade or case.' Corbin suggests the test as being whether the terms are 'so extreme as to appear unconscionable according to the mores and business practices of the time and place.'"

Williams v. Walker-Thomas Furniture Company, 350 F.2d 445, 450 [2 U.C.C. Rep. Serv 955] (D.C. Cir.1965). Accordingly, to determine whether a contract clause is substantively unconscionable, a court asks "whether under the circumstances existing at the time of making of the contract, and in light of the general commercial background and commercial needs of a particular case, clauses are so one-sided as to oppress or unfairly surprise one of the parties." *Barnes v. Helfenbein,* 548 P.2d 1014, 1020 (Okla. 1976).

In the present case, the limitation of consequential damages clause would leave the herbicide user without any substantial recourse for his loss. "One-sided agreements whereby one party is left without a remedy for another party's breach are oppressive and should be declared unconscionable." *Durham v. Ciba-Geigy Corp.,* 315 N.W.2d 696, 700 [33 U.C.C. Rep Serv 588] (S.D. 1982). *See, also, Campbell Soup Co. v. Wentz,* 172 F.2d 80 (3d Cir. 1948). We conclude that the provision excluding consequential damages is substantively unconscionable. The remaining question, therefore, is whether there is evidence of procedural unconscionability. The factors involved in determination of procedural unconscionability have been formulated in *American Nursery v. Indian Wells,* 115 Wash.2d 217, 797 P.2d 477 [12 U.C.C. Rep Serv 2d

928] (1990). In *American Nursery,* the court stated that a clause excluding damages may be found to be conscionable when "the general commercial setting indicates a prior course of dealing or reasonable usage of trade as to the exclusionary clause." *Id.* at 223, 797 P.2d at 481. Otherwise,

> [u]nconscionability is determined in light of all the surrounding circumstances, including (1) the manner in which the parties entered into the contract, (2) whether the parties had a reasonable opportunity to understand the terms of the contract, and (3) whether the important terms were hidden in a maze of fine print.

Id. at 222, 797 P.2d at 481. None of the factors is conclusive; rather, unconscionability is determined under the totality of the circumstances.

Although the evidence supports the conclusion that there is a trade practice among chemical firms related to excluding consequential damages, we find it unreasonable to impose the trade practice on the Adamses. In selecting Prowl herbicide, Adams was merely following the advice of Johnson. He was not independently assessing the risks involved in the use of particular chemicals; and the use of middlemen, as in the case at bar, appears to be a common trade practice in the agricultural industry.

Therefore, we examine the totality of the circumstances. In this case, Adams was in no position to bargain with American Cyanamid. Johnson testified that all herbicide manufacturers place the same disclaimers on their products. Moreover, Adams testified that he did not receive the label containing the exclusion until he had problems with his crops. Even if we disregard the fact that Adams may not have received the contract terms at the time of purchase, the language of the exclusion is not such as to be immediately understandable by a layperson such as Adams. The exclusion specifically excludes "indirect" damages, but allows direct damages without specifying the extent of such damages.

This is a situation where the Adamses had no alternative other than to accept the manufacturer's exclusion. The undisputed evidence is that Adams could not purchase any manufacturer's herbicide without such an exclusion. The Adamses were not in a position to bargain with the defendant for more favorable terms than those set out in the preprinted label. Nor were they in a position to test the effectiveness of the herbicide prior to purchase. As Adams expected, the herbicide he purchased killed the weeds in his crop. However, quite unexpectedly and unfortunately, the herbicide also destroyed his crop.

If the evidence is believed, to permit the defendant to escape all consequential responsibility by inserting a limitation of consequential damage clause, as in this case, would leave a farmer without any substantial recourse for his loss. We conclude that under the circumstances presented here, the exclusion is procedurally unconscionable. Having found the exclusion both substantively and procedurally unconscionable, we decline to enforce it.

NOTES

(1) In *A & M Produce Co. v. FMC Corp.,*186 Cal. Rptr. 114, 135 Cal. App. 3d 473 (1982), decided by the California Court of Appeals, Fourth District, the owner of a small business signed a form contract for the purchase of tomato processing equipment.

Mr. Abatti was informed by Mr. Walker and Mr. Isch of FMC Corporation (FMC) that their equipment was so fast that no hydrocooler was necessary and they bid $15,299.55 for the weightsizer. Mr. Abatti signed a "field order" and made a $5,000 deposit. After plans (including a 20-foot extension of Mr. Abatti's building) were drawn up by FMC's engineers, FMC mailed

Mr. Abatti a form contract with a total price of $32,041.80. The contract contained a disclaimer of warranty in bold print and a disclaimer of consequential damages in smaller print. He signed the contract and returned it with a down payment. The equipment never functioned properly.

The court noted that the principal question involved was:

Whether the trial court erred in concluding that FMC's attempted disclaimer of warranties and exclusion of consequential damages was unconscionable and therefore unenforceable. Before we can answer that question however, we must first concern ourselves with the nature of the unconscionability doctrine.

The Uniform Commercial Code does not attempt to precisely define what is or is not "unconscionable." Nevertheless, "[u]nconscionability has generally been recognized to include an absence of meaningful choice on the part of one of the parties together with contract terms which are unreasonably favorable to the other party." (*Williams v. Walker-Thomas Furniture Company*, (DC Cir 1965) 350 F.2d 445, 449 fn omitted.) Phrased another way, unconscionability has both a "procedural" and a "substantive" element.

The procedural element focuses on two factors: "oppression" and "surprise." "Oppression" arises from an inequality of bargaining power which results in no real negotiation and "an absence of meaningful choice." "Surprise" involves the extent to which the supposedly agreed-upon terms of the bargain are hidden in a prolix printed form drafted by the party seeking to enforce the disputed terms. Characteristically, the form contract is drafted by the party with the superior bargaining position.

Of course the mere fact that a contract term is not read or understood by the non-drafting party or that the drafting party occupies a superior bargaining position will not authorize a court to refuse to enforce the contract. Although an argument can be made that contract terms not actively negotiated between the parties fall outside the "circle of assent" which constitutes the actual agreement, commercial practicalities dictate that unbargained for terms only be denied enforcement where they are also substantively unreasonable. No precise definition of substantive unconscionability can be proffered. Cases have talked in terms of "overly-harsh" or "one-sided" results. One commentator has pointed out, however, that "unconscionability turns not only on a 'one-sided' result, but also on an absence of 'justification' for it," which is only to say that substantive unconscionability must be evaluated as of the time the contract was made. The most detailed and specific commentaries observe that a contract is largely an allocation of risks between the parties, and therefore that a contractual term is substantively suspect if it reallocates the risks of the bargain in an objectively unreasonable or unexpected manner. But not all unreasonable risk reallocations are unconscionable; rather, enforceability of the clause is tied to the procedural aspects of unconscionability (see ante), such that the greater the unfair surprise or inequality of bargaining power, the less unreasonable the risk reallocation which will be tolerated.

Although there is little California precedent directly on point, the importance of both the procedural and substantive elements of unconscionability finds support by analogy in the recent decision by the California Supreme Court.

[The court discussed a California case where a music promoter booked concerts for a group using a standard form contract prepared by the musicians' union providing that all disputes were to be settled by an arbitrator selected by the union. The court found that this was a contract of adhesion since virtually all prominent musicians were in the union. Although the promoter was not surprised by the arbitration clause, the court held it unconscionable since it did not meet the "minimum levels of integrity" that are required for arbitration clauses.]

With these considerations in mind, we must now determine whether the trial court in this case was correct in concluding that the clauses in the FMC form contract disclaiming all warranties and excluding consequential damages were unconscionable. In doing so, we keep in mind that while unconscionability is ultimately a question of law, numerous factual inquiries bear upon that question. The business conditions under which the contract was formed directly affect the parties relative bargaining power, reasonable expectations, and the commercial reasonableness of the risk allocation as provided in the written agreement. To the extent there are conflicts in the evidence or in the factual inferences which may be drawn therefrom, we must assume a set of facts consistent with the court's finding of unconscionability if such an assumption is supported by substantial evidence.

Turning first to the procedural aspects of unconscionability, we note at the outset that this contract arises in a commercial context between an enormous diversified corporation (FMC) and a relatively small but experienced farming company (A & M). Generally, ". . .courts have not been solicitous of businessmen in the name of unconscionability." This is probably because courts view businessmen as possessed of a greater degree of commercial understanding and substantially more economic muscle than the ordinary consumer. Hence, a businessman usually has a more difficult time establishing procedural unconscionability in the sense of either "unfair surprise" or "unequal bargaining power."

Nevertheless, generalizations are always subject to exceptions and categorization is rarely an adequate substitute for analysis. With increasing frequency, courts have begun to recognize that experienced but legally unsophisticated businessmen may be unfairly surprised by unconscionable contract terms and that even large business entities may have relatively little bargaining power, depending on the identity of the other contracting party and the commercial circumstances surrounding the agreement. This recognition rests on the conviction that the social benefits associated with freedom of contract are severely skewed where it appears that had the party actually been aware of the term to which he "agreed" or had he any real choice in the matter, he would never have assented to inclusion of the term.

Both aspects of procedural unconscionability appear to be present on the facts of this case. Although the printing used on the warranty disclaimer was conspicuous, the terms of the consequential damage exclusion are not particularly apparent, being only slightly larger than most of the other contract text. Both provisions appear in the middle of the back page of a long preprinted form contract which was only casually shown to Abatti. It was never suggested to him, either verbally or in writing, that he read the back of the form. Abatti testified he never read the reverse side terms There was thus sufficient evidence before the trial court to conclude that Abatti was in fact surprised by the warranty disclaimer and the consequential damage exclusion. How "unfair" his surprise was is subject to some dispute. He certainly had the opportunity to read the back of the contract or to seek the advice of a lawyer. Yet as a factual matter, given the complexity of the terms and FMC's failure to direct his attention to them, Abatti's omission may not be totally unreasonable. In this regard, the comments of the Indiana Supreme Court in *Weaver v. American Oil Company,* 276 N.E.2d 147-148 (Ind. 1972) are apposite:

> The burden should be on the party submitting [a standard contract] in printed form to show that the other party had knowledge of any unusual or unconscionable terms contained therein.

The principle should be the same as that applicable to implied warranties, namely that a package of goods sold to a purchaser is fit for the purposes intended and contains no harmful materials other than that represented.

Here, FMC made no attempt to provide A & M with the requisite knowledge of the disclaimer or the exclusion. In fact, one suspects that the length, complexity and obtuseness of most form contracts may be due at least in part to the seller's preference that the buyer will be dissuaded from reading that to which he is supposedly agreeing. This process almost inevitably results in a one-sided contract.

Even if we ignore any suggestion of unfair surprise, there is ample evidence of unequal bargaining power here and a lack of any real negotiation over the terms of the contract. Although it was conceded that A & M was a large-scale farming enterprise by Imperial Valley standards, employing five persons on a regular basis and up to fifty seasonal employees at harvest time, and that Abatti was farming some 8,000 acres in 1974, FMC Corporation is in an entirely different category. The 1974 gross sales of the Agriculture Machinery Division alone amounted to $40 million. More importantly, the terms on the FMC form contract were standard. FMC salesmen were not authorized to negotiate any of the terms appearing on the reverse side of the preprinted contract. Although FMC contends that in some special instances, individual contracts are negotiated, A & M was never made aware of that option. The sum total of these circumstances leads to the conclusion that this contract was a "bargain" only in the most general sense of the word.

Although the procedural aspects of unconscionability are present in this case, we suspect the substantive unconscionability of the disclaimer and exclusion provisions contributed equally to the trial court's ultimate conclusion. As to the disclaimer of warranties, the facts of this case support the trial court's conclusion that such disclaimer was commercially unreasonable. The warranty allegedly breached by FMC went to the basic performance characteristics of the product. In attempting to disclaim this and all other warranties, FMC was in essence guarantying nothing about what the product would do. Since a product's performance forms the fundamental basis for a sales contract, it is patently unreasonable to assume that a buyer would purchase a standardized mass-produced product from an industry seller without any enforceable performance standards. From a social perspective, risk of loss is most appropriately borne by the party best able to prevent its occurrence.

Rarely would the buyer be in a better position than the manufacturer/seller to evaluate the performance characteristics of a machine.

In this case, moreover, the evidence establishes that A & M had no previous experience with weight-sizing machines and was forced to rely on the expertise of FMC in recommending the necessary equipment. FMC was abundantly aware of this fact. The jury here necessarily found that FMC either expressly or impliedly guaranteed a performance level which the machine was unable to meet. Especially where an inexperienced buyer is concerned, the seller's performance representations are absolutely necessary to allow the buyer to make an intelligent choice among the competitive options available. A seller's attempt, through the use of a disclaimer, to prevent the buyer from reasonably relying on such representations calls into question the commercial reasonableness of the agreement and may well be substantively unconscionable. The trial court's conclusion to that effect is amply supported by the record before us.

As to the exclusion of consequential damages, several factors combine to suggest that the exclusion was unreasonable on the facts of this case. Consequential damages are a commercially recognized type of damage actually suffered by A & M due to FMC's breach. A party ". . . should be able to rely on their existence in the absence of being informed to the contrary . . ." This factor is particularly important given the commercial realities under which the contract was executed. If the seller's warranty was breached, consequential damages were not merely "reasonably foreseeable"; they were explicitly obvious. All parties were aware that once the tomatoes began to ripen, they all had to be harvested and packed within a relatively short period of time.

Another factor supporting the trial court's determination involves the avoidability of the damages and relates directly to the allocation of risks which lies at the foundation of the contractual bargain. It has been suggested that "[r]isk shifting is socially expensive and should not be undertaken in the absence of a good reason. An even better reason is required when to so shift is contrary to a contract freely negotiated." But as we noted previously, FMC was the only party reasonably able to prevent this loss by not selling A & M a machine inadequate to meet its expressed needs. "If there is a type of risk allocation that should be subjected to special scrutiny, it is probably the shifting to one party of a risk that only the other party can avoid."

In summary, our review of the totality of circumstances in this case, including the business environment within which the contract was executed, supports the trial court's determination that the disclaimer of warranties and the exclusion of consequential damages in FMC's form contract were unconscionable and therefore unenforceable. When non-negotiable terms on preprinted form agreements combine with disparate bargaining power, resulting in the allocation of commercial risks in a socially or economically unreasonable manner, the concept of unconscionability as codified in Uniform Commercial Code § 2-302 and § 2-719, subdivision (3), furnishes legal justification for refusing enforcement of the offensive result.

The majority affirmed the trial court finding of unconscionability. There was also a short concurring opinion which stated:

Facts fly as "thick as autumnal leaves that strow the brooks of Vallombrosa," in support of the trial court's conclusion these contract clauses were oppressive, contrary to oral representations made to induce the purchase, and unreasonably favorable to the party with a superior bargaining position. No experienced farmer would spend $32,000 for equipment which could not process his tomatoes before they rot and no fair and honest merchant would sell such equipment with representations negated in its own sales contract.

(2) In *Industralease Automated & Scientific Equip. Corp. v. R.M.E. Enterprises, Inc.,* 396 N.Y.S.2d 427 (1977), the court considered the issue of whether disclaimers of express or implied warranties are unconscionable under circumstances where the equipment fails to operate. In Industralease, defendant picnic grove owner-operator entered into a lease for the use of rubbish incinerators. Plaintiff subsequently informed defendant that the initial lease was "no good" and asked that he sign "new papers." The new lease contained an unqualified disclaimer of express and implied warranties. The incinerators were delivered and installed properly but did not "then or thereafter work." Defendant then demanded removal of the incinerators from his property, but plaintiff refused to accede and insisted upon timely receipt of the monthly payments. The trial court held that the disclaimer of warranties was not unconscionable as a matter of law. On appeal, the court found that the new contract which eliminated the warranties was entered into

under an "atmosphere [of] haste and pressure" which was "clearly pervasive." The court also found that since the summer season for defendant's operations had already begun, defendant was clearly disadvantaged at this point in the bargaining. The court also explicitly refused to "divorce entirely" events which occur after the time of the making of the contract, even though it recognized that U.C.C. § 2-302 applied only to the time of making of the contract. The court held that the disclaimer of warranties was unconscionable under the circumstances and that the express warranties to the defendant concerning the incinerators had been breached. Judgment for defendant was affirmed.

PROBLEM 1.17

Your senior partner is on the Permanent Editorial Board of the American Law Institute, which has been asked by the Director to consider whether the Article 2 section on unconscionability should be revised so as to parallel the Article 2A unconscionability section. While much of § 2A-108 follows § 2-302, it does contain this addition:

(2) With respect to a consumer lease, if the court as a matter of law finds that a lease contract or any clause of a lease contract has been induced by unconscionable conduct or that unconscionable conduct has occurred in the collection of a claim arising from a lease contract, the court may grant appropriate relief.

In addition, it provides that if the court finds unconscionability, the court shall award the lessee attorney fees. In subsection 4, the court may award the lessor attorney fees if it decides that the lessee knew the claim was groundless. Your senior partner asks for your opinion on the matter. He also gives you an article with the excerpt that follows:

In paragraph 3 of the section on unconscionability, the drafters seem to encourage an attack on unfair and unconscionable lease terms by providing that if one prevails on the unconscionability claim, he or she shall also prevail as to attorney fees. Without this provision, many attorneys might never take an unconscionability case because the amounts involved are often not great enough to justify participation on their part. by assuring attorney fees, paragraph 3 makes it practical for lawyers to attack the unfair contract or lease clauses.

Unfortunately, paragraph 4(b) of the same section destroys the possibility of attacks on unfair clauses by placing the risk of huge attorney fees for the other side on the consumer. This paragraph deals the "death blow" to unconscionability claims. Indeed, it makes the other three sections virtually meaningless. While paragraph 4(b) may seem logical to some on the surface, its impact is disastrous.

Paragraph 4(b) provides that if a judge deems any unconscionability claim to be groundless, then attorney fees may be assessed against the party raising it. "Groundless" is so nebulous and uncertain that it makes it risky for consumers to assert unconscionability. The term is not defined in either the text or comments, and what is "groundless" to one person may not seem so to another. For example, one might view the lease clause as harsh, one-sided, and unconscionable, while another might justify it on the basis of the lessor's need to discipline lessees or to avert any possible risks; one might view the unread and hidden standard form lease clause as "unfair surprise," while another might say consumers have a duty to read the entire contract.

If an attorney asserts a new theory of unconscionability, a judge unfortunately might find it to be groundless. As pointed out in the American Law Institute ("A.L.I.") discussion, would the judges have held the assertion by Brandeis and Warren of the right of privacy as a new theory groundless? Some judges might have! Yet this theory eventually became a major part of the law.

The doctrine of unconscionability has only been used in the last several decades and may still undergo considerable development. In this regard, a number of theories are likely to be asserted and accepted by the courts in the coming years. Also, unconscionability could be recognized in an increasing number of situations. Nevertheless, in this period of uncertainty and development, some courts will hesitate to find unconscionability. Many judges may be conservative and see the unconscionability claim as "groundless." In a fair number of unknown cases, paragraph 4 will indeed be evoked against the party raising unconscionability with a most serious impact.

From King, *Major Problems with Article 2A: Unfairness, "Cutting Off" Consumer Defenses, Unfiled Interests, and Uneven Adoption*, 43 Mercer L. Rev. (1992).

§ 1.07 Further Developments: The Next Millennium

While future developments are never certain, various trends and developments make their occurrence most probable. Reform of the Uniform Commercial Code in several major aspects will take place in the near future. There is already a new U.C.C. Article 5 on Letters of Credit, now contained in the new official text of the code (1995). The work on U.C.C. Article 2 is continuing and the revision of it should be completed around 1998. In addition, Article 2B on the Licensing of Information is proceeding ahead in its draft stages. It also should be promulgated in the official text of the U.C.C. in the next several years. A new section 402A on Strict Liability for Defective Products is also in the process of being formulated.

PROBLEM 1.18

Your law professor in commercial law has been asked to give a talk at a "millennium conference." He has asked you as his research assistant to assist him in formulating some ideas and also in filling out some points of his:

(1) The major reforms of the U.C.C. will finally be in place. With the previous revisions of Articles 3 and 4 on Negotiable Paper and Article 5 on Letters of Credit, the promulgated revised Article 2 on Sales and the new Article 2A on Licensing of Technology will complete current revision efforts. As the states enact them into law, there will be one or two decades without much further activity in this regard. Gradually, of course, there will be some case law interpretation taking place.

(2) The whole area of services will require a review. The Sale of Goods will become proportionately less important and the sale of services will gain. There will need to be a look at that entire area and its relationship to the principles found in the U.C.C.

(3) There will be more comparisons made with the laws of other countries and with developing international standards. Courts will cite the laws and cases in other countries for their persuasive value. Law reform organizations will also undertake more comparative studies and base some of their revisions on developments abroad.

(4) Commercial law attorneys will be more conversive with both U.S. and comparative laws. Many will spend some of their time in offices in the U.S., but also more time travelling or serving in branch offices abroad.

(5) There will be a greater use of mediation and arbitration in solving commercial disputes. In addition, there may be some special commercial courts established to facilitate the settling of disputes.

(6) An international commercial law court, similar to that proposed by Professor King in § 1.04, will be established to oversee court interpretations of the Convention on the International Sale of Goods and other developing commercial law principles.

Please give these matters some thought and also note any ideas of your own.

CHAPTER 2

SCOPE: SUBJECT MATTER OF THE CONTRACT FOR SALE

§ 2.01 Applicability of U.C.C. Article 2—Transactions Included and Excluded

Read: U.C.C. §§ 2-102 (see § 9-206(2)), 2-105, 2-106 (see § 2-304), 2-107, 2-314(1)).

Read also: U.C.C. §§ 2A-102, 2A-103(1)(j) and (h) and (e) and (g), 1-201(37), 9-102(2), 2A-104 (1990); CISG Arts. 1-6, 10, 95.

Article 2 of the Uniform Commercial Code is entitled "Sales." Section 2-102 makes it clear that Article 2 deals with goods: "Unless the content otherwise requires, this Article applies to transactions in goods. . ." The Code does not define "transaction." Arguably, a transaction is broader than a "sale," and therefore includes leases and other arrangements relating to goods which are not technically sales.

Section 2-106 offers a definition of "sale": "A 'sale' consists in the passing of title from the seller to the buyer for a price." Section 2-105 defines "goods": " 'Goods' means all things. . . which are movable at the time of identification to the contract other than the money in which the price is to be paid, investment securities (Article 8) and things in action."

As to the application of the Code by analogy, see § 1.03[D] above and U.C.C. §§ 1-102 Comment 1, 2-105 Comment 1 (last paragraph), and 2-313 Comment 2. See also, Proposed Final Draft of U.C.C. Article 2A Leases.

———

[A] Goods or Services

PROBLEM 2.1

Your client, Robert Rich, recently entered into a contract with the Olympia Pool Company for construction of a pool with a diving board which the company then built. While engaged in diving, Robert fell from the side of the diving board and was badly injured. Robert asserted that the skid resistant material built into the surface of the top of the diving board stopped one inch short of each edge. This condition, he claims, made the board defective. The Olympia Pool Company denies any liability. Is the U.C.C. applicable to this transaction? What possible arguments or theories can be used by the parties in regard to this point? Which do you think will prevail?

(Matthew Bender & Co., Inc.)

(Pub.087)

NOTE

Two major tests, the "Predominant" factor test and the "Gravamen" test have been used by the courts. These were discussed in the *Anthony Pools* case: (295 Md. 285, 455 A.2d 434, 35 U.C.C. Rep. 498, 1983):

> Here, Anthony undertook the construction of an in ground, steel reinforced, gunite swimming pool with hand finished plaster surfacing, tile trim and coping. The Sheehans were not buying steel rods, or gunite, or plaster or tiles. The predominant factor, the thrust, the purpose of the contract was the furnishing of labor and service by Anthony, while the sale of the diving board was incidental to the construction of the pool itself. The question thus resolves itself into whether the predominant purpose test, which we applied in *Burton* for the purpose of determining whether the U.C.C. statute of limitations governed that transaction, should be applied to determine whether the sale of the diving board, included in the Anthony Sheehans transaction, carries an implied warranty of merchantability under § 2-314.

> Were the predominant purpose test mechanically to be applied to the facts of this case, there would be no quality warranty implied as to the diving board. But here the contract expressly states that Anthony agrees not only to construct the swimming pool, but also to sell the related equipment selected by the Sheehans. The Sheehans are described as "Buyer." The diving board itself is not structurally integrated into the swimming pool. Anthony offered the board as an optional accessory, just as Anthony offered the options of purchasing a pool ladder or a sliding board. When identified to the contract, the diving board was movable. See CL § 2-105. The board itself remains detachable from its support, as reflected by a photograph in evidence. The diving board, considered alone, is goods. Had it been purchased by the Sheehans in a transaction distinct from the pool construction agreement with Anthony, there would have been an implied warranty of merchantability.

A number of commentators have advocated a more policy-oriented approach to determining whether warranties of quality and fitness are implied with respect to goods sold as part of a hybrid transaction in which service predominates. See Farnsworth, *Implied Warranties of Quality in Non-Sales Cases,* 57 Colum. L. Rev. 653 (1957); Comment, *Sale of Goods in Service-Predominated Transactions,* 37 Fordham L. Rev. 115 (1968); Note, *Products and the Professional; Strict Liability in the Sale-Service Hybrid Transaction,* 24 Hastings L.J. 111(1972); Note, *Contracts for Goods and Services and Article 2 of the Uniform Commercial Code,* 9 Rut-Cam L.J. 303 (1978); Comment, *Sales-Service Hybrid Transactions. A Policy Approach,* 28 Sw L.J. 575 (1974). To support their position, these commentators in general emphasize loss shifting, risk distribution, consumer reliance and difficulties in the proof of negligence. These concepts underlie strict liability in tort.

A leading case applying a policy approach in this problem area is *Newmark v. Gimbel's Incorporated,* 54 N.J. 585,258 A.2d 697(1969). There the patron of a beauty parlor sued for injury to her hair and scalp allegedly resulting from a lotion used in giving her a permanent wave. Because the transaction was viewed as the rendering of a service, the trial court had ruled that there could be no warranty liability. The intermediate appellate court's reversal was affirmed by the Supreme Court of New Jersey which reasoned in part as follows (*Id.,* at 593, 258 A.2d at 701):

> The transaction, in our judgment, is a hybrid partaking of incidents of a sale and a service. It is really partly the rendering of service, and partly the supplying of goods for a

consideration. Accordingly, we agree with the Appellate Division that an implied warranty of fitness of the products used in giving the permanent wave exists with no less force than it would have in the case of a simple sale. Obviously in permanent wave operations the product is taken into consideration in fixing the price of the service. The no-separate-charge argument puts excessive emphasis on form and downgrades the overall substance of the transaction. If the beauty parlor operator bought and applied the permanent wave solution to her own hair and suffered injury thereby, her action in warranty or strict liability in tort against the manufacturer-seller of the product clearly would be maintainable because the basic transaction would have arisen from a conventional type of sale. It does not accord with logic to deny a similar right to a patron against the beauty parlor operator or the manufacturer when the purchase and sale were made in anticipation of and for the purpose of use of the product on the patron who would be charged for its use. Common sense demands that such patron be deemed a customer as to both manufacturer and beauty parlor operator. [Citations omitted.]

The court was careful to limit its holding to commercial transactions, as opposed to those predominantly involving professional services. *Id.* at 596-97, 258 A.2d at 702-703.

1 R. Anderson, Uniform Commercial Code (1970), § 2-102:5 at 209 refers to *Newmark* as illustrative of a possible trend in the law and states:

> It is probable that a goods-services transaction will come to be subjected to Article 2 of the Code insofar as the contractor's obligations with respect to the goods themselves are involved, at least where the goods involved could have been purchased in the general market and used by the plaintiff-customer.

A warranty of fitness for particular purpose under § 2-315 of the U.C.C.was implied in *Worrell v. Barnes,* 87 Nev. 204, 484 P.2d 573 (1971). In that case a contractor was engaged to do some carpentry work and to connect various appliances in the plaintiff's home to an existing liquified petroleum gas system. The appliances were not supplied by the contractor. Suit was for damage to the plaintiff's home resulting from a fire. The plaintiff produced evidence that the fire was caused by a defective fitting installed by the contractor which had allowed propane to escape. Dismissal of the plaintiff's claims, based on the Nevada version of strict liability in tort and based on implied warranty, was reversed. The court reasoned that, because it had held that the contractor had sold a product so as to bring into operation the doctrine of strict liability, "so also must we deem this case to involve 'goods' within the purview of the Uniform Commercial Code." *Id.* at 208, 484 P.2d at 576.

1 W. Hawkland, Uniform Commercial Code Series (1982), § 2-102:04, at Art. 2, p 12 has suggested what might be called a "gravamen" test in light of the decision in *Worrell.* He writes:

> Unless uniformity would be impaired thereby, it might be more sensible and facilitate administration, at least in this grey area, to abandon the "predominant factor" test and focus instead on whether the gravamen of the action involves goods or services. For example, in *Worrell v. Barnes,* if the gas escaped because of a defective fitting or connector, the case might be characterized as one involving the sale of goods. On the other hand, if the gas escaped because of poor work by Barnes the case might be characterized as one involving services, outside the scope of the U.C.C.

In this state, the provisions of CL § 2-316.1(1) and (2) reflect an implicit policy judgment by the General Assembly which prevents the mechanical application of the predominant purpose test to cases like the one under consideration. Subsection (1) states that § 2-316, dealing in part with the manner in which an implied warranty of merchantability may be excluded or modified, does not apply to "consumer goods. . . services, or both." Under subsection (2) language "used by a seller of consumer goods and services" to exclude or modify implied warranties is unenforceable. The hybrid transaction is covered by, or at least embraced within, those terms.

Under the predominant purpose test, as applied by a majority of the courts, a hybrid transaction must first be classified as a sale of goods in order for there to be U.C.C. based, implied warranties on the goods included in the transaction. If goods predominate and they are consumer goods, an all or nothing classification of the instant transaction under the predominant purpose test would mean there could be no U.C.C. based, implied warranties on the diving board.

The gravamen test of Dean Hawkland suggests the vehicle for satisfying the legislative policy. Accordingly, we hold that where, as part of a commercial transaction, consumer goods are sold which retain their character as consumer goods after completion of the performance promised to the consumer, and where monetary loss or personal injury is claimed to have resulted from a defect in the consumer goods, the provisions of the Maryland U.C.C. dealing with implied warranties apply to the consumer goods, even if the transaction is predominantly one for the rendering of consumer services.

Thus the diving board which Anthony sold to the Sheehans as part of the swimming pool construction contract carried an implied warranty of merchantability under CL § 2-314.

PROBLEM 2.2

Your client, Educational Resources Inc., recently decided to modernize in several ways:

1. it contracted to have its office system computerized and every person's office now has a computer supposedly appropriate for each person's type of work;

2. it contracted for a computer system connecting the main office with the branch operating as to office matters and inventory supplies;

3. it has joined Internet, an information system;

4. it has purchased a software system which is supposedly designed to produce educational tests which Educational Resources can sell.

None of these systems are working satisfactory and it wished to sue for breach of contract. What other facts do you need to know? Would the U.C.C. be applicable?

GEOTECH ENERGY CORP. v. GULF STATES

Court of Appeals of Texas, Houston (14th Dist.)
788 S.W.2d 386 (1990)

CANNON, JUSTICE.

Geotech Energy Corporation [Geotech] appeals from a judgment on the jury's verdict in favor of Gulf States Telecommunications [Gulf States] in a breach of contract case. Geotech alleges the trial court erred (1) by submitting an instruction concerning substantial performance, (2) by refusing to submit an issue on mitigation of damages, (3) by denying Geotech's motion for continuance, (4) by refusing to submit an issue on the effect of reciprocal promises, (5) in awarding damages based on insufficient evidence, and (6) by submitting an issue on bad faith filing of a Deceptive Trade Practices Act claim. We affirm the judgment of the trial court.

On June 27, 1986, Geotech and Gulf States signed a contract. Under the terms of the contract Gulf States was to install a used OKI Spectrum 100A telephone system; Geotech was to arrange for payment to Gulf States through a third-party leasing company. Geotech negotiated a lease agreement with its usual leasing company, Corporate Funding. When Geotech signed a certificate of acceptance for the telephone system, Corporate Funding was then to pay Gulf States.

The equipment was installed and the necessary software written by Chuck Toney, vice president of Gulf States. After a few problems were corrected, the system was verbally accepted by Joel Brown of Geotech. Both Brown and Linda McNaspy, vice president of Geotech, assured Gulf States the certificate of acceptance would be signed by Michael Reedy, one of Geotech's owners, who was in California at the time and the person to whom the certificate was sent.

The record reflects that when Reedy returned from California he was unhappy with the appearance of the telephone, because they did not look sufficiently "high tech." Geotech then began a series of meritless complaints about the phone system. Toney made daily calls at Geotech to attempt to correct the alleged problems. Eventually Gulf States offered to remove the OKI system and replace it with an alternate one, if an inspection by a neutral third-party found it to be defective. Geotech refused to allow such an inspection.

Ultimately, Geotech had the system dismantled and refused to pay Gulf States. Gulf States sued for breach of contract. Geotech answered and counterclaimed against Gulf States for violations of Tex. Bus. & Com. Code Ann. §§ 17.41-17.826 (Vernon 1987 & Supp. 1990) [more commonly referred to as the Deceptive Trade Practices Act, or DPTA].

Geotech's first point of error contends the trial court erred by including an instruction on substantial performance in the jury's charge. Since Geotech raised no objection to the language of the instruction given, we are only concerned with the question of whether an instruction on substantial performance was proper in this case.

Geotech argues the doctrine of substantial performance is inapplicable because this case is controlled by Chapter 2 of Tex. Bus. & Com. Code Ann. (Vernon 1968 & Supp. 1989) [more commonly referred to as the Uniform Commercial Code, or the U.C.C.]; alternatively, it contends that the doctrine is strictly limited to cases involving breach of construction or employment contracts. We disagree with both propositions.

Chapter Two of the U.C.C., by its express terms, applies only to contracts involving the sale of goods. Tex. Bus. & Com. Code Ann. §§ 2.102, 2.106 (Vernon 1968). The contract before us does not fall within its scope.

Appellant concedes the contract involves both goods and services. When faced with such a hybrid contract we must determine whether the essence of the contract is the sale of materials or services. Obviously telephone equipment, the hardware, is a necessary component for the installation of telephone services. However, the hardware alone would be useless to a buyer. The record reveals the telephone system in question is a very sophisticated model. A significant degree of expertise on the part of Gulf States' representative, Chuck Toney, was necessary to install the hardware. Further, even with the equipment installed, Toney's services in writing the

not goods

software were essential to make the phone system operable and to customize it to meet Geotech's specific needs. The contract itself is written as a contract for service: "Gulf States shall perform and/or deliver services on the Customer's premises. . . ." Since the essence of this contract is services, not goods, it does not fall within the scope of the U.C.C.

not a sale

Even if we assume, *arguendo*, that the contract essentially involves goods, the U.C.C. does not apply because the contract does not provide for the sale of goods to Geotech. Section 2-106 of the U.C.C. specifies that a sale "consists in the passing of title from the seller to the buyer for a price." Geotech opted to lease the equipment through a third-part leasing company instead of purchasing it outright. The record reveals Geotech asserted there was no sale, that Geotech would never own the equipment; rather, the leasing company would own it. By Geotech's own admission, title would never pass to it, so no sale was to occur.

Geotech asserted during oral argument that it would have had an option to buy the equipment at the end of the lease term, and that the lease agreement with Corporate Funding assigned to appellant all of Corporate Funding's rights against Gulf States. We note that the copy of the lease agreement between Geotech and Corporate Funding in the record does not contain a purchase option. Further, Geotech did not bring this action as assignee of Corporate Funding's rights. In fact, though its contract with Gulf States required Geotech to enter into a binding lease agreement, Geotech's pleadings refer to the lease as "the proposed lease" and assert that Corporate Funding returned it to Geotech stamped "void" after Geotech refused to sign the certificate of acceptance. Geotech cannot meet the U.C.C. requirement for the passage of title by claiming supposed rights created by an instrument that Geotech has previously asserted is void as a result of its own actions.

Since the U.C.C. is inapplicable, the trial court correctly applied common law principles to the case. Geotech contends that Texas law limits consideration of substantial performance to those cases involving breach of construction and employment contracts. However, a review of the case law reveals that substantial performance is applied to a broad range of contract cases. [cases cited:] (upheld jury finding of substantial performance of a contract for the right of first refusal to purchase property); (applied doctrine to an oil-field drilling contract); (upheld jury finding of substantial compliance with a contract for sale of crops).

Geotech has cited no authority excepting their agreement with Gulf States from the general principles of contract law, which include the doctrine of substantial performance. Gulf States plead full performance, which supports the submission of an instruction on substantial performance. Since both the pleadings and the evidence supported submission of an instruction on substantial performance, the trial court did not err. Point of error number one is overruled.

COMMUNICATIONS GROUPS, INC. v. WARNER COMMUNICATIONS

Civil Court of the City of New York, New York County
138 Misc.2d 80, 527 N.Y.S.2d 341 (1988)

LEONARD N. COHEN, JUDGE.

Plaintiff Communications Groups, Inc. ("CGI") moves to dismiss defendant Warner Communications, Inc.'s ("Warner") first through third counterclaims which are identical to defendant's second through fourth affirmative defenses, respectively, pursuant to CPLR 3211(a)(1), (a)(7) and (b).

This action arises out of an alleged breach of a written agreement dated July 18, 1986 for the licensing, installation and servicing of a certain computer software package (the "Agreement"). Subsequently, the parties entered into two subcontract for additional software and related hardware. As per the Agreement, defendant paid 50% of the amount due upon signing the Agreement. The remaining 50% was to be paid upon installation of the software. It is undisputed that defendant has not paid this remaining amount due under the Agreement.

The complaint, dated October 23, 1987, sets forth three causes of action for breach of contract to recover payment in the total amount of $16,650.00 still due and owing from defendant to plaintiff. Defendant does not dispute nonpayment, but defendant's Answer asserts four affirmative defenses and three counterclaims: breach of an implied warranty of fitness of the computer software for defendant's specified known purposes; breach of an express and/or implied warranty of merchantability of the software system and the good working order of its system and repair services; and the breach of contract in failing to provide support service to keep the system operational and in good working order.

As to the counterclaims alleging implied warranties of merchantability and fitness for a specified known business purpose, the movant, CGI, contends that the Agreement provided for a software system or package which was neither for a tangible and movable product or goods nor a transaction for a sale or lease of either services or goods. Rather, CGI claims the Agreement was a license for computer software as an intangible service for limited use by defendant of "copyrightable information" and for the acquisition of the "abstract right" only "to listen" as with music on a record or disk. As a consequence, CGI argues that since implied warranties of fitness for a particular purpose or merchantability are remedies exclusively for contracts of the sale of goods and because the Agreement herein is not such a transaction of goods, the implied warranty counterclaims lack merit and cannot be maintained either under common law or under the Uniform Commercial Code (U.C.C.).

Moreover, movant contends that even if the contract was for a sale of goods or a lease of goods, the contract, by its terms, provides for an express disclaimer of any implied warranties of fitness and merchantability.

As for the third counterclaim, movant characterizes this claim as a breach of express warranties of the good working order and adequate support services of the computer software. Movant contends that such express warranties are lacking under the terms of the Agreement. Movant argues that any prior or subsequent oral promises or warranties which may have been made by movant cannot be considered part of the agreement based on the parol evidence rules under common law and the U.C.C.

The threshold issue presented is whether the software computer package or system provided issue for under the Agreement involved a transaction of "goods" as defined under U.C.C. 2-105(1) to mean "all things (including specially manufactured goods) which are movable at the time of identification to the contract for sale . . . ."

A review of the Agreement, the sole documentary and evidentiary matter submitted on these motion papers, shows that the computer software referred to therein is not defined. Nor have either of the parties in their motion papers articulated the precise form of the instant software. Software, however, is a widely used term and has several meanings. [cases cited] (software includes programs and computer language listings); (software includes magnetic cards or paper cards programmed to instruct the computer); (software refers to programs used in the computer); see generally, *Note, Computer Programs As Goods Under The U.C.C.*, 77 Mich. L. Rev. 1149 (1979).

Regardless of the software's specific form or use, it seems that computer software, generally, is considered by the courts to be a tangible, and movable item, not merely an intangible idea or thought and therefore qualifies as a "good" under Article 2 of the U.C.C. Moreover, U.C.C. Sec. 1-102 provides that the Act shall be liberally construed and applied to promote its underlying purposes and policies.

Here, the Agreement clearly provides, in part, for the installation by CGI of its specially designed software equipment for defendant's particular telephone and computer system, needs and purposes. This equipment is expressly listed on schedules annexed and made a part of the Agreement. Said schedules clearly reflect installation by CGI of identifiable and movable equipment such as recording, accounting and traffic analysis and optimizations, modules, buffer, directories and an operational user guide and other items. A review of the counterclaim allegations shows that a software computer system and equipment were designed for defendant's special and unique known needs to store data relating to thousand of defendant's monthly telephone calls and to process and print this data on defendant's main computer frame so that defendant's operations would prove more time and labor efficient. Although the ideas and concepts of the CGI designed software system remained its intellectual and copyrightable property under the Agreement, the court finds in the context of the case law and the U.C.C. that the contract terms clearly provided for a transaction of computer software equipment involving movable, tangible and identifiable products or goods and not solely intangible ideas and services and, in fact, such goods were installed by CGI for defendant's special purposes. Therefore, the first and second counterclaims are not dismissable on the ground of an exclusive contractual intangible services transaction as urged by movant.

The next issue raised by movant is that the contractual transaction failed to constitute either a sale or lease but merely was a license to use and service the software, therefore precluding defendant from relying on the common law of the U.C.C. implied warranties of merchantability (U.C.C. Sec. 2-314) and fitness for a particular known purpose (U.C.C. 2-315).

The court finds that the Agreement clearly constituted a lease for the use of CGI's goods despite the terms expressed therein of a "license to use" CGI "proprietary" software for the payment of a one-time perpetual license fee in accordance with attached pricing schedules. The Agreement, although labelled a license agreement, is clearly analogous to a lease for chattels or goods. The movant has not addressed nor presented a distinction, factually or legally, between a license to use goods from an ordinary lease to use goods. Plaintiff's argument is based on an alleged contractual license to provide intangible services which, as hereinabove, the court rejects. Therefore, the court finds the Agreement clearly is a lease for the use of plaintiff's goods, despite the contractual label of a "license."

The law is clear that common law rights exist to state a cause of action or counterclaim for breach of implied warranties of merchantability and/or fitness for a particular known purpose involving the lease of chattels or goods without reliance on the U.C.C. The cases cited by movant suggesting the non-existence of common law rights of implied warranties are inapposite as they involve the provision of contractual services as distinguished form products and goods as found hereinabove.

Therefore, the defendant has sufficiently stated in its first and second counterclaims a common law breach of implied warranties under a contractual lease of goods. However, these counter-claims allege a purchase and sale of the software products. In this regard the contract specifically provided that the CGI software was to be its sole and exclusive property and upon termination of the agreement the defendant would return the software to CGI. Thus, CGI contends the transaction was not a sale within the meaning of U.C.C. Sec. 2-106 (U.C.C. 2-401) as no title passed from seller to buyer for a price and therefore defendant is precluded from asserting U.C.C.'s implied warranties.

However, New York courts have liberally construed the meaning of "transaction" under U.C.C. 2-102, choosing to analyze the underlying facts of the agreement at issue in determining whether it sufficiently resembles a sale.

Courts in this jurisdiction have consistently applied Article 2 of the U.C.C. to the leasing of chattels. Even if the lessor retains title to the goods, where the contract price of a lease is as large as the sales price of the same item, the transaction is analogous to a sale and will be covered by U.C.C.

Therefore, the analysis used by the courts in this jurisdiction to determine whether or not a lease sufficiently resembles a sale so as to bring it within the scope of the U.C.C. may be applicable to the Agreement herein. Although the Agreement specifically provides that plaintiff will retain title to the software, the Agreement appears to have no term and, in fact, is referred to as a "perpetual license." The economic effect of the Agreement is unclear from the sole submitted documentary evidence of the Agreement itself. Despite the Agreement spelling out the fee to be paid by defendant to plaintiff for use of the software, the court lacks information as to the actual value of the software. *But see* Note, op. cit. 77 Mich. L. Rev. 1149, 1156. ("The economic result of a software loan is indistinguishable from a software sale. The price is apt to be the same in either case," *citing United States Leasing Corp., supra.*)

Neither party has submitted an affidavit by a person with knowledge of the transaction at issue nor is the intent of the parties and surrounding circumstances of the whole transaction between the parties clear from the Agreement alone as to whether this transaction was a sale or only a lease of computer software goods. In the context of the case law, as hereinabove, the contractual retention of title to the goods by CGI in and of itself is not determinative of whether this lease transaction resembled a sale for U.C.C. applicability. There are factual triable issues raised in this regard and therefore dismissal of the implied warranty counterclaims for a sale for failure to sufficiently state a counterclaim of affirmative defense is not warranted. The court for purposes of this type of motion must accept the facts as alleged in the counterclaim as true. Here there is a sufficient showing to support legally cognizable counterclaims for the breach of implied warranties of fitness and merchantability for a sale of goods within the scope of the U.C.C.

Finally, as the first and second counterclaims, the CGI contention that the Agreement contains an express and/or implied disclaimer of implied warranties lacks merit. The contractual provision relied on by CGI in this regard fails to alert or call to defendant's attention the exclusion of any warranty of merchantability or fitness for a particular known purpose but relates solely to CGI's maintenance, service and repair obligations for the software systems. Nor does this clause use the words "merchantability," "fitness," "disclaimer," "as is," "warranty," or "all faults."

The courts look to the relevant sections of the U.C.C., and even movant refers to the U.C.C., to test the validity of warranty disclaimers. The above words or other commonly understood language must be set forth in the contract, specifically and conspicuously, to call attention to the exclusion of warranties and make plain that there is no implied warranty in order to validate the exclusion of implied warranties. U.C.C. Sec. 2-316 and Sec. 1-201(10); Therefore the plaintiff's motion to dismiss the first and second counterclaims is denied.

Turning to that branch of the motion to dismiss the defendant's third counterclaim for failure to sufficiently state a cause of action, movant characterizes it as a claim for breach of an express warranty for a "good working order software system and for adequate support services." However, a review of the allegations of this counterclaim shows that it is clearly based on a breach of contract. The Agreement expressly states the CGI will provide "maintenance services" after installation of the system for the "reparation of any failure, malfunction, defects or non-conformity in CGI Software which prevents such CGI software from performing in accordance with the specifications, documentation and criteria set forth in this agreement and any attachments thereto." The Agreement further provides that "The liability of CGI for damages or expenses arising in connection with the failure of CGI software to perform in accordance with its specifications shall be limited to the return of any payments made by the Customer or the actual amount of said damages and expenses, whichever is less."

The court finds that the allegations in the third counterclaim sufficiently set forth a cognizable legal claim for breach of that portion of the Agreement as stated above which clearly imposed a duty on CGI to provide maintenance support services for the adequate functioning and operation of the system. It is noted that no affidavits or other evidence has been submitted relating to the specifications and criteria to be applied for the software operational performance. This appears to raise triable factual issues as to the merits of the alleged contractual breach. It is further noted that there is no explicit language in the Agreement that it is the complete and exclusive statement between the parties. Therefore, plaintiff's branch of the motion to dismiss the third counterclaim is denied.

Accordingly, the plaintiff's motion is denied in its entirety.

PROBLEM 2.3

Your senior partner is a member of the Advisory Board of the Article 2 Revision Committee. Questions have come up as to whether licensing of technology and sale or leasing of computer systems and specialized software should be covered by Article 2. This method would be used rather than having a separate Article 2B for computer or technology law.

He has just heard that the Reporter of Revised Article 2 has included this subject matter into Revised Article 2 with a hub-spoke approach, e.g., some of Article 2 general principles will apply to these just as to all sales of goods (the Hub); others will be fashioned to cover specific peculiar facets of this subject matter (the Spokes). Should he support or oppose this development? At what stages: drafting, debate on floor of ALI, proposal before state legislatures?

[B] Hub-Spoke

The "Hub-Spoke" concept has been described by Professors Nimmer and Speidel in a discussion paper:

Statement of the Idea

The "hub and spoke" idea argues that there are basic contract law principles that apply across all of the types of transactions that might be viewed as commercial transfers of personal property. These principles can be stated separate and apart from contract law applies only to specific types of transactions (*e.g.*, lease, sale license) or particular types of property (*e.g.*, goods, intangibles, services). By stating these basic principles as an identifiable body of contract law rules independent of particular types of transactions, one can facilitate the coordination and symmetry of the current drafting process and establish a more flexible base for inclusion of additional commercial transactions within the Article 2 contract law structure.

In a "hub and spoke" configuration, the general transactional principles would form the "hub" provisions of the revised Article 2. As discussed in more detail below, "hub" provisions include many current Article 2 rules about contract formation and interpretation. Important issues in defining these principles involve (1) delineating which contract law rules should be in this general law hub and (2) specifying the scope of applicability for the hub provisions.

The "spoke" provisions consist of contract law rules that are particularly applicable to specific types of transactions. These could be placed in sub-parts of revised Article 2, defined to apply specifically to the particular subject matter. Thus, for example, one could conceive of current Article 2A as a form of "spoke" applicable to leases. There would be a spoke applicable to sales of goods and a spoke applicable to transfers involving intangibles, including software contracts. Future decisions might include additional spokes to cover transactions in other types of personal property or services as economic and other considerations justify such action.

Excerpts from a memorandum responding by Professor King to this approach and elaborating on it follows:

This approach [Hub-Spoke] permits us to set forth certain basic principles of contract law in Article 2 of the Uniform Commercial Code and to subsequently also set forth from this Hub from these principles in the spokes from other fields of law such as computer software and services law. The scope and importance of this is clearly evident with the increased technological developments and the greater emphasis on service law. Indeed these fields may well eventually surpass the field of sale of goods in terms of economic activity and lawyers' professional activity. It appears that software contracts and some intangible services are to be covered. But what about services? Are services generally to be covered? Now? Or at some distant future time?

"Issue Hub" Approach

It seems to me that the hubs or components of the hub should be thought of in terms of issues when drafting the law. This gives us the necessary flexibility to ask what principles should be set forth in Article 2 of the U.C.C. and also whether they should be set forth in one of the spokes or other fields. It also permits the law to progress and be adopted by states that feel a more progressive or liberal law may be advisable. The *Issue-Hub* component approach would set forth the Hub or its components in terms of an issue rather than in terms of a principle, although certainly there my be alternative statements of principle. For example, a hub may be the issue of the Statute of Frauds (or the issue of a writing). Another hub issue might be the issue of consideration: should there be the requirement of consideration or no consideration necessary? Another might be in terms of the parol evidence rule: should there be a parol evidence rule or not? The value of the *issue-hub* approach is that it permits us to take an issue such as the Statute of Frauds and state it in the sense of whether it is any longer advisable? Indeed, the drafting committee and Reporter for Article 2 are advocating the abolishment of the Statute of Frauds for the sale of goods. Yet it is quite possible that in one of the spokes for one of the specialized subjects it might be retained. In terms of something like the consideration requirement, the *issue-hub* approach permits us to reevaluate that particular requirement and offer alternatives in regard to it, as mentioned in the *dual hub* approach.

While I realize drafters often think of issues while drafting principles, this *issue-hub* approach forces us to do so and to think in terms of alternate possibilities.

Hollow Hubs

Following the *issue-hub* approach, some of the hubs or components of the hub will be *hollow hubs*. The earlier example of Statute of Frauds is case in point. In Article 2, where it will be most probably abolished, it becomes a *hollow hub*, yet it may be part of the spoke of some specialized area of law such as suretyship law, services, or software law. Or it may be that the central *hollow hub* of abolishing the Statute of Frauds will also find it abolished in some of the spokes, if not all.

Dual Hubs

Some of the hubs may be *dual hubs*. For example, take the issue of the parol evidence rule. There may be an Alternative A of the Article 2, which is a continuation of the parol evidence rule in only a slight modified form. There may well be, however, an Alternative B for states to adopt if they want to do away with the parol evidence rule. The same is true for "consideration." Indeed, in Article 2 there are so many inroads on, and modifications of, consideration that it would be relatively easy to do away with it. On the other hand, it might be an important part of one of the fields covered by a spoke of the wheel.

Extent Hubs

The *issue-hub* approach also permits us to have *extent hubs*. There may be some principles of law such as unconscionability or good faith which are so agreed upon that they need not be offered as *dual hubs*. The extent of them, however, may be a matter of concern. For example, good faith is a core type hub because it is a well accepted principle. The extent of that hub may be different in regard to the different spokes. Even in regard to the basic field of sale of goods, there is a question of whether the U.C.C. good faith principle is sufficient. In some countries good faith is being extended to create pre-contractual liability and it is most likely that the question will continue to arise in regard to the good faith requirement of the Code and also in the caselaw.

Domestic-International Hubs

It seems to me that we should try to make the *issue-hubs* which will be placed in to the Uniform Commercial Code compatible with the International hubs that have been developed. In this regard, the wheels should be interchangeable, rather than subjecting our attorneys to two different size hubs. The Convention on International Sale of Goods principles should be generally compatible with the domestic ones and vis-a-versa. In this regard, an *issue-hub* such as consideration should be compatible with the international convention. At the very least it should be a *dual hub* which permits states to adopt an Alternative compatible with the convention. Likewise, parol evidence, Statute of Frauds, good faith, etc. should be basically compatible. This does not mean that they need to be identical, but that we not have them so different that they are not interchangeable or subject to later harmonization or international efforts or uniformity.

Multi-Wheel Hubs

If we think of the hub-spoke concept as containing various hub principle components, then it seems to me that the hubs must be multi-wheel ones. When one thinks of hubs, one often thinks of the old fashioned wagon with four wheels; instead we may be thinking of the "eighteen wheeler" type modern truck. The number of wheels, of course, can be ascertained or decided upon only after our discussion, but we should be open to having a number of hubs so as to create sufficient uniformity both between the U.C.C. and the other fields and also in the international arena.

NOTES ON OTHER AREAS

(1) *Blood Transfusions.* An area of difficulty has been the furnishing of blood by hospitals for transfusions to patients. Recipients of transfusions not infrequently contract homologous serum hepatitis, a serious but usually nonfatal disease, from a virus in the transfused blood. While the patient is generally charged a specific sum for each unit of blood, the courts have frequently refused to apply sales concepts to these transactions, but have instead characterized the furnishing of blood as a service instead of a "sale." The difference, as we shall see in our later discussion of warranty and strict products liability, is that instead of being able to recover from the hospital upon the relatively strict liability of the sales warranty, the patient is forced to allege and prove negligence. Moreover, charitable and governmental tort immunity may, in some jurisdictions, shield hospitals from actions based upon negligence. Logically, the nonsale view is indefensible. But most courts, seeking to protect hospitals from liability, have viewed public policy as justifying this result. A leading case is *Perlmutter v. Beth David Hospital,* 308 N.Y. 100, 123 N.E.2d 792 (1954). When a few courts began to hold the furnishing of blood to be a sale and to impose liability for breach of warranty, state legislatures responded to hospital pressures by enacting statutes declaring the furnishing of blood not to be a sale and to be free from implied warranties. See Fla. Stat. Ann. § 672.316(5) and (6)(Supp. 1985):

(5) The procurement, processing, storage, distribution, or use of whole blood, plasma, blood products, and blood derivatives for the purpose of injecting or transfusing the same, or any of them, into the human body for any purpose whatsoever is declared to be the rendering of a service by any person participating therein and does not constitute a sale, whether or not any consideration is given therefor; and the implied warranties of merchantability and fitness for a particular purpose are not applicable as to a defect that cannot be detected or removed by a reasonable use of scientific procedures or techniques.

(6) The procurement, processing, testing, storing, or providing of human tissue and organs for human transplant, by an institution qualified for such purposes, the rendering of a service; and such service does not constitute the sale of goods or products to which implied warranties of merchantability or fitness for a particular purpose are applicable. No implied warranties exist as to defects which cannot be detected, removed, or prevented by reasonable use of available scientific procedures or techniques.

(2) *Serving of Food. Niskey v. Childs Co.,* 135 A. 805 (N.J. Court of Errors and Appeals 1927), stated the pre-Code general rule that serving food to be immediately consumed on the premises was not a sale of goods but a service. Therefore, no warranty could be implied. Cf. U.C.C. § 2-314(1).

(3) *Electricity as "Goods."* Should a sale of electricity by a utility company be characterized as a sale of "goods" so as to bring Article 2 into play in the relationship between the utility

and its customers? Two recent decisions have reached opposite conclusions. Electricity was held to be "goods" in *Hedges v. Public Service Co. of Indiana,* 396 N.E.2d 933 (Ind. App. 1979), but an opposite result was reached in *Navarro County Electric Cooperative Inc., v. Prince,* 640 S.W.2d 399 (Texas 1982).

(4) *Computer Programs as "Goods." Computer Programs as Goods,* 77 Mich. L. Rev. 1149 (1979).

(5) *Money as "Goods."* Does U.C.C. Article 2 apply to the following: A contracts to purchase from B a rare Liberty Head nickel for $750. See U.C.C. § 2-105; cf. §§ 9-105(1)(h), 9-304(1), 9-305.

(6) *Transactions Excluded.* U.C.C. § 2-102 excludes secured transactions from Article 2 and does not impair or repeal statutes regulating sales to consumers, farmers or other specified classes of buyers. See U.C.C. § 9-206(2); Uniform Consumer Credit Code and see, e.g., Utah Code Ann. 4-24-20 (from Utah Livestock Brand and Anti-theft Act):

Livestock sold at market to be brand inspected — Proceeds of sale may be withheld — Distribution of withheld proceeds — Effect of receipt of proceeds by department

(1) No livestock shall be sold at any livestock market until after they have been brand inspected by the department. Title to purchased livestock shall be furnished the buyer by the livestock market.

(2) Upon notice from the department that a question concerning the ownership of consigned livestock exists, the operator of the livestock market shall withhold the proceeds from the sale of the livestock for a period of 60 days to allow the consignor of the questioned livestock to establish ownership. If the owner or consignor fails within the 60 days to establish ownership to the satisfaction of the department, the proceeds of the sale shall be transmitted to the interested person or to the department as appropriate. Receipt of the proceeds by the department relieves the livestock market from further responsibility for the proceeds.

See *Pugh v. Stratton,* 22 Utah 2d 190, 450 P.2d 463 (1969) (former Utah Code section of this title governed, not Article 2 of the U.C.C.).

[C] Goods or Real Property

Read: U.C.C. §§ 2-105(1), 2-107.

PROBLEM 2.4

Your client owns a small piece of land. Unfortunately, it has a layer of clay just inches below ground level and nothing will grow on it. Fortunately, the Potters Company wants the clay and is willing to purchase it at a high price. Thus, your client's bad fortune has turned out for the good. You are asked to draw up the contract. Will this be governed by the U.C.C.? Does it matter who actually removed the clay as to whether this U.C.C. applies?

PROBLEM 2.5

Your client, August Mellon III, has a large farm. He is a "gentleman farmer" and engages primarily the activities of the "Fox Hunt Society." While some of the family wealth has been used up with these and similar activities, he has the good fortune of having several businesses interested in contracting with him. One is a timber company that wishes to cut some trees in the forested part of the farm. Another is a mining company that wishes to strip-mine a part of his land for coal, but promises to later re-landscape it. The third company wishes to establish some oil pumps at various points on his land, but this will not interfere with the general use of the land. All three are agreeable to not beginning operations until after the fox hunting season. Will these contracts be covered by the U.C.C.? What are the distinctions and rationale? Is it sound or should the code be revised?

NOTES

(1) S owned and operated a sod farm. B entered into an oral contract with S to purchase S's entire crop of sod. B was to remove the sod. Held: a sale of goods within U.C.C. §§ 2-105(1) and 2-107(2). Consequently, the Code Statute of Frauds (§ 2-201) was applicable. See *Barron v. Edwards, 45 Mich. App. 210, 206 N.W 2d 508, 12 U.C.C. Rep. 671(1973).*

(2) A timber lease stated in part: "I, [Lessor], do lease all of my workable timber for turpentine on all lands owned or controlled by me to [Lessee], for a period of five years for a percentage of 30% of each and every dipping . . ." Held: "There is no merit in [Lessee's] contention that the instrument . . . purported to lease or sell only the turpentine itself and thus constituted a contract for the sale of personalty under the Uniform Commercial Code. . . . This writing purported to lease the trees themselves, not merely the product thereof, and therefore was a lease of realty." *Newton v. Allen,* 220 Ga. 681, 141 S.E.2d 417, 2 U.C.C. Rep. 770 (1965).

§ 2.02 Territorial Application of U.C.C. Article 2

Read: U.C.C. §§ 1-105(2), 2A-105, 2A-106; CISG Art. 6.

PROBLEM 2.6

A farmer in Mississippi agrees to sell two thousand head of cattle to a buyer in Tennessee. The buyer is to pick the cattle up at the farm. The farmer-seller and the buyer concluded the transaction on the Delta Queen, a historic paddlewheel steamboat which was docked at Saint Louis, Missouri at that time. Some of the cattle were defective, and the buyer wishes to sue under Tennessee law; the seller asserts that under a special Mississippi Law the U.C.C. warranty of merchant is made inapplicable at this time of transaction. Which law controls?

PROBLEM (Optional-CISG) 2.7

Samson Industries of Michigan entered into a contract to supply logging trucks to the Hudson Bay Timber Company of Canada. There is now a dispute under the contract and a question of whether the U.C.C. enacted in Michigan or the CISG is applicable. In the contract, which had been drafted by Samson, there is a provision that the "law of Michigan" is to be applied. Samson contends that the law of Michigan is the Michigan U.C.C. Hudson Bay contends that the law of Michigan in this setting is the CISG since it is a federal treaty and automatically becomes the law of Michigan for international transactions such as this one. What would be your decision as the judge in this case? Would it make any difference if the case were brought in federal or state court?

CHAPTER 3

THE CONTRACT FOR SALE

§ 3.01 Introduction

Sale of goods law is generally part of the law of contracts. Thus, unless displaced by the U.C.C., the general law of offer and acceptance, consideration, capacity to contract, etc., is applicable. See U.C.C. § 1-103; Restatement, Second, Contracts §§ 9-81(1981). See also, CISG Arts. 14-24.

The law relating to contract formation, consideration and capacity to contract, etc., is given thorough treatment in the first year course in Contracts. This chapter will summarize the Code's effect on this general law.

PROBLEM 3.1

One of your senior partners is on a Law Reform Committee for your jurisdiction. She asks you what you know of contracts and sales law and whether you think there are any major legal doctrines or rules that need changing. While she would like a more detailed response later, she needs a preliminary opinion from you now. She also is interested in whether you have read or thought of any new ideas that merit consideration for law reform.

§ 3.02 Formation of the Contract for Sale

[A] Formation in General

Read: U.C.C. § 2-204.

Read also: U.C.C. § 2A-204; CISG Art. 14, see Art. 55.

Article 2 of the Code, in recognition that commerce depends upon the creation of contracts, has been written to encourage parties to form contracts and to encourage the courts to uphold the creation and existence of contracts whenever the acts of the parties make this rationally supportable. Formality and strictness of interpretation of the parties' words or conduct are minimized. Thus U.C.C. § 2-204 provides that a contract for sale of goods "may be made in any manner sufficient to show agreement." It is not fatal to the existence of a contract that the time of its making is uncertain, or that one or more terms of the agreement have been left open, so long as the intent to contract exists and there is a basis for granting a remedy in case of breach. As to open terms, see U.C.C. §§ 2-305 through 2-311.

It has been proposed that there is a major shift in contract law, much of it surrounding formation:

The new model of contracts consists of five major parts:

I. A contract is primarily a relationship of parties recognized by law. This requires analysis of the setting and the particular relationship in the transaction. Parts of the relationship which are not agreed upon are imposed by law and constitute the "law made" part of the contractual relationship.

II. Agreement is often to a general transaction. Rather than a specific agreement or dovetailing of consensual points, there is only the generalized consent. This spark of generalized consent allows the law to find and enforce a much more thorough and detailed "law made" relationship.

III. A legal framework of reasonableness and fairness is imposed by the law to create the major part of the contract. Principles of trade usage, course of dealing, and course of performance, and Code gap-filling provisions constitute important aspects of contract; good faith, unconscionability and gap-filling terms of reasonableness are also imposed by law. The part drawn from these various sources may be termed "law made," as contrasted to "consensual." In some consumer situations, the contract terms to be used have already been agreed upon previously by a trade association or company negotiating with a consumer representative such as a consumer "ombud" or Ministry of Justice or Attorney General. The making of the contract in this manner before the parties ever actually enter into it, is the "law-made" aspect.

IV. With the generalized consent and the "law made" contract legally enforceable, a contract exists at a very early point in practically all contract situations. In situations where the parties continue to develop the relationship by developing and agreeing on more specific terms, it is in the context of an already existing contractual relationship created by the earlier spark of consent and law made obligations. They are further refining their contract under a legal obligation which is already enforceable.

V. Consideration should no longer be viewed as a major aspect of contract law. Consideration or its substitute can almost always be found, making consideration an over-emphasized part of contract law which should no longer be required. Indeed, the primary question should not be whether there is consideration, but whether there is a relationship which should be recognized.

The new model then is comprised primarily of "relationship" and standards of "reasonableness" and "fairness" which are "law made" and imposed by operation of law. No longer should contracts be viewed as primarily consensual and agreement on specific terms is not necessary. Consideration should no longer be a part of contract law.[1]

[B] Form Contracts Generally

Consider the following new approach:

PROPOSED "REALITY THEORY"

The approach advocated by this article that "dickered upon" or actually agreed upon terms constitute the contract is relatively simple; it is also consistent with true contract theory and with reality and fairness as well. This approach may be called the "Reality Theory" because it recognizes realities without imposing legal fiction. This theory could also be given a more detailed title of the "Only Agreed Upon Terms are Part of the Contract."

---

[1] King, *Death of Contracts, Part One*, 7 J. Con. L. 256 (1994).

Under the proposed theory, only those terms which have been specifically agreed upon by the seller and the buyer are part of the contract. Where there has been an exchange of purchase orders and acknowledgment forms, it is only those particular terms the parties have agreed upon that become part of that contract. This is generally the agreement on the price, the types of goods, and the time and place of delivery. The numerous fine print clauses on the back of the order form, acknowledgment form, or invoice of the seller are simply not part of the contract. If it is a printed form contract signed by both parties, the same approach is taken. It is those specifically negotiated and agreed upon terms that are part of the contract. This is consistent with Karl Llewellyn's analysis of "dickered" terms of a contract. In reality, the only contract between the parties is that dickered upon or the actually agreed upon terms. Thus, if the parties have discussed and negotiated the price of the goods, then this is an agreed term which is part of the contract. If they have discussed delivery of the goods, this, too, is an agreed upon term. All of the terms in the printed form contract which have not been discussed are not a part of the contract.

Thus, the numerous additional terms found in the mass of fine print which was unread and undiscussed by the parties have no legal effect. The large body of printed form contract clauses fails to have any legal significance; instead they simply stand as statements of what the party using them would desire or an initial position which it would like to have, but nothing more. This theory is one which is in line with reality. It is entirely consistent with contract theory which requires mutual assent to the terms of the contracts. They are recognized as making the contract from a meeting of the wills or a meeting of the minds, and clauses not agreed upon are simply not part of the contract. Importantly, there is a contract formed by this meeting of minds in the decision to enter into the general transaction. This also is consistent with the Uniform Commercial Code emphasis on viewing the contract as less of an "entity" or "thing," and instead looking to the relationship of the parties and the overall setting.

It may be asked: If the contract terms in the printed form contract are meaningless and unenforceable by the courts, how will a number of issues covered by them be decided? The answer is that the law with its emphasis on finding a contract from the relationship of the parties and the overall surrounding circumstances already provides for such gaps to be filled in. The Uniform Commercial Code in supporting more general agreements allows a number of terms that are missing to be filled in by the courts. It allows for this in regard to contract formation, contract formalities, contract content, contract performance, and contract remedies. There is a framework of rights or imposition of a legal status upon the parties.

If there is a trade usage which is reasonable and followed by different merchants and known to both, then that may become part of the contract. In the case of merchant transactions, this may be an important gap filler. If the transaction is between a merchant and a consumer, the consumer is generally unaware of trade usages and would not be bound. Further, he is not a member of that trade or engaged in the creation and use of such practices and should not be bound to them. Even if he were, the trade usage would still have to be in good faith and not unconscionable, and would have to conform to consumer protection laws.

The main terms not agreed upon will be filled in by the courts by looking to the Uniform Commercial Code "gap filler terms" found in Part 3 of Article 2. These relate to situations where the parties have not agreed upon things such as price, delivery, payment, and quality of goods, and warranty. These have been discussed in other books and articles at more length.

King, *Standard Form Contracts: A New Perspective*, 1991 Comm. L. Annual 137, 156-8.

[C] Firm Offers

Read: U.C.C. § 2-205.

Read also: U.C.C. § 2A-205; CISG Arts. 15-17.

When an offer is received by the offeree, it is advantageous to the offeree to know how long the offer will be kept open to afford him time in which to decide whether to accept. Where the offer contemplates a complex contract, the offeree may be required to spend much time and effort in determining whether to accept. Prior to the Code, an offer once made might be freely withdrawn by the offeror at any time prior to acceptance unless made irrevocable by a collateral agreement supported by consideration. Rarely, exceptions might also be made through application of the doctrine of promissory estoppel.

U.C.C. § 2-205 modifies prior law to permit a merchant, by means of a signed writing, to make an offer irrevocable, without consideration, for a period of up to three months. This section is intended to relieve the parties of the necessity of forming a collateral contract to keep the offer open. Note that U.C.C. § 2-205 does not prevent the parties from entering into an agreement, supported by consideration, to keep the offer open, and that if they do so, they may agree that the offer remains open for a period of more than three months.

[D] Construing the Offer: Bilateral or Unilateral Contract?

Read: U.C.C. § 2-206.

Read also: U.C.C. § 2A-206(2); CISG Art. 18(3).

The offeree must determine what action upon his part will constitute an acceptance. If the offer by its terms contemplates a bilateral contract, then the offeree will accept by making a promise, in writing or orally. If a unilateral contract is contemplated, then acceptance is through performance of the requested act. The offeree may experience difficulty in ascertaining whether a particular offer contemplates a bilateral contract or a unilateral one. Under pre-Code law, an inappropriate response by the offeree might well result in a failure to form any contract. Code § 2-206 permits acceptance to be made "in any manner and by any medium reasonable in the circumstances" unless the offer unambiguously indicates otherwise; and an order or offer for goods for prompt or current shipment may be accepted either by a promise to ship or by shipment. Note that U.C.C. § 2-206(1)(b) is not without possible complication, however, in that the offeree may accept by the act of shipping non-conforming goods, which results in the seeming anomaly that the very act of acceptance which creates the contract also constitutes a breach of the contract.

[E] Additional Terms in Acceptance or Confirmation

Read: U.C.C. § 2-207.

Read also: CISG Art. 19.

PROBLEM 3.2

Your firm has a number of clients who are sellers and who send their own acknowledgment forms with their own terms in response to any order received. You have been asked for a general position memorandum in regard to the validity of these for contract formation and for effectiveness of special terms contained only in the acknowledgment form. You have been asked to discuss this in light of:

1.   current law

2.   existing and proposed theories

3.   proposed revision to U.C.C. § 2-207

Basic contract law holds that the acceptance must mirror the offer exactly; if the purported acceptance varies in any respect from the offer, then it is not an acceptance, but a counter-offer. In recognition that modern commercial contracts are customarily created through the use of printed forms, with one form often coming from the offeror and a different form coming from the offeree, with the result that frequently there is some disparity in the forms, Code § 2-207(1) provides that a "definite and seasonable expression of acceptance or a written confirmation" operates as an acceptance and a contract is formed, even if it contains terms different from or in addition to those in the offer. U.C.C. § 2-207(2) provides rules for how these additional terms are to be treated; they are "proposals for additions to the contract" and as between merchants may become a part of the contract itself if they do not materially alter the contract and no objection is made by the offeror within a reasonable time. U.C.C. § 2-207(3) seeks to preserve even those exchanges of writings which do not establish a contract, so long as the parties' conduct evidences a belief that they have a contract.

In a report for the Permanent Editorial Board on proposed amendments to Article 2 of the U.C.C., recommendations relating to U.C.C. § 2-207 "Battle of the Forms" were summarized as follows:

> Although the Study Group recommends that § 2-207 be revised, not all agree [on] the form of the revision . . . . For some, that proposed revision is too elaborate and complex. Most of the Study Group favor what might be called a "lean and mean" revision that focuses upon the key issue, under what circumstances should standard form terms which materially alter the standard terms (or "default" rules) of Article 2 be included in the agreement of the parties?[2]

PEB Study Group: *Uniform Commercial Code, Article 2 Executive Summary*, 46 Bus. Law. 1869, 1878-9 (1991) (referred to subsequently as "PEB Study Group Report").

[F]   The Reality of the "Battle of the Forms"[3]

The "battle of the forms" has long received the attention of legal commentators and practitioners. Frequently an order form sent by one company ordering goods will contain a number of fine print clauses. Commonly, this is answered by an acknowledgment, confirming receipt of the order and notification that the goods will be sent, but also containing numerous other printed terms. Quite often the printed terms on the two forms, each drafted by respected attorneys with different interests in mind and seeking to gain the greatest advantage for their clients, will conflict with each other. Karl Llewellyn has noted that in such contracts the attorneys often go much further than the businessmen in seeking to gain a one-sided advantage.

---

[2] Study Group member Robert Weeks articulates the "lean and mean" approach to include in the contract "only those provisions as to which the writings agree, leaving the other terms of the contracts to be determined by the rules of Article 2, including course of business, usage of trade and course of performance." An alternate approach is to repeal § 2-207 and deal with the problem of standard forms in other provisions of Article 2, as they become relevant. Comments of Professor John Honnold, ALI Sales Consultants Meeting, Philadelphia, Pa., Nov. 16, 1990. The Study Group reserved judgment on Professor Honnold's suggestion.

[3] Excerpt from King, *New Perspective on Standard Form Contracts: A Subject Revisited*, Commercial Law Annual pp 91,92 (1993).

Each attorney seeks to have his form control the other. This is done through the "grand defensive" clause and the "grand offensive" clause. The "grand defensive" clause simply states that all the terms mentioned in the order form shall control. The "grand offensive" term in the other answering form simply states that all of its terms shall be controlling. In using the "grand offensive" and the "grand defensive" clauses, each seeks to control the situation.

In terms of the Code, if there is no such clause then the additional term becomes part of the contract provided it is not a material one or is not one objected to subsequently by the other party. In terms of forms which use the "grand defensive" and "grand offensive" clauses, it is the solution of the Code to cancel out each of the extra boilerplate and the terms that have not been agreed upon are viewed as being conditional and are "knocked out" by the other's objecting clause. This is pointed out in the comments.

Thus the Code already has accomplished in a large number of cases, though indirectly, the solution proposed by the Reality Theory. However, the Code does this through an artificial deeming of these conflicting terms to be objections to each other's terms. The Reality Theory is much more direct and simple. It views these terms as never having been agreed upon and hence never part of the contract. In the large number of transactions where the attorneys are alert in using such offensive and defensive clauses, the Reality Theory is already working in effect. It is primarily in those cases where one side is not represented by an attorney who is clever enough to use such terms that the results would differ.

[G]   Sale by Auction

Read: U.C.C. § 2-328.

Read also: CISG Art. 2(b).

A sale by auction is complete when the auctioneer so announces by the fall of the hammer. Such a sale is with reserve unless the goods are explicitly put up without reserve. (In an action with reserve, the auctioneer may withdraw the goods at any time until he announces completion of the sale.) U.C.C. § 2-326(1),(2).

[H]   Home Solicitation Sale

Federal Regulations 16 CFR Part 429 (Cooling Off Period for Door-to-Door Sales) alter the traditional contract concepts of offer, acceptance and repudiation by affording buyers in door-to-door consumer credit sales a limited right to cancel a sale during a cooling-off period ending midnight of the third business day after the date of the transaction. See also Uniform Consumer Credit Code §§ 2.501 *et seq.* (1968), 3.501 *et seq.* (1974).

§ 3.03 Consideration

Read: U.C.C. §§ 2-106(1), 2-304(1), 2-205, 2-209; see § 2-203.

Read also: U.C.C. §§ 2A-103(l)(j), 2A-205, 2A-208, see § 2A-203; CISG Arts. 1(1), 30, 53.

The law relating to consideration as a necessary element of a contract generally receives thorough treatment in the first-year Contracts course. Under the Sales article of the Uniform Commercial Code consideration remains an essential element of a contract for sale. This is made explicit in U.C.C. § 2-106(1): "A 'sale' consists in the passing of title from the seller to the buyer for a price." And U.C.C. § 2-304(1)provides "The price can be made payable in money or otherwise."

The Code has abolished the need for consideration in two areas: firm offers (U.C.C. § 2-205) and modification of contract (U.C.C. § 2-209). Section 2-205 states that a signed written offer by a merchant to buy or sell goods which gives assurance that it will be held open is not revocable for lack of consideration, during the time stated or, if no time is stated, for a reasonable time.

Section 2-209(1) provides that a contract for the sale of goods may be modified by agreement without the necessity of consideration being given. This section represents, then, a departure from the common law of contracts, which requires consideration for a modification to be binding. The section places two limitations upon the power to modify by agreement: under U.C.C. § 2-209(2), if the original agreement was in writing and signed and excluded modification or rescission of the contract except by another signed writing, the contract may be modified or rescinded only by such a signed writing; and under U.C.C. § 2-209(3), if the contract as modified is within the Statute of Frauds, then modification must be accomplished in accordance with the requirements of U.C.C. § 2-201.

Further, U.C.C. § 2-203 abolishes any special effect which affixing a seal to a writing evidencing a sales contract may have had; a seal no longer makes a contract for sale binding without consideration.

PROBLEM 3.3

One of the senior professors has proposed a conference of law professors and practitioners to discuss "Should the requirement of consideration be abolished in regard to Sales Contracts?" He shows you an excerpt from a letter set forth below that he recently received from another professor who is advocating that the doctrine of consideration be abolished. He has asked you as a young professor what arguments you would make on both sides of this issue? Also what do you think in terms of this possible change?

It may well be that consideration should be removed from the law as a contract requirement. As pointed out, it has been eroded away by case law, substitute reliance, and the Code. In business transactions it is nearly always present, serves no usefulness, and has almost no impact on the law generally. Outside of the contracts classroom where it may be given a few weeks of attention, consideration is indeed academic!

Interestingly, in the Convention for the International Sale of Goods, there is no requirement of consideration for the formation of a contract. This is not a matter of validity and therefore is not left to domestic law. It should be remembered that to the extent that the Convention is now part of United States law there already has been the abolition of consideration! While this development has been given little or no attention, it may affect a large number of contracts. It means that already the United States has moved significantly in ending consideration as a contractual requirement. It might be said that, combined with the dilution previously mentioned, consideration has realistically been buried already, even though memories of it remain.

It does not currently appear that any major change will be made in the revised Article 2 on Sales in the Code. While this writer has advocated that a general section be added which would abolish the requirement of consideration, it is quite possible that the longstanding affinity of the American legal profession for the doctrine of consideration is too great. Also, with the present Code exceptions already dispensing with it in a number of situations discussed, it may be felt that there is no need to abolish it. A counter-argument is that this would make its abolition even easier, would do away with its occasional mischiefs, and make the Uniform Commercial Code more consistent with the International Sale of Goods Convention.

King, *Reshaping Contract Theory and Law: Death of Contracts II Part Two: Ending Consideration and Beginning New Performance and Remedies*, 8 J. of Contracts Law 16 (1995).

§ 3.04 Statute of Frauds

Read: U.C.C. §§ 2-201, 2-209(3), 2-326(4), 8-319; see §§ 9-203, 1-206.

Read also: U.C.C. § 2A-201; CISG Arts. 11-13, see Arts. 29, 96.

Background

In 1671, in Old Marston, Oxfordshire, England, defendant Egbert was sued by plaintiff John over an alleged oral promise by Egbert to sell to John a fighting cock named Fiste. John's friend, Harold, claimed he overheard the "deal" and by that dubious means John won, though in fact there apparently was no deal. In 1676, courts did not allow parties to a lawsuit to testify, so Egbert could not testify to rebut Harold's story. Compounding the problem was the fact that courts then could not throw out jury verdicts manifestly contrary to the evidence. So, in response to the plight of the Egberts of this world and to the recurring mischief of the Johns, as well as to combat possible "fraude and perjurie" by the Harolds, Parliament passed in 1677 a "statute of frauds" which required that certain contracts for the sale of goods be in writing to be enforceable.[4]

PROBLEM 3.4

Also Arte, a famous painter, orally agreed to appear on a television fund-raising program for the non-profit Friends of History Society and paint, before the camera, a picture of the Saint Louis Gateway Arch. Arte was then to donate the painting to the Society to be sold to raise funds. The Society alleges that defendant estimated the picture would be worth $25,000. Some pre-program parties and interviews with Arte were thrown by the Society, and considerable newspaper publicity concerning the coming event ensued. When Arte refused at the last moment to appear, the program was canceled and suit was brought by the Society. Among other things, Arte argues that this contract was for a sale of goods in excess of $500 and was, therefore, within the Statute of Frauds (U.C.C. § 2-201). Your client is the Historical Society. What are your possible arguments? What do you thinks Arte's counsel will argue? Who do you think will win? Why?

NOTES AND QUESTIONS

(1) *Writing Signed by Defendant.* The following is an example of a minimal form of contract for sale sufficient to satisfy U.C.C. § 2-201(1) of the Statute of Frauds. It is from 12 West's Legal Forms at § 4.1-Form 1 (2d ed. 1985) and states:[5]

---

[4] From J. White & R. Summers, Handbook of the Law.

[5] Copyright © 1985 by West Publishing Co. Reprinted by permission.

Buyer and seller hereby contract for the sale of 10,000 gallons of 100 octane gasoline.

[Signed]_____Buyer

[Signed]_____Seller

The Comment to the form observes:

Where a writing is required to satisfy the statute of frauds, the writing must (1) identify the parties, (2) indicate that a contract for sale was made, (3) describe the goods which are the subject of the sale, (4) specify the quantity of goods involved and (5) be signed by the party against whom enforcement is sought. The writing in § 4. 1-Form 1 meets these minimal requirements.

Obviously a number of important contract terms are not spelled out in this writing (§ 4. 1-Form 1) but this does not matter for purposes of satisfying the statute of frauds. Once the statute of frauds has been satisfied, a court can enforce the contract because the terms which are left open by the writing can be supplied by parol evidence of agreement between the parties on such terms (U.C.C. § 2-202) or if not agreed upon, the provisions of the Code will fill out the necessary additional terms of the contract. (U.C.C. § 2-204(3)). For example, if the price was not agreed upon by the parties, the price of gasoline will be a reasonable price at the time for delivery (U.C.C. § 2-305). Similarly, the time for delivery of the gasoline will be within a reasonable time after contracting (U.C.C. § 2-309). The place for delivery of the gasoline will be the seller's place of business (U.C.C. § 2-308). The gasoline must be tendered in a single delivery (U.C.C. § 2-307). Payment is due at the time and place at which buyer receives the gasoline (U.C.C. § 2-310).

Would the following language on a scrap of paper satisfy the statute? "Sold 10,000 gal. J.D. (initialed)."

(2) *Writing in Confirmation of Future Agreement. Martco, Inc. v. Doran Chevrolet, Inc.,* 632 S.W. 2d 927, 33 U.C.C. Rep. 1619 at 1620-21 (Texas 1982) states:

The writing in question is on Doran Chevrolet stationery and is signed by Craig Arledge, apparently a sales agent for Doran. The memo is entitled: "Price Worksheet" and indicates that it is a "Competitive Equalization Request." It includes a quantity term (24), but indicates that it is for bid purposes: the only date on the memo is labeled "Bid Opening Date." The affidavit of Martco's own Vice-President confirms that this writing is not in confirmation of the contract but, in fact, formed the basis on which he later claims to have placed an order for the truck chassis. The writing clearly contemplates a contract to be made in the future. The facts and circumstances surrounding these events merely confirm that the writing is not a confirmation of a pre-existing agreement, but constitutes an offer for an agreement that was not entered into until much later, if at all. Our inquiry is whether such a writing will satisfy the statute of frauds. [The Court recites U.C.C. § 2-201(1).] The statute requires that the writing be sufficient to indicate that a contract has been made. Although we are directed to no Texas case, authorities in other jurisdictions uniformly interpret this phrase to disqualify writings which contain "futuristic" language as not confirmatory of a contract already in existence.

(3) *Tape Recording as Writing. Ellis Canning Co. v. Bernstein,* 348 F. Supp. 1212, 11 U.C.C. Rep. 443 at 453-4 (D. Col. 1972) states:

We hold that when the parties agreed to the tape recording of the oral agreement, that tape recording satisfies the requirements of 63 CRS 155-8-319. This conclusion we reach by taking into account the fact that "the purpose of the statute is to prevent fraud and perjury in the enforcement of obligations depending for their evidence on the unassisted memory of witnesses," 37 CJS Statute of Frauds, § 1, p 513. Moreover,'63 CRS 155-1-201, the definition section of the U.C.C. says:

> (46) "Written" or "writing" includes printing, typewriting, or any other intentional reduction to tangible form.

We think and we hold that when the parties to an oral contract agree that the oral contract shall be tape recorded, the contract is "reduced to tangible form" when it is placed on the tape. We do not overlook the requirement for signature contained in the statute, but the clear purpose of this is to require identification of the contracting party, and where, as here, the identity of the oral contractors is established, and, in fact, admitted, the tape itself is enough. So, we hold that even if the signed correspondence were insufficient to get around the statute [which it isn't], the tape recording of the oral contract would be a "reduction to tangible form" under the provisions of the U.C.C. Probably the opposite result would be required under historical statutes of frauds which do not contain the tangible form language of this somewhat unusual definition of the word "written." However, under this statute, we think that the tape recorded agreement meets its requirements.

Contra, see *Roos and Aloi,* 487 N.Y.S.2d 637 (1985) (Tape recording of an oral agreement for the sale of stock did not constitute a "writing" within the meaning of § 8-319 Statute of Frauds). Cf. U.C.C. §§ 2-201, 8-319, see § 8-113 (1994).

(4) The definitional section of the U.C.C. also sets the general standard for what mailrooms "should do":

> An organization exercised due diligence if it maintains reasonable routines for communicating significant information to the person conducting the transaction and there is reasonable compliance with the routines.

U.C.C. §1-201(27). In one case, *Thomson Printing Machinery Co. v. B.F. Goodrich Co.*, 714 F.2d 744 (7th Cir. 1983), the question arose as to whether a letter sent to the company generally containing a purchase order and check, without specifying any particular company official's name, was sufficient notice. The court noted: One cannot say that Goodrich's mailroom procedures were reasonable as a matter of law: if Goodrich had exercised due diligence in handling Thomson Printing's purchase order and check, these items would have reasonably promptly come to Ingram Meyers' attention. First, the purchase order on its face should have alerted the mailroom that the documents referred to a purchase of used printing equipment. Since Goodrich had only one surplus machinery department, the documents' "home" should not have been difficult to find. Second, even if the mailroom would have had difficulty in immediately identifying the kind of transaction involved, the purchase order had Tomson Printing's phone number printed on it and we think a "reasonable routine" in these particular circumstances would have involved at some point in the process a simple phone call to Thomson Printing. Thus, we think Goodrich's mailroom mishandled the confirmatory writings. This failure should not permit Goodrich to escape liability by pleading nonreceipt. See Williston on Sales, supra, §14-8 at 284-85.

We note that the jury verdict for Thomson Printing indicates that the jury found as a fact that the contract had in fact been made and that the Statute of Frauds had been satisfied. Also, Goodrich acknowledges those facts about the handling of the purchase order which we regard as determinative of the "merchants" exception question. We think that there is ample evidence to support the jury findings both of the existence of the contract and of the satisfaction of the Statute.

The district court, in holding as a matter of law that the circumstances failed to satisfy the Statute of Frauds, was impressed by James Thomson's dereliction in failing to specifically direct the purchase order and check to the attention of Ingram Meyers or the surplus equipment department. We agree that Thomson erred in this respect, but, for the reasons we have suggested. Goodrich was at least equally derelict in failing to find a "home" for the well-identified documents. Goodrich argues that in the "vast majority" of cases it can identify checks within a week without contacting an outside party; in the instant case, therefore, if Goodrich correctly states its experience under its procedures, it should presumably have checked with Thomson Printing promptly after the time it normally identified checks by other means—in this case, by its own calculation, a week at most. Under the particular circumstances of this case, we therefore think it inappropriate to set aside a jury verdict on Statute of Frauds grounds.

(5) U.C.C. Article 2A, Leases, has a Statute of Frauds section modeled on § 2-201. The Draft substitutes $1,000 for $500 and does not adopt the "merchant's exception" of § 2-201(2). See § 2A-201.

(6) *Admissions.* In *Garrison v. Piatt*, 113 Ga. App. 74, 147 S.E.2d 374 (1966), the court held that a general demurrer (a motion to dismiss for failure to state a cause of action) could not be sustained on the grounds that the alleged sales contract for a house trailer for a price in excess of $500 was within the Statute of Frauds.

Prior to enactment of U.C.C. § 2-201(3)(b), a defendant could both admit the contract and simultaneously insist on the benefit of the Statute of Frauds. The U.C.C., however, permits enforcement of the contract if the defendant admits it at trial.

A general demurrer must admit, for the purposes of the demurrer only, that all facts in the petition are true—including the existence of the contract. Dismissal at this stage would deprive plaintiff of the opportunity to have the defendant admit the contract otherwise during the course of the trial.

Also, R. Henson, The Law of Sales 6 (1985) observes, "An admission in testimony, even if involuntary, that involves facts which establish the existence of a contract as a matter of law should satisfy the requirements of the statute. If the existence of a contract is denied in testimony and is not otherwise admitted, then it would appear that the statute is not complied with, even though the judge does not find the testimony credible. This gives even an unconvincing liar a break. Query whether the exception for an 'or otherwise in court' admission should not be found in such a case."

(7) *Partial Performance.* In *Williamson v. Martz,* 29 Northumb. L.J. 32 Pa. D. & C.2d 33 (Pa. Court of Common Pleas 1956), defendant paid $100 down on an oral contract for $1,600 for two 200-gallon vats to be manufactured by plaintiff. When finished, defendant refused to accept delivery or make further payments. Plaintiff then sold the vats for $800 and sued for the balance. The court rejected plaintiff's argument that payment of the $100 took the contract out of the Statute of Frauds and held that the complaint failed to state a cause of action since the Statute of Frauds was apparent on the face of the petition. See U.C.C. § 2-201(3)(c).

R. Henson, The Law of Sales 7 (1985), notes that:

[T]here is a problem with partial payments made by buyers and accepted by sellers when the goods have not been delivered. If the quantity of goods allegedly covered by the oral contract can be apportioned so that the goods paid for can be delivered, that would not be difficult case. If the down payment is small and the item or items allegedly covered rather expensive, the problem is acute. One solution is to say that an enforceable contract results if the down payment is less than the cost of any one item. Another solution is to enforce the contract at least to the extent of one unit, which may be all that the contract involves as in the case of such goods as automobiles. The statutory language is reasonably susceptible to either reading.

(8) *Article 2 Proposed Revisions.* Section 2-201. No Formal Requirements. A contract or modification *of a contract* under this Article is enforceable *whether* or not there is a writing signed or *record* authenticated by a party against whom enforcement is sought, even if the contract or modification is *not* capable of performance within one year of its making.

Reporter's Notes — Revised Section 2-201 was approved by the Drafting Committee on March 6, 1993.

PROBLEM 3.5

Your senior partner has just received a copy of the Proposed Article 2 revision. It eliminates the Statute of Frauds! He asks you whether as a member of the American Law Institute he should support or oppose this and reasons therefore. What is your advice?

PROBLEM 3.6

One of your colleagues who is also a young professor has asked you whether you would support her position that the parol evidence rule is generally ineffective because of the many caselaw doctrines used to get around it, and the U.C.C. allowance for trade usage and consistent additional terms, and the cases where courts allow it to show that a word or term which appears to mean one thing can really mean another when either trade usage or course of dealing are used. She also believes that the rule often is asserted so as to prevent companies from being responsible for the oral contemporaneous statements of their own salespersons! She has asked for your opinion on these matters. She also wonders how she might go about trying to reform the law in this regard.

NOTES

(1) See *Omac, Inc. v. Southwestern Machine & Tool Works, Inc.,* Georgia Court of Appeals 189 Ga. App. 39, 374 S.E.2d 829 (1988):

BENHAM, J. Appellant and appellee entered into an agreement whereby appellee manufactured and sold to OMAC certain specified parts made from materials supplied by OMAC. Appellee filed suit to recover monies owed it, and appellant counterclaimed. A jury returned a verdict in favor of appellee, and appellant appeals, contending the trial court erred in charging the jury on the principles espoused in OCGA §§ 11-601; 11-602; and 11-2-606.

The contested instructions are part of the Sales Article of the Uniform Commercial Code which appellant contends is inapplicable because there was no sale involved. "A 'sale' consists in the passing of title from the seller to the buyer for a price." OCGA §11-2-106(1). "Article 2 of the Uniform Commercial Code is expressly limited to transactions involving the sale of goods. [OCGA §11-2-102][A] 'contract for services and labor with an incidental furnishing of equipment and materials' is not a transaction involving 'the sale of goods' and is not controlled by the [U.C.C.]. [Cits.]" *W.B. Anderson Feed & C. Co. v. Ga. Gas Distrib.,* 164

Ga. App. 96 [34 U.C.C. Rep Serv 1509] (296 S.E.2d 395) (1982). The record does not contain a contract outlining the parties' duties and responsibilities, but appellee certified that the work performed by it was done on materials supplied by appellant and conformed to blueprints and revisions. The prices quoted (and presumably charged) by appellee for its work were based upon appellant's supplying the materials. In essence, appellee agreed to perform a service, making appellant's material into the parts appellant needed. Because it used materials supplied by appellant, appellee's prices reflected only the labor cost of making the parts appellant ordered. Inasmuch as appellee sold a service and not goods to appellant, the U.C.C. was inapplicable and the trial court erred in giving the charges excepted to.

Judgment reversed. McMurray, P.J., and Pope, J., concur.

(2) *King Industries, Inc. v. Worlco Data Systems, Inc.,* United States District Court, ED Va. 736 F Supp 114 (1989).

At oral argument, plaintiff's counsel stated that plaintiff's business is in the construction trade, as opposed to retail carpet sales, and that plaintiff relied upon the representations of a Worlco sales agent who stated that the "builder's package" software was compatible with plaintiff's needs; that is, the sale of carpeting and floor covering in the construction trade. Plaintiff's counsel further stated that plaintiff has been unable to use the computer system because it does not comport with plaintiff's business needs.

Defendants Worlco and Copelco argue that plaintiff's claim for breach of express and implied warranties fails as a matter of law because of the disclaimer clauses in both agreements. The disclaimer in the Worlco contract is on the front page of that agreement above the signature line. The disclaimer, in capital letters, states:

WDS MAKES NO WARRANTY OF ANY KIND, EXPRESS OR IMPLIED, INCLUDING WITHOUT LIMITATION WARRANTIES OF MERCHANTABILITY OR FITNESS FOR A PARTICULAR PURPOSE.

In *Hoover Universal, Inc. v. Brockway Imco, Inc.,* 809 F.2d 1039 [3 U.C.C. Rep. Serv. 2d 46] (4th Cir.1987), the Fourth Circuit addressed the effect of a merger clause on the admissibility of extrinsic evidence. In *Hoover,* the buyer of industrial equipment alleged that the seller had misrepresented the cavitation capacity of its equipment. *Hoover,* 809 F.2d at 1041. The misrepresentation was contained in a handout which summarized certain technical data in connection with the equipment. *Id.* The handout had been given to plaintiff's representatives prior to entering the contract. *Id.* The plaintiff alleged in its complaint that the handout created an express warranty. *Id.*

The Fourth Circuit began its analysis by noting that the written contract between the parties contained an enforceable disclaimer clause disclaiming warranties of merchantability, condition or fitness for a particular purpose. *Id.* at 1041-42. The contract also contained a well-drafted merger clause. *Id.* at 1043. The court also noted that the cavitation capacity of the seller's equipment was not mentioned in the final written contract between the parties. *Id.* at 1041. The Fourth Circuit found that the district court did not commit error in finding that the contract between buyer and seller was the "complete and exclusive statement" of their agreement. Accordingly, the Fourth Circuit held that because of the detailed nature of the contract, including the well-drafted merger clause, the Virginia parol evidence rule precluded the admission of the handout in an effort to establish an express warranty.

An effectively worded merger clause can have the same effect as a disclaimer. J. White & R. Summers, Uniform Commercial Code, §12-4 (3d ed. 1988). The *Worlco* contract contains a merger or integration clause, in capital letters above the signature line, which provides:

ALL TERMS AND CONDITIONS WRITTEN ON THE REVERSE SIDE HEREOF AND ON THE FACE HEREOF, INCLUDING SCHEDULE A HERETO, CONSTITUTE THE COMPLETE AND BINDING CONTRACT WHEN ACCEPTED BY WDS. THIS ORDER EXPRESSLY LIMITS ACCEPTANCE TO SUCH TERMS AND CONDITIONS PROPOSED BY THE BUYER ARE REJECTED.

Plaintiff argues that despite the integration clause, the contact is not complete because it contains no description of the "builder's package" and therefore evidence of consistent additional discussions is admissible.

The court finds, however, that the parol evidence rule precludes the admission of oral statements which contradict the terms of a written disclaimer. *Hill v. BASF Wyandotte Corp.*, 696 F.2d 287, 291 [35 U.C.C. Rep Serv 91] (4th Cir. 1982). In *Hill*, a farmer brought suit for breach of warranty and misrepresentation against the manufacturer of an agricultural herbicide. The plaintiff farmer alleged that a sales agent for defendant manufacturer had made false oral representations upon which plaintiff relied to his detriment. Each of the cans of herbicide purchased by plaintiff contained a disclaimer of express and implied warranties. The Fourth Circuit found that the oral representations made by defendant's sales agent were not admissible to vary the terms of sale and warranty on the product label. Additionally, most courts hold that when a disclaimer of warranties is contained in an integrated agreement, parol warranties are "contradictory" within the meaning of parol evidence rule and are therefore inadmissible. J. White & R. Summers, Uniform Commercial Code, § 12-4 n.2 (3d ed. 1988).

Accordingly, this court finds that even if the oral representations made by Worlco's representative became the "basis of the bargain" and therefore constituted an express warranty, those oral statements would not be admissible to contradict or vary the disclaimer of express warranties clause contained in the integrated agreement between Worlco and plaintiff. This parol evidence would be admissible, however, in a properly pleaded fraud in the inducement claim. See, *George Robberecht Seafood, Inc. v. Maitland Bros. Co.*, 220 Va. 109, 255 S.E.2d 682, 683 [26 U.C.C. Rep Serv 669] (1979).

§ 3.05 Terms, Construction and Interpretation of the Contract for Sale

Read: U.C.C. § 1-201(3),(11),(42); §§ 2-202, 1-205, 2-208.

Read also: U.C.C. §§ 2A-103(1)(k) and (1), 2A-202, 1-205, 2A-207; CISG Arts. 8 and 9.

Contracts for sale of goods may contain a variety of terms. U.C.C. § 1-201(3),(11),(42); see § 2-106(1). More common terms relate to description, quantity, quality, price, payment, delivery, inspection, warranties, remedies, risk of loss, circumstances excusing performance, etc.

Please study the following "General Contract for Sale of Goods" and "Check List of Terms to be Included in Contracts for the Sale of Goods."

General Contract for Sale of Goods[6]

[Name of seller], of [address], agrees to sell and [name of buyer], of [address], agrees to buy _____ tons of [describe or identify goods] at $ _____ per ton to be delivered by [name of seller] to [name of buyer] at [address] on or before [date]. In consideration of the premises and of the mutual benefits to each party, it is further agreed as follows:

1. *Description.* The goods subject of this sale and which the seller shall deliver to the buyer and for which the buyer shall pay shall conform to the following specifications:

[here list specifications]

2. *Warranty.* The seller warrants that the goods shall meet the specifications described herein. The foregoing warranty is exclusive, and is in lieu of all other warranties, whether written, oral or implied, including the warranty of merchantability and the warranty of fitness for a particular purpose.

3. *Delivery.* Delivery shall be on or before [date] and shall be to buyer at the seller's place of business. Seller agrees to furnish the facilities and at his cost to load the goods on trucks furnished by the buyer.

4. *Packaging.* Buyer shall give the seller instructions for the packaging of the goods not less than 48 hours prior to the date of delivery, and the reasonable cost of such packaging shall be charged to the buyer.

5. *Title.* Title shall remain with the seller until delivery and actual receipt thereof by the buyer.

6. *Risk of loss.* Identification shall take place on the packaging of the goods, and the risk of loss shall pass on such identification.

7. *Price and time of payment.* The price of the goods shall be $ ____ per ton, and shall be paid at the time of delivery and at the place of delivery in bank draft or cashier's check or certified check.

8. *Inspection.* Inspection shall be made by the buyer at the time and place of delivery.

9. *Claims.* Buyer's failure to give notice of any claim within _____ days from the date of delivery shall constitute an unqualified acceptance of the goods and a waiver by the buyer of all claims with respect thereto.

10. *Remedies.* Buyer's exclusive remedy and seller's limit of liability for any and all losses or damages resulting from defective goods or from any other cause shall be for the purchase price of the particular delivery with respect to which losses or damages are claimed plus any transportation charges actually paid by the buyer.

11. *Assignment and delegation.* Buyer may not assign its rights or delegate its performance hereunder without the prior written consent of the seller, and any attempted assignment or delegation without such consent shall be void.

12. *Choice of law.* This contract is to be construed according to the laws of, and under the Uniform Commercial Code as adopted by, the State of _____.

13. *Integration of contract.* This document constitutes the full understanding of the parties, and no terms, conditions, under standings or agreement purporting to modify or vary the terms

---

[6] Adapted from 12 West's Legal Forms § 17.2-Form 8 (2d ed. 1985); copyright © West Publishing Company, reprinted with permission.

of this document shall be binding unless hereafter made in writing and signed by the party to be bound.

Signed and sealed in triplicate this _____ day of _____, 19_____

_____
Buyer   Seller

Check List of Terms to Be Included in Contracts for the Sale of Goods[7]

Each contract must be tailored to suit the particular transaction but the following check list sets forth terms or items which may be necessary or useful.

a. Description of the parties (§§ 2-103, 2-104).

b. Description of the goods.

    (1) Quantity (§ 2-201).

    (2) Quality (§§ 2-313, 2-314, 2-315).

    (3) Manner of selection (§§ 2-311(2), 2-501).

c. Warranties.

    (1) Title (§ 2-312).

    (2) Quality (§§ 2-313, 2-314, 2-315).

    (3) Disclaimer of warranties (§ 2-316).

    (4) Limitation of liability for breach of warranty (§ 2-719).

d. Title to the goods (§ 2-401).

e. Risk of loss and insurance (§§ 2-303, 2-501, 2-509, 2-510).

f. Seller's obligation to tender delivery of the goods.

    (1) Time of delivery (§§ 2-309, 2-503).

    (2) Place of delivery (§§ 2-308, 2-319 through 2-324,[8] 2-503, 2-504).

    (3) Manner of delivery (§§ 2-311(2), 2-503).

        (a) Delivery in single or several lots (§ 2-307).

        (b) Shipment under reservation (§§ 2-310(b), 2-505).

        (c) Delivery on condition (§ 2-507(2)).

    (4) Seller's right to cure improper tender (§ 2-508).

g. Buyer's obligation to accept goods (§ 2-507).

    (1) Buyer's right to inspect the goods before acceptance (§§ 2-513, 2-606).

    (2) Buyer's right to reject goods (§ 2-601).

        (a) Manner of rejection (§ 2-602).

        (b) Obligation to state reasons for rejection (§ 2-605).

---

[7] From B. Stone, Uniform Commercial Code in a Nutshell, pp. 42-44; copyright © 1995 West Publishing Company, reprinted with permission.

[8] [Abbreviated mercantile terms, such as F.O.B., F.A.S., C.I.F., etc. are often used in contracts involving the shipment of goods.-Ed.]

      (c)   Obligation to care for rejected goods (§§ 2-603, 2-604).

    (3)   Buyer's obligation to notify seller of breach discovered after acceptance (§ 2-607).

    (4)   Buyer's right to revoke his acceptance (§ 2-608).

h.   Buyer's obligation to pay for goods (§§ 2-507, 2-606).

    (1)   Price (§ 2-305).

    (2)   Medium of payment (§§ 2-304, 2-511).

    (3)   Time of payment (§ 2-310).

    (4)   Obligation to pay before inspection of the goods (§ 2-512).

i.   Remedies of seller (§ 2-703).

j.   Remedies of buyer (§§ 2-711, 2-714).

k.   Signature of parties (§ 2-201).

l.   Miscellaneous provisions.

    (1)   Duration and termination of contract term (§§ 2-106(3), 2-309(2)).

    (2)   Provision forbidding parol modification (§§ 2-202, 2-209).

    (3)   Provision relating to waiver of rights by course of performance (§§ 2-208, 2-209).

    (4)   Delegation of performance (§ 2-210).

    (5)   Assignment of rights (§§ 2-210, 9-318(4)).

    (6)   Output and requirements clauses (§ 2-306).

    (7)   Sale on approval terms (§§ 2-326, 2-327).

    (8)   Sale or return (§§ 2-326, 2-327).

    (9)   Consignment sale terms (§§ 1-201(37), 2-326).

    (10)   Seller's rights on buyer's insolvency (§ 2-702).

    (11)   Buyer's rights on seller's insolvency (§ 2-502).

    (12)   Preservation of goods in dispute (§ 2-515).

    (13)   Right to adequate assurance of performance (§ 2-609).

    (14)   Installment contract provisions (§ 2-612).

    (15)   Force majeure (§§ 2-613 through 2-616).

    (16)   Liquidated damages (§ 2-718).

    (17)   Proof of market price (§§ 2-723, 2-724).

    (18)   Clause shortening the statute of limitations period (§ 2-725).

    (19)   Acceleration clauses (§ 1-208).

    (20)   Choice of law clause (§ 1-105).

Construction and Interpretation. The principal problems of construction and interpretation are twofold: (1)(a) what did the parties agree to, and (b) what legal meaning is to be placed thereon;

and (2)(a) what things did the parties fail to agree to, and (b) what will the law supply as "gap-fillers" to round out the contract?

What Parties Agreed to and Legal Meaning. The Code adopts a parol evidence rule in U.C.C. § 2-202 which provides that certain agreed written terms may not be contradicted by evidence of prior agreements or contemporaneous oral agreements. Also, U.C.C. § 1-205(3) provides that a course of dealing[9] between parties and any usage of trade[10] in the vocation or trade in which they are engaged or of which they are or of should be aware give particular meaning to and supplement or qualify terms of an agreement.[11] Further, U.C.C. § 2-208(1) provides that where the contract for sale involves repeated occasions for performance by either party with knowledge of the nature of the performance and opportunity for objection to it by the other, any course of performance accepted or acquiesced in without objection shall be relevant to determine the meaning of the agreement. As Comment 1 to U.C.C. § 2-208 states:

> The parties themselves know best what they have meant by their words of agreement and their action under that agreement is the best indication of what that meaning was. This section thus rounds out the set of factors which determines the meaning of the "agreement."[12]

Further, the Code has rules to determine the meaning of certain terms, for example: output or requirements terms (§ 2-306(1)), exclusive dealing terms (§ 2-306(2)), terms relating to assignment of the contract (§ 2-210(3), (4)); mercantile terms, e.g., F.O.B. (§ 2-319 et seq.); auction with or without reserve terms (§ 2-328(3)); sale on approval and sale of return terms (§§ 2-326, 2-327); option to accelerate "at will" term (§1-208).

Of course, not all terms upon which parties have agreed will necessarily have legal consequences. § 1-201(3), (11). For example, the Code's obligation of good faith in the performance or enforcement of every contract may prevent enforcement of certain terms or agreements. §§1-203, 1-201(19), 2-103(1)(b); see e.g., § 2-209(1) and Comment 2. Further, good faith, diligence, reasonableness and care prescribed by the Code may not be disclaimed by agreement. § 1-102(3) and Comment 3. Also, if a court as a matter of law finds a contract or any clause of the contract to have been unconscionable at the time it was made, the court may: (1) refuse to enforce the contract, or (2) enforce the remainder of the contract without the unconscionable clause, or (3) so limit the application of any unconscionable clause as to avoid any unconscionable result. § 2-302(1); see §§ 2-309(3), 2-719(3).

Parties Failure to Agree and "Gap-Fillers." Where the parties have entered into a contract but have failed to agree on some of the terms (see U.C.C. § 2-204(3)), the Code provides "gap-fillers" to supply the omitted terms. Remember that the Code defines "agreement" to mean the bargain of the parties in fact as found in their language or by implication from other circumstances

---

[9] U.C.C. § 1-205(1) states:

A course of dealing is a sequence of previous conduct between the parties to a particular transaction which is fairly to be regarded as establishing a common basis of understanding for interpreting their expressions and other conduct.

[10] U.C.C. § 1-205(2) provides:

A usage of trade is any practice or method of dealing having such regularity of observance in a place, vocation or trade as to justify an expectation that it will be observed with respect to the transaction in question. The existence and scope of such a usage are to be proved as facts. If it is established that such a usage is embodied in a written trade code or similar writing the interpretation of the writing is for the court.

[11] See Comment 1 to § 1-205.

[12] See U.C.C. § 2-202(a) and Comment 2.

including course of dealing or usage of trade or course of performance as provided in U.C.C. §§ 1-205 and 2-208. U.C.C. § 1-201(3).

The Code gap-fillers include: U.C.C. §§ 2-305 (open price term), 2-306 (output, requirements and exclusive dealings), 2-307 (delivery in single or several lots), 2-308 (place for delivery), 2-309 (absence of specific time provisions), 2-310 (open time for payment), and 2-311 (options and cooperation respecting performance). In addition, other Code provisions will yield to the contrary agreement of the parties, e.g., U.C.C. §§ 2-401(passing of title), 2-509 (risk of loss), 2-513 (buyer's right to inspection). Note that some Code provisions state that they cannot be varied by contrary agreement, e.g., U.C.C. §§ 1-102(3) and (4), 1-105(2), 1-204, 2-210(2), 2-318, 2-718(1).

In summary, the terms of a contract for sale may be supplied by (1) express language of the parties; (2) course of dealing, usage of trade and course of performance; (3) gap-filling rules of the Code (and general law).

The PEB Study Group Report contains the following comments:

Terms of Delivery

Article 2 contains extensive treatment of the context and effect of certain terms of delivery. See §§ 2-319 through 2-324. CISG does not deal with these terms, leaving them to the parties' agreement or such sources as the INCOTERMS or the ICC.

The Study Group discussed whether Article 2 should follow the lead of CISG in this matter, particularly those terms involving international transportation. If that lead were sound, the delivery terms would be deleted from Article 2 and the parties would be free to provide them by contract or to select other alternatives, such as the INCOTERMS. Such a recommendation, however, would be premature without a study of Article 2's current terms, a comparison with those terms used in international trade, and a consideration of how to obtain a continuing, proper mesh between what Article 2 does and does not do and other alternatives.

46 Bus. Lawyer 1869, 1881 (1991).

CHAPTER 4

PROPERTY INTERESTS

§ 4.01 Introduction

In Chapter 3, entitled "The Contract For Sale," we were reminded that U.C.C. Article 2 applies contract law principles to the sale of goods. In this chapter, we see that in certain instances, property principles may be applicable.

The Code recognizes four property interests in goods, namely (1) title, (2) special property, (3) insurable interest, and (4) security interest. Further, the Code deals with the question of risk of loss. This is historically closely related to property interests in goods. These matters are discussed in this chapter.

§ 4.02 Title

Read: U.C.C. § 2-401, see § 2-327(1)(a).

Read also: U.C.C. § 2A-302; CISG Arts. 4(b), 30.

A sale of goods is fundamentally a transaction which brings about a transfer of the property interest in the goods from a seller to a buyer. Section 2-106(1) states, "A 'sale' consists in the passing of title from the seller to the buyer for a price." Given this view of the sale transaction, it is not surprising that pre-Code law, including the Uniform Sales Act (U.S.A.), not only stressed the importance of the passage of title, but also used this concept to solve numerous other problems which arose in the course of the sale. "Has title passed?" was the crucial question in ascertaining the rights and remedies of the parties to the sale contract. For example, U.S.A. § 22 stated in part: "Unless otherwise agreed, the goods remain at the seller's risk until the property therein is transferred to the buyer, but when the property therein is transferred to the buyer the goods are at the buyer's risk." Another example is found at U.S.A. § 66 which reads: "Where the property in the goods has passed to the buyer and the seller wrongfully neglects or refuses to deliver the goods, the buyer may maintain any action by law to the owner of goods of similar kind when wrongfully converted or withheld."

Section 2-401 of the Code abandons the title concept as being the test of the rights, obligations, and remedies of the parties. This abandonment is described by Duesenberg and King as "The single most important conceptual distinction between Article 2 and either the common law or the Uniform Sales Act."[1] Duesenberg and King hasten to point out, however, that the abandonment of the title theory will not bring about a "great purge of the past" or "shocking changes in results achieved under pre-Code law."[2] Instead, while the reasoning of counsel and

---

[1] See the Comment to U.C.C. § 2-101.

[2] Duesenberg & King, Sales and Bulk Transfers Under the Uniform Commercial Code § 8.01.

judges must necessarily be altered, the outcome of sales controversies will not be radically different.

If title is no longer important in determining the rights of the parties to the sales contract, then why do we have U.C.C. § 2-401 with its elaborate distinctions?

NOTES AND QUESTIONS

(1) *Sales tax. State of Alabama v. Delta Airlines, Inc.,* 356 So. 2d 1205, 23 U.C.C. Rep. 1156 (Ala. Civ. App. 1978), states in part:

> Alabama sales tax applies only to sales that are "closed" within the State. Sections 40-23-l(a)(5),-2(1), Code of Alabama (1975). For tax purposes, sales are closed when title to the goods passes to the purchaser. *Hamm v. Continental Gin Co.,* 276 Ala 611, 165 So. 2d 392(1964); *State v. Altec, Inc.,* 46 Ala App 450, 243 So. 2d 713(1971). Actual delivery is of great importance in determining when title passes. *State v. Communication Equip. & Contr. Co.,* 335 So. 2d 123 (Ala Civ App 1976). Title passes, unless otherwise explicitly agreed, at the time and place of completion of performance by physical delivery of the goods. Section 7-2-401(2), Code of Alabama (1975). Under the stated facts, delivery of a meal, if at all, occurs outside Alabama and is in interstate commerce. Delta has no contractual obligation to deliver a meal at all. It maintains possession until actually served. Therefore, the trial court did not improperly conclude that the alleged sale was closed and title passes at the time of delivery without the State and was not subject to Alabama sales tax.

Compare Undercofler v. Eastern Airlines, Inc., 221 Ga. 824,147 S.E.2d 436, 3 U.C.C. Rep. 352 (1966), in which the court held that, while an airline's sale of meals to its passengers is a taxable event:

> such sale occurs when the ticket, the cost of which includes the price of the meal, is purchased. . . . The fact that actual delivery of the meal does not occur until later does not prevent perfection of its sale at the time of purchase of the ticket. . . . [T]he sale is complete when the ticket is bought.

(2) *Criminal Law.* "Whoever . . .steals . . .any . . .thing of value of the United States . . .[s]hall be fined not more than $10,000 or imprisoned not more than ten years, or both." 18 U.S.C. § 641. "Suppose the United States contracts for sale of scrap metal to a buyer. Before delivery of the scrap by the U.S. to buyer, X steals the scrap. Issue: At the time of the stealing was the scrap any thing of value of the United States, *i.e.,* did the U.S. still own or have title to the scrap?" B. Stone, Uniform Commercial Code in a Nutshell 51 (2d ed. 1984).

In a similar vein, Kentucky Revised Statutes § 514.030 (theft by unlawful taking or disposition) provides in part:

> A person is guilty of theft by unlawful taking or disposition when he unlawfully . . .[t]akes or exercises control over movable *property of another* with intent to deprive him thereof. [Emphasis added.]

(3) *Voidable title.* U.C.C. § 2-403(1) states that a person with voidable title has power to transfer a good title to a good faith purchaser for value. This is discussed in Chapter 8 below.

§ 4.03 Special Property

Read: U.C.C. §§ 2-401(1), 2-501(1). Cf. U.C.C. § 2A-217 Comment.

When the contract for sale has proceeded to the point that certain goods are designated the parties as those to which the contract refers, it is important to recognize that the buyer h₊ some interest in the goods. Under pre-Code law, the act of designating the goods was describeɩ as "appropriating them to the contract," and thereafter goods were called "ascertained goods." (See Uniform Sales Act §§ 17-20.) U.C.C. § 2-401(1)(first sentence) and U.C.C. § 2-501(1) use the term "identification" of goods to the contract, and the goods are spoken of as "identified." Generally, identification occurs when goods are designated by the seller as goods to which the contract refers. See U.C.C. § 2-501(1)(b).

The buyer obtains a "special property" by identification of goods. The incidents of this special property are summarized (see U.C.C. § 2-401 Comment 3):

1. *Buyer's Right to Goods on Seller's Insolvency.* A buyer who has paid a part or all of the price of goods in which he has a special property may on making and keeping good a tender of any unpaid portion of their price recover them from the seller if the seller becomes insolvent within ten days after receipt of the first installment on their price. U.C.C. §§ 2-711(2)(a), 2-502. This is discussed at § 7.04[D][1] below.

2. *Buyer's Right to Replevy the Goods.* The buyer has a right of replevin for goods identified to the contract (identification is the event which gives rise to buyer's special property) if after reasonable effort he is unable to cover for such goods. U.C.C. §§ 2-711(2)(b), 2-716(3). This is discussed at § 7.04[D][2] below.

3. *Rights of Seller's Creditors Against Sold Goods.* Generally, rights of unsecured creditors of the seller with respect to goods which have been identified to a contract for sale are subject to the buyer's rights to recover the goods under U.C.C. § 2-502 and U.C.C. § 2-716 summarized in the two preceding paragraphs. This is discussed at § 8.02.

4. *Suit Against Third Parties for Injury to Goods.* Where a third party so deals with goods which have been identified to a contract for sale as to cause actionable injury to a party to that contract, a right of action against the third party is in the party to the contract who has a special property in the goods. U.C.C. § 2-722(a). This is discussed at § 7.07[D] below.

5. *Rights of Good Faith Purchasers.* Certain good faith purchasers, *e.g.*, buyers in the ordinary course of business, may get better title to goods than their transferors had. Will these greater rights arise at the time the goods are identified (which gives rise to a special property) or delivered? See discussion at § 8.02 below.

§ 4.04 Insurable Interest

Read: U.C.C. § 2-501.

Black's Law Dictionary 720 (5th ed. 1979) defines "insurable interest":

Such a real and substantial interest in specific property as will prevent a contract to indemnify the person interested against its loss from being a mere wager policy. Such an interest as will make the loss of the property of pecuniary damage to the insured. . . . Generally, an "insurable interest" exists where insured derives pecuniary benefit or advantage by preservation and continued existence of property or would sustain pecuniary loss from its destruction.[3]

---

[3] Copyright © 1979 by West Publishing Co. Reprinted by permission.

Under the Code, a buyer obtains an insurable interest in goods (as well as a special property) by their identification. U.C.C. § 2-501(1). Special property is discussed at § 4.03 above.

Suppose goods are identified to a contract for sale but remain in the possession of seller. Buyer does not yet "own" the goods since seller has not completed his performance with reference to the physical delivery of the goods. U.C.C. § 2-401(2) discussed at § 4.02 above. Further, risk of loss has not passed to the buyer since buyer has not taken physical possession of the goods. U.C.C. § 2-509(3) discussed at § 4.06 below. Nevertheless, U.C.C. § 2-501(1) states that buyer has an insurable interest in the identified goods. What "pecuniary loss" will buyer sustain from destruction of the goods?

Seller retains an insurable interest so long as title to or any security interest in the goods remains in him. U.C.C. § 2-501(2). See *St. Paul Fire and Marine Insurance Co. v. Toman,* set forth below.

The principal significance of the insurable interest relates to the law of insurance, not the U.C.C. The Code, however, does recognize that a party to a contract for sale of goods with an insurable interest can sue third parties for injury to the goods. See U.C.C. § 2-722.

PROBLEM 4.1

Your client, William Works, recently bought a weekend retreat in the country with an old farm house and also a log barn. While imbued with the "Puritan" work ethic, William has decided he will not spend his weekends raising cattle. He is pleasantly surprised when Gable Gunther comes along and offers to buy the barn for his "historical village" which is a few miles away. Gunther has obtained many historical buildings throughout the country. William sells Gabe the barn and immediately heads for town to celebrate; Gabe returns home. That very day lightning strikes the barn and it burns completely down. William's insurance company, the Fireman's Mutual, refuses to pay on the basis that William no longer had an insurable interest.

Does the U.C.C. apply? Does William still have an insurable interest?

NOTES

(1) In a case similar to Problem 4.1, *St. Paul Fire and Marine Insurance Co. v. Toman,* 351 N.W.2d 146 (1984), the court noted:

In a newspaper display advertisement Toman advertised his public auction for September 23, 1981. Among the items listed for sale was a 24-foot by 40-foot house which was to be removed from Toman's farmstead. Prior to the auction sale, the auctioneer announced that the house had to be removed under terms negotiated by the buyer and Toman.

Van Collins was the successful bidder at the sale. He purchased the residence for $3,250.00, and issued his check to the auctioneer for that amount. No written document evidencing a sale was issued to Van Collins by the auctioneer.

On September 26, 1981, the house had been completely destroyed by fire. Insurer's policy of insurance covering loss by fire of Toman's property insured the residence for $28,000.00.

Insurer admits that if it is liable under the policy, it is liable for the payment of the full amount of the $28,000.00 since the policy was a "valued policy."

Insurer claims, however, that Toman no longer had an insurable interest in the house at the time of the fire loss and that the risk of the loss had passed to Van Collins. Toman contends he did have an insurable interest and payment under the policy provision should be effected.

The trial court concluded that the risk of loss had not yet passed to Van Collins; that there had been no "tender of delivery" as required by SDCL 57A-2-509(3); and, that the sale of the house was a sale of "goods" to which SDCL 57A-2-107(2) of the Uniform Commercial Code applied.

Insurer claims that at the time of the sale the house constituted real property and that title had passed to Van Collins, thereby negating any insurable interest in Toman. Insurer points out that SDCL 5 7A-2-107(1) provides that where "materials [are] to be removed from realty [it] is a contract for the sale of goods . . .if they are to be severed by the seller[,] but until severance a purported present sale thereof which is not effective as a transfer of an interest in land is effective only as a contract to sell." Insurer contends that this represented a contract for the sale of an interest in real property to which U.C.C. provisions have no application. Insurer insists that this conclusion is correct in view of the trial court's finding that title had passed to Van Collins. Such a conclusion is not warranted on an examination of the record. There is no document of any kind entered into evidence indicating a conveyance from Toman to Van Collins of an interest in real property.

Insurer further claims that because the sale of an interest in land was made the provisions of the Uniform Vendor and Purchaser Risk Act, particularly SDCL 43-26-7, are applicable and dispositive of Toman's claim of an insurable interest in the house. However, since we conclude that the sale of the house was not a sale of an interest in land, this contention is without merit.

It is important to note at this juncture that the concept of title under the U.C.C. is of decreased importance.

> No longer is the question of title of any importance in determining whether a buyer or a seller bears the risk of loss. It is true that the person with title will also (and incidentally) often bear the risk that the goods may be destroyed or lost; but the seller may have title and the buyer the risk, or the seller may have the risk and the buyer the title. In short, title is not a relevant consideration in deciding whether the risk has shifted to the buyer.

R. Nordstrom, Handbook of the Law of Sales, 393 (1970) quoted in *Martin v. Melland's Inc.,* 283 N.W.2d 76, 79 (ND 1979). The prevailing view is that the passage of title is not a final determining factor. Under the risk of loss provisions of the U.C.C. the courts should determine the rights of the parties.

Insurer contends that the sale was one for "goods" or personal property for the purpose of determining passage of title and then argues that the provisions of the Uniform Vendor and Purchaser Risk Act should be used to determine the risk of loss. This is a clear contradiction in legal theory. Simply put, insurer has failed to provide evidentiary support in the record and the settled law to support its claim that the sale of an interest in real property resulted when Toman's house was sold.

The provisions of SDCL 57A-2-1 07(2) provide that the sale of "other things attached to realty and capable of severance without material harm thereto. . .is a contract for the sale of goods. . .whether the subject matter is to be severed by the buyer or by the seller even though it forms part of the realty at the time of contracting, and the parties can by identification effect a present sale before severance." Here it is undisputed that Toman and Van Collins mutually identified the property being sold. It was in fact sold at the public auction sale on September 23, 1981.

(Matthew Bender & Co., Inc.)   (Pub.087)

SDCL 57A-2-501(2) recognizes that "[t]he seller retains an insurable interest in goods so long as title to or any security interest in the goods remains in him and where the identification is by the seller alone he may until default or insolvency or notification to the buyer that the identification is final substitute other goods for those identified." In addition SDCL 57A-2-509(3) provides:

> In any case not within subsection (1) or (2), the risk of loss passes to the buyer on his receipt of the goods if the seller is a merchant; otherwise the risk passes to the buyer on tender of delivery.

No one contends Toman as the seller was a "merchant" as defined in SDCL 57A-2-1 04(1). Further, it is clear that Toman never made the "tender of delivery" of the house as required by SDCL 57A-2-509(3). Van Collins knew that Toman was occupying the house at least on a part-time basis; he further knew from the auctioneer's announcement that the removal of the house would have to be negotiated with Toman since Toman not only used the house occasionally, but also retained personal property in it. We agree with the trial court that Toman had an insurable interest, SDCL 58-10-8, in the house at the time of the fire loss and payment by the insurer should be made pursuant to the terms of its policy of insurance.

The trial court awarded Toman prejudgment interest on the $28,000.00 principal sum from September 26, 1981, the date of the fire. Toman is entitled to prejudgment interest only from the date of the refusal of the claim since there was no showing that insurer was dilatory in conducting an investigation of the claim. We note that the summons and complaint was served Toman on December 31, 1981, less than ninety days after the fire loss. Since there was no other evidence about the refusal of the claim, we fix the date of refusal as of December 31, 1981. Interest shall begin to accrue from that date.

Accordingly, the judgment is affirmed in the principal sum with modification only as to the prejudgment interest.

(2) In the case just discussed, the Court states, *inter alia*, "We agree with the trial court that Toman had an insurable interest, SDCL 58-10-8, in the house at the time of the fire loss. . ." This statute reads:

> *58-10-8. Insurable interest in property defined.* "Insurable interest" as used in §§ 58-10-7 and 58-10-9 means any actual, lawful, and substantial economic interest in the safety or preservation of the subject of the insurance free from loss, destruction, or pecuniary damage or impairment.

Further, SDCL 58-10-7 states:

> *58-10-7. Insurance of property—Insurable interest required.* No contract of insurance of property or of any interest in property or arising from property shall be enforceable as to the insurance except for the benefit of persons having an insurable interest in the things insured as at the time of the loss.

See U.C.C. § 2-501(3).

(3) The Uniform Vendor and Purchaser Risk Act, particularly SDCL 43-26-7, and referenced in the case, states as follows:

> *43-26-7. Transfer of subject matter of contract for purchase and sale of realty—Destruction without fault of vendor—Taking by eminent domain—Payment of purchase price.* If, when either the legal title or the possession of the subject matter of the contract has

been transferred, all or any part thereof is destroyed without fault of the vendor or is taken by eminent domain, the purchaser is not thereby relieved from a duty to pay the price, nor is he entitled to recover any portion thereof that he has paid.

§ 4.05 Security Interest

Read: U.C.C. §§ 1-201(37), 9-113 Comment 1.

" 'Security interest' means an interest in personal property or fixtures which secures payment or performance of an obligation. . . . The special property interest of a buyer of goods [see § 4.03 above] on identification of such goods to a contract for sale under U.C.C. § 2-401is not a 'security interest,' but a buyer may also acquire a 'security interest' by complying with Article 9." U.C.C. § 1-201(37).

Security interests can arise under U.C.C. Article 2 Sales, *e.g.*, (1) the rights of a shipper-seller to exercise control over goods in the hands of a carrier when he ships "under reservation" pursuant to U.C.C. § 2-505 (see Chapter 10 below); (2) rights of a buyer who rejects non-conforming goods to hold and resell them if he has paid a part of the price or incurred certain expenses pursuant to U.C.C. § 2-711(3) (see § 7.04[B] below). See U.C.C. § 9-113 Comment 1.

§ 4.06 Risk of Loss

Read: U.C.C. §§ 2-509, 2-510, 2-327(see 2-326(1)), 2-303, 2-319 through 2-322, 2-324; see §§ 2-501 Comment 4, 2-709(1)(a), 7-204, 7-309.

Read also: U.C.C. §§ 2A-219, 2A-220, 2A-221, 2A-529(1)(a); CISG 66-70, see Arts. 25 and 36(1).

PROBLEM 4.2

Your client, Susan Santiago runs a jewelry shop in Oaxaca, Mexico. She agreed to purchase watches from Karen Karinol who operated a wholesale business in Miami. The contract stipulated "Oaxaca Mexico via Belize." There were no provisions allocating risk of loss while the watches were in possession of the carriers and no shipment terms such as FOB or C&F. The shipping cartons were opened in Belize for a customs inspection and no watches were contained therein! Karen's insurance company refuses to pay and Karen refuses to replace the watches. Your client Susan has no insurance covering these watches. Who has the risk of loss? Suppose Karen asks you what shipment term she should put into future contracts? Also she asks what are the meanings of various shipment terms she has encountered in some of her other contracts.

NOTES

In a similar case, *Pestana v. Karinol Corp.,* 367 So. 2d 1096 (1979), the court noted:

There are two types of sales contracts under Florida's Uniform Commercial Code wherein a carrier is used to transport the goods sold: a shipment contract and a destination contract. A shipment contract is considered the normal contract in which the seller is required to send the subject goods by carrier to the buyer but is not required to guarantee delivery thereof at a particular destination. Under a shipment contract, the seller, unless otherwise agreed, must: (1) put the goods sold in the possession of a carrier and make a contract for their transportation as may be reasonable having regard for the nature of the goods and other attendant circumstances, (2) obtain and promptly deliver or tender in due form any document necessary to enable the buyer to obtain possession of the goods or otherwise required by the agreement or by usage of the trade, and (3) promptly notify the buyer of the shipment. On a shipment contract, the risk of loss passes to the buyer when the goods sold are duly delivered to the carrier for shipment to the buyer. §§ 672.503 (Official U.C.C. comment 5), 672.504, 672.509(1), Fla Stat (1977).

A destination contract, on the other hand, is considered the variant contract in which the seller specifically agrees to deliver the goods sold to the buyer at a particular destination and to bear the risk of loss of the goods until tender of delivery. This can be accomplished by express provision in the sales contract to that effect or by the use of delivery terms such as F.O.B. (place of destination). Under a destination contract, the seller is required to tender delivery of the goods sold to the buyer at the place of destination. The risk of loss under such a contract passes to the buyer when the goods sold are duly tendered to the buyer at the place of destination while in the possession of the carrier so as to enable the buyer to take delivery. The parties must explicitly agree to a destination contract; otherwise the contract will be considered a shipment contract. §§ 672.31 9(1)(b), 672.503 (Official U.C.C. comment 5), 672.509(1), Fla Stat (1977).

Where the risk of loss falls on the seller at the time the goods sold are lost or destroyed, the seller is liable in damages to the buyer for non-delivery unless the seller tenders a performance in replacement for the lost or destroyed goods. On the other hand, where the risk of loss falls on the buyer at the time the goods sold are lost or destroyed, the buyer is liable to the seller for the purchase price of the goods sold. [U.C.C. § 2-709(1)(a).]

In the instant case, we deal with the normal shipment contract involving the sale of goods. The defendant Karinol pursuant to this contract agreed to send the goods sold, a shipment of watches, to the plaintiff's decedent in Chetumal, Mexico. There was no specific provision in the contract between the parties which allocated the risk of loss on the goods sold while in transit. In addition, there were no delivery terms such as F.O.B. Chetumal contained in the contract.

All agree that there is sufficient evidence that the defendant Karinol performed its obligations as a seller under the Uniform Commercial Code if this contract is considered a shipment contract. Karinol put the goods sold in the possession of a carrier and made a contract for the goods' safe transportation to the plaintiff's decedent; Karinol also promptly notified the plaintiff's decedent of the shipment and tendered to said party the necessary documents to obtain possession of the goods sold.

The plaintiff Pestana contends, however, that the contract herein is a destination contract in which the risk of loss on the goods sold did not pass until delivery on such goods had been tendered to him at Chetumal, Mexico—an event which never occurred. He relies for this position on the notation at the bottom of the contract between the parties which provides that the goods were to be sent to Chetumal, Mexico. We cannot agree. A "send to" or "ship to" term is a part of every contract involving the sale of goods where carriage is contemplated and has no significance in determining whether the contract is a shipment or destination contract for risk of loss purposes. As such, the "send to" term contained in this contract cannot, without more, convert this into a destination contract.

It therefore follows that the risk of loss in this case shifted to the plaintiff's decedent as buyer when the defendant Karinol as seller duly delivered the goods to the defendant freight forwarder American under a reasonable contract of carriage for shipment to the plaintiff's decedent in Chetumal, Mexico. The defendant Karinol, its agent the defendant American, and its insurer the defendant Fidelity could not be held liable to the plaintiff in this action. The trial court properly entered judgment in favor of all the defendants herein.

Affirmed.

PROBLEM 4.3

Jason sells a hundred thousand pounds of "St. Louis" style barbecue pork ribs to Eckrich, delivery to be effected by a transfer of the ribs from Jason's account in an independent warehouse to Eckrich's account in the same warehouse — which is to say without the ribs actually being moved. On January 13, Jason's phoned warehouse and requested that the ribs be transferred to Eckrich's account. Warehouse noted the transfer on its books immediately and mailed a warehouse receipt which was received by Eckrich on January 24. On January 17 the ribs were destroyed (not barbecued) by a fire at warehouse. Who suffers the risk of loss?

NOTES

(1) In the case from which the problem is drawn, *Jason Foods Inc. v. Peter Eckrich & Sons, Inc.*, 774 F.2d 214 (1985), the court noted that the underlying policies of U.C.C. risk of loss, *i.e.* control and ability to insure, were not helpful:

[L]et us shift now to the plane of policy. The Code sought to create a set of standard contract terms that would reflect in the generality of cases the preferences of contracting parties at the time of contract. One such preference is for assignments of liability—or, what amounts to the same thing, assignments of the risk of loss—that create incentives to minimize—the adverse consequences of untoward events such as (in this case) a warehouse fire. There are two ways of minimizing such consequences. One is to make them less painful by insuring against them. Insurance does not prevent a loss—it merely spreads it—but in doing so it reduces (for those who are risk averse) the disutility of the loss. So if one of the contracting parties can insure at lower cost than the other, this is an argument for placing the risk of loss on him, to give him an incentive to do so. But that as we have seen is not a factor in this case; either party could have insured (or have paid the warehouse to assume strict liability for loss or destruction of the goods, in which event the warehouse would have insured them), and so far as the record shows at equal cost.

The other method of minimizing the consequences of an unanticipated loss is through prevention of the loss. If one party is in a better position than the other to prevent it, this is a reason for placing the risk of loss on him, to give him an incentive to prevent it. It would be a reason for placing liability on a seller who still had possession of the goods, even though title had passed. But between the moment of transfer of title by Jason's and the movement of receipt of the warehouse receipt by Eckrich, neither party to the sale had effective control over the ribs. They were in a kind of limbo, until (to continue the Dantesque image) abruptly propelled into a hotter region. With Jason's having relinquished title and Eckrich not yet aware that it had acquired it, neither party had an effective power of control.

But this is not an argument for holding that the risk of loss shifted at the moment of transfer; it is just an argument for regarding the parties' positions as symmetrical from the standpoint of ability either to prevent or to shift losses. In such a case we have little to assist us besides the language of subsection (b) and its surrounding subsections and the U.C.C. comments; but these materials do point pretty clearly to the conclusion that the risk of loss did not pass at the moment of transfer.

(2) The court then decided the case:

When did it pass? Does "acknowledgment" means receipt, as in the surrounding subsections of § 2-509(2), or mailing? Since the evidence was in conflict over whether the acknowledgment was mailed on January 17 (and at what hour), which was the day of the fire, or on January 18, this could be an important question—but in another case, Jason's waived it. The only theory it tendered to the district court, or briefed and argued in this court, was that the risk of loss passed either on January 13, when the transfer of title was made on the books of the warehouse, or at the latest on January 14, because Eckrich knew the ribs would be transferred at the warehouse sometime between January 10 and 14. We have discussed the immateriality of the passage of title on January 13; we add that the alternative argument, that Eckrich knew by January 14 that it owned the ribs, exaggerates what Eckrich knew. By the close of business on January 14 Eckrich had a well-founded expectation that the ribs had been transferred to its account; but considering the many slips that are possible between cup and lips, we do not think that this expectation should fix the point at which the risk shifts. If you were told by an automobile dealer from whom you bought a car that the car would be delivered on January 14, you would not take out insurance effective that day, without waiting for the actual delivery.

Finally, Jason's argument from trade custom or usage is unavailing. The method of transfer that the parties used was indeed customary but there was no custom or usage on when the risk of loss passed to the buyer.

Affirmed.

(3) *Passage of Risk of Loss on Buyer's Receipt of Goods.* In *Hughes v. Al Green Inc.,* 65 Ohio St.2d 110, 418 N.E.2d 1355, 31 U.C.C. Rep. 890 (1981), buyer of an automobile paid a down payment and took immediate possession. Before leaving the dealership, buyer signed a purchase contract and an application for certificate of title. En route from the dealership to her home, buyer was involved in a collision and the automobile was substantially damaged. Under U.C.C. § 2-509(3), the risk of loss for the damage passed to the buyer on receipt of the goods, since seller was a merchant. Buyer, however, pointed to the Ohio Certificate of Title Act, RC § 4505.04, which provides:

No person acquiring a motor vehicle from the owner thereof, whether such owner is a manufacturer, importer, dealer, or otherwise, shall acquire any right, title, claim, or interest in or to said motor vehicle until such person has had issued to him a certificate of title to said motor vehicle, or delivered to him a manufacturer's or importer's certificate for it; nor shall any waiver or estoppel operate in favor of such person against a person having possession of such certificate of title, or manufacturer's or importer's certificate for said motor vehicle, for a valuable consideration.

No court in any case at law or in equity shall recognize the right, title, claim, or interest of any person in or to any motor vehicle sold or disposed of, or mortgaged or encumbered, unless evidenced:

(A) By a certificate of title or a manufacturer's or importer's certificate issued in accordance with sections 4505.01 to 4505.19, inclusive, of the Revised Code.

(B) By admission in the pleadings or stipulation of the parties.

Buyer's argument was that the car dealer was in breach of contract because when the certificate of title was issued in buyer's name and ownership of the automobile thereby legally transferred to her, the dealer no longer possessed that for which she bargained, i.e., an undamaged automobile.

The court held that risk of loss passed to buyer on receipt of goods per U.C.C. § 2-509(3) and that the Certificate of Title Act was irrelevant to the issue of risk of loss.

The court stated:

> This provision [U.C.C. § 2-509] represents a significant shift away from the prior importance of the concept of title in determining the point at which risk of loss passes from the seller to the buyer. Under the common law, not only did title to the contract goods determine risk of loss, but it also determined the issues of the buyer's right to the goods (through replevin), the seller's right to the purchase price, and the right to proceed against tortfeasors. Under the U.C.C., however, "[e]ach provision . . .with regard to the rights, obligations, and remedies of the seller, the buyer, purchasers, or other third parties applies irrespective of title to the goods except where the provision refers to such title." RC 1302.42 (U.C.C. § 2-401).

Thus, as noted in Nordstrom, Sales, Section 130, at page 393:

> [T]here is. . .one principle which applies to all risk of loss problems. This principle is summarized in one sentence from the Comments:

>> The underlying theory of these sections on risk of loss is the adoption of the contractual approach rather than an arbitrary shifting of the risk with the "property" in the goods.

> No longer is the question of title of any importance in determining whether a buyer or a seller bears the risk of loss. It is true that the person with title will also (and incidentally) often bear the risk that the goods may be destroyed or lost; *but the seller may have title and the buyer the risk*, or the seller may have the risk and the buyer the title. In short, title is not a relevant consideration in deciding whether the risk has shifted to the buyer. (Emphasis added.)

Similarly, in 3A Bender's Uniform Commercial Code Service, Section 8.03, it is stated, at page 8-21, that U.C.C. § 2-509 (RC 1302.53):

> sets forth a contractual approach, as distinguished from the property concept of title, to solving the issues arising when goods are damaged or destroyed. The section focuses on specific acts, such as tender of delivery by the seller, or receipt of the goods or of documents representing the goods by the buyer. Title is relevant under this section only if the parties provide that risk of loss shall depend upon the location of title.

In the instant cause, the appellant-buyer had received possession of the automobile as partial execution of a merchant-seller's obligations under a purchase contract. Thus, unless other statutory provisions make RC 1302.53 inapplicable, the appellant, as a buyer in receipt of goods identified to a contract, must bear the loss of the car's value resulting from the collision.

RC 1302.53 does not conflict with RC 4505.04 [the Certificate of Title Act]. The purpose of the Certificate of Title Act is to prevent the importation of stolen motor vehicles, to protect Ohio bona fide purchasers against thieves and wrongdoers, and to create an instrument evidencing title to, and ownership of, motor vehicles. (Citations omitted). The Act was not adopted to clarify contractual rights and duties, as was RC Chapter 1302.

As stated in *Grogan Chrysler-Plymouth, Inc. v. Gottfried*, (1978), 59 Ohio App. 2d 91, 94-95, 392 N.E.2d 1283:

> RC 4505.04 was intended to apply to litigation where the parties were rival claimants to title, i.e., ownership of the automobile; to contests between the alleged owner and lien claimants; to litigation between the owner holding the valid certificate of title and one holding a stolen, forged or otherwise invalidly issued certificate of title; and to similar situations. (Citations omitted.)

In cases decided prior to the adoption of the Uniform Commercial Code, the Certificate of Title Act was properly consulted in determining whether a buyer or seller bore the risk of loss or could proceed against third-party tortfeasors because determination of those issues was dependent, under the common law, upon a finding of ownership. With ownership no longer being determinative, RC 4505.04 is irrelevant to the issue of risk of loss, and thus does not conflict with a U.C.C. risk of loss analysis.

(4) *Transfer of Title and Risk Under the U.S.A.* Uniform Sales Act § 22 said in part: "[T]he goods remain at the seller's risk until the property therein is transferred to the buyer, but when the property therein is transferred to the buyer the goods are at the buyer's risk. Also, U.S.A. § 19 Rule 1 said: "Where there is an unconditional contract to sell specific goods, in a deliverable state, the property in the goods passes to the buyer when the contract is made."

These provisions were applied in *Radloff v. Bragmus,* 214 Minn. 130, 7 N.W.2d 491 (1943), where plaintiff Radloff on November 9, 1940, sold his flock of turkeys (about 100 hens and 600 toms) to Bragmus. Removal was to be made by Bragmus Nov. 13. On Nov. 11 a blizzard destroyed some 330 of the turkeys and those not destroyed were damaged. The court held that title (and risk) passed to the buyer on Nov. 9 when the contract was made. The goods were "in a deliverable state" on Nov. 9. There was nothing further for plaintiff to do "for the purpose of putting them into a deliverable state." (The counting, weighing and grading of the turkeys were purely matters of routine and of simple computation.)

When would risk of loss pass under the U.C.C.? What policy considerations are relevant? See U.C.C. §§ 2-401, 2-509 and Comment 3.

(5) *Sale on Approval.* In *First Coinvestors, Inc. v. Coppola,* 388 N.Y.S.2d 833, 20 U.C.C. Rep 884 (D. Suffolk City 1976), a coin collector (buyer) submitted an order for certain coins from a coin dealer through a mail order coin collecting club. The dealer mailed the coins to the buyer by registered mail, return receipt requested, on a "sale on approval" basis. See U.C.C. § 2-326(1)(a). The receipt was signed by an unknown person who presumably stole the coins. Held: Risk of loss does not pass to a buyer on a sale on approval until he accepts the goods under U.C.C. § 2-606. Hence, the dealer-seller bore the risk of loss. U.C.C. §§ 2-509(4), 2-327(1)(a).

§ 4.07 Risk of Loss: Breach Settings

Read: U.C.C. § 2-510; see §§ 2-501, 2-508, 2-606, 2-608; cf. § 9-207(2)(b).

PROBLEM 4.4

Prestige Motors delivered a new Jeep Cherokee to your client without the required undercoating. The jeep was returned to Prestige later that day so the coating could be applied. The car was stolen from Prestige's premises and never recovered. Prestige denies any responsibility and says that its insurance company also will not pay. It says your client should have taken out insurance coverage which would cover the theft. What is your argument and position?

NOTE

In a similar case to the fact pattern of the above Problem, *Jakowski v. Carole Chevelet, Inc.,* the court noted:

Given the undisputed facts the operation of § 2-510(1) is inescapable. The goods failed to conform, the buyer never accepted them and the defect was never cured. Accordingly, the risk of loss remained on the seller and judgment is granted for plaintiff. A further note on the law is in order.

It is possible to conjure up a host of hypotheticals leading to seemingly perverse results under § 2-510. The section has been the subject of some scholarly criticism. See *e.g.,* White & Summers, *supra,* § 5.5 at 187. Williston, *The Law of Sales in the Proposed Uniform Commercial Code,* 63 Harv. L. Rev. 561, 583 (1950).

The fact is, however, that those courts considering it have had little difficulty in applying it as written. [Cases cited.]

The rule is simple enough: under NJSA 1 2A: 2-510(1) where goods fail to conform to the contract of sale, the risk of loss remains on the seller until the buyer accepts the goods or until the seller cures the defect. In the aforecited cases, such was the result even though in all of them the goods were still in the buyer's possession at the time of their destruction.

For present purposes it is adequate to hold simply that where a seller obtains possession of the goods in an effort to cure defects in them so as to comply with his end of the bargain, he is under a contractual duty to redeliver them to the buyer. In failing to do so, he has breached the contract.

§ 4.08 Warranty of Title

Read: U.C.C. § 2-312.

Read also: U.C.C. § 2A-211; CISG Arts. 41-44.

PROBLEM 4.5

Your client has just contracted to purchase a modern printing press machine from the News Now Company for $100,000. Your client hopes to resell it to the Current Times Company for $150,000. A computer mechanic, who has his own independent repair services, has filed a $9000 mechanic lien against it.

Your client has asked News Now to pay the mechanic which it had hired and remove the lien. It refuses to do so saying his services were unsatisfactory and it had to hire another mechanic to fix it.

Your client also knows that Current Times will not purchase the machine from it if there is a lien outstanding.

What is your advice to your client?

NOTES

(1) 2 Hawkland, Uniform Commercial Code Series § 2-312:02 (1984), states in part:[4]

> [T]here may be situations where the seller has the power, but not the right, to convey a perfect title to the goods that may expose the buyer unreasonably to the claim of a third person to ownership. In those cases, there is a breach of warranty of title, even though the buyer has the legal ability to defeat the third-party claim. Such a situation might arise, for example, under section 2-403 where a third party delivers goods to a merchant for repair. If the merchant is in the business of selling goods of the kind, he had the power to sell the entrusted goods to a buyer in the ordinary course free and clear of the third party's ownership rights. This new rule is one which many third parties might not be aware of or understand and some third parties might proceed against the buyer in the ordinary course, even though they could not win a lawsuit if he could establish that status. That being the case, the buyer should be able to revoke acceptance, or sue for breach of warranty of title on the ground that the transfer was not rightful. The test is not whether the buyer can win a lawsuit against third-party claimants, but whether he is unreasonably exposed to such a suit.

U.C.C. § 2-403 is discussed at Chapter 8, "Rights of Third Parties-Good Faith Purchase."

Compare the Hawkland quote above with U.C.C. § 3-417 Comment 9.

(2) In *Sunseri v. RKO-Stanley Warner Theaters, Inc.*, 248 Pa Super 111, 374 A.2d 1342 (1977), the following language in a bill of sale for recreational equipment was held insufficiently specific to exclude the warranty of title:

> It is expressly understood and agreed that seller shall in nowise be deemed or held to be obligated, liable, or accountable upon or under guaranties [sic] or warranties, in any manner or form including, but not limited to, the implied warranties of title, merchantability. . .

Note that the warranty of title is not designated as an "implied" warranty, and hence is not subject to U.C.C. § 2-316(3) which deals with the exclusion or modification of implied quality warranties (see Chapter 5 below). Disclaimer of the warranty of title is governed by U.C.C. § 2-312(2), which requires either specific language or the described circumstances. See Comment 6 to U.C.C. § 2-312.

(3) In *Catlin Aviations v. Equilense Corp.*, 626 P.2d 857 (1981), the court said:

> Buyer argues although an aggrieved buyer must mitigate damages, such is inapplicable where the seller has the duty to uphold its warranty of title. However there is no evidence in the record that buyer informed seller of its potential sale and unless the cloud was removed quickly the sale would be lost. Without such knowledge seller should not be held to account for its inaction, especially when buyer could have mitigated easily, quickly and reasonably, and saved its potential sale. We agree with the trial court under the facts of the case in its refusal to grant consequential damages.

---

[4] Copyright © 1984 by American Law Institute. Reprinted by permission.

CHAPTER 5

WARRANTY/PRODUCTS LIABILITY

§ 5.01 Introduction

Read: U.C.C. §§ 2-313, 2-314, 2-315, 2-316, 2-317, 2-318 and Restatement of Torts (Second), § 402A.

Read also: U.C.C. §§ 2A-210, 2A-212 through 2A-216; CISG Arts. 35-40, see Arts. 27, 44.

There is "much more than meets the eye" in sales contracts. A part of the "contract" is found in advertising sales talk, brochures, booklets, and tags which may constitute express warranties. Another part consists of the standards set by implied warranties under the U.C.C., the obligations imposed by the strict liability of § 402A of the Restatement of Torts Second, or federal legislation. Caselaw also has expanded these obligations.

§ 5.02 Historical Development

Some warranty law is found in the time of the fair courts in the thirteenth and fourteenth centuries; the examples in Chapter 1 relating to the defective herring, p. 3 *supra*, reflects this development.

Later, the common law courts predominated and warranty law went through a new development. In the 1600's, it was necessary to use special language to create a warranty. In *Chandelor v. Lopus,* 1 Jac. 1, 79 Eng. Rep. 3 (1625), the plaintiff asserted that the defendant being a goldsmith, and having skill in jewels and precious stones, had a stone which he affirmed to Lopus to be a bezar-stone, and sold it to Lopus for one hundred pounds; but it was not a bezar-stone.

The court held that "the bare affirmation that it was bezar-stone, without warranting it to be so, is no cause for action; and although he knew it to be no bezar-stone, it is not material; for every one in selling his wares will affirm that his wares are good, or the wares which he sells is sound; yet he does not warrant them to be so, it is no cause of action. "

In the late 1700's and early 1800's, implied warranties were developed. While it appears that implied warranty as a cause of action was being argued in the mid-1700's, it was not until 1815 in the case of *Gardiner v. Gray*, 4 Camp. 144, 171 Eng. Rep. (1815), that the cornerstone for the establishment of the implied warranty of merchantability was laid. In that case, the buyer purchased 12 bags of waste silk which was of such an inferior quality that it was not saleable under the denomination of "waste silk." The judge was of the opinion

[t]hat under such circumstances, the purchaser has a right to expect a saleable article answering the description in the contract. Without any warranty, this is an implied term in every such contract. Where there is no opportunity to inspect the commodity, the maxim of *caveat emptor* does not apply. He cannot without a warranty insist that it shall be of any particular quality

of fineness, but the intention of both parties must be taken to be that it shall be saleable in the market under the denomination mentioned in the contract between them. The purchaser cannot be supposed to buy goods to lay them on a dunghill. The question then is whether the commodity purchased by the plaintiff be of such a quality as can be reasonably brought into the market to be sold as waste silk? The witnesses describe it as unfit for the purposes of waste silk, and of such a quality that it cannot be sold under that denomination.

The development of warranty law may be viewed as a pendulum which has swung back and forth — at times favoring the buyer, at times the seller. In its earliest period, it appears to have favored the buyer. Whether it be in the manor court, the church court, or the fair courts, it afforded him some protection. It was not, of course, sophisticated in concept, and practical difficulties of protection also were present.

In the period of *caveat emptor*, the shift was decidedly in favor of the seller. It is somewhat questionable, however, how strong this doctrine was.

With the rebirth of warranty in the late 1700's, the pendulum seemed to swing again, giving the buyer protection against defective goods.

With the establishment of implied warranties, the pendulum began to swing at a slightly faster pace. From the initial protection given the buyer, with the use of disclaimers and the emphasis placed on the "privity" doctrine, it swung to the seller. As some courts began to find reasons to circumvent the then-used disclaimers, the pendulum swung back toward the buyer. The seller, however, merely improved the wording of the disclaimer to take into account the judicial decisions. From disclaimer to circumvention to disclaimer — from seller to buyer to seller — began the pattern. With the assault of the courts on the doctrine of "privity" and their more critical view of "disclaimers," the pendulum has come back somewhat in favor of protecting the buyer against defective products. For the small buyer or consumer, in many instances, there are practical difficulties of securing adequate protection.

The "pendulum" model is somewhat of an oversimplification of legal phenomena since some of the periods of favoring the buyer or seller overlapped. Also, of course, jurisdictional variations existed. Nevertheless, it is helpful in understanding the broader movement of the law in this field. The U.C.C. represented a compromise, permitting the pendulum to swing in favor of the buyer with its warranty sections, and in favor of the seller with its disclaimer section. Its provision on privity also represented only a slight swing toward the buyer, while remaining primarily neutral. It was with § 402A of the Restatement of Torts Second, which eliminated disclaimer and privity as defenses, that the pendulum swung toward the buyer. But, as seen later, the U.C.C. rather than § 402A may apply in some cases involving commercial buyers and sellers.

Warranties also are included in Article 2A on leasing. The drafters noted that:

All of the express and implied warranties of the Article on Sales (Article 2) are included (Sections 2A-210 through 2A-216, revised to reflect differences in lease transactions). The lease of goods is sufficiently similar to the sale of goods to justify this decision. Further, many courts have reached the same decision.

In the mid-1990s, a proposal was drafted and is under consideration in the ALI for the reformulation of § 402A of the Restatement of Torts Second.

§ 5.03 Express Warranties

Read: U.C.C. § 2-313.

Read also: U.C.C. § 2A-210; CISG Art. 35(1), (2)(c), (3) and Arts. 36-40.

PROBLEM 5.1

Your firm is "fortunate" to represent some well known actors and entertainers. One day Brian Keith (once played on TV) comes to the firm with a problem. It seems that even though plaintiff belonged to the Waikiki Yacht Club, had attended a sailing school, had joined the Coast Guard Auxiliary and had sailed on many yachts in order to ascertain his preferences, he had not previously owned a yacht. He attended a boat show in Long Beach during October 1978 and looked at a number of boats, speaking to sales representatives and obtaining advertising literature. In the literature, the sailboat which is the subject of this action, called an "Island Trader 41," was described as a seaworthy vessel. In one sales brochure, this vessel is described as "a picture of sure-footed seaworthiness." In another, it is called "a carefully well-equipped, and very seaworthy live-aboard vessel." Brian says he relied on representations in the sales brochures in regard to the purchase and that he and a sales representative also discussed desire for a boat which was ocean-going and would cruise long distances. Being a cautious individual, Brian asked his friend Buddy Ebsen (who played Jed on the Beverly Hillbillies on TV) who was involved in a boat building enterprise, to inspect the boat. Mr. Ebsen and one of his associates, both of whom had extensive experience with sailboats, observed the boat and advised plaintiff that the vessel would suit his stated needs. A deposit was paid on the boat, a purchase contract was entered into, and optional accessories for the boat were ordered. After delivery of the vessel, a dispute arose in regard to its seaworthiness. The seller refuses to accept the boat back and refuses to return the deposit. What are Brian's rights? What defenses will the Seller raise? Who should win? Why? (See *Keith v. Buchanan*, 220 Cal. Rptr. 392, 42 U.C.C. Rep. 386 (1985).)

NOTES

(1) In *Szajna v. General Motors Corp., 40 U.C.C. Rep. 77 (Ill. App. 1985)*, plaintiff filed a class action suit against defendant General Motors (GMC). In his complaint, plaintiff argued that the trade name "1976 Pontiac Ventura" was a description of the car which created an express warranty that the car would have component parts of a particular kind and quality. The court found that "the use of a trade name, alone, [cannot] be extended to encompass a 'description' of the component parts therein." Compare Szajna to *Kilbourn v. Henderson*, 65 So.2d 533 (1953), where the court affirmed the finding of a breach of express warranty where the car advertised as a "1940 Mercury" was found to have a motor manufactured several years before 1940.

(2) In *Slyman v. Pickwick Farms*, 39 U.C.C. Rep. 1630 (Ohio 1984), the court held that a description given by the seller, or adoption by seller of a third party's opinion, which is a part of the "basis of the bargain," will create a warranty under U.C.C. § 2-313.

David Slyman, plaintiff, attended the Scioto-Tattersalls and Ohio Harness Horse Breeders, Inc. yearling sale. Plaintiff purchased five horses, all consigned by Pickwick Farms. One of the colts, named Masterpoint, purchased for $4,200, occasionally exhibited symptoms of difficulty in breathing. Prior to bids being accepted, a veterinarian, at the request of Pickwick Farms, read the following statement over the public address system:

This animal at very rare intervals will make a slight noise on expiration of air. This is due to the so-called false nasal folds being very slightly more softer than normal. The true nasal openings and nasal cavities are normal in size and in no way is the animal's breathing affected.

A few days after accepting delivery of Masterpoint, William Smith, the trainer, notified plaintiff that the horse was having difficulty breathing and that its training would have to cease.

Plaintiff notified Pickwick Farms, by letter, of the problem and requested that his purchase money plus expenses be returned. Plaintiff also had Masterpoint examined by Dr. Catherine Kohn, a doctor and associate professor of Equine Medicine and Surgery at Ohio State University. Dr. Kohn's examination revealed that Masterpoint's breathing problem was a result of a congenital defect of the ventral meatus and, as a result, Masterpoint could not race in his present condition.

The *Slyman* court, at 39 U.C.C. Rep. 1635-6, stated that:

> As far as the origin of the statement is concerned, regardless of the fact that the description was formulated by a third party, and not by the seller, the statement may still be found to be part of the basis of the bargain and, therefore, constitutes an express warranty. "[T]he seller need only introduce it into the bargaining process so that it becomes part of the basis of the bargain. . ." The major factor to be considered when dealing with a statement originating from a third party is whether or not the description or statement in question became a part of the basis of the bargain. The origin of the statement is not important so long as it is the seller who introduces it into the bargaining process. In the instant case, Knappenberger examined Masterpoint on October 12, 1979 and prepared his evaluation of the horse at the request of Pickwick Farms. It was Pickwick who introduced the statement into the bargaining process by having it read aloud before the sale of the horse. As such, the description given by [Pickwick's veterinarian] concerning the horse's respiratory condition at the time of the sale constituted an express warranty.

(3) Warranties in writing in consumer sales must comply with the provisions of the Magnuson-Moss Act. See § 5.10[A], *infra.*

§ 5.04 Implied Warranties

[A] Merchantability

Read: U.C.C. § 2-314.

Read also: U.C.C. §§ 2A-212, 1-205(1990); CISG. Art. 35(1), (2)(a) and (d) and (3) and Arts. 36-40.

PROBLEM 5.2

Your firm is representing Sara Mayflower, who suffered serious injury from a fish bone which lodged in her throat while eating fish chowder at the Clipper Ship Restaurant. At a small social gathering of several of the firm's members and spouses, the general topic of fish chowder is mentioned. One of the wives mentions that she has an excellent fish chowder recipe her great-grandmother, Mrs. John Standish, used. Another said she has several recipe books with "fish chowder" in them. One of your partners remembers having read about fish chowder in *The House of the Seven Gables* by Hawthorne. Is this conversation of any importance to your case?

NOTES

The courts have split on the issue of liability for injuries suffered from substances in food consumed in a restaurant. Two distinct lines of authority have emerged, the "foreign-natural" test and the "reasonable expectations" test. Although both theories are usually applied to objects found in food, they are also applicable to cases of chemical contamination, such as food poisoning. In *Battiste v. St. Thomas Dining Club,* United States District Court, DVI (1979), plaintiff brought suit for damages resulting from ciguatera fish poisoning contracted after she consumed a fish dinner served by defendant. In addition to an assumption of risk defense, defendant also pleaded that ciguatera fish poisoning is a natural, latent condition in fish; thus, the seller is not liable under the implied warranties in U.C.C. §§ 2-314 and 2-315.

The "reasonable expectations" test holds that "it is a question for the trier of fact whether a buyer could reasonably expect to find the substance in the food consumed" whereas the "foreign-natural" test will bar a buyer from recovery as a matter of law "where the substance in the food which causes the injury was 'natural' to the food served." *Battiste.* The court ruled that the "reasonable expectations" was the better choice, finding that this test was more consistent with Restatement (Second) of Torts § 402A (1965).

[B] Fitness for a Particular Purpose

Read: U.C.C. § 2-315, cf. § 2-314(2)(c); see § 2-317.

Read also: U.C.C. § 2A-213, cf. § 2A-212(2)(c), see § 2A-215 (1990); CISG Art. 35(2)(b), (3) and Arts. 36-40.

PROBLEM 5.3

Two farmers, Richard Warren and James Perry came to your law office in regard to some defective cabbage seed they purchased. The facts and evidence thus far may be summarized as in the statement below. What type of warranties could be asserted? If fitness for particular purpose is asserted, how would it be articulated? Can you have more than one type of warranty from the same facts and can you assert more than one theory?

FACTS OF PROBLEM

In August 1979, plaintiff Richard Warren went to W.S. Clark and Sons and spoke with Murry Fulcher. Mr. Fulcher informed plaintiff that there was a shortage of RioVerde and A-C 5 seed, and offered to sell plaintiff "Sanibel" seed instead. Plaintiff testified as follows:

So I asked him did he know if these cabbage would winter over or had any experience with them, because I had never heard of this type cabbage.

Mr. Fulcher then called the New York seed company that sold the seed. Plaintiff testified:

I asked Mr. Fulcher to ask the man or the woman, whoever it was he was talking to, to be sure to ask him if these cabbage seed would winter over in eastern North Carolina, specifically Carteret County, the area I was concerned with. Mr. Fulcher asked this question and assured me that these cabbage would winter over and do as good, if not better, than the AC 5 or the Rio Verde. Therefore, based upon this conversation and the information Mr. Fulcher had received, I ordered 20 pounds of the Sanibel seeds.

. . . .

I told Mr. Fulcher that if he didn't really know anything about it and he was not sure of these Sanibel seeds, not to even order them, that I would wait and get Florida plants, what I know I could make a crop with. And he stated these cabbage would be all right. Therefore we ordered the seed.

Plaintiff also testified about a later conversation with Mr. Fulcher, in which the following interchange occurred:

I said, "Monk, now are you sure, absolutely sure, have no doubt in your mind that these seeds are going to do well in eastern North Carolina and Carteret County?" And Mr. Fulcher replied to me, said, "I'll guarantee this seed will be as good, if not better, than the AC 5's or the Rio Verde."

Plaintiff planted the seed on 28 September and transferred the plants to fields in January, 1980. In early March, plaintiff observed that the plants "were beginning to look funny." Plaintiff informed Mr. Fulcher of the plants' unusual appearance and his concern that the cabbage was going to "run up." Plaintiff testified:

I told him, I said, "Now, Monk, if there's any doubt in your mind at this point, I have still got time to order plants from Florida and still raise a crop." He said, "No," said, "I don't think you have anything to worry about," said, "that's the way these cabbage grow." He said, "They grow funny and different than your other type cabbage."

As a result of this conversation, plaintiff did not order plants from Florida. More than 50 per cent of the cabbages he raised from Sanibel seed went to seed and were thus unmarketable. Plaintiff James Perry testified as follows:

I asked Monk, I said, "Monk, Richard told me you found some cabbage seed," and he said, "Yes, I couldn't find any Rio Verde or AC 5 but I found a cabbage called Sanibel that I believe will grow just as good a crop if not better than the AC 5 or the Rio Verde, and the only stipulation on them is you can't put them quite as far apart as you do the Rio Verde or they will get big on you and if they get too big you can't market them." So I said, "Murry, you know the type of weather we have in Carteret County." He said, "Jimmy, I believe these cabbage is going to be the cabbage of the future for you boys. You put more plants per acre and I believe they will produce more." I said, "Okay, I want you to order me five pounds."

Mr. Perry also testified to a later conversation with Mr. Fulcher:

I called him and I told him, I said, "Monk, these cabbage don't look right," and I said, "Now we still got time to get the cabbage plants out of Florida." And I said, "What are you thinking about?" He said, "Jimmy, I think that's the way to go. I wouldn't worry with them. I believe they'll be all right." So I didn't do anything.

NOTES

(1) In *El Fredo Pizza, Inc. v. Roto-Flex-Oven Co.*, 261 N.W.2d 358 (1978), plaintiff needed to purchase a new pizza oven for a new El Fredo branch store. Plaintiff negotiated with Roto-Flex, and entered into a contract on September 1, 1973, whereby plaintiff purchased a "Pizza Oven Special" for his new restaurant.

The oven was installed on October 22, 1973, and problems developed immediately. After the oven continued to malfunction plaintiff replaced it with one from a different vendor. The El Fredo court's holding follows:

Roto-Flex contends that the evidence was insufficient to submit the issue of implied warranty of fitness of the oven for a particular purpose to the jury because the evidence did not show that Center Street Pizza had relied on Roto-Flex' skill or judgment in purchasing the oven. Two implied warranties provided for in the Uniform Commercial Code are relevant to this case. Under section 2-314, U.C.C., a warranty that the goods shall be merchantable is implied in a contract for their sale if the seller is a merchant with respect to goods of that kind. In order for goods to be merchantable under section 2-314, they must be at least such as are fit for the ordinary purposes for which such goods are used. Under this implied warranty, no reliance upon the seller need be shown. Under section 2-315, U.C.C., a warranty of fitness for a particular purpose is implied where the seller at the time of contracting has reason to know any particular purpose for which the goods are required and that the buyer is relying on the seller's skill or judgment to select or furnish suitable goods. . . .

Roto-Flex' argument essentially is that Center Street Pizza did not rely on Roto-Flex' skill or judgment in buying the oven, but relied on the judgment of Fred Lennon, who recommended the Roto-Flex oven because his experience with a similar oven had been favorable. This argument misses the mark. Comment 1 to section 2-315, U.C.C., provides that whether or not the warranty of fitness for a particular purpose arises in any individual case is basically a question of fact to be determined by the circumstances of the contracting. Under this section the buyer need not bring home to the seller actual knowledge of the particular purpose for which the goods are intended or of his reliance on the seller's skill and judgment, if the circumstances are such that the seller has reason to realize the purpose intended or that the reliance exists. The buyer, of course, must actually be relying on the seller. If anything, the fact that Center Street Pizza went to Roto-Flex, to purchase an oven because of Lennon's knowledge of past success with a similar oven underscores the fact that Center Street Pizza was relying on Roto-Flex skill to furnish suitable goods for its business. The testimony indicated that Roto-Flex ovens are custom built for Roto-Flex customers, and Roto-Flex was aware of the particular purpose for which the oven was required in this case. Under the circumstances of this case, the evidence was clearly sufficient to raise the factual question of reliance under section 2-315, U.C.C., and it was proper to submit that question to the jury.

Affirmed as modified. [Modifications were to the amount of damages only.—Ed.]

(2) Questions of reliance may arise in U.C.C. § 2-315 cases. The court in *Keith v. Buchanan, supra* Problem 5.1, discussed this matter:

II. Implied Warranty

Appellant also claimed breach of the implied warranty of fitness for a particular purpose in regard to the sale of the subject vessel. An implied warranty of fitness for a particular purpose arises when a "seller at the time of contracting has reason to know any particular purpose for which the goods are required and that the buyer is relying on the seller's skill or judgment to select or furnish suitable goods," which are fit for such purpose. The Consumer Warranty Act makes such an implied warranty applicable to retailers, distributors, and manufacturers. An implied warranty of fitness for a particular purpose arises only where (1) the purchaser at the time of contracting intends to use the goods for a particular purpose, (2) the seller at the time of contracting has reason to know of this particular purpose, (3) the buyer relies on the seller's skill or judgment to select or furnish goods suitable for the particular purpose, and (4) the seller at the time of contracting has reason to know that the buyer is relying on such skill and judgment.

The reliance elements are important to the consideration of whether an implied warranty of fitness for a particular purpose exists. "If the seller had no reason to know that he was being relied upon, his conduct in providing goods cannot fairly be deemed a tacit representation of their suitability for a particular purpose. And if the buyer did not in fact rely, then the principal justification for imposing a fitness warranty disappears." The major question in determining the existence of an implied warranty of fitness for a particular purpose is the reliance by the buyer upon the skill and judgment of the seller to select an article suitable for his needs.

The trial court found that the plaintiff did not rely on the skill and judgment of the defendants to select a suitable vessel, but that he rather relied on his own experts. "Our sole task is to determine 'whether the evidence, viewed in the light most favorable to [respondent], sustains [these] findings.' Moreover, 'in examining the sufficiency of the evidence to support a questioned finding an appellate court must accept as true all evidence tending to establish the correctness of the finding as made, taking into account, as well, all inferences which might reasonably have been thought by the trial court to lead to the same conclusion.' [Citations.] If appellate scrutiny reveals that substantial evidence supports the trial court's findings and conclusions, the judgment must be affirmed."

A review of the record reveals ample evidence to support the trial court's finding. Appellant had extensive experience with sailboats at the time of the subject purchase, even though he had not previously owned such a vessel. He had developed precise specifications in regard to the type of boat he wanted to purchase. He looked at a number of different vessels, reviewed their advertising literature, and focused on the Island Trader 41 as the object of his intended purchase. He also had friends look at the boat before making the final decision to purchase. The trial court's finding that the buyer did not rely on the skill or judgment of the seller in the selection of the vessel in question is supported by substantial evidence.

§ 5.05 Privity

Read: U.C.C. § 2-318.

Read also: U.C.C. §§ 2-607(5), 2A-216, see § 2A-516(4), see also § 2A-209 (1990); CISG Arts. 1(1), and 2(a), 4 and 5.

PROBLEM 5.4

Your law firm represents Mrs. Redblood and plans to appeal. The essential facts are these: Mr. Redblood died on the operating table on March 9, 1976, during open-heart surgery because the heart-lung machine allegedly pumped air into his aorta instead of blood. One of the defenses which the lower court upheld was that there was a lack of privity as to the machine manufacturer, the distributor who sold the machine, the hospital and the doctor held that the hospital and doctors were the ultimate purchasers of the machine, not Mr. Redblood. What causes of action should have been brought? Is privity a valid defense? Should the court make an exception to privity and on what basis?

PROBLEM 5.5

Your client, a restaurant customer, was injured by a defective container of drain opener that came open and splashed on her when it fell from a shelf in the restaurant. The customer was denied recovery by the restaurant under an implied warranty theory because, as a bystander, she had no contractual privity. What is your analysis? Your reply? Your recommendations?

NOTES

(1) In a case similar to the Problem 5.4, the court made the following observations concerning privity:

> Similar issues have been previously addressed by the supreme court, but this application to operating room equipment appears to be a case of first impression. Title 12 OS 1981 §§ 2-314 and 315, provide an implied warranty of fitness and merchantability of goods for their ordinary use. Section 2-318 limits the warranty to "any natural person who is in the family or household of his buyer or who is a guest in his home. . . ." This limitation has been termed a "horizontal" extension of the warranty. See *Hardesty v. Andro Corp.-Webster Div.*, Okla., 555 P.2d 1030 (1976), in which the court refused to permit recovery by the owner of a construction project against the manufacturer of defective air conditioner parts. That decision turned on "lack of privity" between the manufacturer and the ultimate purchaser. It was later declared to be an erroneous decision in *Old Albany Estates, Ltd. v. Highland Carpet Mills, Inc.*, Okla., 604 P.2d 849 (1979), wherein the court declared the ultimate purchaser of defective goods is entitled to recover from the manufacturer for breach of an implied warranty of merchantability regardless of lack of "privity" between it and the manufacturer. the court determined that the ultimate purchaser is properly within the ambit of the "vertical" chain of sale and is entitled, as a mater of policy, to Code protection.

> The protection afforded to the purchaser of defective carpet in Old Albany is an extension of rulings previously made applicable to buyers of pre-packaged edibles.

> "Horizontal" protection, *i.e.*, remedy for those other than the purchaser, has been strictly limited to the statutory confines of the family, invitees, and household of the purchaser under § 2-318.

In a separate opinion, one of the judges made the following suggestion:

> I would also like to point out what I feel is a major flaw in our law pertaining to actions for breach of warranty that possibly our supreme court or the legislature may want to consider. That flaw comes about as to items sold which the purchaser itself will never use as intended, but which will only be "used" by purchaser's patients, clients or customers. This case, in my opinion, is a classic example of what I refer to. The "purchaser" of the heart-lung machine, be it hospital, doctor, clinic, etc., will never be the "consumer" or "user" that would be damaged by a defective machine, but only the unconscious patient will be the party affected. The cases referred to in the main opinion refer to the so-called "vertical" and "horizontal" chain for determining whether a party can maintain an action for breach of warranty. One must be in the "vertical" chain to maintain the action.

> I submit that we need a "diagonal" chain as an exception. The diagonal chain would be an exception wherein the item purchased is one referred to above that virtually no person in the vertical chain would ever be the user/consumer of. Such items normally would be part

of service related occupations or professions where the purchaser buys the item to use on persons other than the purchaser. I would therefore suggest the "diagonal" exception to the cases permitting only "purchasers" in the vertical chain to maintain an action for breach of warranty. Until such exception is recognized or legislated a "warranty" on such items is virtually meaningless. The purchaser (and those in the vertical chain) will never be the ultimate user/consumer of the item. Because the "user consumer" is not in the vertical chain no action for breach of warranty could be maintained by any person — thus any warranty is meaningless.

(2) Can a seller of consumer goods who has given an express warranty limit or exclude consequential damages by the inclusion of an express disclaimer within the contract?

In *Collins v. Uniroyal, Inc.,* 315 A.2d 30 (NJ 1973), Uniroyal, included the following disclaimer: "This Guarantee does not cover consequential damage, and the liability of the manufacturer is limited to repairing or replacing the tire. . . . No other guarantee or warranty, express or implied, is made." The decedent, an entertainer, who with his family traveled extensively throughout the country performing a knife-throwing act, was killed in an automobile accident. Decedent had purchased five new tires for his station wagon from a Uniroyal distributor. While traveling on Interstate Highway 80, in their vehicle laden with personal belongings and "paraphernalia of their act," the right rear tire failed, resulting in loss of control of the vehicle which subsequently rolled over. Decedent died of injuries received in the accident.

Uniroyal argues that the court erred in allowing evidence of Uniroyal's advertisements, and by disallowing the jury to consider the limitation of damages provision of the warranty.

The pertinent language of the warranty is as follows:

The new U.S. Royal Master tire with wrap-around tread and pin stripe (1/2 inch) whitewall design is of such quality and reliability that U.S. Rubber Tire Company makes the following Guarantee:

LIFETIME—Every such U.S. Royal Master tire of our manufacture, bearing our name and serial number, other than "seconds," is guaranteed to be free from defects in workmanship and material for the life of the original tread without limit as to time or mileage.

ROAD HAZARD—In addition, every such U.S. Royal Master tire, when used in normal passenger car service, is guaranteed during the life of the original tread against blowouts, cuts, bruises, and similar injury rendering the tire unserviceable. Tires which are punctured or abused, by being run flat, improperly aligned, balanced, or inflated, cut by chains or obstructions on vehicle, damaged by fire, collision or vandalism, or by other means, and "seconds" are not subject to the road hazard provision of this Guarantee.

If our examination shows that such a U.S. Royal Master tire is eligible for adjustment under either the Lifetime or Road Hazard provision of this Guarantee, we will repair it or provide a new U.S. Royal Master tire at a fractional price computed on percentage of wear of original tread depth and then current U.S. suggested exchange price as follows: [There follows a rate chart and several additional paragraphs not relevant here.]

The jury also had before it copies of Uniroyal tire advertisements used during 1966, received in evidence over the objection of defense counsel. Mrs. Collins testified without objection that about a month before the purchase her husband had shown her a Uniroyal advertisement and had indicated his intent to buy the product. The jury could have inferred from these proofs that the advertisement was like the ones in evidence and that decedent relied upon it when he bought the tires. More importantly, the advertisement helped to explain the scope and intent of the "road hazard" part of the warranty which guaranteed for the life of the original tread every Royal Master tire, when used in normal passenger car service, against blowouts, cuts, bruises, and similar injury rendering the tire unserviceable. Although the term was not defined, the advertisements reflected defendant's concept of what normal passenger car service included. They extolled the virtues of the tire, containing statements such as:

If it only saves your life once, it's a bargain.

. . . It could pay off some day. The day you hit a pothole at 70 miles an hour.

The day you sweep around a tricky, rain-slicked curve. The day it's 90 degrees in the shade and you have to go 600 miles in a hurry. The day you pick up a nail and it's three in the morning. You're getting a brute of a carcass that's so strong, you can practically forget about blowouts.

The court held that in the case of breach of warranty the recovery of consequential damages is permitted. N.J.S.A. 12A:2-714(3). Although consequential damages may be limited or excluded absent unconscionability, "the limitation of consequential damages for injury to the person in the case of consumer goods is prima facie unconscionable." N.J.S.A. 12A:2-719(3).

(3) The PEB Study Group Report contains the following comments:

F. Privity and Related Warranty Issues

In view of the criticisms of the treatment of consumer issues, there was "substantial sentiment" in the Study Group to retreat from two earlier recommendations, namely that Alternative A to § 2-318 and § 2-719(3) be deleted from Article 2. Both of these provisions dealt with personal injuries caused by a breach of warranty and it was our view that remedies for these injuries should be left to the law of torts. On reflection, this imposes an undue restriction upon the options of individuals injured by unmerchantable or defective goods. Thus, buyers and others injured in person or property by a breach of warranty should be able to recover under Article 2, but they should be subject to the same limitations as buyers who suffer only commercial loss, e.g., privity, notice, disclaimers, and statute of limitations, unless those limitations have been modified in the interest of consumers.

The Study Group spent considerable time discussing the "privity" issue and how it should be analyzed.

46 Bus. Lawyer 1869, 1880 (1990).

§ 5.06 Disclaimer

Read: U.C.C. §§ 2-316, 1-201(10); see §§ 2-719, 2-302.

Read also: U.C.C. §§ 2A-108, 2A-214, 2A-503; CISG Arts. 4(a), 6, 7(1), 8(2), 35(2) and (3).

NOTES

(1) *Conspicuous.* One court analyzed this requirement: There is no dispute that the language contained in the contract was in this case sufficient to waive all implied warranties. The issue is whether the disclaimer was "conspicuous." Section 1201(10) [Cal. Comm. Code]. Basic/Four points out that it disclaimed the implied warranties not once but twice, and that the disclaimers were written in italicized print, in contrast to the regular print used on the rest of the contract. Nevertheless, the disclaimers are not conspicuous. In *Dorman v. International Harvester Co.,*

120 Cal. Rptr. 516 (Cal. App. 1975), the California court of appeals noted that under pre-Code California law, disclaimers of warranty are strictly construed, and, applying the code, it found that an attempted disclaimer written in only slightly contrasting print and without a heading adequate to call the buyer's attention to the disclaimer clause was not effective. That decision controls in this case. The two disclaimers in the Office Supply-Basic/Four contract are on the reverse sides of the first two pages of the contract. They are not positioned close to the buyer's signature line. The contracts are printed on pale green paper and the disclaimers are set forth in print which, although italicized, is only slightly contrasting with the remainder of the contract. There are no headings noting the disclaimers of warranty. Since there is only "some slight contrasting set-off" and there is "only a slight contrast with the balance of the instrument," the disclaimers are not conspicuous.

If the disclaimer is not conspicuous, does knowledge of it make it effective?

(2) *Knowledge.* Consider the following testimony:

James Bruno testified during his deposition taken on November 3, 1980, that before he purchased the Basic/Four system, he spent approximately two months comparing it with other systems, and that he drew up a written comparison of the Basic/Four and Qantel systems, including their guarantees: Basic/Four, 90 days; and Qantel had one year. He read the back of the contract before he signed it, when he received the contract from Basic/Four he made out a list of questions to ask Basic/Four before signing and one subject on his list was the ninety-day guarantee and before he signed he showed the warranty provision in the contract to someone he knew in the data processing field. He discussed the warranties with Basic/Four before signing and tried to have them modified:

Q: Did you read the provisions of the warranty?

A: Yes.

Q: And did you discuss those provisions with Basic/Four, or with someone from Basic/Four?

A: Yes.

Q: And what was said to you about those provisions?

A: That that was the condition that I had to accept.

Q: All right. And was that discussion before or after the contract was signed?

A: I would say before.

A: . . .

Q: . . . did you call up Darryl Bannister, for example, and say I want to buy this system but I refuse to agree to the warranty provisions in the contract?

A: Well, I argued with him, but it was to no avail. Nothing.

He also was aware of the warranty limitations before he signed the contract.

Q: Well, were you aware of the provisions of that warranty before you signed the contract?

A: That there were limitations?

Q: That there are limitations to the warranty? Were you aware of that?

A: Certainly.

Q: You were?

A: Yes.

(3) The PEB Study Group Report contains the following comments: p. 168

E. Disclaimer of Warranty

The Study Group agreed in the Preliminary Report that § 2-316 should be revised and placed this revision in the category that justified appointing a Drafting Committee. See Part III(5). After further consideration, the Study Group makes two additional recommendations for revision and retreats from a recommendation made earlier. Rec. A2.2(13).

The additional recommendations for change involve consumer protection and are drawn from the Magnuson-Moss Warranty Act.

First, we recommend that the implied warranty of merchantability should not be disclaimable under § 2-316(2) when the seller makes a written warranty that is subject to MMWA. This is the effect under federal law and there is no good reason why state law should not be the same. Under this recommendation, a revision of the definition of "consumer" in Article 2 would be required.

Second, if a written warranty subject to the MMWA is made, Article 2 should require the same disclosure as that required by federal law. A written warranty which disclaims or limits warranties and provides agreed remedies should clearly and conspicuously state the nature and, perhaps, the effect of the agreement.

The retreat is from our earlier recommendation that a disclaimer should be effective if the buyer knew or had reason to know about it, even though the statutory requirements of form, § 2-316(2), were not met. The Study Group. . . .

46 Bus. Lawyer 1869, 1879-80 (1991).

(4) The New York court in *Rice v. R.M. Burritt Motors, Inc.*, 477 N.Y.S.2d 278 (1984), held that a vehicle sold subject to an as is clause would not be "as is," but rather "as it should be." The plaintiff in *Rice* purchased a vehicle on August 22, 1983. Plaintiff discovered that the heater-defroster unit was inoperable in October of 1983. Defendant in this case did not dispute plaintiff's factual claims, but relied on the traditional interpretation of the contractual "as is" clause. Plaintiff argued that New York State Law gives consumers "additional protection as to used motor vehicles, this being the warranty of serviceability." New York State Law mandates that a dealer furnish the customer a certificate which indicates that the vehicle is in compliance with § 417 of the Vehicle and Traffic Law. 15 NYCRR 78.1 3(c)(9) requires that "all 1964 and later model vehicles must be equipped with a front windshield defrosting device in good working order. . ."

Former law and the apparent intent of the framers of the Uniform Commercial Code was that if one purchases a used car "as is," one gets the car "as is" and one may not be heard to complain, at least in terms of contract, that the vehicle is not what the purchaser in retrospect feels it should have been. Thus, "as is" used to mean "as is."

Now, however, the "warranty of serviceability" which has existed for some time is apparently recognized by the courts as something more than simply a restatement of the implied warranties of merchantability which can be excluded by "as is" clauses. Thus a sale of a used vehicle in New York State "AS IS" no longer means "as is" — but rather it now means "as it should be" under the Vehicle and Traffic Law and the Commissioner's regulations. Whether this be good or bad, it is now certainly the case.

(5) As to unconscionable warranty disclaimers, see Chapter One at § 1.06[D].

§ 5.07 Strict Liability

Read: CISG Arts. 2(a), 5.

[A] Restatement[1]

RESTATEMENT OF TORTS SECOND § 402A

SPECIAL LIABILITY OF SELLER OF PRODUCT
FOR PHYSICAL HARM TO USER OR CONSUMER.[2]

(1) One who sells any product in a defective condition unreasonably dangerous to the user or consumer or to his property is subject to liability for physical harm thereby caused to the ultimate user or consumer, or to his property, if

(a) the seller is engaged in the business of selling such a product, and

(b) it is expected to and does reach the user or consumer without substantial change in the condition in which it is sold.

(2) The rule stated in Subsection (1) applies although

(a) the seller has exercised all possible care in the preparation and sale of his product, and

(b) the user or consumer has not bought the product from or entered into any contractual relation with the seller.

See Reporter's Notes

Caveat:

The Institute expresses no opinion as to whether the rules stated in this Section may not apply

(1) to harm to persons other than users or consumers;

(2) to the seller of a product expected to be processed or otherwise Substantially changed before it reaches the user or consumer; or

(3) to the seller of a component part of a product to be assembled.

Comment b of § 402A describes its history:

b. *History.* Since the early days of the common law those engaged in the business of selling food intended for human consumption have been held to a high degree of responsibility for their products. As long ago as 1266 there were enacted special criminal statutes imposing penalties upon victualers, vintners, brewers, butchers, cooks, and other persons who supplied "corrupt" food and drink. In the earlier part of this century this ancient attitude was reflected in a series of decisions in which the courts of a number of states sought to find some method of holding the seller of food liable to the ultimate consumer even though there was no showing of negligence on the part of the seller. These decisions represented a departure from, and an exception to, the general rule that a supplier of chattels was not liable to third persons in the absence of negligence or privity of contract. In the beginning, these decisions displayed considerable ingenuity in evolving more or less fictitious theories of liability to fit the case. The various devices included an agency of the intermediate dealer or another to purchase for

---

[1] 1964-65 current version. For proposed changes being considered by ALI, see. pp. 5-49.

[2] Copyright © 1968 by American Law Institute. Reprinted by permission.

the consumer, or to sell for the seller; a theoretical assignment of the seller's warranty to the intermediate dealer; a third party beneficiary contract; and an implied representation that the food was fit for consumption because it was placed on the market, as well as numerous others. In later years the courts have become more or less agreed upon the theory of a "warranty" from the seller to the consumer, either "running with the goods" by analogy to a covenant running with the land, or made directly to the consumer. Other decisions have indicated that the basis is merely one of strict liability in tort, which is not dependent upon either contract or negligence.

Recent decisions, since 1950, have extended this special rule of strict liability beyond the seller of food for human consumption. The first extension was into the closely analogous cases of other products intended for intimate bodily use, where, for example, as in the case of cosmetics, the application to the body of the consumer is external rather than internal. Beginning in 1958 with a Michigan case involving cinder building blocks, a number of recent decisions have discarded any limitation to intimate association with the body, and have extended the rule of strict liability to cover the sale of any product which, if it should prove to be defective, may be expected to cause physical harm to the consumer or his property.

Comment c deals with theories underlying § 402A.

c. On whatever theory, the justification for the strict liability has been said to be that the seller, by marketing his product for use and consumption, has undertaken and assumed a special responsibility toward any member of the consuming public who may be injured by it; that the public has the right to and does expect, in the case of products which it needs and for which it is forced to rely upon the seller, that reputable sellers will stand behind their goods; that public policy demands that the burden of accidental injuries caused by products intended for consumption be placed upon those who market them, and be treated as a cost of production against which liability insurance can be obtained; and that the consumer of such products is entitled to the maximum of protection at the hands of someone, and the proper persons to afford it are those who market the products.

The comments to § 402A also deal with contributory negligence and assumption of risk.

n. *Contributory negligence.* Since the liability with which this Section deals is not based upon negligence of the seller, but is strict liability, the rule applied to strict liability cases (see § 524) applies. Contributory negligence of the plaintiff is not a defense when such negligence consists merely in a failure to discover the defect in the product, or to guard against the possibility of its existence. On the other hand the form of contributory negligence which consists in voluntarily and unreasonably proceeding to encounter a known danger, and commonly passes under the name of assumption of risk, is a defense under this Section as in other cases of strict liability. If the user or consumer discovers the defect and is aware of the danger, and nevertheless proceeds unreasonably to make use of the product and is injured by it, he is barred from recovery.

Parties covered by § 402A are termed users or consumers, and are described in the comments:

l. *User or consumer.* In order for the rule stated in this Section to apply, it is not necessary that the ultimate user or consumer have acquired the product directly from the seller, although the rule applies equally if he does so. He may have acquired it through one or more intermediate dealers. It is not even necessary that the consumer have purchased the product at all. He may be a member of the family of the final purchaser, or his employee, or a guest at his table, or a mere donee from the purchaser. The liability stated is one in tort, and does not require any contractual relation, or privity of contract, between the plaintiff and the defendant.

"Consumers" include not only those who in fact consume the product, but also those who prepare it for consumption; and the housewife who contracts tularemia while cooking rabbits for her husband is included within the rule stated in this Section, as is also the husband who is opening a bottle of beer for his wife to drink. Consumption includes all ultimate uses for which the product is intended, and the customer in a beauty shop to whose hair a permanent wave solution is applied by the shop is a consumer. "User" includes those who are passively enjoying the benefit of the product, as in the case of passengers in automobiles or airplanes, as well as those who are utilizing it for the purpose of doing work upon it, as in the case of an employee of the ultimate buyer who is making repairs upon the automobile which he has purchased.

The following comment to § 402A describes some of the basic differences between warranty and strict liability in tort:

m. *"Warranty."* The liability in this Section does not rest upon negligence. The basis of liability is purely one of tort.

A number of courts, seeking a theoretical basis for the liability, have resorted to a "warranty," either running with the goods sold, by analogy to covenants running with the land, or made directly to the consumer without contract. In some instances this theory has proved to be an unfortunate one. Although warranty was in its origin a matter of tort liability, and it is generally agreed that a tort action will still lie for its breach, it has become so identified in practice with a contract of sale between the plaintiff and the defendant that the warranty theory has become something of an obstacle to the recognition of the strict liability where there is no such contract. There is nothing in this Section which would prevent any court from treating the rule stated as a matter of warranty" to the user or consumer. But if this is done, it should be recognized and understood that the "warranty" is a very different kind of warranty from those usually found in the sale of goods, and that it is not subject to the various contract rules which have grown up to surround such sales.

The rule stated in this Section does not require any reliance on the part of the consumer upon the reputation, skill, or judgment of the seller who is to be held liable, nor any representation or undertaking on the part of that seller. The seller is strictly liable although, as is frequently the case, the consumer does not even know who he is at the time of consumption. The rule stated in this Section is not governed by the provisions of the Uniform Sales Act, or those of the Uniform Commercial Code, as to warranties; and it is not affected by limitations on the scope and content of warranties, or by limitation to "buyer" and "seller" in those statutes. Nor is the consumer required to give notice to the seller of his injury within a reasonable time after it occurs, as is provided by the Uniform Act. The consumer's cause of action does not depend upon the validity of his contract with the person from whom he acquires the product, and it is not affected by any disclaimer or other agreement, whether it be between the seller and his immediate buyer, or attached to and accompanying the product into the consumer's hands. In short, "warranty" must be given a new and different meaning if it is used in connection with this Section. It is much simpler to regard the liability here stated as merely one of strict liability in tort.

The following chart illustrates some of the differences between Warranty and Strict Liability.[3]

	Warranty of Merchantability § 2-314	Strict Liability in Tort Restatement, Second, Torts § 402A
1. Condition of goods giving rise to liability	Not merchantable, e.g., not fit for ordinary purpose. 2-314(1), (2)(c).(1).	Defective condition unreasonably dangerous. § 402A
2. Character of defendant	Must be seller who is a merchant with respect to goods of that kind. §§ 2-314(1), 2-104(1).	Must be seller who is engaged in the business of selling such a product § 402A (1)(a).
3. Reliance	No explicit requirement. Such warranty "taken for granted." § 2-314 and Comment 11; see, however, § 2-316(3)(b).	No requirement of "any reliance on the part of the consumer upon the reputation, skill or judgment of the seller." § 402A Comment m.

_____

[3] Excerpt from B. Stone, Uniform Commercial Code in a Nutshell, pp. 74-75; Copyright © 1995, West Publishing Co. Reprinted with permission.

4. Disclaimer	Limitation of consequential damages for injury to the person in the case of consumer goods is prima facie unconscionable. §§ 2-316 (4), 2-719(3), 2-302; but see § 2-316(1)-(3).	Cause of action not affected by any disclaimer or any other agreement. § 402A Comment m.
5. Notice	Buyer must within a reasonable time after he discovers or should have discovered any breach notify seller of breach or be barred from any remedy. Reason of rule to defeat commercial bad faith not to deprive a good faith consumer of his remedy. § 2-607(3) (a) and Comments 4 and 5.	Consumer not required to give notice to seller of his injury within a reasonable time after it occurs § 402A Comment m.
6. Causation	Buyer may recover consequential damages <u>resulting</u> from seller's breach including injury to person or property <u>proximately resulting</u> from any breach of warranty §§ 2-714, 2-715(2)(b) and Comment 5, § 2-314 Comment 13, see § 2-316 (3)(b) and Comment 8.	Seller subject to liability for physical harm <u>caused</u> § 402A(1); see Comment n <u>Contributory negligence</u> Comment p <u>Further process ing or substantial chance;</u> Comment q <u>Component parts;</u> see also Comments g, h, j.
7. Protected persons	Any person who may reasonably be expected to use, consume or be affected by the goods. § 2-318 Alternative C.	Ultimate user or consumer § 402(1), (2)(b) and Comment I.
8. Protected injuries	Injuries to person listed in 7 above or his property. § 2-318 Alternative C and Comment 3; cf. Alternative B.	Physical harm to ultimate user or consumer, or to his property. § 402A(1).
9. Statute of limitations	Four years from tender of delivery. § 2-725(1), (2).	State law varies, e.g. three years from injury.

[B]   Caveats to Restatement (Second) of Torts § 402A

The drafters of U.C.C. § 402A included a "Caveat" limiting its coverage in several ways. One of these dealt with parties injured by the defective products:

o. *Injuries to non-users and non-consumers.* Thus far the courts, in applying the rule stated in this Section, have not gone beyond allowing recovery to users and consumers, as those terms are defined in Comment l. Casual bystanders, and others who may come in contact with the product, as in the case of employees of the retailer, or a passer-by injured by an exploding bottle, or a pedestrian hit by an automobile, have been denied recovery. There may be no essential reason why such plaintiffs should not be brought within the scope of the protection afforded, other than that they do not have the same reasons for expecting such protection as the consumer who buys a marketed product; but the social pressure which has been largely responsible for the development of the rule stated has been a consumer's pressure, and there is not the same demand for the protection of casual strangers. The Institute expresses neither approval nor disapproval of expansion of the rule to permit recovery by such persons.

The following article excerpts discuss this caveat and also give insight into the Restatement processes.

King and Neville, THE BYSTANDER'S RIGHT UNDER STRICT LIABILITY DOES EXIST: A CALL FOR REFORM OF THE RESTATEMENT
25 St. Louis L.J. 543, 546 (1981)[4]

The reason given by the Institute for excluding bystanders is appalling. There is no attempt by the drafters to logically judge whether to include bystanders. Rather the decision to exclude is placed upon grounds that are not logically relevant. Of course bystanders do not have the same reasons for expecting protection from the product as a consumer. However the idea that a bystander does not use or purchase a product, and does not have a consumer's expectation of a reasonably safe product, does not change the fact that he is injured by defective products which are near him or which cause injury to him. Generally, the expectation rationale relating to purchasers is not realistically or judicially sound. In many situations purchasers or users are not consciously examining the safety features of the product when buying or using it. Rather the safety features of the product are quite often only thought of when an accident occurs. Further, the expectations of purchasers and users are not the crucial basis underlying strict liability.

The Restatement position reflects a view of the law from a political pressure perspective, rather than justice. The fact that consumers as a group are more organized and have sought changes in the law should hardly exclude other who are logically entitled to protest from receiving it. The fact that there is not a strong outcry of demand for the protection of "casual strangers" does not justify the failure to extend protection to them which is caused by reason of the defective product.

The term "casual strangers" used by the Institute almost indicates that they are not so important and perhaps should not have been present. Yet in most cases the bystander is legitimately engaged in his own activities when he is injured by the defective product. Furthermore that injured individual is just as important as the injured individual who is a consumer or user and it is just as difficult, if not more difficult, for the bystander to bear the loss which is a central policy

[4] Copyright © 1981 by Saint Louis University Law Journal. Reprinted by permission.

behind § 402A. It is perhaps unfortunate that there is not a "National Association of Bystanders" to put pressure on the Institute for such protection!

The underlying reason why the Institute did not include bystanders in their protection is to be found in its view of its function and the dearth of case law in 1965. When the section was being considered by the Institute, no cases could be found which held in favor of protecting a bystander injured by defective products. In a major survey of cases, the Columbia Law Journal found no support for bystander recovery. Many members of the Institute had believed that the Restatement must reflect the principles found in the majority of the cases. A few members were amenable to looking at trends of cases portending future development in some situations; they would weigh with such trends the desirability of action and consideration of policy. But in 1965 there was not a majority of cases reflecting bystander protection; there was not a trend; there was not a single case! Some persons in the Institute involved with the formulation of § 402A did not feel it was possible to extend recovery under that section to bystanders without even one case to support such a proposition.

The illogic of not covering bystanders was noted in the discussion on the floor of the Institute in the 1965 annual meeting by Witman Knapp, a member from New York. The Reporter, William Prosser, agreed with Knapp's logic but stated that he felt unjustified in broadening the rule since the only cases of strict liability coverage at that time were in terms of consumers or users. A motion was made by Knapp to change the caveat to read that the "Institute expresses approval of the expansion of the rule to permit recovery by such persons." As Professor Wechsler, Director of Institute, who presided over the discussion at the time has said "the motion was defeated, primarily I think on the ground that it was inappropriate in the Restatement (and especially in a caveat) to take a position, without decisional support, that a rule should be extended." Such a view of the function of the Restatement, in the opinion of the Director, is "unfortunate." It should be noted that at this time the views of the Institute as to its function were in a state of flux and that under current views there might have been a chance for such an inclusion of bystanders. Equally unfortunate is the failure to clearly articulate this reason in the comments to the § 402A caveat since this would undoubtedly lead to the Institute's position of neutrality, leaving it up to the courts to extend strict liability coverage.

CONCLUSION

The court decisions overwhelmingly support recovery by the bystander against the seller or manufacturer of a defective product. These decisions are ample in number and of sufficient geographic spread to make this rule applicable throughout the nation. In addition, the courts have had a sufficient number of years to deal with the problem and to reach these conclusions. The reasoning of the courts is sound and reflective of the underlying basis of the Restatement § 402A.

Policy considerations support extending strict liability coverage to bystanders. Risk spreading is just as possible in regard to the bystander as it is for buyers, consumers and users. Deterrence of less than quality production is likewise similar. The need for protecting innocent victims who are unable to bear the burden of loss individually is present.

Authorities who have written on the question of whether strict liability for defective products should extend to bystanders favor such coverage. The illogic of not doing so and the carry-over of the "dead-hand of privity" to include bystanders have been discussed. The commentators generally recognize that the policies underlying strict liability support coverage of bystanders and that the trend of cases favors them.

U.C.C. Alternatives B and C have been adopted by a number of states. These are broadly worded to include not only consumers and users, but those affected by the product and can be applied to cover bystanders. While these Code provisions deal with warranty rather than strict liability, both theories concern defective products liability. Both warranty and strict liability often are raised in a suit by the injured party against the manufacturer or seller of the defective product and the result should be consistent. Furthermore, the policies behind eliminating such privity type requirements and extending such liability to injuries of bystanders are the same for warranty and strict liability in tort; consistency of the law in regard to the elimination of the privity for bystanders is desirable.

It remains only now for the American Law Institute to amend this portion of the Restatement and recognize that fact. In the meantime, bystanders and third persons injured by defective products have been given protection by the courts and this should be recognized in future cases. The right of the bystander exists!

———

Two other caveats to § 402A by the American Law Institute are explained in the following comments:[5]

p. *Further processing or substantial change.* Thus far the decisions applying the rule stated have not gone beyond products which are sold in the condition, or in substantially the same condition, in which they are expected to reach the hands of the ultimate user or consumer. In the absence of decisions providing a clue to the rules which are likely to develop, the Institute has refrained from taking any position as to the possible liability of the seller where the product is expected to, and does, undergo further processing or other substantial change after it leaves his hands and before it reaches those of the ultimate user or consumer.

It seems reasonably clear that the mere fact that the product is to undergo processing, or other substantial change, will not in all cases relieve the seller of liability under the rule stated in this Section. If, for example, raw coffee beans are sold to a buyer who roasts and packs them for sale to the ultimate consumer, it cannot be supposed that the seller will be relieved of all liability when the raw beans are contaminated with arsenic, or some other poison. Likewise the seller of an automobile with a defective steering gear which breaks and injures the driver, can scarcely expect to be relieved of the responsibility by reason of the fact that the car is sold to a dealer who is expected to "service" it, adjust the breaks, mount and inflate the tires, and the like, before it is ready for use. On the other hand, the manufacturer of pigiron, which is capable of a wide variety of uses, is not so likely to be held to strict liability when it turns out to be unsuitable for the child's tricycle into which it is finally made by a remote buyer. The question is essentially one of whether the responsibility for discovery and prevention of the dangerous defect is shifted to the intermediate party who is to make the changes. No doubt there will be some situations, and some defects, as to which the responsibility will be shifted, and others in which it will not. The existing decisions as yet throw no light upon the questions, and the Institute therefore expresses neither approval nor disapproval of the seller's strict liability in such a case.

---

[5] Copyright © 1968 by American Law Institute. Reprinted by permission.

q. *Component parts.* The same problem arises in cases of the sale of a component part of a product to be assembled by another, as for example a tire to be placed on a new automobile, a brake cylinder for the same purpose, or an instrument for the panel of an airplane. Again the question arises, whether the responsibility is not shifted to the assembler. It is no doubt to be expected that where there is no change in the component part itself but it is merely incorporated into something larger, the strict liability will be found to carry through to the ultimate user or consumer. But in the absence of a sufficient number of decisions on the matter to justify a conclusion, the Institute expresses no opinion on the matter.

§ 5.08 Interaction of Warranty and Strict Liability

Read: CISG Arts. 2(a), 5.

PROBLEM 5.6

Your client, Interstate Movers, a major trucking company, recently purchased twenty Transnational Company "20 wheeler" trucks (and trailers). These are longer than the current "18 wheelers" and can haul more freight. Unfortunately, the twenty transnational trucks were defective in several respects. The motor size was not sufficient to pull the larger trucks up many hills and mountain pass highways; the wheels were made with defective metals; and the design of the coupling of the truck cabs and trailers were defective. The Interstate Company has suffered considerable losses in regard to these defects in the sense of repairs, lost days of use, need to take longer routes in some situations, and compensation to customers for delays.

Transnational has refused to remedy these problems or compensate Interstate in anyway. It points to the disclaimers in the contract, which appear to meet U.C.C. disclaimer standards. What theories can you use in regard to these losses?

PROBLEM 5.7

Another of your clients, Robert Roader, recently bought a Transnational "twenty wheeler" with the same defects. On one of his "runs" he was badly injured when one set of wheels broke loose causing the truck to crash. Transnational denies any liability based on its disclaimer. What theories can be used and what type of losses can be recovered?

———

NOTES

(1) In *Sanco Inc. v. Ford Motor Co.*, 579 F. Supp. 893 (1984), the court noted:

"Economic loss" designates the diminution in the value of a product and consequent loss of profits because the product is inferior in quality and does not work for the general purposes for which it was manufactured and sold. See Comment, *Manufacturers' Liability to Remote Purchasers for "Economic Loss" Damages-Tort or Contract?*, 114 U. Pa. L. Rev. 539, 541(1966). Some definitions further limit economic loss to costs of repair and replacement of the product and consequent loss of profits — "without any claim of personal injury or damage to other property." Note, *Economic Loss in Products Liability Jurisprudence*, 66 Colum. L. Rev. 917, 918 (1966). For reasons which will appear hereafter, we believe that economic loss is better defined without this limitation.

The only indication of the way Indiana courts would view the issue of whether such losses should be recoverable in a negligence action is provided in *Babson Bros. Co. v. Tipstar Corporation*, 446 N.E.2d 11 (Ind. App. 1983) (transfer denied August 31, 1983), where the Indiana Court of Appeals cited with approval the leading case in Illinois, *Moorman Mfg. Co. v. National Tank Co.*, 435 N.E.2d 443 (Ill. 1982), holding that economic losses cannot be recovered in a tort action. The *Babson* court, however, went on to affirm an award of lost profits as consequential damages for negligently performed services. This apparent contradiction renders that decision of limited value to our inquiry.

Since our effort to determine whether the Indiana law of negligence is compatible with recovery of economic losses has not been aided by any other opinions of Indiana courts, we have referred to decisions from other jurisdictions and to the works of scholarly commentators to determine the better rule of law.

The majority of jurisdictions which have considered this issue have not permitted the recovery of economic loss in a negligence action.

Dean Prosser summarized the majority rule with respect to recovery of economic losses as follows:

> There can be no doubt that the seller's liability for negligence covers any kind of physical harm, including not only personal injuries, but also property damage to the defective chattel itself, as where an automobile is wrecked by reason of its own bad brakes, as well as damage to any other property in the vicinity. But where there is no accident, and no physical damage, and the only loss is a pecuniary one, through loss of the value or use of the thing sold, or the cost of repairing it, the courts have adhered to the rule . . .that purely economic interests are not entitled to protection against mere negligence, and so have denied the recovery.

W. Prosser, *Handbook on the Law of Torts*, § 101 at 665 (4th ed 1971).

One of the most fully articulated discussions of the considerations underlying this rule is found in [Chief] Justice Traynor's majority opinion in *Seely v. White Motor Co.*, 63 Cal. 2d 9, 45 Cal. Rptr. 17, 403 P.2d 145 (1965). In *Seely* the plaintiff sought to recover lost profits and a refund of the purchase price of a defective truck. The California Supreme Court ruled that such damages, although recoverable in a breach of warranty action, were not recoverable in strict liability in tort. The following passage from the majority opinion is pertinent to this case:

> The distinction that the law has drawn between tort recovery for physical injuries and warranty recovery for economic loss is not arbitrary and does not rest on the "luck" of one plaintiff in having an accident causing physical injury. The distinction rests, rather, on an understanding of the nature of the responsibility a manufacturer must undertake in distributing his products. He can appropriately be held liable for physical injuries caused by defects by requiring his goods to match a standard of safety defined in terms of conditions that create unreasonable risks of harm. He cannot be held for the level of performance of his products in the consumer's business unless he agrees that the product was designed to meet the consumer's demands. A consumer should not be charged at the will of the

manufacturer with bearing the risk of physical injury when he buys a product on the market. He can, however, be fairly charged with the risk that the product will not match his economic expectations unless the manufacturer agrees that it will. Even in actions for negligence, a manufacturer's liability is limited to damages for physical injury and there is no recovery for economic loss alone.

45 Cal. Rptr. at 23, 403 P.2d at 151 (Citations omitted).

We think that the rule embraced by the majority of the jurisdictions is sound for the reasons articulated by [Chief] Justice Traynor in *Seely*. A tort action traditionally presupposes that the plaintiff has been exposed to an unreasonable risk of injury to his person or his property. Qualitative defects which merely disappoint the buyer's expectations of the product's performance do not expose the user or his property to any risk of physical harm. When a product does not perform as expected, the buyer's remedy should be governed by the rules of contract, which traditionally protect expectation interests.

We are aware that this argument loses some of its appeal when the plaintiff is an ordinary consumer faced with the usual "take-it-or-leave-it" disclaimed warranties from all of the potential sellers. The effect of these disclaimers is that a consumer may have purchased a worthless product and yet be left without a remedy. In his dissent in *Seely* Justice Peters recognized this problem and suggested that consumer buyers in particular should have a tort cause of action to cover purely economic losses.

However, the consumer is not entirely remediless in such situations. The Uniform Commercial Code has several provisions which provide courts with room for the exercise of judicial discretion to ensure that substantial justice results in particular cases. See Ind Code 26-1-2-302 and Ind Code 26-1-2-719(3) concerning unconscionable clauses and contracts, and Ind Code 26-1-1-203 imposing a general obligation of good faith. The fact that courts are reluctant to invoke these provisions does not justify the application of tort theory to resolve a problem of sales law.

Imposing tort liability on a manufacturer, and thus increasing the cost of doing business, is justified when a product causes personal injury or even when it causes damage to itself or other property under circumstances in which the absence of personal injury is merely fortuitous, such as when an object explodes but does not inflict personal injuries on anyone. Society has a great interest in spreading the cost of such injuries. We believe, however, that the Supreme Court of Indiana would concur in the opinion of most courts that when a plaintiff has suffered only economic loss, as first above defined, the societal interest in cost spreading is insufficient to justify requiring "the consuming public to pay more for their products so that a manufacturer can insure against the possibility that some of his products will not meet the . . . needs of some of his customers." *Seely v. White Motor Co.*, 403 P.2d at 151.

Justice Traynor stated another reason why subjecting a manufacturer to liability under a tort theory for economic loss is inappropriate: it would encroach on the decision of the legislature to enact the carefully articulated sales provisions of the Uniform Commercial Code. Ind Code 26-1-2-101 to 26-1-2-725. See *Seely v. White Motor Co.*, 403 P.2d 145,150. Thus, in the present case, if a negligence cause of action were available, Sanco could recover despite any effective disclaimer of warranty under Ind Code 26-1-2-316, or any failure of Sanco to adhere to the notice requirements of Ind Code 26-1-2-607.

We agree that this result would represent an unwarranted extension of the traditional boundaries of tort law into an area that our legislature, by enactment of the Uniform

Commercial Code, has provided with a finely tuned mechanism for dealing with the rights of parties to a sales transaction with respect to economic losses. We are confident that the Supreme Court of Indiana would view unfavorably any encroachment of tort law on the sales scheme of the Uniform Commercial Code.

Finally, we note that the Restatement (Second) of Torts, § 395 (1965) is in apparent agreement with the majority rule. The Restatement states that a manufacturer is to be liable for "physical harm" caused by its negligence in the manufacture of a chattel dangerous unless carefully made. That section, however, does not extend the manufacturer's liability to encompass purely economic loss.

As indicated above, however, not every instance of damage to the defective product itself is a case of economic loss. Sometimes such damage is properly characterized as physical harm susceptible to tort recovery. In some such circumstances it is difficult to determine which theory of recovery is appropriate. The line between tort and contract must then be drawn "by analyzing the interrelated factors such as the nature of the defect, the type of risk, and the manner in which the injury arose." Although this analysis sometimes demands fine line drawing, the proper view of the distinction between tort and contract theories requires that the line be drawn, even in close cases.

Two cases decided by the Alaska Supreme Court illustrate the difference in types of damage and the necessity of distinguishing between tort and warranty causes of action. In *Morrow v. New Moon Homes, Inc.*, 548 P.2d 279 (Alaska 1976), the plaintiff purchased a mobile home and proceeded to occupy it. He soon discovered that the roof leaked continually and that it had numerous other defects. He sued the manufacturer under a strict liability theory to recover for the defects. The Alaska Supreme Court noted that the defects merely reduced the value of the product below the price actually paid for it. The defects did not create a situation potentially dangerous to persons or other property; they only disappointed the buyer's expectations of the product's performance. The court therefore refused to allow Morrow to proceed under a strict liability in tort theory and instead relegated him to his rights under contract theory embodied in the Uniform Commercial Code.

In contrast, fire destroyed a mobile home in *Cloud v. Kit Manufacturing Co.*, 563 P.2d 248 (Alaska 1977). Padding stored under the mobile home had been ignited by a heating unit mounted under the structure to keep pipes from freezing. The fire did not result in personal injury and damaged only the mobile home. However, the fire was a sudden event which reduced the product's value in a manner entirely different than in *Morrow*. The defect in *Cloud* created a situation potentially dangerous to persons or other property and the loss occurred as a result of that danger. Recovery in tort was therefore held to be appropriate, even though the damage was confined to the product itself.

It may therefore be said, as a general rule, that when damage is sudden and calamitous, resulting from an occurrence hazardous to human safety, recovery may be had in tort, but damage resulting merely from deterioration, internal breakage, depreciation, failure to live up to expectation, and the like, will be considered economic loss, as to which recovery may be had only on a contract theory.

Although the revised definition refers to "economic losses" without defining them, and fails to make clear whose property is referred to in the first sentence, we believe that a fair construction of the act, as amended, would lead to precisely the result which we have elaborated in the foregoing pages. The new definition would not, of course, have any retroactive effect but does tend to show that the Indiana legislature and this court are in agreement as to the distinction which we have attempted to make clear as to what type of defect does, and what does not, properly give rise to an action in tort for damage caused to the defective property itself, and for consequential damages approximately caused by sudden, major damage.

(2) *Sanco, Inc.*, appealed but the appellate court affirmed at 7871 F.2d 1081(7th Cir. 1985). The appellate court found that Indiana's enactment of the U.C.C. precluded recovery for purely economic interests in a negligence action. Court cites: (Court denied recovery of lost profits and refund of purchase price in a strict liability case, although they would be recoverable in a breach of warranty action). The appellate court in *Sanco* also found that the warranty booklets formed a part of the sale agreement as a matter of law since the warranty disclaimers were known by the president of Sanco to be the routine and only way in which Ford warranted its trucks and engines.

(3) In *Salt River Project Agricultural Improvement & Power v. Westinghouse Elec. Corp.*, 694 P.2d 198 (Ariz. 1984), the Arizona Supreme Court dealt with the issue of whether tort law or contract law is to govern claims arising from the malfunction of a product. In December 1971, Salt River Project (SRP) purchased and accepted for commercial operation a gas-turbine generator unit from Westinghouse, to be installed at the Kyrene Power Plant in Tempe, Arizona. In April 1972, SRP notified Westinghouse that the generator had a number of problems, including "frequent computer malfunctions" with the one-word P-50 control computer. SRP further suggested that "an improvement could be made if there was a means of operating the turbine manually." Westinghouse wrote to SRP and advised them that Westinghouse was developing a device (LMC) which "would permit manual operation of . . .gas turbine plants during maintenance of the [P-50]." On March 2, 1973, SRP sent a standard purchase order to Westinghouse. The purchase order contained SRP's standard boilerplate "terms and conditions" which included the following:

> 1. Acceptance of Purchase Order. . . . Acceptance of this Purchase Order must be made on its exact terms and if additional or different terms are proposed by Seller such response will constitute a counter-offer, and no contract shall come into existence without Buyer's written assent to the counter-offer. Buyer's acceptance or payment for material shipped shall constitute acceptance of such material subject to the provisions herein, only, and shall not constitute acceptance of any counter-offer by Seller not assented to in writing.

On March 15, 1973, Westinghouse responded to SRP's purchase order with a standard acceptance form of its own, which stated: "Your order has been entered as our general order number as shown above." The form also referred the purchaser to the reverse side where Westinghouse's "terms and conditions" of the sale were printed as follows:

TERMS AND CONDITIONS

The conditions stated below shall take precedence over any conditions which may appear on your standard form, and no provisions or condition of such form except as expressly stated herein, shall be binding on Westinghouse.

WARRANTY—. . .Westinghouse warrants that the products sold hereunder shall be of the kind and quality described in this quotation and shall be free of defects in workmanship or materials . . . THIS WARRANTY . . . IS EXCLUSIVE AND IN LIEU OF ANY WARRANTY OF MERCHANTABILITY, FITNESS FOR PURPOSE, OR OTHER WARRANTY OF QUALITY, WHETHER EXPRESS OR IMPLIED. (Emphasis in original.)

LIMITATION OF LIABILITY—Neither party shall be liable for special, indirect, incidental or consequential damages. The remedies of the Purchaser set forth herein are exclusive, and the liability of Westinghouse with respect to any contract or sale or anything done in connection therewith, whether in contract, in tort, under any warranty or otherwise, shall not, except as expressly provided herein, exceed the price of the product or part on which such liability is based.

The LMC was delivered to SRP's Kyrene plant in February 1974. Westinghouse employees assisted in the installation and testing of the LMC. On May 16, 1976, an accident destroyed the rotating blades in sections one through four of the gas turbine unit. Damages were calculated to be in excess of $1.9 million. SRP alleges that the accident was a result of an explosion and fire due to a malfunction in the LMC unit. In the alternative, SRP alleged that Westinghouse breached an implied warranty of fitness.

With respect to the "battle of the forms" the court held that Westinghouse prevailed since SRP had "accepted the LMC device nearly a year later without protesting any of the terms in the Westinghouse boilerplate." The rationale behind this result is that the U.C.C. recognizes that merchants may merely exchange forms without ever "engaging in actual negotiations concerning a knowledgeable allocation of risks." The court also rejected SRP's assertions that Westinghouse's boiler-plate "terms and conditions" were unconscionable, stating that, "although a commercial purchaser is not doomed to failure in pressing an unconscionability claim, . . . findings of unconscionability in a commercial setting are rare."

SRP then contended that even if relief were unavailable under the U.C.C., it still may proceed against Westinghouse under a tort doctrine of strict liability. In determining whether SRP can invoke a strict liability theory, the court turned to the question of whether SRP's claim was a "claim governed by tort law, or a contract claim governed by the U.C.C., or partly one and partly the other."

The Westinghouse court emphasized the policy considerations which underlie contract and tort law.

Strict liability "is not based upon traditional concepts of fault," *Reader v. General Motors Corp.*, 107 Ariz. 149, 154, 483 P.2d 1388, 1393 (1971), but is imposed in an attempt to make the products safer.

> The "prophylactic" factor of preventing future harm has been quite important in the field of torts. The courts are concerned not only with compensation of the victim, but with admonition of the wrongdoer. When the decisions of the courts become known, and defendants realize that they may be held liable, there is of course a strong incentive to prevent the occurrence of the harm. Not infrequently one reason for imposing liability is the deliberate purpose of providing that incentive. . . . [T]he manufacturer who is made liable to the consumer for defects in a product will do what can be done to see that there are no such defects.

Thus, preventing accidents by deterring the distribution of unsafe products is one of the prime goals of tort law.

A basic policy of contract law, on the other hand, is to preserve freedom of contract and thus promote the free flow of commerce. This policy is best served when the commercial law permits parties to limit the redress of a purchaser who fails to receive the quality of product he expected. When a defect renders a product substandard or unable to perform the functions for which it was manufactured, the purchaser's remedy for disappointed commercial expectations is through contract law.

Division One of the Arizona Court of Appeals has aptly summarized the difference between tort and contract:

> [T]he rationale for making a distinction is that traditional contract remedies are designed to redress loss of the benefit of the bargain while tort remedies are — designed to protect the public from dangerous products.

In making the determination of whether a claim to recover damages alleged to have been caused by a defect in the goods is governed by the doctrine of strict liability or by the U.C.C., the court outlined three relevant factors to be considered. These factors are (1) the nature of the product defect that caused the buyer's loss, (2) the manner in which the loss occurred, and (3) the type of loss for which redress is sought.

The type of product that will trigger tort liability is one which is defective in a way that poses an unreasonable danger to those who use or consume it. In contrast, the type of product defect contemplated by the U.C.C. is a qualitative one; the Code provides that a merchant impliedly warrants that his goods are "merchantable," that is, fit for the ordinary purposes for which such goods are used.

Though the manner in which loss occurs will not often be determinative, in a particular case it may be relevant. In discussing this factor, courts have distinguished between losses resulting from a sudden accident and those occurring from a slow process of deterioration.

These courts have allowed tort recovery only in instances where an accident has occurred and have relegated the plaintiff to commercial remedies where the property loss was of a non-accidental nature and where, for example, there was "no evidence of violence, fire, collision with external objects, or other calamity."

In discussing the type of loss or damage, the court utilized the hypotheticals:

A few hypotheticals will be useful to illustrate the problems to be addressed in determining whether certain types of loss should be recoverable in tort or under the U.C.C. In all five hypotheticals, a new LMC unit with an unreasonably dangerous and undiscovered defect was installed in the previously purchased turbines. Subsequently the LMC malfunctioned, causing the losses and damage illustrated below.

At Plant # 1, the defect caused the LMC to malfunction at a time when the plant engineer was aloft on a catwalk inspecting one of the turbines controlled by the LMC. The force of the resulting explosion (accident) knocked the engineer to the floor, injuring him.

At Plant #2, the same malfunction affected only one turbine, which accidentally caught on fire and was completely destroyed.

At Plant #3, the defect caused the LMC to malfunction and burn. The fire department responded quickly, so none of the turbines or other property located near the LMC was damaged in the accident.

At Plant #4, the plant engineer discovered the defect in the LMC and was able to shut down the turbines and replace the LMC before any damage occurred. However, the LMC replacement cost to SRP is $50,000, including shutdown, start-up and testing costs.

At Plant #5, during a peak demand period, the LMC malfunctioned and failed to start all four of the gas turbines. The plant was down for twenty-four hours. As a result, SRP could not deliver electricity to its numerous commercial and residential users. SRP not only lost all the profits anticipated from the sales to those consumers but must replace the LMC and faces lawsuits by some of its large commercial users.

By unanimous authority, the personal injuries suffered by the engineer at Plant #1 and the property damage at Plant #2 are recoverable in a strict tort liability action. Restatement (Second) of Torts § 402A. The defect was unreasonably dangerous to person or property and caused accidental damage to other property.

There is a split in authority on whether to allow recovery in tort for physical harm to or destruction of only the defective product itself, the situation at Plant #3. The defect was unreasonably dangerous and caused an accident. However, the only "loss" was the product itself. No person or other property was damaged. Cases which have held such losses not recoverable in tort have done so on the rationale that the aggrieved buyer has lost only the benefit of his bargain, that the loss is purely economic, and that the buyer therefore may seek redress only through the U.C.C. Courts which have allowed tort recovery for such losses generally have done so on a policy basis, reasoning that a manufacturer's responsibility to market safe products should not depend on the fortuity of whether the full extent of the unreasonable danger posed — personal injury or damage to property other than the defective product — has actually occurred. It is in the realm of this direct property damage that we believe the unreasonably dangerous nature of the product defect and the occurrence of the loss in a sudden, accidental manner would tip the balance in favor of strict tort liability even though the damage fortuitously was confined to the product itself. *Russell v. Ford Motor Co., supra; Berg v. General Motors Corp., supra.* However, where the loss to a defective product alone occurs in such a way as to pose no unreasonable danger of harm to person or other property, then U.C.C. remedies will generally be appropriate and exclusive for recovery of the damage to the defective product itself.

The majority rule holds that economic losses such as those at Plants #4 and #5 are not recoverable in tort. There was no accident; the danger remained latent, even though the loss is attributable to a defect that could have become unreasonably dangerous. The loss is only economic in nature. The rule denying recovery in tort for such losses had its genesis in *Seely v. White Motor Co., supra,* and has been applied by courts to deny tort recovery for repair and replacement costs, as well as lost profits.

The immediate case was remanded for further proceedings not inconsistent with this opinion.

(4) In *Vaugh v. General Motors Corp.,* 102 Ill. 2d 432 (1984), the court considered the interaction of tort liability for economic loss and the legislative scheme of the U.C.C. Defendant contended that product liability law was developed to overcome problems of privity of contract. Defendant also contended that where privity is not a problem and where the purchaser is not injured, the General Assembly intended that the rights of the parties be determined by the Uniform Commercial Code (§ 1-101 *et seq.*). In ruling that economic damages were recoverable under tort theory the court stated:

> "There can be no doubt that the seller's liability for negligence covers any kind of physical harm, including not only personal injuries, but also property damage to the defective chattel itself, as where an automobile is wrecked by reason of its own bad brakes." Prosser, *Torts* Sec. 101, at 665 (4th ed. 1971).

91 Ill. 2d 69, 86.

The court thus rejected the argument that recovery must be under the U.C.C. only.

(5) In *Santor v. A.M. Karagheusian, Inc.*, 44 N.J. 52, 207 A.2d 305 (1965), the court upheld recovery under strict liability for "economic loss" to the extent that the defect caused the product to diminish in value. The case involved a consumer purchase of a defective carpet. The manufacturer of the carpet had asserted the defense of lack of privity. The court noted that a cause of action based on strict liability in tort and that this liability was not subject to such a defense, since that cause of action arose simply from marketing the product. The court thereby recognized consumer rights to the economic loss resulting from the goods being defective under strict liability, rather than limiting consumer rights to only U.C.C. warranties.

(6) In questions of recovery for the economic loss caused the buyer when the product turns out to be defective, some courts have distinguished between situations where the product defect causes "violent" damage to the product as opposed to deterioration of the product. In the former, these courts would allow recovery under Restatement of Torts, Second, § 402A; in the latter they would not allow a U.C.C. § 402-A action, but only a U.C.C. warranty action which is subject to privity and disclaimer defenses. In a Missouri case, a car was bought new; after only 23,500 miles there was a heater core rupture that allowed coolant to escape, causing severe damage to the engine. The court of appeals said that in order to claim damages under § 402A there must be a violent occurrence causing damage and that here there was not. Warranty law, not strict liability, governed.

§ 5.09 Special Problems

[A] Design

A defect in design of a product may cause harm, giving rise to a product liability action. The following notes indicate some of the problems that may arise.

———

NOTES

(1) In *Bowman v. General Motors Corporation*, 427 F. Supp. 234 (E.D. Pa. 1977), plaintiff suffered extremely serious and disfiguring burns when his 1966 Oldsmobile Toronado burst into flames after being struck in the rear by another vehicle. The front of the vehicle which struck Mr. Bowman's vehicle underrode the Toronado's rear bumper and pierced its fuel tank. Plaintiff's crashworthiness allegation is that the Toronado was not designed to minimize the risk of injury to the vehicle's occupants in the event of accident. Factually, plaintiff's case rests on the following claims of defective design: (1) the fuel tank was positioned too close to the rear bumper; (2) the angle of the rear bumper invited a striking vehicle to underride it, thus exposing the fuel tank to trauma; and (3) openings in the Toronado's structure (especially the plenum drain) unnecessarily allowed flames to invade the passenger cabin.

Plaintiff founded his design defect claim upon Restatement (Second) of Torts, § 402A. Section 402A of the Restatement provides:

> One who sells any product in a defective condition unreasonably dangerous to the user or consumer . . .is subject to liability for physical harm thereby caused to the ultimate user.

The *Bowman* court, with reference to Professor Henderson's article, *Judicial Review of Manufacturer's Conscious Design Choices: The Limits of Adjudication*, 73 Colum. L. Rev. 1531, 1548 (1973), wrote:

At one end of the spectrum are risks of harm which originate in the inadvertent failure of the design engineer to appreciate adequately the implications of the various elements of his design, or to employ commonly understood and universally accepted engineering techniques to achieve the ends intended with regard to the product. At the other end of the spectrum are risks of harm which originate in the conscious decision of the design engineer to accept the risks associated with the intended design in exchange for increased benefits or reduced costs which the designer believes justify conscious acceptance of the risks.

427 F. Supp. at 241.

In order for a trier of fact to determine the existence of a "defect," the only standard alluded to in § 402A is that of "unreasonably dangerous." The *Bowman* court concluded that in a conscious design choice case, where the trade-off among safety, utility, and cost is weighed against that which is acceptable to the consumer, "defect" should be defined in terms of "unreasonableness of danger."

(2) In developing the balancing test in *Bowman* the court relied heavily upon the works of Dean Wade [Court's footnote 18] in which

Dean Wade proposed a set of criteria by which the reasonableness of product danger can be measured, which reflects a . . .realization that all products involve some degree of danger; and that what is being censured is the manufacturer's failure to strike a proper balance between design safety and social desire for utility and aesthetics. They include:

(1) The usefulness and desirability of the product — its utility to the user and to the public as a whole.

(2) The safety aspects of the product — the likelihood that it will cause injury, and the probable seriousness of the injury.

(3) The availability of a substitute product which would meet the same need and not be as unsafe.

(4) The manufacturer's ability to eliminate the unsafe character of, the product without impairing its usefulness or making it too expensive to maintain its utility.

(5) The user's ability to avoid danger by the exercise of care in the use of the product.

(6) The user's anticipated awareness of the dangers inherent in the product and their avoidability because of general public knowledge of the obvious condition of the product, or of the existence of suitable warnings or instructions.

(7) The feasibility, on the part of the manufacturer, of spreading the loss by setting the price of the product or carrying liability insurance. [footnote omitted]

Wade, *On the Nature of Strict Tort Liability Products*, 44 Miss. L. J. 825 837-38 (1973).

Professor Fisher [sic] has also suggested some factors which could be used in a balancing test:

In deciding when to impose strict liability courts should consider, in light of the facts of the particular case, the merits of the policies underlying strict liability and balance these considerations against countervailing factors. Some of the factors that should be considered are as follows:

I. Risk Spreading

A.   From the point of view of consumer.

    1.   Ability of consumer to bear loss.

    2.   Feasibility and effectiveness of self-protective measures.

        a.   Knowledge of risk.

        b.   Ability to control danger.

        c.   Feasibility of deciding against use of product.

B.   From point of view of manufacturer.

    1.   Knowledge of risk.

    2.   Accuracy of prediction of losses.

    3.   Size of losses.

    4.   Availability of insurance.

    5.   Ability of manufacturer to self-insure.

    6.   Effect of increased prices on industry.

    7.   Public necessity for the product.

    8.   Deterrent effect on the development of new products.

II. Safety Incentive.

A.   Likelihood of future produce improvement.

B.   Existence of additional precautions that can presently be taken.

C.   Availability of safer substitutes.

Fischer, *The Meaning of Defect*, 39 Mo. L. Rev. 339, 359 (1974).

In appropriate cases other factors listed by Wade and/or Fischer [sic] could be incorporated into the unreasonably dangerous charge.

Bowman, 427 F. Supp. at 234.

[B]   Comparative Negligence and Strict Liability

PROBLEM 5.8

The plaintiff had the duty of operating a planing machine in the course of his employment. The blades of the machine were protected by a metal guard which was designed to close after the board being planed had cleared the cutterhead. A board slipped out of the plaintiff's hand and he reached down to catch it as it fell. The guard plate had not covered the blades as it should have and his hand engaged the blades, resulting in the loss of two fingers and severe laceration of others.

The plaintiff alleged that the planing machine was defective and unreasonably dangerous and that inadequate warning of the danger had been given and that there is breach of warranty and strict liability. The defendant asserts a percentage of fault should be assessed against the plaintiff that his negligence had contributed to his injury.

You are counsel for the plaintiff. What arguments will you make?

You are the judge. What is your decision on this issue?

NOTES

(1) In *Correlia v. Firestone Tire & Rubber Co.*, 446 N.E. 2d 1033 (1983), involving the issue of whether contributing negligence should be considered in a strict liability § 402A action, the court noted:

As Restatement (Second) of Torts § 402A, comment n, indicates, actions for strict liability are not actions in negligence. The defendant may be liable "even though he has exercised all possible care in the preparation and sale of the product. . . ."

If the comparative negligence statute does not literally apply, the question remains whether its underlying principles should be given effect by judicial adoption. This is the course of action most strongly urged by Firestone. We decline to take such action. To do so would be to meld improperly the theory of negligence with the theory of warranty as expressed in G.L. c. 106, §§ 2-314–2-318, and thereby to undercut the policies supporting these statutes.

Simply stated, the policy of negligence liability presumes that people will, or at least should, take reasonable measures to protect themselves and others from harm. This presumption justifies the imposition of a duty on people to conduct themselves in this way. A person harmed by one whose conduct "falls below the standard established by law for the protection of others against unreasonable risk" may recover against the actor. However, if the injured person's unreasonable conduct also has been a cause of his injury, his conduct will be accounted for in apportioning liability or damages.

Strict liability is justified on a much different basis.

On whatever theory, the justification for the strict liability has been said to be that the seller, by marketing his product for use and consumption, has undertaken and assumed a special responsibility toward any member of the consuming public who may be injured by it; that the public has the right to and does expect, in the case of products which it needs and for which it is forced to rely upon the seller, that reputable sellers will stand behind their goods; that public policy demands that the burden of accidental injuries caused by products intended for consumption be placed upon those who market them, and be treated as a cost of production against which liability insurance can be obtained; and that the consumer of such products is entitled to the maximum of protection at the hands of someone, and the proper persons to afford it are those who market the products.

Recognizing that the seller is in the best position to ensure product safety, the law of strict liability imposes on the seller a duty to prevent the release of "any product in a defective condition unreasonably dangerous to the user or consumer," into the stream of commerce. This duty is unknown in the law of negligence and it is not fulfilled even if the seller takes all reasonable measures to make his product safe. The liability issue focuses on whether the product was defective and unreasonably dangerous and not on the conduct of the user or the seller. Given this focus, the only duty imposed on the user is to act reasonably with respect to a product which he knows to be defective and dangerous. When a user unreasonably proceeds to use a product which he knows to be defective and dangerous, he violates that duty and relinquishes the protection of the law. It is only then that it is appropriate to account for his conduct in determining liability. Since he has voluntarily relinquished the law's protection, it is further appropriate that he be barred from recovery. The absolute bar to the user for breach of his duty balances the strict liability placed on the seller. Other than this instance, the parties are not presumed to be equally responsible for injuries caused by defective products, and the principles of contributory or comparative negligence have no part in the strict liability scheme. Given this focus, the user's negligence does not prevent recovery except when he unreasonably uses a product that he knows to be defective and dangerous. In such circumstances, the user's conduct alone is the proximate cause of his injuries, as a matter of law, and recovery is appropriately denied. In short, the user is denied recovery, not because of his contributory negligence or his assumption of the risk but rather because his conduct is the proximate cause of his injuries.

The policies of negligence and warranty liability will best be served by keeping the spheres in which they operate separate until such time as the Legislature indicates how and to what extent they should be melded. The standards of care and the duties are well defined in each sphere. The comparative negligence statute defined no standard of behavior and imposed no duty not previously recognized under the traditional theories of contributory negligence. It merely adjusted the manner in which unreasonable conduct which caused injury would be treated in a negligence action. There is no reason to presume that by passage of the comparative negligence statute the Legislature intended to merge negligence liability with warranty liability. Even if we were convinced that some restructuring of the Massachusetts law of warranty was necessary, we ordinarily would leave that restructuring to the Legislature, given the wide variety of possible solutions it might reasonably adopt.

Restatement (Second) of Torts § 402A, comment n (1965), states the essence of our position. To paraphrase and elaborate on that comment, we conclude that the plaintiff in a warranty action under G.L. c. 106, § 2-314, may not recover if it is found that, after discovering the product's defect and being made aware of its danger, he nevertheless proceeded unreasonably to make use of the product and was injured by it. No recovery by the plaintiff shall be diminished on account of any other conduct which might be deemed contributorily negligent.

(2) Consider the following from *Lippard v. Houdaville Indus., Inc.*, 715 S.W.2d 491 (Mo. Supr. Ct. 1986):

Products liability law, essentially, is to socialize the losses caused by defective products.

Inasmuch as negligence is not an element of a products liability case, we have consistently held that the claimant's contributory negligence does not operate as a bar to recovery.

Gustafson v. Benda, supra, introduced the concept of comparative fault into Missouri negligence law.

. . . .

The respondent argues eloquently, however, that the rule of comparative fault is a fair one in products liability cases just as in negligence cases, that it gives product users a motive for being more careful, and that it states a good rule for decision. Authorities in other states are divided on the point. We therefore make the choice for ourselves, based on our doctrines of products liability, as expounded in our numerous cases.

We conclude that there should be no change in the Missouri common law rule, as established in the *Keener* opinion that the plaintiff's contributory negligence is not at issue in a products liability case. It should neither defeat nor diminish recovery. The defendant may sometimes make use of the plaintiffs alleged carelessness in support of arguments that the product is not unreasonably dangerous, or that the alleged defects in a product did not cause the injury, but these are traversing claims not appropriate for instruction. If the defective product is a legal cause of injury, then even a negligent plaintiff should be able to recover.

. . . .

The judgment is reversed and the cause is remanded with directions to enter judgment for the plaintiff for the full amount of damage determined by the jury.

(3) In the *Lippard* case, *supra*, the defendants raise an assumption of risk defense, but the court found no evidence in support of this defense. If it had, what would have been the result? Would this be desirable?

(4) How should assumption of risk, in the sense of choosing to encounter a known risk, be treated in states which adopt comparative fault? In the Uniform Comparative Fault Act, it is treated as "fault."

PROBLEM 5.9

You are a member of the legislature. The courts of your state have followed the rational of the *Correlia* case and the *Lippard* case. You are now asked to consider on a bill which would make warranty and strict liability actions subject to comparative fault.

If you are for it, what arguments would you make?

If you oppose it, what arguments?

You are a legislator who has heard arguments both ways. Which way do you vote?

NOTES

(1) The determination of whether the comparative negligence doctrine should apply to products liability cases may ultimately be decided by state legislatures. After the *Lippard* case, the Missouri legislature enacted the following:

Section 36.

1. Contributory fault, as a complete bar to plaintiff's recovery in a products liability claim, is abolished. The doctrine of pure comparative fault shall apply to products liability claims as provided in this section.

2. Defendant may plead and prove the fault of the plaintiff as an affirmative defense. Any fault chargeable to the plaintiff shall diminish proportionately the amount awarded as compensatory damages but shall not bar recovery.

3. For purposes of this section, "fault" is limited to:

(1) The failure to use the product as reasonably anticipated by the manufacturer;

(2) Use of the product for a purpose not intended by the manufacturer;

(3) Use of the product with knowledge of a danger involved in such use with reasonable appreciation of the consequences and the voluntary and unreasonable exposure to said danger;

(4) Unreasonable failure to appreciate the danger involved in use of the product or the consequences thereof and the unreasonable exposure to said danger;

(5) The failure to undertake the precautions a reasonably careful user of the product would take to protect himself against dangers which he would reasonably appreciate under the same or similar circumstances; or

(6) The failure to mitigate damages.

(2) The trend in states with applicable statutes is to apply comparative negligence principles to strict liability and implied warranty actions. The court in *Fiske v. MacGregor*, 464 A.2d 719 (R.I. 1983), noted that:

> Our decision today to apply comparative negligence principles to strict liability and implied warranty is well supported by other jurisdictions. [The court cites cases in Kansas, Alaska, California and Florida.]

> The state of Mississippi, which has the same comparative-negligence statute as our own, has had that statute interpreted by a federal court to allow its application to strict-liability claims. Moreover, there are jurisdictions that have applied comparative negligence principles to strict-liability claims despite the presence of comparative-negligence statutes that are limited by their terms to actions for negligence. (held that Strict liability in torts is the equivalent of negligence per se; therefore, application of comparative negligence in such cases would be appropriate); contra (held that the comparative negligence statute did not apply to strict-liability cases because it is confined by its term to actions for negligence; however, the court further held that strict liability is a judicially created doctrine to which the principle of comparative causation will apply); (held that phrase, "in an action. . .for negligence" should not be read literally so as to refer only to traditional negligence tort actions). Fortunately, because of the broad language in our comparative negligence statute, we do not need to engage in any such creative analysis. Nonetheless, the existence of these cases can only lend support to our decision.

Fiske, 464 A.2d at 728.

(3) The rationale behind the trend to apply comparative negligence principles to strict liability actions is founded on the desire for a fair and equitable result. In *Fiske v. MacGregor, supra,* the court stated:

> If the comparative-negligence statute only applied to negligence actions, a defendant manufacturer found liable in strict liability or implied warranty could not have the damages apportioned because of plaintiff's culpable conduct. Ironically, defendant manufacturers found liable in negligence would have the damages apportioned, despite the fact that their conduct was clearly more culpable than the conduct of those defendants found liable in strict liability or implied warranty. We believe that the just outcome of a case should not be determined by adroit pleading or semantical distinctions. A defendant's culpability is the basis for an award of damages, whether that culpability is denominated negligence, strict liability, or breach of warranty. Similarly, a plaintiff's culpable conduct is the basis for an apportionment of those damages. In the present case there is a finding of fact by the jury in regard to plaintiff's culpability which cannot be dismissed by adverting to semantics.

464 A.2d at 728.

(4) In *Gagnon v. Dresser Industries Corp.*, 344 N.W.2d 582 (Mich. 1984), plaintiff argued that a defense of comparative negligence did not apply to his action under a theory of implied warranty. Plaintiff based his allegation on U.C.C. § 2-314 (MCL 440.2314; MSA 19.2314).

The court in *Gagnon* noted that plaintiff's implied warranty theory was not contractual in nature, but a products liability action as defined by MCL 600.2945; MSA 27A.2945. The court held that comparative negligence is a defense to any claim of inadequate safety devices. "Accordingly, given that plaintiff's claim is contractual in nature . . .comparative negligence was . . .applicable regardless of whether the claim is characterized as a products liability action for breach of implied warranty on the one hand, or a claim of inadequate safety devices on the other."

PROBLEM 5.10

Your firm handles a number of products liability cases for a variety of clients (though always avoiding conflicts of interest). These include manufacturers, metal sellers, and consumers who have suffered personal or economic injury. Your senior partner is aware of the proposed § 402A revision and asks your opinion as to how each of these client groups may be affected? Also should he vote for or against the proposal at the ALI annual meeting?

§ 1   Commercial Seller's Liability for Harm Caused by Defective Products

(a) One engaged in the business of selling products who sells a defective product is subject to liability for harm to persons or property caused by the product defect.

(b) A product is defective if, at the time of sale, it contains a manufacturing defect, is defective in design, or is defective because of inadequate instructions or warnings.

Comment:

a. History. The Section states a rule of tort liability applicable to commercial sellers of products. The types of products defects referred to in § 1(b) are defined in § 2. The liability established in this Section draws on both warranty law and tort law. Historically, the focus of products liability law was on manufacturing defects. A manufacturing defect is a physical departure from a product's intended design that poses risks of harm to persons or property. Typically manufacturing defects occur in only a small percentage of units in a product line. Courts early began imposing liability without fault on product sellers for harm caused by such defects. When holding a seller liable for harm caused by manufacturing defects even though all possible care had been exercised by the seller in the preparation and marketing of the product, courts relied on the concept of warranty, in connection with which fault has never been a prerequisite to liability.

The imposition of liability for manufacturing defects has a long history in the common law. As early as 1266, criminal statutes imposed liability upon victualers, vintners, brewers, butchers, cooks, and other persons who supplied contaminated food and drink. By the early 1960s, American courts recognized that a seller of any product having a manufacturing defect should be liable in tort for harm caused by the defect regardless of the plaintiff's ability to maintain a traditional negligence or warranty action. Liability would attach even if the manufacturer's quality control in producing the defective product was reasonable. Furthermore, it had been held that a plaintiff need not be in direct privity with the defendant seller to bring an action. A cause of action in tort for defectively manufactured products, recognized by American courts since the early 1960s, merges the concept of implied warranty, in which negligence is not required, with the concept of negligence in tort, in which contractual privity is not required.

Questions of design defect and defects based on inadequate instructions or warnings arise when the specific product unit conforms to the intended design but the intended design itself, or its sale without adequate instructions or warnings, renders the product not reasonably safe. If these forms of defect are found to exist, then every unit in the same product line is potentially defective. See § 2, Comments c and d. Liability for design defects and for defects based on inadequate instructions or warnings occurred relatively infrequently until the late 1960s and early 1970s. A number of limited-duty rules made recovery for such defects, especially design defects, difficult to obtain. Following the erosion of these restrictive rules, courts sought to impose liability without fault for design defects and defects due to inadequate instructions or warnings, accepting the invitation of § 402A of the Restatement, Second, of Torts. It soon became evident that § 402A, created to deal with liability for manufacturing defects, could not readily be applied to cases of design defects or defects based on inadequate instructions or warnings. A product unit that fails to meet the manufacturer's own design specifications thereby fails to perform its intended function and is, almost by definition, defective. However, when the product unit meets the manufacturer's own design specifications it is necessary to go outside those specifications to determine whether the product is defective.

Sections 2(b) and (c) and 4(b)(2), (3), and (4) recognize that the rule developed for manufacturing defects is inappropriate for the resolution of claims of defective design and defects based on inadequate instructions or warnings. The latter categories of cases require determinations that the product could have reasonably been made safer by a better design or instruction or warning. Sections 2(b) and (c) and 4(b)(2), (3), and (4) rely on a reasonableness test traditionally used in determining whether an actor has been negligent. See Restatement, Second, Torts §§ 291-293. Nevertheless, many courts insist on speaking of liability based on the standards described in §§ 2(b)(2) and (3) and 4(b)(2), (3), and (4) as being "strict."

Several factors help to explain this rhetorical preference. First, in many cases dealing with design defects, if the product causes injury while being put to a reasonably foreseeable use, the seller is held to have known of the risks that attend such use. See § 2, Comment i. Second, some courts have sought to limit the defense of comparative fault in certain products liability contexts. In furtherance of this objective, they have avoided characterizing the liability test as based in negligence, thereby affording freedom to fashion comparative or contributory fault doctrine in a more restrictive fashion. See § 7, Comment d. Third, some courts are concerned that a negligence standard might be too forgiving of a small manufacturer who might be excused for its ignorance of risk or for failing to take adequate precautions to avoid risk. Negligence, which focuses on the conduct of the defendant-manufacturer, might allow a finding that a defendant with meager resources was not negligent because it was too burdensome for the defendant to discover some risks or to design or warn against them. Strict liability language, which focuses on the product rather then the conduct of the manufacturer, may help make the point that a defendant is held to the standard of knowledge available to the relevant manufacturing community at the time the product was manufactured. Finally, the liability of nonmanufacturing sellers in the distributive chain is strict. It is no defense that they acted reasonably and were not aware of a defect in the product, be it manufacturing, design, or failure to warn.

Thus, "strict products liability" is a term of art that reflects the judgment that products liability is a discrete area of tort law which borrows piecemeal from negligence and warranty. It is not fully congruent with classical tort or contract law. Rather than perpetuating confusion spawned by existing doctrinal categories, §§ 1 and 2 define the liability for each form of defect in functional terms. As long as the functional criteria are met, courts may utilize the doctrines of negligence, strict liability, or the implied warranty of merchantability, or simply define liability in the functional terms set forth in the black letter. See § 2, Comment *j*.

b. *Product sellers*. The rule stated in this Section applies not only to sales transactions but also to other forms of product distribution that are the functional equivalent of product sales. Commercial lessors of products for consumer use are thus liable for injuries caused by defective products that they lease to consumers. The rule in this Section also applies to housing, although sales of real property historically have not been within the ambit of product sales. Providers of services unaccompanied by products are not product sellers. See the rules governing providers of services who provide or install products while performing their services.

c. *One engaged in the business of selling*. The rule stated in this Section applies only to commercial sellers who are engaged in the business of selling or distributing the type of product that harmed the plaintiff. The rule does not apply to an occasional seller of such products. Thus, it does not apply to one who occasionally sells jam or other foodstuffs to neighbors, nor does it apply to the noncommercial private owner of an automobile who sells it to another.

It is not necessary that the seller be engaged exclusively or even primarily in selling the type of product that injured the plaintiff. Thus the rule applies to a motion picture theater that sells popcorn or ice cream, either for consumption on the premises or in packages to be taken home.

A service station that does mechanical repair work on cars may also sell tires and automobile equipment. Such sales are subject to the rule in this Section. However, the rules does not cover occasional sales outside the regular course of business (frequently referred to as "casual sales"). Thus, an occasional sale of surplus equipment by a business does not fall within the ambit of this rule. Whether the defendant is a commercial seller is ordinarily a question of law to be determined by the court.

d. *Harm to persons or property*. The rule stated in this Section applies only to harm to persons or property, commonly referred to as personal injury and property damage. In this context, property damage does not include harm to the product itself. See rules governing emotional upset, for economic loss.

§ 7 Apportionment of Liability Between Negligent Plaintiff and Seller of a Defective Product

When the conduct of the plaintiff combines with a product defect to cause harm to the plaintiff's person or property and the plaintiff's conduct fails to conform to an applicable standard of care, liability for harm to the plaintiff is apportioned between the plaintiff and the product seller pursuant to the applicable rules governing apportionment of liability.

Comment:

a. *Rationale*. The rules governing apportionment of liability are frequently referred to as the rules governing "comparative responsibility" or "comparative fault." Those rules impose on users and consumers responsibility they should bear for safe product use and consumption. The premise is that it would be unfair to impose the costs of substandard plaintiff conduct on manufacturers, who will be impelled to pass on those costs to all users and consumers, including those who use and consume products safety and reasonably. See § 2, Comment a. Shifting injury costs to plaintiffs who properly should bear those costs is not considered to significantly diminish a manufacturer's incentive to produce and sell reasonably safe products. Theoretically, a manufacturer might reduce the level of its investment in product safety to take into account its reduced exposure by reason of comparative responsibility. However, such a calculation would be entirely speculative on the manufacturer's part. Hence, any diminished incentive effect is likely to be insignificant.

b. Conduct of the plaintiff. The applicable rules of apportionment of liability vary among jurisdictions. Some states have adopted "pure" comparative fault. Others follow some variant of modified comparative fault. The apportionment of liability principles as they have developed in each jurisdiction should be applied to products liability cases. With respect to whether special exceptions should be made in products liability cases for certain categories of plaintiff conduct, see Comment d.

Illustration:

1. Roger was driving his car manufactured by the ABC Motor Co. when he noticed the temperature light flashing. The instruction manual warned drivers that when the temperature light flashes it is a sign that the car is seriously overheating and that the car should be brought to a stop and the motor shut off. The overheating in this instance was caused by a hose that was defective at the time of sale by ABC and was leaking coolant. Roger had not read the instruction manual and paid no attention to the flashing temperature light. He continued driving for 30 minutes. The overheating of the car was so intense that it brought about an electrical fire in the car causing Roger serious personal injury. Roger's conduct in failing to read the manual and failing to pay attention to the flashing temperature light may be considered by the trier of fact to be negligent conduct warranting a reduction of Roger's recovery against ABC based on the percentage of fault attributed to him.

c. Misuse, alteration, and modification. When plaintiff's misuse, alteration, or modification of a product constitutes substandard plaintiff conduct, and that conduct combines with a product defect to bring about harm to the plaintiff, liability is apportioned between plaintiff and the product defendant under the rule of this Section.

Illustration:

ABC Machine Tools, Inc. manufactures and sells pelletizer machines, which draw strands of plastic into position for cutting into very small pellets. The pelletizer comes equipped with a removable guard. It is necessary periodically to dismantle the guard so that the inside of the machine can be cleaned. Fred, an employee, removed the guard on an ABC pelletizer to perform the cleaning but neglected to reinstall it. Fred resumed operation of the machine without the guard. Shortly thereafter a strand of plastic caught his hand and pulled it into the rollers of the machine. Fred lost four fingers. Fred alleges that the pelletizer should have been equipped with an interlock mechanism that would have prevented it from operating without the safety guard in place. On the evidence presented, a trier of fact may conclude that the pelletizer was defectively designed and also that Fred's failure to replace the safety guard was a foreseeable alteration of the machine. The trier of fact may also find that Fred's conduct in failing to reinstall the safety guard and operating the machine without the guard constitute negligent conduct on his part that should reduce his recovery based on the percentage of fault attributed to him.

d. Particular forms of plaintiff conduct. Some decisions hold that when the plaintiff's negligence consists in the failure to discover a product defect, there should be no reduction of damages on the basis of apportionment of liability. The premise is that a consumer has a right to expect a defect-free product and should not be burdened with a duty to inspect for defects. Other decisions hold that apportionment of liability is inappropriate where the product lacked a safety feature that would protect against the risk that resulted in the injury in question. The premise is that liability should not be diminished when the plaintiff engages in the very conduct that the product design should have prevented. On the other hand, some decisions hold that assumption of the risk should be a complete defense to a products liability action, not merely a basis for apportionment of liability.

Section 7 states that all forms of plaintiff's failure to conform to applicable standards of care should be presented to the trier of fact for the purpose of apportioning liability between the plaintiff and the product seller. How much responsibility to attribute to a plaintiff will vary with the circumstances. When the plaintiff's conduct is failure to discover a defect, or inattention to a danger that should have been eliminated by a safety feature, a trier of fact may decide to allocate little or no responsibility to the plaintiff. Conversely, when the plaintiff voluntarily and unreasonably encounters a risk, the trier of fact may decide to attribute all or a substantial percentage of responsibility to the plaintiff. All forms of plaintiff misconduct should be the subject of apportionment by the trier of fact. The relative innocence or seriousness of plaintiff's fault should be taken into account by the trier of fact in apportioning liability between the plaintiff and the product seller, but should not serve automatically to absolve the plaintiff from fault or bar the plaintiff from recovery.

Several justifications support the position that plaintiff fault should not be separated into discrete categories. Recognition of such special categories tends to result in either a plaintiff being absolved from responsibility or being completely barred from recovery. The litigation becomes involved in competing efforts to fit plaintiff's conduct into one or another of the categories. This, in turn, spawns appellate litigation seeking precise definition of the category boundaries. That effort has proven costly and largely futile. By and large, the trier of fact should be able fairly to assess the appropriate percentages of responsibility in the circumstances of a case. Such fact-sensitive evaluations are better adapted to apportioning liability that is reliance on discrete categories of plaintiff conduct. Courts always retain the power to review whether the percentage of responsibility assigned to a plaintiff is unreasonable.

Another significant reason to eschew separate categories of plaintiff conduct is that products liability cases often involve parties other than the plaintiff and the product seller, who are either joined by the plaintiff or impleaded by the defendant for contribution purposes. Establishing special categorical rules governing the apportionment of liability between the plaintiff and the product seller creates difficulties when the fault of other parties must be taken into account. These non-seller parties can legitimately insist that plaintiff's fault be determined in assessing their liability. Using different systems for allocating liability, one for the plaintiff and product seller and another for plaintiff and non-seller parties, makes it difficult to adjudicate such a case in a coherent and consistent manner.

§ 8   Disclaimers, Litigations, Waivers, and Other Contract-Based Defenses to Products Liability Claims for Harm to persons.

Disclaimers and limitations of remedies by product sellers, waivers by product purchasers, and other similar contractual exculpations, oral or written, do not bar or reduce otherwise valid products liability claims for harm to persons.

Comment:

a. Effect of contract defenses on products liability tort claims for harm to persons. A commercial seller of a product is not permitted to escape liability for harm to persons through limiting terms in a contract governing the sale of a product. It is presumed that the plaintiff lacked sufficient information, bargaining power, or bargaining position necessary to execute a fair contractual limitation of rights to recover. For a limited exception to this general rule, see Comment d. The rule in this Section applies only to "product sellers," a term defined to include only sellers of new products. See the rule governing sellers of used products and whether they may rely on disclaimers, waivers, and other contractual defenses.

b. Distinguishing disclaimers from warnings. This Section invalidates disclaimers and contractual exculpations of liability by sellers of new products when they are raised to bar or limit claims by plaintiffs for personal injury. Disclaimers should be distinguished from warnings. Warnings usually convey specific information to the buyer about avoiding risk in using the product. In some cases warnings inform the consumer of risks that cannot be avoided. Both types of warnings provide consumers with valuable information concerning the risks attendant to using the product. A product sold with reasonable instructions or warnings may be nondefective. See § 2, Comments f, g, and h. Disclaimers attempt contractually to avoid liability for defective products. For the reasons set forth in Commend a, courts refuse to enforce disclaimers to deny recovery for personal injury caused by new products that were defective at the time of sale.

c. Effect of disclaimers on claims for harm to property or for economic loss. See the effect of disclaimers on tort claims for defect-caused harm to property or for economic loss.

d. Waiver of rights in non-adhesive contracts. The rule in this Section applies to cases in which commercial product sellers attempt to disclaim or otherwise limit their liability to persons who are presumed to lack information and bargaining power adequately to protect their interests. This Section does not address whether consumers, especially when represented by consumer groups or intermediaries, with full information and sufficient bargaining power, may contract with product sellers to accept curtailment of liability for concomitant benefits, or whether such consumers might be allowed to agree to substitute alternative dispute resolution mechanisms in place of traditional adjudication. When such contracts are accompanied by alternative non-tort remedies that serve as an adequate quid pro quo for reducing or eliminating rights to recover in tort, especially when authorized by statute, persuasive argument support giving effect to such agreements. Such contractual arrangements raise policy questions different from those raised by this Section and require careful consideration by the courts.

§ 5.10 Proposed Federal Legislation

PROBLEM 5.11

Your senior partner also is interested in how this particular proposed federal legislature will affect the firm's clients. It would override and replace state law products liability. Please advise as to how manufacturers, retail sellers, and consumers will be affected. He also asks you whether he should as a matter of professional responsibility and good citizenship support such legislation.

H.R. 10 104th Congress, 1st Session to reform . . . product liability law

(1) GENERAL RULE. — Except as provided in paragraph 2, in a product liability action, a product seller shall be liable to a claimant for harm only if the claimant establishes that —

(A)(i) the product which allegedly caused the harm complained of was sold by the product seller,

(ii) the product seller failed to exercise reasonable care with respect to the product, and

(iii) such failure to exercise reasonable care was a proximate cause of the claimant's harm,

(B)(i) the product seller made an express warranty applicable to the product which allegedly caused the harm complained of, independent of any express warranty made by the manufacturer as to the same product,

(ii) the product failed to conform to the warranty, and

(iii) the failure of the product to conform to the warranty caused the claimant's harm, or

(C) the product seller engaged in intentional wrongdoing as determined under applicable State law and such intentional wrongdoing was a proximate cause of the harm complained of by the claimant.

For purposes of subparagraph (A)(ii), a product seller shall not be considered to have failed to exercise reasonable care with respect to a product based upon an alleged failure to inspect a product where there was no reasonable opportunity to inspect the product in a manner which would, in the exercise of reasonable care, have revealed the aspect of the product which allegedly caused the claimant's harm.

(2) SPECIAL RULE — In a product liability action, a product seller shall be liable for harm to the claimant caused by such product as if the product seller were the manufacturer of such product if —

(A) the manufacturer is not subject to service of process under the laws of the State in which the claimant brings the action, or

(B) the court determines that the claimant would be unable to enforce a judgment against the manufacturer.

CHAPTER **6**

PERFORMANCE

§ 6.01 Rights and Obligations of the Parties

[A] In General

Read: U.C.C. § 2-301.

Read also: U.C.C. § 2A-103(1)(j); CISG Arts. 30, 53.

Generally, the obligation of a seller of goods is to transfer and deliver them, and that of a buyer is to accept and pay for them. See U.C.C. §§ 2-301, 2-503, 2-606, 2-310. Buyer has a right to inspection of goods. U.C.C. § 2-513. Buyer's rights on improper delivery include the right to reject the goods. U.C.C. § 2-601. Seller may have a right to cure an improper tender or delivery. U.C.C. § 2-508. These and other rights and obligations will be explored in this Chapter.

[B] Good Faith

Read: U.C.C. § 1-203.

Read also: CISG Arts. 7(1), 60(a), 65.

Every contract within the Uniform Commercial Code imposes an obligation of good faith in its performance. U.C.C. § 1-203. Such obligation may not be disclaimed. U.C.C. § 1-102(3). Good faith is discussed in Chapter 1 at § 1.04[C].

PROBLEM 6.1

S contracts to sell 600 pens to *B; B* has the option of choosing styles and colors desired but *B* refuses to so choose. What remedies has *S*? U.C.C. § 2-311, *see* § 2-305(3).

[C] Right to Unimpaired Expectation of Proper Performance

Read: U.C.C. §§ 2-609, 2-610, 2-611.

Read also: U.C.C. §§ 2A-401, 2A-402, 2A-403; CISG Arts. 71, 72, see Arts. 25-27.

Adequate Assurance of Performance. Section 2-609(1) states: "A contract for sale imposes an obligation on each party that the other's expectation of receiving due performance will not be impaired." Comment 1 observes: "The section rests on the recognition of the fact that the essential purpose of a contract between commercial men is actual performance and they do not bargain merely for a promise, or for a promise plus the right to win a lawsuit and that a continuing sense of reliance and security that the promised performance will be forthcoming when due, is an important feature of the bargain. If either the willingness or the ability of a party to perform

(Matthew Bender & Co., Inc.)   (Pub.087)

declines materially between the time of contracting and the time for performance, the other party is threatened with the loss of a substantial part of what he has bargained for." See U.C.C. §§ 2-210(5), 2-311(3), 2-611(2), 2-612(2).

Anticipatory Repudiation. Comment 1 to U.C.C. § 2-610 reads: "With the problem of insecurity taken care of by the preceding section [U.C.C. § 2-609, Right to Adequate Assurance of Performance] . . ., anticipatory repudiation [U.C.C. § 2-610] centers upon an overt communication of intention or an action which renders performance impossible or demonstrates a clear determination not to continue with performance."

––––

CREUSOT-LOIRE INTERNATIONAL, INC. v. COPPUS ENGINEERING CORP.

United States District Court, Southern District of New York
585 F. Supp. 45, 39 U.C.C. Rep. 186 (1983)

CANNELLA, DISTRICT JUDGE. Plaintiff's motion for summary judgment is granted.

BACKGROUND

Plaintiff commenced this diversity action alleging breach of contract and warranty. Simply stated, in January 1979, plaintiff purchased five type DG-26 fanmix burners [the "burners"] from defendant for installation in an ammonia plant in Kutina, Yugoslavia. According to plaintiff in February 1981, before the burners were installed, it learned that serious problems developed concerning the operation of similar burners manufactured by defendant in ammonia plants in Syria and Sri Lanka. Thereafter, plaintiff claims it sought reasonable assurances from defendant that its burners would perform satisfactorily. Plaintiff asserts that defendant repudiated its contract by failing to give adequate assurances, thus, justifying plaintiff's revocation and its demand for rescission. Plaintiff now moves for summary judgment contending that defendant is liable for the purchase price of the burners plus plaintiff's incidental damages.

FACTS

Plaintiff is a wholly-owned subsidiary of Creusot-Loire, S.A. ["Creusot-Loire"], a French manufacturing and engineering concern. Creusot-Loire Enterprises ["CLE"] is a contracting subsidiary of Creusot-Loire. CLE is the project engineer for the ammonia plants in Yugoslavia and Syria. The design process engineer for all three ammonia plants—Yugoslavia, Syria and Sri Lanka—is M.V. Kellogg ["Kellogg"], an American engineering firm with affiliated offices in Europe. As design process engineer, Kellogg designated defendant's burners for the auxiliary steam boiler in all three plants.

In the fall of 1978, plaintiff sent Kellogg's burner specifications to defendant. In response, defendant mailed plaintiff both technical specifications and price information on the burners. Defendant expressly warranted that the burners were capable of continuous operation using heavy fuel oil with combustion air preheated to 260 degrees Centigrade. Defendant further guaranteed that this warranty would extend for one year from the start-up of the plant but not exceeding three years from the date of shipment.

After receiving several technical clarifications, on January 3, 1979 plaintiff issued a purchase order for the burners. Subsequently, the purchase order was amended on two occasions to include additional components. Plaintiff paid $175,586 for the burners and additional parts. In November 1979, the burners were shipped to Yugoslavia. The Kutina plant originally was scheduled for start-up in 1981, however, for reasons not pertinent to the instant motion, the plant will not be operational until the end of 1983.

In 1981 after the burners were shipped, plaintiff became aware of operational difficulties with the burners at the Syrian and Sri Lankan ammonia plants. With respect to the Sri Lankan plant,[1] it became clear that the burners overheated when using heavy fuel oil with combustion air preheated to 316 degrees C. Moreover, as plaintiff later learned, efforts to modify the burners proved futile. Indeed, even when the operating conditions at Sri Lanka were substantially relaxed, the burners still failed to function properly. In May 1981, Kellogg terminated defendant's attempts to rectify the problems with the Sri Lankan burners and replaced them with a competitor's burner which apparently satisfied all performance specifications.

In February 1981, plaintiff wrote to defendant expressing its concern that the burners purchased for Yugoslavia, like the Sri Lankan burners, would be unable to perform satisfactorily. In June 1981, defendant told plaintiff that the problems with the Syrian burners were being resolved. Defendant, however, did not inform plaintiff of the difficulties experienced in Sri Lanka. In September 1981, defendant suggested to plaintiff several modifications in the burners. These modifications were necessary to insure that the Yugoslavian operational specifications could be met. Defendant also indicated that plaintiff would be billed for these modifications.

In response, plaintiff demanded proof that the burners delivered to Yugoslavia would satisfy the contract specifications. Thereafter, on November 6, 1981, defendant informed plaintiff that it had no experience operating burners under conditions comparable with the specifications for the Yugoslavia plant. Defendant suggested, however, that plaintiff consider altering the contract specifications with respect to the preheat temperature and the type of fuel. Defendant did not disclose that the same modifications proved unsuccessful in Sri Lanka.

In December 1981, after Kellogg withdrew its approval for installing defendant's burners, representatives from CLE, Kellogg and defendant met in London. At this meeting, the difficulties with the Sri Lankan burners were discussed. In addition, Kellogg informed defendant that the decision to withdraw prior approval for the Yugoslavian burners was based on the problems encountered at Sri Lanka. CLE also requested that defendant take back the burners and refund the purchase price to plaintiff. Defendant declined this request. On December 15, 1981, plaintiff also demanded that defendant take back the burners.

On December 23, 1981 and again on January 13, 1982, representatives of plaintiff and defendant met in New York. At these meetings, plaintiff stated that it would accept the burners only if defendant provided contractual and financial assurances of performance. Plaintiff requested that defendant extend its contractual guarantee because of a delay in the start-up of the Yugoslavian plant and that defendant post an irrevocable letter of credit for the purchase price of the burners. Defendant refused this request and plaintiff's further demand for a refund.

---

[1] . . .Apparently there is no dispute that the specifications for the Syrian plant were less onerous than the specifications for the Sri Lankan and Yugoslavian plants because the Syrian burners used light weight fuel without combustion air being preheated.

Defendant's correspondence and internal memoranda reveal that it was less than candid with plaintiff. For example, in May 1981 defendant knew that the modifications it would propose in September to plaintiff proved unsuccessful in Sri Lanka. Moreover, after suggesting the modifications, defendant failed to tell plaintiff that the modifications met with limited success under conditions less rigorous than those specified for Yugoslavia.[2] Further, defendant's documents recognize that the representations in its technical offering were misleading because they failed to disclose that defendant had no experience with preheated Kellogg burners. Finally, the documents disclose that from at least September 1981, defendant decided to stall or delay plaintiff's efforts to obtain assurances and to cajole plaintiff into purchasing burners from a competitor.

DISCUSSION

To grant the instant motion, the court must be convinced, after viewing the facts and circumstances in a light most favorable to defendant, that no genuine issues exist for trial. . . . Moreover, merely because a "factual dispute *may* exist, without more, is not sufficient to overcome a convincing presentation by the moving party." *Quinn v. Syracuse Model Neighborhood Corp.*, 613 F.2d 438, 445 (2d Cir. 1980) (emphasis in original). Plaintiff contends that defendant's failure to give adequate assurances after plaintiff learned that the burners probably could not perform as warranted constitutes a repudiation, thus, justifying plaintiff's revocation and demand for a refund. Defendant, on the other hand, argues that summary judgment is inappropriate because (1) the burners substantially conformed to contract specifications; (2) plaintiff's request for assurances was unreasonable; (3) plaintiff did not revoke its acceptance within a reasonable time; and (4) defendant needs further discovery.[3]

As defendant correctly observes, because the Yugoslavian burners were never installed, to establish that these burners did not conform to specifications, plaintiff must show that the Yugoslavian and Sri Lankan specifications and operating conditions were similar and that the Sri Lankan burners did not perform satisfactorily. After reviewing the record, the court concludes that defendant has not raised a genuine question of fact in this area.

First, defendant's documents reveal the scope of the problems encountered with the Sri Lankan burners and defendant's inability to correct them. Moreover, defendant's assertion that the Sri Lankan burners operated at ninety-three percent capacity does not raise a material question of fact. This capacity only was attained for a short period of time and under conditions less rigorous than that contracted for at either Sri Lanka or Yugoslavia.

Second, the court agrees with plaintiff that the operating specifications for Sri Lanka and Yugoslavia were sufficiently similar to give plaintiff reasonable grounds for insecurity. Three of defendant's employees have stated or represented that the operating conditions for the

---

[2] . . .The telexes relied upon by defendant indicate that the Sri Lankan burners were operating (1) at 50 to 90% capacity; (2) with significant down-time for repairs and adjustments; and (3) at preheat temperatures less than that called for in the specifications. . . . There is no dispute that defendant did not make these facts known to plaintiff.

[3] Initially, defendant cross-moved for summary judgment or, alternatively, to add CLE as a party-plaintiff. In essence, defendant asserted that CLE was the real party-in-interest and that plaintiff suffered no damages. Further, defendant claimed that it was necessary to add CLE as a party to avoid multiple litigation. Relying on Fed R Civ P 17 and the language of the contract, plaintiff in response argued that it rather than CLE is the proper party to bring this action. In addition, plaintiff obtained an assignment from CLE for all claims it may have had against defendant. . . . Upon receiving a copy of this assignment, defendant withdrew its motion. Neither party disputes the applicability of New York law to this action.

Yugoslavian and Sri Lankan plants are similar; thus, the court finds unpersuasive defendant's sales engineer's claim that the two plants are different. While the court recognizes that several technical differences between the two plants' specifications exist, defendant has failed to demonstrate the materiality of these differences to the determination of the instant motion. Indeed, with respect to the preheating requirement, the record shows that the burners could not perform adequately at temperatures below that required for Yugoslavia.[4]

Turning to defendant's claim that plaintiff's request for assurances was unreasonable, the court notes that defendant promised to do more than just deliver the burners. The contract plainly states that defendant was obligated to provide burners which would operate under certain conditions. The present record establishes that plaintiff was justified in seeking assurances that the burners were able to meet the Yugoslavian operating specifications. As the Official Comment to NYUCC § 2-609 (McKinney 1964) recognizes, a buyer of precision parts has reasonable grounds for insecurity "if he discovers that his seller is making defective deliveries of such parts to other buyers with similar needs." *Id.*, Comment 3. As stated previously, defendant's own documents indicate that the burners delivered to Sri Lanka did not conform to specifications; thus plaintiff was justified in seeking assurances from defendant.

With respect to defendant's claim that the assurances sought by plaintiff were unreasonable, the court initially observes that after being asked for technical assurances in February, defendant did not respond until September,[5] thereby heightening plaintiff's suspicions. . . . Further, the court finds that the assurances later sought by plaintiff—an extension of contractual guarantee and the posting of a letter of credit—were not unreasonable in light of the circumstances. First, plaintiff's contention that its demand for a letter of credit comported with accepted international business practice is not seriously contested.[6] Second, the record demonstrates that defendant's stalling and lack of candor forced plaintiff to request security in the form of a letter of credit as an extension of the warranty. Third, while it understands that defendant bargained for a contract that included a limited warranty, in view of the strategy adopted to meet plaintiff's demand for assurances, the court concludes that plaintiff's request to extend its warranty also was reasonable. Thus, defendant's failure to provide any assurances save its statement that the burners would work if installed, constitutes a repudiation of the contract. NYUCC § 2-609(4). . . .

Defendant's claim that plaintiff did not timely revoke its acceptance is also without merit. What constitutes a reasonable time for plaintiff to revoke its acceptance depends upon the nature, purpose and circumstances of the case. NYUCC § 1-204(2) (McKinney 1964). While case law indicates that as a matter of law revocation within the warranty period, which occurred in this case, is timely, see *White Devon Farm v. Siahl*, 88 Misc 2d 961, 965, 389 NYS2d 724, 727-28 (Sup Ct 1976), the evidence establishes that plaintiff timely revoked its acceptance. After plaintiff sought assurances in February 1981, it did not receive an answer until September. Moreover, defendant's September response indicates that further assurances were forthcoming. Thus, it was

---

[4] . . ."Combustion air temperature had to be limited to 150 deg C and they could not reach target 316 deg C, or problems mounted".

[5] While defendant did communicate with plaintiff before its September 8 telex, nothing in these communications can be construed as providing reasonable assurances that the Yugoslavian burners would meet contract specifications.

[6] Defendant's reliance on paragraph seven of Peter Horstmann's affidavit to raise a question of fact in this regard is misplaced. Horstmann's affidavit does not indicate that the request for a letter of credit failed to comport with "commercial standards," rather, the affidavit indicates that defendant disputed the basis upon which plaintiff sought the letter of credit. Thus, plaintiff's claim that its demand for a letter of credit was consistent with international business dealings stands unrefuted. . . .

not until November that plaintiff learned that defendant had no experience with burners operating under "Yugoslavian-like" conditions and that it was unlikely that the burners could satisfy the contract specifications. Accordingly, the court concludes that any delay in revoking acceptance occurred because plaintiff reasonably relied on defendant's assurances that the burners would work. Moreover, it is clear that after it learned that defendant had been less than candid with its assurances, plaintiff revoked its acceptance within a reasonable time. Finally, as plaintiff correctly observes, defendant has not shown that it was prejudiced by this alleged delay.

Defendant further argues that plaintiff's motion must be denied because defendant needs more discovery. In response, plaintiff contends that defendant (1) has knowledge of all the facts and circumstances relevant to the instant motion, and (2) declined to seek the information allegedly pertinent to its defense of the instant motion during the discovery period established by the court. Because the court finds merit to both these arguments, the application for further discovery is denied.

The court finds unavailing defendant's protestation that it had no knowledge of the operation of the Sri Lankan burners. Similarly, defendant's claim that it has no information concerning the workings of the Yugoslavian plant or the relationship between plaintiff, CLE and Kellogg as it relates to this action is belied by defendant's own evidence. Moreover, as stated previously, at least three of defendant's employees acknowledged the similarities between the Yugoslavian and Sri Lankan plants; thus, further discovery in this area is unwarranted.

Defendant's failure to seek either informally or by motion information it now claims is necessary also militates against ordering further discovery. Several avenues of discovery were available to defendant to obtain information from plaintiff CLE or Kellogg. Defendant, however, declined to do so. Accordingly, it would be inequitable for the court, at this time, to order further discovery.

Plaintiff claims that it is entitled to recover the price it paid for the burners as well as incidental damages. Plaintiff asserts that this is an appropriate measure of damages because the burners are of no value to it. Thus, plaintiff claims it is entitled to a full refund which represents the difference between the value of the burners as accepted and the value of the burners if they meet the contract specifications. *City of New York v. Pullman Inc.*, 662 F.2d 910, 916 [31 U.C.C. Rep 1375] (2d Cir 1981), *cert. denied*, 454 US 1164 (1982); see NYUCC § 2-714(2) (McKinney 1964). Initially, the court observes that defendant does not seriously dispute the *amount* of money plaintiff seeks to recover.[7] Moreover, nothing in the present record justifies a smaller award because defendant failed to replace the burners or give adequate assurances. See *Tokio Marine & Fire Insurance Co. v. McDonnell Douglas Corp.*, 617 F.2d 936, 941 (2d Cir 1980). With respect to incidental damages, it is clear that the transportation, inspection and storage costs incurred by plaintiff are recoverable, NYUCC § 2-715(1) (McKinney 1964). In addition, as was the case with plaintiff's other claim for damages, defendant does not dispute the amount. Accordingly, the court concludes that plaintiff is entitled to recover damages in the sum of $242,335.58.

. . . .

[7] . . .Defendant initially claimed that CLE, not plaintiff; incurred the loss but did not dispute the amount sought.

CONCLUSION

In accordance with the foregoing, plaintiff's motion for summary judgment is granted.

Plaintiff is awarded the sum of $242,335.58 and shall submit a proposed judgment forthwith because the court finds that there is no just reason for delay. This is done without prejudice to plaintiff seeking further incidental and consequential damages unknown at this time.

Plaintiff's and defendant's applications for attorneys' fees are denied.

———

OPTIONAL QUESTION

How would *Creusot-Loire* be resolved under CISG Articles 71 and 72?

§ 6.02 Seller's Obligation to Deliver

Read: U.C.C. §§ 2-301, 2-507(1).

Read also: U.C.C. §§ 2A-508(1), 2A-509(1); CISG Arts. 30-34.

Seller's basic obligation is to tender delivery of conforming goods to buyer. U.C.C. §§ 2-301, 2-507(l), 2-503(1); §§ 2-601(a), 2-106(2), 2-511(l). "Tender" connotes such performance by the tendering party as puts the other party in default if he fails to proceed in some manner. See U.C.C. § 2-503 Comment 1 and § 2-301.

Significance of Tender. If seller duly tenders conforming goods and buyer does not accept them (U.C.C. § 2-606), buyer is in breach; if seller does not duly tender delivery of conforming goods, seller is in breach. U.C.C. § 2-507(1); see §§ 2-703, 2-601(a), 2-612(3), 2-711.[8] Seller's and buyer's damages may be measured by the market price at the time and place for tender (U.C.C. § 2-708(1)), or the market price as of the place for tender (U.C.C. § 2-713(2)). A cause of action under the Statute of Limitations may accrue when tender of delivery is made. U.C.C. § 2-725(2).[9] The risk of loss may pass to the buyer on tender of delivery. U.C.C. § 2-509(3).[10]

PROBLEM 6.2

In the absence of agreement (§ 1-201(3)) otherwise:

1.   What is the time and place for tender and delivery?

2.   Are specifications or arrangements relating to shipment at the seller's or buyer's option?

3.   Is delivery to be made in a single lot or several lots?

---

[8] Buyer generally will have the right to inspect the goods before payment or acceptance. U.C.C. § 2-513. (Unless otherwise agreed, payment is due at the time and place at which the buyer is to receive the goods. U.C.C. § 2-310(a).) Inspection, acceptance and payment are discussed at § 6.03, below.

[9] Damages are discussed at Chapter 7, below.

[10] Risk of loss is discussed at § 4.06, above.

See U.C.C. §§ 2-307, 2-308, 2-309, 2-311.

———

Manner of Tender. Tender of delivery requires that (1) the seller put and hold conforming goods at the buyer's disposition and (2) give the buyer any notification reasonably necessary to enable the buyer to take delivery. Study U.C.C. § 2-503(1). The manner of tender of delivery (1) where goods are to be delivered by carrier or (2) where goods are in the possession of a bailee and are to be delivered without being moved, are explored below.

———

PROBLEM 6.3

What are the tender of delivery requirements in the following cases:

1.   In a "shipment" contract? U.C.C. § 2-503(2).

2.   In a "destination" contract? U.C.C. § 2-503(3).

3.   Where the following mercantile terms are used: "F.O.B. Seller City"; or "F.O.B. Buyer City"; or, "C.I.F. Buyer City?"[11] U.C.C. §§ 2-319 through 2-325. Documents of Title are discussed in Chapter 10.

———

HALSTEAD HOSP., INC. v. NORTHERN BANK NOTE CO.

United States Court of Appeals
680 F.2d 1307, 33 U.C.C. Rep. 1665 (10th Cir. 1982)

SETH, CHIEF JUDGE.

———

[11] Where goods were sold "F.O.B. Cambridge, Massachusetts," Massachusetts was the place of delivery for conflict of laws purposes. *Travenol Laboratories, Inc. v. Zotal, Ltd.*, 394 Mass. 95, 474 N.E.2d 1070, 40 U.C.C. Rep. 487(1985).

In international transactions, note "Incoterms" codified by the International Chamber of Commerce. For information contact: ICC Publishing Company, Inc., 156 Fifth Avenue, New York, NY 10010.

In any contract or communication involving agricultural commodities within the scope of the Perishable Agricultural Commodities Act, 7 U.S.C. §§ 499a-499s, certain trade terms and definitions are construed in accordance with 7 C.F.R. § 46.43. *See, e.g.,* such terms as "Shipping-point inspection," "Shipping-point inspection final," etc.

Halstead Hospital, Inc. commenced a diversity suit alleging breach of contract by the failure of Northern Bank Note Company to deliver printed bond forms in time for a bond closing in New York City. Trial was to the district judge and Halstead obtained a judgement. . . .

Halstead is a nonprofit corporation with its principal place of business in Halstead, Kansas. Northern is an Illinois corporation with a nationwide business of printing bonds and other securities. Northern's principal place of business is located near Chicago. Halstead planned new Hospital facilities to be financed by industrial revenue bonds. A New York City law firm was retained to serve as bond counsel and agent in the bond offering. Halstead's bond counsel on behalf of the Hospital placed an order with Northern by telephone for the printing of bonds. A subsequent letter from bond counsel to Northern confirmed the order and stated that the bond closing was scheduled for December 18, 1975. Northern in turn accepted the order, and by letter stated, "[W]e will complete our work for shipment December 16." The parties agreed that the bonds were to be at the Signature Company in New York on December 17 so that they could be inspected and signed prior to the formal closing on December 18.

Northern printed the bonds and boxed them in four separate cartons. Northern arranged for a common carrier or courier to pick up the four cartons on the afternoon of December 16 and deliver them to New York the next morning. However, one of the boxes of bonds did not arrive in New York until after December 18, 1975. This delay necessitated cancellation of the December 18 closing.

As to the contract matter the parties agree that it is governed by the Uniform Commercial Code. The basic question is whether the contract to provide the bonds was a destination contract requiring shipment and timely delivery by the defendant at a particular place (U.C.C. § 2-503(3), K.S.A. § 84-2-503(3)) or a shipment contract which required only that the goods be put on a carrier with no further responsibility on the seller. Recognizing that a shipment contract is regarded as normal and a delivery contract is viewed as variant (U.C.C. § 2-503, Official Comment 5, K.S.A. § 84-2-503), the trial court concluded that the Halstead-Northern contract was a destination contract. We agree with the trial court's determination that the contract was a destination contract.

Northern's pivotal role in arranging for the delivery of the bond forms to a specific location in New York City, the Signature Company, indicates that the parties intended a destination contract. Furthermore, the obvious deadline provided by the closing date, accepted by Northern, created an obligation beyond placing the bonds on a common carrier. Northern paid the carrier it had selected for its services. The "Carrier" was apparently a courier. The trial court's finding that Northern breached its contract with Halstead when it failed to deliver the fourth box of bond forms in time for the scheduled closing in New York is supported by the evidence.

[Ruling of district court is affirmed.]

PROBLEM 6.4

S agrees to sell certain goods to *B*. The goods are stored in *W* warehouse. It is anticipated that *B* will not immediately remove the goods from *W* but rather B anticipates leaving them in storage for a period. *W* has issued to *S* a warehouse receipt engaging to deliver the goods "to *S*." What is the manner of S's tender of delivery?" What if the warehouse receipt read "to the order of *S*?" U.C.C. §§ 7-104, 2-503(4). *See North Dakota Public Service Commission v. Valley Farmers Bean Association, 365 N.W.2d 528, 40 U.C.C. Rep. 1847 (1985)* (§ 2-503(4)(a) involves a situation in which a bailee merely holds possession of the goods and the sales transaction occurs between a seller and buyer *unrelated* to the bailee. In this case *buyer* is also the bailee who has physical possession of the goods).

NOTE

Proposed U.C.C. § 2-503(d)(1) clarifies § 2-503(4)(a) by requiring that the seller procure an acknowledgment by the bailee *to the buyer* of the buyer's right to possession of the goods.

PROBLEM 6.5

S sold and delivered nonmerchantable quality goods to *B*. *S* asserts that U.C.C. § 2-725 provides: (1) An action by *B* for breach of contract must be commenced within four years after the cause of action occurred. (2) A cause of action accrues when the breach occurs. (3) A breach of warranty occurs when *tender of delivery* is made. Since B did not commence its action within the four years, B's claim is barred by the statute of limitations. U.C.C. § 2-725(1), (2).

B contends that there was never a proper tender of delivery and therefore the limitations period of § 2-725 has never expired. *B* bases this argument on § 2-503(1) which states, "Tender of delivery *requires* that the seller put and hold *conforming* goods at the buyer's disposition." [Emphasis added.] In this respect, § 2-106(2) provides that goods are conforming to the contract "when they are in accordance with the obligations under the contract." Here, the goods did not conform and, consequently, the statute has not run.

As *S*'s counsel, kindly counter this argument. What would be the consequence if the court bought *B*'s position? See U.C.C. § 2-503 Comment 1.

NOTES

(1) See *Eades Commodities, Inc. v. Hoeper*, 825 S.W.2d 34, 17 U.C.C. Rep. 2d 771 (Mo. App. 1992) (seller's delivery of grain to buyer excused when buyer refused to accept deliveries due to limited storage capacity; also, seller called in advance for delivery time which was denied them).

(2) *Mercantile Terms. In re Isis Foods, Inc.*, 38 BR 48, 38 U.C.C. Rep. 1134 (WD Mo. 1983): According to buyer's purchase order, shipment was to be made "F.O.B. St. Louis. St. Louis was the destination of the shipment and the location of the buyer. Held: " 'F.O.B. St. Louis' in the purchase order is clear and unequivocal in its importing a 'destination' contract under which the duty to pay arises as of the terms of receipt of the shipment. . . . Any contrary or additional terms then unilaterally laid down by [seller] in its invoice could only become provisions of the

contract if they were accepted by [buyer]." 38 U.C.C. Rep. at 1136. U.C.C. §§ 2-319, 2-503, 2-507; see § 2-207.

Steuber Co., Inc. v. Hercules, Inc., 646 F.2d 1093, 31 U.C.C. Rep. 508, 510-11(5th Cir. 1981):

The Uniform Commercial Code has codified the well-settled principles of commercial law relating to C.I.F. contracts. A contract containing the phrase C.I.F. plus a destination requires the seller to deliver goods meeting the contract description on an appropriate carrier, obtain prepaid bills of lading and appropriate insurance certificates for the goods, and then tender these documents plus an invoice to the buyer. Upon tender of these documents, the buyer must pay the full C.I.F. price to the seller. Delivery and possession of conforming goods then becomes a matter between the buyer and the carrier and/or insurer of the goods, but the seller's involvement in the transaction is at an end. In other words, under C.I.F. terms, the buyer pays on delivery of documents; the risk of loss during shipment and the responsibility for delivery and unloading of the goods are for the buyer. However, terms or conditions agreed to by the parties must control over the general reference to C.I.F. contained on the face of the document. This fact is recognized, not only in the commentary but also the express language, "unless otherwise agreed," of the sections of the Uniform Commercial Code. [See U.C.C. §§ 2-320, 2-504.]

(3) *Delay in Shipping. In Harlow & Jones, Inc. v. Advance Steel Co.*, 424 F. Supp. 770, 21 U.C.C. Rep. 410 (E.D. Mich. 1976). Advance contracted to buy steel from Harlow to be imported from a West German mill for shipment C.I.F. during "September-October." The first two shipments were accepted and paid for. The third shipment was shipped from Antwerp on November 14 and arrived in Detroit on November 27. On October 29, Advance by letter canceled because of "late delivery." (According to an accepted steel importing trade usage, shipment in "September-October" meant delivery in October-November.) Thus the situation: seller breached a contractual shipment term but still managed to make timely delivery. The court cited an Ohio case (*Van Decker Packing Co. v. Armour and Co.*, 184 NE 2d 548 (Ohio Ct of Comm Pl 1967)) which noted that delivery time, not shipment time, was the primary concern of the parties and that a delay in shipment was therefore not of such material importance as to justify buyer's cancellation. The court then remarked:

U.C.C. [§§] 2-320 and 2-504 have not really departed from nor modified traditional contract doctrine regarding shipment contracts. A material delay in shipment has traditionally been required before a buyer under a C.I.F. agreement is allowed to cancel his order, and a merely technical delay or a delay which is later cured by timely delivery has never by itself justified cancellation. . . .

Compare U.C.C. § 1-201(38).

(4) *Contract for Successive Performances But Indefinite in Duration.* Such a contract is valid for a reasonable time but, unless otherwise agreed, may be terminated at any time by either party. U.C.C. § 2-309(2), (3). But see Federal and state legislation: 15 U.S.C. § 1221 *et seq.* (Chapter 27—Automobile Dealer Suits Against Manufacturers—The policy behind enactment of this chapter was to correct abuses of arbitrary termination and nonrenewal of dealer's franchises by automobile manufacturers. *Blenke Bros. v. Ford Motor Co.*, 203 F. Supp. 670 (D.C. Ind. 1962)); Mich. Comp. Laws Ann. § 445. 1561 et seq. (Fair Trade and Business—Motor Vehicles) (445.1580 is captioned, "Termination, failure to renew or discontinuance of dealer agreement for other than good cause; action and damages"). See Comment, *Franchise Termination and Nonrenewal*, 26 S.D.L. Rev. 321(1981).

§ 6.03 Buyer's Right to Inspect and Obligation to Accept and Pay

Read: U.C.C. §§ 2-301, 2-310, 2-507, 2-511, 2-512, 2-513, 2-606.

Read also: U.C.C. §§ 2A-515, 2A-516; CISG Arts. 35(3), 38, 53-60.

Inspection. Unless otherwise agreed, "where goods are tendered or delivered . . .the buyer has a right before payment or acceptance to inspect them." U.C.C. § 2-513(1). The buyer does not have a right to inspect the goods before payment of the price when the contract provides for delivery C.O.D. or for payment against documents. U.C.C. § 2-513(3), see § 2-512.

Acceptance. "If the seller has made a tender which in all respects conforms to the contract, the buyer has a positive duty to accept U.C.C §§ 2-602 Comment 3, 2-507(1).[12] In some instances, buyer will be obligated to accept goods even though they are nonconforming. *See, e.g.,* U.C.C. § 2-504 (postamble), see also § 2-326(1).[13]

Payment. "Unless otherwise agreed payment is due at the time and place at which the buyer is to receive the goods." U.C.C. § 2-310(a). Unless otherwise agreed, tender of payment is a condition to the seller's duty to tender and complete any delivery, tender of delivery is a condition to the buyer's duty to pay for them. U.C.C. §§2-511(1) and Comment 2, 2-507(1). The requirement of payment against delivery has no application to the great body of commercial contracts which carry credit terms. U.C.C. § 2-511 Comment 1. In such instances the buyer need not tender payment as a condition to the seller's duty to tender and complete delivery.

———

An early case involving a buyer's right of inspection where payment is due at the time and place buyer is to receive the goods is *Imperial Products Co. v. Capitol Chemical Co.*, 187 App. Div. 599, 176 N.Y.S. 49 (1919). Here, B agreed to purchase and accept from S one car of standard quality white naphthalene flakes in barrels at a certain price per pound, f.o.b. West Elizabeth, N.J., prompt shipments from S's plant at Birmingham, Ala. The question involved was whether B had the right to inspect the goods shipped to it by S pursuant to the agreement of sale. The court stated:

In this case there was no agreement that the shipment should be made "collect on delivery" nor was there any agreement that the buyer would pay the purchase price by sight draft to be attached to the bill of lading. No terms of payment were specified in the agreement between the parties. Under such a contract, delivery and payment are concurrent obligations. [*Cf.* U.C.C. §§ 2-310(a), 2-507(1), 2-511(1) and Comment 1.] This is very different from payment of the purchase price by sight draft with bill of lading attached. In the first, the buyer has the right of inspection to ascertain whether the goods are in conformity with the contract, when the seller tenders delivery, before he is required to accept and pay for the goods. In the latter, payment is a condition precedent to delivery, and hence inconsistent with the right of

---

[12] " 'Acceptance' . . .means that the buyer, pursuant to the contract, takes particular goods . . .as his own, whether or not he is obligated to do so, and whether he does so by words, action, or silence when it is time to speak." U.C.C. § 2-606 and Comment 1. See U.C.C. § 2-607(2) and (4).

[13] Discussion of the "perfect tender rule" and exceptions is found below at § 6.04, Buyer's Rights on Improper Delivery.

inspection. . . . Inasmuch as there was no provision in the agreement between the parties inconsistent with the right of inspection before acceptance and payment, the seller could not deprive the buyer of that right by adopting a method of collection not provided in the agreement. . . .

PROBLEM 6.6

Resolve *Imperial Products* case assuming the Uniform Commercial Code is applicable. *See* U.C.C. §§ 2-310 and Comments, 2-513 and Comment 2, *see* § 2-503 Comment 2.

———

PROBLEM 6.7

Chapman was the prime contractor for the plumbing work in the construction of a dormitory for Pacific Lutheran University. On January 10, Chapman purchased from Cervitor Kitchens four kitchen units to be installed in the dormitory for a price of $1,284, f.o.b. job site. On May 4 Chapman received from Cervitor four kitchen units enclosed in shipping crates. The units were not inspected. Chapman's manager then caused the units enclosed in their shipping crates to be stored in a separate room at the dormitory then under construction.

About August 5, Chapman removed the units from the crates and installed them without further inspection in the dormitory. Shortly thereafter it was determined by the University architect that the units were of poor quality and did not comply with specifications. The defects included chipped and rough edges on the stove sections which did not fit properly with the adjoining surface, poorly fitted doors, a poorly installed aluminum panel along one side of the unit, and inadequate hinges on the refrigerator section. Consequently, Chapman rejected the units and caused them to be shipped back to Cervitor who refused to accept them. They were then stored and ultimately sold for storage charges.

Cervitor contends that Chapman waited too long to inspect and reject the units and his installation of the units without inspection further precludes him from rejecting them. Chapman asserts that it was well known by both parties: (1) that the units were to be installed in a building then under construction; (2) that Cervitor knew that the units would not be installed until the building had reached the proper stage of completion; (3) that it would have been uneconomical and would have exposed the units to unnecessary risk of damage to have unpacked them until just before installation.

The question is whether Chapman must be deemed to have accepted the kitchen units because of his failure to inspect and reject them for a period of approximately 3 months after delivery and because of his installation of the units without prior inspection and rejection. *See* U.C.C. §§ 2-513, 2-601, 2-602(1), 2-606; *Cervitor Kitchens, Inc. v. Chapman*, 513 P.2d 25, 13 U.C.C. Rep. 458 (Wash. 1973).

NOTES

(1) *Inspection v. Examination.* " 'Inspection' under [§ 2-513] has to do with the buyer's check-up on whether the seller's *performance* is in accordance with a contract previously made and is not to be confused with the 'examination' of the goods or of a sample or model of them at the *time* of *contracting* which may affect the warranties involved in the contract." [Emphasis added.] (*See* U.C.C. § 2-316(3)(b).) U.C.C. § 2-513 Comment 9. See *E.L.E.S.C.O. v. Northern States Power Co.,* 370 N.W.2d 700 (Minn. App. 1985). *Cf.* CISG Arts. 35(3), 38, 58.

(2) *Sufficiency of Tender of Payment.* In *Armfield v. Poretsky Mgmt., Inc.,* 39 U.C.C. Rep. 883, 884 (D.C. 1984), the court observed:

> The use of checks in today's economy is so common as to spawn a belief that there is a right to pay by check. Yet a check is not legal tender and a debtor pays by check only at the sufferance of the creditor. Where the creditor objects to the use of a check, the debtor must pay in legal tender—cash. [The court cited U.C.C. § 2-511(2).]

For discussion of payment by check in a "cash sale" transaction, see U.C.C. §§ 2-507(2), 2-511(3) and § 7.03 entitled, "Seller's Remedies (1) on Discovery of Buyer's Insolvency, (2) in a " 'Cash Sale.' "

(3) *Payment Against Documents of Title.* The sales contract may require the buyer to pay the price before he inspects the goods. The typical example of this is where delivery is COD or where the buyer is required to pay against documents, such as an order bill of lading. As we shall see later in greater detail, this practice is one solution to one of the great dilemmas in dealings between parties who either do not quite trust one another or are unwilling to rely upon the other's fulfillment of the contractual obligation in unquestioned fashion. The seller wants to be assured of payment before he will relinquish the goods to the buyer; if he delivers without payment he may end up getting no payment at all, or at best payment only after a long delay. Also, the unpaid seller who has delivered the goods is particularly vulnerable to claims on the part of the buyer that the goods are defective or otherwise fail to conform to the contract—accompanied of course, by a demand that there be a corresponding deduction from the balance due on the purchase price. The buyer, on the other hand, does not want to pay for goods unless he has some assurance that conforming goods actually will be delivered to him. He may find that after he has paid the price the seller will turn a deaf ear to his claims that the goods do not conform. If the parties are in the same locality, the buyer may inspect the goods at the seller's place of business and ascertain that they are indeed the goods he has contracted to purchase before he pays for them and secures delivery. Likewise, the seller can be assured of payment before he delivers the goods to the buyer.

But if the parties are dealing at a distance and the goods must travel by carrier, some further arrangements must be made. The seller wants to be protected against the possibility that he will ship goods to Desolation, North Dakota only to have them refused there on the basis of some minor alleged discrepancy from the sale contract terms. The buyer, on the other hand, wants to assure himself that the goods he pays for do conform to the contract—to the buyer in Desolation a cause of action against the seller in Moosetrack, Maine may have little value.

Some compromise is necessary. It may be reached through the seller's shipment of the goods under an order bill of lading, which bill of lading will be turned over to the buyer upon payment of a draft for the sale price. Here, the seller is assured of payment before the goods will be delivered to the buyer. The buyer is assured that goods will be delivered—because the carrier has issued its bill of lading describing the goods generally. However, the buyer will not be certain that the goods conform to the sale contract before paying for them, because he will not have opportunity to inspect the goods. Either he will pay for the goods before they arrive, precluding inspection before payment, or will not be permitted by the carrier to inspect after arrival, in accordance with the terms of the bill of lading: "The surrender of this Original ORDER Bill of Lading properly indorsed shall be required before the delivery of the property. Inspection of property covered by this bill of lading will not be permitted unless provided by law or unless permission is indorsed on this original bill of lading or given in writing by the shipper." Thus, to a degree, the buyer is buying a pig in a poke. Yet the seller continues to bear the risk that the buyer, when the draft for the purchase price is presented to him for payment, will not pay it, leaving the seller with a carload of goods at Desolation, North Dakota. One solution is to use a documentary letter of credit. See Chapter 10, below, entitled "Documentary Transactions."

§ 6.04 Buyer's Rights on Improper Delivery: Reject or Accept

[A] Rejection or Acceptance

Read: U.C.C. §§ 2-601 through 2-607.

Read also: U.C.C. §§ 2A-509 through 2A-512, 2A-514 through 2A-516; CISG Arts. 45-52, 81-84 (see Arts. 49, 25-27), 86-88.

U.C.C. § 2-601 states in part: "[I]f the goods or the tender of delivery fail in any respect to conform to the contract, the buyer may (a) reject the whole; or (b) accept the whole . . ." This is often referred to as the "perfect tender rule." The policy considerations underlying this rule are stated by Professors Braucher and Riegert: (1) buyer should not be required to guess at his peril whether a breach is material, (2) proof of materiality would sometimes require disclosure of buyer's private affairs (e.g., secret formulas or processes).[14]

The perfect tender rule is, however, subject to certain limitations or exceptions, summarized as follows:[15]

1. In a shipment contract, failure to make a proper contract for transportation or to notify buyer is a ground for rejection only if material delay or loss ensues. U.C.C. § 2-504.

2. Where an agreed manner of delivery becomes commercially impracticable, a commercially reasonable substitute must be tendered and accepted. U.C.C. § 2-614(1).

3. In an installment contract, a buyer may not reject any installment which is non-conforming if the non-conformity does not substantially impair the value of that installment. U.C.C. § 2-612(2).

---

[14] R. Braucher & R. Riegert, Introduction to Commercial Transactions 305-6 (1977).

[15] B. Stone, Uniform Commercial Code in a Nutshell 93-94 (4th ed. 1995). Copyright © by West Publishing Co. Reprinted by permission.

4. There may be an enforceable agreement that buyer will accept goods even though there is a non-conformity. U.C.C. § 2-601.

5. Course of dealing, usage of trade, course of performance and the obligation of good faith may afford some leeway. U.C.C. §§ 1-205, 2-208, 1-203, 2-508 Comment 4, 2-106 Comment 2.

Further, the perfect tender rule is undercut by:

6. Seller in appropriate circumstances has the right to cure an improper tender or delivery. U.C.C. § 2-508. This is discussed at [§ 6.05, below].

7. Buyer, if he does not meet certain procedural requirements, *e.g.*, timely notice of rejection, will have accepted the goods. U.C.C. §§ 2-602(1), 2-606(1)(b). Buyers frequently will accept by not timely rejecting. [See this § 6.04[A], below.]

8. Buyer, after accepting, may revoke his acceptance (which gives buyer the same rights as if he had rejected them), but only if the non-conformity *substantially* impairs the value of the goods to buyer. U.C.C. § 2-608. Other requirements for revocation of acceptance are discussed [at § 6.04[C], below].

The "perfect tender rule" in Proposed § 2-601 has been preserved, but rejection is subject to the seller's expanded power to cure under Proposed § 2-508.

———

BORGES v. MAGIC VALLEY FOODS, INC.

Idaho Supreme Court
616 P.2d 273, 29 U.C.C. Rep. 1282 (1980)

SHEPARD, J. This is an appeal from a judgment following a jury verdict which awarded plaintiffs-respondents Borges and G & B Land and Cattle Company $12,832.00 for potatoes received by defendant-appellant Magic West pursuant to a contract with respondents. We affirm.

In 1975, respondents grew and harvested approximately 45,000 c.w.t. of potatoes, which were stored in a cellar near Buhl, Idaho. Magic West inspected those potatoes and, although their inspection indicated that some contained a "hollow heart" defect, Magic West agreed to purchase them for $3.80 per c.w.t. "Hollow heart" indicates a vacant space in the middle of the potato. The purchase contract provided that "if internal problems develop making these potatoes unfit for fresh pack shipping, this contract becomes null and void." It was agreed that the cost of transporting the potatoes from the storage cellar to the processing plant would be borne by Magic West. Examination of the potatoes by State inspectors would occur at the plant to determine that the number of potatoes affected by the hollow heart defect did not exceed the limit prescribed for shipping under the fresh pack grade.

The potatoes were transported to the processing plant, where more than 30,000 c.w.t. were processed and shipped under the fresh pack grade. In March, 1976, State inspectors declared the remaining 4,838.77 c.w.t. of potatoes unfit for the fresh pack grade because of the increased incidence of hollow heart condition.[16] On March 31, 1976, the parties met to discuss the problem of the remaining potatoes and it was apparently agreed that Magic West should attempt to blend them with other potatoes of a higher grade in the hope that such a blend would meet fresh pack grade standards. That experiment failed and Magic West, without notifying the respondents, processed the remaining 4,838.77 c.w.t. of potatoes into flakes and sold them for $1.25 per c.w.t. The evidence in the record disclosed that the remaining potatoes could not be removed from the processing plant without destroying at least one-third of the potatoes.

Respondents demanded the contract price of $3.80 per c.w.t. for the potatoes sold as flakes. Magic West refused, and instead offered to pay $1.25 per c.w.t. This action resulted. The jury returned a general verdict to the respondents of $12,832.00 and the trial court also awarded $6,975.00 as and for attorney fees and costs to the respondents.[17]

Magic West's basic contention is that the 4,838.77 c.w.t. of potatoes were clearly defective and that they were never accepted. It is claimed that when Magic West processed the potatoes into flakes and sold them for $1.25 per c.w.t., they were only following respondents' instructions.

The potatoes in the instant case were clearly movable at the time they were identified in the contract, IC § 28-2-105, and, hence, were "goods" within the purview of the Idaho Uniform Commercial Code, IC §§ 28-2-101 to -2-725, and the dispute is governed by the provisions of the Uniform Commercial Code.

It is clear and undisputed that Magic West had the responsibility of transporting the potatoes from the storage cellar to the processing plant and that State inspection would occur at the plant. It is also clear that the 4,838.77 c.w.t. of potatoes, unable to make the fresh pack grade, did not conform to the contract and gave Magic West the right of rejection. IC § 28-2-601(a). Also, it is not disputed that when Magic West determined that the potatoes would not meet fresh pack grade, Magic West so notified the respondents and met with them to determine what disposition should be made of the potatoes. The record is unclear as to precisely what was decided at that March 31, 1976 meeting, but respondents apparently approved of Magic West's proposal to blend the defective potatoes with those with higher quality in an attempt to meet the fresh pack grade. However, it is clear that no agreement on price was reached at that meeting.

A buyer must pay the contract rate for any goods accepted. IC § 28-2-607(1). Generally, a buyer is deemed to have accepted defective goods when, knowing of the defect, he resells the goods without notifying the seller. See White & Summers, Uniform Commercial Code, §8-2 (2d ed 1980); 67 Am Jur2d Sales (1973). A buyer accepts goods whenever he does any act inconsistent with the seller's ownership. IC §28-2-606(1)(c). Respondents assert that Magic West's processing of the remaining potatoes into flakes and the subsequent sale constituted acts inconsistent with the respondents' ownership.

---

[16] There were also potatoes still in storage which Magic West never paid for due to the hollow heart problems. There is no dispute with regard to those potatoes. Respondents eventually sold them for $3.00 per c.w.t. to be used as french fries. There were also 702 c.w.t. of defective potatoes in transit to the plant on March 31, 1977. The respondents agreed to accept $1.25 per c.w.t. for those potatoes from Magic West.

[17] Both parties agreed that the jury had apparently awarded respondents the full contract price of $3.80 per c.w.t. for the potatoes in dispute. If no deductions were made, a jury award of $3.80 per c.w.t. would have resulted in a jury verdict of $18,387.32 [$3.80 x 4838.77]. Obviously, some deductions were made although they are not apparent from the record and were not explained or challenged by counsel. For purposes of this appeal, we assume, as counsel do, that the jury awarded $3.80 per c.w.t. for the potatoes in dispute.

Magic West argues, however, that their processing of the potatoes into flakes and their subsequent sale did not constitute an acceptance, but rather was a permissible resale under the provisions of either IC § 28-2-603(1) or IC § 28-2-604. [The court cites IC §§ 28-2-603(1) and 28-2-604.] [Read U.C.C. §§ 2-603(1), 2-604; see § 2-602(2).]

We note that both IC § 28-2-603(1) and IC §28-2-604 were given in their entirety as instructions to the jury. We find it unclear from the record whether the respondents had agents or a place of business at the "market of rejection." Also, the duty to resell under IC § 28-2-603(1) is triggered by an absence of instructions from a seller. Here, given the state of the record and its lack of clarity and the conflicting evidence, the jury could have reasonably found that the respondents did instruct Magic West to attempt to blend the potatoes, but did not instruct them to process the potatoes into flakes. While IC § 28-2-604 allows a buyer an option to resell rejected goods if the seller gives no instructions within a reasonable time after the notification of rejection, the jury could have reasonably found that respondents' instructions were only to blend the potatoes in hope of accomplishing fresh pack grade and that Magic West's processing of the potatoes into flakes and subsequent resale thereof was a precipitate action taken before the lapse of a reasonable time within which respondents could give further instructions.

In addition, even if a reasonable time had elapsed, thus permitting Magic West to resell the potatoes, the jury properly could have concluded that processing of the potatoes by Magic West was an acceptance rather than a resale. There was no evidence presented either of an attempt to resell the potatoes in the bins to an independent third party, or of the value of the potatoes in the bins, less damage caused by removal, should it have been effected. Absent any evidence that the $1.25 per c.w.t. offered by Magic West was the highest value obtainable for the potatoes, Magic Valley's use of the potatoes in the ordinary course of its own business (presumably for profit) was an act inconsistent with the seller's ownership, and constituted an acceptance of the goods. IC § 28-2-606(1)(c).

The jury was adequately and correctly instructed regarding the provisions of IC § 28-2-603(1) and IC § 28-2-604, which constituted Magic West's theory of its duty or option of resale because of an absence of instructions from respondents. The jury was at liberty to reject Magic West's theory of defense based on substantial, albeit conflicting, evidence that Magic West's resale of the potatoes after processing them into flakes constituted an acceptance and Magic West was hence liable for the full contract price.

We have examined appellants' remaining assignments of error and find them to be without merit.

Affirmed. Costs to respondents.

NOTES

(1) *Use After Rejection as Acceptance.* J. White & R. Summers, Uniform Commercial Code § 8-2 at 352 (3d ed. 1988), observe: "[T]here may be cases in which continued use is inevitable (for instance, a carpet nailed to the floor), and in such cases use should not be regarded as

inconsistent with seller's ownership" [under U.C.C. § 2-606(l)(c)]. *See, e.g., Garfinkel v. Lehman Floor Covering Co., 302 N.Y.S.2d 167, 6 U.C.C. Rep. 915 (1969)* (carpet on floor of buyer's house). Of course, one may have trouble drawing a line between those cases where the buyer must use the goods (*e.g.,* a rug) and those where it would be very convenient but not necessary for him to do so (*e.g.,* commuting by "rejected" car rather than by bus). Cases involving the rejection of motor homes, the revocation of acceptance of motor homes, or both, have been especially difficult to classify. The courts have come to divergent conclusions. [*See, e.g., Twin Lakes Mfg. v. Coffey, 281 S.E.2d 864, 32 U.C.C. Rep. 770 (1981)*]."

(2) *Payment as Acceptance.* In *Klockner, Inc. v. Federal Wire Mill Corp.,* 663 F.2d 1370, 32 U.C.C. Rep. 1097, 1107 (7th Cir. 1981), the court stated that seller would have been justified in believing that full payment ($504,853.98) made after arrival of the goods and five days after a meeting between the parties constituted acceptance under U.C.C. § 2-606(1)(a). (The court noted that buyer attempted to cancel purchase order 5836 *following* the precipitous decline in rod prices.) See U.C.C. § 2-512(2).

(3) *Reasonable Time for Rejection.* Rejection of goods must be within a reasonable time after their delivery or tender and is ineffective unless buyer seasonably notifies seller. U.C.C. § 2-601(2). When the buyer fails to make an effective rejection under U.C.C. § 2-602(1), acceptance of the goods occurs. U.C.C. § 2-606(1)(b). In *Bowlin's Inc. v. Ramsey Oil Co., Inc.,* 662 P.2d 661, 36 U.C.C. Rep. 1110, 1123 (N.Mex. 1983), the court quoted White and Summers:

[F]our "circumstances" which will always have relevance to the determination of whether a reasonable time has passed before the buyer took his action to reject or revoke:

(1)   the difficulty of discovering the defect,

(2)   the terms of the contract,

(3)   the relative perishability of the goods, and

(4)   the course of performance after the sale and before the formal rejection[.]

White and Summers, Uniform Commercial Code § 8-3 (3d ed. 1988), also comment:

The obvious policies behind the notice provisions are to give the seller an opportunity to cure, to permit seller to assist the buyer in minimizing the buyer's losses, and to return the goods to seller early, before they have substantially depreciated. If the seller can step in and cure the difficulty and so save the sale and prevent several months' lost profit that the buyer might otherwise suffer, the policy has been fulfilled. Even if seller's inspection discloses that the goods are defective and he agrees to take them back, the entire loss from the transaction may be minimized by early action, because the seller may be able to resell the goods to another party shortly after the sale at a higher price than the goods would command after they had depreciated over a period of time.

In *Bowlin's,* the provision of the contract for the purchase of gasoline which provided a two-day period after each delivery for buyer to report any shortages was not unconscionable under U.C.C. § 2-302 in light of the fact that the buyer had established by memo to its gasoline outlets a procedure to verify the quantities of gasoline delivered *within* the two-day period.

(4) *Particularize Reasons for Rejection.* It is important that the buyer state with particularly all defects which are ascertainable by reasonable inspection when he gives notice of rejection. A buyer that does not do so runs the risk of being precluded from relying on unstated defects

to justify the rejection where the seller could have cured the defect if notified thereof. U.C.C. § 2-605(l)(a). 12 West's Legal Forms § 9.9-Form 6 (2d ed. 1985) illustrates:[18]

———

[*Date*]

Seller Company

[*Address*]

We have rejected the goods which you have delivered to us today under our contract dated [*date*].

We have rejected the goods for the following reasons among others: (1) the goods, which are of a seasonal character were delivered _____ days later than the date set forth in our contract; (2) the quantities for the various colors ordered do not conform to those set forth in our contract, there being shortages in quantity as to some colors and overages as to quantities in other colors; and (3) the goods are of quality number 2, whereas the contract calls for quality number 1.

Kindly advise as to disposition of these goods.

Buyer Company

By _____

(5) *Acceptance and Rejection Under the Perishable Agricultural Commodities Act.* The Act, 7 U.S.C. § 499a *et seq.*, is intended to prevent agricultural commodities from becoming distress merchandise and to protect sellers, who often are at a great distance from a buyer. Accordingly, in certain instances, a buyer's remedy is by recovery of damages from a seller and not by rejection of a shipment. See 7 C.F.R. § 46.43 which construes certain trade terms, for example:

(m) "F.o.b. acceptance final" or "Shipping point acceptance final" means that the buyer accepts the produce at shipping point and has no right of rejection. Suitable shipping condition does not apply under this trade term. The buyer does have recourse for a material breach of contract, providing the shipment is not rejected. The buyer's remedy under this type of contract is by recovery of damages from the seller and not by rejection of the shipment.

[B] Notice of Breach

Read: U.C.C. § 2-607(3), (5), (6).

Read also: U.C.C. § 2A-516(3)-(5); CISG Arts. 27, 39, 40, 44.

Article 2 of the U.C.C. has many provisions where notification is necessary or desirable. *See, e.g.*, 13 West's Legal Forms Chs. 18-23 (2d ed. 1985). Here, we look particularly at § 2-607(3)(a) which states that "[w]here a tender has been accepted the buyer must within a reasonable time after he discovers or should have discovered any breach notify the seller of breach or be barred from any remedy." This provision was considered in *Eastern Air Lines v. McDonnell-Douglas*

---

[18] Copyright © 1985 by West Publishing Co. Reprinted by permission.

Corp., 532 F.2d 957 (5th Cir. 1976). The jury awarded Eastern damages of approximately 25 million dollars against McDonnell Douglas for breach of contract to deliver jet aircraft. The Fifth Circuit found error and reversed, ruling that the question of timely and adequate notice under U.C.C. § 2-607 should have been submitted to the jury.

———

CITY OF WICHITA, KAN. v. U.S. GYPSUM, CO.

United States District Court, District of Kansas
828 F. Supp. 851, 23 U.C.C. Rep.2d 96 (1993)

BELOT, DISTRICT JUDGE.

This matter is before the court on the joint motion of defendants for partial summary judgment; summary judgment; and the motion of plaintiff for partial summary judgment. The City of Wichita ("the City") brings this action to recover damages for the costs of removing asbestos from two City buildings—the Century II Civic Cultural Center ("Century II"), and the Wichita Public Library. Plaintiff seeks recovery against defendant U.S. Gypsum Company as the manufacturer of asbestos products used in the construction of both buildings. Plaintiff alleges that asbestos products manufactured by the remaining two defendants—U.S. Mineral Products Company and Asbestospray—were used in the construction of the Public Library. Plaintiff seeks recovery under theories of negligence, strict liability, implied warranty, and fraud for defendants' alleged misrepresentations as to the characteristics and health hazards associated with their products. Plaintiff also seeks punitive damages.

* * * *

1. *Partial Summary Judgment*

Defendants seek partial summary judgment on plaintiff's claims based upon negligence, strict liability, and implied warranty.

A. *Negligence and Strict Liability*

* * * *

B. *Implied Warranty*

Defendants seek summary judgment on plaintiff's claim of breach of implied warranty, arguing that plaintiff failed to give defendant notice of the claimed breach.

The parties agree that K.S.A. § 84-2-607 is applicable to plaintiff's implied warranty claim. Under this statute, "the buyer must within a reasonable time after he discovers or should have discovered any breach notify the seller of breach or be barred from any remedy; . . . ." *Id.* § 84-2-607(3)(a). The Kansas Comment makes clear that under this provision, "the buyer may waive any claim for defect against the seller by failing to give notice to the seller of any defect." As defendants observe, notice of the alleged breach has been held to be a condition precedent to suit, and the burden is on the party claiming the breach to plead and prove notice within a reasonable time. *Dold v. Sherow*, 220 Kan. 350, 351-52, 552 P.2d 945, 947 (1976). However, this general rule has its exceptions.

The Kansas Court of Appeals has recognized three general purposes served by the notice requirement:

> First, notice provides the seller a chance to correct any defect. Second, notice affords the seller an opportunity to prepare for negotiation and litigation. Third, notice provides the seller a safeguard against stale claims being asserted after it is too late for the manufacturer or seller to investigate them.

Carson v. Chevron Chem. Co., 6 Kan. App. 2d 776, 784, 635 P.2d 1248, 1255 (1981) (citations omitted; quoting *Prutch v. Ford Motor Co.*, 618 P.2d 657, 661 (Colo. 1980)). "[T]he rule of requiring notification is designed to defeat commercial bad faith, not to deprive a good faith consumer of his remedy.' " *Dold*, 220 Kan. at 352, 552 P.2d at 948 (quoting comment 4 to Official U.C.C. Comment).

Plaintiff concedes that prior to filing suit, it did not give notice to defendant. Plaintiff argues, however, that this is not fatal to its claim.

The court agrees. Kansas law requires the court to focus on the purposes of giving notice under the totality of the circumstances. In *Smith v. Stewart*, 233 Kan. 904, 914, 667 P.2d 358, 366 (1983), the Kansas Supreme Court considered whether K.S.A. § 84-2-607(3) was an "absolute bar" to a plaintiff who failed to give pre-suit notice of an alleged breach of express warranty. 233 Kan. at 910, 667 P.2d at 363. The court quoted favorably from several sources indicating that pre-suit notice is not required in all cases. For example, *"[a] comparably strict application of the notice requirement . . .may not be appropriate in a case involving a consumer's claim of breach.' "* 233 Kan. at 912, 667 P.2d at 365 (emphasis supplied by *Stewart* court; quoting *Armco Steel Corp. v. Isaacson Struct. Steel*, 611 P.2d 507, 513 n.15 (Alaska 1980)). Thus, "[t]he defendant's lawyer whose client is sued *not by merchant-buyer but by a consumer*, especially by a consumer who suffered personal injury or property damage, should not rely heavily on a lack of notice defense.' " *Stewart*, 233 Kan. at 913, 667 P.2d at 366 (emphasis added; quoting White & Summers, Uniform Commercial Code § 11-10, at 423 (2d ed. 1980)). In addition, *Stewart* also recognized that "[a] commonly utilized exception to the requirement of giving notice of the defect within a reasonable time is involved in situations where the defective produce has caused personal injury." 233 Kan. 912, 667 P.2d at 365. In these cases, courts typically require no pre-suit notice, because the damage has already been done, and notice would not serve the purpose of allowing the seller to cure the defect. *Id*. at 913, 667 P.2d at 365 (quoting *Maybank v. Kresge Co.*, 302 N.C. 129, 134, 273 S.E.2d 681 (1981)). *See also Graham v. Wyeth Laboratories*, 666 F.Supp. 1483, 1500 (D.Kan.1987) (filing of lawsuit sufficient notice in personal injury action). Because "none of the purposes of the notice within a reasonable time requirement of K.S.A. § 84-2-607(3)(a) [were] served by blind adherence to the generally appropriate 'condition precedent' concept," 233 Kan. at 914, 667 P.2d at 366, the *Stewart* court concluded that plaintiff's express warranty claim was not barred for failure to give pre-suit notice of the defect. Thus, *Stewart* interprets pre-suit notice as a "requirement" only to the extent that notice would serve the underlying purpose of this "condition precedent." *See also Unified Sch. Dist. No. 500 v. U.S. Gypsum Co.*, 788 F.Supp. 1173, 1176 (D.Kan.1992).

As applied to the facts of this case, the court finds that notice prior to filing suit would have accomplished none of the purposes of K.S.A. § 84-2-607(3)(a). The defect in this case is not restricted to a single instance of improper performance of an otherwise safe product. As alleged in this case and numerous other asbestos-contamination cases across the country involving these same defendants, the defect *is* the product, not because it fails to perform its function as a fire retardant, but rather because it presents a health hazard. Defendants have disputed the health hazard allegation from the outset of this litigation, and it is highly doubtful that defendants would have utilized earlier notice to cure a defect that they vigorously contend, here and elsewhere, does not even exist.[19] Defendants do not suggest otherwise. Moreover, defendants have not alleged or demonstrated any prejudice to their litigation posture as a result of plaintiff's failure to give earlier notice. Finally, it is significant that plaintiff is not a merchant-buyer, but a consumer, to whom the notice requirement does not strictly apply.

Thus, as to this issue, the court finds no material facts in substantial controversy, Fed.R.Civ.P. 56(d), and concludes as a matter of law that plaintiff's failure to give presuit notice does not bar its implied warranty claim.

* * *

———

NOTES AND QUESTIONS

(1) Do you agree with the court's analysis? See U.C.C. § 1-102 Comment 1 (text accompanying *Fiterman v. J.N. Johnson & Co.* citation). Note that Proposed U.C.C. § 2-606(c)(1) adds the language: "However, a failure to give proper notice does not bar the buyer from any remedy that does not prejudice the seller."

(2) *Timeliness of Notice. In Mazur Bros. & Jaffe Fish Co., Inc.*, 3 U.C.C. Rep. 419 (VACAB 1965), Appellant-seller sought recovery of the purchase price of raw shrimp ordered and received by a Government hospital (buyer). The shrimp was inspected by buyer's inspector at seller's plant then delivered to buyer on July 23. On July 24 buyer cooked the shrimp and noticed an unwholesome odor and a discoloration. On July 29 buyer notified seller by telephone and telegram that the shrimp were rejected because unfit for service to patients. In sustaining seller's appeal the Board said:

> Conversion of virtually the entire order of shrimp from a raw to a cooked state in preparation for service to patients far exceeded the testing necessary for inspection purposes. This alteration of the product rendered it incapable of return to Appellant in the condition in which it had been delivered, and in our opinion constituted an act of dominion inconsistent with Appellant's ownership. . . . In addition, we believe the Government's delay of five days in notifying Appellant of the rejection was unreasonable because of the perishable nature of the commodity and must therefore be regarded as an additional act of implied acceptance. Appellant was a local supplier and could have been notified of any defects the same day they were discovered. Prompt rejection is necessary in order that the contractor may have a fair opportunity to show that the supplies complied with the contract or to correct any deficiencies. . . . Under the facts of this case Appellant had no opportunity to do either.

---

[19] As indicated in part III, *infra*, U.S. Gypsum has declined to admit that it manufactured the asbestos material found in the Public Library. It seems doubly doubtful that Gypsum would have agreed to cure the alleged defect.

. . . .

As an additional defense the Government contends that Appellant breached an implied warranty that the shrimp would be of merchantable quality, suitable for cooking, and fit for service to hospital patients. Under the Universal [sic] Commercial Code and the Universal [sic] Sales Act such a warranty exists where the seller is a dealer in the goods described and is aware of the purposes for which they are required by the buyer. U.C.C. Secs 2-314, 2-315; USA, Sec 15. Both the Code and the Sales Act provide, however, that the seller shall not be liable under an implied warranty if the buyer, after acceptance, fails to give notice of a breach within a reasonable time after its discovery. U.C.C. Sec 2-607. The hospital's failure in this case to give reasonable notice of rejection after performing an act of acceptance thus stands as a bar to the Government's defense of breach of warranty.

We find no basis under the facts of law for the Government's rejection of the shrimp and conclude that Appellant is entitled to payment in full.

(3) Contractual Time Limitation. In *Q. Vandenberg & Sons, N.V. v. Siter, 204 A.2d 494, 2 U.C.C. Rep. 383 (Pa. 1964),* a Netherlands seller sued defendants (buyers) for the balance of the purchase price of certain tulip and hyacinth bulbs; defendants in Pennsylvania counterclaimed for breach of warranty that bulbs were sound and healthy. The contract provided: "The seller warrants the goods to be sound and healthy at the time of shipment but does not otherwise warrant flowering or other planting, growing or forcing results. . . . All claims hereunder shall be deemed waived unless presented within eight (8) days after receipt of the goods." The goods were delivered on October 18, 1960. Defendants offered testimony that most of the bulbs were planted shortly thereafter; about a month later some of the unplanted bulbs were examined and broken open and found by "Mr. Rotteveel, the expert" to be worthless; the defective character of the remaining bulbs could not be discovered until flowering time shortly before Easter 1961. Plaintiff objected to the reception of any testimony as to occurrences more than eight days after delivery. Should defendants' evidence be admitted? See U.C.C. §§ 2-607(3)(a), 1-204.

(4) Content of Notice. In *Mountain-Aire Refrigeration & Air Conditioning Co., Inc. v. General Electric Co.,* 703 P.2d 577,41 U.C.C. Rep. 1304, 1308 (Arizona 1985), the court quoted White & Summers on the sufficiency of the notice requirement:

Finally, what constitutes sufficient notice under § 2-607(3)(a)? How explicit must it be? May it be oral? Must it threaten litigation? Quite clearly the drafters intended a loose test; a scribbled note on a bit of toilet paper will do:

> The content of the notification need merely be sufficient to let the seller know that the transaction is still troublesome and must be watched. There is no reason to require that the notification which saves the buyer's rights under this section must include a clear statement of all the objections that will be relied on by the buyer, as under the section covering statements of defects upon rejection (Section 2-605). Nor is there reason for requiring the notification to be a claim for damages or of any threatened litigation or other resort to a remedy. The notification which saves the buyer's rights under this Article need only be such as informs the seller that the transaction is claimed to involve a breach, and thus opens the way for normal settlement through negotiation.

Under this comment, it is difficult to conceive of words which, if put in writing, would not satisfy the notice requirement of 2-607. Indeed, a letter containing anything but the most exaggerated encomiums would seem to tell that the transaction "is still troublesome and must be watched." [J. White & R. Summers, Uniform Commercial Code § 11-10 at 484 (3d ed. 1988).

The content of a possible notice of discovery of breach is illustrated by 13 West's Legal Forms § 21.13-Form 2:[20]

[*Date*]

Seller Company

[*Address*]

We hereby notify you that you have breached our agreement dated [*date*] for our purchase from you of 10,000 precision steel fittings, to be delivered to us in one lot on [*date*], in the following respects:

(1)   The delivery was twenty (20) days subsequent to that specified in the contract, which has occasioned a readjustment of our production schedule at considerable expense;

(2)   The quantities shipped, based upon a tentative count, are 1500 units less than the contract amount;

(3)   Express and implied warranties of quality and fitness for purpose have been breached in that a spot-check has disclosed the following defects among a substantial number of the units inspected:

(a)   rust spots,

(b)   uneven surfaces,

(c)   improper threading.

Our hurried inspection in the one day that has elapsed since delivery has disclosed these breaches. We are continuing our inspection and will promptly advise you of any additional breaches which we intend to assert.

Buyer Company

By _____

(5) *Magnuson-Moss Warranty Act.* The Act, in 15 U.S.C. § 2304, sets forth federal minimum standards for "full" warranty. Generally, a warrantor can not impose any duty (*other than notification*) upon any consumer as a condition of securing remedy of any consumer product which malfunctions, is defective, etc. See U.C.C. §§ 2-602(1), 2-607(3)(a), 2-608(2).

(6) *Strict Liability in Tort.* Restatement (Second) of Torts § 402A, Comment m states in part:

The rule stated in this Section is not governed by the provisions of the Uniform Sales Act, or those of the Uniform Commercial Code, as to warranties; and it is not affected by limitations on the scope and content of warranties, or by limitation to "buyer" and "seller" in those statutes. Nor is the consumer required to give notice to the seller of his injury within a reasonable time after it occurs, as is provided by the Uniform Act.

[C]   Revocation of Acceptance

Read: U.C.C. § 2-608, see § 2-607(2).

----

[20] Copyright © 1985 by West Publishing Co. Reprinted by permission.

Read also: U.C.C. 2A-517; see § 2A-516(2); CISG Arts. 45, 49, 81-84 (see Arts. 25-27).

————

COLONIAL DODGE, INC. v. MILLER

Michigan Supreme Court
420 Mich. 452, 362 N.W.2d 704, 40 U.C.C. Rep. 1 (1984)

issue

KAVANAGH, J. This case requires the court to decide whether the failure to include a spare tire with a new automobile can constitute a substantial impairment in the value of that automobile entitling the buyer to revoke his acceptance of the vehicle under MCL 440.2608; MSA 19.2608.

We hold it may and reverse.

On April 19, 1976, defendant Clarence Miller ordered a 1976 Dodge Royal Monaco station wagon from plaintiff Colonial Dodge which included a heavy-duty trailer package with extra wide tires.

On May 28,1976, defendant picked up the wagon, drove it a short distance where he met his wife, and exchanged it for her car. Defendant drove that car to work while his wife returned home with the new station wagon. Shortly after arriving home, Mrs. Miller noticed that their new wagon did not have a spare tire. The following morning defendant notified plaintiff that he insisted on having the tire he ordered immediately, but when told there was no spare tire then available, he informed the salesman for plaintiff that he would stop payment on the two checks that were tendered as the purchase price, and that the vehicle could be picked up from in front of his home. Defendant parked the car in front of his home where it remained until the temporary ten-day registration sticker had expired, whereupon the car was towed by the St. Clair police to a St. Clair dealership. Plaintiff had applied for license places, registration, and title in defendant's name. Defendant refused the license plates when they were delivered to him.

According to plaintiff's witness, the spare tire was not included in the delivery of the vehicle due to a nation-wide shortage caused by a labor strike. Some months, later, defendant was notified his tire was available.

Plaintiff sued defendant for the purchase price of the car. On January 13, 1981, the trial court entered a judgment for plaintiff finding that defendant wrongfully revoked acceptance of the vehicle. The Court of Appeals decided that defendant never accepted the vehicle under MCL 440.2606; MSA 19.2606 of the Uniform Commercial Code and reversed. 116 Mich App 78, 85; 322 NW2d 549; 34 UCCRS 123 (1982). On rehearing, the Court of Appeals, noting the trial court found the parties had agreed that there was a valid acceptance, affirmed the trial court's holding there was not a substantial impairment in value sufficient to authorize defendant to revoke acceptance of the automobile.

Defendant argues that he never accepted the vehicle under MCL 440.2606; MSA 19.2606, claiming mere possession of the vehicle is not sufficient according to the U.C.C. Plaintiff contends defendant did accept the vehicle by executing an application for Michigan title and driving the vehicle away from the dealership. The trial court stated "[t]he parties agree that defendant Miller made a valid acceptance of the station wagon under § 2.606 of the Uniform Commercial Code. . . ."[21]

We are not persuaded that, had the matter been contested in the trial court, a finding of acceptance would be warranted on this record. However, since defendant did not submit the question to the trial judge, but in effect stipulated to acceptance, we will treat the matter as though there was acceptance.

We are satisfied defendant made a proper revocation under MCL 440.2608(1)(b); MSA 19.2608(1)(b). This section reads:

. . . .

Plaintiff argues the missing spare tire did not constitute a substantial impairment in the value of the automobile, within the meaning of MCL 440.2608(1); MSA 19.2608(1). Plaintiff claims a missing spare tire is a trivial defect, and a proper construction of this section of the U.C.C. would not permit defendant to revoke under these circumstances. It maintains that since the spare tire is easy to replace and the cost of curing the nonconformity very small compared to the total contract price, there is no substantial impairment in value.

However, MCL 440.2608(1); MSA 19.2608(1) says "[t]he buyer may revoke his acceptance of a lot or commercial unit whose non-conformity substantially impairs its value *to him*. . . . (Emphasis added.) Number two of the Official Comment to MCL 440.2608; MSA 19.2608 attempts to clarify this area. It says that

> [r]evocation of acceptance is possible only where the nonconformity substantially impairs the value of the goods to the buyer. For this purpose the test is not what the seller had reason to know at the time of contracting; the question is whether the nonconformity is such as will in fact cause a substantial impairment of value to the buyer though the seller had no advance knowledge as to the buyer's particular circumstances.

We cannot accept plaintiff's interpretation of MCL 440.2608(1); MSA 19.2608(1). In order to give effect to the statute, a buyer must show the nonconformity has a special devaluing effect on him and that the buyer's assessment of it is factually correct. In this case, the defendant's concern with safety is evidenced by the fact that he ordered the special package which included special tires. The defendant's occupation demanded that he travel extensively, sometimes in excess of 150 miles per day on Detroit freeways, and often in the early morning hours. Mr. Miller testified that he was afraid of a tire going flat on a Detroit freeway at 3 a.m. Without a spare, he testified, he would be helpless until morning business hours. The dangers attendant upon a stranded motorist are common knowledge, and Mr. Miller's fears are not unreasonable.[22]

---

[21] The basis for the statement by the trial court appears to be the argument in defendant's brief to the trial court, which stated: "Mr. Miller contends that the provisions of MCLA 440.2608(1) and (b) have been clearly met due to the fact that he accepted the vehicle in question . . ." The first opinion of the Court of Appeals, 116 Mich App 78, 85, held that the trial court clearly erred in finding acceptance. However, on rehearing the plaintiff pointed out the statement cited above and the Court of Appeals found a valid acceptance. 121 Mich. App. 466; 328 N.W.2d 678 (1982).

[22] [Judge Deming, in the first opinion of the Michigan Court of Appeals, 116 Mich.App. 78, 82, 322 N.W.2d 549 (1982), remarked:

> We take judicial notice of the fact that Detroit area freeways and expressways have been the scene of violent crime and that many citizens justifiably fear automobile breakdowns while traveling on the expressways and the danger attendant thereto.—Ed.]

holding

We hold that under the circumstances the failure to include the spare tire as ordered constituted a substantial impairment in value to Mr. Miller, and that he could properly revoke his acceptance under the U.C.C.

That defendant did not discover this nonconformity before he accepted the vehicle does not preclude his revocation. There was testimony that the space for the spare tire was under a fastened panel, concealed from view. This out-of-sight location satisfied the requirement of MCL 440.2608(1)(b); MSA 19.2608(1)(b) that the nonconformity be difficult to discover.

MCL 440.2608(2); MSA 19.2608(2) requires that the seller be notified of the revocation of acceptance and that it occur within a reasonable time of the discovery of the nonconformity. Defendant notified plaintiff of his revocation the morning after the car was delivered to him. Notice was given within a reasonable time.

Plaintiff argues that defendant failed to effectively revoke acceptance because he neglected to sign over title to the car to plaintiff.

Defendant, however, had no duty to sign over title absent a request from plaintiff that he do so. Under MCL 440.2608(3); MSA 19.2608(3), "[a] buyer who so revokes has the same rights and duties with regard to the goods involved as if he had rejected them." And a buyer who has rejected goods in his possession "is under a duty . . .to hold them with reasonable care at the seller's disposition for a time sufficient to permit the seller to remove them; but the buyer has no further obligations with regard to the goods. . . ." MCL 440.2602(1)(b) and (c); MSA 19.2602(1)(b) and (c). Defendant's notice to plaintiff and holding of the car pending seller's disposition was sufficient under the statute, at least in the absence of evidence that defendant refused a request by the plaintiff to sign over title.

Plaintiff contends defendant abandoned the vehicle, denying it any opportunity to cure the nonconforming tender as prescribed in MCL 440.2508; MSA 19.2508. We find that defendant's behavior did not prevent plaintiff from curing the nonconformity. Defendant held the vehicle and gave notice to the plaintiff in a proper fashion; he had no further duties.

Reversed.

RYAN, J. (dissenting). I dissent.

While I agree that MCL 440.2608(1)(b); MSA 19.2608(1)(b) establishes what is essentially a subjective test to measure the buyer's authority to revoke an acceptance of nonconforming goods, the requisite impairment of the value of the goods to the buyer must be *substantial*. It is not sufficient that the nonconformance be worrisome, aggravating, or even potentially dangerous. It must be a nonconformity which diminishes the value of the goods to the buyer to a substantial degree. The mere possibility that the new car in this case would have a flat tire in the early hours of the morning in an unsafe area of the City of Detroit, leaving its driver with no spare tire, although real, is unlikely. In all events, it is not a possibility which can reasonably be said to elevate the absence of a spare tire, a temporary deficiency easily remedied, to the level of a "substantial impairment" of the value of the new automobile for its ordinary use as a motor vehicle.

Consequently, I would reverse the judgment of the Court of Appeals and affirm the finding of the trial court on this issue.

BOYLE, J. (dissenting). I disagree with the conclusion reached by the majority for the reasons stated by Judge Cynar in his dissent in the Court of Appeals. 116 Mich App 78, 87; 322 NW2d

549 (1982) (Cynar, P.J., dissenting). I agree with Judge Cynar's analysis of the law of substantial impairment and its application to the facts in this case. As he succinctly summarized:

> A buyer may properly revoke acceptance where the nonconformity substantially impairs its value. The existence of such nonconformity depends on the facts and circumstances of each case. *Jorgensen v. Pressnall*, 274 Or 285; 545 P.2d 1382 (1976). The determination of substantial impairment has been made from the buyer's subjective view, considering particular needs and circumstances. See Summers & White, Handbook of the Law Under the Uniform Commercial Code (2d ed), § 8-3, p 308; committee Comment 2 to MCL 440.2608; MSA 19.2608. An objective approach was utilized in *Fargo Machine & Tool Co. v. Kearney & Trecker Corp.*, 428 F Supp 364 (ED Mich, 1977), and an objective and subjective test was employed in *Jorgensen, supra*.

> The purpose of the requirement of substantial impairment of value is to preclude revocation for trivial defects or defects which may be easily corrected. . . .

> The trial judge's determination that the temporarily missing spare tire did not constitute a substantial impairment in value under either the subjective or objective test was not clearly erroneous.

> Therefore, I do not agree that defendant Miller properly rejected the vehicle, and I would affirm the trial court's finding on that issue.

CAVANAGH, J., concurs.

——

NOTES AND QUESTIONS

(1) Both Michigan Court of Appeals opinions and a dissent referenced *Zabriskie Chevrolet, Inc. v. Smith*, 99 N.J. Super. 441, 240 A.2d 195, 5 U.C.C. Rep. 30 (1968). Here, buyer (B) signed a purchase order form on February 2 for a "brand-new car that would operate perfectly." B made a $124 deposit followed by a check representing the balance of the purchase price. In the evening of February 10, B's wife took delivery of the car. En route home, about 2-1/2 miles away, and after having gone about 7/10 of a mile from the showroom, the car stalled at a traffic light, stalled again within another 15 feet and again each time the vehicle was required to stop. When about half-way home the car could not be driven in "drive" gear at all, and B's wife was obliged to then propel the vehicle in "low-low" gear at a rate of about five to ten miles per hour, its then maximum speed. In great distress, B's wife was fearful of completing the journey home and called B, who thereupon drove the car in "low-low" gear about seven blocks home. B immediately called his bank (which was open in the evening), stopped payment on the check given in payment, and called S to notify them that they had sold him a "lemon," that he had stopped payment on the check and that the sale was canceled. The next day S sent a wrecker to B's home, brought the vehicle to its repair shop and after inspection determined that the transmission was defective. S replaced the transmission with another one removed from a vehicle then on S's showroom floor, notifying B thereafter of what had been done. B refused to take delivery of the vehicle as repaired and reasserted his cancellation of the sale. S sued on the check and the purchase order for the balance of the purchase price, and B counterclaimed for return of his deposit.

In rendering judgment for B the court said, *inter alia*:

[W]e hold that the vehicle. . .was substantially defective and constituted a breach of the contract and the implied warranty of merchantability [U.C.C. § 2-314]. . . . It is clear that a buyer does not accept goods until he has had a "reasonable opportunity to inspect." [U.C.C. § 2-606(l).] Defendant [B] sought to purchase a new car. He assumed . . .that his new car, with the exception of very minor adjustments, would be mechanically new and factory-furnished, operate perfectly, and be free of substantial defects. . . . How long the buyer may drive the new car under the guise of inspection of new goods is not an issue in the present case. It is clear that defendant [B] discovered the non-conformity within 7/10 of a mile and minutes after leaving plaintiff's [S's] showroom. Certainly this was well within the ambit of "reasonable opportunity to inspect". . . . [D]efendant never accepted the vehicle.

Even if defendant [B] had accepted the automobile tendered, he had a right to revoke [acceptance] under [U.C.C. § 2-608]: "(1) The buyer may revoke his acceptance of [goods] whose non-conformity *substantially impairs its value* to him. . . ."

[The court related that B properly rejected the car under U.C.C. §§ 2-601 and 2-602.]

(2) In assessing U.C.C. §§ 2-601, 2-602 and 2-608 it should be evident that it is more difficult for a buyer to revoke acceptance of goods than to have rejected them. Why this is the case is stated in J. White & R. Summers, Uniform Commercial Code § 8-4 (3d ed. 1988):

[First],. . .the longer the buyer has the goods, the higher the probability that the alleged defect was caused by him or aggravated by his failure properly to maintain the goods. Secondly, the longer the buyer holds the goods (if he uses them), the greater the benefit he will have derived from them. All of these factors support a rule which makes it difficult for the buyer who has once accepted to cast the goods and attendant loss from depreciation and market factors back on the seller.

(3) *Continued Use After Revocation of Acceptance.* In *McCullough v. Bill Swad Chrysler-Plymouth, Inc.*, 449 N.E.2d 1289, 36 U.C.C. Rep. 513, 518-20 (1983), the court said:

In ascertaining whether a buyer's continued use of an item after revocation of its acceptance was reasonable, the trier of fact should pose and divine the answers to the following queries: (1) Upon being apprised of the buyer's revocation of his acceptance, what instructions, if any, did the seller tender the buyer concerning return of the now rejected goods? (2) Did the buyer's business needs or personal circumstances compel the continued use? (3) During the period of such use, did the seller persist in assuring the buyer that all nonconformities would be cured or that provisions would otherwise be made to recompense the latter for the dissatisfaction and inconvenience which the defects caused him? (4) Did the seller act in good faith? (5) Was the seller unduly prejudiced by the buyer's continued use?

It is manifest that, upon consideration of the aforementioned criteria, appellee [buyer] acted reasonably in continuing to operate her motor vehicle even after revocation of acceptance. First, the failure of the seller to advise the buyer, after the latter has revoked his acceptance of the goods, how the goods were to be returned entitles the buyer to retain possession of them. . . . Appellant [seller], in the case at bar, did not respond to appellee's request for instructions regarding the disposition of the vehicle. Failing to have done so, appellant can hardly be heard now to complain of appellee's continued use of the automobile.

Secondly, appellee, a young clerical secretary of limited financial resources, was scarcely in position to return the defective automobile and obtain a second in order to meet her business and personal needs. A most unreasonable obligation would be imposed upon appellee were she to be required, in effect, to secure a loan to purchase a second car while remaining liable for repayment of the first car loan.

Additionally [third], appellant's successor (East), by attempting to repair the appellee's vehicle even after she tendered her notice of revocation, provided both express and tacit assurances that the automobile's defects were remediable, thereby, inducing her to retain possession. Moreover [fourth], whether appellant acted in good faith throughout this episode is highly problematic, especially given the fact that whenever repair of the car was undertaken, new defects often miraculously arose while previous ones frequently went uncorrected. Both appellant's and East's refusal to honor the warranties before their expiration also evidences less than fair dealing.

Finally [fifth], it is apparent that appellant was not prejudiced by appellee's continued operation of the automobile. Had appellant retaken possession of the vehicle pursuant to appellee's notice of revocation, the automobile, which at the time had been driven only 12,000 miles, could easily have been resold. Indeed, the car was still marketable at the time of trial, as even then the odometer registered less than 35,000 miles. In any event, having failed to reassume ownership of the automobile when requested to do so, appellant alone must bear the loss for any diminution of the vehicle's resale value occurring between the two dates.

[U.C.C. § 2-711(3)] provides an additional basis for appellee's retention after revocation of the automobile. A buyer who possesses, as appellee does in the instant action, a security interest in the rejected goods may continue to use them even after revoking his acceptance. . . . Consequently, appellee's continued use of the defective vehicle was a permissible means of protecting her security interest therein.

In *Computerized Radiological Services v. Syntax Corp.*, 786 F.2d 72, 42 U.C.C. Rep. 1656 (2d Cir. 1986), buyers of CAT scanner continued to use it for some 22 months after the letter of revocation. The court said:

The continued use of goods is inconsistent with the seller's ownership and may be found to constitute an acceptance. U.C.C. § 2-606(1)(c). If so, such use would be at odds with a revocation of acceptance and could be held to have invalidated an earlier attempt at revocation. *Gasque v. Mooers Motor Car Co.*, 227 Va. 154, 313 S.E.2d 384 (1984) (buyer cannot use automobile after revocation).

CRS argues, however, that continued use for a reasonable period of time to allow buyers to seek an alternative or to avoid substantial hardship may be allowed. *Minsel v. El Rancho Mobile Home Center, Inc.*, 32 Mich. App. 10, 188 N.W. 2d 9 (1971) (use of mobile home for six weeks after revocation while searching for another dwelling held reasonable); *Fablok Mills, Inc. v. Cocker Machine & Foundry Co.*, 125 N.J. Super. 251, 310 A.2d 491(1973) (continued use of machines reasonable where seller is only manufacturer and alternative is going out of business).

Under the U.C.C., a buyer who revokes acceptance rather than relying solely upon an action for breach of warranty must begin the search for replacement goods with reasonable dispatch and may not put off purchase until a seller offers ideal financial terms. CRS' desultory search for another scanner simply belies its revocation claim, much as the long delay in the hope of avoiding personal liability implies that CRS continued to use the Syntex scanner because continued use was more advantageous than the existing alternatives. CRS' extended use of the defendant's scanner thus invalidates the purported revocation of acceptance.

(4) *Offset for Buyer's Use.* In *Johnson v. General Motors Corp., Chevrolet Motor Division, 233 Kan. 1044, 668 P.2d 139, 36 U.C.C. Rep. 1089,1097-98 (1983),* the buyers revoked acceptance of a pickup truck. The principal issue was whether the trial court erred in allowing a setoff from the purchase price of the truck for the buyers' continued use of the truck after the buyers' revocation of acceptance. The court said:

> The purpose of allowing revocation after acceptance is to restore the buyer to the economic position the buyer would have been in if the goods were never delivered. . . . After revocation of acceptance any significant use by the buyer should allow the seller to recover from the buyers restitution for the fair value of any benefit obtained resulting from such use. . . . The proper setoff is the value of use of the goods received by the buyer after his revocation of acceptance.

> [GMC introduced into evidence a Federal Highway Administration booklet entitled, "Cost of Owning Automobiles and Vans 1982." The booklet] stated the cost of owning and operating a similar vehicle to the truck purchased by the buyers is calculated at 33.2 cents per mile. After deduction of maintenance, gas and oil, parking and tolls, insurance and state and federal taxes, expenses the buyers have already paid, the booklet concluded the original vehicle cost to operate is 10.7 cents per mile. Since buyers drove the vehicle 14,619 miles at 10.7 cents per mile after revocation, the setoff would be $1,564.23. From the evidence presented in this case, GMC is entitled to the sum of$1,564.23 as a setoff for the buyers' use of the truck after revocation of acceptance.

In *Stridiron v. I.C., Inc.,* 578 F.Supp. 997, 37 U.C.C. Rep. 1568, 1575 (D. Virgin Islands 1984), the court said:

> Even though offset seems to be inconsistent with 11A VIC § 2-608 which precludes revocation where there has been a substantial change in the condition of the goods, many courts and commentators have recognized and permitted sellers to offset the purchase price returned to revoking buyers in order to reflect the use of the goods made by the buyers. See G. Priest, *Breach & Remedy for the Tender of Non-Conforming Goods Under the U.C.C.: An Economic Approach*, 91 Harv. L. Rev. 960 (1978); . . .Although we recognize that there is authority to award an offset, we cannot say that the trial court erred by refusing to do so.

State "lemon laws" may provide for offset. *See, e.g.,* New York General Business Law § 198-a. Under subdivision (c)(1), any refund from the manufacturer or dealer may be reduced by:

> an allowance for the consumer's use of the vehicle in excess of the first twelve thousand miles of operation pursuant to the mileage deduction formula defined in paragraph four of subdivision (a) of this section, and a reasonable allowance for any damage not attributable to normal wear or improvements.

Paragraph four of subdivision (a) reads:

> "Mileage deduction formula" means the mileage which is in excess of twelve thousand miles times the purchase price, or the lease price if applicable, of the vehicle divided by one hundred thousand miles.

[D]   Installment Contracts

Read: U.C.C. § 2-612.

Read also: U.C.C. § 2A-510; CISG Art. 73, see Arts. 25-27, 81-84.

An "installment contract" is one which requires or authorizes the delivery of goods in separate lots to be separately accepted. U.C.C. § 2-612(1). See the references to U.C.C. § 2-612in U.C.C. §§ 2-703 (Seller's Remedies in General), 2-711(1) (Buyer's Remedies in General). Remedies are discussed in the next chapter. Under Proposed U.C.C. § 2-611, the definition has been revised to include installment contracts by operation of law (§ 2-307) and clarify that an installment contract exists where the delivery of goods is in separate lots to be separately accepted even though payment is not in installments.

TRANS WORLD METALS, INC. v. SOUTHWIRE CO.

United States Court of Appeals
769 F.2d 902, 41 U.C.C. Rep. 453 (2nd Cir. 1985)

JON O. NEWMAN, CIRCUIT JUDGE: This appeal requires us to resolve an expensive dispute arising out of the repudiation of a long-term commodity supply contract. Southwire Company ("Southwire") appeals from a judgment of the District Court for the Southern District of New York (Charles E. Stewart, Jr., Judge) entered in this diversity action following a four-week jury trial. The jury awarded plaintiffs Trans World Metals, Inc., Trans-World Metals & Co., Ltd., and Trans World Metals, Ltd. (collectively "Trans World") approximately $7.1 million in damages. Southwire challenges the finding that it is liable to Trans World under the contract, the measure of damages awarded to Trans World, and various rulings by the District Court. We affirm.

BACKGROUND

On April 7, 1981, Trans World and Southwire negotiated by telephone for the purchase and delivery in 1982 of approximately $20.4 million of aluminum. The parties confirmed the contract by exchanging unsigned, standard form documents: Trans World sent Southwire both a confirming telex and a similarly worded "sales contract"; Southwire sent Trans World a "purchase contract confirmation." The contract documents reflect an agreement for the sale and delivery of twelve thousand metric tons of primary aluminum at an average price of $.77 per pound. The "delivery time" clause of the Trans World sales contract and the "shipment schedule" clause of the Trans World telex both state that delivery shall occur "[a]t the rate of 1000 mt [metric tons] per month from January 1982 through December 1982." The Southwire purchase contract confirmation indicates that the quantity and "expected date" under the agreement is 2,205,000 lbs. (one thousand metric tons) "Per Month." The standard printed form on the reverse side of the purchase contract confirmation indicates, in the "Delivery" clause, that "Time is hereby made of the essence, any late delivery shall be a default, and Seller shall be fully responsible for any cost occasioned Buyer thereby."

Also pertinent to the delivery obligation is the following clause in the Trans World sales contract:

Delivered Railhead, usual midwest U.S.A. destinations *as per buyer's instructions, which are to be submitted no later than the 15th of the month of shipment*. Any tonnage not released by that date is to be invoiced on the last day of month on net 30 days terms.

(Emphasis added.) The purchase contract confirmation contained similar language.

The Southwire purchase contract confirmation contained a "termination" clause with the following provision regarding untimely delivery:

(a) Buyer may, by written notice of default, cancel this contract in whole or in part if:

(1) Seller fails to make timely delivery, time being of the essence; or

(2) Seller fails to comply with any provision thereof; and

Seller fails to cure such failure within ten (10) days, or such longer period as may be specified in the notice, from the date of receiving the notice.

Pursuant to the delivery terms of the contract, Southwire sent Trans World several delivery instruction "releases" during January 1982. Trans World shipped about three-fourths of the first month's one thousand metric tons of aluminum during January. The remaining one-fourth of the first one thousand tons of metal was shipped between February 1 and February 11, 1982. On February 17, 1982, representatives of Trans World attended a meeting at Southwire's request in Carrollton, Georgia, at which Southwire sought to extend the length of the contract to two years without altering the total quantity of aluminum to be delivered. The parties did not discuss the late delivery of the aluminum ordered in January. Southwire sent no delivery instruction releases to Trans World after January 1982.

Between April 1981, when the contract was negotiated, and March 1982, the price of aluminum fell dramatically. On March 4, 1982, Southwire sent Trans World a telex repudiating the entire contract, pursuant to the termination clause of the purchase contract confirmation. The telex stated:

Pursuant to [the termination clause] of our contract . . .Southwire Company hereby notifies you of default in your performance of said contract and cancels the same because of your failure to make timely delivery of material called for by said contract.

Please advise us how to dispose of material you have late shipped, which we hold for your instruction.

The "failure to make timely delivery" refers to shipments to be made during the first month of the twelve-month contract. The "late shipped" material consists of the $419,232.84 worth of aluminum shipped by Trans World in early February 1982.

On May 3, 1982, Trans World brought suit in New York state court against Southwire for breach of the aluminum supply contract.[23] Southwire removed the action to federal court and unsuccessfully sought to transfer the case to Georgia. At the conclusion of the trial the jury answered special interrogatories in addition to rendering a general verdict in favor of Trans World. The jury found that the parties had entered into a contract but that the "time is of essence" and "termination" clauses of Southwire's "purchase contract confirmation" were not a part of the

---

[23] Southwire had earlier brought a similar action against Trans World in the Northern District of Georgia. The day after repudiating the supply contract, Southwire field suit seeking a declaratory judgment that the contract was of no force and effect. The District Court for the Northern District of Georgia dismissed for lack of personal jurisdiction. The Eleventh Circuit reversed that judgment after the action in the Southern District of New York had gone to trial. See *Southwire Co. v. Trans World Metals & Co., Ltd.*, 735 F.2d 440 (11th Cir. 1984).

contract. The jury could not agree whether the aluminum shipments made in early February were timely but found that, even if the shipments were late, they were accepted by Southwire and that there was no substantial impairment of the value either of any particular shipment or of the contract as a whole. The jury awarded Trans World total damages of $7,122,141.84, consisting of $6,702,529.00 for repudiation of the remaining purchase obligations of the contract and $419,232.84 for shipments accepted without payment by Southwire in February.[24] The District Court applied the New York prejudgment interest rate and awarded Trans World $1,304,804.88 in prejudgment interest, for a total of $8,426,946.72. The District Court denied Southwire's motions for judgment notwithstanding the verdict and for a new trial. This appeal followed.

DISCUSSION

I.

Southwire challenges the jury's finding that it is liable for repudiation of the contract, arguing that the District Court should have ruled as a matter of law that Trans World breached the contract by failing to complete the first month's shipments in January. Southwire argues, in essence, that the deliveries made in February violated the "delivery" and "termination" clauses of its purchase contract confirmation and therefore that it was error for the District Court to permit Trans World to introduce evidence regarding trade practices in order to show that the February deliveries were timely. Even if we ignore the jury's finding that the "time is of the essence" and "termination" clauses were not part of the contract between the parties, Southwire's argument fails.

First, because the provisions governing the timing of delivery are somewhat ambiguous, the District Court correctly admitted parol evidence regarding the contract meaning of the terms. See *Rose Stone & Concrete, Inc. v. County of Broome*, 429 N.YS.2d 295, 296 (3d Dep't 1980) ("[T]rade terms may be shown by parol evidence to have acquired a meaning by usage."); cf. *Long Island Airports Limousine Service Corp. v. Playboy-Elsinore Associates*, 739 F.2d 101, 103-04 (2d Cir. 1984) (non-U.C.C. case; parol evidence admissible when contract susceptible of at least two fairly reasonable meanings); *Schering Corp. v. Home Insurance Co.*, 712 F.2d 4, 9 (2d Cir. 1983) (same). The contract provides for delivery at a rate of 1,000 metric tons per month, but the apparent certainty of this provision is undermined by the provision regarding delivery instructions from the buyer. It is not self-evident from reading both provisions whether 1,000 metric tons are to be delivered precisely within each calendar month or whether some part of each month's shipment may be delivered in the following month so long as it is shipped within a reasonable time after receipt of delivery instructions. At a minimum the delivery provisions were permissibly "explained or supplemented" by evidence of trade usage. N.Y.U.C.C. Law § 2-202(a) (McKinney 1964); see . . . N.Y.U.C.C. Law § 1-205(3).

Second, the termination clause in Southwire's purchase contract confirmation explicitly affords Trans World a right to cure "within ten (10) days. . .from the date of receiving [written] notice" of default. Southwire provided no written notice of default before March 4, when it sent Trans World the telex repudiating the contract. Because Trans World had cured any potential default by completing all requested deliveries before the period for cure expired, the contract does not permit Southwire to terminate on the basis of the shipments made in February.

---

[24] The component figures total $380 less than the aggregate figure awarded by the jury. The discrepancy has not been noticed by the parties, which we take to be a waiver of any complaint.

Finally, the Uniform Commercial Code offers Southwire no ground to repudiate the contract. The agreement at issue is an "installment contract" within the meaning of N.Y.U.C.C. Law § 2-612(1) because it "requires or authorizes the delivery of goods in separate lots to be separately accepted." Therefore, Southwire may treat a late shipment of one installment as a breach of the entire contract only if the "default with respect to one or more installments substantially impairs the value of the whole contract." *Id.* § 2-612(3). The jury's finding, not challenged by Southwire on appeal, that there was no substantial impairment of the value of either the shipments received in February or the contract as a whole supports the ultimate finding that Southwire breached the contract. The District Court properly refused to overturn the jury verdict against Southwire.

II. & III.

[The court evaluated the damage award per U.C.C. § 2-708. With respect to fixed price contracts, the court observed: "Because Trans World accepted the risk that prices would rise, it is entitled to benefit from their fall." 41 U.C.C. Rep. at 461.]

. . . .

We have considered Southwire's remaining claims and find them to lack merit. The judgment of the District Court is affirmed.

§ 6.05 Seller's Right to Cure

Read: U.C.C. §§ 2-508, 2-608(1)(a).

Read also: U.C.C. §§ 2A-513, 2A-517(1)(a); CISG Arts. 34, 37, 48, see Art. 46.

———

T.W. OIL, INC. v. CONSOLIDATED EDISON CO. OF NEW YORK, INC.

New York Court of Appeals
443 N.E.2d 932, 35 U.C.C. Rep. 12 (1982)

FUCHSBERG, J. In the first case to wend its way through our appellate courts on this question, we are asked, in the main, to decide whether a seller who, acting in good faith and without knowledge of any defect, tenders nonconforming goods to a buyer who properly rejects them, may avail itself of the cure provision of § 2-508 (subd [2]) of the Uniform Commercial Code. We hold that, if seasonable notice be given, such a seller may offer to cure the defect within a reasonable period beyond the time when the contract was to be performed so long as it has acted in good faith and with a reasonable expectation that the original goods would be acceptable to the buyer.

The factual background against which we decide this appeal is based on either undisputed proof or express findings at trial term. In January 1974, midst the fuel shortage produced by the oil embargo, the plaintiff (then known as Joc Oil, USA, Inc.) purchased a cargo of fuel oil whose sulfur content was represented to it as no greater than 1%. While the oil was still at sea en route to the United States in the tanker MT Khamsin, plaintiff received a certificate from the foreign refinery at which it had been processed informing it that the sulfur content in fact was .52%. Thereafter, on January 24, the plaintiff entered into a written contract with the defendant (Con Ed) for the sale of this oil. The agreement was for delivery to take place between January 24 and January 30, payment being subject to a named independent testing agency's confirmation of quality and quantity. The contract, following a trade custom to round off specifications of sulfur content at, for instance, 1%, .5% or .3%, described that of the Khamsin oil as .5%.[25] In the course of the negotiations, the plaintiff learned that Con Ed was then authorized to buy and burn oil with a sulfur content of up to 1% and would even mix oils containing more and less to maintain that figure.

When the vessel arrived, on January 25, its cargo was discharged into Con Ed storage tanks in Bayonne, New Jersey.[26] In due course, the independent testing people reported a sulfur content of. 92%. On this basis, acting within a time frame whose reasonableness is not in question, on February 14 Con Ed rejected the shipment. Prompt negotiations to adjust the price failed; by February 20, plaintiff had offered a price reduction roughly responsive to the difference in sulfur reading, but Con Ed, though it could use the oil, rejected this proposition out of hand. It was insistent on paying no more than the latest prevailing price, which, in the volatile market that then existed, was some 25% below the level which prevailed when it agreed to buy the oil.

The very next day, February 21, plaintiff offered to cure the defect with a substitute shipment of conforming oil scheduled to arrive on the SS Appolonian Victory on February 28. Nevertheless, on February 22, the very day after the cure was proffered, Con Ed, adamant in its intention to avail itself of the intervening drop in prices, summarily rejected this proposal too. The two cargos were subsequently sold to third parties at the best price obtainable, first that of the Appolonian and, sometime later, after extraction from the tanks had been accomplished, that of the Khamsin.[27]

[handwritten margin note: seller's offer to cure]

There ensued this action for breach of contract,[28] which, after a somewhat unconventional trial course, resulted in a non-jury decision for the plaintiff in the sum of $1,385,512.83, essentially the difference between the original contract price of $3,360,667.14 and the amount received by the plaintiff by way of resale of the Khamsin oil at what the court found as a matter of fact was a negotiated price which, under all the circumstances,[29] was reasonably procured in the open market. To arrive at this result, the trial judge, while ruling against other liability theories advanced by the plaintiff; which, in particular, included one charging the defendant with having failed to act in good faith in the negotiations for a price adjustment on the Khamsin oil (Uniform Commercial Code, § 1-203), decided as a matter of law that Uniform Commercial Code § 2-508(subd [2]) was available to the plaintiff even if it had no prior knowledge of the nonconformity. Finding that in fact plaintiff had no such belief at the time of the delivery, that

---

[25] Confirmatorily, Con Ed's brief describes .92% oil as "nominally" 1% oil.

[26] The tanks already contained some other oil, but Con Ed appears to have had no concern over the admixture of the differing sulfur contents. In any event, the efficacy of the independent testing required by the contract was not impaired by the commingling.

[27] Most of the Khamsin oil was drained from the tanks and sold at $10.75 per barrel. The balance was retained by Con Ed in its mixed form at $10.45 per barrel. The original price in January had been $17.875 per barrel.

[28] The plaintiff originally also sought an affirmative injunction to compel Con Ed to accept the Khamsin shipment or, alternatively, the Appolonian substitute. However, when a preliminary injunction was denied on the ground that the plaintiff had an adequate remedy at law, it amended its complaint to pursue the latter remedy alone.

[29] These circumstances included the fact that the preliminary injunction was not denied until April so that, by the time the Khamsin oil was sold in May, almost three months had gone by since its rejection.

what turned out to be a .92% sulfur content was "within the range of contemplation of reasonable acceptability" to Con Ed, and that seasonable notice of an intention to cure was given, the court went on to hold that plaintiff's "reasonable and timely offer to cure" was improperly rejected (*sub nom Joc Oil USA, Inc. v. Consolidated Edison Co. of NY*, 107 Misc 2d 376 [Shanley N. Egeth, J.]). The Appellate Division having unanimously affirmed the judgment entered on this decision, the case is now here by our leave.

In support of its quest for reversal, the defendant now asserts that the trial court erred (a) in ruling that the verdict on a special question submitted for determination by a jury was irrelevant to the decision of this case, (b) in failing to interpret Uniform Commercial Code, § 2-508(subd [2]) to limit the availability of the right to cure after date of performance to cases in which the seller knowingly made a nonconforming tender and (c) in calculating damages on the basis of the resale of the nonconforming cargo rather than of the substitute offered to replace it. For the reasons which follow, we find all three unacceptable.

. . . .

II

We turn then to the central issue on this appeal: Fairly interpreted, did subdivision 2 of § 2-508 of the Uniform Commercial Code require Con Ed to accept the substitute shipment plaintiff tendered? In approaching this question, we, of course, must remember that a seller's right to cure a defective tender, as allowed by both subdivisions of § 2-508, was intended to act as a meaningful limitation on the absolutism of the old perfect tender rule, under which, no leeway being allowed for any imperfections, there was, as one court put it, just "no room for the doctrine of substantial performance" of commercial obligations (*Mitsubishi Goshi Kaisha v. J. Aron & Co., Inc.*, 16 F2d 185, 186 [Learned Hand, J.]).

In contrast, to meet the realities of the more impersonal business world of our day, the Code, to avoid sharp dealing, expressly provides for the liberal construction of its remedial provisions (§1-102) so that "good faith" and the "observance of reasonable commercial standards of fair dealing" be the rule rather than the exception in trade (see § 2-103 subd [1], par [b]), "good faith" being defined as "honesty in fact in the conduct or transaction concerned" (Uniform Commercial Code, § 1-201, subd [19]). As to § 2-508 in particular, the Code's Official Comment advises that its mission is to safeguard the seller "against surprise as a result of sudden technicality on the buyer's part" (Uniform Commercial Code, § 2-106, Official Comment 2).

Section 2-508 may be conveniently divided between provisions for cure offered when "the time for performance has not yet expired" (subd [1]), a pre-Code concept in this State, and ones which, by newly introducing the possibility of a seller obtaining "a further reasonable time to substitute a conforming tender" (subd [2]), also permit cure beyond the date set for performance. In its entirety the section reads as follows: [The court quotes U.C.C. § 2-508.]

Since we here confront circumstances in which the conforming tender came after the time of performance, we focus on subdivision (2). On its face, taking its conditions in the order in which they appear, for the statute to apply (1) a buyer must have rejected a non-conforming tender, (2) the seller must have had reasonable grounds to believe this tender would be acceptable (with or without money allowance) and (3) the seller must have "seasonably" notified the buyer of the intention to substitute a conforming tender within a reasonable time.[30]

In the present case, none of these presented a problem. The first one was easily met for it is unquestioned that, at .92%, the sulfur content of the Khamsin oil did not conform to the .5% specified in the contract and that it was rejected by Con Ed. The second, the reasonableness of the seller's belief that the original tender would be acceptable, was supported not only by unimpeached proof that the contract's .5% and the refinery certificate's .52% were trade equivalents, but by testimony that, by the time the contract was made, the plaintiff knew Con Ed burned fuel with a content of up to 1%, so that, with appropriate price adjustment, the Khamsin oil would have suited its needs even if, at delivery, it was, to the plaintiff's surprise, to test out at .92%. Further, the matter seems to have been put beyond dispute by the defendant's readiness to take the oil at the reduced market price on February 20. Surely, on such a record, the trial court cannot be faulted for having found as a fact that the second condition too had been established.

As to the third, the conforming state of the Appolonian oil is undisputed, the offer to tender it took place on February 21, only a day after Con Ed finally had rejected the Khamsin delivery and the Appolonian substitute then already was en route to the United States, where it was expected in a week and did arrive on March 4, only four days later than expected. Especially since Con Ed pleaded no prejudice (unless the drop in prices could be so regarded), it is almost impossible, given the flexibility of the Uniform Commercial Code definitions of "seasonable" and "reasonable," to quarrel with the finding that the remaining requirements of the statute also had been met.

Thus lacking the support of the statute's literal language, the defendant nonetheless would have us limit its application to cases in which a seller *knowingly* makes a nonconforming tender which it has reason to believe the buyer will accept. For this proposition, it relies almost entirely on a critique in Nordstrom, Law of Sales (§105), which rationalizes that, since a seller who believes its tender is conforming would have no reason to think in terms of a reduction in the price of the goods, to allow such a seller to cure after the time for performance had passed would make the statutory reference to a money allowance redundant.[31] Nordstrom, interestingly enough, finds it useful to buttress this position by the somewhat dire prediction, though backed by no empirical or other confirmation, that, unless the right to cure is confined to those whose nonconforming tenders are knowing ones, the incentive of sellers to timely deliver will be undermined. To this it also adds the somewhat moralistic note that a seller who is mistaken as to the quality of its goods does not merit additional time (Nordstrom, *loc cit*). Curiously, recognizing that the few decisions extant on this subject have adopted a position opposed to

---

[30] Essentially a factual matter, "seasonable" is defined in Uniform Commercial Code, § 1-204(subd [3]) as "at or within the agreed time or if no time is agreed at or within a reasonable time." At least equally factual in character, a "reasonable time" is left to depend on the "nature, purpose and circumstances" of any action which is to be taken (Uniform Commercial Code, § 1-204, subd [2]).

[31] The premise for such an argument, which ignores the policy of the Code to prevent buyers from using insubstantial remediable or price adjustable defects to free themselves from unprofitable bargains (Hawkland, Sales and Bulk Sales, 120-122), is that the words "with or without money allowance" apply only to sellers who believe their goods will be acceptable with such an allowance and not to sellers who believe their goods will be acceptable without such an allowance. But, since the words are part of a phrase which speaks of an otherwise unqualified belief that the goods will be acceptable, unless one strains for an opposite interpretation, we find insufficient reason to doubt that it intends to include both those who find a need to offer an allowance and those who do not.

the one for which it contends, Con Ed seeks to treat these as exceptions rather than exemplars of the rule (*e.g., Wilson v. Scampoli*, 228 A2d 848 [goods obtained by seller from their manufacturer in original carton resold unopened to purchaser; seller held within statute though it had no reason to believe the goods defective]; *Appleton State Bank v. Lee*, 33 Wis 2d 690 [seller mistakenly delivered sewing machine of wrong brand but otherwise identical to one sold; held that seller, though it did not know of its mistake, had a right to cure by substitution]).[32]

That the principle for which these cases stand goes far beyond their particular facts cannot be gainsaid. These holdings demonstrate that, in dealing with the application of § 2-508 (subd [2]), courts have been concerned with the reasonableness of the seller's belief that the goods would be acceptable rather than with the seller's pre-tender knowledge or lack of knowledge of the defect (*Wilson v. Scampoli, supra;* compare *Zabriskie Chevrolet, Inc. v. Smith*, 99 NJ Super 441).

It also is no surprise then that the aforementioned decisional history is a reflection of the mainstream of scholarly commentary on the subject (*e.g.,* 1955 Report of NY Law Rev Comm, p 484; White and Summers, Uniform Commercial Code [2d ed], § 8-4, p 322; . . .

White and Summers, for instance, put it well, and bluntly. Stressing that the Code intended cure to be "a remedy which should be carefully cultivated and developed by the courts" because it "offers the possibility of conforming the law to reasonable expectations and of thwarting the chiseler who seeks to escape from a bad bargain" (*supra,* at 322, 324), the authors conclude, as do we, that a seller should have recourse to the relief afforded by Uniform Commercial Code, § 2-508(subd [2]) as long as it can establish that it had reasonable grounds, tested objectively, for its belief that the goods would be accepted (*ibid.,* at 321). It goes without saying that the test of reasonableness, in this context, must encompass the concepts of "good faith" and "commercial standards of fair dealing" which permeate the Code (Uniform Commercial Code, §§1-201, subd [19]; 1-203; 2-103, subd [l], par[b]).[33]

III

As to the damages issue raised by the defendant, we affirm without reaching the merits. . . .

For all these reasons, the order of the Appellate Division should be affirmed, with costs.

---

[32] The only New York case to deal with this section involved a seller who knowingly tendered a "newer and improved version of the model than was actually ordered" on the contract delivery date. The court held he had reasonable grounds to believe the buyer would accept the newer model (*Bartus v. Riccardi*, 55 Misc 2d 3).

[33] Except indirectly, on this appeal we do not deal with the equally important protections the Code affords buyers. It is as to buyers as well as sellers that the Code, to the extent that it displaces traditional principles of law and equity (U.C.C. § 1-103), seeks to discourage unfair or hypertechnical business conduct bespeaking a dog-eat-dog rather than a live-and-let-live approach to the marketplace (*e.g.,* U.C.C. §§ 2-314, 2-315, 2-513, 2-601, 2-608). Overall, the aim is to encourage parties to amicably resolve their own problems (*Ramirez v. Autosport*, 88 NJ 277, 285; compare Restatement, Contracts, 2d, Introductory Note to Chapter 10, p 194 [". . . the wisest course is ordinarily for the parties to attempt to resolve their differences by negotiations, including clarification of expectations [and] cure of past defaults . . ."]). See also U.C.C. § 2-605 Comment 2—Ed.]

PROBLEM 6.8

On September 5, Gappelberg (B) purchased a large screen Advent television set from The Video Station owned by Landrum (S). B paid $2,231.25 in cash and was allowed a $1,500 credit on the trade-in of his old set. B immediately experienced numerous and different problems with the new set. S and Alpha Omega, the authorized repair agency, made several house calls in an effort to repair the set. On September 26, the set totally ceased operating. B allowed the television set to be removed from his home, but refused offers to make further repairs on the set, saying he simply wanted his money and his old set returned to him. S felt he was in no position to return the old set, as he had promised it as a prize for a promotional sweepstakes, and offered B another Advent as replacement. B refused to accept the substitute and brought suit against S for return of his consideration.

The trial court held that B had duly revoked acceptance under U.C.C. § 2-608: (1) B accepted the TV without knowledge of the defects (which were discovered later); (2) B revoked acceptance within a reasonable time after the defects were discovered and before any change in the condition of the set occurred not caused by such defects; (3) B timely notified S of the revocation; (4) the set's faulty convergence (thereby causing color shadowing around the screen's images), the constant projection of a red dot on one corner of the screen when the set was in operation, and the complete power failure of the set, were each defects which substantially impaired the set. Nevertheless, the trial court concluded that revocation of acceptance was subject to S's right to cure under U.C.C. § 2-508. Consequently, the court denied relief to B because B prevented S from curing the nonconforming goods by B's refusal to accept a replacement Advent set.

On appeal what is S's argument that it has the right to cure after revocation of acceptance? See U.C.C. § 2-608(3). As B's counsel, what is your argument that S does *not* have the right to cure after B has revoked acceptance. Could you distinguish between cure by *repair* and cure by *replacement*? See *Gappelberg v. Landrum*, 654 S.W.2d 549 (Tex. App. 1983), 666 S.W.2d 88 (Tex. 1984).

NOTES

(1) Proposed U.C.C. § 2-508 expands the seller's right to cure to include cases where acceptance is rightfully revoked. Cure will not be available if acceptance was revoked because the seller had failed seasonably to cure a nonconformity that the buyer assumed would be cured. Proposed § 2-607(c) modifies § 2-608(3) by stating that a buyer who justifiably revokes acceptance has the same rights and duties, with regard to the goods involved under §§ 2-603 and 2-604, as if they had been rejected. Would these proposed sections change the analysis or result of Problem 6.8?

(2) With respect to cure, *Zabriskie Chevrolet, Inc. v. Smith*, 5 U.C.C. Rep. 30 at 42 (1968), cited at § 6.04[C] Notes and Questions (1), states:

The "cure" intended under . . .the Code does not, in the court's opinion, contemplate the tender of a new vehicle with a substituted transmission, not from the factory and of unknown lineage from another vehicle in plaintiff's possession. It was not the intention of the Legislature that the right to "cure" is a limitless one to be controlled only by the will of the seller. A "cure" which endeavors by substitution to tender a chattel not within the agreement or contemplation of the parties is invalid.

(3) See *Olmstead v. General Motors Corp., Inc.,* 500 A.2d 615, 619 (Del. Super. 1985):

Though neither the Federal nor State laws specify how many failed attempts at repair are necessary before a buyer is justified in revoking acceptance, it would appear from caselaw that at a minimum there must be more than one or two attempts, or there must be an outright refusal to repair.

See also Travalio, *The U.C.C.'s Three "R's": Rejection, Revocation and (The Seller's) Right to Cure,* 53 Cin. L. Rev. 931 (1984) (strong policy reasons support seller's right to cure following revocation of acceptance).

(4) *Federal Magnuson-Moss Warranty Act.* With respect to "full" warranties under the Act, see 15 U.S.C. § 2304(a)(1) and (4).

(5) *State Automobile/Consumer Goods "Lemon Laws."* Illustrative of such a law is the Missouri statute at V.A.M.S. § 407.560 *et seq.*

§ 6.06 Preserving Evidence of Goods in Dispute

Read: U.C.C. § 2-515.

NOTE

The purpose of U.C.C. § 2-515 is "[t]o meet certain serious problems which arise when there is a dispute as to the quality of goods and thereby perhaps to aid the parties in reaching a settlement . . ."; "to afford either party an opportunity for preserving evidence . . . and thereby to reduce the uncertainty in any litigation, and in turn perhaps, to promote agreement." U.C.C. § 2-515 Comments 1 and 2. When litigation has been commenced, the applicable rules of procedure govern discovery, including inspections. *See Fenway Cambridge Motor Hotel, Inc. v. American Contract Designers, Inc. v. Milliken & Co.,* 39 U.C.C. Rep. 1263 (D. Mass. 1984).

§ 6.07 Excuse of Performance

Read: U.C.C. §§ 2-613 (see U.C.C. § 2-509), 2-614, 2-615, 2-616; see U.C.C. § 2-311(3)(a).
Read also: U.C.C. §§ 2A-221, 2A-404, 2A-405, 2A-406; CISG Arts. 79, 80, see Art. 27.

The Code contains three sections which state general principles relieving the seller from full performance of his contractual obligations.[34] They can be rationalized within the law of contracts in several ways. They can be explained under language of excuse, impossibility, impracticability, or even implied promise or condition. The most accurate way, however, to explain these sections is to consider the risks which the parties shifted by their agreement.[35]

Section 2-615, Excuse by Failure of Presupposed Conditions, states in subsection (a) that delay in delivery or non-delivery is not a breach of seller's duty under a contract for sale "if performance as agreed has been made impracticable by the occurrence of a contingency the non-occurrence

---

[34] U.C.C. §§ 2-613, 2-614, 2-615.

[35] R. Nordstrom, Handbook of the Law of Sales § 107 at 324 (1970).

of which was a basic assumption on which the contract was made." The issue of "commercial impracticability" as a basis for excusing performance can arise in many situations including those (1) where costs to seller have increased and (2) where there is a crop failure. *See* U.C.C. § 2-615 Comments 3 and 4.

Increased cost. In *Publicker Industries, Inc. v. Union Carbide Corp.*, 17 U.C.C. Rep. 989 (E.D. Pa. 1975), the defendant Union Carbide had contracted in 1972 to sell ethanol in specified quantities over a three year period to the plaintiff. The price was set by a formula, adjusted annually to reflect the seller's cost for raw materials, and subject to a ceiling on adjustment increases. The raw materials were derivatives of natural gas; their price soared beginning in 1973. The seller's costs for ethanol rose from 21.2 cents a gallon in 1973 to 37.2 cents per gallon in mid-1974. The ceiling contract sales price was then 26.5 cents per gallon. The seller's loss of 10.7 cents per gallon led to a projected aggregate loss of $5.8 million. The court refused to relieve the seller. It found that the ceiling provision constituted an intentional allocation of the "risk of a substantial and unforeseen rise in cost" to the seller. It based this finding in part on the twenty-five percent rise in prices by OPEC in 1971 which made future cost increases highly foreseeable.

Other commonly cited cases, where seller's performance was not excused, include: *Eastern Air Lines, Inc. v. Gulf Oil Corp.*, 415 F. Supp. 429 (S.D. Fla. 1975) (increase of price of jet fuel); *Iowa Elec. Light & Power Co. v. Atlas Corp.*, 467 F. Supp. 129 (N.D. Iowa 1978), *rev'd. on other grounds*, 603 F.2d 1301 (8th Cir. 1979) *cert. denied*, 445 U.S. 911 (1980) (increase of price of uranium); *Maple Farms, Inc. v. City School Dist.*, 352 N.Y.S.2d 784 (1974) (radical increase in milk costs); *Transatlantic Financing Corp. v. United States*, 363 F.2d 312 (D.C. Cir. 1966) (increased costs to carrier shipping goods via Cape of Good Hope upon closing of Suez Canal).

A particularly noteworthy case is *Aluminum Company of America v. Essex Group, Inc.*, 499 F. Supp. 53, 29 U.C.C. Rep. 1 (W.D. Pa. 1980). Here, ALCOA and Essex were parties to a long term toll conversion *service contract* where Essex would supply ALCOA with alumina which ALCOA would convert into molten aluminum that would be picked up by Essex for further processing. The price provisions of the contract contained an escalation formula which indicated that: (1) $.03 per pound of the original price escalated in accordance with changes in the Wholesale Price Index — Industrial Commodities (WPI) and (2) $.03 per pound escalated in accordance with an index based on the average hourly labor rates paid to ALCOA employees at a designated plant. The price term also included a cap. Assisting in the preparation of this formula was economist Alan Greenspan. The WPI did not take into account subsequent material increases in energy costs and the contract became unprofitable to ALCOA who stood to lose $75 million over the life of the contract. ALCOA sought relief on the basis of commercial impracticability because the non-occurrence of an extreme deviation of the WPI was a basic assumption on which the contract was made. *See* Restatement, Second, Contracts §§ 261, 265, 266. The court did not excuse ALCOA's performance, rather, it reformed the contract and fashioned its alternative price schedule. For a critique, see Dawson, *Judicial Revision of Frustrated Contracts: The United States,* 64 B.U.L. Rev. 1 (1984); *cf.* Speidel, *Court-Imposed Price Adjustments Under Long-Term Supply Contracts,* 76 Nw.U.L. Rev. 369 (1981).

Crop failure. Study Comments 4, 5 and 9 to U.C.C. § 2-615 and the following case.

ALIMENTA (U.S.A.), INC. v. CARGILL INCORPORATED

United States Court of Appeals
861 F.2d 650, 7 U.C.C. Rep.2d 1100 (11th Cir. 1988)

NESBITT, DISTRICT JUDGE:

In July 1980, Alimenta (U.S.A.), Inc. ("Alimenta") entered into seven contracts with Cargill, Incorporated ("Cargill") under which Cargill promised to deliver to Alimenta shelled, edible peanuts. The peanut crops were still in the field at the time the contracts were entered into. Later that summer there was a drought, the severity of which is disputed, which reduced the peanut crop yield.

Due to the decrease in the crop yield, Cargill notified Alimenta that it would proceed under U.C.C. § 2-615,[36] that is, Cargill would allocate deliveries of the 1980 peanut crop among its customers, distributors of peanuts with whom they had contracted. Alimenta was advised that it would receive approximately 65% of the peanuts for which they had contracted. Alimenta accepted their allocated share of the peanuts, but later filed suit for breach of contract against Cargill alleging that Cargill acted in bad faith in opting to proceed under Section 2-615. At trial the jury rendered a verdict for Defendant Cargill.

I.

At the inception of the trial, the trial court granted Cargill's motion *in limine* thus barring Alimenta from referring to Cargill's size in any respect.[37] Alimenta urges the exclusion of this evidence was error entitling Alimenta to a new trial because the excluded evidence of Cargill's size and financial resources was relevant to the issue of commercial impracticability. This Court has previously stated that the standard by which impracticability should be judged is an objective one, *Alimenta (U.S.A.), Inc. v. Gibbs Nathaniel (Canada) Ltd.,* 802 F.2d 1362 (11th Cir. 1986). Commercial impracticability under Section 2-615 focuses upon the "the reasonableness of the expenditure at issue, not upon the ability of a party to pay the commercially unreasonable expense." *Asphalt International, Inc. v. Enterprise Shipping Corp.,* 667 F.2d 261 (2nd Cir. 1981); *Transatlantic Financing Corp. v. United States,* 363 F.2d 312, 319 n. 13 (D.C. Cir. 1966) ("the issue of impracticability should no doubt be 'an objective determination of whether the promise can reasonably be performed rather than a subjective inquiry into the promisor's capability of performing as agreed.' "). Under this objective standard, the focus of the impracticability analysis is upon the nature of the agreement and the expectations of the parties, not to the size and financial ability of the parties. The fact that Cargill has grain elevators in Minnesota and barges on the Mississippi is irrelevant to the contract at issue and the expectations of the parties with respect to that contract. Cargill's net sales or net worth has no bearing upon the reasonableness of Cargill's decision to allocate production of peanuts. Accordingly, the trial court was correct in excluding evidence as to Cargill's size inasmuch as such evidence was not relevant to the issue of impracticability.

---

[36] Section 2-615 of the Uniform Commercial Code provides as follows: [Read § 2-615.]

[37] Cargill is a large agriprocessing and trading company based in Minneapolis, Minnesota. Cargill had between 30 and 40 billion dollars in sales in 1980.

This objective standard applies to both parties. A dealer opting under U.C.C. § 2-615 may not represent itself to the jury as a small company beset by circumstances with which it does not have the financial resources to contend. Just as Alimenta was barred from portraying Cargill as a large company who could have financially met its obligations, Cargill could not portray itself as a small company. The statements made by Cargill addressed the contracts at issue and the expected profits at the time of contracting and not, as Alimenta contends, the size of the Cargill peanut business. Thus Cargill did not improperly mislead the jury as to the issue they were to resolve: whether or not their performance was made impracticable by the crop failure.[38] *issue*

II.

The District Court held that under Georgia law, in order to preclude reliance on the allocation remedy of O.C.G.A. § 11-2-615, the seller need expressly assume a greater obligation in the contract. This Court had previously dealt with this issue in *Alimenta (U.S.A.), Inc. v. Gibbs Nathaniel (Canada) Ltd.*, 802 F.2d 1362 (11th Cir. 1986):

> In this diversity action we are bound by the Georgia Supreme Court's interpretation of this statute:

> We therefore construe Code Ann. Sec. 109A-2-615 to mean that in order for there to be an expectation to and an exemption from the rule of allocation applicable to a contract of sale, such a contract must contain an affirmation provision that the seller will perform the contract even though the contingencies which permit an allocation might occur.

Mansfield Propane Gas Co., Inc. v. Folger Gas Company 231 Ga. 868, 870, 204 S.E.2d 625, 628 (1974).

> Since neither of the contracts contained such an affirmative provision, Gibbs was entitled to allocate if it could satisfy the jury by a preponderance of the evidence that the occurrence of the contingency (drought) was not reasonably foreseeable when the contracts were entered into and that performance as agreed was made impractical thereby. Obviously, its burden entailed the production of persuasive factual evidence.

Gibbs, 802 F.2d at 1363-64. As required under *Erie R.R. Co. v. Tompkins*, 304 U.S. 64, 58 S.Ct. 817, 82 L.Ed. 1188 (1938), the trial court sitting in diversity applied the law of Georgia. Inasmuch as this court is bound by the law of Georgia and prior opinions of this court, plaintiff's lengthy arguments citing authority and rationale of other jurisdictions are without effect.

III.

Alimenta raises three separate errors relating to the trial court's failure to make factual findings as a matter of law, apparently contending that the court should have directed a verdict in their favor. In reviewing the district court's decision to deny a motion for directed verdict, the evidence must be viewed in a light most favorable to the prevailing party. *Prudential Insurance Company of America v. Schreffler*, 376 F.2d 397, 399 (5th Cir. 1967). This court cannot delve into any conflicts of the evidence, but must assume that all such conflicts have been resolved by the jury in favor of the prevailing party. *Id.; Russell v. Baccus*, 707 F.2d 1289, 1292 (11th Cir. 1983).

---

[38] Cargill has expected $3,000,000.00 in profits. Projected loses after the drought reduced the crop yield amounted to $47,000,000.00.

A. Foreseeability of the Peanut Crop Failure

Alimenta first argues that the issue of foreseeability of crop failure should not have gone to the jury. We find that there was sufficient evidence to submit this case to the jury. First, the evidence demonstrated that for the twenty years preceding the 1980 crop there had been a surplusage of domestic peanuts. Secondly, there was evidence that pre-harvest forward sales contracts are customary in the peanut industry. This contracting practice reflects the need to sufficiently schedule production to comport with the capacity of peanut shelling plants. In this manner, such contracts enable production capacity to be pre-committed and deliveries of the plant's output can be scheduled throughout the harvest season. The shelling plant can run more economically; the peanuts are shipped rather than stored; and the plant generated a steady cash flow from sales. Thirdly, improved agronomic and irrigation methods contributed to the industry's expectations of a continued surplusage of peanuts. There was evidence that the shortage of peanuts in 1980 was unprecedented and unforeseen by many if not all experts. The unforeseeability was also demonstrated by the effect of the drought on the peanut market prices: price of peanuts increase often exceeded one dollar per pound. In view of the evidence introduced during trial, it was proper for the trial court to submit the issue of the foreseeability of the crop failure to the jury for its determination.

B. Fairness of Peanut Allocation under § 2-615

Alimenta contends the trial court erred by refusing to rule as a matter of law that Cargill's allocation to its distributors of the available peanuts was both unfair and unreasonable. O.C.G.A. § 11-2-615 provides that the seller may allocate in any manner which is fair and reasonable. Upon a review of the record it appears that there was sufficient evidence to submit this issue to the jury. *See Cosden Oil & Chemical Co. v. Carl O. Helm Aktiengesellschaft*, 736 F.2d 1064 (5th Cir. 1984).

C. Seasonable Notice

Thirdly, Alimenta claims that the trail court erred by refusing to rule as a matter of law that Cargill failed to give reasonable notice of its intention to allocate the peanuts under O.C.G.A. § 11-2-615. Section 11-2-615(c) provides that "the seller must notify the buyer seasonably that there will be delay or non-delivery and, when allocation is required under paragraph (b) of this Code section, of the estimated quota thus made available for the buyer." O.C.G.A. § 11-2-615(c). Action is taken seasonably when it is taken within a reasonable time period, O.C.G.A. § 11-1-204(3), and the reasonable time for taking any action depends upon the nature, purpose and circumstances of such action, O.C.G.A. § 11-1-204(2). From a review of the record in this case there was sufficient evidence to submit the issue of seasonable notice to the jury for determination.

IV.

Alimenta charges as error the trial court's refusal to give its instruction on the definition of good faith. In addition to the definition of good faith stated in the commercial code, Alimenta requested the following:

This obligation applies in determining whether Cargill acted in good faith in its dealings with customers prior to the time Cargill notified Alimenta of its intention to allocate, whether Cargill acted in good faith in making its decision to allocate, whether Cargill acted in good faith in deciding to discontinue all efforts to acquire peanuts as of November 12, 1980, and whether Cargill acted in good faith in dividing up peanuts among its customers.

In evaluating the instructions given to the jury, we consider the charges given as a whole. *Lacaze v. Olendorff*, 526 F.2d 1213, 1220, *reh'g en banc granted*, 526 F.2d 1223 (5th Cir. 1976). The instructions given are reviewed in light of the evidence given, the pleadings in the cause and the arguments presented to counsel. *See First Virginia Bankshares v. Benson*, 559 F.2d 1307, 1316 (5th Cir. 1977). To determine whether the trial court was in error in refusing to give Alimenta's particular instruction, we look to whether the jury was misled by the instructions given and whether the jury understood the issues. *See id.* We find that the requested charge by Alimenta was mere surplusage, redundant to the charges given by the court on O.C.G.A. §§ 11-2-615 and 11-2-616. The jury was instructed that Cargill had to prove that they had allocated in a fair and reasonable manner, that the law requires good faith on the part of Cargill, and that Cargill could allocate only if the crop failure was not reasonably foreseeable by commercial standards. While a general instruction as to the definition of good faith, *i.e.,* honesty in fact, O.C.G.A. § 11-2-203 [§ 1-203—Ed.], may have been helpful to the jury, the failure to give such a charge, viewing the instructions as a whole, was not error.

For these reasons, the rulings of the District Court are hereby *affirmed.*

———

Suppose in *Alimenta* buyer either wants all the peanuts ordered or no peanuts; it does not want an allocation. What, if anything, can buyer do? *See* U.C.C. § 2-616.

———

NOTES

(1) *Excuse of Buyer's Performance. In International Minerals & Chemical Corp. v. Llano, Inc.*, 770 F.2d 879, 41 U.C.C. Rep. 347 (10th Cir. 1985), IMC (buyer) (owner of a potash mine and processing facility) was obligated to buy natural gas from Llano (seller) under a "take or pay" requirements contract. Subsequently, the New Mexico Environmental Improvement Board (EIB) promulgated Regulation 508 which limited emissions from potash processing equipment. There was no technically suitable way for buyer to comply with EIB's Regulation 508 without shutting down the gas-powered boilers with the concomitant decrease in natural gas consumption. Held: Performance by buyer was excused when made impracticable by having to comply with a supervening governmental regulation. See U.C.C. § 2-615 and Comments 9 and 10. *Cf.* CISG Art. 79.

As to impracticability of performance under a fixed price contract to purchase pinto beans where there was a radical drop in market price, see *Lawrence v. Elmore Bean Warehouse, Inc.*, 702 P.2d 930, 41 U.C.C. Rep. 358 (Idaho App. 1985).

(2) *Substituted Performance. In Jon-T Chemicals, Inc. v. Freeport Chemical Co.*, 704 F.2d 1412, 36 U.C.C. Rep. 154 (5th Cir. 1983), John-T (buyer) agreed to buy several thousand short tons of phosphoric acid from Freeport (seller). When the Chicago area (buyer's location) was crippled by severe snowstorms, the railroad embargoed shipments from seller into Chicago. Under the *force majeure* clause seller's performance was excused by "adverse weather condition . . .or any contingency or delay or failure or cause beyond the reasonable control of Seller." 36 U.C.C. Rep. at 157; see U.C.C. § 2-615. As to substituted performance the court said:

> The sales agreement between Jon-T and Freeport expressly provided that delivery of the phosphoric acid was to be made by *rail unless otherwise agreed.* On its face, this language expresses the intention of the parties who negotiated and entered into the contract that delivery was to be by rail unless both parties *mutually* agreed to make delivery by another carrier. It was thus not error for the district court to decline to instruct the jury that Freeport should have considered delivery by truck when delivery by rail became impossible.

> Despite the provisions of the contract terms, Jon-T argues that since the parties did not contract to make delivery by *rail only* then Texas Business and Commerce Code, § 2.614 imposes a duty upon the seller to tender delivery by a commercially reasonable substitute. This contention might have merit were there no contract between the parties relating to the manner of delivery and the absence of such an agreement created a vacuum or an apparent ambiguity; however, the parties' agreement to deliver the acid by rail *unless otherwise agreed* does not create a gap for the relevant provisions of the Code to fill.

> . . . .

To summarize, we hold that (i) Freeport was not required to seek an alternative method of delivery under the contract, (ii) the force majeure clause in the contract excused Freeport's obligation to deliver the balance of the acid under the contract. . . .

36 U.C.C. Rep. at 158,59,61.

(3) *Casualty to Identified Goods.* In *Emery v. Weed, 494 A.2d 438, 41 U.C.C. Rep. 115 (Pa. Super. 1985),* buyer signed an agreement on June 7 to purchase from seller for $25,000 a Chevrolet "Pacer Corvette," serial number 1Z87L85901303, and paid $10,000 toward the purchase price. On June 27, July 12, August 10 and September 28, he made additional payments totaling $2,229.90. On or about November 5 the Pacer Corvette was stolen from seller's premises. On November 15 buyer died. Father, as his son's administrator, sought to cancel his son's agreement for the purchase of the Pacer and demanded a refund of the $12,229.90 paid toward its purchase. The court affirmed for buyer's father and stated that all the requirements of U.C.C. § 2-613 were satisfied: (1) the Pacer Corvette "suffer[ed] casualty without fault of either party" prior to delivery to the buyer, (2) the casualty was "total" and occurred "before the risk of loss [had] pass[ed] to the buyer" [U.C.C. § 2-509(3)], (3) "the contract requir[ed] for its performance goods identified [see U.C.C. § 2-501] when the contract [was] made." As to the requirement of identification the court observed:

> Quite apart from its identification in the agreement by serial number, the Pacer was identified by being removed from the display showroom, after the agreement was signed, and being covered and locked. From this it may be inferred that there was "a meeting of the minds as to the particular or actual goods designated."

41 U.C.C. Rep. at 121.

CHAPTER 7

REMEDIES

§ 7.01 Remedies Generally

Read: U.C.C. § 1-106.

Read also: CISG Art. 74.

Make Aggrieved Party Whole. In examining Article 2 remedies set forth in this Chapter, consider whether the Code drafters have achieved "the end that the aggrieved party may be put in as good a position as if the other party had fully performed." U.C.C. § 1-106(1). Further, observe that Article 2 "rejects any doctrine of election of remedy as a fundamental policy and thus the remedies are essentially cumulative in nature and include all of the available remedies for breach." U.C.C. § 2-703 Comment 1; cf. §§ 2A-508 Comment 2, 2A-523 Comment 1. For example, in *Tinker v. De Maria Porsche Audi, Inc.*, 459 So. 2d 487, 37 U.C.C. Rep. 1519 at 1528 note 8 (Fla. App. 1984), it was noted:

> Although not made an issue in this case we note that Section 672.721 [U.C.C. § 2-721, discussed at § 7.07[C], *infra*], Florida Statutes (1981), the Florida version of the Uniform Commercial Code, provides that in an action based on material misrepresentation or fraud, neither rescission of the contract nor rejection or return of the goods bars or is deemed inconsistent with a claim for damages or other remedies. The comment to the Uniform Commercial Code following this section states that an action for rescission does not bar other remedies (such as damages) unless the circumstances make the remedies incompatible. This provision is a change from pre-Code Florida law which required a defrauded buyer to make a choice between the remedies of rescission and damages.
>
> Maintaining a suit in equity to obtain rescission of a sales agreement induced by fraud does not necessarily preclude plaintiff from later suing for damages or other relief inconsistent with rescission if rescission is inadequate, unavailable or useless. . . .

Waiver of Remedies. "Any claim or right arising out of an alleged breach can be discharged. . .without consideration by a written waiver or renunciation signed and delivered by the aggrieved party." U.C.C. § 1-107; see §§ 1-207, 2-720.

§ 7.02 Seller's Remedies for Breach by Buyer

Read: U.C.C. §§ 2-703, 2-709(1)(a).

Read also: U.C.C. §§ 2A-523, 2A-532; CISG Art. 61.

Buyer breaches its obligations under the sales contract when it: (1) wrongfully rejects goods, (2) wrongfully revokes acceptance of goods, (3) fails to make a payment due on or before delivery, or (4) repudiates. Seller's remedies in such instances are indexed in U.C.C. § 2-703. Where buyer accepts and retains the goods, but fails to make payment due after delivery, see U.C.C. § 2-709(1)(a). With regard to rejection, acceptance and revocation of acceptance, see U.C.C. §§ 2-601 through 2-608. These matters are discussed above at § 6.04, Buyer's Rights on Improper Delivery.

[A] Cancellation

Read: U.C.C. §§ 2-703(f), 2-106(3) and (4); cf. § 2-711(1).

Read also: U.C.C. §§ 2A-523(1)(a), 2A-103(1)(b) and (z), cf. § 2A-508(1)(a); CISG Arts. 64, 25-27, 81-84, cf. 49.

A case which draws a distinction between "termination and cancellation" is *Camfield Tires, Inc. v. Michelin Tire Corp.*, 719 F.2d 1361(8th Cir. 1983). There, tire manufacturer (Michelin) had a dealership contract with plaintiff dealer (Camfield). The court said:

> Camfield, the district court found from the record, was chronically in debt to Michelin and "substantially in breach of the dealership agreement as early as January of 1980." When Michelin canceled in April of 1980, the account remained unpaid, more than half of it over 180 days.
>
> Camfield argues that . . . its agreement with Michelin did not allow Michelin to terminate the contract until after the first anniversary date of the contract and upon 120 days written notice. Camfield further argues that under U.C.C. § 1-102(3) which permits parties to vary by agreement provisions of the U.C.C., the contract's termination provision supersedes Michelin's power to cancel under Section 2-703. We disagree. The U.C.C. explicitly draws a distinction between "termination" and "cancellation."
>
> "Termination" occurs when either party pursuant to a power created by agreement or law puts an end to the contract *otherwise than for its breach.* . . . "Cancellation" occurs when either party puts an end to the contract for breach by the other and its effect is the same as that of "termination" except that the canceling party also retains any remedy for breach of the whole contract or any unperformed balance.
>
> N.Y.U.C.C. § 2-106 (McKinney 1964) (emphasis supplied). Thus, the contract's limitation applies only to the "termination" remedy, not to a party's right to cancel for breach by the other party.

[B] Take Action as to the Goods

[1] Withhold or Stop Delivery

Read: U.C.C. §§ 2-703(a) and (b), 2-705.

Read also: U.C.C. §§ 2A-523(1)(c) and (d), 2A-525(1), 2A-526; CISG Arts. 58(2), 64, 71, 72.

BUTTS v. GLENDALE PLYWOOD CO.

United States Court of Appeals
710 F2d 504, 36 U.C.C. Rep. 545 (9th Cir. 1983)

NORRIS, CIRCUIT JUDGE.

The question presented by this appeal is whether Glendale Plywood Co. (Glendale) had the right to stop a shipment of plywood to Summit Creek Plywood Company (Summit Creek) after Summit Creek resold the plywood to a third party and ordered its destination changed. The district court held that, under § 2-705 of the Uniform Commercial Code, the redirection of a shipment at the order of a buyer, without the seller's knowledge, constitutes a reshipment that cuts off the seller's right to stop the goods in transit. We affirm.

I

Summit Creek ordered two railroad carloads of lumber from Glendale Plywood in March, 1978. On April 15, Glendale was instructed to ship the cars to "Summit Creek Forest Products, Murray, Utah." On April 17, Glendale shipped the cars. The railroad issued a [straight (nonnegotiable)] bill of lading showing Glendale as the shipper, Summit Creek as the consignee, and Summit Creek at Murray, Utah as the destination. On April 19, while the goods were in transit, Summit Creek sold its interest in the lumber to Davidson Lumber Sales (Davidson). At the request of Summit Creek, the railroad changed the waybills to show Summit Creek as the shipper, Davidson as the consignee, and Davidson at Murray, Utah as the destination. Summit Creek then sold this account receivable from Davidson, and others, to Walter E. Heller Western, a factoring agent.

The railroad, following Summit Creek's instructions, sent the cars on their way to Davidson at Murray. On April 28, having learned that Summit Creek might be insolvent and before the cars had reached Murray, Glendale ordered the railroad to stop both cars. The railroad complied with Glendale's orders and Glendale then sold the lumber directly to Davidson. The lumber was delivered to Davidson at Murray on May 3.

On May 3, Summit Creek was adjudicated a bankrupt. Thereafter, Summit Creek's trustee in bankruptcy sued Glendale, claiming it had no right to stop the shipment. The bankruptcy court held for Glendale. The district court reversed, holding that Glendale was not allowed to stop the shipment and that Summit Creek, not Glendale was entitled to payment from Davidson. Glendale appeals. The only issue on appeal is whether, under § 2-705 of the Uniform Commercial Code, Glendale had the right to stop the shipment while it was in transit.

II

Section 2-705 of the Uniform Commercial Code provides that: [the Court quotes § 2-705(1), (2)(a)-(c)] . . . The dispute in this case is whether the railroad's redirection of the cars from Summit Creek to Davidson at Summit Creek's request constituted a reshipment which cut off Glendale's right to stop delivery under § 2-705(2)(c). The legal question we must thus decide is whether a re-routing of a shipment from a purchaser to a subpurchaser (a buyer from the original purchaser) upon the instructions of the purchaser and without the knowledge of the seller should constitute a reshipment under § 2-705(2)(c). We hold that it should.

The purpose of § 2-705(2)(c) is to protect transactions between original buyers and subpurchasers. See *Interlake, Inc. v. Kansas Power & Light Co.*, 79 Ill App 3d 679, 685-86, 34 Ill Dec 954, 959, 398 NE2d 945, 950, 28 U.C.C. Rep 689, 695-96 (1979). Section (2)(c) protects a subpurchaser from being affected by disputes between the buyer and the seller by ensuring that the goods he orders are delivered regardless of the financial condition of his seller (the original buyer). Whether the original seller has knowledge of the transaction between his buyer and the sub-purchaser has no effect on the subpurchaser's need for protection. To read into § 2-705 a requirement of seller knowledge or permission for reshipment would endanger subpurchasers and discourage resale transactions of the sort conducted here.[1]

Moreover, defining reshipment as the point at which the seller's right to stop shipment ceases provides a time at which the rights of all parties are fixed. Disputes between sellers, buyers, and subpurchasers as to whether permission was ever granted or what the seller intended in his grant of permission, which would result if the seller's permission was required to reship, are avoided.

We find unpersuasive Glendale's argument that the rule we adopt today will cause sellers to demand payment before shipment in order to ensure that they will be paid. While it is true that our interpretation of § 2-705 gives the buyer the power, by reshipping, to cut off the seller's right to stop shipment, the seller's right to stop transit is cut off once the goods are received by the buyer in any event. In most instances the seller has not been paid at this point and still runs the risk of being unable to collect. Yet sellers have not, as a response, shipped only on a C.O.D. basis. There is no reason to believe that they will begin demanding prepayment under our interpretation of § 2-705(2)(c).[2]

The interpretation of § 2-705 adopted by the district court is consistent with the goals of predictability in commercial transactions and providing protection for buyers and sellers alike. The judgment is thus affirmed.

PROBLEM 7.1

In *Butts* what if the railroad had issued a negotiable bill of lading wherein the plywood was "Consigned to ORDER of Summit Creek Plywood Company" and Glendale retained possession of the bill. How would this affect the analysis and outcome of the case? *See* U.C.C. §§ 2-705, 7-104, 7-303.

---

[1] Glendale argues that, while § 2-705 is designed to protect subpurchasers, the subpurchaser here needed no protection because he was able to buy the goods directly from the seller when shipment was stopped. It is true that the subpurchaser in this case was able to mitigate his damages by buying from the seller (though we do not know at what price). However, that may not be the situation in other cases, for example when the subpurchaser has already paid his seller (the buyer). To allow the seller to stop transit after the buyer has made a bargain with a subpurchaser forces the shipment to the subpurchaser to be delayed and the subpurchaser to renegotiate his deal, possibly at a higher price, through no fault of his own. Moreover, an interpretation of § 2-705 that would allow a seller in a rising market to stop transit of the goods and resell them to the subpurchaser at a higher price would allow the seller, merely by claiming a fear of buyer insolvency, to deprive the buyer of the benefit of an advantageous bargain with the subpurchaser. Such a result would be both inequitable and inconsistent with the goals of protection of the contractual rights of all the parties.

[2] Glendale also contends that it is inequitable to establish a rule under which a buyer, without the seller's knowledge, can cut off the seller's right to stop shipment by merely shipping the goods to a third party. While it is true that a buyer can cut off the seller's right to collect by reshipment, to do so he has to sell the goods to someone else and give up the right to receive and use them. If he only has them shipped to himself at another location, his action would be a mere diversion which would not rise to the status of a reshipment, U.C.C. § 2-705 Official Comment 3, and would not cut off the seller's rights.

[2] Identify Goods to the Contract or Salvage Unfinished Goods

Read: U.C.C. §§ 2-703(c), 2-704.

Read also: U.C.C. §§ 2A-523(1)(b), 2A-524; CISG Art. 77.

MODERN MACHINERY v. FLATHEAD COUNTY

Montana Supreme Court
656 P2d 206, 36 U.C.C. Rep. 395 (1982)

HARRISON, JUSTICE.

Plaintiff brought this action for breach of contract in the Eleventh Judicial District in Flathead County. A jury trial commenced in Kalispell, Montana, on February 24, 1982. On February 26, 1982, the jury returned a verdict awarding plaintiff $10,000. Plaintiff and defendant appeal from the judgment entered upon the jury's verdict.

On or about July 30, 1979, the Flathead County commissioners issued a call for bids for the purchase of a jaw-type rock crusher to be used by the Flathead County road department. The commissioners received three bids in response to the call, one from plaintiff in the amount of $305,725 and two from another Kalispell distributor, Westmont; one for $201,193 and the other for $200,870. On August 22, 1979, the day the bids were opened, the commissioners voted to take the bids under advisement pending recommendation of the county road department. Representatives from the road department and Commissioner Frank Guay then flew to Cedar Rapids, Iowa, with plaintiff's agent, Jim Fox, to view plaintiff's crusher. Commissioner Guay and the representatives from the road department were impressed with features contained on plaintiff's crusher which were not available on Westmont's models.

On September 14, 1979, the commissioners met with members of the road department and Jim Fox to discuss the crusher bids. The road department recommended that the commissioners purchase plaintiff's crusher. Commissioner Guay then made a motion to accept the road department's recommendation. The motion was seconded by Commissioner Joan Deist. The motion was recorded in the minutes of the meeting as follows:

> Motion to Guay to accept the Road Department's recommendation to purchase gravel crusher from Modern Machinery for $305,725. The only other bid being received having been for used power plant generator contained in a second unit not attached to the crusher itself, thereby creating operational problems. Motion seconded by Joan A. Deist, motion carried. Note: Mel Wollan votes no on crusher bid as the lower bid for a jaw crusher was very adequate and a savings of $100,000.

Everyone in attendance at the meeting who testified at the trial felt that the county was going to eventually purchase plaintiff's crusher. On September 17, the following Monday, an attorney representing Westmont delivered a letter to commissioner Frank Guay which requested that the award to plaintiff be vacated or he would seek to enforce Westmont's rights in the matter by whatever means permitted by law. Guay then called Jim Fox in Missoula and told him if the crusher had been ordered from the factory, to have the order stopped.

On Wednesday, Fox and another representative for plaintiff, Larry Exe, met Guay in Helena, Montana, to discuss the crusher. Guay testified at trial that he again told Fox and Exe to stop order on the crusher if it had, in fact, been ordered. Fox and Exe testified that the meeting in Helena was mainly to discuss the political ramifications to Guay should the sale be completed. After the meeting in Helena, Exe called the factory to see how far they had progressed on the order. Exe told the factory to let him know how much expense would be incurred if plaintiff was to stop order on the crusher at that time. That was the last contact plaintiff had with the factory concerning a stop order on the crusher.

Fox, Guay and Exe then met with Assistant County Attorney, Charles Kuether, at the Flathead County commissioner's office. Again, Guay told plaintiff's representatives not to order the crusher. Guay stated that the bid award was not final until the clerk and recorder's office issued a letter accepting plaintiff's bid and rejecting all other bids. A second meeting with Kuether followed attended by Fox, Exe, Guay and plaintiff's attorney. Again, Guay stated the bid award was not final until the clerk and recorder's office issued notice of the successful bid. Plaintiff's counsel requested a letter directing plaintiff to either order or stop order on the crusher. Guay refused to draft such a letter stating that since the commissioners had not formally ordered the crusher it was not necessary to rescind an order. That was the last meeting between plaintiff and the commissioner's office.

On November 11, 1979, plaintiff tendered the crusher to Flathead County pursuant to the statement in the call for bids that delivery must be within forty-five days from date of order. The county refused to accept delivery of the machine. On November 20, 1979, the commissioners met and issued a letter to plaintiff stating they had decided to reject all bids received in response to its call for bids on the rock crusher. Plaintiff subsequently transported the crusher to Tempe, Arizona, where it was finally sold. On December 11, 1979, plaintiff filed a complaint in the District Court of the Eleventh Judicial District, in and for the County of Flathead, against Flathead County alleging breach of contract. After a jury trial commencing February 24, 1982, the jury returned a verdict in favor of plaintiff assessing damages in the amount of $10,000. Plaintiff then filed this appeal and defendant cross-appeals.

The substance of the appeals is as follows:

1. Whether there was a valid contract.

2. Whether the jury was properly instructed on the measure of damages.

3. Whether the jury verdict was supported by substantial credible evidence.

[The court held that there was a valid contract not barred by the Statute of Frauds.]

The next issue is whether the jury was properly instructed on the measure of damages. First, plaintiff argues the giving of court's instruction No. 7 was in error. The instruction states:

If you find that the Plaintiff is entitled to damages, you may award any of the following: 1) Lost net profits; 2) Incidental damages such as expenses incurred in the transportation of goods after the buyer's breach.

The measure of damages when a buyer wrongfully rejects or revokes acceptance of goods is governed by the Uniform Commercial Code. Section 30-2-703, MCA, states: "Where the buyer wrongfully rejects or revokes acceptance of goods. . .the aggrieved seller may: (d) resell and recover damages as hereinafter provided (30-2-706); (e) recover damages for nonacceptance (30-2-708). . . ." Pursuant to § 30-2-706, MCA: "the seller may recover the difference between the resale price and the contract price together with any incidental damages . . . less expenses saved in consequence of the buyer's breach." Pursuant to § 30-2-708, MCA: "the measure of damages for nonacceptance or repudiation by the buyer is the difference between the market price at the time and place for tender and the unpaid contract price together with any incidental damages . . . less expenses saved in consequence of the buyer's breach," or "If the measure of damages provided in subsection (2) is inadequate to put the seller in as good a position as performance would have done, then the measure of damages is the profit . . . which the seller would have made from full performance by the buyer together with any incidental damages . . ., due allowance for costs reasonably incurred and due credit for payments or proceeds of resale."

We find court's instruction no. 7 was not a correct statement of the law as stated by the U.C.C. The possible measures of damages under the U.C.C. are not stated in permissive language, but rather, are mandatory and specifically state the amount of recoverable damage depending upon the remedy seller has pursued. The District Court's use of the words "may award any of the following" in instruction no. 7 implied to the jury that they were not required by law to award specific damages. Thus, the giving of the District Court's instruction no. 7 was in error as being in contradiction of the U.C.C.

Plaintiff also claims the giving of the following instruction was in error:

A party who alleges that it has been damaged by the breach of contract by another party is bound to exercise reasonable care and diligence to avoid loss and to minimize its damage. A party may not recover for losses which could have been prevented by reasonable efforts on its part.

We find the giving of this instruction was in error. In this case a method of mitigating damages is addressed by § 30-2-704(2), MCA. The section states:

Where the goods are unfinished an aggrieved seller may in the exercise of reasonable commercial judgment for the purposes of avoiding loss and of effective realization either complete the manufacture and wholly identify the goods to the contract or cease manufacture and resell for scrap or salvage value or proceed in any reasonable manner.

This section is better understood by looking to the Official Comment [2] to § 30-2-704(2), MCA:

Under this Chapter the seller is given express power to complete manufacture or procurement of goods for the contract unless the exercise of reasonable commercial judgment as to the facts as they appear at the time he learns of the breach makes it clear that such action will result in a material increase in damages. The burden is upon the buyer to show the commercially unreasonable nature of the seller's action in completing manufacture.

Here, Commissioner Guay expressed concern about the contract at an early date, but the board of commissioners refused to repudiate the contract. The county has power to contract, and its contracts are the contracts of its board of county commissioners, not of the individual members thereof. Commissioner Guay did not have the authority to individually revoke the contract, and when plaintiff asked that the board take some action, it refused. Thus, plaintiff was acting in a commercially reasonable manner to fulfill its obligation under the contract. If plaintiff had not delivered the crusher within forty-five days, it would have breached the contract and exposed itself to legal liability. Had the board taken some action at an early date, plaintiff could have mitigated its damages under § 30-2-704, MCA. The District Court's instruction unfairly placed the entire burden to mitigate damages upon plaintiff whereas the comments to § 30-2-704, MCA, state: "the burden is upon the buyer [Flathead County] to show the commercially unreasonable nature of the seller's action in completing manufacture." Thus, the giving of the court's instruction was in error.

The last issue is whether the jury verdict was supported by substantial credible evidence. As stated above, the measure of damages is governed by § 30-2-706, MCA, and § 30-2-708, MCA. Under § 30-2-706, MCA, the damages would be the contract price ($305,725) plus incidental damages less the resale price ($186,499.86) and expenses saved in consequence of the buyer's breach. Under § 30-2-708(2) the damages would be plaintiff's anticipated profit ($78,879.56) plus incidental damages less credit for payments made or proceeds of resale. Using either section in this instance the record shows plaintiff's damages were far in excess of $10,000 and there is no substantial credible evidence which can support the jury verdict.

We affirm the case as to county's liability and judgment is reversed and the case is remanded to the District Court for a hearing on damages by following the applicable statutes.

NOTE

Comment 1 to U.C.C. § 2-704 reads:

This section gives an aggrieved seller the right at the time of breach to identify to the contract any conforming finished goods, regardless of their resalability, and to use reasonable judgment as to completing unfinished goods. It thus makes the goods available for resale under the resale section [U.C.C. § 2-706, see § 2-708] the seller's primary remedy, and in the special case in which resale is not practicable, allows the action for the price [U.C.C. § 2-709(1)(b)] which would then be necessary to give the seller the value of his contract. [*Cf.* U.C.C. §§ 2A-527, 2A-528, 2A-529. CISG Arts. 62, 75, 76.]

U.C.C. §§ 2-706, 2-708 and 2-709 are discussed at § 7.02[C] immediately below.

[C] Recover Monies

[1] Resell and Recover Damages

Read: U.C.C. §§ 2-703(d), 2-706; cf. § 2-712.

Read also: U.C.C. §§ 2A-523(1)(e), 2A-527, cf. § 2A-518; CISG Arts. 61(1)(b), 74, 75.

APEX OIL CO. v. THE BELCHER CO. OF NEW YORK, INC.

United States Court of Appeals
855 F.2d 997 (2d Cir. 1988)

WINTER, CIRCUIT JUDGE

This diversity case, arising out of an acrimonious commercial dispute, presented the question whether a sale of goods six weeks after a breach of contract may properly be used to calculate resale damages under Section 2-706 of the Uniform Commercial Code, where goods originally identified to the broken contact were sold on the day following the breach. Defendants The Belcher Company of New York, Inc. and Belcher New Jersey, Inc. (together "Belcher") appeal from a judgment, entered after a jury trial before Judge McLaughlin, awarding plaintiff Apex Oil Company ("Apex") $432,365.04 in damages for breach of contract and fraud in connection with an uncompleted transaction for heating oil. Belcher claims that the district court improperly allowed Apex to recover resale damages and that Apex failed to prove its fraud claim by clear and convincing evidence. We agree and reverse.

BACKGROUND

Apex buys, sells, refines and transports petroleum products of various sorts, including No. 2 heating oil, commonly known as home heating oil. Belcher also buys and sells petroleum products, including No. 2 heating oil. In February 1982, both firms were trading futures contracts for No. 2 heating oil on the New York Mercantile Exchange ("Merc"). In particular, both were trading Merc contracts for February 1982 No. 2 heating oil—*i.e.*, contracts for the delivery of that commodity in New York Harbor during that delivery month in accordance with the Merc's rules. As a result of that trading, Apex was short 315 contracts, and Belcher was long by the same amount. Being "short" one contract for oil means that the trader has contracted to deliver one thousand barrels at some point in the future, and being "long" means just the opposite—that the trader has contracted to purchase that amount of oil. If a contract is not liquidated before the close of trading, the short trader must deliver the oil to a long trader (the exchange matches shorts with longs) in strict compliance with Merc rules or suffer stiff penalties, including disciplinary proceedings and fines. A short trader may, however meet its obligations by entering into an "exchange for physicals" ("EFP") transaction with a long trader. An EFP allows a short trader to substitute for the delivery of oil under the terms of a futures contract the delivery of oil at a different place and time.

Apex was matched with Belcher by the Merc, and thus became bound to produce 315,000 barrels of No. 2 heating oil meeting Merc specifications in New York Harbor. Those specifications required that oil delivered in New York Harbor have a sulfur content no higher than 0.20%. Apex asked Belcher whether Belcher would take delivery of 190,000 barrels of oil in Boston Harbor in satisfaction of 190 contracts, and Belcher agreed. At trial, the parties did not dispute that, under this EFP, Apex promised it would deliver the No. 2 heating oil for the same price as that in the original contract—89.70 cents per gallon—and that the oil would be lifted from the vessel *Bordeaux*. The parties did dispute, and vigorously so, the requisite maximum sulfur content. At trial, Belcher sought to prove that the oil had to meet the New York standard of 0.20%, while Apex asserted that the oil had to meet only the specifications for Boston Harbor of not more than 0.30% sulfur.

The *Bordeaux* arrived in Boston Harbor on February 9, 1982, and on the next day began discharging its cargo of No. 2 heating oil at Belcher New England, Inc.'s terminal in Revere, Massachusetts. Later in the evening of February 10, after fifty or sixty thousand barrels had been offloaded, an independent petroleum inspector told Belcher that tests showed the oil on board the *Bordeaux* contained 0.28% sulfur, in excess of the New York Harbor specification. Belcher nevertheless continued to lift oil from the ship until eleven o'clock the next morning, February 11, when 141,535 barrels had been pumped into Belcher's terminal. After pumping had stopped, a second test indicated that the oil contained 0.22% sulfur—a figure within the accepted range of tolerance for oil containing 0.20% sulfur. (Apex did not learn of the second test until shortly before trial.) Nevertheless, Belcher refused to resume pumping, claiming that the oil did not conform to specifications.

After Belcher ordered the *Bordeaux* to leave its terminal, Apex immediately contacted Cities Service. Apex was scheduled to deliver heating oil to Cities Service later in the month and accordingly asked if it could satisfy that obligation by immediately delivering the oil on the *Bordeaux*. Cities Service agreed, and that oil was delivered to Cities Service in Boston Harbor on February 12, one day after the oil had been rejected by Belcher. Apex did not give notice to Belcher that the oil had been delivered to Cities Service.

Meanwhile, Belcher and Apex continued to quarrel over the portion of the oil delivered by the *Bordeaux*. Belcher repeatedly informed Apex, orally and by telex, that the oil was unsuitable and would have to be sold at a loss because of its high sulfur content. Belcher also claimed, falsely, that it was incurring various expenses because the oil was unusable. In fact, however, Belcher had already sold the oil in the ordinary course of business. Belcher nevertheless refused to pay Apex the contract price of $5,322.200.27 for the oil it had accepted, and it demanded that Apex produce the remaining 48,000 barrels of oil owing under the contract. On February 17, Apex agreed to tender the 48,000 barrels if Belcher would both make partial payment for the oil actually accepted and agree to negotiate as to the price ultimately to be paid for that oil. Belcher agreed and sent Apex a check for $5,034.997.12, a sum reflecting a discount of five cents per gallon from the contract price. However, the check contained an endorsement stating that "[t]he acceptance and negotiation of this check constitutes full payment and final settlement for all claims" against Belcher. Apex refused the check, and the parties returned to square one. Apex demanded full payment; Belcher demanded that Apex either negotiate the check or remove the discharged oil (which had actually been sold) and replace it with 190,000 barrels of conforming produce. Apex chose to take the oil and replace it, and on February 23 told Belcher that the 142,000 barrels of discharged oil would be removed on board the *Mersault* on February 25.

By then, however, Belcher had sold the 142,000 barrels and did not have an equivalent amount of No. 2 oil in its entire Boston terminal. Instead of admitting that it did not have the oil, Belcher told Apex that a dock for the *Mersault* was unavailable. Belcher also demanded that Apex either remove the oil *and* pay terminalling and storage fees, or accept payment for the oil at a discount of five cents per gallon. Apex refused to do either. On the next day, Belcher and Apex finally reached a settlement under which Belcher agreed to pay for the oil discharged from the *Bordeaux* at a discount of 2.5 cents per gallon. The settlement agreement also resolved an unrelated dispute between an Apex subsidiary and a subsidiary of Belcher's parent firm, The Coastal Corporation. It is this agreement that Apex now claims was procured by fraud.

After the settlement, Apex repeatedly contacted Belcher to ascertain when, where and how Belcher would accept delivery of the remaining 48,000 barrels. On March 5, Belcher informed Apex that it considered its obligations under the original contract to have been extinguished, and that it did not "desire to purchase such a volume [the 48,000 barrels] at the offered price." Apex responded by claiming that the settlement did not extinguish Belcher's obligation to accept the 48,000 barrels. In addition, Apex stated that unless Belcher accepted the oil by March 20, Apex would identify 48,000 barrels of No. 2 oil to the breached contract and sell the oil to a third party. When Belcher again refused to take the oil, Apex sold 48,000 barrels to Gill & Duffus Company. This oil was sold for delivery in April at a price of 76.25 cents per gallon, 13.45 cents per gallon below the Belcher contract price.

On October 7, 1982, Apex brought this suit in the Eastern District, asserting breach of contact and fraud. The breach-of-contract claim in Apex's amended complaint contended that Belcher had breached the EFP, not in February, but in March, when Belcher had refused to take delivery of the 48,000 barrels still owing under the contract. The amended complaint further alleged that "[a]t the time of the breach of the Contract by Belcher the market price of the product was $.7625 per gallon," the price brought by the resale to Gill & Duffus on March 23. In turn, the fraud claim asserted that Belcher had made various misrepresentations—that the *Bordeaux* oil was unfit, and unusable by Belcher, and that consequently Belcher was suffering extensive damages and wanted the oil removed—upon which Apex had relied when it had agreed from the *Bordeaux*. Apex asserted that as a result of the alleged fraud it had suffered damages of 2.5 cents per gallon, the discount agreed upon in the settlement.

The case went to trial before Judge McLaughlin and a jury between February 3 and February 13, 1986. As it had alleged in its pleadings, Apex asserted that its breach-of-contract claim was based on an alleged breach occurring *after* February 11, 1982, the day Belcher rejected the oil on board the *Bordeaux*. Judge McLaughlin, however, rejected this theory as a matter of law. His view of the case was that Belcher's rejection of the *Bordeaux* oil occurred under one of two circumstances: (i) either the oil conformed to the proper sulfur specification, in which case Belcher breached; or (ii) the oil did not conform, in which case Apex breached. Judge McLaughlin reasoned that, if Belcher breached on February 11, then it could not have breached thereafter. If on the other hand Apex breached, then, Judge McLaughlin reasoned, only under the doctrine of cure, *see* N.Y.U.C.C. § 2-508 (McKinney 1964), could Belcher be deemed to have breached. Apex, however, waived the cure theory by expressly disavowing it (perhaps because it presumes a breach by Apex). Instead, Apex argued that, regardless of whether the *Bordeaux* oil had conformed, Belcher's refusal throughout February and March 1982 to accept delivery of 48,000 barrels of conforming oil, which Belcher was then still demanding, had constituted a breach contract. Judge McLaughlin rejected this argument, which he viewed as simply "an attempt to reintroduce the cure doctrine."

In a general verdict, the jury awarded Apex $283,752.94 on the breach-of-contract claim, and $148,612.10 on the fraud claim, for a total of $432,365.04. With the addition of prejudgment interest, the judgment came to $588,566.29.

Belcher appeals from this verdict. Apex has not taken a cross-appeal from Judge McLaughlin's dismissal of its post-February 11 breach theories, however. The parties agree, therefore, that as the case comes to us, the verdict concerning the breach can be upheld on the theory that, if Belcher breached the contract, it did so only on February 11, 1982, and that the oil sold to Gill & Duffus on March 23 was identified to the broken contract.

DISCUSSION

[Here the court cited U.C.C. § 2-706 and italicized the following in subjection (2): *The resale must be reasonably identified as referring to the broken contract. . . .*"]

Belcher's principal argument on appeal is that the district court erred as a matter of law in allowing Apex to recover resale damages under Section 2-706. Specifically, Belcher contends that the heating oil Apex sold to Gill & Duffus in late March of 1982 was not identified to the broken contract. According to Belcher, the oil identified to the contract was the oil aboard the *Bordeaux*—oil which Apex had sold to Cities Service on the day after the breach. In response, Apex argues that, because heating oil is a fungible commodity, the oil sold to Gill & Duffus was "reasonably identified" to the contract even though it was not the same oil that had been on board the *Bordeaux*. We agree with Apex that, at least with respect to fungible goods, identification for the purposes of a resale transaction does not necessarily require that the resold goods be the exact goods that were rejected or repudiated. Nonetheless, we conclude that as a matter of law the oil sold to Gill & Duffus in March was not reasonably identified to the contract breached on February 11, and that the resale was not commercially reasonable.

holding

Resolving the instant dispute requires us to survey various provisions of the Uniform Commercial Code. The first such provision is Section 2-501, which defines "identification" and states in pertinent part:

[The court recites U.C.C. § 2-501(1)(a) and (b).]

The *Bordeaux* oil was unquestionably identified to the contract under Section 2-501(1)(b), and Apex does not assert otherwise. Nevertheless, Apex argues that Section 2-501 "has no application in the context of the Section 2-706 resale remedy," because Section 2-501 defines identification only for the purpose of establishing the point at which a buyer "obtains a special property and an insurable interest in goods." N.Y.U.C.C. § 2-501. This argument has a facial plausibility but ignores Section 2-103, which contains various definitions, and an index of other definitions, of terms used throughout Article 2 of the Code. With regard to "[i]dentification," Section 2-103(2) provides that the "definition[] applying to *this Article*" is set forth in Section 2-501. *Id.* § 2-103 (emphasis added).

Section 2-501 thus informs us that the *Bordeaux* oil was identified to the contract. It does not end our inquiry, however, because it does not exclude as a matter of law the possibility that a seller may identify goods to a contract, but then substitute, for the identified goods, *identical* goods that are then identified to the contract.

. . .

Belcher relies upon Section 2-706's statement that "the seller may resell the *goods concerned*," N.Y.U.C.C. § 2-706(1) (emphasis added), and upon Section 2-704, which states that "[a]n aggrieved seller . . . may . . . identify to the contract conforming goods *not already identified* if at the time he learned of the breach they are in his possession or control." *Id.* § 2-704(1) (emphasis added). According to Belcher, these statements absolutely foreclose the possibility of reidentification for the purpose of a resale. Apex, on the other hand, points to section 2-706's statement that "it is not necessary that the goods be in existence or that any or all of them have been identified to the contract before the breach." *Id.* § 2-706(2). According to Apex, this language shows that "[t]he relevant inquiry to be made under Section 2-706 is whether the resale transaction is reasonably identified to the breached contract and not whether the goods resold were originally identified to the contract."

None of the cited provisions are dispositive. First, Section 2-706(1)'s reference to reselling "the goods concerned" is unhelpful because those goods are the goods identified to the contract, but which goods are so identified is the question to be answered in the instant case. Second, as to Section 2-704, the fact that an aggrieved seller may identify goods "not already identified" does not mean that the seller may not identify goods as substitutes for previously identified goods. Rather, Section 2-704 appears to deal simply with the situation described in Section 2-706(2) above, where the goods are not yet in existence or have not yet been identified to the contract. Belcher thus can draw no comfort from either Section 2-704 or Section 2-706(1). Third, at the same time, however, Section 2-706(2)'s reference to nonexistent and nonidentified goods does not mean, as Apex suggests, that the original (pre-breach) identification of goods is wholly irrelevant. Rather, the provision regarding nonexistent and nonidentified goods deals with the special circumstances involving anticipatory repudiation by the buyer. *See* N.Y.U.C.C. § 2-706 comment 7. Under such circumstances, there can of course be no resale remedy unless the seller is allowed to identify goods to the contract after the breach. That is obviously not the case here.

. . .

[F]ungible goods resold pursuant to section 2-706 must be goods identified to the contract, but need not always be those *originally* identified to the contract. In other words, at least where fungible goods are concerned, identification is not always an irrevocable act and does not foreclose the possibility of substitution.

. . .

Nevertheless, as [§ 2-706] expressly states, "[t]he resale must be *reasonably* identified as referring to the broken contract," and "every aspect of the sale including the method, manner, time, place and terms must be commercially reasonable." N.Y.U.C.C. § 2-706(2) (emphasis added). Moreover, because the purpose of remedies under the Code is to put "the aggrieved party . . . in as good a position as if the other party had fully performed," *id.* § 1-106(1), the reasonableness of the identification and of the resale must be determined by examining whether the market value of, and the price received for, the resold goods "accurately reflects the market value of the goods which are subject of the contract." *Servbest*, 82 Ill. App.3d at 671, 37 Ill. Dec. at 952, 403 N.E.2d at 8.

. . .

[A]n example of an unreasonable identification and resale would be to claim as a resale the sale of goods located where they would have a significantly lower value than the originally identified goods. For example, had Apex purported to identify and resell 48,000 barrels of No. 2 oil contained in a storage tank in the Virgin Islands, where heating oil is presumably less useful and valuable than in Boston, while simultaneously delivering the same amount to Cities Service in Boston, the identification and resale would be unreasonable.

The most pertinent aspect of reasonableness with regard to identification and resale involves timing. As one treatise explains:

[T]he object of the resale is simply to determine exactly the seller's damages. These damages are the difference between the contract price and the market price at the time and place when performance should have been made by the buyer. The object of the resale . . . is to determine what the market price in fact was. *Unless the resale is made at about the time when performance was due it will be of slight probative value, especially if the goods are of a kind which fluctuate rapidly in value.* If no reasonable market existed at this time, no doubt a delay may be proper and a subsequent sale may furnish the best test, though confessedly not a perfectly exact one, of the seller's damage.

4 R. Anderson, Anderson on the Uniform Commercial Code § 2-706:25(3d ed. 1983); *see also Servbest*, 82 Ill. App.3d at 671, 37 Ill. Dec. at 952, 403 N.E.2d at 8. The issue of delay between breach and resale has previously been addressed only in the context of determining commercial reasonableness where the goods resold are the goods originally identified to the broken contract. However, the principles announced in that context apply here as well.

What is . . .a reasonable time [for resale] depends upon the nature of the goods, the condition of the market and other circumstance of the case; its length cannot be measured by any legal yardstick or divided into degrees. Where a seller contemplating receives a demand from the buyer for inspection under the section of [sic] preserving evidence of goods in dispute, the time for resale may be appropriately lengthened.

N.Y.U.C.C. § 2-706 comment 5. . . .

Here, Apex's delay of nearly six weeks between the breach on February 11, 1982 and the purported resale on March 23 was clearly unreasonable, even if the transfer to Cities Service had not occurred. Steven Wirkus, of Apex, testified on cross-examination that the market price for no. 2 heating oil on February 12, when the *Bordeaux* oil was delivered to Cities Service, was "[p]robably somewhere around 88 cents a gallon or 87." (The EFP contract price, of course, was 89.70 cents per gallon.) Wirkus also testified on redirect examination that the market price fluctuated throughout the next several weeks:

> **Q:** Sir, while you couldn't remember with particularity what the price of oil was on a given day four years ago, is it fair to say that prices went up and down?
>
> **A:** Definitely that's fair to say.
>
> **Q:** From day-to-day?
>
> **A:** Yes.
>
> **Q:** Towards the end of February prices went down?
>
> **A:** That's correct.
>
> **Q:** Then in early March it went back up?
>
> **A:** In early March, yes.
>
> **Q:** Then they went back down again towards the middle of March; isn't that correct?
>
> **MR. GILBERT:** I object to the form of this, your Honor, on redirect.
>
> **THE COURT:** Yes.
>
> **Q:** Did they go back down in mid March, Mr. Wirkus?
>
> **A:** My recollection, yes.
>
> **Q:** In late March what happened to the price?
>
> **A:** Market went back up.

Moreover, Wirkus testified that, on March 23, in a transaction unrelated to the resale, Apex purchased 25,000 barrels of No. 2 oil for March delivery at 80.50 cents per gallon, and sold an equivalent amount for April delivery at 77.25 cents per gallon. Other sales on March 22 and 23 for April delivery brought similar prices: 100,000 barrels were sold at 76.85 cents, and 25,000 barrels at 76.35 cents. The Gill & Duffus resale, which was also for *April* delivery, fetched a price of 76.25 cents per gallon—some eleven or twelve cents below the market price on the day of the breach.

rationale

In view of the long delay and the apparent volatility of the market for No. 2 oil, the purported resale failed to meet the requirements of Section 2-706 as a matter of law. The delay unquestionably prevented the resale from "accurately reflect[ing] the market value of the goods." *Servbest*, 82 Ill. App.3d at 671, 37 Ill. Dec. at 952, 403 N.E.2d at 8. Indeed, in the analogous context of the securities markets (which are arguably not much more liquid or volatile than today's centralized and computerized commodities markets), we have upheld a district court's conclusion that thirty days was a maximum time for the commercially–reasonable resale of securities after the breach of a tender offer. [Citation.]

Nor do we find Apex's delay justified on any other ground. Apex does not assert, for example, that "the time for resale [should] be appropriately lengthened" because Belcher sought an "inspection . . .[to] preserv[e] evidence of [the] goods in dispute," N.Y.U.C.C. § 2-706 comment 5; Belcher of course made no such request, and Apex immediately disposed of the *Bordeaux* oil in any event. Apex's only asserted justification, which the district court accepted in denying Belcher's motion for judgment notwithstanding the verdict, was that the delay was caused by continuing negotiations with Belcher. We find that ruling to be inconsistent with the district court's view that Belcher's breach, if any, occurred on February 11. The function of a resale was to put Apex in the position it would have been on that date by determining the value of the oil Belcher refused. The value of the oil at a later date is irrelevant because Apex was in no way obligated by the contract or by the Uniform Commercial Code to reserve 48,000 gallons for Belcher after the February 11 breach. Indeed, that is why Apex's original theory, rejected by the district court and not before us on this appeal, was that the breach occurred in March.

The rule that a "resale should be made as soon as practicable after . . .breach," *Bache*, 339 F.Supp. at 352 should be stringently applied where, as here, the resold goods are not those originally identified to the contract. In such circumstances, of course, there is a significant risk that the seller, who may perhaps have already disposed of the original goods without suffering any loss, has identified new goods for resale in order to minimize the resale price and thus to maximize damages. That was not the case in *Servbest*, for example, where the resale consisted of the first sales made after the breach. *See* 82 Ill. App.3d at 675, 37 Ill. Dec. at 955, 403 N.E.2d at 11. Here, by contrast, the oil originally identified to the contract was sold the day after the February 11, 1982 breach, and no doubt Apex sold ample amounts thereafter in the six weeks before the purported resale. . . . Because the sale of the oil identified to the contract to Cities Service on the next day fixed the value of the goods refused as a matter of law, the judgment on the breach-of-contract claim must be reversed.

We turn finally to Apex's fraud claim. [The court held that the reliance element of fraud was not established in view of the acknowledgment by Apex's president that he did not believe Belcher's misrepresentations.]

Reversed.

NOTES

(1) The case of *Afram Export Corp. v. Metallurgiki Halyps, S.A.*, 772 F.2d 1358, 41 U.C.C. Rep. 1709 (7th Cir. 1985), involved U.C.C. § 2-706. The pertinent portion of the court's opinion states:

Afram Export Corporation, the plaintiff, is a Wisconsin corporation that exports scrap metal. Metallurgiki Halyps, S.A., the defendant, is a Greek corporation that makes steel. In 1979, after a series of trans-Atlantic telephone and telex communications, the parties made a contract through an exchange of telex messages for the purchase by Metallurgiki of 15,000 tons of clean shredded scrap, at $135 per ton, F.O.B. Milwaukee, delivery to be made by the end of April. Metallurgiki apparently intended to use the scrap to make steel for shipment to Egypt, pursuant to a contract with an Egyptian buyer. Afram agreed to pay the expenses of an agent of Metallurgiki—Shields—to inspect the scrap for cleanliness before it was shipped.

The scrap for the contract was prepared, in Milwaukee, by Afram Metal Processing Company. Both Afram Metal Processing and the plaintiff Afram Export are wholly owned subsidiaries of Afram Brothers. All three are Wisconsin corporations, and have the same officers and directors. Unless otherwise indicated, when we say "Afram" we mean "Afram Export."

Shields arrived to inspect the scrap on April 12. He told Afram that the scrap was clean but that Metallurgiki would not accept it, because the price of scrap had fallen. Sure enough, Metallurgiki refused to accept it. Afram brought this suit after selling the scrap to other buyers. Metallurgiki unsuccessfully challenged the court's jurisdiction over it, then filed a counterclaim alleging that Afram had broken the contract and had thereby made it impossible for Metallurgiki to fulfill its contract with the Egyptian purchaser.

After a bench trial, the district judge gave judgment for Afram for $425,149 and dismissed the counterclaim. Metallurgiki has appealed from the judgment for Afram, and Afram has cross-appealed, contending that the judge should have given it the full damages it sought—$483,750—plus incidental damages of $40,665, prejudgment interest, the cost of a so-called public sale, and attorney's fees for defending against the counterclaim.

. . . .

This completes our consideration of Metallurgiki's appeal and we turn to Afram's cross-appeal. Afram claims that it sold all of the scrap rejected by Metallurgiki at a public sale on June 15, 1979, and that its damages should therefore be based on the price of that sale, which was $102.75 per ton. The district judge disagreed. He found that two-thirds of the scrap had been sold at a substantially higher price to Luria Brothers on June 4 ($118—actually somewhat less, because Afram defrayed some freight costs) and the other third to International Traders on September 15 at a price of $103. Afram points out that the sale on June 4 actually was made by its affiliate, Afram Metal Processing Company, and further argues that since all Afram scrap is sold from the same pile in Milwaukee it is arbitrary to treat the first sale after the breach of contract as the cover transaction, rather than the sale that Afram designated as that transaction.

We agree with the district judge that the sale on June 4 was a cover transaction, even though the nominal seller was a different corporation from the plaintiff. Not only are both corporations wholly owned subsidiaries of another corporation, not only do all three corporations have the same officers and directors, but the record indicates substantial commingling of assets and operation of the three corporations as a single entity. Shortly after Metallurgiki's rejection, Zeke Afram, an officer of both Afram Export (the party to the contract with Metallurgiki) and Afram Metal Processing (the nominal owner of the scrap sold on June 4), called Luria Brothers and explained that he had extra scrap for sale because of a buyer's breach; apparently he did not bother to indicate which Afram corporation he was calling on behalf of. The June 4 sale followed shortly. The conversation and the timing of the sale are powerful evidence that the breach enabled the sale—that it would not have occurred but for the breach—and hence that the revenue from the sale must be subtracted from the contract price to determine Afram's loss.

But this does not dispose completely of the issue of the cover price. If the sale on June 15 was "made in good faith and in a commercially reasonable manner," it fixed Afram's damages on the remaining one-third of the scrap. U.C.C. § 2-706(1), Wis. Stat. § 402.706(1). The question may seem less than earthshaking since the June sale price and the September sale price which the district court used as the cover price for the remaining third were only 25 per ton apart. But the bona fides of the June 15 sale casts additional light on the intercorporate relations of the Afram group and hence on the proper interpretation of the sale to Luria Brothers. In any event, the district judge was entitled to find that neither condition in § 2-706(1) was satisfied. . . . The June 15 "sale" was about a pure a bookkeeping transaction—as empty of economic significance—as can be imagined. It consisted of a transfer of the scrap on the books of one affiliated corporation to the books of another. The transferor and transferee were not only under common ownership but were operated as if they were limbs of a single organism. The scrap itself was not moved; it remained on the scrap heap till sold later on. No invoice or check for the sale was produced at trial. The inference that the sale was designed simply to maximize the enterprise's damages, leaving it free to resell the scrap at higher prices later on, is overpowering. The sale of the scrap three months later to International Traders at a (slightly) higher price provided better evidence of what the enterprise actually lost, so far as the scrap not sold to Luria Brothers is concerned, by Metallurgiki's breach of contract.

(2) *Person in Position of Seller.* In *Hart v. Sims*, 702 F.2d 574, 35 U.C.C. Rep. 1517 (5th Cir. 1983), an art dealer had become responsible for the balance of the purchase price of a painting on behalf of her principal. Held: She was a "person in the position of a seller," and entitled to remedies available to a seller, *e.g.*, those under U.C.C. § 2-706. U.C.C. § 2-707.

(3) Under proposed § 2-706, except where a buyer with a security interest in the seller's goods sells the goods under § 2-711, notice is no longer required for a private resale under § 2-706(b).

[2]   Recover Damages for Non-Acceptance or Repudiation

Read: U.C.C. §§ 2-703(e), 2-708; see §§ 2-723, 2-724, 2-503; cf. § 2-713.

Read also: U.C.C. §§ 2A-523(1)(e), 2A-528, 2A-507, cf. § 2A-519(1) and (2); CISG Arts. 61(1)(b), 74, 76.

Comment 2 to U.C.C. § 2-706 states in part: "Failure to act properly under this section deprives the seller of the measure of damages here provided [difference between resale price and contract price] and relegates him to that provided in Section 2–708." In *Apex*, above, how would damages be calculated under § 2-708(1)?

———

PROBLEM 7.2

Seller contracts to sell certain goods to buyer for $10,000. Buyer repudiates. In accordance with U.C.C. § 2-706, Seller resells the goods to X for $8,000. Under U.C.C. § 2-708(1), however, the market price for the goods at the time and place for tender is $6,000. Seller wishes to recover damages based on the 2-708(1) formula rather than that under 2-706. May it do so? *See* §§ 1-106, 2-712 Comment 3. *See also, Tesoro Petroleum Corp. v. Holborn Oil Company, Ltd.*, 547 N.Y.S.2d 1012 (1989).

handwritten marginalia: holding applies only to sellers who are middlemen & bear no risk of price fluctuation

UNION CARBIDE CORP. v. CONSUMERS POWER CO.

United States District Court
636 F.Supp. 1498, 1 U.C.C. Rep.2d 1202 (E.D. Mich. 1986)

JOINER, DISTRICT JUDGE.

This dispute arises out of a contract between Union Carbide Corporation ("Union Carbide") and Consumers Power Company ("Consumers") for the purchase of large quantities of residual fuel oil. Plaintiff Union Carbide alleges that Consumers breached this contract by refusing to accept further deliveries of the oil. Both parties have filed motions asking this court to determine the appropriate measure of damages to be applied if a breach is determined to have occurred.

FACTUAL BACKGROUND

The facts of the case which are relevant to these motions are largely agreed upon. There are two major contracts involved: one between Union Carbide and Consumers, and the other between Petrosar Limited ("Petrosar") and Union Carbide. On September 5, 1980, Union Carbide and Consumers entered into a contract whereby Union Carbide would deliver, and Consumers would purchase, 10,000 barrels of residual fuel oil per day until December 31, 1987. Union Carbide's oil supplier was Petrosar.

After the contract was signed, and deliveries begun, there was a dramatic drop in the price of residual fuel oil which was not passed through to Consumers. Thus, Consumers was paying prices well in excess of the market price for the oil it received from Union Carbide. In late 1981, Consumers announced that it would refuse to take any further deliveries of residual fuel oil after December 31, 1981. Union Carbide made sporadic efforts to resell the oil Consumers refused until August 27, 1982. Union Carbide then canceled the contract under the terms of Uniform Commercial Code (U.C.C.) § 2-703(f) [Mich. Comp. Laws. Ann. § 440.2703]. In lieu of accepting further deliveries of oil previously sold to Consumers, Union Carbide paid Petrosar to keep the oil. These payments were called residual oil reduction payments (RORP). They continued making these payments until July 1, 1983, when Union Carbide and Petrosar terminated their contract.

The pricing mechanism for the Union Carbide-Consumers contract insured that Union Carbide was guaranteed to profit on each barrel of oil that Consumers accepted. Using the price Union Carbide paid to Petrosar as a base, Consumers' price was calculated by multiplying the base price by a fixed percentage and adding in certain fixed costs. The net result was that Consumers always paid Union Carbide more per barrel than Union Carbide paid to Petrosar, with the difference between these two prices amounting to a certain net profit.

The second contract involved in this case is Union Carbide's 1974 contract with Petrosar to purchase 27,000 barrels of residual fuel oil per day. Since it had no use for the oil in its own operations, Union Carbide sought to dispose of it through resale contracts or on the spot market.

In addition to the Consumers contract, Union Carbide had contracted with Niagara Mohawk Power and Light (Mohawk) for the resale of 5,000 barrels per day. As noted above, Union Carbide terminated its contract with Petrosar on July 1, 1983. Union Carbide's termination of its Petrosar contract was the result of many factors, only one of which was Consumers' refusal to accept further deliveries of residual fuel oil after 1981. As a result of its decision to end this contract, Union Carbide negotiated a settlement of its contractual obligations with Petrosar. The terms of this settlement required Union Carbide to assign the Mohawk contract to Petrosar and pay it approximately $20 million (Canadian).

There is no dispute over the measure of damages to be applied for all shipments of oil which Union Carbide resold. Both parties agree that U.C.C. § 2-706(1) dictates that damages for this oil should be measured by the difference between the resale price and the contract price plus allowable incidental damages minus expenses saved in consequence of the buyer's breach.

The parties disagree over the proper measure of damages to be applied for the oil which Consumers refused that Union Carbide did not attempt to resell. This includes the oil identified to the Consumers' contract which Union Carbide paid RORP to Petrosar to not deliver to it plus the amount of oil that would have been identified to the Consumers' contract if Union Carbide had not terminated its contract with Petrosar. While the parties concur that U.C.C. § 2-708 applies, they differ over which section of that provision should be utilized.

The text of § 2-708 provides that: [the Court quotes U.C.C. § 2-708].

Union Carbide claims that the appropriate measure of damages is governed by section 1 (market price differential). It urges that the court award market price damages. These were estimated at oral argument to amount to approximately $120 million (U.S.).

Consumers responds that section 2 (lost profits) damages are more appropriate in this case because they give Union Carbide what it would have received if the contract had been performed. Consumers believes that market price damages would greatly overcompensate Union Carbide for the riskless role it assumed in this contract. It says this would violate U.C.C. § 1-106. Lost profit damages were estimated at oral argument to amount to $30 million (U.S.).

LEGAL ANALYSIS

Turning first to the language of the statute, the court must interpret the first phrase of § 2-708(2), which says: "If the measure of damages provided in subsection (1) is *inadequate* to put the seller in as good a position as performance would. . ." The key to understanding this passage's meaning is the word "inadequate."

Union Carbide claims that the language of the statute supports reading inadequate to mean insufficient. Thus, whenever market price damages undercompensate the seller (relative to contract performance), the seller can, under Union Carbide's interpretation, elect lost profits damages. This reading of the statute ignores the question of what measure of damages is appropriate where market price damages greatly over-compensate the seller vis-a-vis what it would receive if the contract had been performed. Presumably, Union Carbide would claim the seller somehow deserved this exorbitant award as the premium for standing ready to perform in the face of the buyer's breach.

This position is contrary to the clear intention of the U.C.C. that remedies should place the parties in the same position as if the contract had been performed. U.C.C. § 1-106, for example, provides that the remedies of the U.C.C. should be ". . .liberally administered to the end that the aggrieved party may be put in as good a position as if the other had performed . . ." and that neither penal, special, nor consequential damages be awarded except where specifically provided by law. This court is reluctant to endorse any position that runs counter to this policy.

Instead, the court believes that inadequate should be interpreted to mean incapable or inadequate to accomplish the stated purpose of the U.C.C. remedies of compensating the aggrieved person but not overcompensating that person or specially punishing the other person. The measure of damages provided in section 1 will be incapable of putting the seller in as good a position as performance whenever it does not fairly measure the damages suffered by the aggrieved party. This interpretation is more flexible in that it provides the damages under section 1 can be too great or too small.

Moreover, the language of 2-708(2) states the seller should be put in "as good as" a position as performance would have done. "As good as" does not include better than. The statute should not authorize awards of damages which put the seller in a better position than performance would have put them. This view is supported by the policy behind U.C.C. § 1-106, discussed above.

Existing case law supports the court's reading of the statute. There is no Michigan case law which addresses this issue. However, since the U.C.C. is intended to be interpreted uniformly across the country, it is appropriate to look to the decisions of other courts in other states for guidance. The Fifth Circuit has examined a factual situation very similar to this one and held that U.C.C. § 2-708(2) applies when the buyer can prove that damages under 2-708(1) would overcompensate the seller. *Nobs Chemical, USA, Inc. v. Koppers Co., Inc.*, 616 F.2d 212 (5th Cir. 1980).

Nobs Chemical involved a suit by the disappointed sellers of 1000 metric tons of cumene (a colorless oily hydrocarbon used as an additive for high-octane gasoline) against the breaching buyer. The sellers had not yet actually purchased, or contracted in a binding fashion to purchase, the cumene. They had contacted their manufacturer in Brazil and arranged to get the cumene with another shipment of 3000 tons that they had ordered for some clients.

In district court, the seller requested market price damages under 2-708(1). The buyer objected that these damages would overcompensate the seller and asked the court to award lost profits. The district court awarded lost profits and the Court of Appeals affirmed.

The Court of Appeals relied on White and Summers treatise on the U.C.C. J. White and R. Summers, Uniform Commercial Code (1st Ed. 1972). The court examined White and Summers' analysis of section 2-708, saying:

Professors White and Summers, recognizing that § 2-708(b) [§ 2-708(2)] is not the most lucid or best-drafted of the sales article sections, decided that the drafters of the Uniform Commercial Code intended subsection (b) to apply to certain sellers whose losses would rarely be compensated by the subsection (a) [§ 2-708(1)] market price-contract price measure of damages, and for these sellers the lost profit formula was added in subsection (b). One such type of seller is a "jobber," who, according to the treatise writers, must satisfy two conditions: "[f]irst, he is a seller who never acquires the contract goods. Second, his decision not to acquire those goods after learning of the breach was not commercially unreasonable. . . ."

. . . .

The plaintiffs argue, however, that in this case the measure of damages under subsection (a) would adequately compensate them and therefore, according to the terms of subsection (a), subsection (b) does not control. This is an intriguing argument. It appears that the drafters of § 2708(a) did not consider the possibility that recovery under that section may be more than adequate. White & Summers, *supra*, § 7-12, at 232-233. It is possible that the code drafters intended subsection (a) as a liquidated damage clause available to a plaintiff-seller regardless of his actual damages. There have been some commentators who agree with this philosophy. . . . But, this construction is inconsistent with the code's basic philosophy, announced in Tex. Bus. & Com. Code Ann. § 1.106(a) (Vernon), which provides "that the aggrieved party may be put in as good a position as if the other party had fully performed" but not in a better posture. White & Summers, *supra*, § 7-12, at 232.

   . . . .

Moreover, White and Summers conclude that statutory damage formulas do not significantly affect the practices of businessmen and therefore "breach deterrence," which would be the purpose of the statutory liquidated damages clause, should be rejected in favor of a standard approximating actual economic loss. White & Summers, *supra*, § 7-12, at 232. No one insists, and we do not think they could, that the difference between the fallen market price and contract price is necessary to compensate the plaintiffs for the breach. Had the transaction been completed, their "benefit of the bargain" would not have been affected by the fall in market price, and they would not have experienced the windfall they otherwise would receive if the market price-contract price rule contained in § 2-708(a) is followed. Thus, the premise contained in § 1.106 is a strong factor weighing against application of § 2.708(a).[3]

Id. at 215-216. (citations to the official text of the U.C.C. added). The figures referred to in footnote 3 showed that lost profits damages amounted to $95,000 (U.S.), while market price damages would have come to approximately $300,000 (U.S.).

Union Carbide can be described as a middleman or jobber in this case, at least for the period in which it did not accept the residual fuel oil which it had contracted to sell to Consumers. As the middleman between Petrosar and Consumers, Union Carbide's role was simply to get the oil, transport it to Consumers and receive its guaranteed profit. Once it stopped reselling the oil identified to the Consumers' contract, Union Carbide's decision not to acquire further quantities of oil from Petrosar was a commercial reasonable one. Thus, for the period of time in which Union Carbide claims it should be awarded market price damages, it was a middleman.

This court agrees with the *Nobs Chemical* court that allowing section 1 damages where they overcompensate the plaintiff is equivalent to awarding liquidated damages to Union Carbide. This would be inconsistent with the code's basic philosophy as expressed in U.C.C. § 1-106(1). Neither does this court believe that breach deterrence justifies granting such a disproportionate award.

Most importantly, this court finds that here, as in *Nobs Chemical*, had the transaction between Union Carbide and Consumers been completed, Union Carbide's "benefit of the bargain" would not have been affected by changes in the market price of oil. The price formula which set the contract price paid by Consumers tracked the price that Union Carbide paid to Petrosar. No matter what happened to Petrosar's prices, Union Carbide could pass through the change in prices to Consumers. It was guaranteed its fixed profit on the contract and no more. Any windfall gains

---

[3] White and Summers condition forcing the damage formula of subsection (b) on the plaintiff-seller. They would require the defendant to prove that the measure of damages in subsection (a) would overcompensate the plaintiff. We do not find this to be a problem here, as the figures themselves refute any contention that the market price-contract rule is anything but over-adequate compensation for the plaintiffs. White & Summers, *supra*, § 7-12, at 232-233.

that might arise from rapid price changes would be realized by Petrosar, not Union Carbide. For this court to fundamentally alter this allocation of contractual benefits between the parties by giving Union Carbide vastly greater returns than were provided for by its contract with Consumers would fly in the face of the U.C.C.'s basic premises and be manifestly unjust. In short, Union Carbide was guaranteed a riskless, fixed profit under the terms of the contract and they should not receive the benefit of price fluctuations whose risk they did not assume.

Finally, the court finds that market price damages will overcompensate Union Carbide. By overcompensation, the court means that Union Carbide would receive greatly more than the riskless benefit of the bargain they would have received if the contract had been performed.[4] At oral argument, the court heard uncontested evidence that Union Carbide would have earned approximately $30 million (U.S.) if the contract had been performed. These were its lost profits. Its damages under the market price measure of damages would be four times as great, or roughly $120 million (U.S.).[5] This is sufficient to establish overcompensation.

Union Carbide relies on the Second Circuit's decision in *Trans World Metals, Inc. v. Southwire Company*, 769 F.2d 902 (2d Cir.1985), to support its argument that it should be able to elect market price damages if it prefers them. This court finds that *Trans World* is distinguishable.

In that case, Southwire, the buyer, repudiated a short-term supply contract for the provision of aluminum that it had entered into with Trans World, the seller. The contract ran from January to December, 1982. It was negotiated in April of 1981. Between that time and March 1982, the price of aluminum dropped dramatically. Southwire repudiated the entire contract in March 1982, alleging that the supplies for February had been delivered late in violation of a "time-is-of-the-essence" clause. The jury held for Trans World in special interrogatories finding that the "time-is-of-the-essence" clause was not part of the contract and therefore the repudiation was a total breach. The court of appeals held that the jury's findings were supported by the evidence. They then reviewed the alleged errors of the district court.

The court considered the defendant's argument that the award of contract price damages overcompensated the plaintiff-seller. It held that market price damages should be awarded. *Id.* at 907.

The court was unconvinced that Trans World would be overcompensated by the award of damages under 2-708(1). They believed that the parties had consciously assumed different risks of price variations: Southwire assumed the risk that prices would fall and Trans World assumed the risk that the price would rise. It would deny Trans World the benefit of its bargain if they were not allowed to gain from the drop in prices.

The *Trans World* court distinguished the *Nobs Chemical* decision. They said the seller in *Nobs Chemical* was a middleman who had fixed its supply price prior to entering into the contract with the buyer Koppers Company. The seller had therefore protected itself against the risk of market price fluctuations and it would have been unfair to allow them to reap a riskless benefit. This was not the case in *Trans World* because the parties had expressly bargained for the allocation of the risk of price changes.

Similarly in this case, the focus of the decision must center on the fundamental allocation of risk between the parties. The price mechanism in the contract insured that Union Carbide

---

[4] The court does not imply that this same standard of overcompensation would apply if Union Carbide bore the risks of price fluctuations.

[5] In *Nobs Chemical*, the Fifth Circuit found that market price damages three times greater than lost profits were overcompensation: 616 F.2d at 216, n. 3.

could pass through all of its costs to Consumers. This means Union Carbide, the middleman, assumed no risk of price changes. *Trans World* is therefore inapplicable; *Nobs Chemical* should be applied instead.

One other matter should be resolved. Under U.C.C. § 2-708(2), Union Carbide is entitled to incidental damages. Counsel for Consumers represented at oral argument that the RORP payments which Union Carbide made to Petrosar would fall within the rubric of incidental damages. Consumers' counsel further stated that Union Carbide's payments to Petrosar in settlement of its contractual obligations with them would be incidental damages at least to the extent they can be apportioned to the loss of the Consumers contract. The court finds that U.C.C. § 2-710 defining a seller's incidental damages can be reasonably interpreted to cover these costs. They are commercially reasonable expenses incurred by the seller as a result of the buyer's breach.

In summary, the limited applicability of this decision should be reemphasized. The seller in this case was a middleman who assumed none of the risks of price variations. The contract provided that the seller would be guaranteed a profit on all goods accepted by the buyer. Moreover, the buyer proved that market price damages would overcompensate the seller. Given these limiting facts, the court holds that the seller's damages should be calculated under § 2-708(2).

So Ordered.

———

NOTES AND QUESTIONS

(1) Proposed U.C.C. § 2-703 states that it is subject to § 2-701. Section 2-701(c) states that Article 2 remedies must be liberally administered to put the aggrieved party in as good a position as if the other party had fully performed. If those remedies fail to place the aggrieved party in that position, damages may be awarded measured by the loss resulting in the ordinary course of events from the breach as determined in any manner which is reasonable. Thus, courts may protect not only the expectation interest but reliance and restitution interests where appropriate.

Proposed § 2-701(e) reinforces the idea that the rights and remedies provided by Article 2 are cumulative. But the subsection goes on to say that a court may deny or limit a remedy if it would put an aggrieved party in a substantially better position than if the other party had fully performed.

Proposed § 2-708(a) measures damages based on market price in two ways: (1) for breach other than repudiation, damages are the "contract price less the market price of comparable goods at the time and place for tender;" (2) for breach by repudiation, damages are "the contract price less the market price of comparable goods prevailing at the place for tender and at the time when a commercially reasonable period after the seller learned of the repudiation has expired."

Proposed § 2-708(b) measures damages based on other than market price, including (1) lost profits (including reasonable overhead) resulting from the breach determined in any reasonable manner (plus incidental and consequential damages, less expenses avoided) and (2) reasonable unreimbursed expenditures made in preparing for or performing the contract. A seller may choose this remedy rather than market price damages unless the choice puts it in a substantially better position than full performance under § 2-701(e).

(2) How would Proposed §§ 2-701, 2-703 and 2-708 affect the analysis and result of *Union Carbide*?

————

R. E. DAVIS CHEMICAL CORP. v. DIASONICS, INC.

United States Court of Appeals
826 F.2d 678 (7th Cir. 1987)

[Davis contracted to purchase a piece of medical diagnostic equipment from Diasonics. Subsequently, Davis wrongly refused to take delivery of the equipment. Diasonics later resold the equipment to a third party for the same price at which it was to be sold to Davis. Davis sued Diasonics asking for restitution of its $300,000 downpayment under U.C.C. § 2-718(2); Diasonics claimed that it was entitled to an offset under § 2-718(3). Diasonics' position was that it was entitled to lost profits as a "lost volume seller" under U.C.C. § 2-708(2). The district court held that Diasonics was limited to recovering damages under §2-706. Diasonics appealed.]

We consider . . .Diasonics' claims that the district court erred in holding that Diasonics was limited to the measure of damages provided in 2-706 and could not recover lost profits as a lost volume seller under 2-708(2). Surprisingly, given its importance, this issue has never been addressed by an Illinois court, nor, apparently, by any other court construing Illinois law. Thus, we must attempt to predict how the Illinois Supreme Court would resolve this issue if it were presented to it. Courts applying the laws of other states have unanimously adopted the position that a lost volume seller can recover its lost profits under 2-708(2). Contrary to the result reached by the district court, we conclude that the Illinois Supreme Court would follow these other cases and would allow a lost volume seller to recover its lost profit under 2-708(2).

. . .

Article 2 contains four provisions that concern the recovery of a seller's general damages (as opposed to its incidental or consequential damages): 2-706 (contract price less resale price); 2-708(1) (contract price less market price); 2-708(2) (profit); and 2-709 (price). The problem we face here is determining whether Diasonics' damages should be measured under 2-706 or 2-708(2). To answer this question, we need to engage in a detailed look at the language and structure of these various damage provisions.

The Code does not provide a great deal of guidance as to when a particular damage remedy is appropriate. The damage remedies provided under the Code are catalogued in section 2-703, but this section does not indicate that there is any hierarchy among the remedies. One method of approaching the damage sections is to conclude that 2-708 is relegated to a role inferior to that of 2-706 and 2-709 and that one can turn to 2-708 only after one has concluded that neither

2-706 nor 2-709 is applicable.[6] Under this interpretation of the relationship between 2-706 and 2-708, if the goods have been resold, the seller can sue to recover damages measured by the difference between the contract price and the resale price under 2-706. The seller can turn to 2-708 only if it resells in a commercially unreasonable manner or if it cannot resell but an action for the price is inappropriate under 2-709. The district court adopted this reading of the Code's damage remedies and, accordingly, limited Diasonics to the measure provided in 2-706 because it resold the equipment in a commercially reasonable manner.

The district court's interpretation of 2-706 and 2-708, however, creates its own problems of statutory construction. There is some suggestion in the Code that the "fact that plaintiff resold the goods [in a commercially reasonable manner] does *not* compel him to use the resale remedy of § 2-706 rather than the damage remedy of § 2-708." Harris, *A Radical Restatement of the Law of Seller's Damages: Sales Act and Commercial Code Results Compared*, 18 Stan.L.Rev. 66, 101 n. 174 (1965) (emphasis in original). Official comment 1 to 2-703, which catalogues the remedies available to a seller, states that these "remedies are essentially cumulative in nature" and that "[w]hether the pursuit of one remedy bars another depends entirely on the facts of the individual case." *See also State of New York, Report of the Law Revision Comm'n for 1956*, 396-97 (1956).[7]

Those courts that found that a lost volume seller can recover its lost profits under 2-708(2) implicitly rejected the position adopted by the district court; those courts started with the

---

[6] Evidence to support this approach can be found in the language of the various damage sections and of the official comments to the U.C.C. *See* § 2-709(3) ("a seller who is held not entitled to the price under this Section shall nevertheless be awarded damages for non-acceptance under the preceding section [§ 2-708]"); U.C.C. comment 7 to § 2-709 ("[i]f the action for the price fails, the seller may nonetheless have proved a case entitling him to damages for non-acceptance [under § 2-708]"); U.C.C. comment 2 to § 2-706 ("[f]ailure to act properly under this section deprives the seller of the measure of damages here provided and relegates him to that provided in Section 2-708"); U.C.C. comment 1 to § 2-704 (describes § 2-706 as the "primary remedy" available to a seller upon breach by the buyer); *see also Commonwealth Edison Co. v. Decker Coal Co.*, 653 F.Supp. 841, 844 (N.D. Ill.1987) (statutory language and case law suggest that "§ 2-708 remedies are available only to a seller who is not entitled to the contract price" under § 2-709); Childres & Burgess, *Seller's Remedies: The Primacy of U.C.C. 2-708(2)*, 48 N.Y.U.L.Rev. 833, 863-64 (1973). As one commentator has noted, 2-706

is the Code section drafted specifically to define the damage rights of aggrieved reselling sellers, and there is no suggestion within it that the profit formula of section 2-708(2) is in any way intended to qualify or be superior to it.

Shanker, *The Case for a Literal Reading of U.C.C. Section 2-708(2) (One Profit for the Reseller)*, 24 Case W.Res. 697, 699 (1973).

[7] U.C.C. comment 2 to 2-708(2) also suggests that 2-708 has broader applicability than suggested by the district court. U.C.C. comment 2 provides:

This section permits the recovery of lost profits in all appropriate cases, which would include all standard priced goods. The normal measure there would be list price less cost to the dealer or list price less manufacturing cost to the manufacturer.

The district court's restrictive interpretation of 2-708(2) was based in part on U.C.C. comment 1 to 2-704 which describes 2-706 as the aggrieved seller's primary remedy. The district court concluded that, if a lost volume seller could recover its lost profit under 2-708(2), every seller would attempt to recover damages under 2-708(2) and 2-706 would become the aggrieved seller's residuary remedy. This argument ignores the fact that to recover under 2-708(2), a seller must first establish its status as a lost volume seller.

The district court also concluded that a lost volume seller cannot recover its lost profit under 2-708(2) because such a result would negate a seller's duty to mitigate damages. This position fails to recognize the fact that, by definition, a lost volume seller cannot mitigate damages through resale. Resale does not reduce a lost volume seller's damages because the breach has still resulted in its losing one sale and a corresponding profit.

assumption that 2-708 applied to a lost volume seller without considering whether the seller was limited to the remedy provided under 2-706. None of those courts even suggested that a seller who resold goods in a commercially reasonable manner was limited to the damage formula provided under 2-706. We conclude that the Illinois Supreme Court, if presented with this question, would adopt the position of these other jurisdictions and would conclude that a reselling seller, such as Diasonics, is free to reject the damage formula prescribed in 2-706 and choose to proceed under 2-708.

Concluding that Diasonics is entitled to seek damages under 2-708, however, does not automatically result in Diasonics being awarded its lost profit. Two different measures of damages are provided in 2-708. Subsection 2-708(1) provides for a measure of damages calculated by subtracting the market price at the time and place for tender from the contract price.[8] The profit measure of damages, for which Diasonics is asking, is contained in 2-708(2). However, one applies 2-708(2) only if "the measure of damages provided in subsection (1) is inadequate to put the seller in as good a position as performance would have done. . . ." Ill.Rev.Stat. ch. 26, para. 2-708(2) (1985). Diasonics claims that 2-708(1) does not provide an adequate measure of damages when the seller is a lost volume seller. To understand Diasonics' argument, we need to define the concept of the lost volume seller. Those cases that have addressed this issue as one that has a predictable and finite number of customers and that has the capacity either to sell to all new buyers or to make the one additional sale represented by the resale after the breach. According to a number of courts and commentators, if the seller would have made the sale represented by the resale whether or not the breach occurred, damages measured by the difference between the contract price and market price cannot put the lost volume seller in as good a position as it would have been in had the buyer performed.[9] The breach effectively cost the seller a "profit," and the seller can only be made whole by awarding it damages in the amount of its "lost profit" under 2-708(2).

We agree with Diasonics' position that, under some circumstances, the measure of damages provided under 2-708(1) will not put a reselling seller in as good a position as it would have been in had the buyer performed because the breach resulted in the seller losing sales volume. However, we disagree with the definition of "lost volume seller" adopted by other courts. Courts awarding lost profits to a lost volume seller have focused on whether the seller had the capacity to supply the breached units in addition to what it actually sold. In reality, however, the relevant questions include, not only whether the seller could have produced the breached units in addition to its actual volume, but also whether it would have been profitable for the seller to produce both units. Goetz & Scott, *Measuring Sellers' Damages: The Lost-Profits Puzzle,* 31 Stan.L.Rev. 323, 332-33, 346-47 (1979). As one commentator has noted, under

---

[8] There is some debate in the commentaries about whether a seller who has resold the goods may ignore the measure of damages provided in 2-706 and elect to proceed under 2-708(1). Under some circumstances in the contract-market price differential will result in overcompensating such a seller. *See* J. White & R. Summers, Handbook of the Law under the Uniform Commercial Code § 7-7, at 271-73 (2d ed. 1980); Sebert, *Remedies Under Article Two of the Uniform Commercial Code: An Agenda for Review,* 130 U.Pa.L.Rev. 360, 380-83 (1981). We need not struggle with this question here because Diasonics has not sought to recover damages under 2-708(1).

[9] According to one commentator,

Resale results in loss of volume only if three conditions are met: (1) the person who bought the resold entity would have been solicited by plaintiff had there been no breach and resale; (2) the solicitation would have been successful; and (3) the plaintiff could have performed that additional contact.

Harris, *supra,* text accompanying n.7, at 82 (footnotes omitted).

the economic law of diminishing returns or increasing marginal costs[,] . . .as a seller's volume increases, then a point will inevitably be reached where the cost of selling each additional item diminishes the incremental return to the seller and eventually makes it entirely unprofitable to conclude the next sale.

Shanker, *supra* at 705. Thus, under some conditions, awarding a lost volume seller its presumed lost profit will result in overcompensating the seller, and 2-708(2) would not take effect because the damage formula provided in 2-708(1) does place the seller in as good a position as if the buyer had performed. Therefore, on remand, Diasonics must establish, not only that it had the capacity to produce the breached unit in addition to the unit resold, but also that it would have been profitable for it to have produced and sold both. . . .

One final problem with awarding a lost volume seller its lost profits was raised by the district court. This problem stems from the formulation of the measure of damages provided under 2-708(2) which is "the profit (including reasonable overhead) which the seller would have made from full performance by the buyer, together with any incidental damages provided in this Article (Section 2-710), due allowance for costs reasonably incurred and due credit for payments or *proceeds of resale.*" (emphasis added). The literal language of 2-708(2) requires that the proceeds from resale be credited against the amount of damages awarded which, in most cases, would result in the seller recovering nominal damages. In those cases in which the lost volume seller was awarded its lost profit as damages, the courts have circumvented this problem by concluding that this language only applies to proceeds realized from the resale of uncompleted goods for scrap. *See, e.g., Neri,* 30 N.Y.2d at 399 & n. 2, 334 N.Y.S.2d at 169 & n.2, 286 N.E.2d at 314 & n. 2; *see also* J. White & R. Summers, Handbook of the Law under the Uniform Commercial Code § 7-13, at 285 ("courts should simply ignore the 'due credit' language in lost volume cases") (footnote omitted). Although neither the text of 2-708(2) nor the official comments limit its application to resale of goods for scrap, there is evidence that the drafters of 2-708 seemed to have had this more limited application in mind when they proposed amending 2-708 to include the phrase "due credit for payments or proceeds of resale." We conclude that the Illinois Supreme Court would adopt this more restrictive interpretation of this phrase rendering it inapplicable to this case.

We therefore reverse the grant of summary judgment in favor of Davis and remand with instructions that the district court calculate Diasonics' damages under 2-708(2) if Diasonics can establish, not only that it had the capacity to make the sale to Davis as well as the sale to the resale buyer, but also that it would have been profitable for it to make both sales. Of course, Diasonics, in addition, must show that it probably would have made the second sale absent the breach.

. . .

NOTES

(1) On remand, the district court found that Diasonics' profit would have been $453,050. (The contract price was $1,500,000.) The 7th Circuit held that the method of calculating damages was not unreasonable. 924 F.2d 709 (1991).

(2) The Reporter's Notes to proposed § 2-708 states that no attempt was made to provide a detailed solution to the lost volume problem. Whether a seller is a lost volume seller and the measure of lost profits if it is, are left to the courts.

[3] Recover the Price

Read: U.C.C. §§ 2-703(e), 2-709; cf. § 2-716(3).

Read also: U.C.C. §§ 2A-523(1)(e), 2A-529, cf. § 2A-521(3); CISG Arts. 61(1)(a), 62; see Arts. 28, 78, cf. Art. 45(1).

SCHUMANN v. LEVI

United States Court of Appeals
728 F.2d 1141, 38 U.C.C. Rep. 131 (8th Cir. 1984)

Before LAY, CHIEF JUDGE, AND ROSS AND MCMILLIAN, CIRCUIT JUDGES.

PER CURIAM.

[Pursuant to an auction sale, Schumann (plaintiff-appellee) sold some items of personal property, including a Bobcat loader, to Levi (defendant-appellant). Levi breached the contract to buy and Schumann rejected Levi's offer of settlement. United States Magistrate Boline entered a judgment for Schumann, awarding him the price of the Bobcat plus interest. Levi appeals, arguing that the magistrate erred in ordering specific performance of the contract and in his calculation of pre-judgment interest.]

Specific Performance/Action for the Price

The pertinent part of the magistrate's order states:

CONCLUSIONS OF LAW

1. That defendant entered into a valid contract with plaintiff on March 14, 1981 to purchase a Bobcat loader, backhoe attachment and trailer for the sum of $11,600.00, and that defendant has breached the contract.

2. That plaintiff is entitled to specific performance to obtain the benefit of his bargain.

3. That plaintiff is entitled to the sum of $11,600.00 because of the breach of contract.

4. That plaintiff suffered additional damages consisting of interest costs from March 15, 1981 through October 7, 1981 in the amount of $851.09 less the reasonable rental for machinery in the amount of 300.00.

5. That plaintiff is not entitled to an award of punitive and exemplary damages.

ORDER FOR JUDGMENT

1. That plaintiff is awarded $11,600.00 plus interest in the amount of $551.09.

2. That plaintiff shall tender possession and title of the Bobcat loader, backhoe attachment and trailer to defendant at the time defendant satisfies this judgment.

Appellant contends that the magistrate ordered specific performance of the contract, and that this was in error. Citing cases that speak specifically to the traditional division of law and equity, appellant argues that under the doctrine of election of remedies, specific performance was unavailable to plaintiff because he only brought a legal claim for damages. In response, appellee argues that specific performance is not the issue here; he claims that the court awarded him his legal remedy of the price pursuant to Minn Stat § 336.2-709 (1966). That section reads in pertinent part: [the court quotes U.C.C. § 2-709(1)(b), (2)].

The facts as found by the magistrate meet the requirements for recovery of the price. Appellant failed to pay the price when it was due. The goods were identified to the contract, and appellee presented evidence of his unsuccessful attempts to resell. Appellee's contention that he was awarded his legal remedy is persuasive. The equitable remedy of specific performance and the Uniform Commercial Code's action for the price are virtually identical, and the court's order appears to be a judgment for the price.

Appellant also argues that the magistrate abused his discretion in awarding Schumann the price because his complaint did not allege an action for the price or cite the Minnesota statute. Schumann's complaint alleged a breach of contract, and in his prayer for damages, he asked for "an amount necessary to compensate for his loss of bargain." Because a trial court must grant the relief to which a prevailing party is entitled, the court can award such relief, even though the party has not demanded it: Fed. R. Civ. P. 54(c). . . . Here, the parties stipulated to the breach of contract prior to trial and proceeded to litigate the damages issues. As stated above, the evidence adduced at trial provided the support for an award of the price.

. . . .

For the foregoing reasons, the magistrate's judgment is affirmed in part and reversed and remanded in part.

NOTES

In *Rowland Meledandi, Inc. v. Kohn*, 7 U.C.C. Rep. 34 (N.Y. Civ. Ct. 1969), buyer ordered a custom-made suit from seller. Seller cut the pattern in accordance with the buyer's particular measurements and specifications, ordered the cloth, and on receipt of the latter, cut it, along with the lining. Buyer then stopped payment on his $100 check. The court said:

When [seller] learned that payment had been stopped on [buyer's] check, it treated this as a repudiation and ceased further work on the suit (on which it had spent no more than six hours, including several hours selling time). Nonetheless, [seller] seeks to recover the full contract price, relying, inter alia, on § 2-704 of the U.C.C. That section must be read in conjunction with §§ 2-709 and 2-708. When a seller, in the process of manufacturing goods which are not resalable when finished, elects to cease manufacture on the buyer's repudiation, the seller does not have an action for the full purchase price (see Bender U.C.C. Service, Vol. 3, Sales & Bulk Transfer sec. 13.07(4) p. 13-85. . . . He does retain his action for damages (U.C.C. § 2-709(3)).

U.C.C. § 2-704 is discussed at § 7.02[B][2], *supra*.

SWIFT & CO. v. REXTON, INC.

Connecticut Supreme Court
187 Conn. 540, 447 A.2d 9, 34 U.C.C. Rep. 558 (1982)

PER CURIAM.

The single issue presented by this appeal is the sufficiency of the evidence relied upon by the trial court in ruling for the plaintiff in an action to recover the purchase price of goods allegedly sold to the defendants.

From the evidence presented at trial, the trial court could reasonably have found the following facts. From November, 1977, through September, 1978, the plaintiff, Swift and Company (hereinafter Swift), sold goods in the form of meat products to the defendant, Rexton, Inc. d/b/a Chicago Beef and Provision Company (hereinafter Rexton), on an open account basis. The plaintiff's witness, a salesman with Swift for 27 years, testified that because Rexton was his account, he visited and sold it products on a regular basis. In his capacity as a salesman, he prepared invoices at the time orders were taken from which a ledger card was prepared for each account, including Rexton. These ledger cards were periodically updated by Swift, indicating dates, charges, credits and balances due. All charges by the plaintiff and payments by the defendant were included on the ledger cards.

The ledger cards for the Rexton account from November 4, 1977, to September 21, 1978, were introduced as evidence by the plaintiff. The second to last entry, showing a payment of $300, left a balance due Swift of $8728.04. The last entry, however, marked "J/E" for journal entry, indicated a credit of $8728.04 and left the balance column blank. The plaintiff's witness testified that this last entry was an accounting procedure utilized to clear the ledger and suspend the account as a prerequisite to collection proceedings by Swift's legal department.

In this appeal from the judgment of the trial court rendered against it in the amount of $8728.04, the defendant asserts that the findings of fact were unsupported by sufficient competent evidence. We disagree.

When a buyer accepts goods and fails to tender payment when due, the seller may recover the purchase price. General Statutes § 42a-2-709(1)(a). As prerequisites to recovery, therefore, a seller must establish acceptance by the buyer of goods sold and delivered, as well as the failure of the buyer to fulfill his payment obligation.

In the ordinary civil action, while the plaintiff must establish every element of a claim by a fair preponderance of the evidence, there need not be direct evidence of each material fact. It is sufficient if the evidence presented establishes circumstances "from which logical and reasonable inferences of other material facts can be fairly drawn." Moreover, the plaintiff's evidence need not be so overwhelming that every other possible result is excluded; it is sufficient if the evidence "induces in the mind of the trier a reasonable belief that it is more probable than otherwise that the fact in issue is true."

It is the province of the trier of fact to weigh the evidence presented and determine the credibility and effect to be given the evidence. On appellate review, therefore, we will give the evidence the most favorable reasonable construction in support of the verdict to which it is entitled.

Viewed within these principles, the evidence, although scant, supports the judgment rendered by the trial court. The plaintiff's witness testified that as a salesman for Swift he sold the defendant products on a regular basis, from which invoices and subsequently ledger cards were prepared. The ledger cards show charges and payments made against and by the defendant. From this uncontroverted evidence it is reasonable and logical to infer the sale, delivery and acceptance of the plaintiff's goods by the defendant. Moreover, the final balance due of $8728.04 as shown on the ledger cards, although disputed, reasonably establishes the failure by the defendant to tender payment to the plaintiff. Thus, on the foregoing facts and reasonable inferences therefrom, we conclude that the judgment of the trial court was adequately supported by the evidence presented.

There is no error.

———

NOTES

(1) Would U.C.C. § 2-606(1)(b) be of relevance in this case?

(2) U.C.C. § 2-709(1)(a) states that seller may recover the price of conforming goods lost or damaged within a commercially reasonable time after risk of their loss has passed to the buyer. Risk of loss is discussed at § 4.06, *supra*. See U.C.C. § 2-509.

[4] Incidental Damages

Read: U.C.C. § 2-710.

Read also: U.C.C. § 2A-530; CISG Art. 74.

At § 7.02, we have been evaluating seller's remedies for breach by buyer. In particular, § 7.02[C][1] discussed that the seller may recover the difference between the resale price and the contract price "together with any incidental damages allowed . . ." U.C.C. § 2-706, cf. § 2A-527(2).

Section § 7.02[C][2] recited that the measure of damages for non-acceptance or repudiation by the buyer is the difference between the market price and the unpaid contract price "together with any incidental damages. . . ." U.C.C. § 2-708(1). Further, U.C.C. § 2-708(2) states the measure of damages as the profit which the seller would have made "together with any incidental damages. . . ." *Cf.* U.C.C. § 2A-528(1) and (2).

Section § 7.02[C][3] explained that when the buyer fails to pay the price as it becomes due, the seller may recover the price in enumerated circumstances, "together with any incidental damages . . ." U.C.C. § 2-709(1), *cf.* U.C.C. § 2A-529(1).

Because Section 2-710 [Seller's Incidental Damages] does not include recovery for consequential damages, it is not surprising that some courts may be willing to include that which might be considered consequential damages within the "or otherwise resulting from the breach" language of § 2-710. Representative cases are surveyed below.

In *Bulk Oil (U.S.A.), Inc. v. Sun Oil Trading Co.*, 697 F.2d 481, 35 U.C.C. Rep. 23 (2d Cir. 1983), seller contracted to sell $4,000,000 worth of fuel oil to buyer. Seller bought the oil from a third party supplier and financed the transaction by borrowing almost all the cost from Chase Manhattan Bank. Buyer accepted delivery of the oil from seller but refused to pay. After the breach, seller incurred further interest charges on the Chase loan which it paid on a monthly basis. The court held that seller's post breach interest payments to Chase were incidental damages.

In *Ernst Steel Corp. v. Horn Construction Division, Haliburton Co.,104 A.D.2d 55, 481 N.Y.S.2d 833, 40 U.C.C. Rep. 145 at 152-3 (1984)* the court commented:

In an appropriate case a seller is entitled to recover commercially reasonable finance and interest charges incurred as a result of a buyer's breach as a proper item of incidental damages (see Uniform Commercial Code, § 2-710; *Neri v. Retail Mar. Corp.*, 30 NY2d 393 [10 U.C.C. Rep 950]). For the most part, however, interest expenses have only been awarded to sellers for indebtedness specifically identified to goods intended for resale to the breaching party and who, as a result of the breach, cannot repay the loans (*see, e.g., Bulk Oil [USA], Inc. v. Sun Oil Trading Co.*, 697 F2d 481; *Intermeat, Inc. v. American Poultry, Inc.*, 575 F2d 1017; *Neri v. Retail Mar. Corp., supra; Hoffman v. Stoller*, 320 NW2d 786, 792; *Gray v. West*, 608 SW2d 771, 781). In the case of *Atlas Concrete Pipe, Inc. v. Roger J. Au & Son, Inc.* (467 F Supp 830, rev'd 668 F2d 905) relied upon by the trial court, interest expenses were awarded. Although in that case there was no proof of a loan specifically covering the contract goods, the seller proved instead that it was virtually insolvent and had financed fully 100% of its operations. While there is no requirement in the code that interest expenses must be identified to indebtedness specifically covering the contract goods, where a seller cannot link the claimed damages to the contract it clearly has a more difficult burden of proof.

In *S.C. Gray Incorporated v. Ford Motor Company*, 92 Mich. App. 789, 286 N.W.2d 34 (1979), Gray sought to recover for interest it paid on loans taken out to maintain the business when Ford failed to pay the money Gray claimed was due. The court concluded (1) that the interest paid fell within the category of consequential damages, not incidental damages, and (2) that the U.C.C. does not allow a seller to recover consequential damages, U.C.C. §§ 1-106(1), 2-710. The court quoted the *Petroleo Brasileiro* case, which was cited in court's footnote 6 to *Bulk Oil (U.S.A.) v. Sun Oil Trading Co., supra.*

The difference between incidental and consequential damages was highlighted in *Petroleo Brasileiro, SA v. Ameropan Oil Corp*, 14 U.C.C. Rep. 661, 667 (E.D.N.Y., 1974), wherein the court stated:

> While the distinction between the two is not an obvious one, the Code makes plain that incidental damages are normally incurred when a buyer (or seller) repudiates the contract or wrongfully rejects the goods, causing the other to incur such expenses as transporting, storing, or reselling the goods. On the other hand, consequential damages do not arise within the scope of the immediate buyer-seller transaction, but rather stem from losses incurred by the nonbreaching party in its dealings, often with third parties, which were a proximate result of the breach, and which were reasonably foreseeable by the breaching party at the time of contracting.

In *Afram Export Corp. v. Metallurgiki Halyps, S.A.*, 772 F.2d 1358, 41 U.C.C. Rep. 1709 (1985), seller was allowed prejudgment interest. The court observed at 41 U.C.C. Rep. 1716-18:

> Looking first to general principles, we point out that while at one time a plaintiff in a contract suit could obtain an award of prejudgment interest only if the suit was for a fixed amount, as in a suit to collect a promissory note, this is no longer required; it is nowadays quite enough that the amount of damages be ascertainable by reference to an objective standard of value, such as market value where "readily ascertainable." . . . In other fields of law, too, courts increasingly award prejudgment interest, noting for example that a failure to award such interest gives defendants an incentive to prolong litigation. . . .

> The Wisconsin cases seem generally in accord with the position outlined above, though we can find no case on point. Provided that there is "a reasonably certain standard of measurement by the correct application of which [the party who breaks the contract] can

ascertain the amount he owes," prejudgment interest will be awarded, *Dahl v. Housing Authority*, 54 Wis. 2d 22, 31, 194 N.W.2d 618, 623 (1972), unless the damage claim is "substantially inflated," *Wyandotte Chemicals Corp. v. Royal Electric Mfg. Co*, 66 Wis. 2d 577, 586, 225 N.W.2d 648, 653 (1975). Afram [seller] passes this two-part test (the second part of which may be special to Wisconsin). The test of ready ascertainability is satisfied by so much of Afram's claim as seeks simply the difference between the contract price, a fixed amount, and the market value at the date of breach. [See U.C.C. § 2-708(1).]

. . . .

What must give us pause through is the statement in *Congress Bar & Restaurant* that, "As long as there is a genuine dispute about the amount that is due, the insurer should not have to pay interest until the amount has been determined and judgment entered thereon." 42 Wis. 2d at 71, 165 N.W.2d at 417. Like all judicial language, however, this must be read in context. The case involved fire damage which proved difficult to estimate, and as mentioned the plaintiff's estimate was way too high. There was no contract price to provide a lodestar. The court in *Congress Bar & Restaurant* quoted approvingly the statement made in many Wisconsin opinions that "before interest can be recovered the amount claimed must be fixed or determined *or readily determinable*," . . .and the words we have italicized described this case.

See also North American Foreign Trading Corp. v. Direct Mail Specialist, 697 F.2d 163 (S.D.N.Y. 1988).

In *Nobs Chemical, U.S.A., Inc. v. Koppers Co.*, 616 F.2d 212 (5th Cir. 1980), seller contracted to sell cumene (an additive for high-octane motor fuel) to buyer. Buyer breached the contract. Seller was forced to pay its Brazilian supplier an extra $25 per ton when the price per ton increased because its total order with the supplier was reduced from 4,000 metric tons to 3,000 because of buyer's breach. The court affirmed the district court and decided this lost quantity discount amounted to consequential damages and therefore not recoverable.

See also Atlanta Paper Box Co. v. Whitman's Chocolates, 23 U.C.C. Rep. 2d 361, 844 F. Supp. 1038 (E.D. Pa. 1994). (When buyer cancelled a million dollar order for candy boxes and seller brought suit alleging that this decreased the value of seller's business, and thereby caused a potential purchaser of seller's business to withdraw its offer, this was clearly an impermissible attempt to obtain consequential damages); *Jelen & Son, Inc. v. Brandimere*, 801 P.2d 1182, 13 U.C.C. Rep. 2d 344 (Colo. 1990). (Absent other statutory or contractual provisions to the contrary, attorney's fees are not incidental damages under U.C.C. § 2-710).

Of particular interest is *Associated Metals & Minerals Corp. v. Sharon Steel Corp.*, 590 F. Supp. 18, 39 U.C.C. Rep. 892 (S.D.N.Y. 1983), where the seller sought to recover interest for delayed payment of the purchase price by the buyer. The court allowed recovery of the interest as consequential damages. It recognized that consequential damages are not awarded to seller under § 2-710, but it applied the common law of Pennsylvania to award consequential damages under § 1-103 and Restatement, Second, Contracts § 347, which gives "the injured party" incidental or consequential loss caused by the breach. See U.C.C. §1-106(1): "Consequential damages. . .may not be had except as specifically provided in this Act *or by other rule of law*." [Emphasis added.]

NOTE

Proposed § 2-710 is captioned, "Seller's Incidental and Consequential Damages." The consequential damages provision is drafted to parallel § 2-715(2)(a) (Proposed § 2-715(b)(1)).

§ 7.03 Seller's Remedies (1) on Discovery of Buyer's Insolvency, (2) in a "Cash Sale" Transaction

Read: U.C.C. § 2-702, cf. § 2-502; §§ 2-507(2), 2-511(3).

Read also: U.C.C. §§ 2A-523(1)(c), 2A-525, cf. 2A-522; CISG Arts. 81(2), 84(2).

Discovery of Buyer's Insolvency. Section 2-702(2) provides in part: "Where the seller discovers that the buyer has received goods on credit while insolvent he may reclaim the goods upon demand made within ten days after the receipt . . ." This right to reclaim is subject to the rights of certain good faith purchases under U.C.C. § 2-403. See U.C.C. § 2-702(3). See discussion at Chapter 8, Rights of Third Parties: Good Faith Purchase of Goods.

Cash Sale Transaction. L. Vold, The Law of Sales § 29 (2d ed. 1959) summarizes the common law: [10]

> Technical cash sales at common law differ from ordinary sales. In technical cash sales the property interest does not pass until the price is paid. Example: over-the-counter cash deal in the old-fashioned retail store. Such a deal involves no credit. The goods are handed over in exchange for the price then paid at about the same time.
>
> . . . .
>
> Cumbersome details often make exactly simultaneous exchange of goods for price impossible. . . . The delay that is involved may not exceed what the practical circumstances require for exchanging goods for price paid. If so, the parties often treat this exchange as if it were "substantially simultaneous." Where the parties have done so, the courts, seeking justice between the parties, often treat the deal the same way. . . .
>
> Waiver of expected cash payment may be shown in various ways: agreement or usage showing giving of credit; permitting the buyer without objection after delivery to retain the goods for a considerable time; failure promptly to reclaim possession.
>
> Where payment is made by check, Vold at § 30 observes:
>
> Our American authorities commonly treat payment by check as only conditional payment until cashed. Receiving the buyer's check for the price therefore does not waive cash payment. Making and receiving payment here includes not only the issue of the check but its cashing at the drawee bank. The routine time involved in check collection is thus included in the time that is treated as "substantially simultaneous." Payment by check thus usually is not regarded as an extension of credit for the time needed to cash the check.
>
> Suppose on the other hand, the seller takes a promissory note for the price, or a postdated check. What then? This clearly amounts to an extension of credit. It thereby waives immediate cash payment.
>
> A no-fund check will "bounce." It will not be paid on presentation at the drawee bank. If paid by mistake in the first instance, it will promptly be charged back to the holder on discovery

---

[10] Copyright © by West Publishing Co. 1959. Reprinted by permission.

of this mistake. Such a check therefore not only is not completed payment when given but never becomes completed payment.

On this basis American common law usually holds, in cases of this kind, that the goods still belong to the seller; that is, unless the seller is shown to have accepted the check itself as absolute payment.

Vold summarizes:

Payment by check, unless otherwise agreed, is usually treated as merely conditional payment until the check is cashed. In technical cash sale deals, therefore, though the goods be delivered, the property interest does not pass until the check is cashed. If the check "bounces," the unpaid seller can reclaim his goods.

How is the "cash sale" transaction handled under the Code? See U.C.C. §§ 2-507(2) and Comment 3, 2-511(3) and Comments 4-6 and PEB Commentary No. 1, U.C.C. § 2-507(2) (March 10, 1990). See also U.C.C. § 2-403(1)(b) and (c) and Chapter 8, Rights of Third Parties: Good Faith Purchase of Goods.

—

IN RE CHARTER CO.

United States Bankruptcy Court, Middle District of Florida
52 BR 263, 42 U.C.C. Rep. 192 (1985)

GEORGE L. PROCTOR, BANKRUPTCY JUDGE.

The amended complaint in this adversary proceeding sets forth two factually related but theoretically distinct claims for relief, *i.e.* reclamation and constructive trust, both arising from a sale of crude oil by Pratt to the defendant Charter Crude Oil Company (CCOC). A trial was held on April 18, 1985, and the parties have submitted post-trial briefs. The facts as stipulated lead the court to conclude that Charter International Oil Company (CIOC) is merely a nominal party, and references to "the defendant" throughout the text of the opinion will be to CCOC. The essential facts are subject to a stipulation entered into by the parties, and we will draw on that stipulation, as well as evidence adduced at trial, for our summary of the material facts.

Prior to April 20, 1984, the defendant had, on a regular basis, purchased crude oil from leases operated by the plaintiff. Throughout this course of dealing, the defendant only was responsible for payment for oil it purchased. Between April 3 and April 14, 1984, crude oil with a value of $32,410.41 was produced by Pratt and delivered for the account of the defendant to Mobil Oil Corporation. Between April 15 and April 18, 1984, crude oil with a value of $73,594.98 was delivered in the same manner.

On April 24, 1984, Pratt sent the defendant notice of reclamation as to all of the oil delivered on or after April 3, 1984.

The defendant and Mobil Oil Corporation had entered into the exchange agreement whereby Mobil was to purchase oil from the defendant in November 1983. The plaintiff was not a party to this agreement.

On or about April 3, 1984, Larry Golden, president of the defendant, sent the plaintiff a letter, which appears to be a form letter sent to all operators and producers with which the defendant had a business relationship. The letter appears to be intended to amplify on an announcement that had been made publicly by the defendant on April 2, 1984, to no longer "run crude oil on a sustained basis . . .at the Houston division." The second paragraph of the letter reads in pertinent part as follows:

> As to the impact this has on the operations, organization, and financial condition of the Crude Oil Gathering Company, we anticipate that there will be no changes. This segment of our business continues to be one in which we take great pride and anticipate continuing for many years to come.

Delivery of the crude oil was made from trucks operated by Pratt via either trucks leased by Mobil or via the facilities of Mobil Pipe Line Company and was not in the custody or possession of CCOC at any time.

On April 16, 1984, the Charter Company and various of its subsidiaries including the defendant filed in this court for protection under Chapter 11 of the Bankruptcy Code. On May 8 and 18, 1984, the defendant billed Mobil in the amount of $109,540.00 for the subject crude oil. No payment pursuant to the contract has been made; rather, pursuant to the court's order of February 21, 1985, granting relief from the automatic stay and allowing offset of mutual debts in the bankruptcy cases to which this adversary proceeding is related, Mobil has placed the funds in a segregated interest bearing account and has agreed to distribute it as provided by court order or agreement of the parties. It is undisputed that, to the extent that state law governs the outcome of this proceeding, Kansas law applies.

Section 546[(c)] of the Bankruptcy Code defines the rights of reclaiming creditors where the defaulting buyer has filed for bankruptcy protection. It provides in pertinent part that

> . . . the rights and powers of a trustee under sections 544(a), 545, and 549 of this title are subject to any statutory or common-law right of a seller that has sold goods to the debtor, in the ordinary course of such seller's business, to reclaim such goods if the buyer has received such goods while insolvent, but — (1) such a seller may not reclaim any such goods unless such seller demands in writing reclamation of such goods before ten days after receipt of such goods by the debtor. . . .

Uniform Commercial Code § 2-702(2) as adopted in Kansas provides [the Court quotes U.C.C. § 2-702(2)].

Subsection (3) makes the seller's right to reclaim subject to

> . . . the rights of a buyer in the ordinary course of business or other good faith purchaser or lien creditor under this chapter.[11]

By agreement of the parties, the issue of the alleged insolvency of the defendant has been reserved for a separate trial at a later time.

We first must confront the issues created by the debtor's nonpossession of the goods at the time of the reclamation demand or indeed at any time. The defendants treat as dispositive their non-possession at the time of reclamation, citing case law to the effect that where the goods sought to be reclaimed are not in the hands of the buyer at the time reclamation is sought there is nothing to reclaim and thus that remedy is foreclosed. Cases which treat possession by the

---

[11] [This is the 1962 version of U.C.C. § 2-702(3). In 1966 § 2-702(3) was amended to delete "or lien creditor."—Ed.]

buyer as an absolute prerequisite to the right of reclamation have generally not arisen in the factual context of the defaulting buyer, by agreement, *never* having had possession of the goods; they rather appear to arise from the situation in which the buyer had possession but relinquished it to a third party before a timely reclamation demand. This court does not specifically disavow but is unwilling to adopt the sweeping proposition that non-possession by the defaulting buyer at the time of reclamation demand is *invariably* a bar to reclamation. The case law makes abundantly clear, however, that if the goods sought to be reclaimed are not in the hands of the buyer and are in the hands of a good faith purchaser, no reclamation remedy can lie.

Had there been no bankruptcy, the plaintiff would have been able to pursue any rights created by state law, i.e. principally, if not exclusively, the provisions of U.C.C. § 2-702. In the context of bankruptcy, the reclaiming seller would have no rights against a debtor-in-possession exercising the rights of a trustee, but for the provision of § 546(c). Section 546(c), however, places a crucial limitation on a reclaiming seller's pursuit of state law reclamation rights. According to its plain language, no reclamation is to be had unless the seller has made a reclamation demand before ten days after receipt of the goods. The state law with which § 546(c) was drafted to harmonize sets forth *two* sets of circumstances under which a seller may reclaim from an insolvent buyer — the seller may make timely demand or the demand may be excused where a written misrepresentation as to the debtor's solvency has been made by the debtor. The plaintiff urges that the letter from Mr. Golden of February 21, 1984, constitutes such a written misrepresentation and that § 546 permits use of the written misrepresentation-as-to-solvency route to reclamation. The case law and this court's unambivalent reading of § 546(c) do not support the plaintiff's position. *In re Gibson Distributing Co.*, 40 B.R. 767 (Bkrtcy.W.D.Tex.1984), *In re L.T.S., Inc.*, 32 B.R. 907(Bkrtcy.D.Idaho 1983), and I*n re Ateco Equipment*, 18 B.R. 917(Bkrtcy.W.D.Pa 1982) have all held that the § 546 requirement for written demand for reclamation within ten days is absolute and cannot be waived on the ground of the buyer's written misrepresentation as to solvency. Our conclusion that, as a matter of law, any written misrepresentation as to solvency is immaterial determines that we need not consider whether Mr. Golden's letter constituted such a misrepresentation. Thus failure to make a timely reclamation demand in itself cuts off the plaintiff's rights in the oil delivered more than 10 days before demand was made.

With respect to that oil for whose reclamation a timely demand *was* made, U.C.C. § 2-702 provides that the reclaiming seller's rights are cut off by the rights of a good faith purchaser. We must determine then, with respect to that portion of the oil for which the plaintiff made a timely reclamation demand, whether Mobil was a good faith purchaser. The plaintiff contests good faith purchaser status on Mobil's part in that, 1) it alleges knowledge on Mobil's part of the defendant's insolvency prior to the plaintiff's reclamation demand, and, 2) because Mobil has, rather than actually paying for the oil, placed the agreed-upon price in a segregated fund subject to this court's order. The facts as stipulated do not suggest that Mobil intended to be other than a buyer in the ordinary course of business. We can find that Mobil is not a good faith purchaser if and only if some additional fact stipulated or shown has the legal effect of affirmatively disqualifying Mobil for good faith purchaser status.

The vast majority of published cases which address the rights of the reclaiming seller vis-a-vis those of a third party concern themselves with a lien creditor of the debtor and are not applicable in this instance. The case most factually analogous to that before us appears to be *In re Coast Trading Co., Inc.*, 31 B.R. 667(Bkrtcy.D.Ore. 1982). There, three growers sold grain to Coast which in turn sold it to Ralston Purina. Ralston "did not pay for the grain as it was in doubt as to which party was entitled to payment," *Id.* at 668. Ralston did later pay the agreed upon price into the registry of the bankruptcy court pursuant to an interpleader action which it filed, i.e. it followed a course of behavior similar to that of Mobil in the instant case. The Coast court holds that "[w]hether the ultimate purchaser has yet paid for the goods . . .is clearly immaterial," *Id.* A finding of good faith purchaser status on Ralston's part is clearly implicit in the slightly earlier language, "[i]f the buyer, before reclamation, has already sold the goods to *a good faith purchaser for value,* there is nothing to reclaim as the seller cannot demand a return of the goods from the ultimate purchaser." (*Id.,* emphasis added). The *Coast* court clearly, in predicating its ultimate holding on good faith purchaser status, did not believe that mere non-payment of the purchase price by the ultimate purchaser does negate good faith status where, as the facts in *Coast* and the case before us indicate, it cannot be said that the ultimate purchaser has received, or attempted to receive, a windfall.

We see no merit in the position that Mobil is not in good faith because of some knowledge it may have had of financial instability of the defendant's part—the facts indicate no reason to believe that Mobil sought any unfair advantage or expected to be anything other than a buyer for value in the ordinary course of business. Thus we find Mobil Oil to be a good faith purchaser. Its good faith purchaser status cuts off reclamation rights which the plaintiff would otherwise have to oil delivered within ten days before the reclamation demand.

Our holding in favor of the defendant on the statutory reclamation count of the amended complaint renders moot for this particular adversary proceeding the issue of the defendant's solvency at the time of receipt of the goods.

The second count of the plaintiff's amended complaint urges that this is an appropriate instance for imposition of a constructive trust. It is apparent to this court, however, that it was the intent of the drafters of the Uniform Commercial Code to create U.C.C.-based reclamation as the exclusive remedy to sellers to insolvent defaulting buyers. As we have discussed *supra* it was equally clearly the intent of Congress to further limit the rights of such parties in a bankruptcy context by the restrictions of 11 U.S.C. § 546. We cannot reconcile with such strictly limited statutory remedies, the concept that recourse may be had to a vaguely defined equitable remedy.

. . . .

For the reasons set forth above, a judgment in favor of the defendant on both counts will be entered with this opinion.

Final judgment for defendants and order directing turnover of property of the estate

Ordered as follows:

1. Judgment is hereby entered in favor of the defendants on both counts of the amended complaint;

2. Mobil Oil Corporation holds funds which, by the terms of this judgment, become property of the bankruptcy estate and it appearing that those funds have been held in an interest bearing account and that Mobil Oil Corporation asserts no interest in the funds other than that of a stakeholder, Mobil shall forthwith turnover to the debtor-in-possession all principal and interest so held.

———

NOTES

Section 546(c) of the Bankruptcy Code, 11 U.S.C. § 546(c), reads in full:

(c) Except as provided in subsection (d) of this section, the rights and powers of a trustee under sections 544(a), 545, 547, and 549 of this title are subject to any statutory or common-law right of a seller of goods that has sold goods to the debtor, in the ordinary course of such seller's business, to reclaim such goods if the debtor has received such goods while insolvent, but—

(1) such a seller may not reclaim any such goods unless such seller demands in writing reclamation of such goods

(A) before 10 days after receipt of such goods by the debtor; or

(B) if such 10–day period expires after the commencement of the case, before 20 days after receipt of such goods by the debtor; and before ten days after receipt of such goods by the debtor; and

(2) the court may deny reclamation to a seller with such a right of reclamation that has made such a demand only if the court—

(A) grants the claim of such a seller priority as a claim of a kind specified in section 503(b) of this title; or

(B) Secures such claim by a lien.

———

PROBLEM 7.3

On May 20, Braxton Motor Company sold and delivered to Richard Taggart a new brown four-door Cadillac for a cash price of $29,864.30. Taggart paid Braxton by a check dated May 20. Before the check cleared, Taggart moved the car out of town. On June 1 the check was returned to Braxton for lack of sufficient funds.

Meanwhile, Taggart owed Citizens Bank $30,000 pursuant to two promissory notes. He defaulted on the notes and the bank brought suit in the Placer County Superior Court and secured judgment against Taggart for an amount in excess of $30,000. A writ of execution was issued and on July 15 the Placer County Sheriff levied on the Cadillac registered in Taggart's name. Braxton was unable to locate the Cadillac until notified by the Placer County Sheriff that the vehicle had been seized.

Braxton asserts a cash seller's reclamation rights under U.C.C. §§ 2-507(2) and 2-511(3). Citizens Bank concedes that an unpaid cash seller prevails over an attaching lien creditor. But it asserts that Braxton waived its reclamation rights by not demanding reclamation within ten days after the receipt of the Cadillac by Taggart. Bank's authority is Comment 3 to § 2-507 (1989) which reads in part: "The provision of this Article for a ten day limit within which the seller may reclaim goods delivered on credit to an insolvent buyer [§ 2-702(2)] is also applicable here."

Who prevails, Braxton or Citizens Bank? See § 2-507 Comment 3 (1990) and PEB Commentary No. 1, dated March 10, 1990; *Citizens Bank of Roseville v. Taggart*, 143 Cal. App. 3d 318, 191 Cal. Rptr. 729, 36 U.C.C. Rep. 529 (1983).

NOTES

(1) Proposed § 2-702 combines in one place the right of a seller to reclaim goods delivered to a buyer (1) in a cash sale where payment is not made or (2) in a credit sale where the buyer was insolvent. The credit sale provision follows essentially present § 2-702(2); the cash sale provision is: "If payment is due and demanded on delivery to the buyer, a seller may reclaim the goods delivered upon demand made within a reasonable time after the seller discovers or should have discovered that payment was not made."

(2) U.C.C. § 2-403 is discussed at Chapter 8, Rights of Third Parties: Good Faith Purchase of Goods.

§ 7.04 Buyer's Remedies for Breach Where Goods Not Accepted or Acceptance Justifiably Revoked

Read: U.C.C. § 2-711.

Read also: U.C.C. § 2A-508, CISG Art. 45.

The remedies dealt with in this section are those available to a buyer who has not accepted the goods or who has justifiably revoked his acceptance. These remedies are indexed in U.C.C. § 2-711, cf. § 2A-508.

The remedies available to a buyer with regard to goods finally accepted appear in the next section, § 7.05, and at U.C.C. § 2-714, Buyer's Damages in Regard to Accepted Goods. See U.C.C. § 2-711Comment 1.[12] Cf. §§ 2A-508(3) and (4), 2A-519(3) and (4).

For discussion of rejection, acceptance and revocation of acceptance, see § 6.04, Buyer's Rights on Improper Delivery, and U.C.C. §§ 2-601 through 2-608. Cf. §§ 2A-509 through 2A-512, 2A-514 through 2A-517.

The buyer's right to proceed as to all goods when the breach is as to only some of the goods is determined by the section on breach in installment contracts, U.C.C. §§ 2-612, cf. § 2A-510. See § 6.04[D] above. As to partial acceptances, see U.C.C. § 2-601(c). U.C.C. § 2-711Comment 1.

[A] Cancellation

Read: U.C.C. §§ 2-711(1), 2-106(3) and (4); cf. § 2-703(f).

---

[12] Simply, the buyer's remedies for breach of the sale contract by the seller fall into two functional categories: those remedies available where the buyer does not receive and retain the goods, as where seller fails to deliver, or where buyer rejects or revokes acceptance; and those remedies available where the buyer has received and retained the goods. The first category is contained in § 2-711; the second in § 2-714.

Read also: U.C.C. § 2A-508(1)(a), 2A-103(1)(b) and (z), 2A-505(1)-(3), cf. § 2A-523(1)(a); CISG Arts. 49, 25-27, 81-84, cf. Art. 64.

ROYCO, INC. v. COTTENGIM

Florida District Court of Appeal
427 So. 2d 759, 35 U.C.C. Rep. 465 (1983)

SHARP, J.

Royco, Inc., d/b/a Uncle Roy's Mobile Home Sales, appeals from a judgment, entered after a non-jury trial, which allowed the Cottengims (purchasers of a mobile home from Royco) to cancel a contract for the purchase of a mobile home and to recover the sums they had paid Royco. The trial court ruled the Cottengims had not accepted the mobile home; Royco had materially breached the sales contract; and the Cottengims could cancel the contract under § 672.711, Florida Statutes (1981), even though they had an adequate remedy at law (damages). We affirm.

The trial court found Royco had breached the sales contract in three respects: failure to provide a mobile home with a beamed living room ceiling, as in the model shown to the purchasers when they ordered the home; failure to provide ceramic tile in the bathrooms, as in the model they were shown; and failure to provide a 36 inch-wide entry door to the mobile home. Mr. Cottengim is physically handicapped, and his wheelchair requires 36 inches for passage — a fact made known to Royco's salesman. The record is also clear that Royco refused to remedy these defects after the mobile home was delivered to the Cottengims, although it was given adequate time and opportunity to do so.

Although some pre-Code Florida cases held that rescission was not an available remedy to a buyer if the breach was curable by an award of damages, the rule is clearly otherwise under § 672.711. It provides: [the court quotes U.C.C. § 2-711(1)]. This section imposes no condition or qualification on the buyer's right to cancel the contract where he rightfully rejects or justifiably revokes acceptance. He is no longer required to bring an equitable action for rescission, and, as part of that remedy, prove that damages are an inadequate remedy.

Affirmed.

[B] Recover Price Paid; Security Interest in Rejected Goods

Read: U.C.C. § 2-711(1) and (3), see § 2-706, especially (6).

Read also: U.C.C. § 2A-508(1)(b) and (5); CISG Art. 81, 84.

U.C.C. § 2-711(1) allows the buyer to recover so much of the price as has been paid. Subsection (3) is intended to make it clear that the buyer may hold and resell rejected goods if he has paid part of the purchase price or incurred expenses of the type specified. U.C.C. § 2-711 Comment 3.

IN RE ADAMS PLYWOOD, INC.

United States Bankruptcy Court, Western District of Tennessee
48 BR 719, 41 U.C.C. Rep. 830 (1985)

WILLIAM B. LEFFLER, BANKRUPTCY JUDGE.

Champion Building Products ("Champion") purchased from Adams Plywood, Inc. ("Debtor") 708 sheets of one-fourth inch four-by-eight natural birch plywood along with 61 sheets of one-fourth inch four-by-eight red oak plywood. Champion paid the Debtor $6,656.93 upon delivery of the plywood. On August 22, 1984, nine days after delivery, Champion inspected the plywood and exercised its right to reject all the goods because they did not conform to the contract. Tenn. Code Ann. § 47-2-601. Champion returned the plywood to the Debtor on August 22, 1984, the same day that the Debtor filed a Chapter 11 Petition in Bankruptcy. The plywood was sold or otherwise disposed of before this matter was filed with this Court.

Champion is now before this court by virtue of what it calls a "Petition to Require Debtor to Relinquish in and Return Equipment to Petitioner." In this petition, Champion prays for the following: an injunction against the Trustee selling or otherwise disposing of goods; an order allowing Champion to reclaim the goods; an order allowing Champion's claim for $6,656.93, including $2,218.98 in attorney fees.[13]

Champion takes the position that it has a right to reclaim the goods pursuant to 11 U.S.C. § 546(c).[14] The court finds that Champion's position is without merit. Section 546(c) grants the right of reclamation to a *seller* of goods. Champion is clearly a buyer that exercised its right to reject the goods. Therefore, Section 546(c) is unavailable to Champion.

The remedies available to Champion once it discovered that the goods shipped by the Debtor did not conform to the contract are found at Tenn. Code Ann. § 47-2-711. Section 47-2-711(3) reads in pertinent part as follows:

---

[13] This should have been filed as an adversary proceeding pursuant to Bankruptcy Rule 7001.

[14] Champion sent a written demand for reclamation of the plywood within ten days after the Debtor received the plywood. Section 546(c) states as follows:

(c) Except as provided in subsection (d) of this section, the rights and powers of a trustee under sections 544(a), 545, and 549 of this title are subject to any statutory or common-law right of a seller of goods that has sold goods to the debtor, in the ordinary course of such seller's business, to reclaim such goods if the debtor has received such goods while insolvent, but—

(1) such a seller may not reclaim any such goods unless such seller demands in writing reclamation of such goods before ten days after receipt of such goods by the debtor; and

(2) the court may deny reclamation to a seller with such a right of reclamation that has made such a demand only if the court—

(A) grants the claim of such a seller priority as a claim of a kind specified in section 503(b) of this title; or

(B) secured such claim by a lien.

(3) On rightful rejection . . .of acceptance a buyer has a security interest in goods *in his possession* or control for any payments made on their price and any expenses reasonably incurred in their inspection, receipt, transportation, care and custody and may hold such goods and resell them in like manner as an aggrieved seller.

(Emphasis added.)

Champion could have protected itself by properly exercising its remedies under Tenn. Code Ann. § 47-2-711. Under § 47-2-711(3), Champion could have rejected the plywood yet kept the goods and maintained a security interest in the goods. By sending the plywood back to the Debtor, Champion is left with a mere unsecured claim against the Debtor in the amount of $6,656.93.

Although the result reached by the Court in this case seems inequitable at first glance, when one views the case in the context of the entire bankruptcy proceeding and from the perspective of all the other creditors involved, the holding can be justified.

There are two principal goals underlying the Bankruptcy Act. The first goal is to ". . . relieve the honest debtor from the weight of oppressive indebtedness and permit him to start afresh . . ." *Local Loan Co. v. Hunt*, 292 U.S. 234, 244 (1934). The other principal goal is to provide for equitable distribution of a debtor's estate among all his creditors . . . .

Therefore, under the particular facts and circumstances of the case, the court must hold that Champion holds an unsecured claim against the Debtor in the amount of $6,656.93.

[C]   Recover Money Damages

[1]   Cover and Have Damages

Read: U.C.C. §§ 2-711(1)(a), 2-712; cf. § 2-706.

Read also: U.C.C. §§ 2A-508(1)(c), 2A-518, 2A-520, cf. § 2A-527, CISG Arts. 75, 77.

MARTELLA v. WOODS

United States Court of Appeals
715 F.2d 410, 36 U.C.C. Rep. 1200 (8th Cir. 1983)

BRIGHT, CIRCUIT JUDGE.

James H. Woods, Jr., d/b/a Chaumiere Farms, appeals the judgment of the district court awarding Fred H. Martella, Robert M. Berry, Robert M. Lee and William J. Mouren, d/b/a Arkavalley Farm $43,248 in damages for cover and $64,529.60 in damages for the nondelivery of certain heifers. Arkavalley Farm cross-appeals, arguing that the district court erred in failing to award $ 129,391.50 in damages for lost profits. For the reasons outlined below, we affirm on the merits, but reverse and remand to the district court for recomputation of damages.

I. Background.

On or about December 2, 1976, Woods and Ralston Purina Company, d/b/a Arkavalley Farm, executed the "Arkavalley Farm Heifer Growing Contract." The contract provided that Woods would purchase from Arkavalley Farm an unspecified number of three and four month-old heifers. Woods would feed these heifers and allow them to breed with bulls furnished by Arkavalley. The contract also provided that when these heifers reached approximately 24 to 30 months of age Woods would sell them back to the Arkavalley Farm at a price determined by the weight of each heifer. The then-pregnant heifers would be used to replace the less productive heifers in Arkavalley's dairy farm.[15]

Pursuant to this contract, Woods purchased 190 Holstein heifer calves from Arkavalley. Woods expected that the calves would reach 900 pounds between 18 and 19 months of age. At that time, the parties expected to place the heifers with a bull. Waiting until the calves reached 900 pounds before breeding them would benefit both parties because Woods could produce heavier bred heifers thereby obtaining the maximum contract price of 48 cents per pound and Arkavalley would receive replacement heifers capable of producing more milk than could smaller heifers.

Problems arose, however, because the heifers did not grow fast enough. None of the first 36 heifers ultimately placed with bulls reached 900 pounds between 18 and 19 months of age. Indeed, 34 of the 36 heifers did not reach 900 pounds until they were 22 months or older.

Between March 26 and May 8, 1979, Woods sold 41 bred heifers to Arkavalley. These heifers averaged slightly more than 30 months of age.

In April of 1979, Ralston Purina sold Arkavalley Farm to Martella, Berry, Lee and Mouren, and assigned them its interest in the 1976 contract.

On May 5, 1979, Woods informed Arkavalley that, because the heifers were not progressing normally and were causing the Chaumiere Farm to lose money, he was going to sell the heifers. Arkavalley offered Woods 46 cents per pound for the 144 heifers.[16] Woods rejected this offer. Woods then proceeded to sell the remaining 144 heifers, which were supposed to have been sold to the dairy, to third persons.

To compensate for the heifers that Woods failed to supply, Arkavalley purchased 50 pregnant heifers from third parties. Arkavalley then sued Woods in federal district court for breach of contract. Arkavalley contended that Woods breached the contract by failing to resell 144 of the 186 heifers to Arkavalley Farm. Woods failed to dispute that his sale of the 144 heifers to third parties did not conform to the requirements of the contract. Rather, Woods argued in the district court that the contract was rescinded by failure of consideration. Woods asserted that no consideration for the contract existed because Arkavalley breached expressed and implied warranties concerning the quality of the heifers provided to him.

---

[15] Specifically, the contract provided in pertinent part:

1. Feeder [Woods] will purchase from Dairy [Arkavalley Farm] a mutually agreeable number of replacement heifers weighing approximately 200 pounds. . . .

. . . .

3. Feeder will transport these replacement heifers to his farm . . .where Feeder will care for and raise them, allow them to breed with the bull(s) furnished by Dairy. . . .

4. When these heifers reach approximately 24-30 months of age, Feeder will sell these heifers back to the Dairy using the following formula:

1. Those heifers weighing less than 1,100 pounds at forty (40) cents per pound.

2. Those heifers weighing over 1,100 pounds but less than 1,200 pounds at forty-four (44) cents per pound.

3. Those heifers weighing over 1,200 pounds at forty-eight (48) cents per pound.

[16] As we noted earlier in the text, Woods purchased 190 heifer calves from Arkavalley. One calf died and three others were viewed as unfit and sold on the open market. Between March 26 and May 8, 1979, Woods sold 41 bred heifers to Arkavalley. Woods also resold to Arkavalley a single "freemartin," which is a heifer incapable of reproduction. Thus, by mid-May 1979, Woods still had 144 of the original 190 heifers purchased from Arkavalley.

The district court found that: (1) the assignment of the contract from Ralston Purina to Martella, Berry, Lee and Mouren was effective because it did not materially change the duties, burdens or risks of Woods; (2) Arkavalley made no express warranties as to the quality of the heifers Woods purchased; (3) there existed no implied warranties as to the calves because it is impossible to determine the growth and breeding potential of heifer calves at three or four months of age, when they were purchased by Woods; (4) the fact that the heifers had grown slowly and thus were incapable of being dairy replacement heifers at 24 to 30 months of age was not a condition precedent to Woods' performance of the contract, making the contract unenforceable; and finally, (5) the contract was not, therefore, rescinded because of failure of consideration.

On the issue of damages, the district court: (1) awarded Arkavalley $43,248 in damages for cover; (2) awarded Arkavalley $64,529.60 in damages for nondelivery; and (3) determined that Arkavalley was not entitled to damages for lost profits.

On appeal, Woods urges that the district court erred in: (1) concluding that no express or implied warranties of the quality of the heifer calves existed; (2) concluding that growth of the heifers and their development into dairy replacement heifers within the time frame specified in the contract was not a condition precedent; (3) concluding that the conduct of the parties did not demonstrate mutual rescission of the contract; and (4) awarding damages. . . .

II. Discussion.

A. The Merits.

After a careful review of the briefs and record in this case, we conclude that the district court did not err in any of its rulings on the merits. However, the district court's award of damages presents more substantial questions, and it is to those issues we now turn.

B. Damages for Cover.

The district court found that Arkavalley had partially covered Woods' breach by purchasing 50 heifers at $63,088. The court observed that the contract price for the 50 heifers would have been $19,840. The district court concluded that the difference, $43,248, was recoverable as cover costs by Arkavalley. The court rejected Woods' argument that the 50 replacement heifers purchased by Arkavalley were not like-kind substitutes for the heifers Woods had sold to third parties. The court stated that "[i]t is irrelevant what the **state of** the heifers was when defendant Woods sold them to third parties." We disagree.

The Uniform Commercial Code, as adopted in Missouri, provides: [the court quotes U.C.C. § 2-712].

Section 400.2-712 allows a buyer the right to purchase reasonable substitutes and recover the difference between the cost to obtain the substitute goods and the contract price. To recover under this section, the buyer must act in good faith and in a reasonable manner in purchasing substitute goods, and the goods must be a like-kind substitute. However, the buyer may not utilize cover to put himself in a better position than he would have been had the contract been performed. . . .

We note initially that the contract did not require Woods to deliver pregnant heifers of a certain weight and quality to Arkavalley. The contract merely required Woods to sell and Arkavalley to buy those heifers between 24-30 months of age.[17] Therefore, a breach of that contract only

---

[17] We note that specifically the contract did not require Woods to deliver to Arkavalley pregnant heifers. The contract provided that "Feeder will transport these replacement heifers to his farm . . .where Feeder will care for and raise

permits Arkavalley to cover with the quality and size of heifers Woods was obligated to sell Arkavalley. The 50 heifers purchased by Arkavalley were not like-kind substitutes for the heifers Woods sold to third parties. The district court found that Arkavalley covered by purchasing 50 pregnant heifers, weighing between 1,100 to 1,200 pounds each. In contrast, the evidence establishes that, at best, only a third of the 144 heifers Woods sold to third parties could have been pregnant. The district court found, for example, that only 84 of the 190 heifers Woods possessed had been bred with Arkavalley bulls. Moreover, according to the district court's findings, the average weight of the 50 heifers Arkavalley purchased as cover was 1,100 to 1,200 pounds, which was substantially higher than Woods' 144 heifers. As the district court found, only 110 of Woods' 144 heifers weighed 900 pounds or more.

Arkavalley was only entitled to cover what Woods had to sell. By purchasing heifers seven and a half to eight months pregnant, weighing 1,100 to 1,200 pounds, Arkavalley placed themselves in a better position than they would have been had Woods resold his heifers to them. Arkavalley's cover was not a reasonable like-kind substitute for Woods' heifers. Accordingly, we determine that the district court erred in awarding cover damages.

[The case is continued and concluded at § 7.04[C][2] immediately below.]

NOTES

(1) In *Dangerfield v. Markel*, 278 N.W.2d 364, 26 U.C.C. Rep. 419 (N.D. 1979), seller breached a contract to deliver chipping potatoes to buyer. Buyer completed "covering" the contract on March 21, 1973, which was 38 days after the date of breach. During the first 18 days of this cover period, the buyer's purchases averaged $4.41 per cwt. During the remaining 20 days, the buyer's purchases averaged over $5.41 per cwt., with many purchases made at $6.00 per cwt. Seller argues that 38 days for the buyer to cover in a rapidly rising market is improper under U.C.C. § 2-712; therefore U.C.C. § 2-713 should have been used to compute damages. Held: for buyer. He covered in good faith and without unreasonable delay under U.C.C. § 2-712.

The court cited *Farmer's Union Co-op of Mead v. Flamme Bros.*, 196 Neb. 699, 245 N.W.2d 464 (1976), where the Supreme Court of Nebraska was presented with a similar situation in which the seller argued that the buyer should not have been allowed to cover a breached corn contract over a 15-day period in a rising market. The Nebraska court rejected the argument:

them, allow them to breed with the bull(s) furnished by the Dairy . . . ." Thus, the plain language of the contract imposes upon Arkavalley the responsibility for breeding the heifers, and merely requires Woods to permit breeding. Indeed, Charles N. Brock, who had been the director of operations at Arkavalley Farms from 1969 to 1979, stated during direct examination:

Q What was your understanding with respect to these one hundred and forty-four heifers, if some of them were not bred?

[Brock] Under the terms of the contract, we always took the heifers back, whether they were bred or not.

Q If they were not bred, what did Arkavalley do with them, if anything?

[Brock] We would breed them.

Arkavalley does not argue on appeal that Woods thwarted or in any way hampered Arkavalley's attempt to impregnate the heifers.

In the case at bar, the appellee did not go into the market and buy corn specifically to cover the contracts, but appellee did continue buying corn from its members, as was its normal practice until the three contracts were fulfilled. The trial court determined, as inherent in its verdict and judgment for appellee, that appellee did "cover" the contract "without unreasonable delay," and under all the circumstances of this case, we affirm the trial court's judgment. Appellee did between the dates of January 2 and January 15, 1974, purchase over 111,000 bushels of corn and applied such purchases to the unfulfilled contracts. The comment following section 2-712, U.C.C., is particularly applicable to this case. That comment states, in part: "2. The definition of 'cover' under subsection (1) envisages a series of contracts or sales, as well as a single contract or sale; . . . and contracts on credit or delivery terms differing from the contract in breach, but again reasonable under the circumstances. The test of proper cover is whether at the time and place the buyer acted in good faith and in a reasonable manner, and it is immaterial that hindsight may later prove that the method of cover used was not the cheapest or most effective."

The offended party is not bound by hindsight, and the practice used by appellee might have resulted in lower damages if the price over the time period had declined. Instead, the price fluctuated and the net result was that the damages were slightly higher than if the entire volume of corn had been purchased on January 2, 1974, at the $2.32 price. Appellee acted in good faith and made the 'cover' purchases without unreasonable delay, within the meaning of the Uniform Commercial Code. 196 Neb. at 706, 245 N.W.2d at 468. The court also noted White and Summers's comment on U.C.C. § 2-712:

If 2-712 is to be the remedy used by more aggrieved buyers than any other remedy, then the courts must be chary of finding a good faith buyer's acts unreasonable. The courts should not hedge the remedy about with restrictions in the name of "reasonableness" that render it useless or uncertain for the good faith buyer. Indeed, one may argue that the courts should read very little substance into the reasonableness requirement and insist only that the buyer proceed in good faith. A question a lawyer might put to test his client's good faith under 2-712 is this: "How, where, and when would you have procured these goods if you had not been covering and had no prospect of a court recovery from another?" If the client can answer truthfully that he would have spent his own money in the same way, the court should not demand more.

J. White & R. Summers, Handbook of the Law under the Uniform Commercial Code, at p. 178.

(2) U.C.C. § 2-712(1) provides that cover must be "without unreasonable delay" and that the purchase of substitute goods must be "reasonable." As seen in the foregoing cases, where the buyer has covered, the seller will often raise one or both of these reasonableness questions. Professors White and Summers lament that the Code furnishes little guidance. After quoting U.C.C. § 1-204(2) that "What is a reasonable time for taking any action depends on the nature, purpose and circumstances of such action," they continue:

The drafters have hardly left us with a solid basis upon which to predict whether a given act was or was not "reasonable"; each new sentence of the Comment is like an additional bucket of muck thrown into a quagmire. Of course the drafters were not dummies, and their vagueness was doubtless purposeful.

J. White & R. Summers, Uniform Commercial Code § 6-3 at 246 (3d ed. 1988).

[2]   Recover Damages for Non-Delivery or Repudiation

Read: U.C.C. §§ 2-711(1)(b), 2-713; see §§ 2-723, 2-724, 2-503; cf. § 2-708.

Read also: U.C.C. §§ 2A-508(1)(c), 2A-519(1) and (2), 2A-507, 2A-520, cf. § 2A-528; CISG Arts. 45(1)(b), 76, 77.

MARTELLA v. WOODS

United States Court of Appeals
715 F2d 410, 36 U.C.C. Rep. 1200 (8th Cir. 1983)

[This case is continued from § 7.04[C][1] immediately above.]

C. Damages for Nondelivery.

The district court also awarded Arkavalley $64,529.60 in damages for Woods' failure to deliver 94 of the 144 heifers. This award represented the difference between the fair market price, at the time of the breach, of 89 pregnant heifers and 5 non-pregnant heifers, and the contract price. After a careful review of the record and briefs in this case, we conclude that the district court erred in awarding nondelivery damages.

Missouri law provides for damages for nondelivery: [the Court recites U.C.C. § 2-713].

The contract merely required Woods to sell and Arkavalley to buy those heifers between 24-30 months of age. Therefore, a breach of that contract only permits recovery of the difference between the lower contract price and the higher market price of those heifers Woods was obligated but did not sell to Arkavalley. As we noted earlier, the evidence establishes that only a third of the 144 heifers Woods sold to third parties could have possibly been pregnant, and only 110 of Woods' 144 heifers weighed 900 pounds or more. Accordingly, we remand to the district court for a recomputation of damages based on the difference between the contract price and the market price for those heifers Woods had previously sold to third parties as of the time Arkavalley learned of the breach.

III. Conclusion

We affirm the district court's decision on the merits. . . . However, we conclude that the district court erred in calculating damages for cover [U.C.C. § 2-712] and nondelivery [U.C.C. § 2-713]. We determine that Arkavalley is entitled to damages only for the difference between the fair market price of the 144 heifers Woods sold to third parties and the lesser contract price, said differential to be determined as of the time that Arkavalley learned of the breach.

We observe that there exists some evidence in the record regarding the fair market price of the 144 heifers Woods sold to third parties. The district court, however, did not engage in any substantial factfinding on this issue. Accordingly, on remand, the district court may, at its discretion, hold a new hearing for additional factfinding before proceeding to recalculate damages.

Affirmed in part, reversed in part, and remanded to the district court for proceedings consistent with this opinion.

Read: U.C.C. §§ 2-610, 2-713.

Read also: U.C.C. §§ 2A-402, 2A-519(1) and (2); CISG Arts. 71, 72, 76, 25-27, 81-84.

COSDEN OIL & CHEMICAL CO. v. KARL O. HELM AKTIENGESELLSCHAFT

United States Court of Appeals
736 F.2d 1064, 38 U.C.C. Rep. 1645 (5th Cir. 1984)

REAVLEY, CIRCUIT JUDGE.

We must address one of the most difficult interpretive problems of the Uniform Commercial Code—the appropriate time to measure buyer's damages where the seller anticipatorily repudiates a contract and the buyer does not cover. The district court applied the Texas version of Article 2 and measured buyer's damages at a commercially reasonable time after seller's repudiation. We affirm, but remand for modification of damages on another point.

I. Case History

This contractual dispute arose out of events and transactions occurring in the first three months of 1979, when the market in polystyrene, a petroleum derivative used to make molded products, was steadily rising. During this time Iran, a major petroleum producer, was undergoing political turmoil. Karl O. Helm Aktiengesellschaft (Helm or Helm Hamburg), an international trading company based in Hamburg, West Germany, anticipated a tightening in the world petrochemical supply and decided to purchase a large amount of polystyrene. Acting on orders from Helm Hamburg, Helm Houston, a wholly-owned subsidiary, initiated negotiations with Cosden Oil & Chemical Company (Cosden), a Texas-based producer of chemical products, including polystyrene.

Rudi Scholtyssek, general manager of Helm Houston, contacted Ken Smith, Cosden's national sales coordinator, to inquire about the possibility of purchasing quantities of polystyrene. Negotiating over the telephone and by telex, the parties agreed to the purchase and sale of 1250 metric tons[18] of high impact polystyrene at $.2825 per pound and 250 metric tons of general purpose polystyrene at $.265 per pound. The parties also discussed options on each polystyrene type. On January 18, 1979, Scholtyssek met with Smith in Dallas, leaving behind two purchase confirmations. Purchase confirmation 04 contained the terms for high impact and 05 contained the terms for general purpose. Both confirmations contained the price and quantity terms listed above, and specified the same delivery and payment terms. The polystyrene was to be delivered during January and February in one or more lots, to be called for at Helm's instance. Confirmation 04 specified that Helm had an option for an additional 1000 metric tons of high impact, and

---

[18] One metric ton equals approximately 2,204.5 pounds.

confirmation 05 expressed a similar option for 500 metric tons of general purpose. The option amounts were subject to the same terms, except that delivery was to be during February and March. The options were to be declared, at the latest, by January 31, 1979.

On January 22, Helm called for the first shipment of high impact under order 04, to be delivered FAS at a New Jersey port to make a January 29 shipping date for a trans-Atlantic voyage. On January 23, Helm telexed Cosden to declare the options on purchase orders 04 and 05, designating the high impact option quantity as order 06 and the general purpose option quantity as order 07. After exercising the options, Helm sent purchase confirmations 06 and 07, which Cosden received on January 29. That same day Helm Houston received confirmations 04 and 05, which Smith had signed.

Cosden shipped 90,000 pounds of high impact polystyrene to Helm on or about January 26. Cosden then sent an invoice for that quantity to Helm Houston on or about January 31. The front of the invoice stated, "This order is subject to the terms and conditions shown on the reverse hereof." Among the "Conditions of Sale" listed on the back of the invoice was a force majeure provision. Helm paid for the first shipment in accordance with the agreement.

As Helm had expected, polystyrene prices began to rise in late January, and continued upward during February and March. Cosden also experienced problems at two of its plants in late January. Normally, Cosden supplied its Calumet City, Illinois, production plant with styrene monomer, the "feed stock" or main ingredient of polystyrene,[19] by barges that traveled from Louisiana up the Mississippi and Illinois Rivers to a canal that extended to Cosden's plant. Due to the extremely cold winter of 1978-79, however, the Illinois River and the canal froze, suspending barge traffic for a few weeks. A different problem beset Cosden's Windsor, New Jersey, production plant. A new reactor, used in the polystyrene manufacturing process, had recently been installed at the Windsor plant. A manufacturing defect soon became apparent, however, and Cosden returned the reactor to the manufacturer for repair, which took several weeks. At the time of the reactor breakdown, Cosden was manufacturing only general purpose at the Windsor plant. Cosden had planned on supplying Helm's high impact orders from the Calumet City plant.

Late in January Cosden notified Helm that it was experiencing problems at its production facilities and that the delivery under 04 might be delayed. On February 6, Smith telephoned Scholtyssek and informed him that Cosden was canceling orders 05, 06, and 07 because two plants were "down" and it did not have sufficient product to fill the orders. Cosden, however, would continue to honor order 04. Smith confirmed the cancellation in a letter dated February 8, which Scholtyssek received on or about February 12. After Helm Hamburg learned of Cosden's cancellation, Wolfgang Gordian, a member of Helm's executive board, sent an internal memorandum to Helm Houston outlining a strategy. Helm would urge that Cosden continue to perform under 04 and, after receiving the high impact polystyrene, would offset amounts owing under 04 against Helm's damages for nondelivery of the balance of polystyrene. Gordian also instructed Helm Houston to send a telex to Cosden. Following instructions, Scholtyssek then requested from Cosden "the relevant force majeure certificate" to pass on to Helm Hamburg. Helm also urged Cosden to deliver immediately several hundred metric tons of high impact to meet two February shipping dates for which Helm had booked shipping space.

---

[19] Styrene monomer comprises approximately 90% of high impact polystyrene and a larger percentage of general purpose polystyrene.

In mid-February Cosden shipped approximately 1,260,000 pounds of high impact to Helm under order 04. This shipment's invoice, which also included the force majeure provision on the reverse side, specified that Helm owed $355,950, due by March 15 or 16. After this delivery Helm requested that Cosden deliver the balance under order 04 for shipment on a vessel departing March 16. Cosden informed Helm that a March 16 delivery was not possible. On March 15, citing production problems with the 04 balance, Cosden offered to sell 1000 metric tons of styrene monomer at $.41 per pound. Although Cosden later lowered the price on the styrene monomer, Helm refused the offer, insisting on delivery of the balance of 04 polystyrene by March 31 at the latest. Around the end of March, Cosden informed Scholtyssek by telephone that it was canceling the balance of order 04.

Cosden sued Helm, seeking damages for Helm's failure to pay for delivered polystyrene. Helm counterclaimed for Cosden's failure to deliver polystyrene as agreed. The jury found on special verdict that Cosden had agreed to sell polystyrene to Helm under all four orders. The jury also found that Cosden anticipatorily repudiated orders 05, 06, and 07 and that Cosden canceled order 04 before Helm's failure to pay for the second 04 delivery constituted a repudiation. The jury fixed the per pound market prices for polystyrene under each of the four orders at three different times: when Helm learned of the cancellation, at a commercially reasonable time thereafter, and at the time for delivery.

The district court, viewing the four orders as representing one agreement, determined that Helm was entitled to recover $628,676 in damages representing the difference between the contract price and the market price at a commercially reasonable time after Cosden repudiated its polystyrene delivery obligations and that Cosden was entitled to an offset of $355,950 against those damages for polystyrene delivered, but not paid for, under order 04.

II. Time for Measuring Buyer's Damages

Both parties find fault with the time at which the district court measured Helm's damages for Cosden's anticipatory repudiation of orders 05, 06, and 07.[20] Cosden argues that damages should be measured when Helm learned of the repudiation. Helm contends that market price as of the last day for delivery — or the time of performance — should be used to compute its damages under the contract-market differential. We reject both views, and hold that the district court correctly measured damages at a commercially reasonable point after Cosden informed Helm that it was canceling the three orders.

Article 2 of the Code has generally been hailed as a success for its comprehensiveness, its deference to mercantile reality, and its clarity. Nevertheless, certain aspects of the Code's overall scheme have proved troublesome in application. The interplay among §§ 2.610, 2.711, 2.712, 2.713, and 2.723, Tex Bus & Com Code Ann (Vernon 1968), represents one of those areas, and has been described as "an impossible legal thicket." J. White & R. Summers, Uniform Commercial Code § 6-7 at 242 (2d ed 1980). The aggrieved buyer seeking damages for seller's anticipatory repudiation presents the most difficult interpretive problem.[21] Section 2.713 describes the buyer's damages remedy:

---

[20] The damages measurement problem does not apply to Cosden's breach of order 04, which was not anticipatorily repudiated. The time Helm learned of Cosden's intent to deliver no more polystyrene under 04 was the same time as the last date of performance, which had been extended to the end of March.

[21] The only area of unanimous agreement among those that have studied the Code provisions relevant to this problem is that they are not consistent, present problems in interpretation, and invite amendment.

Buyer's Damages for Non-Delivery or Repudiation

(a) Subject to the provisions of this chapter with respect to proof of market price (Section 2.723), the measure of damages for non-delivery or repudiation by the seller is the difference between the market price *at the time when the buyer learned of the breach* and the contract price together with any incidental and consequential damages provided in this chapter (Section 2.715), but less expenses saved in consequence of the seller's breach.

(Emphasis added).

Courts and commentators have identified three possible interpretations of the phrase "learned of the breach." If seller anticipatorily repudiates, buyer learns of the breach:

(1) When he learns of the repudiation;

(2) When he learns of the repudiation plus a commercially reasonable time; or

(3) When performance is due under the contract.

See, e.g., *First National Bank of Chicago v. Jefferson Mortgage Co.*, 576 F2d 479 (3d Cir 1978); *Cargill, Inc. v. Stafford*, 553 F2d 1222 (10th Cir 1977); J. White & R. Summers § 6-7 at 240-52; Note, U.C.C. § 2-713: *Anticipatory Repudiation and the Measurement of an Aggrieved Buyer's Damages*, 19 Wm & Mary L Rev 253 (1977).

We would not be free to decide the question if there were a Texas case on point, bound as we are by Erie to follow state law in diversity cases. We find, however, that no Texas case has addressed the Code question of buyer's damages in an anticipatory repudiation context. Texas, alone in this circuit, does not allow us to certify questions of state law for resolution by its courts. . . .

Fredonia Broadcasting Corp. v. RCA Corp., 481 F2d 781(5th Cir 1973) (*Fredonia I*), contains dicta on this question. The court merely quoted the language of the section and noted that the time for measuring market price — when buyer learns of the breach — was the only difference from pre-Code Texas law.[22] *Id.* at 800. . . . We have found no Texas case quoting or citing *Fredonia I* for its dicta on damages under § 2.713. Although *Fredonia I* correctly stated the statutory language, it simply did not address or recognize the interpretive problems peculiar to seller's anticipatory repudiation.[23]

Since *Fredonia I*, four Texas courts have applied § 2.713 to measure buyer's damages at the time he learned of the breach. In all of these cases the aggrieved buyer learned of the breach at or after the time of performance.

Two recent Texas cases indicate that appropriate measure for buyer's damages in the anticipatory repudiation context has not been definitively decided. In *Aquamarine Associates v. Burton Shipyard*, 645 SW2d 477 (Tex App-Beaumont 1982), affd, 659 SW2d 820 (Tex 1983),

---

[22] Before Texas adopted the Code, its courts applied the traditional time-of-performance measure of damages in repudiation cases. By interpreting the time buyer learns of the breach to mean a commercially reasonable time after buyer learns of the repudiation, we depart from pre-Code law, although in a different manner than suggested by the dicta of *Fredonia I*. This panel, however, is not bound by dicta of a previous panel.

[23] In *Fredonia I*, the buyer, a television station, brought contract claims against the seller of broadcasting equipment. Fredonia claimed that delays in delivery and delivery of defective equipment by RCA caused Fredonia to miss its initial broadcast date and to suffer interruptions in broadcasting service. The jury found that RCA repudiated the contract by several acts or omissions — the same acts that supported other jury findings that RCA breached the contract. The *Fredonia I* court reversed the judgment on both the breach and repudiation claims. On remand, since Fredonia's contract claims were precluded by terms of the contract, the case was tried on a fraud theory. . . .

seller anticipatorily repudiated its obligation to construct and deliver ships. After seller learned of the repudiation, it covered by contracting with another party to complete the vessels. Since buyer covered under § 2.712, the jury's answer to the section 2.713 damages issue was properly disregarded. Referring to comment 5 of § 2.713, however, the Texas Court of Civil Appeals cited two cases that measured buyer's damages for anticipatory repudiation at different times. *Id.* at 479 & n 8. *Cargill, Inc. v. Stafford*, 553 F2d 1222 (10th Cir 1977), held that buyer's damages for anticipatory repudiation should be measured at a commercially reasonable time after he learned of the repudiation if he should have covered, and at the time of performance if buyer had a valid reason for failure or refusal to cover. *Id.* at 1226-27. In *Ralston Purina Co. v. McFarland*, 550 F2d 967 (4th Cir 1977), the court measured buyer's damages at the market price prevailing on the day seller anticipatorily repudiated. *Id.* at 971. The two citations in *Aquamarine* reveal uncertainty concerning the applicable time for measuring damages.

Hargrove v. Powell, 648 SW2d 372 (Tex App-San Antonio 1983, no writ), also indicates that the interpretation of § 2.713 in an anticipatory repudiation case has not been settled in Texas. In referring to the hypothetical case of seller's repudiation, the *Hargrove* court cited *Cargill* and Professor Anderson's article, which presents the argument that "time when the buyer learned of the breach" means the time for performance or later. *Id.* at 377; see Anderson, *supra.*

We do not doubt, and Texas law is clear, that market price at the time buyer learns of the breach is the appropriate measure of § 2.713 damages in cases where buyer learns of the breach at or after the time for performance. This will be the common case, for which § 2.713 was designed. See Peters, *Remedies for Breach of Contracts Relating to the Sale of Goods Under the Uniform Commercial Code: A Roadmap for Article Two*, 73 Yale LJ 199, 264 (1963). In the relatively rare case where seller anticipatorily repudiates and buyer does not cover, see Anderson, *supra*, at 318, the specific provision for anticipatory repudiation cases, § 2.610, authorizes the aggrieved party to await performance for a commercially reasonable time before resorting to his remedies of cover or damages.[24]

In the anticipatory repudiation context, the buyer's specific right to wait for a commercially reasonable time before choosing his remedy must be read together with the general damages provision of § 2.713 to extend the time for measurement beyond when buyer learns of the breach. Comment 1 to § 2.610 states that if an aggrieved party "awaits performance beyond a commercially reasonable time he cannot recover resulting damages which he should have avoided." This suggests that an aggrieved buyer can recover damages where the market rises during the commercially reasonable time he awaits performance. To interpret § 2.713's "learned of the breach" language to mean the time at which seller first communicates his anticipatory repudiation would undercut the time that § 2.610 gives the aggrieved buyer to await performance.

The buyer's option to wait a commercially reasonable time also interacts with § 2.611, which allows the seller an opportunity to retract his repudiation. Thus, an aggrieved buyer "learns of the breach" a commercially reasonable time after he learns of the seller's anticipatory repudiation. The weight of scholarly commentary supports this interpretation. See J. Calamari & J. Perillo, Contracts § 14-20 (2d ed 1977); Sebert, *Remedies Under Article Two of the Uniform Commercial Code: An Agenda for Review*, 130 U Pa L Rev 360, 372-80 (1981); Wallach, *Anticipatory Repudiation and the U.C.C.*, 13 U.C.C.LJ 48 (1980); Peters, *supra*, at 263-68.

Typically, our question will arise where parties to an executory contract are in the midst of a rising market. To the extent that market decisions are influenced by a damage rule, measuring

---

[24] Section 2.610 provides: [the court recites U.C.C. § 2-610].

market price at the time of seller's repudiation gives seller the ability to fix buyer's damages and may induce seller to repudiate, rather than abide by the contract. By contrast, measuring buyer's damages at the time of performance will tend to dissuade the buyer from covering, in hopes that market price will continue upward until performance time.

Allowing the aggrieved buyer a commercially reasonable time, however, provides him with an opportunity to investigate his cover possibilities in a rising market without fear that, if he is unsuccessful in obtaining cover, he will be relegated to a market-contract damage remedy measured at the time of repudiation. The Code supports this view. While cover is the preferred remedy, the Code clearly provides the option to seek damages. See § 2.712(c) [U.C.C. § 2-712(3)] & comment 3. If "[t]he buyer is always free to choose between cover and damages for non-delivery," and if § 2.712 "is not intended to limit the time necessary for [buyer] to look around and decide as to how he may best effect cover," it would be anomalous, if the buyer chooses to seek damages, to fix his damages at a time before he investigated cover possibilities and before he elected his remedy. *See id.* comment 2 & 3; *Dura-Wood Treating Co. v. Century Forest Industries, Inc.*, 675 F2d 745, 754 (5th Cir), cert. denied, 459 US 865, 103 S Ct 144, 74 L Ed 2d 122 (1982) ("buyer has some time in which to evaluate the situation"). Moreover, comment 1 to § 2.713 states, "The general baseline adopted in this section uses as a yardstick the market in which the buyer would have obtained cover had he sought that relief." See § 2.610 comment 1. When a buyer chooses not to cover, but to seek damages, the market is measured at the time he could have covered-a reasonable time after repudiation. See §§ 2.711 & 2.713.

Persuasive arguments exist for interpreting "learned of the breach" to mean "time of performance," consistent with the pre-Code rule. See J. White & R. Summers, *supra*, § 6-7; Anderson, *supra*. If this was the intention of the Code's drafters, however, phrases in § 2.610 and § 2.712 lose their meaning. If buyer is entitled to market-contract damages measured at the time of performance, it is difficult to explain why the anticipatory repudiation section limits him to a commercially reasonable time to await performance. See § 2.610 comment 1. Similarly, in a rising market, no reason would exist for requiring the buyer to act "without unreasonable delay" when he seeks to cover following an anticipatory repudiation. See § 2.712(a) [U.C.C. § 2-712(1)].

The interplay among the relevant Code sections does not permit, in this context, an interpretation that harmonizes all and leaves no loose ends. We therefore acknowledge that our interpretation fails to explain the language of § 2.723(a) insofar as it relates to aggrieved buyers. We note, however, that the section has limited applicability — cases that come to trial before the time of performance will be rare. Moreover, the comment to § 2.723 states that the "section is not intended to exclude the use of any other reasonable method of determining market price or of measuring damages. . . ." In light of the Code's persistent theme of commercial reasonableness, the prominence of cover as a remedy, and the time given an aggrieved buyer to await performance and to investigate cover before selecting his remedy, we agree with the district court that "learned of the breach" incorporates § 2.610's commercially reasonable time.[25]

---

[25] We note that two circuits arrived at a similar conclusion by different routes. In *Cargill, Inc. v. Stafford*, 553 F2d 1222 (10th Cir 1977), the court began its discussion of damages by embracing the "time of performance" interpretation urged by Professors White and Summers. *Id.* at 1226. Indeed, the court stated that "damages normally should be measured from the time when performance is due and not from the time when the buyer learns of repudiation." *Id.* Nevertheless, the court

conclude[d] that under § 4-2-713 a buyer may urge continued performance for a reasonable time. At the end of a reasonable period he should cover if substitute goods are readily available. If substitution is readily available

VI. "Cover" as a Ceiling

At trial Cosden argued that Helm's purchases of polystyrene from other sources in early February constituted cover. Helm argued that those purchases were not intended to substitute for polystyrene sales canceled by Cosden. Helm, however, contended that it did cover by purchasing large amounts of high impact polystyrene from other sources late in February and around the first of March. Cosden claimed that these purchases were not made reasonably and that they should not qualify as cover. The jury found that none of Helm's purchases of polystyrene from other sources were cover purchases.

Now Cosden argues that the prices of polystyrene for the purchases that Helm claimed were cover should act as a ceiling for fixing market price under § 2.713. We refuse to accept this novel argument. Although a buyer who has truly covered may not be allowed to seek higher damages under § 2.713 than he is granted by § 2.712, see § 2.713 comment 5; J. White & R. Summers, *supra*, § 6-4 at 233-34, in this case the jury found that Helm did not cover. We cannot isolate a reason to explain the jury's finding: it might have concluded that Helm would have made the purchases regardless of Cosden's nonperformance or that the transactions did not qualify as cover for other reasons. Because of the jury's finding, we cannot use those other transactions to determine Helm's damages.

NOTES AND QUESTIONS

(1) Proposed U.C.C. § 2-711 states that it is subject to § 2-701. Section 2-701(c) states that Article 2 remedies must be liberally administered to put the aggrieved party in as good a position as if the other party had fully performed. If those remedies fail to place the aggrieved party in that position, damages may be awarded measured by the loss resulting in the ordinary course of events from the breach as determined in any manner which is reasonable. Thus, courts may protect not only the expectation interest but reliance and restitution interests where appropriate.

---

and buyer does not cover within a reasonable time, damages should be based on the price at the end of that reasonable time rather than on the price when performance is due.

Id. at 1227. The *Cargill* court would employ the time of performance measure only if buyer had a valid reason for not covering.

In *First Nat'l Bank of Chicago v. Jefferson Mortgage Co.*, 576 F2d 479 (3d Cir 1978), the court initially quoted with approval legislative history that supports a literal or "plain meaning" interpretation of New Jersey's § 2-713. Nevertheless, the court hedged by interpreting that section "to measure damages within a commercial reasonable time after learning of the repudiation." *Id.* at 492. In light of the unequivocal repudiation and because cover was "easily and immediately . . .available . . .in the well-organized and easily accessible market," *id.* at 493 (quoting *Oloffson v. Coomer*, 11 Ill App 3d 918, 296 NE2d 871(1973)), a commercially reasonable time did not extend beyond the date of repudiation.

We agree with the *First National* court that "the circumstances of the particular market involved should determine the duration of a 'commercially reasonable time.' " 576 F2d at 492; see Tex Bus & Com Code § 1.204(b). In this case, however, there was no showing that cover was easily and immediately available in an organized and accessible market and that a commercially reasonable time expired on the day of Cosden's cancellation. We recognize that § 2.610's "commercially reasonable time" and § 2.712's "without unreasonable delay" are distinct concepts. Often, however, the two time periods will overlap, since the buyer can investigate cover possibilities while he awaits performance. See Sebert, *supra*, at 376-77 & n 80.

Although the jury in the present case did not fix the exact duration of a commercially reasonable time, we assume that the jury determined market price at a time commercially reasonable under all the circumstances, in light of the absence of objection to the form of the special issue.

Proposed § 2-701(e) reinforces the idea that the rights and remedies provided by Article 2 are cumulative. But the subsection goes on to say that a court may deny or limit a remedy if it would put an aggrieved party in a substantially better position than if the other party had fully performed.

Under proposed § 2-713 the measure of market damages for the buyer depends upon the type of breach by the seller. For breach other than by repudiation, the measure is that provided by present § 2-713(1). For breach by repudiation, the measure is that provided in proposed § 2-708(a)(2), that is, damage is the "market price for comparable goods prevailing at the time when a commercially reasonable period after the seller learned of the repudiation has expired less the contract price" determined at the place stated in subsection (b). Under (b) market price is determined at the place for tender; in case of rejection after arrival or revocation of acceptance, it is determined at the place of arrival.

(2) How would Proposed §§ 2-701, 2-711 and 2-713 affect the analysis and result of *Cosden Oil*?

[D]   Reach the Goods Themselves

[1]   Recover Identified Goods on Seller's Insolvency

Read: U.C.C. §§ 2-711(2)(a), 2-502, see § 2-501; cf. § 2-702.

Read also: U.C.C. §§ 2A-508(2)(a), 2A-522, 2A-217, cf. § 2A-525(2); CISG Arts. 45(1)(a), 46(1), 28, cf. Art. 62.

IN RE CSY YACHT CORP.

United States Bankruptcy Court, Middle District of Florida
42 BR 619, 39 U.C.C. Rep. 879 (1984)

ALEXANDER L. PASKAY, CHIEF JUDGE.

This is a Chapter 11 case and the matter under consideration is an objection by the Debtor, CSY Yacht Corporation (CSY) to claim number 72 filed by Alan R. Jaegar and Katherine Jaegar (Jaegars). The claim under challenge was filed as a priority claim in the amount of $900 and as secured in the amount of $39,100. CSY does not object to the priority claim asserted under § 507(a)(5) of the Bankruptcy Code nor to the allowance of an unsecured claim for $37,000, but does object to the claim as secured. The Jaegars claim secured status of this claim on the basis that they have a special property interest in CSY's materials, supplies and parts inventory pursuant to Fla Stat § 672.502 (1981).

The matter came on for hearing and the parties, by stipulation, created the record through submission of depositions. The facts as adduced from the record as created and pertinent to resolution of the matter may be summarized as follows:

At the time pertinent to the transaction under consideration, CSY was engaged in the business of manufacturing and selling sailing yachts. The Jaegars became interested in purchasing a yacht from CSY after attending a sailing school conducted by one of CSY's affiliates. Before executing the sales contract, the Jaegars paid an initial deposit of $1,000 to CSY in August of 1980 and a second deposit of $4,000 on February 5, 1981 toward the purchase of a 44 foot cutter to be constructed by CSY for a total purchase price of $176,111. On February 24, 1981, the Jaegars executed the sale purchase agreement with CSY and pursuant to the agreement paid an additional $35,000 towards the purchase price of the yacht.

CSY was in poor financial condition and by the spring of 1981 following the receipt of the Jaegars' $35,000, CSY ceased constructing any new yachts. The Jaegars' yacht was one of several yachts which were never started.

On August 28, 1981, CSY filed its petition for relief pursuant to Chapter 11 of the Bankruptcy Code. While operating as a debtor in possession, CSY completed the yachts which were already under construction at the time of the commencement of the case and then proceeded to sell its unneeded inventory. Notice of Sale was sent to all interested parties and creditors of CSY. The Notice provided that the items would be sold free and clear of all liens and any liens or claims against the items sold would attach to the proceeds of the sale. In February, 1982, the sale was concluded.

The Jaegars did not file their claim contending a secured position until March 29, 1982. It is without dispute that the Jaegars do not have a security agreement nor did they file a financing statement pursuant to § 679.302 in order to perfect a security interest under Article 9 of the U.C.C. as adopted in this state by Florida Statute § 679.101. The basis for the Jaegars' asserted secured claim is based on paragraph 14 of the sales and purchase agreement which provides as follows:

The boat and all materials, engines and equipment attached to the boat or any material in the possession of the builder and designated for use on the boat shall become the property of the purchaser upon the payment of the first installment. The boat and all the materials, engines and equipment in the possession of the builder shall be subject to a lien in favor of the builder as against the purchaser. In the event of any rejection of any materials or equipment by the purchaser, title to such goods will revest in the builder.

It is Jaegars' position that they have a right to recover goods from CSY as an insolvent seller under Fla Stat § 672.502 and that this right was transferred to the proceeds of the sale under the notice of the sale. Fla Stat § 672.502 provides as follows: [the Court quotes U.C.C. § 2-502].

In order for a buyer to recover goods in the seller's possession after the seller has become insolvent, several elements must be present. The buyer must (1) have a special property interest in the goods under Fla Stat 672.501; (2) have paid part or all of the purchase price; and (3) keep good a tender of any unpaid portion of the purchase price. Additionally, the seller must become insolvent within ten days following the receipt of the first installment of the purchase price. 3A Bender's Uniform Comm Code Serv, § 14.03[2] (1983).

There is no dispute that the Jaegars paid part of the purchase price or that they were willing to keep good a tender for the remaining balance. The only issues to be resolved are whether the Jaegars have a special property interest in the goods and whether CSY became insolvent within ten days of receiving the $35,000 installment.

In order to determine if the Jaegars have a special property interest in the goods, it is necessary to refer to Fla Stat § 672.501 (1)(a) and (b) which provides as follows: [the Court quotes U.C.C. § 2-501(a) and (b)].

According to Fla Stat § 672.501, the buyer obtains a special property interest when the goods are identified. In the present case the Jaegars contracted to purchase a yacht to be built in the future. Pursuant to paragraph 14 of that contract, the boat and all materials, engines and equipment attached to the boat would become property of the Jaegars upon payment of the first installment. Since construction of the boat never commenced there were obviously no materials, engines or equipment attached to the boat.

As noted earlier, Paragraph 14 of the contract further provides that any materials designated for use on the boat shall become property of the Jaegars upon payment of the first installment. The Jaegars contend that this provision is inconsistent with Paragraph 3(b) which requires the installment to be paid at least 30 days prior to construction of the hull, unless CSY designated the materials to be incorporated into the boat from its inventory when it received the first installment.

Paragraph 3(b) merely requires that 30% of the purchase price be paid before construction will begin. Identification is governed by paragraph 14 which occurs when the materials were "designated" by CSY Nothing in the record indicates that the materials were set aside or ever designated for the Jaegars' yacht.

In the alternative, the Jaegars take the position that the materials and inventory of CSY constitute a tangible bulk and that reference to the materials in the contract is for an undivided share of the fungible bulk which is sufficient to establish identification for purposes of U.C.C. § 2-501. In support of their position, the Jaegars rely on Comment 5 of U.C.C. § 2-501 which provides as follows:

> 5. Undivided shares in an identified fungible bulk, such as grain in an elevator or oil in a storage tank, can be sold. The mere making of the contract with reference to an undivided share in an identified fungible bulk is enough under subsection (a) to effect an identification if there is no explicit agreement otherwise.

The Jaegars' reliance on Comment 5 is misplaced. The contract did not refer to an identified fungible bulk such as 35,000 pounds of fiberglass and resin. Rather, the contract explicitly referred to those materials "designated" for use on the Jaegars' yacht. As a result, this court is satisfied that the Jaegars' contention is without merit.

In light of the foregoing, the court is satisfied that the materials were never identified so as to create a special property interest pursuant to U.C.C. § 2-501. As a result, the Jaegars cannot recover any property from CSY under U.C.C. § 2-502.

This being the case, it is unnecessary to address the question of whether CSY became insolvent within ten days after it received the $35,000 installment from the Jaegars.

A separate final judgment will be entered in accordance with the foregoing.

———

NOTE

The scope of proposed § 2-502 has been expanded. Under revised § 2-502 a pre-paying buyer can recover identified goods, whether or not conforming, from a seller, whether or not insolvent, who repudiates or fails to deliver upon making and keeping a tender of full performance.

[2]   Obtain Specific Performance or Replevy the Goods

Read: U.C.C. §§ 2-711(2)(b), 2-716; see §§ 2-306, 2-501; cf.§ 2-709(1)(b).

Read also: U.C.C. §§ 2A-508(2)(b), 2A-521, 2A-217, cf. § 2A-529(1)(b); CISG Arts. 45(1)(a), 46(1), 28, cf. Art. 62.

SEDMAK v. CHARLIE'S CHEVROLET, INC.

Missouri Court of Appeals
622 S.W.2d 694, 31 U.C.C. Rep. 851 (1981)

Satz, J.

This is an appeal from a decree of specific performance. We affirm.

In their petition, plaintiffs, Dr. and Mrs. Sedmak (Sedmaks), alleged they entered into a contract with defendant, Charlie's Chevrolet, Inc. (Charlie's), to purchase a Corvette automobile for approximately $15,000.00. The Corvette was one of a limited number manufactured to commemorate the selection of the Corvette as the Pace Car for the Indianapolis 500. Charlie's breached the contract, the Sedmaks alleged, when, after the automobile was delivered, an agent for Charlie's told the Sedmaks they could not purchase the automobile for $15,000.00 but would have to bid on it.

The trial court found the parties entered into an oral contract and also found the contract was excepted from the Statute of Frauds. The court then ordered Charlie's to make the automobile "available for delivery" to the Sedmaks.

Charlie's raises three points on appeal: (1) the existence of an oral contract is not supported by the credible evidence; (2) if an oral contract exists, it is unenforceable because of the Statute of Frauds; and (3) specific performance is an improper remedy because the Sedmaks did not show their legal remedies were inadequate. . . .

[T]he record reflects the Sedmaks to be automobile enthusiasts, who, at the time of trial, owned six Corvettes. In July, 1977, "Vette Vues," a Corvette fancier's magazine to which Dr. Sedmak subscribed, published an article announcing Chevrolet's tentative plans to manufacture a limited edition of the Corvette. The limited edition of approximately 6,000 automobiles was to commemorate the selection of the Corvette as the Indianapolis 500 Pace Car. The Sedmaks were interested in acquiring one of these Pace Cars to add to their Corvette collection. In November, 1977, the Sedmaks asked Tom Kells, sales manager at Charlie's Chevrolet, about the availability of the Pace Car. Mr. Kells said he did not have any information on the car but would find out about it. Kells also said if Charlie's were to receive a Pace Car, the Sedmaks could purchase it.

On January 9, 1978, Dr. Sedmak telephoned Kells to ask him if a Pace Car could be ordered. Kells indicated that he would require a deposit on the car, so Mrs. Sedmak went to Charlie's and gave Kells a check for $500.00. She was given a receipt for that amount bearing the names of Kells and Charlie's Chevrolet, Inc. At that time, Kells had a pre-order form listing both standard equipment and options available on the Pace Car. Prior to tendering the deposit, Mrs. Sedmak asked Kells if she and Dr. Sedmak were "definitely going to be the owners." Kells replied, "yes." After the deposit had been paid, Mrs. Sedmak stated if the car was going to be theirs, her husband wanted some changes made to the stock model. She asked Kells to order the car equipped with an L82 engine, four speed standard transmission and AM/FM radio with tape deck. Kells said that he would try to arrange with the manufacturer for these changes. Kells was able to make the changes, and, when the car arrived, it was equipped as the Sedmaks had requested.

Kells informed Mrs. Sedmak that the price of the Pace Car would be the manufacturer's retail price, approximately $15,000.00. The dollar figure could not be quoted more precisely because

Kells was not sure what the ordered changes would cost, nor was he sure what the "appearance package" — decals, a special paint job — would cost. Kells also told Mrs. Sedmak that, after the changes had been made, a "contract" — a retail dealer's order form — would be mailed to them. However, no form or written contract was mailed to the Sedmaks by Charlie's.

On January 25, 1978, the Sedmaks visited Charlie's to take delivery on another Corvette. At that time, the Sedmaks asked Kells whether he knew anything further about the arrival date of the Pace Car. Kells replied he had no further information but he would let the Sedmaks know when the car arrived. Kells also requested that Charlie's be allowed to keep the car in their showroom for promotional purposes until after the Indianapolis 500 Race. The Sedmaks agreed to this arrangement.

On April 3, 1978, the Sedmaks were notified by Kells that the Pace Car had arrived. Kells told the Sedmaks they could not purchase the car for the manufacturer's retail price because demand for the car had inflated its value beyond the suggested price. Kells also told the Sedmaks they could bid on the car. The Sedmaks did not submit a bid. They filed this suit for specific performance.

Mr. Kells' testimony about his conversations with the Sedmaks regarding the Pace Car differed markedly from the Sedmaks' testimony. Kells stated that he had no definite price information on the Pace Car until a day or two prior to its arrival at Charlie's. He denied ever discussing the purchase price of the car with the Sedmaks. He admitted, however, that after talking with the Sedmaks on January 9, 1978,[26] he telephoned the zone manager and requested changes be made to the Pace Car. He denied the changes were made pursuant to Dr. Sedmak's order. He claimed the changes were made because they were "more favorable to the automobile" and were changes Dr. Sedmak "preferred." In ordering the changes, Kells said he was merely taking Dr. Sedmak's advice because he was a "very knowledgeable man on the Corvette." There is no dispute, however, that when the Pace Car arrived, it was equipped with the options requested by Dr. Sedmak.

Mr. Kells also denied the receipt for $500.00 given him by Mrs. Sedmak on January 9, 1978, was a receipt for a deposit on the Pace Car. On direct examination, he said he "accepted a five hundred dollar ($500) deposit from the Sedmaks to assure them the first opportunity of purchasing the car." On cross-examination, he said: "We were accepting bids and with the five hundred dollar ($500) deposit it was to give them the first opportunity to bid on the car." Then after acknowledging that other bidders had not paid for the opportunity to bid, he explained the deposit gave the Sedmaks the "last opportunity" to make the final bid. Based on this evidence, the trial court found the parties entered into an oral contract for the purchase and sale of the Pace Car at the manufacturer's suggested retail price.

Charlie's first contends the Sedmaks' evidence is "so wrought with inconsistencies and contradictions that a finding of an oral contract for the sale of a Pace Car at the manufacturer's suggested retail price is clearly against the weight of the evidence." We disagree. The trial court chose to believe the Sedmaks' testimony over that of Mr. Kells and the reasonableness of this belief was not vitiated by any real contradictions in the Sedmaks' testimony. Charlie's examples of conflict are either facially not contradictory or easily reconcilable.

Although not clearly stated in this point or explicitly articulated in its argument, Charlie's also appears to argue there was no contract because the parties did not agree to a price. The

---

[26] According to Kells' testimony, both Mr. and Mrs. Sedmak visited Charlie's on January 9, 1978. Mrs. Sedmak testified only she visited Charlie's on that date.

trial court concluded "[t]he price was to be the suggested retail price of the automobile at the time of delivery." Apparently, Charlie's argues that if this were the agreed to price, it is legally insufficient to support a contract because the manufacturer's suggested retail price is not a mandatory, fixed and definite selling price but, rather, as the term implies, it is merely a suggested price which does not accurately reflect the market and the actual selling price of automobiles. Charlie's argument is misdirected and, thus, misses the mark.

Without again detailing the facts, there was evidence to support the trial court's conclusion that the parties agreed the selling price would be the price suggested by the manufacturer. Whether this price accurately reflects the market demands on any given day is immaterial. The manufacturer's suggested retail price is ascertainable and, thus, if the parties choose, sufficiently definite to meet the price requirements of an enforceable contract. Failure to specify the selling price in dollars and cents did not render the contract void or voidable. . . . See also, § 400.2-305 RSMo 1978. As long as the parties agreed to a method by which the price was to be determined and as long as the price could be ascertained at the time of performance, the price requirement for a valid and enforceable contract was satisfied. See . . .§ 400.2-305 RSMo 1978. This point is without merit.

Charlie's next complains that if there were an oral contract, it is unenforceable under the Statute of Frauds. . . .

. . . .

We hold, therefore, that where, as here, there is no dispute as to quantity, part payment for a single, indivisible commercial unit validates an oral contract under § 400.2-201(3)(c) RSMo 1978.

Finally, Charlie's contends the Sedmaks failed to show they were entitled to specific performance of the contract. We disagree. Although it has been stated that the determination whether to order specific performance lies within the discretion of the trial court, this discretion is, in fact, quite narrow. When the relevant equitable principles have been met and the contract is fair and plain, "specific performance goes as a matter of right." Here, the trial court ordered specific performance because it concluded the Sedmaks "have no adequate remedy at law for the reason that they cannot go upon the open market and purchase an automobile of this kind with the same mileage, condition, ownership and appearance as the automobile involved in this case, except, if at all, with considerable expense, trouble, loss, great delay and inconvenience." Contrary to defendant's complaint, this is a correct expression of the relevant law and it is supported by the evidence.

Under the Code, the court may decree specific performance as a buyer's remedy for breach of contract to sell goods "where the goods are unique or in other proper circumstances." § 400.2-716(1) RSMo 1978. The general term "in other proper circumstances" expresses the drafters' intent to "further a more liberal attitude than some courts have shown in connection with the specific performance of contracts of sale." § 400.2-716, U.C.C., Comment 1. This Comment was not directed to the courts of this state, for long before the Code, we, in Missouri, took a practical approach in determining whether specific performance would lie for the breach of contract for the sale of goods and did not limit this relief only to the sale of unique goods. *Boeving v. Vandover*, 218 SW2d 175 (Mo App 1945). In *Boeving*, plaintiff contracted to buy a car from defendant. When the car arrived, defendant refused to sell. The car was not unique in the traditional legal sense but, at that time, all cars were difficult to obtain because of war-time shortages. The court held specific performance was the proper remedy for plaintiff because a new car "could not be obtained elsewhere except at considerable expense, trouble or loss, which cannot be estimated in advance and under such circumstances [plaintiff] did not have an adequate remedy at law." *Id.* at 177-178. Thus, *Boeving* presaged the broad and liberalized language of § 400.2-716(1) and exemplifies one of the "other proper circumstances" contemplated by this subsection for ordering specific performance. § 400.2-716, Missouri Code Comment 1. The present facts track those in *Boeving*.

The Pace Car, like the car in *Boeving*, was not unique in the traditional legal sense. It was not an heirloom or, arguably, not one of a kind. However, its "mileage, condition, ownership and appearance" did make it difficult, if not impossible, to obtain its replication without considerable expense, delay and inconvenience. Admittedly, 6,000 Pace Cars were produced by Chevrolet. However, as the record reflects, this is limited production. In addition, only one of these cars was available to each dealer, and only a limited number of these were equipped with the specific options ordered by plaintiffs. Charlie's had not received a car like the Pace Car in the previous two years. The sticker price for the car was $14,284.21. Yet Charlie's received offers from individuals in Hawaii and Florida to buy the Pace Car for $24,000.00 and $28,000.00 respectively. As sensibly inferred by the trial court, the location and size of these offers demonstrated this limited edition was in short supply and great demand. We agree, with the trial court. This case was a "proper circumstance" for ordering specific performance.

Judgment affirmed.

NOTES

(1) In *Schweber v. Rallye Motors, Inc,* 12 U.C.C. Rep. 1154 (N.Y. Sup. Ct. 1973), buyer sought specific performance and an injunction to restrain seller from selling or transferring to a third party a 1973 Rolls Royce Corniche auto. The court believed the circumstance of the case justified the relief of specific performance, citing U.C.C. § 2-716(1), "where the goods are unique, *or in other proper circumstances.*" *Cf. Bander v. Grossman,* 611 N.Y.S.2d 985, 23 U.C.C. Rep. 2d 1159 (1994) where buyer contracted to purchase a rare Astin-Martin automobile. The court held that it would be inequitable and improper to grant specific performance in the form of a constructive trust upon the proceeds of the sale of the auto to a third party.

In *Scholl v. Hartzell*, 33 U.C.C. Rep. 951 (Pa. Ct. Com. Pl. 1981), the court stated that although a 1962 Chevrolet Corvette may be considered by many a collector's item, it is not one of the unique goods contemplated by U.C.C. § 2-716(1). Also, buyer did not allege he was unable to cover; accordingly, buyer's action did not lie in replevin per U.C.C. § 2-716(3).

In *Tatum v. Richter*, 373 A.2d 923 (Md. 1977), Richter contracted to purchase a 1971 Ferrari Daytona coupe for $17,500, paying more than $15,000 down in the form of a personal check for $7,500 and a bank cashier's check for $7524.10. Both checks referred to the 1971 Ferrari by its serial number. When the car arrived in the hands of the dealer, excuses were made for nondelivery. Richter secured possession of the car in a replevin action. "Once the car was identified to the contract, § 2-716(3), Richter had a right of replevin, because he was unable to effect cover, and there was no other way to protect himself against the loss of his deposit." 373 A.2d at 926. *See also, King Aircraft Sales, Inc. v. Lane*, 846 P.2d 550, 22 U.C.C. Rep. 2d 515 (Wash. App. 1993) (The airplanes, although not necessarily unique, were rare enough to make the ability to cover virtually impossible).

(2) The energy crisis, with its attendant shortages of commodities such as oil and natural gas and unprecedented price increases, resulted in threats by suppliers to cease deliveries, particularly under contracts entered into at a time when the suppliers failed to foresee the magnitude of price increases. The courts have been willing to grant specific performance of these contracts, not because the goods are unique, but because of "other proper circumstances," *i.e.*, that "chaos and irreparable damage" would result, or that it would be difficult or impossible to find another supplier willing to enter into a long-term supply contract. *See, e.g., Laclede Gas Co. v. Amoco Oil Co.*, 522 F.2d 33 (8th Cir. 1975); *Iowa Electric Light & Power Co. v. Atlas Corp.*, 467 F. Supp. 129 (N.D. Iowa 1978); *Eastern Air Lines, Inc. v. Gulf Oil Corp.*, 415 F. Supp. 429 (S.D. Fla. 1975); *Missouri Public Service Co. v. Peabody Coal Co.*, 583 S.W.2d 721 (Mo. App. 1979); compare *Columbia Gas Transmission Corp. v. Larry H. Wright, Inc.*, 443 F. Supp. 14 (S.D. Ohio 1977).

(3) U.C.C. § 2-716(2) states: "The decree for specific performance may include such terms and conditions as to payment of the price, damages, or other relief as the court may deem just." In *Iowa Electric Light & Power Co. v. Atlas Corp.*, 467 F. Supp. 129, 135 (N.D. Iowa 1978), an action resulting from an enormous increase in the market price of uranium concentrate ("yellowcake"), the court at first indicated that this section "would allow this court to equitably adjust the price of the disputed U308." In a supplemental opinion the court reversed itself, declaring that this section does not permit the court "to adjust the price in favor of seller to balance the equities of specific performance." 467 F. Supp. at 138.

(4) Under proposed § 2-716(a), a court may order specific performance if the parties have expressly agreed in the contract for sale. *Cf.* CISG Articles 28 and 46.

§ 7.05 Buyer's Remedies Where Goods Finally Accepted

[A] Buyer's Damages for Breach

Read: U.C.C. § 2-714; see § 2-607(1).

Read also: U.C.C. §§ 2A-508(3) and (4), 2A-519(3) and (4), 2A-520, see § 2A-516(1); CISG Arts. 50, 74.

WINCHESTER v. McCULLOCH BROTHERS GARAGE, INC.

Alabama Supreme Court
388 So. 2d 927 30 U.C.C. Rep. 212 (1980)

TORBERT, CHIEF JUSTICE.

This is a breach of warranty case under the Alabama version of the Uniform Commercial Code. The facts in this case are stated in the dissenting opinion of Mr. Justice Faulkner and need not be repeated.

Code 1975, §§ 7-2-316(4), -719(1), provides that a seller may contractually limit his buyer's remedies for breach of warranty. The warranty given by the defendants in this case was the type typically given — the vehicle warranty expressly limited the buyer's remedy to repair or replacement of defective parts and disclaimed liability for incidental and consequential damages. As a result of the limitation sanctioned by § 7-2-719, the jury must find that the limited warranty failed of its essential purpose before it can proceed to award damages other than as provided in the limited warranty. See Code 1975, § 7-2-719(2).

Since testimony revealed that the cost to repair the Jeep was around $1,200, we believe that the jury concluded the warranty failed of its essential purpose. Furthermore, we find the facts reasonably support the jury's conclusion. Where a seller refused to honor its own limited warranty, that warranty may properly be found to fail by reason of § 7-2-719(2).

Because the jury presumably found the contractual remedy ineffective, the buyer is entitled to other remedies provided in the Code. Code 1975, § 7-2-714(2), (3), sets down the general rule in breach of warranty cases: [the court quotes U.C.C. § 2-714(2), (3)]. According to the statute, damages are normally the difference between the value of the goods as warranted and the value as delivered, plus incidental and consequential damages.

The purchase price is evidence of the value of the goods as warranted. However, it is often difficult to ascertain the value of the goods as delivered. For this reason, where the goods are repairable, cost to repair is a useful measure of the difference in values. See J. White & R. Summers, Handbook of The Law Under The Uniform Commercial Code § 10-2(1972) [§10-2 (2d ed. 1980)].

Under the authority of §§ 7-2-714(3), -715, plaintiff buyer may also claim consequential damages. Evidence adduced at trial shows the plaintiff spent $1,000 for an expert witness. Here, however, expenses of trial preparation are not consequential damages.

Plaintiff also produced evidence that the reasonable rental value of an automobile was $15 per day, but plaintiff did not rent an automobile. He borrowed an automobile for two days, and then he purchased a substitute means of transportation. Although the plaintiff's purchase of the replacement automobile may have been more than was reasonably required at the time, plaintiff chose to buy the substitute car. Recovery for consequential damages is allowed only to the extent the buyer suffers actual damage, and since the plaintiff borrowed, then bought, another car, the rental cost of a substitute car is not an item of damage.

Applying the foregoing rules to this case, it is apparent the jury verdict was excessive. We recognize the amount of damages is left largely to the jury, but the jury may not ignore the statutory standards by which to measure plaintiff's damages. In the unlikely event the truck could not be repaired and had no salvage value, the difference in the value of the truck as accepted and its value as warranted can be no more than $8,225, the cost of the truck. Since no includable consequential damage was shown, the total award could not exceed $8,225, and the jury award of $20,000 was certainly improper.

The trial judge recognized the impropriety of the jury award and ordered a new trial unless the plaintiff consented to remittitur. Under the facts, his order was undoubtedly not an abuse of discretion; The order is due to be affirmed.

Affirmed.

MADDOX, ALMON, SHORES, EMBRY AND BEATTY, JJ., concur.

FAULKNER, J., with whom JONES, J., concurs, dissents.

FAULKNER, JUSTICE (dissenting).

This is an appeal from a judgment of the Circuit Court of Lawrence County granting a motion for new trial unless Winchester remitted $15,100 of a jury verdict of $20,000 damages awarded him in a suit for breach of warranty of a Jeep motor vehicle. I would reverse and render.

In February, 1978, James Winchester traded a 1978 Chevrolet four-wheel drive vehicle with one of the McCulloch brothers, owners of McCulloch Brothers Jeep dealership in Decatur, for a 1978 Jeep Honcho vehicle. He paid, in cash the day of the sale, the difference in price between the two vehicles, $485.00. This vehicle was used to drive back and forth to work each day, a trip between Hillsboro and Decatur. Mr. Winchester owned no other automobile.

On March 4, while driving the Jeep, having only 692 miles on it, Winchester felt a hard jolt and the Jeep fell down in the rear. It pulled to the left-hand side of the road and ran off the road into a ditch and hit a mailbox. He finally got it straightened up and went directly up the ditch. While the Jeep was being removed by the wrecker, he noticed that the rear leaf spring on the driver's side had broken completely loose from where it was attached to the frame and was hanging loose. The drive shaft had come out of the Jeep, having been broken at the universal joint and having slipped out of the transmission. The vehicle was taken to Moulton and after McCulloch Brothers was called and Hoss McCulloch was told of the problem, the Jeep was taken to McCulloch Brothers dealership. After talking with McCulloch Brothers later, he was told the North Alabama adjuster had told them not to fix the Jeep. He called the adjuster in Nashville and the factory in Detroit and received no satisfaction. Two days after this incident in which the Jeep was wrecked, Winchester purchased a 1975 car and paid $2,556.00 for it in order to have a car to drive to work. Rental cost of a car would have been $15.00 a day and at the time of the trial, 435 days after the wreck, rental could have been $6,525.00.

On May 18, Winchester filed suit against the McCulloch Brothers, AMC, American Motors Sales Corporation, and Jeep Corp., for breach of warranty. The complaint was later amended to include a count under the Alabama Extended Manufacturers Liability Doctrine. At trial Winchester presented expert testimony that the leaf spring was defectively made. The jury returned a verdict for Winchester in the amount of $20,000.00. Defendants filed a motion for new trial and in the alternative for judgment notwithstanding the verdict, asserting that the excessive verdict exhibited bias against the defendants and the damages were not supported by the evidence. The trial judge ordered a remittitur as to all defendants in the amount of $15,000.00 or a new trial. Winchester initially accepted the remittitur, believing the amount remitted was to be $4,900.00, but later struck consent to the remittitur and appeals.

The sole issue before this Court is whether the trial judge abused his discretion by ordering the remittitur.

The evidence shows the following proof relating to damages: Winchester purchased the Jeep for $8,225.00. To pay this, he traded in a Chevrolet, and paid $485.00 cash. Two days after the accident, Winchester bought another automobile for $2,556.00. He introduced evidence that the fair rental value of a vehicle was $15.00 per day, and he claimed loss of 435 days $6,525.00 The cost to repair the Jeep was estimated to be $1,200.00. (It was never repaired.) Winchester paid a metallurgist $1,000.00 to testify as an expert witness at the trial.

Section 7-2-714, Code 1975, provides that the measure of damages for breach of warranty is the difference at the time and place of acceptance between the value of the goods accepted, and the value they would have had if they had been as warranted. Here, the only evidence presented as to the value of the Jeep when accepted was its purchase price. The Court of Civil Appeals held that the purchase price of personal property is admissible as going to the value of the property, and in the absence of other evidence, it is sufficient. In *Riley v. Ford Motor Company,* 442 F.2d 670 (1971), the Fifth Circuit permitted evidence of purchase price as going to the value, but there the owner testified that the property made the basis of a breach of warranty action was useless to him.

Because there was no evidence of value introduced other than the purchase price of the Jeep, we take that as a starting point to assess damages. The purchase price was $8,225.00, and it was obviously useless in its present condition at the time of the trial. In fact it was sitting on jacks — none of the defendants would agree to repair it. Therefore, I would find that the purchase price is an element of damages. Next, Winchester, when he had no automobile to go to his place of employment, had to buy another vehicle as a substitute means of transportation. I opine that this is another element of damages. Cf. *Riley*, where substitute transportation was permitted as an element of damages.

I would hold that Winchester's damages should be $10,781.00 instead of $4,900.00 as found by the trial judge. With this award he would be placed in the same economic condition as he was in at the time he purchased the Jeep.

JONES, J., concurs.

NOTES

(1) Several states have enacted automobile "lemon laws." Note particularly Mich.Comp.Laws Ann. § 257.1403, subsection (1):

(1) If a defect or condition which was reported to the manufacturer or new motor vehicle dealer pursuant to section 2 continues to exist and the new motor vehicle has been subject to a reasonable number of repairs as determined under subsection (3), the manufacturer shall within 30 days have the option to either replace the new motor vehicle with a comparable replacement motor vehicle currently in production and acceptable to the consumer or accept return of the vehicle and refund to the consumer the full purchase price including the cost of any options or other modifications installed or made by or for the manufacturer, and the amount of all other charges made by or for the manufacturer, less a reasonable allowance for the consumer's use of the vehicle not exceeding 10 cents per mile driven at the time of the initial report of the same defect or conditions or 10%, of the purchase price of the vehicle, whichever is less, and less an amount equal to any appraised damage that is not attributable to normal use or to the defect or condition. A reasonable allowance for use is that amount directly attributable to use by the consumer and any previous consumer prior to his or her first report of a defect or condition that impairs the use or value of the new motor vehicle to the manufacturer, its agents, or the new motor vehicle dealer. Whenever a vehicle is replaced or refunded under the provisions of this section, in those instances in which towing services and rental vehicles were not made available without cost to the consumer, the manufacturer shall also reimburse the consumer for those towing costs and reasonable costs for a comparable rental vehicle that were incurred as a direct result of the defect or condition.

(2) *See Davis Industrial Sales, Inc. v. Workman Construction Co.,* 856 S.W.2d 355, 21 U.C.C. Rep. 2d 607 (Mo. App. 1993) (Section 2-714(2) formula is the difference between the value

of goods as accepted and the value of goods as warranted. Value of forklift in the condition warranted was its sales price of $8,400; cost of repair was $3,500. A useful objective measurement of the difference in values is the cost of repair or replacement).

(3) The court in *Nelson v. Logan Motor Sales, Inc.*, 370 S.E.2d 734 at 737 (W.Va. 1988) remarked:

Our ruling in *Mountaineer Contractors* is in accord with the generally accepted view that the damage formula provided in Code, 46-2-714(2) "works fairly smoothly where the buyer replaces the defective goods. The cost of repair is strong evidence of the difference between the value they would have had if they had been as warranted . . . . In most cases damages can be determined based on estimates of what it would cost to repair or replace." 3 W. Hawkland, U.C.C. Series § 2-174:04 and cases cited therein (1984).

(4) *But see Santor v. A and M Karagheusian, Inc.*, 207 A.2d 305, 2 U.C.C. Rep. 599 (N.J. 1965) (defective carpeting — purchase price $14 per square yard; salvage value $3 to $4 per square yard. Measure of damages: difference between price paid and actual market value of defective carpeting at the time buyer knew or should have known that it was defective).

———

HILL v. BASF WYANDOTTE CORP.

Supreme Court of South Carolina
311 S.E.2d 734 (1984)

LITTLEJOHN, JUSTICE:

This case comes before us as a certified question from the United States District Court, District of South Carolina.

The question presented is as follows:

Given the distinction between (1) actual or direct and (2) consequential damages as set forth in §§ 36-2-714 and 36-2-715 of the South Carolina Code of Laws, 1976, as amended, what is the measure of actual damages in a herbicide failure case where there is a valid limitation of consequential, special or indirect damages?

This is a breach of warranty case involving an alleged herbicide failure which caused crop damage.

Plaintiff Hill (Farmer) purchased a quantity of the herbicide, Basalin, from a retail distributor. Basalin is manufactured by defendant BASF Wyandotte Corporation (BWC).

Among other things, to each can of Basalin there were attached the following statements:

1) "BWC" warrants that this product conforms to the chemical description on the label and is reasonably fit for the purpose referred to in the Directions for Use subject to the inherent risks to above.

2) In no case shall "BWC" or the Seller be liable for consequential, special or indirect damages resulting from the use or handling of this product, and

3) Read "CONDITIONS OF SALE AND WARRANTY" before buying or using. If terms are not acceptable, return product at once, unopened.

Farmer alleges that he used Basalin on approximately 1,450 acres of soybeans and another herbicide, Treflan, on approximately 200 acres. He further alleges that although there was a severe drought that year, the Treflan treated crops were significantly better than the Basalin crops both in quality and yield per acre.

Farmer initially brought suit in United States District Court on oral and written warranties for damages. A jury awarded him $207,725.00. BWC appealed and the Fourth Circuit Court of Appeals reversed and remanded the case, holding that only the written warranties on the labels of the product apply and that the limitation of remedies quoted above is valid. *Hill v. BASF Wyandotte Corp.*, 696 F.2d 287 (4th Cir. 1982).

In footnote 6 the court stated:

We express no opinion as to whether under subsections (1) and (2) of § 36-2-714 and on the evidence that may be adduced on retrial the appropriate measure of damages would be the purchase price of the herbicide or some other measure.

This question was certified to us by the trial court after remand.

Ordinarily, *S.C. Code Ann.* § 36-2-714(2) (1976) is controlling as the measure of damages in a breach of warranty case. This section provides:

(2) The measure of damages for breach of warranty is the difference at the time and place of acceptance between the value of the goods accepted and the value they would have had if they had been as warranted, *unless special circumstances show proximate damages of a different amount.* (Emphasis added.)

We find that the formula in this subsection is inapplicable to a herbicide failure case. This formula is most appropriate where the nonconforming good can be repaired or replaced and value (both as warranted and as accepted) can be defined with certainty.

A herbicide failure is a latent defect in the product. There is no reasonable way a farmer can determine in advance whether a herbicide will perform as warranted. Discovery of the problem must await the development of the crop at which time it is usually too late to correct.

The value of a herbicide as warranted is difficult to define. Price and value are not equivalents. From the farmer's perspective, the value of the herbicide is a healthy crop at maturity. In the manufacturer's viewpoint, the value is its selling price.

The value as accepted is equally uncertain and difficult to define. There is no market for such goods and thus no market price. If anything, it has a negative value.

In our view, the inability of a court to ascertain with certainty the value of goods both as warranted and as accepted creates a special circumstance within the meaning of § 36-2-714(2). It is this special circumstance which removes cases of this type from the § 36-2-714(2) measure of damages into subsection (1).

Subsection (1) provides: [The court cites U.C.C. § 2-714(1).]

Official Comment 2 to § 36-2-714 indicates that subsection (1) is applicable in breach of warranty cases.

It has consistently been held by this Court that the measure of actual damages, in cases similar to this, is the value the crop would have had if the product had conformed to the warranty less the value of the crop actually produced, less the expense of preparing for market the portion of the probable crop prevented from maturing. [Citations.] We hold this formula to be appropriate in the present case.

BWC has argued that this formula includes lost profits and that lost profits are a consequential damage barred by the limitation of remedies on the cans of Basalin. We disagree.

In *W.R. Grace and Co., supra*, it was noted that the ". . .destruction or loss of a mature crop, which has a realizable value in excess of the cost of harvesting, processing and marketing, results in a monetary loss to the owner, regardless of whether the farming operation would, otherwise, have been profitable."

If the measure of damages we have adopted includes an element of lost profits, such inclusion is merely coincidental as the measure covers the direct loss resulting in the ordinary course of events from the alleged breach of the warranty. See, § 36-2-714(1).

The foregoing is the order of this Court.

LEWIS, C.J., and NESS, GREGORY and HARWELL, J.J., concur.

NOTES

(1) "Special circumstances" under § 2-714(2) have also been found where after acceptance of defective goods by the buyer, the seller has repaired some of the defects. Thus, in *Stutts v. Green Ford, Inc.*, 267 S.E.2d 919, 926 (N.C.App. 1980), the court said:

> [T]he date of acceptance preceded the time when numerous repairs were made in full compliance with the warranty. At the end of the warranty period, the only nonconformity of which plaintiff complains and of which there is evidence of defective parts or workmanship is the oil leakage. Under the special facts of this case, we hold, then, that an appropriate measure of damages would be the difference in the fair market value of the truck in its condition at the time and place of acceptance, increased by the value of repairs and replacements made in compliance with the warranty, and its fair market value had it been as warranted. . . . This, in effect, would permit plaintiff to recover damages compensating him for the loss in value due to the persistent oil problem, while preventing him from receiving windfall damages for defects which were subsequently successfully repaired.

(2) *Nelson v. Logan Motor Sales Inc.*, 370 S.E.2d 734 at 378 note 8 (W.Va. 1988), points out other "special circumstances":

> Examples of true "special circumstances" cases, where the formula was found wholly inadequate and other means of proving damages were approved are: *Hirst v. Elgin Metal Casket Co.*, 438 F. Supp. 906 (D.C.Mont.1977) (Damages for breach of expressed warranty for a "leak-proof casket" are the pain and suffering of the decedent's relatives when viewing a moldy corpse upon exhumation); *Baden v. Curtiss*, 380 F. Supp. 243 (D.C.Mont.1977) (Damages

for breach of implied warranty of merchantability of defective bull semen are the value of the first calf crop that would have been produced.)

(3) Reported decisions are legion in which counsel for buyer, having successfully crossed the hurdles of proving the existence of a warranty and the breach thereof by seller, has then failed to marshal sufficient evidence to prove damages. Typical language appears in *Chrysler Corp. v. Marinari,* 177 Ga. App. 304, 42 U.C.C. Rep. 1310 at 1311-12 (1985), where the court said with regard to damages:

> With regard to the award of compensatory damages for breach of warranty, appellant [seller] contends that the evidence was not sufficient to authorize the jury's verdict of "the estimated $4,000.000. . . ."

> "The measure of damages for breach of warranty is the difference *at the time and place of acceptance* between the value of the goods accepted and the value they would have had if they had been as warranted. . . ." (Emphasis supplied.) OCGA § 11-2-714(2). Appellee [buyer] did testify as to the purchase price of the van, and, thus, he established *one* of the two figures for calculating the amount of damages recoverable for breach of warranty. However, a review of the transcript reveals that appellee's testimony failed further to establish the second figure, which is "the value of the vehicle delivered in a defective condition." The evidentiary basis upon which the jury obviously arrived at its "estimated" verdict is a portion of appellee's testimony concerning the difference between the "as warranted" value and the actual value of the allegedly defective van *at the approximate time of trial,* some years *after* the time of original delivery and acceptance. The transcript reveals no competent evidence of the value of the van in its defective state *at the time and place of delivery.* When the entirety of appellee's testimony is considered, it is clear that he was *never* able to establish any value for the van at the time and place of delivery except that value indicated by the price that he paid for it. In order to recover for breach of warranty, it was necessary for appellee to produce evidence of the actual value of the *defective* van at the time of delivery. In the absence of such evidence, it was error to enter judgment on the jury's award of compensatory damages for the breach of warranty count.

. . . .

Judgment reversed.

The burden to prove damages is not, however, insuperable. "The damage award need not be absolutely exact; a reasonable estimate based on relevant data is sufficient to support an award." *District Concrete Co., Inc. v. Bernstein Concrete Corp.,* 418 A.2d 1030, 1038 (D.C. Ct. App.1980).

[B]   Deduction of Damages From Price

Read: U.C.C. § 2-717.

Read also: U.C.C. § 2A-508(6); CISG Arts. 45(1)(a), 50.

PROBLEM 7.4

In April-May 1993, Forsythe Racing, Inc. entered into an oral agreement with Hector Rebaque and his son under which the son was to serve as a race driver for an Indy-type race car owned by Forsythe for the 1993 Indy Car World Series. Forsythe agreed to provide the equipment and support staff for the racing team. Forsythe asserted that Rebaque agreed to furnish it in turn with $675,000 in sponsorship funds for the 1993 season. Rebaque maintained that he was obligated to furnish only $500,000. The amount actually paid to Forsythe by Rebaque was $500,000.

On July 19, 1993, Rebaque purchased in Italy a Lamborghini sports car. It was shipped from Italy on July 27, 1993. Prior to the automobile's arrival in the United States, Rebaque and Forsythe orally agreed that Forsythe would purchase the automobile from Rebaque for $72,000.

On June 2, 1993, Forsythe paid Rebaque $36,000 toward the purchase price. Upon the automobile's arrival in the United States, Forsythe took immediate possession. On August 2, 1993, Forsythe issued a check to Rebaque for the $36,000 balance owing on the sales agreement. Forsythe stopped payment on the check. It never paid the balance of $36,000 to Rebaque. Forsythe withheld the balance due as a $36,000 credit against an amount it believed Rebaque owed to it under the sponsorship agreement. Despite repeated requests, Forsythe refused either to complete payment or to relinquish the Lamborghini.

Rebaque filed suit against Forsythe to recover the $36,000 balance due on the automobile. Forsythe, in an attempt to set off the amount it alleged Rebaque owed it under the sponsorship agreement, filed a counterclaim against Rebaque seeking $175,000. It claimed that its liability for the balance of the automobile purchase agreement would be more than offset by the damages it claimed under the sponsorship agreement.

On March 20, 1995, Rebaque moved for summary judgment in the amount of $36,000 (plus prejudgment interest), arguing that Forsythe had no right to set off its debt to him against its claim against him because such set-off was prohibited by U.C.C. § 2-717. Forsythe also moved for summary judgment in its favor as to seeking declaratory relief to confirm its right to assert a set-off. It further argued that any judgment — or at a minimum any enforcement of judgment — should await trial of its counterclaim seeking $175,000 against Rebaque.

On May 15, 1995, the trial court entered judgment for Rebaque for $36,000 (plus prejudgment interest) and ordered Rebaque to furnish and execute all documents necessary for registration and domestication of the automobile by Forsythe. The court found that there was no just cause to delay its order.

On May 23, 1995, Forsythe moved for modification of the May 15 order by deletion of the finding making that order immediately enforceable. It argued that it would be inequitable to permit Rebaque to immediately collect his judgment against it — while its claim against him remained pending — since Rebaque was a nonresident alien without assets in the United States sufficient to satisfy any judgment which might be ultimately entered against him. In its motion Forsythe offered to post a letter of credit or set aside sufficient funds under court supervision to ensure payment to Rebaque of any net judgment which might be entered in his favor. The court denied this motion to modify.

Forsythe on appeal argues that the trial court improperly refused to allow a set-off from the automobile purchase price based on its claim under the sponsorship agreement. What result? *See Rebaque v. Forsythe Racing Inc.*, 480 N.E.2d 1338, 42 U.C.C. Rep. 222 (Ill. App. 1985); *see also, Berdex International, Inc. v. Milfico Prepared Foods, Inc.*, 630 N.E.2d 998, 23 U.C.C. Rep. 2d 1167 (Ill. App. 1994).

§ 7.06 Buyer's Incidental and Consequential Damages

Read: U.C.C. § 2-715.

Read also: U.C.C. § 2A-520; CISG Arts. 45(1)(b), 74, 77, 78.

At § 7.04, we evaluated remedies available to a buyer who has not accepted the goods or who has justifiably revoked his acceptance. In particular, § 7.04[C][1] recited buyer's right to cover and to recover from seller as damages the difference between the cost of cover and the contract price "together with incidental or consequential damages." U.C.C. § 2-712. Section 7.04[C][2] recited buyer's right to recover damages for non-delivery or repudiation by the seller measured by the difference between the market price and the contract price "together with any incidental and consequential damages." U.C.C. § 2-713. Cf. U.C.C. §§ 2A-518, 2A-519(1) and (2).

Further, at § 7.05, we evaluated the remedies available to a buyer with regard to goods finally accepted. In particular, § 7.05[A] recited buyer's measure of damages as the difference between the value of the goods accepted and the value they would have had if they had been as warranted. Also, in a proper case "any incidental and consequential damages . . .may . . .be recovered." U.C.C. § 2-714. Cf. U.C.C. § 2A-519(3) and (4).

In this section we evaluate buyer's incidental and consequential damages under U.C.C. § 2-715.

HORIZONS, INC. v. AVCO CORP

United States Court of Appeals
714 F2d 862, 36 U.C.C. Rep. 1207 (8th Cir. 1983)

Ross, Circuit Judge.

This diversity action was instituted by Horizons, Inc. alleging a breach of express and implied warranties of fitness for an ordinary purpose and fitness for a particular purpose in connection with the purchase by Horizons of an airplane engine which was remanufactured by Avco Corporation. Horizons claimed that it suffered ordinary, incidental and consequential damages as a result of backfiring which occurred in the engine shortly after installation. Following a bench trial, the district court found that Avco had breached an implied warranty of merchantability and awarded Horizons $9,974.37 in general damages, $619.84 in incidental damages, and $56,265.00 in consequential damages. Horizons cross-appeals alleging that the failure to award damages for the cost of "cover" was error.

Horizons is a South Dakota corporation in the business of providing aerial photographic and photogrammetric services, including topographic surveying and mapping. Avco does not sell its remanufactured engines directly to the public, but does so only through its authorized domestic distributors. Aviation Sales, Inc. of Denver, Colorado, is an authorized distributor of Avco engines. James Spell, president of Horizons, contacted purchasing an Avco remanufactured engine for one of its company airplanes. Aviation Sales advised Spell that Horizons would be better off to order the engine through an Avco "fixed base operator," such as Casper Air Service, a dealer located in Casper, Wyoming. In December of 1977, Horizons ordered an Avco engine from Casper Air Service for a price of $12,767.00.

Robert Collett, Horizons' pilot, installed the engine in a Cessna 310 aircraft owned by Horizons about mid-June of 1978. After the engine was installed and ground-tested, Horizons' personnel attempted to operate the aircraft. A series of mechanical failures and breakdowns occurred primarily because of backfiring in the engine. Horizons notified Avco, in writing, of the engine malfunctions. In order to correct the backfiring problems, Horizons incurred numerous expenses and ultimately had to overhaul the engine. The district court found that expert testimony established that there was a defect in the valve train which existed at the time the engine was remanufactured and was not caused by normal engine wear.

The district court held that an award of consequential damages was proper because Aviation Sales was the ostensible agent of Avco who had "reason to know" of the requirements of Horizons' business and the knowledge of an agent is imputed to the principal under South Dakota law. The district court found that in 1977 and 1978, Horizons had sufficient contract work available to occupy the aircraft on every available flight day. Horizons lost eleven flight days (57.7 hours) in 1978 due to the defective condition of the Avco engine. The court found that consequently, Horizons was unable to complete its 1978 contracts and was forced to utilize flight days in late 1978, 1979 and 1980 to complete those contracts. The court held that the evidence at trial established, to a reasonable degree of certainty, that had Horizons been able to complete flights on those days it would have received net earnings of $56,265.00, which was then awarded as consequential damages for the "down time" experienced by the aircraft during repair of the defective valve train.

On appeal, Avco contends that the district court erred in its award of consequential damages and also in its computation of the proper amount of consequential damages. Horizons, as cross-appellant, contends that the district court erred in failing to award damages for the cost of "cover." We find that the district court correctly awarded consequential damages but failed to award the proper amount of such damages. We also find that the district court correctly denied an award of damages for the cost of "cover." We accordingly affirm in part and reverse in part.

The district court based its determination that an award of consequential damages was proper in this case upon SD Codified Laws Ann § 57A-2-715(2)(a), providing as follows [the Court quotes U.C.C. § 2-715(2)(a)].

Avco alleges that the district court erred when it found that Avco had "reason to know" of Horizons' requirements. Avco traced the reasoning of the district court as finding: (1) that Horizons communicated its requirements to Aviation Sales; (2) Aviation Sales was the ostensible agent[27] of Avco; and (3) that knowledge of Horizons' requirements are imputed to Avco, the principal, under South Dakota law, thereby giving Avco "reason to know" as required under the statute. Avco argues that each of the three steps in the district court's reasoning is flawed and allowed an erroneous award of consequential damages. We disagree.

Avco contends that the first step of the court's analysis is erroneous because Horizons never put on evidence that it actually communicated its requirements to anyone at Aviation Sales. Avco alleges that the district court should not have relied on the fact that Horizons' president, James Spell, habitually explained the nature of Horizons' business to people that he spoke to on the telephone. Avco argues that such testimony does not establish that Spell actually told Aviation Sales of its business requirements. We conclude that the district court's finding that Avco had

---

[27] Agency is ostensible when by conduct or want of ordinary care the principal causes a third person to believe another, who is not actually appointed, to be his agent. SD Codified Laws Ann § 59-1-5.

knowledge of Horizons' requirements is not clearly erroneous under Fed R Civ P 52(a). The record in this case fully supports the court's finding and demonstrates that, at every level of the transaction, knowledge of Horizons' business use of its airplane engines was either communicated to or previously known by Avco. We find three instances of communication to Avco of Horizons' requirements. First, Avco sent mailings to Horizons' business address which identified Horizons as an aerial photographer. Second, it is doubtful that James Spell departed from his habit of identifying himself and his company's line of work when he talked to Aviation Sales about purchasing the engine. Third, Casper Air Service, the Avco dealer which sold the engine to Horizons, had previously modified Horizons' plane for aerial photography. Thus, it is clear that Avco knew, both directly from its own mailing list and indirectly through its distributors, of Horizons' business requirements.

In *Lewis v. Mobil Oil Corporation*, 438 F2d 500, 510-11 [8 U.C.C. Rep 625] (8th Cir 1971) we held that

> [w]here a seller provides goods to a manufacturing enterprise with knowledge that they are to be used in the manufacturing process, it is reasonable to assume that he should know that defective goods will cause a disruption of production, and loss of profits is a natural consequence of such disruption. Hence, loss of profits should be recoverable under those circumstances.

We find the analysis in *Lewis* controlling in this case. Avco provided Horizons, a company it knew through its own mailing list to be an aerial photographer, with a remanufactured engine to be used in its photograph business. It is now unreasonable for Avco to contend that it was unaware that a defective engine could disrupt Horizons' photograph business and cause a loss of profits.

Since we have previously held that Avco had "reason to know" of Horizons' requirements because of Horizons' presence on Avco's own mailing list, we deem it unnecessary to reach the district court's findings that Aviation Sales was the ostensible agent of Avco and its knowledge is thereby imputed to Avco.

The district court awarded Horizons $56,265.00 in consequential damages as compensation for the value of productive capacity lost during the engine's down time. Horizons calculated its lost production claim by utilizing a formula approved in *Clark v. International Harvester Co.*, 581 P2d 784, 805 (Idaho 1978). To arrive at the total claim amount of $56,265.00, Horizons multiplied the contract payment rate per square mile times the number of square miles the aircraft could have covered with the engine functioning properly and subtracted from that figure the operation costs of the plane and the cost of materials. Horizons did not deduct the overhead expense of maintaining the film processing personnel as it felt that this was a cost incurred by Horizons without the benefit of income to meet the expenses during the down time. Although Horizons was ultimately paid the full contract price for both of its contracts which had to be completed at a later date due to the engine's down time, the district court found that 57.7 hours of productive time lost can never be recovered in a company which has sufficient work to keep busy on every available flight day. The district court viewed this loss as similar to the loss suffered by a volume seller: even though the goods are later purchased by another, the supply is endless and a loss of profits has still occurred. We agree with the district court that a loss of profits has occurred. However, we disagree with the amount of consequential damages suffered by Horizons.

In general, expected profits of a commercial business are too remote, speculative and uncertain to permit a recovery of damages for their loss. *Cargill, Inc. v. Taylor Towing Service, Inc.*, 642 F2d 239, 241 (8th Cir 1981). Proof of lost profits must be sufficient to remove the question of profits from the realm of speculation and conjecture. *Rogers v. Allis-Chalmers Credit Corp.*, 679 F2d 138, 142 (8th Cir 1982). The burden of proving the extent of loss incurred by way of consequential damage is on the plaintiff but mathematical precision is not required, only that the loss can be shown in a manner reasonable under the circumstances. *Karlen v. Butler Mfg. Co.*, 526 F2d 1373, 1380 (8th Cir 1975). The sufficiency of the evidence of lost profits is dependent upon whether the financial information contained in the record is such that a just or reasonable estimate can be drawn. *Cargill, supra*, 642 F2d at 241. The law in South Dakota concerning recovery of lost profits mirrors the position taken by the Eighth Circuit. See *Drier v. Perfection, Inc.*, 259 NW2d 496 (SD 1977); *Olson v. Aldren*, 170 NW2d 891 (SD 1969).

In reviewing the consequential damage award, we are convinced that the amount of loss suffered by Horizons was not calculated in a manner reasonable under the circumstances. However, because of the quality of the financial information contained in the record, we feel that a just and reasonable estimate can be drawn by adopting reasonable accounting procedures on gross receipts and expenses for the year of 1978.

Trial Exhibit 67 discloses that in 1978 Horizons' gross receipts amounted to $402,239.12, while expenses amounted to $348,792.00. This results in a net profit of $53,447.12 for the year 1978. This figure includes payment in full on the two contracts which had to be completed at a later date due to the defective engine. Thus, it seems grossly excessive to award Horizons $56,265.00 for 57.7 hours of lost flying time when they only made $53,447.12 for a total of 855.05 hours of flying time in 1978. We find that the most reasonable method of calculating Horizons' loss of profits is to employ a rate of average hourly profit. In 1978 Horizons flew 855.05 hours and made a net profit of $53,447.12. Thus, Horizons' 1978 average hourly profit was $62.51. In multiplying the average hourly profit and the 57.7 hours of down time, we find that the amount of Horizons' loss of profits is $3,606.83. Although this is a far cry from the original award of $56,265.00, we find it quite reasonable considering that the two contracts which had to be completed at a later date were not completely profitable ventures for Horizons. In sum, we hold that Horizons is entitled to $3,606.83 in consequential damages.

On cross-appeal, Horizons contends that the district court erred in failing to award damages for the cost of "cover" incurred when Horizons purchased substitute engines to use during the period of down time. The district court held that Horizons could not recover its claim for the cost of "cover" as Horizons had never rejected or revoked its acceptance of the Avco engine. We agree.

SD Codified Laws Ann § 57A-2-711(1)(a) provides that: [the court cites § 57A-2-711(1)(a)]. Thus, the district court was correct in finding that Horizons was not entitled to damages for the cost of "cover."

In summary, we affirm the district court's decision to award consequential damages and deny the claim for the cost of "cover." However, we reverse the amount of the consequential damage award and order that the total damage award be reduced to $14,201.04.

NOTES

(1) This case may bring to mind *Hadley v. Baxendale*, 9 Exch. 341, 156 Eng. Rep. 145 (1854). Illustration 1 to Restatement, Second, Contracts § 351(1981) is based on Hadley and reads:[28]

A, a carrier, contracts with B, a miller, to carry B's broken crankshaft to its manufacturer for repair. B tells A when they make the contract that the crankshaft is part of B's milling machine and that it must be sent at once, but not that the mill is stopped because B has no replacement. Because A delays in carrying the crankshaft, B loses profit during an additional period while the mill is stopped because of the delay. A is not liable for B's loss of profit. That loss was not foreseeable by A as a probable result of the breach at the time the contract was made because A did not know that the broken crankshaft was necessary for the operation of the mill.

(2) *Duracote Corp. v. Goodyear Tire & Rubber Co.*, 2 Ohio St. 3d 160, 443 N.E.2d 184, 35 U.C.C. Rep. 471, 472-73 (1983), quotes as follows:

Professors White and Summers have observed that U.C.C. § 2-715(2). . ."imposes two restrictions on the recovery of consequential damages in addition to the foreseeability requirement: they must be reasonably ascertainable, and the plaintiff cannot recover for losses he reasonably could have prevented." White & Summers, Uniform Commercial Code (2 Ed 1980), 396, § 10-4.

See, e.g., *Prutch v. Ford Motor Co.*, 618 P.2d 657, 29 U.C.C. Rep. 1507 (Colo. 1980) (The court reasoned that plaintiffs, in deciding to continue farming with the knowledge that their Ford tractor, plow, disc harrow and hay baler might continue to malfunction, actually mitigated their losses. This they were required to do by U.C.C. § 2-715(2)(a). Their decision to try to produce at least part of a normal crop, rather than no crop at all, was required by their duty to lessen, rather than increase, their damages).

(3) It is clear from the outcome in numerous cases that consequential damages are often difficult to establish. Occasionally the courts will give some concrete indication of how difficult the task may be. Thus, in *Farmers Mutual Exchange of Baxley, Inc. v. Dixon*, 146 Ga. App. 663, 247 S.E.2d 124, 126 (1978), where plaintiff sought consequential damages in the form of lost profits from lost crops, the court said:

In the present case there is no uncertainty that the alleged cause of damage was defective seed corn. If plaintiffs can establish by comparison to corn crops grown on land in the same planted field, with the same soil, the same brand of seed, fertilized and cultivated in the same manner, and planted at the same time and under identical weather conditions, then the damages would not be too speculative and conjectural for a jury to determine.

(4) In *Tremco, Inc. v. Valley Aluminum Products Corp.*, 831 S.W.2d 156, 18 U.C.C. Rep.2d 168 (Ark. App. 1992), seller sold window assembly gaskets to buyer, a manufacturer of window

---

[28] Copyright © 1981 by American Law Institute. Reprinted by permission.

assemblies. Buyer had contacted to provide window assemblies to Win-Wall, Inc., a glazing subcontactor, for two commercial buildings. The gaskets were defective and buyer sought recovery for consequential damages. Held: For buyer: (1) substantial evidence was introduced as to loss of profits and amount of loss so as to support an award of consequential damages, and (2) award of damages for cost of replacing gaskets was not speculative. Note regarding lost profits: Win-Wall's president testified that he had refused to allow buyer the opportunity to bid on subsequent projects and that buyer would receive no further business as long as the gasket problem existed. The president listed ten contracts he had awarded since the gasket incident totaling $1,408,000, which required materials of the kind supplied by buyer. He was "very confident" that he would have sublet at least half of them to buyer but for the problem experienced with the gaskets.

———

DAKOTA GRAIN CO., v. EHRMANTROUT

Supreme Court of North Dakota
502 N.W.2d 234, 23 U.C.C. Rep.2d 402 (1993)

LEVINE, JUSTICE.

. . . .

During the Spring of 1989, Ehrmantrout orally agreed to sell [to Dakota Grain Co., Inc. (the Elevator)] some of his Lenn variety hard red spring wheat. The Elevator intended to sell this wheat to other farmers for seeding and insists that Ehrmantrout was informed that the wheat would be used as seed. Ehrmantrout claims that he was neither told nor had reason to believe that the Elevator intended to resell his wheat for seed. Ehrmantrout delivered four truck loads of spring wheat to the Elevator in April 1989.

In early May 1989, the Elevator manager asked Ehrmantrout if he would agree to sell more of his spring wheat to the Elevator. Ehrmantrout agreed and on May 9, 1989, he delivered to the Elevator two truck loads of wheat, totaling 629.49 bushels. The Elevator cleaned this wheat and sold about 585 bushels of it to four different farmers for seeding. The farmers planted the seed, but none of the crops matured. It was ultimately determined that the wheat planted by the four farmers was not Lenn spring wheat, but a winter wheat which, by its nature, will not produce a crop when seeded during the spring of the year. The Elevator paid the four farmers a total of $22,201 as damages for selling them winter wheat to seed instead of spring wheat. The Elevator then filed this action for damages against Ehrmantrout, alleging various theories of recovery, including breach of contract, breach of warranty, negligence and fraud.

The parties made this case much more complex and confusing than was necessary by trying the case on mixed principles of tort and contract law. Yet, this is a classic breach of warranty case, resolvable by application of Chapter 41-02, N.D.C.C., our codification of the Article 2— Sales provisions of the Uniform Commercial Code. Despite the lack of clarity in the parties' presentation of their respective legal theories, the trial court's analysis was close to the mark and, in fact, its resolution of the case, except for some ambiguity in its findings regarding consequential damages, is in accord with Chapter 41-02, N.D.C.C.

The trial court concluded that Ehrmantrout breached his oral sale contract with the Elevator by delivering winter wheat instead of Lenn spring wheat. Using comparative fault principles, the court concluded that Ehrmantrout was 51 percent responsible and the Elevator was 49 percent responsible for the consequential damages arising from the sale of the wheat to the four farmers for spring seeding. The trial court entered judgment awarding the Elevator $125.90 in general damages, representing the difference in the value of the spring wheat Ehrmantrout contracted to sell the Elevator and the value of the winter wheat that he actually delivered to the Elevator. In addition, the trial court awarded the Elevator consequential damages of $11,332.51, representing 51 percent of the total damages incurred by the Elevator in its settlement with the four farmers. Ehrmantrout filed a post-trial motion to amend the trial court's findings of fact, conclusions of law and judgment and filed an alternative motion for a new trial. These post-trial motions were denied by the court, and Ehrmantrout appealed.

Ehrmantrout asserts on appeal that the trial court erred by not specifying what act or omission by Ehrmantrout constituted negligent conduct. The parties unnecessarily complicated this case by using negligence terminology to describe Ehrmantrout's breach of his express warranty to deliver Lenn spring wheat. Under the Uniform Commercial Code, a bargain that includes a description of the goods to be sold creates an express warranty that the goods will conform to that description. Section 41-02-30(1)(b), N.D.C.C. [U.C.C. § 2-313(1)(b)]. The contract is breached when the delivered goods do not conform to the description, irrespective of whether the seller acted negligently or otherwise. Section 41-02-93(1), N.D.C.C. So, the seller's negligence, or lack of negligence, is not relevant to the question of whether the seller breached his or her express warranty to delivery conforming goods. . . .

Ehrmantrout also asserts that the trial court's findings that Ehrmantrout delivered to the Elevator winter wheat instead of spring wheat and that the wheat purchased by the four farmers was wheat sold to the Elevator by Ehrmantrout are not supported by the evidence. We disagree. . . .

Ehrmantrout also asserts that the trial court erred in awarding consequential damages in this case. The appropriate measure of damages for a breach of warranty is set forth under Section 41-02-93(2) and (3), N.D.C.C. [U.C.C. 2-714(2) and (3)]: . . .

The trial court awarded general damages to the Elevator of $125.90 based upon a 20 cent per bushel difference in value between the spring wheat for which Ehrmantrout was paid and the winter wheat that he actually delivered (629.49 bushels delivered X $.20 per bushel price difference = $125.90). Section 41-02-93(2), N.D.C.C. Ehrmantrout does not object to this award of general damages.

However, Ehrmantrout does object to the court's award of consequential damages. In awarding consequential damages, the trial court compared the "fault" of Ehrmantrout and the Elevator that caused those damages and apportioned them accordingly. Before we discuss the elements necessary to award consequential damages, we must first determine whether the court erred in applying comparative fault principles here.

Our comparative fault law, Chapter 32-03.2, N.D.C.C., defines the term "fault" to include "breach of warranty . . .and failure to exercise reasonable care to avoid an injury or to mitigate damages." Section 32-03.2-01, N.D.C.C. Under Section 32-03.2-03, N.D.C.C., "fault" is expressly defined to mean "product liability or *breach of warranty* for product defect." (Emphasis added.) So, under this section pure comparative fault applies in a breach of warranty action and damages are diminished in proportion to the amount of contributing fault of the person recovering the damages. Section 32-03.2-03, N.D.C.C.

Clearly the, the trial court did not err in comparing fault for purposes of awarding consequential damages in this case. *See Peterson v. Bendix Home Systems, Inc.,* 318 N.W.2d 50 (Minn. 1982) (comparative fault applies to consequential damages in a breach of warranty action).

Ehrmantrout also argues that in awarding consequential damages, the trial court did not first determine whether those damages were foreseeable by Ehrmantrout and, if foreseeable, whether the Elevator could reasonably have prevented them. Consequential damages are defined under 41-02-94(2), N.D.C.C. [U.C.C. 2-715(2)]:

> "2. Consequential damages resulting from the seller's breach include:
>
> a. Any loss resulting from general or particular requirements and needs of *which the seller at the time of contracting had reason to know and which could not reasonably be prevented by cover or otherwise;* and
>
> b. Injury to person or property proximately resulting from any breach of warranty." (Emphasis added.)

Under this provision, the primary factor for awarding consequential damages is whether the losses were foreseeable by the seller at the time he or she entered the contract. *Schneidt v. Asbey Motors, Inc.* 248 N.W.2d 792 (N.D. 1976); White & Summers, Uniform Commercial Code § 10-4(1988). The Official Comment to this section of the Uniform Commercial Code is instructive:

> "Subsection (2) operates to allow the buyer, in an appropriate case, any consequential damages which are the result of the seller's breach. The 'tacit agreement' test for the recovery of consequential damages is rejected. Although the older rule at common law which made the seller liable for all consequential damages of which he had 'reason to know' in advance is followed, the liberality of that rule is modified by refusing to permit recovery unless the buyer could not reasonably have prevented the loss by cover or otherwise." Uniform Commercial Code (U.L.A.) Section 2-715 p.418 (1989).

Following the requirements of this uniform provision on consequential damages, the Idaho Supreme Court upheld an award of consequential damages under factual circumstances nearly identical to those in this case. *Nezperce Storage Co. v. Zenner*, 105 Idaho 464, 670 P.2d 871 (1983). The Zenners, wheat farmers in Idaho, agreed to sell spring wheat to Nezperce but instead delivered winter wheat, which was subsequently resold to farmers, who planted it in the springtime and experienced complete crop failures. Nezperce paid for the farmers' damages and then sued the Zenners for reimbursement. The court, based upon a jury verdict, required the Zenners to reimburse Nezperce. In making this award of consequential damages, the court concluded that there was evidence supporting the jury's finding that the Zenners had reason to know that the wheat they sold Nezperce was intended to be resold as wheat seed.

The same analysis for awarding consequential damages applies in this case. As a prerequisite to awarding consequential damages against Ehrmantrout in favor of the Elevator, one must find that Ehrmantrout either knew or had reason to know when he entered the contract, that the spring wheat was going to be resold as seed. Unfortunately, the trial court's findings on this issue are unclear.

In its findings of fact, the court stated that prior to delivering the wheat, "Ehrmantrout brought a sample of the grain to Dakota Grain to be germination tested." Ehrmantrout's testimony indicates that he was aware that the only reason for doing a germination test was to determine whether the grain was useable for seed. The court also found that the Elevator manager "called Ehrmantrout and told him the germination was acceptable and that he could use the wheat," and that Ehrmantrout orally contracted with the Elevator on or about May 9, 1989, "to deliver two loads of Lenn spring wheat, which was subsequently to be sold to local farmers for seeding purposes." The implication of these findings is that Ehrmantrout either knew or had reason to know that the wheat he was selling to the Elevator was intended to be resold as seed.

However, in its order denying the post-trial motions, the court made the following relevant statements:

> "While there certainly is some evidence that [Ehrmantrout] knew or reasonably should have known that the [Elevator] intended to resell his wheat as seed wheat, I did not find that such evidence was sufficient to prove by a preponderance that Ehrmantrout had such personal knowledge. . . . [B]y the application of comparative negligence, the [Elevator] has already been 'penalized' for its inability to prove that Ehrmantrout actually knew or should have known that the wheat involved was intended for resale as seed stock."

These seemingly inconsistent statements by the trial court on this issue leave unresolved the question of whether Ehrmantrout either knew or should have known when he entered the contract, that his wheat was intended to be resold by the Elevator for seed. The resolution of that question is the key element in determining whether an award of consequential damages is appropriate in this case. So, we must remand this case for clarification of the court's findings on this issue.

Ehrmantrout argues that the Elevator's actions are the sole cause of the consequential damages and the trial court erred in apportioning fault. The apportionment of fault for purposes of awarding consequential damages only becomes an issue in this case if the trial court finds that Ehrmantrout either knew or had reason to know that his wheat was intended to be resold for seed. In the absence of that finding, it would be inappropriate for the court to award consequential damages. Section 41-02-94(2)(a), N.D.C.C. [U.C.C. § 2-715(2)(a)].

 If, however, the court does find that Ehrmantrout had reason to know that the wheat was intended to be resold for seed, then the second element, *i.e.*, whether the Elevator could have reasonably prevented the consequential damages, must be resolved because it, too, is a prerequisite to awarding consequential damages. Section 41-02-94(2)(a), N.D.C.C. We conclude that the court's findings with regard to this element of consequential damages are clear and that on remand the court does not have to redetermine this issue. The trial court found that the Elevator was 49 percent responsible for the consequential damages and deducted that percentage from the award of consequential damages. The court stated in its memorandum opinion, that the elevator "failed to take reasonable measure [sic] to mitigate or reduce to a minimum the losses which eventually resulted." In discussing the Elevator's failure to mitigate, the court stated that, "there was no testing of any kind of the wheat delivered on May 9." Unless reasonable persons could not disagree, the court's allocation of fault is a finding of fact that will not be overturned on appeal, unless we are convinced that the court has made a mistake. *See Jones v. Ahlberg*, 489 N.W.2d 576 (N.D.1992). We conclude that the trial court's finding of 49 percent causation of the consequential damages by the Elevator is not clearly erroneous.

We affirm the trial court's determination that Ehrmantrout breached his contract with the Elevator and the court's award of $125.90 in general damages. However, we hold that, as a necessary element of consequential damages, the Elevator was required to prove that Ehrmantrout either knew or should have known when he entered the contract, that his wheat was intended to be resold by the Elevator for seed. The trial court's findings on this key element are unclear and need to be clarified in order to resolve the consequential damages issue. Accordingly, we reverse the award of consequential damages and remand for clarification of the findings and a redetermination on that issue.

Affirmed in part, reversed in part, and remanded.

VANDE WALLE, C.J., and NEUMANN, SANDSTROM AND MESCHKE JJ., concur.

NOTES AND QUESTIONS

(1) E. Farnsworth, Contracts § 12.17 at 931-33 (2d ed. 1990), comments on the requirements of *foreseeability* and *certainty* (footnotes omitted):

> Sometimes a court is confronted with a large damage claim that seems greatly disproportionate to the modest consideration received by the party in breach. It may not seem just to require the party in breach to pay for all loss caused by the breach, even though that loss was foreseeable and has been proved with reasonable certainty. . . .

> For a time many courts overtly used the tacit agreement test to justify their refusal to award damages to the full extent of the loss in such cases. . . . However, the tacit agreement test has now generally been discarded and no longer affords a vehicle for limiting recovery in such cases.

> Nevertheless, there remains a judicial reluctance to impose on a contracting party liability in an amount greatly disproportionate to the consideration received. . . . Courts have covertly expressed their reluctance by so applying the test of foreseeability as to find that what was foreseeable becomes "unforeseeable." They have also shown their reluctance by a particularly rigorous application of the requirement of certainty. Use of the requirements of foreseeability and certainty as surrogates for some other principle, however, has not contributed to clarity in dealing with this problem. What is the principle for which these limitations are surrogates?

> Restatement Second § 351(3) gives the following answer: "A court may limit damages for foreseeable loss by excluding recovery for loss of profits, by allowing recovery only for loss incurred in reliance, or otherwise if it concludes that in the circumstances justice so requires in order to avoid disproportionate compensation.". . .Section 351(3). . .invites the court to make a frank evaluation of the proper allocation of risks in determining what justice requires.

In *Native Alaskan Reclamation and Pest Control, Inc. v. United Bank Alaska*, 685 P.2d 1211 (Alaska 1984), action was instituted against a bank for breach of a loan agreement made by a corporation in connection with a plan to purchase and convert planes for use in fire fighting. The court held that damages were recoverable if the corporation's inability to obtain replacement financing and resulting loss of profit were foreseeable as a probable result of the bank's breach at the time of contracting. Restatement, Second, Contracts § 351(1). On remand, though, the court stated that the trial court should reconsider its award in light of § 351(3) (a court may limit damages for foreseeable loss if in the circumstances justice so requires).

Proposed U.C.C. § 2-715(2)(a) conforms to Restatement, Second, § 351: The seller must still have reason to know at the time of contracting of the particular needs or requirements of the buyer. In addition the seller must have reason to know that the loss would "probably result from the breach" and the court has power, where justice requires, to limit disproportionate consequential loss.

(2) *Injury to Person or Property.* U.C.C. §§ 2-714(3) and 2-715(2)(b) allow recovery of consequential damages resulting from seller's breach and include injury to person or property proximately resulting from any breach of warranty. This is discussed in Chapter 5 at § 5.08, Interaction of Warranty and Strict Liability.

(3) *Incidental Damages.* U.C.C. §§ 2-714(3) and 2-715(1) set forth buyer's incidental damages. Cf. U.C.C. § 2-710. The following are recent noteworthy cases: *Frank B. Bozzo, Inc. v. Electric Weld Division of Spang Industries, Inc.*, 498 A.2d 895, 42 U.C.C. Rep. 213 (Pa. 1985) (buyer of steel mesh could recover prejudgment interest as an incidental damage resulting from the seller's breach if the interest represented a reasonable expense incident to the delay); *Fast v. Southern Offshore Yachts*, 587 F. Supp. 1354, 38 U.C.C. Rep. 1569 (Conn. 1984) (buyer entitled to incidental damages in the form of statutory interest on the monies paid by him running from the date of breach through judgment); *Happy Dack Trading Co., Ltd. v. Agro-Industries, Inc.*, 602 F. Supp. 986, 41 U.C.C. Rep. 1718 (S.D.N.Y. 1984) (buyer may recover as incidental damages expenses reasonably incurred in inspection of goods rightly rejected; thus, where plaintiff intermediate buyers had sent a representative to the People's Republic of China to investigate claims of nonconformity made by the ultimate buyer, plaintiff intermediate buyers were entitled to the travel and testing expenses incurred by the representative); *Devore v. Bostrom*, 632 P.2d 832, 31 U.C.C. Rep. 984 (Utah 1981) (allowed as incidental damages in an action revoking acceptance of a new car which seller refused to repair were expenses associated with car insurance, license plates, lost wages and interest on the purchase price of the automobile; attorney's fees were not allowable (with dissent)).

In *Ohline Corp. v. Granite Mill*, 849 P.2d 602, 21 U.C.C. Rep.2d 49 (Utah App. 1993), seller agreed to sell window shutters to buyer to be used in remodeling suites at the Las Vegas Hilton. Seller was late in delivering the shutters and buyer had to pay $9405 in overtime pay to install the shutters before an August 4 deadline buyer had with Hilton. Held: Buyer was entitled to recover from seller the overtime charges, regardless of whether the overtime damages were considered incidental or consequential damages under U.C.C. § 2-715.

———

PROBLEM 7.5

You represent Heat Treater Inc., a firm which manufactures and heat treats bolts, nuts and reinforcing rods. Heat Treater sold and delivered to Essex Auto Co., an automobile manufacturer, 50,000 bolts for use in steering mechanisms of Essex automobiles. One bolt is used in each steering mechanism. The price of the 50,000 bolts is 4 cents each, or a total of $2,000.

When the bolt sale was made, Heat Treater's sales manager recognized that if defects appeared in the bolts after they were installed in the automobiles, a recall of Essex automobiles might occur pursuant to the National Traffic and Motor Vehicle Safety Act. For this reason, pains were taken to ensure that due care was exercised in the manufacture of the bolts. However, at the time of the sale Heat Treater was unable: (1) to assess the magnitude of the risk that defects might appear in the bolts and that a recall would occur; (2) to purchase insurance against losses which might ensue if recall did occur; (3) to add to the price of the bolts sold to Essex an amount commensurate with the risk; (4) to spread the risk among all buyers of Heat Treater bolts; or (5) to set aside and deduct from corporate taxable income a fund to pay any recall expenses which might occur. At the same time, when the sale was made, Heat Treater dealt rather informally with Essex Auto Co., and no attempt was made to allocate the risks, whether by warranty disclaimer, limitation of damages or otherwise.

After the 50,000 Essex automobiles containing Heat Treater bolts were manufactured and sold to consumers, it was discovered that some of the bolts were defective, causing a dangerous condition. The result was that the 50,000 vehicles were recalled pursuant to the Act, at a cost to Essex Auto Co. of $820,000.

Essex has now brought suit against Heat Treater for the $820,000 in recall expenses. What defenses, if any, can you raise for Heat Treater? Could (should) Restatement, Second, Contracts § 351(3) and proposed § 2-715(2)(a), cited in Note (1) above, affect the outcome of the Essex suit?

See B. Stone, *Recovery of Consequential Damages for Product Recall Expenditures*, 1980 B.Y.U.L. Rev. 485. See also, *Taylor & Gaskin v. Chris-Craft Industries*, 732 F.2d 1273, 38 U.C.C. Rep. 858 (6th Cir. 1984) (expenses of recall of defective fuel tanks which buyer had installed in power boats were recoverable as consequential damages); *Upjohn Co. v. Rachelle Laboratories, Inc.*, 661 F.2d 1105, 32 U.C.C. Rep. 747 (6th Cir. 1981) (cost to buyer of drug tablet recall and lost sales of drug tablets before recall were recoverable as damages).

§ 7.07 Remedies Applicable to Sellers and Buyers

[A] Liquidated Damages

Read: U.C.C. §§ 2-718, 2-719(1), 2-302; see § 1-106.

Read also: U.C.C. §§ 2A-504, 2A-108; CISG Arts. 4(a), 6.

An early U.C.C. case was *Denkin v. Sterner*, 10 Pa. D.&C.2d 203, 1 U.C.C. Rep. 173 (Pa. 1956). Here defendants (buyers) agreed to purchase from plaintiff (seller) certain refrigerated cases and equipment for a food market. Buyers by letter canceled the order before delivery of any of the goods. Judgment was entered for the full amount of the purchase price. The court observed the sales agreement and stated:

> Perusal of the agreement disclosed some peculiar features which would indicate that it was undoubtedly prepared by the sellers. In paragraph 16 it provides: "This agreement may be canceled by seller at any time before delivery of the property to purchaser," but nowhere in the agreement is there any similar right extended to the purchaser. On the contrary, paragraph 11 provides: "In the event of default by purchaser, seller shall have the following rights in addition to any and all other rights under the Uniform Commercial Code and/or any other applicable law." Then follows the authority to enter judgment in replevin for the goods in question and also the authority to enter judgment for the full amount of the unpaid purchase price plus interest and costs, with 15 percent added for attorney's fees.

> Why anyone would sign such a biased and one-sided agreement is difficult to understand. . . .

While there seems little doubt from the depositions taken under the rule issued in this case that plaintiff is entitled to damages, for defendants admit that they canceled the agreement because they found out after checking that they could buy more equipment for less money elsewhere, yet it also seems evident under all the circumstances that to permit plaintiff to recover the full amount of the purchase price without showing what goods, if any, have been identified to the contract, what goods were standard items and readily salable and what goods had actually been specially manufactured prior to the cancellation by defendants, as well as what goods have been or can be readily resold, would be in effect "unreasonably large liquidated damages" and, therefore, unconscionable and void.

. . . .

We therefore hold that the judgment in this case should be opened to permit defendants to defend as to the amount due plaintiff. Incidentally, it would seem that well-intentioned counsel, informed of all the actual pertinent facts involved, might be in a much better position to resolve this question than would the customary 12 good men and true [jury].

A liquidated damages term which takes into account the elements to be considered as set forth in U.C.C. § 2-718(1) is illustrated by 12 West's Legal Forms § 15.1 — Form 1 (2d ed. 1985):[29]

Inasmuch as the failure of the seller to deliver the quantity of commodities specified herein, in accordance with the terms of this agreement will, because of the urgent need for the commodities by the buyer, arising from the present emergency conditions, cause serious and substantial damages to the buyer, and it will be difficult, if not impossible to prove the amount of such damages, the seller agrees to pay to the buyer, [amount] as liquidated damages for failure to deliver, which sum is computed as follows:

[number] cents per pound for [identify or designate article];

[number] cents per pound for [identify or designate article];

[etc.]

The sum is agreed upon as liquidated damages and not as a penalty. The parties hereto have computed, estimated and agreed upon the sum as an attempt to make a reasonable forecast of probable actual loss because of the difficulty of estimating with exactness the damages which will result.

———

STOCK SHOP, INC. v. BOZELL & JACOBS, INC.

New York Supreme Court, New York County
126 Misc. 2d 95, 481 N.Y.S.2d 269, 39 U.C.C. Rep. 1295 (1984)

SAXE, J.

---

[29] Copyright © 1985 by West Co. Reprinted by permission.

In this motion for summary judgment, I am asked to decide whether an unusual liquidated damage clause in a contract is valid or instead, a penalty.

The underlying facts are these: On three occasions during November and December 1979, the plaintiff delivered to defendant 697 stock photographs for the defendant's consideration for possible use as part of a slide show for one of its advertising clients. The photographs depicted various cities, and other points of interest in the United States. It appears that 39 of the 40 photographs that the defendant agreed to license were never returned. The plaintiff argues that each of the 39 photographs has a value of at least $1,500. The principal basis for this contention lies in paragraph "3" of the delivery memoranda between the parties which states:

> The monetary damage for loss or damage of an original color transparency or photograph shall be determined by the value of each individual photograph. Recipient agrees however, that the reasonable minimum value of such tort or damaged photographs or transparency shall be no less than fifteen hundred ($1,500.00) dollars.

The plaintiff claims that this clause is a proper liquidated damage provision and that they are entitled to summary judgment in an amount representing the total number of photographs not returned multiplied by $1,500.00.

The defendant's main argument is that even if it is liable for the non-return of 39 photographs, the $1,500 per photograph liquidated damage demand bears no relationship to the actual or fair or reasonable value of the photographs and is therefore a penalty.

In early English legal history, parties used penal bonds to secure performance of a contract. Upon a breach, the entire amount of the bond was due immediately, regardless of the actual damages suffered (S. Williston, Contracts, 3d Ed § 774 (1961)). Courts sitting in equity, however, had jurisdiction to intervene and mitigate the harsh results where the breach did not cause any actual damage (*Id*).

American courts recognized the parties' right to set damages in advance of a breach, and distinguished valid clauses from penalties. These courts allowed recovery where the parties had attempted to reasonably estimate in advance the damages that might result from a breach. *United States v. Bethlehem Steel Co.*, 205 US 105 (1907).

In contrast, where the preset damages were "disproportionate to the damage which could have been anticipated from breach of the contract, and which [were] agreed upon in order to enforce performance. . ." (*Bignall v. Gould*, 119 US 495 (1886)), the court labeled the clause an "unenforceable penalty." *Caesar v. Rubinson*, 174 NY 492 (1903).

The controlling principle of law is contained in § 2-718(1) of the Uniform Commercial Code ("U.C.C.") which reads:

> Damages for breach by either party may be liquidated in the agreement but only at an amount which is reasonable in the light of the anticipated or actual harm caused by the breach, the difficulties of proof of loss, and the inconvenience or nonfeasibility of otherwise obtaining an adequate remedy. A term fixing unreasonably large liquidated damages is void as a penalty.

The first sentence of subdivision (1) of U.C.C. § 2-718 focuses on the situation of the parties both at the time of contracting and at the time of breach. So, a liquidated damage provision will be valid if reasonable with respect to either (1) the harm which the parties anticipate will result from the breach at the time of contracting or (2) the actual damages suffered by the nondefaulting party at the time of breach (*See, Equitable Lumber Corp. v. IPA Corp.*, 38 NY2d 516 (1976)).

The plaintiff contends that the $1,500 per photograph liquidated damage provision is an industry wide standard or custom. The defendant disputes this. But, the fact remains that even assuming that his amount is accepted throughout the industry, U.C.C. § 2-718(1) requires that an examination be made to determine the reasonableness of the sum from the aspect of anticipated harm determined at the time of entry into the contract or actual harm determined at the time of breach.

The plaintiff has not made a successful demonstration under either prong of this test. The $1,500 per photograph figures may bear no relationship to the actual value of a photograph which (a) may never have generated any past revenue; (b) is neither unique or novel, and (c) may be able to be duplicated by the photographer who submitted the photograph.

In terms of assessing the reasonableness of the anticipated harm, depending upon the nature and quality of the photograph, an amount required for the loss of one or more of them would, of necessity, vary. I conclude, therefore that the liquidated damage provision is invalid because it is not reasonable with respect to the anticipated or actual harm.

Alternatively, the provision in question is indefinite, rendering it unenforceable. The $1,500 figure is a minimum value and permits the plaintiff to prove a greater value if disposed to do so. There is therefore, no true liquidation of damages since the plaintiff is given the option to disregard the liquidated sum and sue for actual damages. Such a clause is invalid. *Jarro Building Industries Corp. v. Schwartz*, 54 Misc 2d 13.

In *Jarro*, the so-called liquidated damage clause permitted the plaintiff to recover 25% of the total agreed contract price but also afforded the plaintiff the option to disregard the clause and sue for damages if they exceeded the amount stipulated. The court had no trouble finding this clause invalid noting that a valid liquidated damages provision must fix the damages in advance and be for a sum certain.

But here, the clause under scrutiny operates a bit more subtly. It establishes a minimum recovery with the option to seek more by way of a suit for actual damages. A similar clause was invalidated in *Dalston Const. Corp. v. Wallace*, 26 Misc 2d 698, 214 NYS2d 19 (Dist Ct Nassau Co, 2nd Dist 1960), where the court said:

> A liquidated damage clause must always be examined rather closely. The policy of the law is to approve such clauses where they are reasonable. The underlying purpose is to permit parties to look to the future, anticipate that there may be a breach and make a settlement in advance. This implies two things: (1) that the amount specified be a fixed amount and (2) that both parties be bound to that amount. The clause here does not disclose a fixed amount. In essence it fixes a minimum which must be paid by the home owner to the contractor, but leaves the door wide open to him to prove actual damage in addition to the so-called liquidated damage. This is no settlement at all and it permits the contractor to have his cake and eat it too.

214 NYS2d at 193.

The clause here would allow the plaintiff to have its cake and eat it too. Accordingly, it is no liquidated damage clause at all and therefore, plaintiffs motion for summary judgment is denied. Settle order.

BAKER v. INTERNATIONAL RECORD SYNDICATE, INC.

Texas Court of Appeals
812 S.W.2d 53, 15 U.C.C. Rep.2d 875 (1991)

ENOCH, C.J. The opinion of this court issued April 15, 1991 is withdrawn. This is the opinion of the court. Jeff Baker, d/b/a/ Jeff Baker Photography (Baker), appeals a judgment rendered in his favor in a breach of contract case. The trial court determined that a liquidated damages provision was unenforceable and awarded damages to Baker based on jury findings. We reverse the trial court's judgment and render judgment for Baker.

International Record Syndicate (IRS) hired Baker to take photographs of the musical group Timbuk-3. Baker mailed thirty-seven "chromes" (negatives) to IRS via the business agent of Timbuk-3. When the chromes were returned to Baker, holes had been punches in thirty-four of them. Baker sued for the damages to these chromes. The trial court submitted the issues of actual damages and attorney's fees to the jury. The jury found $15,000 in actual damages and $5000 for attorney's fees. The trial court rendered judgment awarding $51,000 in actual damages and $5000 for attorney's fees. The damage award was pursuant to a liquidated damages clause, which set damages at $1500 per chrome. The trial court later modified the judgment, awarded Baker the $15,000 actual damages found by the jury, and eliminated the attorney's fee award.

Liquidated Damages

The provision printed on Baker's invoice states: "[r]eimbursement for loss or damage shall be determined by a photograph's reasonable value which shall be no less than $1500 per transparency." A liquidated damages clause is meant to be the measure of recovery in the event of nonperformance or breach of a contract. . . . The determination of whether a contractual clause is enforceable as a liquidated damages provision or void as a penalty is a question of law. . . .

The Uniform Commercial Code provides:

[Read U.C.C. § 2-718(1).]

Under Texas law, a liquidated damages provision will be enforced when the court finds (1) the harm caused by the breach is incapable or difficult of estimation, and (2) the amount of liquidated damages is a reasonable forecast of just compensation. . . . This might be termed the "anticipated harm" test. The party asserting that a liquidated damages clause is, in fact, a penalty provision has the burden of proof. . . . Evidence related to the difficulty of estimation and the reasonable forecast must be viewed as of the time the contract was executed.

Baker testified that he had been paid as much as $14,000 for a photo session, which resulted in twenty-four photographs and that several of these photographs had also been resold. Baker further testified that he had received as little as $125 for a single photograph. Baker also testified he once sold a photograph for $500. Subsequently, he sold reproductions of the same photograph three additional times at various prices; the total income from this one photo was $1500. This particular photo was taken in 1986 and was still producing income in 1990. Baker demonstrated, therefore, that an accurate determination of the damages from the loss of a single photograph is virtually impossible.

Timbuk-3's potential for fame was an important factor in the valuation of the chromes. At the time of the photo session, Timbuk-3's potential was unknown. In view of the inherent difficulty in determining the value of a piece of art, the broad range of values and long-term earning power of photographs, and the unknown potential for fame of the subject, $1500 is not an unreasonable estimate of Baker's actual damages.

Additionally, liquidated damages must not be disproportionate to actual damages. If the liquidated damages are shown to be disproportionate to the actual damages, then the liquidated damages can be declared a penalty and recovery limited to actual damages proven. . . . This might be called the "actual harm" test. The burden of proving this defense is upon the party seeking to invalidate the clause. *Id.* The party asserting this defense is required to prove the amount of the other party's actual damages, if any, to show that the actual loss was not an approximation of the stipulated sum. . . .

While evidence was presented that showed the value of several of Baker's other projects, this was not evidence of the value of the photographs in question. The evidence clearly shows that photographs are unique items with many factors bearing on their actual value. Each of the thirty-four chromes may have had a different value. Proof of this loss is difficult; where damages are real but difficult to prove, injustice will be done the injured party if the court substitutes the requirements of judicial proof for the parties' own informed agreement as to what is a reasonable measure of damages. The evidence offered to prove Baker's actual damages lacks probative force. IRS failed to establish Baker's actual damages as to these particular photographs.

Even assuming that the jury's findings as to damages are an accurate assessment, we do not agree that that sum is so disproportionate to the stipulated sum so as to abrogate the parties' agreement. Consequently, we conclude that the facts and circumstances of this case require that we reach a decision contrary to the one made by the trial court. We sustain Baker's first point of error and hold that the liquidated damages clause is enforceable.

. . . .

We reverse the judgment of the trial court. We render judgment for Baker in the amount of $51,000 for actual damages and $5000 for attorney's fees.

NOTES

(1) In *Grumman Flexible Corp. v. City of Long Beach*, 505 F. Supp. 623, 31 U.C.C. Rep. 1248 (E.D. N.Y 1980), a contract for purchase of buses contained a liquidated damages provision whereby a charge of $35 per day per bus was to be assessed if the total contract price per bus was not paid within a twenty-day time frame. Held: The provision was consistent with U.C.C. § 2-718(1). "The court . . .finds that the liquidated damages mandated by said agreement are reasonable under the circumstances."

(2) A liquidated damage clause may make a "lease" one intended as security. U.C.C. §§ 1-201(37), 2A-103(1)(j), 9-102(2). See *In re Zerkle Trucking Co.*, 132 B.R. 316 (Bkrtcy, S.D.W.Va. 1991) (Equipment leases with "terminal rent adjustment clauses" (TRAC) were leases intended for security, and not true leases, where agreement provided creditor a guarantee of receiving on default the full cost of equipment plus its anticipated profit).

(3) Proposed U.C.C. § 2-718(a) deletes the word "actual" from 2-718(1) (first sentence), and deletes the second sentence. Proposed subjection (a) goes on to say that in consumer contracts a term fixing unreasonably large or small liquidated damages is unenforceable. The last sentence states that if a liquidated damage term is unenforceable, the aggrieved party has the remedies provided in Article 2. In sum, proposed § 2-718 increases the chances that an otherwise conscionable liquidated damage clause will be enforceable in a commercial contract.

PROBLEM 7.6

Buyer ordered a quantity of wood from Seller for $895 and made a down payment in the amount of $400. Seller accepted the order. There was no understanding with respect to liquidated damages. Three weeks later — and before the wood was delivered — Buyer canceled the order, *i.e.*, repudiated the contract.

Buyer institutes a small claims action for return of the $400 down payment. Is Buyer entitled to recover the down payment or any part thereof? *See* U.C.C. § 2-718 and *Feinberg v. J. Bongiovi Contracting*, 442 N.Y.S.2d 399, 32 U.C.C. Rep. 139 (1981).

NOTE

Proposed U.C.C. § 2-718(b) and (c) has deleted the 20%/$500 formula of § 2-718(2).

WENDLING v. PULS

Kansas Supreme Court
610 P2d 580, 28 U.C.C. Rep. 1362 (1980)

HERD, J.

This is a civil action to recover damages for breach of an oral contract for the purchase and sale of cattle. The case was tried to the court which rendered judgment for the plaintiff-appellee seller [Wendling] in the amount of $14,755.02. . . .

Appellants' second issue is as follows: after Wendling accepted and cashed a down payment check of $1000, can he claim damages in excess of that sum in light of KSA 84-2-718 or in light of the custom and usage in the cattle trade?

Appellants argue custom and usage in the livestock industry considers all down payments on livestock purchase contracts to be liquidated damages, thereby eliminating the need for a specific agreement.

We held in *McSherry v. Blanchfield*, 68 Kan 310, 75 Pac 121 (1904), that custom and usage cannot be shown to create a contract where none existed, but rather its use is restricted to the explanation of technical or trade terms in a contract. This court went on to point out that it must first be shown either that the other party had knowledge of such a custom or that the knowledge among those in the business or industry was so notorious as to furnish a presumption that the other party had knowledge of it. These principles have often been applied.

In *Radio Station KEH Co. v. Local No. 297*, 169 Kan at 603, we discussed the standard of proof required in custom and usage cases as follows:

> The requisites of a good custom must all be established by evidence which is clear and convincing.

The trial court found the evidence of custom and usage was insufficient to show such a custom exists in the cattle trade. We find the appellants failed to meet the required standard of proof and we will not disturb the trial court's findings and conclusions of law as to this issue.

KSA 84-2-718 provides parties to a sales contract may agree to a reasonable amount of liquidated damages in the event of breach. That statute states: [the Court quotes U.C.C. § 2-718].

Appellants argue "if the contract provides for a down payment but not for liquidation of damages, this section [KSA 84-2-718] in effect liquidates them." Appellants argue they are entitled to a refund of their down payment in excess of $500, except that Wendling can offset any damages he proves he has the right to recover. Appellants claim that Wendling may take only $952.70. They arrive at this figure by subtracting $500 [they claim Wendling would keep $500 of the original $1000, pursuant to KSA 84-2-718(2)(b)], from $1452.70, a figure they claim represents the true difference between the market price on the date of delivery and the contract price. They measure the date of delivery from August 23, 1973, rather than September 21, 1973. We do not agree with this construction of KSA 84-2-718. First, there is no written agreement between the parties regarding the amount of liquidated damages to be recovered in the event of breach by the parties. The down payment check itself does not serve as a clear agreement and there is no evidence the parties intended it to indicate a firm agreement regarding damages. Second, we agree that where a seller withholds delivery of the goods because of a buyer's breach, the buyer is entitled to restitution of his down payment, pursuant to KSA 84-2-718(2)(a), or, in the absence of an agreement, pursuant to the formula set forth in KSA 84-2-718(2)(b). The appellants seem to have overlooked, however, the next section of the statute which states the buyer's right to restitution is subject to offset to the extent the seller establishes "(a) a right to recover damages under the provisions of this article other than subsection (1)." The seller in this case has his remedy under KSA 84-2-708. The entire down payment must be applied to the amount recovered pursuant to that statute. In this case, we have already determined the date upon which to base the seller's damages. That date is September 21, 1973, rather than August 23, 1973.[30] Therefore, appellants' proposed recovery formula will not stand. This issue is without merit.

[B]   Contractual Modification or Limitation of Remedy

Read: U.C.C §§ 2-719, 2-302; cf. §§ 2-316, 7-204(2), 7-309(2).

Read also: U.C.C. §§ 2A-503, 2A-108, Cf. § 2A-214; CISG Arts. 4(a), 6, 8(2).

IN RE FEDER LITHO-GRAPHIC SERVICES, INC.

United States Bankruptcy Court, Eastern District of Michigan
40 BR 486, 39 U.C.C. Rep. 495 (1984)

GEORGE BRODY, BANKRUPTCY JUDGE.

On March 16, 1978, Rockwell International Corporation (Rockwell) entered into a contract to sell a Miehle Roland Four Color Offset Press to Feder Litho-Graphic Services, Inc. (debtor) for $381,970.[31] Feder Litho-Graphic Services made a down payment of $50,000, and granted Rockwell a security interest to secure the payment of the balance due under the contract. The contract provided for some warranties and excluded others. The warranties and exclusions were as follows:

WARRANTY: Seller warrants for a period of twelve (12) months from date of initial shipment that new Machinery erected under Seller's supervision is free from defects in material and workmanship at the date of shipment.

THERE IS NO WARRANTY OF MERCHANTABILITY THERE ARE NO WARRANTIES WHICH EXTEND BEYOND THE DESCRIPTION ON THE FACE HEREOF. THERE ARE NO WARRANTIES EXPRESS OR IMPLIED OR ANY AFFIRMATION OF FACT OR REPRESENTATION EXCEPT AS SET FORTH HEREIN.

REMEDY: Seller's sole responsibility and liability and Purchaser's exclusive remedy under this agreement shall be limited to the repair or replacement at Seller's option, of part or parts, not so conforming to the warranty. . . .

DAMAGES: In no event shall Seller be liable for damages of any nature, including incidental, consequential damages, including but not limited to any damages resulting from nonconformity, defect in material or workmanship, services provided or delay of shipment for whatever reason.

On December 22, 1980, Feder Litho-Graphic Services, Inc. filed a chapter 11 proceeding. At the time of the filing of the petition in bankruptcy, the debtor was in default on the payments required under the purchase agreement. Rockwell, accordingly, moved to have the stay vacated to permit it to recover the press, which secured its obligation. Feder counterclaimed, alleging

---

[30] [The court found defendants breached the contract when they failed to take delivery of the cattle on or before September 21, 1973. Plaintiffs damages were computed, pursuant to KSA 84-2-708 to be the difference between the contract price computed as to the weight of the cattle on September 21 ($50,533.59) and the fair market value of the cattle on that date ($34,849.08), plus plaintiffs incidental damages incurred in the way of freight costs ($70.51), but less the amount of the down payment tendered by the defendants ($1,000.00).

28 U.C.C. Rep. at 1366-7.-Ed.]

[31] Rockwell entered into the contract with David Feder individually. Thereafter, the business was incorporated.

that Rockwell breached its repair warranty and, therefore, the debtor was entitled to recover damages for such breach and additionally to recover consequential damages for lost profits resulting from the breach.[32]

Rockwell denies that it failed to repair the machine, but contends that even if the repair warranty was breached, such breach would not reinstate the consequential damage remedy. To facilitate the progress of the case and in the interest of economy, the parties agreed to submit prior to trial the question whether an exclusion of consequential damages clause survives if a limited remedy fails of its essential purpose. In deciding the preliminary question submitted, the court will assume that the limited repair remedy was breached but that the failure to repair was not willful—that the failure was due to Rockwell's inability to satisfactorily repair the machine.

Initially it is necessary to decide whether Michigan or Illinois law governs the construction of the contract. Subject to certain conditions, the Uniform Commercial Code, adopted in both Illinois and Michigan, permits parties to a contract covered by the Code to designate the law to govern the rights and duties expressed in the agreement. U.C.C. § 1-105(1).[33] The contract provided that the "agreement shall be governed by the laws of the state of Illinois.". . .Accordingly, the contract is to be construed by reference to Illinois law.

The basic provisions of Illinois' U.C.C. governing the merits of this controversy are not in dispute.[34] The debtor and Rockwell agree that parties to a contract of sale may "limit or alter the measure of damages recoverable," § 2-719(1)(a), and that "[c]onsequential damages may be limited or excluded unless the limitation or exclusion is unconscionable," § 2-719(3). Nor is there any question that if the exclusion of consequential damages is unconscionable the court may disregard the exclusionary clause. § 2-302(1). Finally the parties recognize that "[w]here circumstances cause an exclusive or limited remedy to fail of its essential purpose, remedy may be had as provided in this act." § 2-719(2).

The debtor does not contend that the exclusion of consequential damages was unconscionable when the contract was negotiated. The debtor's sole contention is that since Rockwell failed to repair the press, the limited remedy of repair failed of "its essential purpose" and, therefore, by virtue of § 2-719(2), it may recover not only damages for breach of the warranty to repair[35] but may also recover consequential damages despite the contract provision excluding such recovery.

The debtor's argument is simplistic, isolates § 2-719(2) to the exclusion of other related provisions, and is contrary to existing construction of Illinois law. Courts applying Illinois law have consistently held that the failure of a limited remedy to repair does not automatically nullify a contractual provision excluding consequential damages as a remedy. . . .[36]

---

[32] The case was converted to Chapter 7 on August 23, 1982, and the press was sold pursuant to court order for $315,000.

[33] Section 1-105(1) of the U.C.C. reads in pertinent part: "[W]hen a transaction bears a reasonable relation to this state and also to another state or nation the parties may agree that the law either of this state or of such other state or nation shall govern their rights and duties." U.C.C.§ 1-105(1).

[34] Actually, the U.C.C. of every state has essentially the same provisions. However, not all states have reached the same result as to the construction to be given these provisions.

[35] The measure of damages for breach of warranty to repair is the difference between "the value of the goods accepted and the value they would have had if they had been as warranted." § 2-714(2).

[36] For an analysis of the cases dealing with this issue, see Eddy, *On "Essential Purposes" of Limited Remedies: The Metaphysics of U.C.C. Section 2-719(2)*, 65 Calif. L. Rev. 28 (1977).

These holdings harmonize the statutory provisions that relate to this controversy. The Code was intended to encourage and facilitate the allocation of risks associated with the sale of goods. "By limiting the warranties available and the remedies under the warranties, parties are able to provide a consensual allocation of risks in accordance with sound business practices." *AES Technology Systems Inc.*, 583 F2d at 939. Courts, therefore, absent circumstances that warrant their intrusion, ought not to "rewrite contracts by ignoring parties' intent; rather, [they should] interpret the existing contract as fairly as possible when all events did not occur as planned." *Id.* at 941. "The limited remedy of repair and a consequential damages exclusion are two discrete ways of attempting to limit recovery for breach of warranty. The Code, moreover, tests each by a different standard. The former survives unless it fails of its essential purpose, while the latter is valid unless it is unconscionable." *Chatlos Systems, Inc.*, 635 F2d at 1086 (citations omitted). No reason exists, therefore, to hold, "as a general proposition, that the failure of the limited remedy provided in the contract, without more, invalidates a wholly distinct term in the agreement excluding consequential damages. The two are not mutually exclusive." *Id.* Whether the preclusion of consequential damages as a remedy is to be nullified when a limited warranty fails "depends upon the circumstances involved." *Id.* Essentially, the question "narrows to the unconscionability of the buyer retaining the risk of consequential damages upon the failure of the essential purpose of the exclusive repair remedy." *Id.* at 1087. *See also Adams v. J.I. Case Co.*, 125 Ill. App 2d 388,261 NE2d 1(1970). Absent the presence of factors that make the exclusion of consequential damages unconscionable at the inception of the contract or in its performance, the buyer's recovery for the breach of a warranty to repair is limited to the damages flowing from the breach of such warranty.

The cases construing Illinois law relied upon by the debtor, *Adams v. J.I. Case Co.*, 125 Ill App 2d 388, 261 NE2d 1 (1970); *Custom Automated Machinery v. Penda Corp.*, 537 F Supp 77 (D ND Ill 1982); *KKO, Inc. v. Honeywell -Inc.*, 517 F Supp 892 (D ND Ill 1981), do not support the debtor's position. In *Adams*, the court did refuse to give effect to the contract provision excluding consequential damages when the warranty to repair clause was breached, but did so only because the complaint alleged facts "that would constitute a repudiation by the defendants of their obligations under the warranty, that repudiation consisting of their wilful failure or their careless and negligent compliance." 261 NE2d at 7-8. The court made it clear that had the sellers "reasonably complied with their agreement contained in the warranty they would be in a position to claim the benefits of their stated limited liability and to restrict plaintiff to his stated remedy." *Id.* at 7.

The contract in *Penda* did not expressly exclude consequential damages. Therefore, the court had no reason to, and did not, address the question presented here.

Honeywell also offers no aid to the debtor. *Honeywell* does not hold, as the debtor maintains, that the breach of a limited warranty automatically entitles a buyer of goods to recover consequential damages when the contract specifically excludes such damages. *Honeywell* merely holds, as this court now holds, that, although consequential damages are not automatically recoverable, "factual circumstances may permit an award of consequential damages where a remedy has failed its essential purpose, notwithstanding an exclusion clause." 517 F Supp at 898.

. . .

An order consistent with this opinion has been previously entered.

NOTES AND QUESTIONS

(1) The court in *Middletown Concrete Products, Inc. v. Black Clawson Co.*, 802 F. Supp. 1135 at 1151-52 (D. Del. 1992) comments:

The courts from various jurisdictions are divided on the issue of whether a clause disclaiming liability for consequential damages is automatically ineffective when a repair and replacement remedy has failed of its essential purpose. Some courts have read subsection (2) and (3) of § 2-719 as being interdependent, thus permitting recovery of consequential and incidental damages when a limitation of remedy contained in a contract has failed of its essential purpose. [Citations.] Special Project, *Article Two Warranties in Commercial Transactions: An Update*, 72 Cornell L.Rev. 1159, 1307 (1987) (noting a majority of cases have concluded that the failure of an exclusive remedy voids the consequential damages exclusion when an exclusive remedy fails).

These "interdependent" courts find support for their position in the straightforward application of § 2-719(2) which reads, "[w]here circumstances cause an exclusive or limited remedy to fail of its essential purpose, the remedy may be had as provided in this chapter." Focusing solely on the language of subsection (2), the interdependent courts conclude that when a limited remedy fails of its essential purpose, the plain language of subsection (2) entitles plaintiff to consequential and incidental damages as remedies available "in this chapter."

Further support for this position is found in the comments to § 2-719. Comment 1 to Iowa's equivalent of § 2-719, for instance, reads in pertinent part, "[U]nder subsection (2), where an apparently fair and reasonable clause because of circumstances fails in its purpose or operates to deprive either party of the substantial value of the bargain, it must give way to the general remedy provisions of this Article." Since consequential and incidental damages are permitted under the general remedy provisions of the Iowa Code, it can be argued they are, therefore, permitted when the limited remedy of repair and replace fails of its essential purpose. Explaining the underlying assumptions of this approach, one student commentator has observed, interdependent courts "conclude that the parties intended the validity of the consequential damage exclusion to depend on the effectiveness of the limited remedy; if the limited remedy fails, so does the consequential damage exclusion." Murtagh, *U.C.C. Section 2-719: Limited Remedies and Consequential Damage Exclusions,* 74 Cornell L.Rev. 359, 369 (1989).

Other courts, however, have reached different conclusions based on the language in subsection (3). [Citations.] Subsection (3) reads, "Consequential damages may be limited or excluded unless the limitation or exclusion is unconscionable. Limitation of consequential damages for injury to the person in the case of consumer goods is prima-facie unconscionable but limitation of damages where the loss is commercial is not." The courts relying on subsection (3) view it as "independent" from subsection (2). Accordingly, these "independent" courts "see no reason to hold, as a general proposition, that the failure of the limited remedy provided in the contract, without more, invalidates a wholly distinct term in the agreement excluding consequential damages. The two are not mutually exclusive." [Citation.] That the two subsections are independent is supported by the Code which tests each by a different standard: a limited remedy of repair or replace survives under subsection (2) unless it fails of its essential purpose; a limitation of consequential damages survives under subsection (3) unless it is unconscionable. Because the tests for the two subsections are different, the "independent" courts conclude the two subsections are wholly distinct.

Further support for this approach can also be found in the comments to § 2-719. Comment 1 to the Iowa equivalent of § 2-719 reads, "Under this section parties are left free to shape their remedies to their particular requirements and reasonable agreements limiting or modifying remedies are to be given effect." . . . Consistent with this sentiment, independent courts have concluded the purpose of § 2-719 is to encourage and facilitate allocation of risk between contracting parties. . . . Accordingly, independent courts will not preclude a limitation of consequential damages unless it is unconscionable. . . .

Having weighed both positions, the Court concludes the latter line of cases is more thoroughly reasoned and consistent with the general purposes of the Uniform Commercial Code. . . . According to Professors James White and Robert Summers, the cases treating the two subsections as independent,

> seem most true to the Code's general notion that the parties should be free to contract as they please. When the state intervenes to allocate the risk of consequential loss, we think it more likely that the loss will fall on the party who cannot avoid it as the lowest cost. This is particularly true when a knowledgeable buyer is using an expensive machine in a business setting. It is the buyer who operates the machine, adjusts it, and understands the consequences of its failure. Sometimes flaws in such machines are inherent and attributable to the seller's faulty design or manufacture. But the fault may also lie in buyer neglect, inadequate training and supervision of the operators or in intentional use in ways forbidden by the seller. Believing the parties to know their own interests best, we would leave the risk allocation to the parties.

(2) In *Rudd Construction Equipment Co., Inc. v. Clark Equipment Co.*, 735 F.2d 974, 38 U.C.C. Rep. 873 (6th Cir. 1984), Rudd purchased a tractor shovel from Clark. The machine was destroyed by a fire caused by fluid from a ruptured hydraulic hose which ignited upon contact with heat from the turbochargers. (The hose was part of the original equipment of the machine.) The contract for sale had provisions (1) disclaiming warranties (with exceptions) (2) limiting remedies to replacing or repairing defective parts and (3) excluding liability for consequential damages. Held: Repair-replace and consequential damages exclusion clauses were ineffective to limit liability; buyer was entitled to the net replacement value of the machine. "[W]here the failure of a part of the machine has resulted directly in the loss of the whole, the machine is considered 'one big defective part.' " 38 U.C.C. Rep. at 876. Alternatively, "any limitation which would deny this recovery would also fail of its essential purpose under [U.C.C. § 2-719(2)]." *Id.*

(3) See *Adams v. American Cyanamid Co.*, 498 N.W.2d 577, 21 U.C.C. Rep.2d 962 (Neb. App. 1992) (conspicuous requirement imposed by U.C.C. § 2-316(2)for warranty disclaimers should be read into § 2-719 for remedy limitations); cf. *American Dredging Co. v. Plaza Petroleum, Inc.*, 799 F.Supp. 1335, 18 U.C.C. Rep.2d 1101 (E.D. N.Y. 1992) (U.C.C. § 2-719 provides that parties to a contract may agree to exclude consequential damages so long as the limitation is not unconscionable, but it does not require that the clause be conspicuous. Conspicuousness, however, is a factor to consider when determining unconscionability).

(4) The Magnuson-Moss Federal Warranty Act applies to written warranties as to "consumer products." 15 U.S.C. § 2301 et seq.; 16 C.F.R. 700. Generally, the act does not affect state law regarding consequential damages for injury to the person or other injury. § 2311 (b)(2). However, under § 2304(a)(3), a "warrantor may not exclude or limit consequential damages for breach of any written or implied warranty on such product, unless such exclusion or limitation conspicuously appears on the face of the warranty." Further, 16 CFR § 701.3(a)(8)(see § 2302(a)) requires disclosure of any exclusions of or limitations on relief such as incidental or consequential damages, accompanied by the following statement:

> Some states do not allow the exclusion or limitation of incidental or consequential damages, so the above limitation or exclusion may not apply to you.

(5) Proposed U.C.C. § 2-719(b) clarifies the effect when an agreed, exclusive remedy fails of its essential purpose: The aggrieved party has remedies provided in Article 2 to the extent that the agreed remedy has failed, but agreed remedies outside the scope of and not dependent on the failed agreed remedy are enforced as provided in § 2-719. Under subsection (c) a limitation or exclusion of consequential damages for commercial loss is presumed to be conscionable. Subsection (d) provides special rules for consumer contracts, e.g., if an exclusive remedy fails of its essential purpose, the consumer buyer may revoke acceptance, obtain a refund or replacement of the goods from the seller. A term limiting or excluding consequential damages is inoperative unless the seller proves by clear and convincing evidence that the buyer understood and expressly agreed to the term. Exclusion or limitation of consequential damages for injury to the person is unconscionable as a matter of law.

[C]   Remedies for Fraud

Read: U.C.C. § 2-721.

Read also: § 2A-505(4) and (5); CISG Art. 4(a).

PROBLEM 7.7

Tinker purchased for investment purposes a used Jaguar automobile from DeMaria who orally represented to Tinker, prior to making the sale, that the Jaguar was in good operating condition, was powered by its original engine, and had never been involved in a major collision. Tinker relied on these representations and DeMaria intended for Tinker to act on the representations.

Tinker had problems with the Jaguar immediately after its purchase. In addition to the misrepresentation with respect to the automobile's operating condition at the time of purchase, it was not powered by its original engine when sold, had previously been involved in a major collision and was considered a total loss by its previous owner's insurance company. DeMaria knew of and concealed the true history of the automobile which constituted intentional misrepresentation.

Tinker seeks to obtain recision of the sales agreement induced by DeMaria's intentional misrepresentation (fraud) and seeks in addition to recover consequential damages for loss of its investment. DeMaria asserts that the state's fraud law requires defrauded Tinker to make a choice between the remedies of recision and damages. May Tinker rescind *and* have damages? See U.C.C. §§ 1-103, 2-608, 2-711, 2-715, 2-721 and *Tinker v. DeMaria Porsche Audi, Inc.*, 459 So. 2d 487, 37 U.C.C. Rep. 1519 (Fla. App. 1984). See also, *South Hampton Co. v. Stinnes Corp.*, 733 F.2d 1108, 38 U.C.C. Rep. 1137 (5th Cir. 1984).

[D] Who Can Sue Third Parties for Injury to Goods?

Read: U.C.C. § 2-722.

Read also: U.C.C. § 2A-531; CISG Art. 4.

INTERNATIONAL HARVESTER CREDIT CORP v. VALDEZ

Washington Court of Appeals
42 Wash. App. 189, 42 U.C.C. Rep. 337 (1985)

MUNSON, J.

International Harvester Credit Corporation (International) appeals a summary judgment in favor of Santiago Valdez. The sole issue is whether the holder of a security interest in a motor vehicle is barred from bringing suit against a tortfeasor, who had destroyed the secured vehicle, after the tortfeasor's settlement with the registered owner. We answer in the affirmative.

In 1980, David Valle purchased a used truck tractor and potato bed for $14,375.84. He made a substantial down payment and received a trade-in allowance; the remainder of the purchase price was financed by the seller, who assigned the contract to International. Valle was to make four payments, due in July and December 1981 and 1982 respectively. International's perfected security interest was shown on the certificate of title. See RCW 62A.9-302; RCW 46.12.095.

In October 1981, the tractor was involved in a collision with a truck owned by Santiago Valdez and driven by his employee. The tractor was apparently damaged beyond repair. Valdez's insurance carrier paid Valle approximately $14,000 in full settlement of his property damage claim. Neither Valdez nor his insurance carrier had actual knowledge of the security interest; neither contacted the Department of Licensing to examine the certificate of title.

Valle failed to make the 1982 payments, totaling approximately $4,000. International first learned of the accident and settlement when it began its collection effort.

International commenced this action against Valdez for the damages to its security interest. The trial court granted summary judgment for Valdez, stating: (1) Valdez had no duty to protect International's security interest and (2) International's suit was barred by Valdez's settlement in full with Valle. International appeals.

We assume arguendo that Valdez was responsible for the 1981 accident. Initially, both the debtor and secured party have a cause of action against the tortfeasor who damages the secured property. RCW 62A.2-722;[37] . . .

In *Stotts v. Puget Sound Traction, Light & Power Co.*, *supra*, the court noted a tortfeasor with actual notice of security interest in the damaged property could protect himself by bringing in the secured party as an additional party. However, the court went on to hold the secured party had waived his right to recover by appearing as a witness on the debtor's behalf and not seeking to formally intervene. Neither Stoss [sic] nor articles 2 and 9 of the Uniform Commercial Code speak to whether a settlement between the debtor and tortfeasor releases the tortfeasor from liability to the secured party. See 69 Am. Jur. 2d Secured Transactions, § 267 at 97 (1973); Weinberg, *Secured Party's Right to Sue Third Persons for Damage to or Defects in Collateral*, 81 Com. L.J. 445 (1976).

---

[37] RCW 62A.2-722 provides: [the Court quotes U.C.C. § 2-722].

The majority rule is that only one cause of action arises out of the tortfeasor's misconduct; therefore settlement in full between the tortfeasor and debtor for all property damage, absent fraud or collusion, bars a subsequent suit by the secured party.

International vigorously argues the certificate of title constituted constructive notice to Valdez of its security interest. Thus, Valdez had a duty to notify International of the accident, and include it as a party to any settlement of the claim.

Nationwide Ins. Co. v. Bank of Forest, 368 S.2d 1273 (Miss. 1979), supports International's position. There it was held the tortfeasor's insurer acted without reasonable prudence when it settled with the owner of the other vehicle without first checking the certificate of title. Therefore, the secured party was entitled to maintain an action, subsequent to the settlement, against the tortfeasor and her insurer to recover the amount of its lien. The court reasoned the purpose of the Mississippi Motor Vehicle Title Law was to establish a central source of information regarding motor vehicle titles, affording protection to the public, including secured parties. The court referred to statutes which provide the certificate of title constitutes prima facie evidence of the facts appearing on it, and that notation on the certificate of title is the exclusive method of perfecting a security interest.

Nationwide, at 1276, rejected the majority rule, stating:

We acknowledge the rule but do not think it persuasive. The numerous business and credit transactions directly related to motor vehicles are common knowledge. The protection of business through registration of title under the Motor Vehicle Title enactment, in our opinion, outweighs the barring of either a mortgagor or mortgagee from bringing suit against a tortfeasor who has settled with either one or the other with total disregard for the lien rights of others. We think the very purpose of the Motor Vehicle Title Law was to afford a central place and a designated official so that essential information concerning title to motor vehicles might be readily available to anyone with legitimate needs therefor. It seems to us that ordinary prudence, at the very minimum, would require a cursory investigation of title before an owner was paid the full value of the vehicle, less salvage value, in settlement of a claim. Had this been done both the Bank of Forest and Nationwide would have been protected.

However, the court restricted its holding to cases where the collateral has been destroyed:

The present factual situation does not permit discussion of the many claims that might arise from minor accidents, "fender benders," which, it is contended, might inundate the motor vehicle comptroller's office with multiple inquiries, thereby disturbing its normal business activities. Moreover, the repair of a vehicle as distinguished from a sale for salvage has the likelihood of maintaining the value of the security and thereby protecting the lien rather than obliterating it. We presently speak only to facts wherein a vehicle was demolished leaving the residue of salvage value only.

Nationwide, at 1275.

We adopt the majority rule for the following reasons. First, the purpose of the Certificate of Title Act is to protect secured parties as those parties are identified and defined in the Uniform Commercial Code. See RCW 46.12.005; RCW 46.12.095 (procedure for protecting security interest in motor vehicle). Official Comment 1, RCW 62A.9-303 states that the result of perfecting a security interest is that the secured party is protected against *creditors, transferees*, and creditors' representatives in insolvency. Tortfeasors are not among those given record notice of properly perfected security interests.

Second, RCW 62A.2-722 contemplates one settlement in which the settling party holds the proceeds in trust for the secured party to the extent of the outstanding obligation. The underlying rationale is that the debtor has the right to possession and is entitled to recover the full amount of damage. Thus, a tortfeasor would not necessarily have a duty to join the secured party even if he had actual notice of the security interest. But cf. . . . (where tortfeasor's insurer assured secured party that settlement would not affect his rights, tortfeasor estopped from raising settlement with debtor as bar to subsequent action by secured party). This comports with the common law of bailment and the public policy favoring compromise and settlement.

In applying the above concepts to the facts presented here, we conclude the tortfeasor, Valdez, did not owe any duty to the secured party, International. First, International's perfection of its security interest in the tractor did not provide Valdez or his insurer with notice of that interest. Neither Valdez nor his insurer was required to ascertain whether there were any liens upon Valle's tractor prior to the settlement of the claim. Official Comment 1, RCW 62A.9-303. Moreover, International's contract does not obligate Valle to give the secured party notice of any damage to the collateral. International is seeking to impose a higher duty upon Valdez than it imposed upon its own debtor, Valle.

Second, Valle and not International was in possession of the tractor at the time the accident occurred. Valle was not in default and, in fact, made one payment after the accident. Valdez's wrongful act created only once cause of action for property damage, and Valle as vendee was entitled to recover for the full value of the damage. *Universal Credit Co. v. Collier, supra; Ellis v. Snell, supra*; RCW 62A.2-722.

The judgment is affirmed.

NOTES

(1) *Security Interest Under Article 2 Sales.* In *Johnson v. Conrail-Amtrak Federal Credit Union, 37 U.C.C. Rep. 933 (D.C. Super. 1983)*, the court asserted that any security interest, whether it is a security interest which arises by a security agreement under Article 9, or a security interest by virtue of Article 2, is a security interest within U.C.C. § 2-722 so as to justify suit by the secured party against the third person tortfeasor. See U.C.C. §§ 2-703(a), 9-113 and Comment 1; see also § 4.05 Security Interest.

(2) *Special Property.* In *Ross Cattle Co. v. Lewis, 415 So. 2d 1030, 34 U.C.C. Rep. 913 (Miss. 1982)*, Lewis contracted to sell identified cattle to Ross. Lewis then sold some of the animals through Cow Palace, Inc., an auction sales corporation. With respect to Ross's rights against Cow Palace, and its officers Delony and Reeves, the court said:

In substance, § 75-2-722 [U.C.C. § 2-722], provides for a cause of action against a third person who deals with goods that have been identified to a contract in such a way as to cause an actionable injury to a party to the contract. The right of action is given to either the seller or the buyer who has title to or a security interest in, or a special property or insurable interest in the goods. 67 Am Jur 2d, Sales § 236 (1973). The effect of § 75-2-722 is that third parties will be liable for conversion, physical damage to goods, or interference with the buyer's rights in goods. Mississippi Code Annotated § 75-2-103 (1972) defines a buyer as a person who buys or contracts to buy the goods.

Upon the evidence we think Ross had a right of action under this section against Cow Palace, Delony, and Jim Reeves. There can be no doubt that Ross had a special property interest in the animals because the company had contracted to buy them and the animals had been identified to the contract.[38]

. . . .

The plain black letter language of § 75-2-722 means that Ross having a "special property" interest in the animals has a right of action against the third parties (Cow Palace, Delony, and Jim Reeves) because they were "converting" the animals after they were shown or given knowledge of Ross's contract vesting in Ross the special property interest in the animals. These three defendants/appellees, with full knowledge of Ross's claim against the animals, actively and knowingly aided and abetted Lewis in disposing of the animals contrary to his contract with Ross.

See § 4.03 Special Property.

[E] Statute of Limitations

Read: U.C.C. § 2-725; see §§ 2-313, 2-314, 2-315, 2-503.

Read also: U.C.C. § 2A-506; see §§ 2A-210, 2A-212, 2A-213; Convention on the Limitation Period in the International Sale of Goods (1974 and 1980 Protocol of Amendment).

NEW ENGLAND POWER CO. ET AL. v. RILEY STOKER CORP.

Massachusetts Appeals Court
20 Mass. App. Ct. 25, 477 N.E.2d 1054, 40 U.C.C. Rep. 1735 (1985)

PERRETTA, J.

In 1969, the plaintiffs (referred to herein, in the singular, as NEP) entered into two contracts with the defendant (Riley) for the design, manufacture, and installation of two boilers for NEP's facilities at Salem and Brayton Point (Fall River). A detailed description of the boilers is unnecessary. It is sufficient to state, as did NEP in its amended complaint, that "[b]oilers such as these are technologically complex and sophisticated and . . .are entirely dissimilar from the small, residential or commercial units with which the public is generally familiar." Almost as soon as the boilers were put into use, it became apparent that they suffered from serious defects. Then began an extended period, from 1972 through 1976, during which Riley, working along with independent consultants and engineers retained by NEP, made repeated but unsuccessful attempts to repair the boilers. By 1978, Riley was no longer participating in any repair attempts. On March 11, 1980, NEP brought this action, alleging breaches of warranties and of promises to repair, as well as negligence. Riley affirmatively pleaded that the action was time-barred under GL c 106, § 2-725(1), and c 260, § 2A, and moved for summary judgment. NEP appeals from

---

[38] Under Miss Code Ann § 75-2-501 identification of goods occurs when existing goods are designated or agreed upon as the goods to which the contract refers, which happened in the instant case at the time the contract was signed.

the judgment entered on Riley's motion and argues that its action was not commenced beyond the time allowed by those statutes and, in the alternative, that Riley is estopped by its conduct from asserting that defense. We affirm.

I. Breaches of Warranties [39]

If NEP were to commence timely its action for breaches of warranties under the contract, it was required by GL c 106, § n 2725(1), as appearing in St 1957,c 765, § 1, to bring its action "within four years after the cause of action has accrued." Paragraph (2) of § 2-725 provides, in full: [the Court quotes U.C.C. § 2-725(2)]. [40]

When Riley tendered delivery of the boilers is the issue in dispute. By way of definition, GL c 106, § 2-503(1), as appearing in St 1957, c 765, § 1, provides that tender of delivery "requires that the seller put and hold conforming goods at the buyer's disposition." The judge found that the Salem and Brayton Point boilers were put into "commercial use" on August 24, 1972, and December 18, 1974, respectively, and concluded that delivery had to have been completed prior to March, 1976. [41] Suit was commenced on March 11, 1980.

NEP argues that there was no tender of delivery prior to March of 1976 and that, in fact, delivery has never been tendered. As support for this contention, NEP extracts two sentences from the first paragraph of the official comment to GL c 106, § 2-503: "The term 'tender' is used in this Article in two different senses. In one sense it refers to 'due tender' which contemplates an offer coupled with a present ability to fulfill all the conditions resting on the tendering party and must be followed by actual performance if the other party shows himself ready to proceed." [42] Uniform Laws Comment, GL c 106, § 2-503, Ann Laws of Mass, at 69. Defining tender as "due tender," NEP argues that there was no tender of delivery within the meaning of § 2-725(2), because when the boilers were "delivered," both Riley and NEP knew that they were defective and had to be repaired. Extending this theory, NEP takes the position that since the boilers are still defective, there has been no tender of delivery.

---

[39] Counts one and seven of the amended complaint allege breaches of express and implied warranties under the two contracts of sale, count one as to Salem, count seven as to Brayton Point. The arguments in NEP's brief are diffuse and scattered, but, as we understand them, NEP now argues only as to implied warranties. Its claims based on breaches of express warranties under those contracts have been transformed, as will be seen *infra*, to claims of breaches of promises to repair, as alleged in counts two and eight. . . .

[40] We are not dealing with warranties as to future performance. (See *e.g.*, *Mittasch v. Seal Lock Burial Vault, Inc.*, 42 AD2d 573 [NY 1973], where the court held that the statement that the casket and burial vault "will give satisfactory service at all times" was a warranty which explicitly extended to future performance.) Were we, NEP would have no claim, since it does not argue express warranties, and "an implied warranty, by its very nature cannot explicitly extend to future performance. . . .

[41] In its brief, NEP states that in the utility industry the term "commercial use" means that the boiler is generating steam and that the term is "strictly a financial and rate-making consideration unrelated to compliance or non-compliance with the contract." This contention would be material and in dispute only if we accept NEP's definition of "tender of delivery," which, as will be seen, *infra*, we do not.

[42] That paragraph continues: "Unless the context unmistakably indicates otherwise this is the meaning of 'tender' in this Article and the occasional addition of the word 'due' is only for clarity and emphasis. At other times it is used to refer to an offer of goods or documents under a contract as if in fulfillment of its conditions, even though there is a defect when measured against the contract obligation. *Used in either sense, however, 'tender' connotes such performance by the tendering party as puts the other party in default if he fails to proceed in some manner.*" (Emphasis added.)

A similar, if not identical, argument was unsuccessfully made in *Standard Alliance Indus. v. Black Clawson Co.*, 587 F2d 813, 819 (6th Cir 1978),[43] i.e., that "tender" of new, highly complex machinery should not be held to have occurred until the machine is made to operate properly. We also do not accept this claim, for to do so would "extend the statute of limitations indefinitely into the future since a defect at the time of delivery would prevent proper 'due tender' from taking place until it was corrected." *Id. See also Ontario Hydro v. Zallea Sys., Inc.*, 569 F Supp 1261, 1267 (D Del 1983) ("If the court were to apply the phrase ['due tender'] as [the plaintiff] suggests, then until the seller tenders conforming goods, the limitation period provided in § 2-725 would never apply. This would circumvent the very purpose of § 2-725, which . . .is to provide a finite period in time when the seller knows that he is relieved from liability for a possible breach of contract for sale or breach of warranty"). We conclude that the definition of tender of delivery urged by NEP is inconsistent with the purpose of § 2-725(2), as well as with the final sentence of the first paragraph of the official code comment to § 2-503. *See note 6, supra.*

We are not dissuaded from our conclusion by NEP's argument that acceptance of "due tender" as the controlling definition is compelling where the seller and buyer acknowledge at the time of delivery that the goods are defective. We see no reason to apply a more rigorous rule to an unwitting buyer than to a fully informed one. Simply put, although knowledge may be relevant to a buyer's acceptance of goods, see GL c 106, § 2-607, it is irrelevant to the running of the time period set out in § 2-725, except where, unlike here, there is a warranty as to future performance.

II. PROMISES TO REPAIR.[44]

Both contracts entered into in 1969 contain the following clause:

Notwithstanding the other continuing obligations of the Contractor under this Agreement, the Contractor shall repair and make good, without cost to the Purchaser, any damages, defects or faults resulting from imperfect or defective work done or unsound or improper materials furnished by the Contractor which develop during the period of one year (or during a longer period if so stipulated in the specifications) from date of the certification by the Engineer that the work has been completed.

NEP argues that language constitutes "a promise rather than a warranty," and that this cause of action could not have accrued until Riley, in 1978, refused or failed to repair the boilers. However, promises to repair or to replace are generally viewed as specifications of a remedy rather than as an independent or separate warranty. See *Standard Alliance Indus. v. Black Clawson Co.*, 587 F2d at 818 n 10; *Ontario Hydro v. Zallea Sys., Inc.*, 569 F Supp at 1266-1267; *Centennial Ins. Co. v. General Elec. Co.*, 74 Mich App 169, 171-172 (1977); *Commissioners of Fire Dist. No. 9 v. American La France*, 176 NJ Super 655, 573 (1980); *Owens v. Patent Scaffolding Co.*, 77 Misc 2d 992, 998-999 (1974), rev'd on other grounds, 50 AD2d 866 (NY 1975). Those cases instruct that when there are a warranty and a promise to repair, the remedy of first resort is the promise to repair. If that promise is not fulfilled, then the cause of action is the underlying breach of warranty.

[43] Cases from jurisdictions other than Massachusetts deal with the relevant parts of § 2-725 of the Uniform Commercial Code which are in a form identical to those found in GL c 106.

[44] Counts two and eight of the amended complaint speak in terms of breaches of express warranties. NEP now couches its claims in terms of promises distinct from warranties.

The reasoning is sound and particularly pertinent here, where NEP's argument seems structured to avoid the consequences of its failure timely to commence suit. As pointed out in *Centennial Ins. Co. v. General Elec. Co.*, 77 Mich App at 172: "Plaintiff's argument is in essence that by failing to remedy its first breach, the defendant committed a second breach, giving rise to a brand new cause of action and starting anew the limitations period. The fallacy of this approach is apparent. If we adopted plaintiff's position, limitations periods could be extended for virtually infinite time. We doubt that the Legislature intended such a result." It follows from this that what we have stated in part one of this option is applicable to NEP's claims of breaches of the promises to repair.

III. TOLLING AND ESTOPPEL.

NEP next contends that Riley's repeated efforts to repair and assurances that the boilers would be fixed either tolled the running of § 2-725(1) or estopped Riley from relying upon it as a defense.

a. Tolling. Whether repeated repair efforts toll the running of § 2-725(1) depends upon our tolling statutes, as found in GL c 260, §§ 7 through 12, since § 2-725 "does not alter the law on tolling of the statute of limitations. . . ." GL c 106, § 2-725(4), as appearing in St 1957, c 765, § 1. There is nothing in our tolling statutes which would allow NEP to commence suit as late as sometime in 1982, in other words, four years after Riley ceased its efforts to repair the boilers. Nor is it open to us to enlarge upon those statutes.[45] See *Del Grosso v. Board of Appeal of Revere*, 330 Mass 29, 32(1953), and cases therein cited.

b. Estoppel. If NEP is to escape the consequence of its lack of diligence in bringing its action, it must be by way of proof that Riley wrongfully lulled NEP into the delay. See *White v. Peabody Constr. Co.*, 386 Mass 121, 134 (1982) ("[E]stoppel would require proof that the defendants made representations they knew or should have known would induce the plaintiffs to put off bringing a suit and that the plaintiffs did in fact delay in reliance on the representations"). The judge concluded that the facts alleged by NEP to estop Riley, even if proved, were insufficient as matter of law because: (1) NEP made no allegation of fraud or misrepresentations by Riley which would show that Riley "purposely prolonged the time for repairs beyond the running of the statute of limitations"; (2) any assurance given by Riley that the boilers would be fixed did not rise to the level of "lulling" NEP into "foregoing suit"; and (3) "both parties are large corporations with equal access to legal advice."

There are no rigid criteria to apply in determining whether a defendant's conduct was such as to give rise to an estoppel. The test, if it can be so called, is that the "doctrine of estoppel is not applied except when to refuse it would be inequitable." We think it appropriate then, when looking to the facts offered by NEP to show an estoppel, that they be viewed in the context in which they took place, *i.e.*, "Here . . .we have two corporate behemoths, well able to look out for themselves. . . ."

NEP contends that whether it was lulled into inaction by Riley presents a material factual dispute. The conduct NEP relies upon is correspondence between NEP and Riley in 1974. NEP wrote to Riley suggesting that arbitration would be a reasonable course of action "at this time." NEP's letter pointed out: "While arbitration is not the nicest place to end up, it seems preferable

---

[45] NEP relies upon *Colorado-Ute Elec. Assn. v. Envirotech Corp.*, 524 F Supp 1152, 1155-1156 (D Col 1981), for the proposition that repair efforts generally toll § 2-725(1). However, there the court cited and relied upon *Kniffin v. Colorado Western Dev. Co.*, 622 P2d 586 (Col App 1980), as indicative of Colorado's acceptance of the theory that repair efforts operate to toll the running of a limitation period.

to an open-break between our companies, and the unpleasant events that will inevitably follow
. . . ." Riley responded, and swiftly, that Riley and NEP were more competent than an arbitrator
to analyze the problems with the boilers. Riley added that it "has in the past and will in the
future stand behind all of its warranties" and that "[s]hould there be design deficiencies,
Riley. . .corrects them without further cost to the customer." Riley pointed out that there were
"major questions" as to whether problems with the boilers were in fact caused by improper
operation rather than any design deficiencies. The letter concluded with Riley voicing "concerns"
of its own regarding NEP's failure to release certain monies owed to Riley.

Reading this correspondence as favorably as possible to NEP, we do not see how, in the absence
of distortion, Riley's statements could give rise to an estoppel.[46] When we couple these statements
with Riley's repeated efforts to repair (1972 through 1976, when the efforts tapered off; they
ceased altogether by 1978), NEP's argument loses rather than gains force. The undisputed facts
show that it was Riley's position from the outset that it would repair the boilers and that it
continuously tried to do so. NEP does not allege that Riley's repair efforts were insincere or
a mere pretext, only that they were unsuccessful.

That NEP may have behaved in a commercially reasonable manner in relying upon Riley's
efforts (in the belief that because Riley designed, manufactured, and installed the boilers, it was
best able to repair them) does not become material until it is first shown that Riley engaged
in some conduct, such as insincere effort, which would make it unfair to allow Riley to rely
upon § 2-725(1). We do not view the fact of honest, genuine repair efforts, standing alone, as
sufficient basis for application of the doctrine of estoppel. In our view, to conclude otherwise
would be to hold that repair efforts toll § 2-725.

Judgment affirmed.

—

NOTES AND QUESTIONS

(1) *Tender of Delivery.* With respect to a breach of warranty, proposed U.C.C.
§ 2-725(c)(1)[Alternative 1] provides that a claim for relief accrues when the seller has tendered
delivery of *nonconforming* goods. Further, Subsection (c)(2) states that if a warranty expressly
extends to performance of the goods after delivery, a claim for relief accrues thereafter when
the buyer discovers or should have discovered the breach. Subsection (c)(3) provides that if the
seller, after delivery, attempts to conform goods to the contract and fails, the period of limitation
is tolled during the time of the attempt.

---

[46] NEP also relies upon oral statements alleged by NEP's general purchasing agent by way of affidavit to have
been made by Riley in response to the purchasing agent's complaints that if the boilers were not fixed, litigation
would be commenced. The purchasing agent set out Riley's response as, "Riley repeatedly assured me that it would
repair the boilers and that litigation was not necessary." It does not appear from the judge's memorandum of decision
that he took these statements into account. He was, however, free to disregard them. Conspicuously missing from
the affidavit are any factors to show who from Riley gave these assurances.

(2) *Warranty of Future Performance.* Compare the "tender of delivery" rule with the "discovery of the breach" rule of U.C.C. § 2-725(2). Which rule do you prefer from seller's standpoint; from buyer's? Now read the following excerpt.

Nationwide Insurance Co. v. General Motors Corporation/ Chevrolet Motor Division, 625 A.2d 1172, 21 U.C.C. Rep.2d 277 (Pa. 1993), held that GM's automobile warranty which provided that the dealer would repair or make adjustments to the automobile for the first 12 months or 12,000 miles, whichever came first, was a warranty which explicitly extended to future performance of the automobile and the cause of action accrued at the time the breach of warranty was or should have been discovered, rather than the date of delivery of the automobile, even though GM claimed that the commitment was not a warranty but an undertaking to repair or replace. See U.C.C. § 2-725(2). A dissent observed:

> Here, the promise to repair or adjust defective parts for 12 months or 12,000 miles. This is not the same as a promise that the car and its parts will remain free of defects for 12 months or 12,000 miles. The latter promise "explicitly extends to future performance of the goods;" the former promise does not.

With respect to implied warranties the majority stated:

> Although we find the express warranty to explicitly extend to future performance of the goods, we cannot find that the implied warranties of merchantability and fitness for a particular purpose so extend. The warranty contains the following language: "ANY IMPLIED WARRANTY OF MERCHANTABILITY OR FITNESS FOR A PARTICULAR PURPOSE APPLICABLE TO THIS CAR IS LIMITED IN DURATION TO THE DURATION OF THIS WRITTEN WARRANTY." We do not read this language as explicitly extending the terms of any implied warranties, because the document states that any implied warranties are of a duration *no longer than* that of the express warranty and not that they are of a duration *equal to* that of the express warranty. The quoted language does not create implied warranties, because such warranties are created not by contract language but by operation of law in certain circumstances. *See* [U.C.C. §§ 2-314, 2-315]. The legal effect of the quoted language is merely to limit the protection that the law might otherwise impose. Therefore, it cannot be read as the type of language that "explicitly extends to future performance" for purposes of § [2-725(2)]. In addition, the great weight of authority takes the position that an implied warranty, by nature, cannot "explicitly" extend to future performance.

But a dissent stated:

> I would hold that the implied warranties of merchantability and fitness for a particular purpose also extend to the future performance of the vehicle because these implied warranties are expressly linked temporally to the express warranty by the [above] language contained in the express warranty at issue.

See *Tittle v. Steel City Oldsmobile GMC Truck, Inc.*, 544 So.2d 883 (Ala. 1989) (New car limited warranty which covered "any repairs and needed adjustments to correct defects in material or workmanship" was warranty to repair, and not warranty extending to future performance).

(3) *Proposed U.C.C. § 2-725(c).* Proposed § 2-725(c) [Alternative 1] is summarized at Notes and Questions (1) above. Alternative 2 states that if a breach of warranty occurs, a claim for relief accrues when the buyer discovers or should have discovered the breach. The Reporter's Notes state that § 2-725(c) provides a choice for the Drafting Committee in breach of warranty cases between the tolling principle now found in § 2-725(2) and a discovery principle, *i.e.*, the

cause of action does not accrue until the buyer "discovers or should have discovered the breach." Which Alternative would you recommend to the Drafting Committee and why?

(4) *Tolling*. West's Ann.Cal.Civ.Code § 1795.6 (Tolling or expiration of warranty period during time of repairs) states that every warranty period relating to an implied or express warranty accompanying a sale of consumer goods (bought for personal, family or household purposes) selling for $50 or more shall be automatically tolled for the period as set forth in the statute. See also, *e.g.*, Mich.Comp.Laws Ann. § 440.2313b (Express warranty, extension of period for repaired goods).

As to tolling of the statute for mental incapacity, see *Curlee v. Mock Enterprises Inc.*, 173 Ga. App. 594, 327 S.E.2d 736, 41 U.C.C. Rep. 63 (1985); as to tolling of the statute for fraudulent concealment in a personal injury case, see *Freiberg v. Atlas Turner, Inc.*, 1984 WL 178948, 37 U.C.C. Rep. 1592 (D. Minn. 1984).

See Proposed U.C.C. § 2-725(c)(3)[Alternative 1] at Notes and Questions (1) above.

(5) *Tort versus Contract*. A recurrent question arising in actions for defective goods is whether the cause of action arises in tort or in contract. If the action can be characterized as tort, whether on the basis of negligence or strict liability, the statute of limitations will often be only two or three years, but the statute will not begin to run until the plaintiff has been injured by the defect. If the action is a contract action, on the other hand, U.C.C. § 2-725 will apply, the period of limitation will be four years (unless shortened by agreement), but the statute will begin to run upon breach of the sale contract, which will normally occur when tender of delivery is made. Some courts have permitted the plaintiff to characterize the action as tort or contract through allegations in the complaint. See, *e.g., Cochran v. Buddy Spencer Mobile Homes Inc.*, 618 P.2d 947 (Okla. 1980); *Colvin v. FMC Corp.*, 43 Ore. App. 709, 604 P.2d 157 (1979). Other courts have held that all personal injury actions arising from defective products must be treated as tort actions. See, *e.g.,Witherspoon v. General Motors Corporation*, 535 F. Supp. 432, 33 U.C.C. Rep. 583 (WD. Mo. 1982). The Delaware Supreme Court, on the other hand, has held that enactment of the U.C.C. sales provisions preempted the entire field of sales cases, and therefore strict tort liability has no application. *Cline v. Prowler Industries of Maryland, Inc.*, 418 A.2d 968, 29 U.C.C. Rep. 461 (Del. 1980). Accordingly, the four-year statutory period of U.C.C. § 2-725is applicable in all actions arising from the sale of goods. *Johnson v. Hockessin Tractor, Inc.*, 420 A.2d 154, 29 U.C.C. Rep. 477 (Del. 1980). (For a catalogue of the different approaches taken to this question by the various state and federal courts, see *Ogle v. Caterpillar Tractor Co.*, 716 P.2d 334, 42 U.C.C. Rep. 1668 (Wyo. 1986)).

In *R. W. Murray Co. v. Shatterproof Glass Corp.*, 697 F.2d 818, 35 U.C.C. Rep. 477 (8th Cir. 1983), it was held that the U.C.C. § 2-725 four-year statute of limitations applied to an implied warranty action by a remote purchaser for economic loss arising in the sale of goods. The court at 35 U.C.C. Rep. 487, note 9, observed:

> We do not believe this result is in conflict with the recent decision in *Witherspoon v. General Motors Corp.*, 535 F. Supp. 432 (WD Mo 1982). *Witherspoon* did not address the question of the statute of limitations applicable in Missouri to an implied warranty suit by a remote purchaser for *economic loss*. Instead, the court held only that under Missouri law an action for *personal injuries* arising out of a breach of an implied warranty is not governed by the four year Uniform Commercial Code statute of limitations, but by the five year statute of limitations for actions for personal injuries not arising on contract and not otherwise enumerated. See Mo Ann Stat § 516.120 (Vernon 1952).

For discussion of strict liability and interaction of warranty and strict liability, see §§ 5.07 and 5.08, *supra.*

(6) *Products Liability Action.* Some states have adopted a statute of limitations for "products liability actions," that is, those which involve injuries to person or property. For example, Mich. Comp. Laws Ann. § 600.2945 defines such action:

> As used in . . .section 5805, "products liability action" means an action based on any legal or equitable theory of liability brought for or on account of death or injury to person or property caused by or resulting from the manufacture, construction, design, formula, development of standards, preparation, processing, assembly, inspection, testing, listing, certifying, warning, instructing, marketing, advertising, packaging, or labeling of a product or a component of a product.

Mich. Comp. Laws Ann. § 5805(1) and (9) sets forth the relevant period of limitations:

> (1) A person shall not bring or maintain an action to recover damages for injuries to persons or property unless, after the claim first accrued to the plaintiff or to someone through whom the plaintiff claims, the action is commenced within the periods of time prescribed by this section.

> . . . .

> (9) The period of limitations is 3 years for a products liability action. However, in the case of a product which has been in use for not less than 10 years, the plaintiff, in proving a prima facie case, shall be required to do so without benefit of any presumption.

For discussion of product liability statutes, see §§ 5.09 and 5.10, *supra.*

(7) *Privity.* If the doctrine of privity of contract has been abolished, so that a consumer may bring a breach of warranty action against the manufacturer, does the statute of limitations begin to run when the manufacturer tenders delivery of the goods to the wholesaler or retailer, or when the consumer receives tender of delivery from the retailer? *Patterson v. Her Majesty Industries, Inc.*, 450 F. Supp. 425, 23 U.C.C. Rep. 1198 (E.D. Pa. 1978), gives the latter answer, reasoning that maximum protection should be accorded the ultimate user.

In *Heller v. U.S. Suzuki Motor Corp.*, 64 N.Y.2d 407, 488 N.Y.S.2d 132, 477 N.E.2d 434, 40 U.C.C. Rep. 917 (1985), distributor Suzuki sold a motorcycle to Bakers on March 30, 1978, who transferred it to retailer Moroney, who in turn, sold it to plaintiff on April 21, 1979. Plaintiff was injured July 7, 1979, and brought suit against Suzuki on February 15, 1983, for breach of warranty that the motorcycle was safe, merchantable and fit for its intended use. (Note that New York had adopted Alternative B to U.C.C. § 2-318. Also note that the tort causes of action were barred by the three-year statute of limitations.) The court held that under U.C.C. § 2-725, the cause of action against distributor Suzuki accrued on the date the party charged tendered delivery of the product to Bakers (March 30, 1978), not on the date some third party (Moroney) sold it to plaintiff (April 21, 1979). Thus plaintiff's failure to commence the action within the four-year period from March 30, 1978, barred his action against Suzuki. (*See also Rissew v. Yamaha Motor Co., Ltd.*, 493 N.Y.S.2d 78, 41 U.C.C. Rep. 1740 (1985).)

For discussion of privity, see § 5.05, *supra.*

(8) *Reduction of Period of Limitation.* U.C.C. § 2-725(1) provides: "By the original agreement the parties may reduce the period of limitation to not less than one year but may not extend it." See *Burroughs Corporation v. Suntogs of Miami, Inc.*, 472 So. 2d 1166, 41 U.C.C. Rep.

498 (Fla. 1985) (effect of § 95.03, Florida Statutes, which provides: "Any provision in a contract fixing the period of time within which an action arising out of the contract may be begun at a time less than that provided by the applicable statute of limitations is void.").

————

CITY OF WOOD RIVER v. GEER-MELKUS CONSTRUCTION COMPANY, INC.

Supreme Court of Nebraska
444 N.W.2d 305 (1989)

WITTHOFF, DISTRICT JUDGE.

This is an appeal from an order of the Hall County District Court finding the third-party action of Geer-Melkus Construction Company, Inc., and United States Fidelity & Guarantee Company (Geer-Melkus) against Geo. A. Hormel & Company (Hormel) was barred by the statute of limitations.

FACTS

Appellant Geer-Melkus contracted with the City of Wood River to construct a waste water treatment facility. Appellee Hormel manufactured and supplied the rotating media aeration system for the facility. The media system was delivered on or about September 14, 1976, and the plant became operational in the summer of 1977. In the following years, many repairs were made to the media system, and in December 1982 the system broke down completely and could not be repaired.

Wood River filed an action for breach of contract against Geer-Melkus on July 6, 1981. With the court's consent, on December 22, 1981, Geer-Melkus filed a third-party complaint against Hormel, alleging that if it was found liable to Wood River, Hormel was liable to it for breach of warranty.

Specifically, Geer-Melkus complained (1) Hormel warranted the rotating media aeration system would, without further modification, provide a minimum of 22,000 square feet of biological support media in each of the first two stages and 33,000 square feet in the final two stages, for a total of 110,000 square feet of biological support media; (2) Geer-Melkus installed the waste water treatment facility in exact accordance with the plans and specifications; (3) the waste water treatment facility was made operational on or about July 27, 1977; (4) the media rotary disk unit deteriorated and shifted on its shaft; (5) the deterioration and shifting subsequently caused damage to the bearings of the shaft and the shaft itself; (6) the shifting and deterioration required Wood River to replace portions of the waste water treatment system; and (7) the deterioration and shifting were contrary to the specifications for the fixed media rotating disk unit. Geer-Melkus attached, and incorporated by reference, a copy of Wood River's petition as an exhibit to their third-party complaint, and alleged that if the allegations of the Plaintiff's Petition are found to be true and if the Plaintiff recovers a judgment against the Defendants and Third Party Plaintiffs, the Third Party Defendant would be liable to the Defendants and Third Party Plaintiffs for the entire amount of the Plaintiffs [sic] claim against them for the reason that said allegations constitute a breach of the Third Party Defendant's express warranty set forth in paragraph 8 hereof.

On February 12, 1982, Hormel filed a demurrer, based primarily upon the statute of limitations defense, which the court overruled. Hormel filed an answer to the third-party complaint on March 5, 1982, admitting it manufactured and supplied the rotating system and stating the system was delivered on February 12, 1978. Hormel raised as affirmative defenses that (1) the action was barred by the statute of limitations; (2) the amount of the claim exceeded the coverage of the warranty; (3) Wood River failed to properly operate and maintain the system; (4) Hormel was not notified of the alleged breach of warranty; and (5) the warranty expired on February 12, 1978. Geer-Melkus filed a reply, alleging the statute of limitations had not run because they were asking for indemnity.

Hormel then moved for summary judgment, once again asserting the statute of limitations. The motion for summary judgment was overruled.

On November 12, 1985, a separate trial was held on the issue of the statute of limitations. At trial, Hormel demurred ore tenus, which demurrer the court also overruled. At the conclusion of this trial, the judge ruled the statute of limitations was tolled because of repairs and replacements made by Hormel.

Trial on the merits was held on October 28, 1986. The court found for Wood River and against Geer-Melkus in the amount of $57,379.54 on the original petition. On the third-party petition, the court found for Hormel and against Geer-Melkus, holding that the third-party action was barred by the statute of limitations. Pursuant to statute, the court allowed attorney fees of $19,000 to Wood River against Geer-Melkus. Geer-Melkus appeals the court's ruling on their third-party complaint and Hormel cross-appeals the earlier failures to dismiss the action.

ASSIGNMENTS OF ERROR
ON APPEAL

Geer-Melkus assigns as error (1) the trial court's failure to direct a verdict in favor of Geer-Melkus and against Hormel at the close of the evidence; (2) the trial court's entry of judgment generally in favor of Hormel and against Geer-Melkus; (3) the trial court's failure to enter judgment against Hormel on the theory of indemnity; (4) the trial court's finding, after the trial on merits, that Geer-Melkus' claim was barred by Neb. U.C.C. § 2-725 (Reissue 1980), and reversing its previous finding in favor of Geer-Melkus following a separate trial on the issue of the statute of limitations; and (5) the trial court's failure to determine Neb.Rev.Stat. § 25-224(3) (Reissue 1985) applied to Geer-Melkus' claim.

On cross-appeal, Hormel claims the trial court erred (1) in overruling Hormel's demurrer and (2) in denying Hormel's demurrer ore tenus and admitting evidence at trial on the nature of the statute of limitations issue, over Hormel's objection.

LOSS OF JURISDICTION BY THE
DISTRICT COURT TO MODIFY
ITS OWN ORDERS

The term of court ended after the trial on the statute of limitations and the court's ruling against Hormel. Geer-Melkus claims the court was therefore without authority to modify this ruling after the trial on the merits.

. . . .

[Discussion.]

In conclusion, the district court had jurisdiction to modify its earlier orders on the statute of limitations issue.

ISSUE OF INDEMNITY RAISED BY
THE PLEADINGS

Before we can determine whether the statute of limitations bars Geer-Melkus' third party claim, we must determine whether Geer-Melkus seeks damages on a breach of warranty or seeks indemnification. Geer-Melkus does not specifically ask for "indemnity," but, instead, asks for damages for breach of warranty. The third-party complaint specifically set forth the problems with the "rotating media aeration system" manufactured by Hormel. It incorporated Wood River's petition and all its allegations. Finally, the third-party complaint alleged that if Wood River recovered a judgment against Geer-Melkus, Hormel would be liable to Geer-Melkus for the entire amount of Wood River's claim because of the expressed warranty.

While the term "indemnity" is not specifically used,

[t]he essential character of a cause of action or the remedy of relief it seeks, as shown by the allegations of the complaint, determines whether a particular action is one at law or in equity, unaffected by conclusions of the pleader or what the pleader calls it, or the prayer for relief.

Waite v. Samson Dev. Co., 217 Neb. 403, 408, 348 N.W.2d 883, 887 (1984); *Brchan v. The Crete Mills*, 155 Neb. 52 N.W.2d 333 (1952).

Even if the pleading mistakenly identified a cause of action, the right to recover under the facts alleged is not affected.

In order to decide the form of the redress, whether contract or tort, it is necessary to know the source or origin of the duty or the nature of the grievance. Attention must be given to the cause of the complaint; in other words, the character of the action must be determined from what is asserted concerning it in the petition in the cause. It is not important what the plaintiff calls his action. If he does attempt to identify it and is mistaken, that is immaterial. This is the rationale of the code provision that a petition is a statement of facts constituting a cause of action in ordinary and concise language.

Fuchs v. Parsons Constr. Co., 166 Neb. 188, 192, 88 N.W.2d 648, 651 (1958).

It is evident from the pleadings Geer-Melkus claims that (1) appellant Geer-Melkus purchased the rotary system from Hormel; (2) Hormel manufactured the same to meet certain specifications; (3) the system did not meet those specifications; and (4) if Geer-Melkus suffered damages because of the failure of Hormel to fulfill its contractual obligation, they would look to Hormel for payment of their loss. The third-party complaint sets out specifically what Hormel's aeration system did wrong. A duty to indemnify will always arise out of another more basic obligation whether it arises on contract or tort. Although Utah chose to bring sales indemnification actions within § 2-725 of the Uniform Commercial Code, the Utah Supreme Court identified an allegation of a breach of warranty as raising the issue of indemnification.

> Perry argues that [§ 2-725] does not apply because his action is in reality one for indemnity, not one for breach of warranty. We consider this argument in the context of the undeniable fact that the subject matter of this entire lawsuit is the sale of goods, which will be governed where applicable by the Utah version of the Uniform Commercial Code. . . . *The underlying action was for breach of contract, and the amended third-party complaint alleges only a cause of action for breach of warranty. It nowhere mentions indemnity. Nonetheless, we look to the substance of Perry's claim, regardless of what he chose to call it.*

(Emphasis supplied.) *Perry v. Pioneer Wholesale Supply Co.*, 681 P.2d 214, 217 (Utah 1984).

Hormel cannot claim that it did not understand the theory upon which the third-party complaint was predicated or that it had no warning in time to defend itself. The motion for leave to file a third party complaint against Hormel specifically stated that "a rotating media aeration system manufactured by George A. Hormel & Co. was defective and was not merchantable and if such allegations are true these Defendants would be entitled to indemnification from George A. Hormel & Co."

In addition thereto, the reply filed by Geer-Melkus specifically addressed § 2-275 and alleged that it did not apply

> for the reason that under the substantive law of the State of Nebraska the periods of limitation set forth in the foregoing statues, if applicable in the instant case, do not start to run upon a claim for indemnity until such time as the indemnitee's liability has been fixed and discharged.

Therefore, the third-party complaint raised an indemnification cause of action.

APPLICABILITY OF § 2-725 TO INDEMNIFICATION CAUSES OF ACTION

All parties agree the sale which is the subject matter of the third-party complaint is a sale of goods within the meaning of the Uniform Commercial Code. As such, the original contract and warranty were covered by the statute of limitations of contracts for sale.

In examining the statute and the proposed scope of the statute, it should be noted that any action for breach of contract must be commenced within 4 years after the cause of action has accrued. The statute further specifically defines accrual of a cause of action by saying that the breach occurs when a tender of delivery is made, except where a warranty specifically extends to future performance of the goods, and discovery of the breach must await time of such performance. In this case the warranty did not specifically extend to future performance.

We have not previously addressed the question of whether the limitation set out in § 2-725 applies to an indemnity claim. Other jurisdictions have split on the issue.

Georgia, Utah, Illinois, and Idaho have held indemnity claims are controlled and limited by § 2-725. [Citations.] These jurisdictions view the strict application of § 2-725 as necessary to avoid the problem of unending litigation.

> The four-year statute applicable to the indemnity theory does not apply in this case because a sale of goods occurred in 1974 with observable defects (if any), and any cause of action against Third-Party Defendants arose at that time. Otherwise, anyone buying defective goods could resell them before or after the statute had run, and upon being sued for the original defects, file a third-party complaint for indemnity and thus defeat the policy of repose underlying the statute of limitation.

Perry v. Pioneer Wholesale Supply Co., 681 P.2d 214, 217 n. 1 (Utah 1984).

Maryland, New Hampshire, Missouri, Maine, North Carolina, and New York have ruled indemnity claims do not come under the time limitation found in § 2-725. [Citations.] These jurisdictions follow the reasoning advanced by the New York Court of Appeals in *McDermott v. City of N.Y., supra* 50 N.Y.2d at 216-17, 406 N.E.2d at 462, 428 N.Y.S.2d at 646:

> Conceptually, implied indemnity finds its roots in the principles of equity. It is nothing short of simple fairness to recognize that "[a] person who, in whole or in part, has discharged a duty which is owed by him but which as between himself and another should have been discharged by the other, is entitled to indemnity" (Restatement, Restitution, § 76). To prevent unjust enrichment, courts have assumed the duty of placing the obligation where in equity it belongs. [Citations.]

In deciding the statute of limitations question was governed by the indemnity rule rather than the contract or warranty rule, the Maryland Court of Special Appeals stated:

> In approaching this issue, both sides have focused their attention on when limitations begins to run in an action for indemnification and have given but scant consideration to the nature of the indemnity claim actually made by appellant. As to the limitations question, we think that appellant is correct in her view that an action for indemnification accrues and the limitations period commences not at the time of the underlying transaction but when the would-be indemnitee pays the judgment arising from the underlying transaction. That seems to be the majority view, and it is certainly in keeping with the nature of an indemnity action.

(Citations omitted.) *Hanscome v. Perry, supra* 75 Md.App. at 614, 542 A.2d at 425.

In applying the Missouri rule, the U.S. District Court used the same rationale. In *City of Clayton v. Grumman Emer. Prod.,* [576 F. Supp. 1122 (E.D. Mo. 1983)], the issue was which party was financially responsible for cracks in a firetruck frame. The firetruck was purchased by the city from Howe Fire Apparatus Co., Inc., which was subsequently merged into Grumann Emergency Products, Inc. The frame was manufactured by The Warner and Swayse Company. Clayton sued Grumman as the successor in interest to Howe, which brought in Warner and Swayse as third party defendants. Warner and Swayse responded by pleading the statute of limitations.

> Although Grumman raises the issue of the future performance exception to § 2-725, the Court need not address that question. Counts I and III of Grumann's third-party complaint state causes of action for indemnity based on breaches of express and implied warranties. The statue of limitations for indemnity does not start to run until the indemnitee is found liable to a third party. *See Simon v. Kansas City rug Co.,* 460 S.W.2d 596, 600 (Mo.1970). Therefore, Grumman's claims for indemnity from Warner are not time barred. This result does not imprudently enlarge the statute of limitations for breach of warranty. A party who buys and

then resells a product is not in a position to discover the latent defect within the warranty's limitation period because the product is in the hands of the consumer during that time. Only when the consumer sues the retailer does the retailer gain notice of the latent defect. *See Walker Manufacturing Co. v. Dickerson, Inc.*, 619 F.2d 305, 310 (4th Cir.1980) (North Carolina U.C.C. law).

City of Clayton, supra at 1127.

Nebraska has long held a claim for indemnity accrues at the time the indemnity claimant suffers loss or damage. *City of Lincoln v. First Nat. Bank of Lincoln,* 67 Neb. 401, 93 N.W. 698 (1903).

In *Waldinger Co. v. P & Z Co., Inc.,* 414 F.Supp. 59 (D.Neb. 1976), the trial court held the underlying statute of limitations dealing with political subdivision tort claims did not apply to actions seeking contribution or indemnification. Waldinger Co. instituted an action on January 16, 1976, against P & Z, Metropolitan Utilities District of Omaha, and the City of Omaha, alleging negligence proximately resulting in the collapse of a slurry trench wall which surrounded the Omaha-Douglas Civic Center. On May 3, 1976, the City of Omaha filed a third-party complaint against Hawkins Construction Company, Leo A. Daly Company, and Omaha-Douglas Public Commission for indemnification or contribution. Thereafter, the commission moved to dismiss the third-party complaint for failure to file a tort claim pursuant to the Political Subdivisions Tort Claims act, Neb.Rev.Stat. § 23-2401 et seq. (Reissue 1974). The commission argued that any claims not filed within 1 year of the injury were extinguished.

In interpreting Nebraska law on contribution and indemnity, the trial court held:

These decisions are based on sound equitable principles. Contribution and indemnification are inchoate rights which do not arise until one tort feasor has paid more than his share of the damages or judgment. A plaintiff may sue one tort feasor or he may join all tort feasors in one suit. He may also wait more than a year to file his suit. To accept the Commission's argument that the claim for contribution or indemnification arises when the injury is incurred would allow plaintiff to choose which defendant would bear the burden by simply filing his lawsuit after the one year statute of limitations has run. The defendant joint tort feasor, having no prior knowledge of a claim, would be unable to file a claim prior to being joined in the lawsuit.

Waldinger Co. v. P & Z Co., Inc., supra at 60.

The reasoning in *McDermott, Hanscome,* and *City of Clayton* is consistent with Nebraska law. If we were to adopt the opposite position, a party who might have a claim for indemnification would have to bring his action before the underlying claim was brought to avoid the running of the statue of limitations. Therefore, we hold § 2-725 does not apply where a party is seeking indemnification.

The present case is a classic example of the inequity which would result from adopting the theory advanced by Hormel. Geer-Melkus could not have brought their cause of action for indemnity until the original suit was brought by Wood River on July 6, 1981. The statute of limitations on the indemnity action would have expired on December 14, 1980. Geer-Melkus would be left with no recourse under these circumstances.

It is generally recognized that the party seeking indemnification must have been free of any wrongdoing, and its liability is vicariously imposed. Therefore, it should recover from another. [Citations.] In this case, the product was manufactured and sold by Hormel. The evidence in the record indicates any problems with the product were directly attributable to Hormel, not to Geer-Melkus.

The trial court found that the statute of limitations questions was resolved by *Grand Island School Dist. #2 v. Celotex Corp.,* 203 Neb. 559, 279 N.W.2d 603 (1979). This action was to recover damages arising from a leaky roof installed upon a junior high school. The school district sued the general contractor, the architect, the subcontractors, and various and sundry bonding companies. One of the defendants was dismissed on a demurrer and the others on motions for summary judgment, on the basis that the various statutes of limitations had run. Because none of the defendants were liable, there was no issue of indemnity.

Geer-Melkus asserts the proper statute governing limitation of this action is Neb.Rev.Stat. § 25-224 (Reissue 1985). In the event § 25-224 were deemed applicable, subsection (3) removes the limitation on indemnity claims. We therefore need not address the question of whether the third-party complaint comes within § 25-224.

For the foregoing reasons, we find the statute of limitations does not bar the third-party complaint brought by Geer-Melkus.

CONCLUSION

The trial court's findings that the pleadings and evidence establish that Geer-Melkus Construction Company, Inc., and United States Fidelity & Guarantee Company's claim was for a breach of warranty and not for a claim of indemnification and that the claim was barred by the statute of limitations, § 2-275, are reversed. As noted above, the uncontroverted evidence establishes that the loss was directly attributable to Hormel. The action is therefore remanded with instruction to enter judgment against Hormel.

Reversed and remanded with direction.

NOTES AND QUESTIONS

(1) Proposed U.C.C. § 2-725(c)[Alternative 2] provides that if a breach of warranty or *indemnity* occurs, a claim for relief accrues when the buyer discovers or should have discovered the breach. How would this affect the *Wood River* case? Cf. U.C.C. § 2A-506(2)(second sentence).

(2) Statutes that address the question of indemnity include West's Ann.Cal.Civ.Code § 1792:

> Unless disclaimed in the manner prescribed by this chapter, every sale of consumer goods that are sold at retail in this state shall be accompanied by the manufacturer's and the retail seller's implied warranty that the goods are merchantable. The retail seller shall have a right of indemnity against the manufacturer in the amount of any liability under this section.

Further, § 1795.7 (Liability of manufacturer; extension upon tolling of warranty period) states:

> Whenever a warranty, express or implied, is tolled pursuant to Section 1795.6 as a result of repairs or service performed by any retail seller, the warranty shall be extended with regard to the liability of the manufacturer to a retail seller pursuant to law. In such event, the

manufacturer shall be liable in accordance with the provisions of Section 1793.5 for the period that an express warranty has been extended by virtue of Section 1795.6 to every retail seller who incurs obligations in giving effect to such express warranty. The manufacturer shall also be liable to every retail seller for the period that an implied warranty has been extended by virtue of Section 1795.6, in the same manner as he would be liable under Section 1793.5 for an express warranty. If a manufacturer provides for warranty repairs and service through its own service and repair facilities and through independent repair facilities in the state, its exclusive liability pursuant to this section shall be to such facilities.

See discussion of tolling at Notes and Questions (4) following the New England Power Co. case, *supra*.

§ 7.08 Punitive Damages

Read U.C.C. § 1-106

Traditionally, punitive damages were not allowed by the courts in breach of contract cases. However, in recent years, punitive damages have played an increasingly important role in contract and other commercial law cases. In some cases throughout this casebook, you may note that the damages asserted or given include punitive damages.

Some courts have required that in addition to breach of contract, there be an independent tort show such as fraud. Others have simply allowed punitive damages because the circumstances so warrant (*e.g.*, bad faith, outrageous conduct) and note it as an exception to the traditional rule. The basic code section on remedies, § 1-106, generally is viewed as permitting punitive damages under the "otherwise in law" part. Caselaw has established the doctrine of punitive damages over many decades.

The student of commercial law will find punitive damages in cases where there has been intentional and outrageous conduct by one of the parties. Willfulness or wanton reckless disregard of others are elements of the requirement of intentionalness, There may be various degrees of outrageousness. Some of these will involve sales contracts. Punitive damages also arise in other areas. For example, it may arise in regard to the wrongful dishonor of a customer's checks in Article 3, or in regard to a wrongful repossession under a security agreement in Article 9.

PROBLEM 7.8

A.R. Jones, a car dealer for the Fuji Car Company, often receives some of its luxury "Diamond" cars with minor scratches on a fender incurred during shipment. It is able to repaint these without it being noticed and has the approval of the Fuji Company on doing this. It does not tell the customer and generally it is never noticed.

Mr. Robert Rich has found out that this happened to a Diamond car he recently purchased from A.R. Jones Company.

Suppose you are representing Mr. Rich. What damages would you assert? What evidence would be relevant? What dollar amount would you suggest as appropriate?

PROBLEM 7.9

Suppose you are representing A.R. Jones Company with the facts as stated above. What arguments and damages would you anticipate ? What are your arguments?

PROBLEM 7.10

The A.R. Rich Company also sells s streaking Star sports car with the "Rocket" engine. Out of rocket engines, Fuji substitutes one of its other car engines which is used in the Diamond car. This engine has just as much horsepower, as much quality, and a similar design. It advises A.R. Jones company not to mention this to customers.

You have been consulted by A.R. Jones. What is your advice? What are the possible damages? What are Fuji Company's possible damages? Suppose the Fuji Company carries out this plan and you represent a Streaking car buyer. What damages and what amount would you assert?

NOTES

(1) In a U.S. Supreme Court case with facts similar to Problem 7.8, *BMW of North America, Inc. v. Gore*, 116 S. Ct. 1589 (1996), it was held that the state had a legitimate interest in allowing punitive damages but that the gross excessiveness violated elementary fairness as reflected in due process. For the undisclosed minor repainting of the new car ($ 600 on a $ 40,000 car) the jury assessed compensated damages of $ 4,000 and $ 4 million in punitive damages. The Alabama Supreme Court had reduces punitive damages to $ 2 million. The U.S. Supreme Court found this to be excessive. It looked at:

(1)   the degree of reprehensibility,

(2)   the disparity of harm or potential harm suffered and the punitive damage award,

(3)   the difference between this remedy and civil penalties in comparable areas.

It found no evidence of deliberate false statements or concealment with improper motive.

Three justices in a concurring opinion noted the difficulties in ascertaining just when the punitive damage amount is excessive and exceeds the state's legitimate interests, but that this award lies in the line's far side.

(2) How does one measure the degree of outrageousness or reprehensibility? Can you devise some standards?

(3) One of the purposes of punitive damages is to punish or "slap" the wrongdoer to such an extent that it takes notice and revises its practices. It has long been recognized that the more wealthy the company involved, the harder the "slap" necessary. A very wealthy company is not hurt as badly y a couple million dollar punitive damage award. Evidence of a company's net worth is often brought into such cases for this very purpose. The Supreme Court in the *Gore* case noted that there was no evidence that a more modest sanction would not be sufficient to motivate BMW to make full disclosure thereafter.

(4) Some states require that a part of punitive damage awards (*e.g.*, one half) go the state or a special state government fund to help others. Should this make a difference in evaluating the amount?

CHAPTER 8

RIGHTS OF THIRD PARTIES:
GOOD FAITH PURCHASE OF GOODS

§ 8.01 Introduction

The general common law rule was that where goods were sold by a person who was not the owner, and who did not sell them under the authority or with the consent of the owner, the buyer acquired no better title to the goods than the seller had.[1] This rule is reflected in the maxims: Nemo dare protest quod non habet (No man can give that which he has not), Nemo dat qui non habet (He who hath not cannot give), etc. To this rule there were exceptions, notably (1) the doctrine of market overt;[2] and (2) estoppel — the owner of the goods by his conduct may be precluded from denying the seller's authority to sell.[3]

The classic case of *O'Connor's Administratrix v. Clark*, 170 Pa. 318, 32 A. 1029 (1895), is illustrative. There, O'Connor owned a wagon. Tracy, a piano mover, with the knowledge and consent of O'Connor had his name and occupation printed upon the side of the wagon to create the public impression that he was the owner as follows: "George Tracy-Piano Mover" and proceeded to use the same. Thereafter, Tracy, without the knowledge and consent of O'Connor, the owner of the wagon, sold the wagon to Clark. O'Connor sought to recover possession of the wagon from Clark. In holding for Clark the court stated:

> While the soundness of the general rule of law that a vendee of personal property takes only such title or interest as his vendor has and is authorized to transfer cannot for a moment be doubted, it is not without its recognized exceptions. One of these is where the owner has so acted with reference to his property as to invest another with such evidence of ownership, or apparent authority to deal with and dispose of it, as is calculated to mislead, and does mislead, a good-faith purchaser for value. In such cases the principle of estoppel applies, and declares that the apparent title or authority, for the existence of which the actual owner was responsible, shall be regarded as the real title or authority, at least so far as persons acting on the apparent title or authority, and parting with value, are concerned. Strictly speaking, this is merely a special application of the broad equitable rule that, where one of two innocent persons must suffer loss by reason of the fraud or deceit of another, the loss should fall upon

---

[1] See Uniform Sales Act § 23(1) at note c below.

[2] The English Sale of Goods Act § 22(1) provided: "Where goods are sold in market overt, according to the usage of the market the buyer acquires a good title to the goods provided he buys them in good faith and without notice of any defect or want of title on the part of the seller." This doctrine has not been recognized in the United States.

[3] Uniform Sales Act § 23(1) stated:

> [W]here goods are sold a person who is not the owner thereof, and who does not sell them under the authority or with the consent of the owner, the buyer acquires no better title to the goods than the seller had, unless the owner of the goods is by his conduct precluded from denying the seller's authority to sell.

him by whose act or omission the wrongdoer has been enabled to commit the fraud. Assuming, in this case, that a jury, under the evidence, should find — as we think they would be warranted in doing — that such marks of ownership were placed on the property by direction of O'Connor, the real owner, as were not only calculated to deceive, but actually intended to deceive, the public, and that by reason thereof and without any fraud or negligence on his part, the defendant was misled into the belief that Tracy was the real owner, and he accordingly bought and paid him for the property, can there be any doubt, as between the real owner and the innocent purchaser, that the loss should fall upon the former, by whose act Tracy was enabled to thus fraudulently sell and receive the price of the property? We think not. In *Bannard v. Campbell*, . . . a well-considered case, involving substantially the same principle it was held that to create an estoppel by which an owner is prevented from asserting title to and is deprived of his property by the act of a third person, without his assent, two things must concur: (1) The owner must have clothed the person assuming to dispose of the property with the apparent title to or authority to dispose of it. (2) The person alleging the estoppel must have acted and parted with value upon the faith of such apparent ownership or authority, so that he will be the loser if the appearances to which he trusted are not real.

————

ANDERSON CONTRACTING CO., INC. v. ZURICH INSURANCE CO.

Florida District Court of Appeal
448 So. 2d 7, 38 U.C.C. Rep. 108 (1984)

BARFILED, J.

Anderson Contracting Company, Inc. (Anderson) appeals a summary judgment in favor of Zurich Insurance Company (Zurich) in which Zurich was awarded immediate possession of property. . . . We affirm the summary judgment for Zurich.

The issues raised on this appeal are whether the trial court erred in (1) failing to apply the law of Louisiana in determining the property rights of the parties; (2) granting a motion for summary judgment in favor of defendants on their respective "counterclaims" when no notice of hearing on the motion was given to plaintiff; and (3) granting a summary judgment as to Zurich simultaneously with the filing of the counterclaim and motion for summary judgment thereon. We find no merit in Anderson's arguments as to issues (2) and (3). As to issue (1), our affirmance of the trial court's holding that Florida law applies is based on the public policy of Florida.

Each of the appellees, Zurich and Fireman's Fund, insured a Caterpillar tractor. Both of the tractors were stolen in Texas and were sold to Southeast Equipment Company (Southeast), a Louisiana company which sells used heavy equipment. Southeast subsequently sold both tractors to Ring Power Corporation (Ring Power), which sells new and used heavy Caterpillar equipment. Ring Power had the tractors transported to Florida where they were sold to Anderson. The insurance companies paid the claims on the stolen tractors. When the tractors were found in Florida, this litigation ensued.

Anderson argues that, under the rule of comity, the trial court should have applied Louisiana law, which Anderson asserts would require the true owner to reimburse the subsequent purchaser upon recovery of the stolen property. Comity does not require Florida public policy to be supplanted by foreign law. Comity is not a rule of law, but of practice, convenience and expediency. Where it would be contrary to the statutory law or contravene some established and important policy of the forum state, it is not applied; (New Hampshire's law enforcing "other insurance" clauses in auto policies contrary to Florida public policy against such clauses); (contract not to compete repugnant to Florida's public policy, therefore unenforceable in Florida); (waiver of homestead exemption as to debt contrary to policy of Florida's exemption laws); (both concerned with gambling debts unenforceable in Florida). [Citations omitted.]

It has generally been held by Florida courts that the old English common law principle of title acquired by purchase and sale in open market does not apply in this country and that, in the absence of some intervening principle of estoppel, one cannot convey a better title than he has and conversely, one cannot claim a better title than he, in fact, receives. [Citations omitted.]

Where an owner has voluntarily parted with possession of his chattel, even though induced by a criminal act, a bona fide purchaser can acquire good title, under the theory that where one of two innocent parties must suffer because of the wrongdoing of a third person, the loss must fall on the party who by his conduct created the circumstances which enabled the third party to perpetuate the wrong. [Citations omitted.] However, no such estoppel argument can be advanced against an owner of property that is stolen and subsequently sold to an innocent purchaser. It is the public policy of Florida that one in possession of stolen property, even if he has innocently purchased it from a "dealer," has no possessory or ownership right to the property as against the rightful owner from whom the property was stolen, since the dealer could convey no better title than he received from the thief.

Affirmed.

NOTE

Study U.C.C. § 2-403(1)(first sentence) and Comment 1.

PROBLEM 8.1

One night Carr stole 24 bales of cotton from a gin where the cotton had been processed and tagged. All the cotton was owned by Lineburger. Early the next morning Carr carried the cotton to Warehouse and after weighing had a receipt issued "to the order of Carr" and delivered to him. Carr took the receipt to a nearby town where he indorsed and delivered it to Hodge who purchased it in good faith. Carr then disappeared and has not since been located.

Lineburger discovered the theft and determined the location of the cotton and the existence of the receipt in the hands of Hodge. Both Lineburger and Hodge demand the cotton from

Warehouse and Warehouse interpleads. Who is entitled to the cotton, Lineburger or Hodge? See U.C.C. § 7-503(1).

§ 8.02 Entrusting

Read: U.C.C. § 2-403(2) and (3); see §§ 2-702(3), 7-205, 9-307(1).

Read also: U.C.C. §§ 2A-304(2), 2A-305(2), 2A-103(3)(§ 2-403(3)); CISG Arts. 1(1), 4(b).

A common law case which dealt with entrustment is *Levi v. Booth, 58 Md. 305 (1882).* In this case, plaintiff was the owner of a diamond ring. He placed the ring in the hands of De Wolff, a dealer and trader in jewelry, for the purpose of obtaining a match for it, or failing that to get an offer for it. There was nothing to show that it was given to De Wolff for any other purpose or that he was in any manner authorized to sell it. Subsequently, De Wolff sold the ring to Levi who was a good faith purchaser. In holding for plaintiff-owner the court said:

> [I]t is very clear, upon the principles that we have already stated, that the *bare possession* of goods by one, though he may happen to be a *dealer* in that class of goods, does not clothe him with power to dispose of the goods as though he were owner, or as having authority as agent to sell or pledge the goods, to the preclusion of the right of the real owner. If he sells *as owner* there must be some other *indicia* of property than mere possession. There must . . . be some act or conduct on the part of the real owner whereby the party selling is clothed with the apparent ownership, or authority to sell, and which the real owner will not be heard to deny or question to the prejudice of an innocent third party dealing on the faith of such appearances. If it were otherwise, people would not be secure in sending their watches or articles of jewelry to a jeweller's establishment to be repaired, or cloth to a clothing establishment to be made into garments.

PROBLEM 8.2

How would *the Levi v. Booth* case be resolved under U.C.C. § 2-403(2), assuming Levi to be a buyer in ordinary course of business?

———

THORN v. ADAMS

Court of Appeals of Oregon
125 Or. App. 257, 865 P.2d 417 (1993)

LEESON, JUDGE.

Defendant purchased a car in 1989. On April 15, 1992, her son-in-law, Richard, took the car to Gateley's Fairway Motors (Gateley's), a car dealership that also performed repairs. As defendant's authorized agent, Richard requested an estimate of the car's value, and left it for repairs. Several days later, plaintiff saw the car on Gateley's lot, next to several cars for sale. Gateley's allowed her to take the car for a test drive, and later sold it to her. Gateley's never informed plaintiff that it had no authority to sell the car, nor did it indicate that the car was anything other than inventory.

When Richard learned of the sale, he demanded that plaintiff return the car. She refused, and brought this action for an injunction requiring defendant to deliver the certificate of title to her. She also sought damages for conversion, based on defendant's refusal to surrender the certificate of title. Defendant counterclaimed for an order requiring plaintiff to surrender possession of the car, or, in the alternative, to require plaintiff to pay defendant the reasonable market value of the car.

Both parties moved for summary judgment. The trial court denied defendant's motion and granted plaintiff's motion. It ordered defendant to surrender the certificate of title and to take such other actions as reasonably necessary to register the vehicle in plaintiff's name.

Summary judgment should be granted only when there is no genuine issue of material fact and the moving party is entitled to judgment as a matter of law. [Citation.] The parties agree that there is no genuine issue of material fact. The only dispute in which party was entitled to judgment as a matter of law.

Plaintiff bases her claim of legal ownership on ORS 72.4030, the provision of the Oregon Uniform Commercial Code commonly known as the "entrustment principle." ORS 72.-4030(3) provides:

[Read U.C.C. § 2-403(2).]

Under ORS 72.4030(4),

[Read U.C.C. § 2-403(3).]

Plaintiff contends that defendant entrusted the car to Gateley's, which was a merchant that dealt in goods of that kind, and, therefore, that Gateley's had the power to transfer all rights in the car to her as a buyer in the ordinary course of business.

Defendant concedes that the entrustment principle gives merchants the power to pass good title even when the merchant has no authority to sell the goods, but argues that that principle does not apply. She contends that ORS 803.094(1) provides the exclusive method for transferring legal title to a vehicle that has a certificate of title. That statute provides, in part:

> "Except as otherwise provided in this section, *upon the transfer of any interest* shown on an Oregon certificate of title any person whose interest is released, terminated, assigned or transferred, shall release or assign that interest on the title certificate." (Emphasis supplied.)

Nothing in the plain language of the statute describes or limits the methods that may be used to transfer an interest shown on an Oregon certificate of title. Rather, the statute describes what must be done *once the transfer has occurred.* By its terms, ORS 803.094(1) does not prevent or invalidate a transfer of interest that takes place under ORS 72.4030(3).[4]

---

[4] The result would be different under two former statutes, which explicitly described the methods for transferring *any* interest in a vehicle. *Former* ORS 481.405 provided, in part:

> "(1) . . . To transfer title *or any interest* in a motor vehicle, trailer or semitrailer issued a certificate of title under this chapter, the transferor shall sign the certificate and fill in any information required by the division in the appropriate places on the certificate." (Emphasis supplied.)

Former ORS 481.405 was repealed effective January 1, 1986. Or Laws 1983, ch. 338, § 978. It was replaced by *former* ORS 803.095, which provided, in part:

Defendant argues that, even if the entrustment principle of ORS 72.4030 applies, plaintiff still was not entitled to judgment as a matter of law, because she was not a buyer in the ordinary course of business. According to ORS 71.2010(9),

> "[b]uyer in ordinary course of business" means a person who in good faith and without knowledge that the sale to the person is in violation of the ownership rights . . . of a third party in the goods buys in ordinary course from a person in the business of selling goods of that kind . . . .

Good faith is defined as "honesty in fact in the conduct or transaction concerned." ORS 71.2010(19).

Defendant argues that plaintiff could not have acted with honesty in fact, because no legal title can be conveyed at the time of the purchase without a concurrent transfer of the certificate of title. She contends that plaintiff was put on notice that there was something unusual in the transaction when she failed to obtain a certificate of title at the same time she purchased the vehicle.

We disagree. Nothing in the motor vehicle statutes required plaintiff to take possession of the certificate of title at the moment she purchased the car in order to acquire legal title.[5] Absent such a requirement, plaintiff's "failure" to obtain the certificate of title at the moment that she purchased the car is not unreasonable, and does not put plaintiff on notice that the transaction was "unusual." Defendant provides no other support for her contention that plaintiff was not a buyer in the ordinary course of business.

Finally, defendant argues that it is unfair to place motor vehicle owners at the mercy of the entrustment principle. That choice was made by the legislature when it adopted ORS 72.4030(3), which mirrors section 2-402(3) of the Uniform Commercial Code. 1 Bailey, Oregon Uniform Commercial Code § 2.92 (2d ed. 1990). The entrustment principle promotes one of the basic goals of commerce:

> "In most cases the equities between the entruster-owner and the buyer in the ordinary course are equal, and the balance is tipped in favor of the latter because that frees the marketplace and promotes commerce. This goal, called 'security of transactions[,]' is an ideal of the commercial law. The protection of property rights . . . is not an ideal of the commercial law. . . . On the assumption that both the entruster and buyer have been equally victimized by the dishonesty of the merchant-dealer, section 2-403(2) resolves the issue so

---

"This section establishes the procedures for transferring title *or an interest in a vehicle* for which the division has issued a certificate of title. . . . Except as provided in ORS 803.110, the following procedures are for the described type of transfer of an interest:

"(1) Transfer of title *or any interest in a vehicle* requires completion of . . . the following:

"(a) The transferor shall sign the certificate of title in the appropriate place provided on the certificate." (Emphasis supplied.)

Former ORS 803.095 was repealed by Oregon Laws 1989, chapter 148 section 20, and the present version of ORS 803.094 was added. Or Laws 1989, ch. 148, § 2.

[5] We are not persuaded by defendant's citation to cases from other jurisdictions whose statutes are different. For example, defendant cites *Ballard v. Associates* Investment Co., 368 S.W.2d 232, 233-34 (Tex. Civ. App. 1963), in which the court applied the then existing Texas certificate of title act, which provided that "no title to any motor vehicle shall pass or vest" until the transfer of the certificate of title occurred. We are equally unpersuaded by defendant's citation to *Ellsworth v. Worthey*, 612 S.W.2d 396, 400 (Mo. App. 1981), in which the court cited several pre-U.C.C. cases and concluded that Kansas law provided that the sale of a used vehicle without concurrent delivery of the signed certificate was "fraudulent and void."

as to free the marketplace, rather than protect the original owner's property rights." 2 Hawkland, U.C.C. Series § 2.403:07 (1992).

The trial court did not err in granting plaintiff's motion for summary judgment and in denying defendant's motion.

Affirmed.

PROBLEM 8.3

Big Knob Volunteer Fire Department contracted to purchase a fire truck from Hamerly Custom Productions. (Hamerly was in the business of assembling component parts into fire trucks.) Big Knob paid $48,000 toward the purchase price of $51,836. Subsequently, Hamerly ordered a chassis for the truck from Lowe & Moyer who reserved a security interest in the chassis. Hamerly began work on transforming the chassis into a fire truck and painted Big Knob's name on the cab. However, Hamerly neither paid Lowe & Moyer for the chassis nor did it complete and deliver the truck to Big Knob.

Lowe & Moyer seeks possession of the chassis pursuant to its rights under the default provisions of U.C.C. § 9-503. Big Knob seeks possession of the fire truck because it was unable to effect cover for the truck. *See* U.C.C. § 2-716(3).

Big Knob asserts that, as a buyer in ordinary course of business, it takes free of the security interest created by Hamerly in favor of Lowe & Moyer. *See* U.C.C. § 9-307(1). The issue arises as to the point at which a person becomes a buyer in ordinary course of business. Is it when:

(1)   *title* to the truck passes to buyer? *See* U.C.C. §§ 2-106(1), 2-401?

(2)   the truck is *delivered* to Big Knob? See predecessor Uniform Trust Receipts Act § 9(2) which protected "a buyer in the ordinary course of trade" defined as a person "to whom goods are sold and *delivered.*"

(3)   the truck is *identified* to the contract? (Hamerly painted Big Knob's name on the cab.) See U.C.C. §§ 2-501, 2-716(3), 2-401 Comment 3 and Point 3 of Cross References.

See Big Knob Volunteer Fire Co. v. Lowe & Moyer Garage, Inc., 487 A.2d 953, 40 U.C.C. Rep. 1691 (1985).

PROBLEM 8.4

Bailor delivers several tons of grain to Warehouse who not only stores grain but also sells it. Warehouse issues to Bailor a warehouse receipt engaging to deliver "to the order of Bailor." Bailor signs and delivers the receipt to Adams who takes by "due negotiation." Warehouse sells and delivers the grain to Baker who buys in the ordinary course of business. Is Adams or Baker entitled to the goods? See U.C.C. § 7-205.

———

NOTES AND QUESTIONS

(1) *Merchant as Buyer in Ordinary Course of Business.* In *Sherrock v. Commercial Credit Corp.*, 290 A.2d 648, 10 U.C.C. Rep. 523 (Del. 1972), car-dealer Sherrock agreed to purchase

two automobiles from Dover Motors. Held: a merchant-buyer may be a buyer in ordinary course of business (BOCB) under U.C.C. § 9-307(1); this section is not limited to consumer buyers. BOCB means a person who in *good faith* buys in ordinary course. U.C.C. § 1-201(9) and (19). With respect to U.C.C. Article 2, " 'good faith' in the case of a merchant means honesty in fact and the observance of reasonable commercial standards of fair dealing in the trade." U.C.C. § 2-103(1)(b). Clearly, a merchant BOCB under § 2-403(2) must observe reasonable commercial standards of fair dealing. Is the merchant BOCB of U.C.C. § 9-307(1) required to observe these standards? The court in *Sherrock, supra,* said: "We find no basis anywhere for the conclusion that the drafters of the Code intended to make it permissible to 'cross-over' to Article 2 for the definition of the term 'good faith' as incorporated by reference in Article 9." Should we not direct the Court's attention to U.C.C. § 1-102 Comment 1?

(2) *Seller in Possession.* Entrusting of possession of goods to a merchant who deals in goods of the kind includes any acquiescence in retention of possession by the merchant. U.C.C. § 2-403(2), (3). In *Metalworking Machinery Co., Inc. v. Fabco, Inc.,* 17 Ohio App. 3d 91, 477 N.E.2d 634 (1984), East Coast sold a metalworking machine to Metalworking, who never picked it up. Later, Yoder purchased the same machine from East Coast. (East Coast was a manufacturing company and the machine was not sold by East Coast in the ordinary course of its business.) Subsequently, Yoder sold the machine to Fabco. Held: Money judgment for Metalworking against Fabco. Per U.C.C. § 2-403(2) and (3), the machine was not left in possession of a merchant who dealt in goods of that kind and machine was not sold in ordinary course of East Coast's business. (Further, money judgment was granted to Fabco against Yoder.)

See also U.C.C. § 2-503(4)(b).

(3) *Warranty of Title under* U.C.C. § 2-312. 2 Hawkland, Uniform Commercial Code Series § 2-312:02 (1992) states in part:

> [T]here may be situations where the seller has the power, but not the right, to convey a perfect title to the goods that may expose the buyer unreasonably to the claim of a third person to ownership. In those cases, there is a breach of warranty of title, even though the buyer has the legal ability to defeat the third-party claim. Such a situation might arise, for example, under section 2-403 where a third party delivers goods to a merchant for repair. If the merchant is in the business of selling goods of the kind, he had the power to sell the entrusted goods to a buyer in the ordinary course free and clear of the third party's ownership rights. This new rule is one which many third parties might not be aware of or understand and some third parties might proceed against the buyer in the ordinary course, even though they could not win a lawsuit if he could establish that status. That being the case, the buyer should be able to revoke acceptance, or sue for breach of warranty of title on the ground that the transfer was not rightful. The test is not whether the buyer can win a lawsuit against third-party claimants, but whether he is unreasonably exposed to such a suit.

Cf. U.C.C. § 3-416 Comment 3. Warranty of title is discussed in Chapter 4, Property Interests.

(4) See U.C.C. §§ 2A-304(2), 2A-305(2)(entrusters to merchants lose to "lessees in the ordinary course of business").

§ 8.03 Voidable Title

Read: U.C.C. §§ 2-403(1), 2-702(3); cf. § 3-404(a).

Read also: U.C.C. §§ 2A-304(1) and (3), 2A-305(1) and (3); CISG Arts. 1(1), (4)(b).

A leading common law case with respect to voidable title is *Phelps v. McQuade*, 220 N.Y. 232, 115 N.E. 441 (1917). In this case, Walter J. Gwynne falsely represented to plaintiffs that he was Baldwin J. Gwynne, a man of financial responsibility. Relying on the truth of this statement, plaintiffs delivered to him upon credit a quantity of jewelry. Gwynne in turn sold it to defendant, who bought it without notice of any defect in title and for value. Learning of the deception practiced upon them, the plaintiffs began an action in replevin to recover the goods. The court stated as follows:

> The only question before us is whether under such circumstances, the vendor of personal property does not retain title thereto after he has parted with possession thereof. . . . Where the vendor of personal property intends to sell his goods to the person with whom he deals, then title passes, even though he be deceived as to that person's identity or responsibility. Otherwise it does not. It is purely a question of the vendor's intention.

> The fact that the vendor deals with the person personally rather than by letter is immaterial, except in so far as it bears upon the question of intent.

> Where the transaction is a personal one, the seller intends to transfer title to a person of credit, and he supposes the one standing before him to be that person. He is deceived. But in spite of that fact his primary intention is to sell his goods to the person with whom he negotiates.

> Where the transaction is by letter the vendor intends to deal with the person whose name is signed to the letter. He knows no one else. He supposes he is dealing with no one else. And while in both cases other facts may be shown that would alter the rule, yet in their absence, in the first, title passes; in the second, it does not. Two cases that illustrate the distinction are [1] *Edmunds v. Merchants' Dispatch Transportation Company*, 135 Mass. 283, and [2] Cundy v. Lindsay, 3 App. Cas. 463.

Id. at 234-5.

> In *Cundy v. Lindsay*, one Blenkarn, signing himself Blenkiron & Co., bought goods by letter of Lindsay & Co. The latter shipped the goods to Blenkiron & Co. They knew of the firm of Blenkiron & Son; believed the letter came from that firm and that the goods were shipped to it. Blenkiron & Son were the persons with whom Lindsay & Co. intended to deal and supposed they were dealing. Under those circumstances it was held that, although Blenkiron obtained possession of the goods, he never acquired title thereto.

> In *Edmunds v. Merchants' Transportation Company*, a swindler, representing himself to be one Edward Pape, personally bought goods of the plaintiff on credit. The court held that the title passed. "The minds of the parties met and agreed upon all the terms of the sale, the thing sold, the price and time of payment, the person selling and the person buying. The fact that the seller was induced to sell by fraud of the buyer made the sale voidable, but not void. He could not have supposed that he was selling to any other person; his intention was to sell to the person present, and identified by sight and hearing; it does not defeat the sale because the buyer assumed a false name, or practised any other deceit to induce the vendor to sell."

. . .

(The Court held for defendant.)

NOTES AND QUESTIONS

Simply, if plaintiff dealt personally with the impostor (face to face), the impostor acquired voidable title and could pass good title to a good faith or bona fide purchaser. If plaintiff dealt with the impostor through the mails, the impostor acquired void title (no title) and could not pass good title even to a bona fide purchaser. Query: Does U.C.C. § 2-403(1)(a) recognize this distinction?

SHERIDAN SUZUKI, INC. v. CARUSO AUTO SALES, INC.

New York Supreme Court, Erie County
110 Misc. 2d 823, 442 N.Y.S.2d 957, 32 U.C.C. Rep. 1127 (1981)

JOSEPH J. SEDITA, JUSTICE.

The court finds itself in the position of having to choose where to place the burden of loss as between two apparently innocent parties. The basic facts of this case are essentially not in dispute. Only the application of the law to those facts is in serious question. Both parties have moved for summary judgment. To the best of this court's knowledge, this is a case of the first impression in New York State.

On May 26, 1981, the plaintiff, Sheridan Suzuki, Inc., (hereinafter Suzuki) "sold" a motorcycle to one Ronald Bouton. Incident to this sale they gave him possession of the motorcycle, a signed bill of sale marked paid in full and registration of the vehicle in said Bouton's name. Additionally, they filed an application for an original Certificate of Title (pursuant to requirements of Article 46 of the New York State Vehicle and Traffic Law). Said certificate was never received by Bouton. Its processing in Albany was interrupted when they were notified by Suzuki of subsequent developments. In return for the subject motorcycle, the plaintiff was given Bouton's check for $3,559.44 in satisfaction of the purchase price. Said check was later dishonored. Bouton has disappeared from the area.

On May 27,1981, (one day after the initial sale), Bouton offered to sell the vehicle to Caruso Auto Sales, Inc. (hereinafter Caruso). After examining the papers that Bouton had "in hand," but before Bouton had received the Certificate of Title from Albany, Caruso "purchased" the motorcycle from Bouton for $2,000.00. Bouton gave Caruso possession of the motorcycle, signed over the registration and assured Caruso that he would transfer the Certificate of Title upon receipt of the title documents from the State. Before accepting the transaction, Caruso had called Suzuki and they had confirmed Bouton's assertion of prior purchase (not yet having notice of the dishonored check). Justice Norman Stiller has granted a preliminary order placing the motorcycle with Suzuki pending a determination of the legal issues raised here.

To unravel and resolve the controversy presented here, we must examine closely the fabric of law designed to regulate these types of relationships.

At common law, a thief could pass no title whatsoever to stolen goods.

However, § 2-403(2) of the Uniform Commercial Code supplanted the common law rule as to goods received "in exchange for a check which is later dishonored . . ." or "delivery was criminal law."[6] This motorcycle was transferred as part of a transaction involving a bad check, rather than as a result of a direct larceny or burglary and therefore it cannot be asserted that any title received by a "bona fide purchaser for value" would be void. The law is clear that a person receiving goods incident to a transaction involving a dishonored check and a fraud receives only voidable title, at best.[7] (See U.C.C. § 2-403, *supra*.) A "bona fide purchaser for value" can receive good title from a person with "voidable" title under the Uniform Commercial Code.

The crucial question at this point becomes the effect of the State Uniform Vehicle Certificate of Title Act (hereinafter UVCTA) on the species of "title" received by Bouton. The courts have an obligation to give effect to all acts of the legislature and to avoid interpretations which result in a conflict between statutes. Where a general statute and a more particular statute overlap, the courts will usually give greater effect to the more particularized statute.

This court takes note of the fact that the Uniform Commercial Code establishes a general rule for commercial transactions. The Uniform Vehicle Certificate of Title Act does not seek to abrogate the U.C.C., but merely seeks to add additional requirements for transactions involving this unique area of "goods," due to unique problems of fraud and theft experienced with motor vehicles. Section 2113(c) of the UVCTA expressly states in part:

. . . a transfer by an owner is not perfected so as to be valid against third parties generally until the provisions of this section . . . have been complied with.

Section 2105 of the UMVTA sets forth the procedures for making an application for the first Certificate of Title. This section makes clear that the requirements of this act are more than ministerial record keeping. The commissioner is required to make a "quasi-judicial" determination as to ownership. (See section 2105(d) of the UMVTA.)

"Title" under this act is not an automatic result once the bureaucratic process is triggered, but is a result of a *determination* of the Department after examining the documents submitted to it. The process of obtaining title is not complete, and the provisions of this statute are not fully complied with until the Department is satisfied that title was in the alleged owner/applicant.

Since the Department suspended the issuance of a title certificate due to its knowledge of the fraud perpetrated herein, the voidable "title" received by Bouton was never perfected as required by the statute (sec 2113, (c), cited *supra*) and could not be successfully passed to a "bona fide purchaser for value." The object of this section is clearly to effectuate the intent of the UVCTA, which is to make transfers of improperly obtained motor vehicles more difficult by requiring a "perfected" title before a successful transfer of a vehicle can be made. An interpretation which

[6] [The Court undoubtedly intended to cite U.C.C. § 2-403(1)(b) and (d).—Ed.]

[7] [For a discussion of seller's right to reclaim goods exchanged for a check which was later dishonored, see Chapter 7, Remedies, at § 7.03; see U.C.C. §§ 2-507(2), 2-511 (3).—Ed.]

avoids this requirement would in effect "extract" the "teeth" built into this legislation and circumvent its clear purpose.

If Bouton had obtained a valid Certificate of Title, his title would have still been voidable, but would have been "perfected" according to the requirements of the law. He could then have successfully passed good title to a "bona fide purchaser for value." (As for example in *White v. Pike*, 240 Iowa 596, 36 N.W.2d 761, where the perpetrator of the fraud had obtained a Certificate of Title in addition to the other usual indicia of ownership.)

Since Bouton never had a perfected title, he could not pass good title to Caruso.

Defendant alleges that Suzuki is equitably estopped from denying Caruso's title because of Suzuki's representation that Bouton had properly received ownership of the vehicle in question. Caruso alleges that he relied upon those representations to his detriment. Equitable estoppel, however, does not operate to create rights which are nonexistent. It may only operate to preclude the denial of a right claimed otherwise to have arisen.

Since Bouton never received the Certificate of Title, he never had perfected title as required under New York Law to enable him to transfer good title. Caruso therefore never got any legal title or right to the vehicle, and therefore has no claim to assert in seeking equitable estoppel against Suzuki's claim.

Buyers who purchase from a seller who does not have a Certificate of Title, do so at their own risk. Caruso took that risk in the hope of making a substantial profit by obtaining a brand new $3,500.00 motorcycle for $2,000.00. The risk he took backfired, and this court cannot protect him from his loss. The law is clear and intended to protect society against exactly the type of fraud perpetrated herein. The duty of this court is to enforce the express mandate of that law.

Accordingly, plaintiff's motion for summary judgment is granted and defendant's motion for summary judgment is denied.

NOTES AND QUESTIONS

(1) In *Kotis v. Nowlin Jewelry*, Inc., 844 S.W.2d 920 (Tex. App. 1992), Nowlin sold a Rolex watch to Sitton who paid with a forged check. Sitton then sold the watch to Kotis. Held: For Nowlin. While Sitton acquired voidable title under U.C.C. § 2-403(1), Kotis was not a good faith purchaser.

(2) *Goods Subject to Certificate of Title.* R. Henson, The Law of Sales 103 (1985) comments (footnotes omitted):

When the goods sold are subject to a certificate of title, as motor vehicles would be in most states, then the application of Section 2-403 is somewhat less clear. The problems basically arise in sales of used vehicles when the seller may not have had "title" and so may be held unable to convey good title to a purchaser, no matter what the purchaser paid and without regard to good faith. It is possible to conclude that Section 2-403 is subject to the operation of the state's certificate of title law [the *Sheridan Suzuki* case, *supra,* is cited], or it may be found that Section 2-403 controls; but this seems unlikely in a state having a certificate of title law specifically covering the problem.

In *Inmi-Etti v. Aluisi*, 492 A.2d 917, 40 U.C.C. Rep. 1612 (Md. Ct. Spec. App. 1985), Appellant Inmi-Etti purchased a new car. Butler converted the car, obtained a certificate of title in his name from the State of Maryland and sold it to car-dealer Pohanka. Inmi-Etti sued Pohanka for conversion. In holding for Inmi-Etti the court said:

> Under the undisputed facts of the present case Butler possessed void title when Pohanka dealt with him. Although the record simply is not sufficient for us to decide whether Butler actually stole the appellant's vehicle, it is undisputed that the appellant at no time made a voluntary transfer to Butler. Thus, Pohanka obtained no title, and its sale of the vehicle constituted a conversion of the appellant's property. We believe the above analysis sufficient to impose liability upon Pohanka. We will nevertheless answer certain of Pohanka's collateral arguments.

> . . . .

> Implicit in all that we have said so far is the fact that Butler did not obtain title (voidable or otherwise) merely from the fact that he was able to convince the Motor Vehicle Administration to issue a certificate of title for the automobile to him. Although "[a] certificate of title issued by the Administration is prima facie evidence of the facts appearing on it," Md Code (1977, 1984 Repl Vol), § 13-107 of the Transportation Article, the erroneous issuance of such a certificate cannot divest the title of the true owner of the automobile.

> Likewise, we find unpersuasive Pohanka's argument that since Butler had possession of the automobile and a duly issued certificate of title in his name, Pohanka should be protected as a "good faith purchaser for value" under § 2-403 of the Commercial Law Article, *supra.* Such status under that section of the Uniform Commercial Code is relevant in situations where the seller (transferor) is possessed of voidable title. It does not apply to the situation presented by the instant case where the seller had no title at all.

> . . . .

Cf. U.C.C. §§ 2A-304(3), 2A-305(3).

(3) *Seller's Right to Reclaim Under U.C.C. § 2-702.* Section 2-702(2) states in part: "Where the seller discovers that the buyer has received goods on credit while insolvent he may reclaim the goods upon demand made within ten days of the receipt." Subsection (3), however, states: "The seller's right to reclaim under subsection (2) is subject to the rights of a buyer in ordinary course or other good faith purchaser [or lien creditor (1962 Code)] under this Article (Section 2-403). . . ."

For discussion see Chapter 7, Remedies, at § 7.03. As to seller's rights against buyer's trustee in bankruptcy, see Bankruptcy Code § 546(c).

(4) *Secured Party and Lien Creditor as Good Faith Purchaser.* A person with a voidable title has power to transfer a good title to a good faith *purchaser* for value. U.C.C. § 2-403(1). "Purchaser" means a person who takes by "purchase," *i.e.*, any . . . voluntary transaction creating an interest in property." U.C.C. § 1-201(32), (33). A U.C.C. Article 9 secured party has engaged in a voluntary transaction (U.C.C. § 9-102(2)) creating an interest (security interest, § 1-201(37)) in property. See U.C.C. § 9-103 Comment 7 (third paragraph). See *Genesee Merchants Bank & Trust Co. v. Tucker*, 143 Mich. App. 339, 372 N.W.2d 546, 42 U.C.C. Rep. 150 (1985) (unpaid

cash seller's right to reclaim goods from buyer subordinate to "floating lien" of buyer's secured creditor); *In re Misco Supply Co.*, 42 U.C.C. Rep. 150 (Mich. 1986) (secured parties which had "floating lien" on debtor's inventory and after-acquired property were good faith "purchasers" for "value").

Lien creditors (creditors who have acquired a lien on the property involved by attachment, levy or the like, U.C.C. § 9-301(3)) are not "purchasers" and consequently cannot qualify as "good faith purchasers for value." U.C.C. § 2-403(1). A "purchaser" is involved in a voluntary transaction; an attaching or levying creditor is involved in an involuntary transaction. The debtor whose property is seized by the sheriff cannot be said to have given his assent. This result reflects the common law position that "a creditor as such is not protected against latent equities against the judgment debtor and that he stands in all respects in the shoes of the judgment debtor." S. Riesenfeld, Creditors' Remedies and Debtors' Protection 130 (4th ed. 1987). The rationale for the common law position is well stated in *Oswego Starch Factory v. Lendrum*, 57 Iowa 573, 10 N.W. 900(1881), with respect to the rights of an attaching creditor:

> The title of the property was not divested by the attachment, but remained in the vendees. The seizure conferred upon the creditors no right to the property as against plaintiff other or different from those held by the vendee. The sole effect of the seizure was to place the property in the custody of the law, to be held until the creditors' claims had been adjudicated and the property could be sold on execution. They parted with no consideration in making the attachment, and their condition as to their claims were in no respect changed. Their acts were induced by no representation or procurement originating with plaintiff which would in law or equity give them rights to the property as against plaintiff. Plaintiff's right to rescind the sale inhered in the contract and attached to the property. It could not be defeated except by a purchaser for value without notice of fraud. . . .

> Our position is simply this, that as an attaching creditor parts with no consideration, and does not change his position as to his claim, to his prejudice, he stands in the shoes of the vendee. . . . The innocent purchaser for value occupies a different position, and his rights are, therefore, different.

See *Citizens Bank of Roseville v. Taggart*, 143 Cal. App. 3d 318,191 Cal. Rptr. 729, 36 U.C.C. Rep. 529 (1983) (bank as lien creditor did not have status of good faith purchaser for value; its rights in an auto on which it had levied were subordinate to the reclamation rights of the unpaid seller. Bank had not given value for the auto nor had it relied on the ostensible ownership or voidable title of the debtor to the auto).

See U.C.C. §§ 2-402, 2A-301, 2A-307, 2A-308.

§ 8.04 A Note on Bulk Transfers

Former Article 6 of the Uniform Commercial Code dealt with what were termed "bulk transfers"—defined as a transfer in bulk and not in the ordinary course of business of a major part of the inventory of an enterprise whose principal business is the sale of merchandise from stock. Former U.C.C. §§ 6-102, 6-103. The purpose of Article 6 was to protect the unsecured creditors of such enterprises against the possibility that the owner might suddenly and without notice sell out and disappear, leaving the unsecured creditors without any recourse against the purchaser of the business. To this end, Article 6 required that when a bulk transfer occurred, a schedule of property to be transferred and a list of the seller's creditors must be prepared, ·

and notice of the proposed transfer must be sent to the seller's creditors at least ten days before the buyer takes possession of the goods, or pays for them. See former U.C.C. §§ 6-104 through 6-107. The transfer was ineffective against any creditor of the seller unless the notice was given. Former U.C.C. § 6-104. It is important to note that Article 6 did not protect the seller's creditors by requiring that the buyer pay them, or that the seller use the purchase price for their benefit. The article was primarily a notice provision.

Under the 1989 Code Article 6 was renamed "Bulk Sales." Alternative A repealed Article 6; Alternative B revised Article 6. The Comment to revised § 6-101 recites the major changes from former Article 6, e.g., buyer's noncompliance does not render the sale ineffective, rather, the liability of a noncomplying buyer is for damages. Most states thus far have chosen Alternative A.

CHAPTER 9

LEASES OF GOODS

§ 9.01 Introduction

Read: Forward to Article 2A and U.C.C. § 2A-101 Comment.

Article 2A deals with leases. U.C.C. §§ 2A-102, 2A-104. A lease is defined as "a transfer of the right to possession and use of goods for a term in return for consideration, but a sale . . . or retention or creation of a security interest is not a lease." U.C.C. §§ 2A-103(1)(j) and Comment (j), 1-201(37), 2-106(1), 9-102(2).

Chapters 1 through 8 deal with sales of goods: contract formation, warranties, performance, remedies, and rights of third parties. Throughout these chapters there are references to analogous lease provisions. Consequently, it is anticipated that discussion of leases will be made in association with their sales counterpart.

One area for discussion in this chapter involves warranties with respect to the "finance lease." Read U.C.C. §§ 2A-210 through 2A-216, then proceed to § 9.02 immediately below.

§ 9.02 Warranties in Finance Leases

Read: U.C.C. §§ 2A-103(1)(g), 2A-209, 2A-407, 9-206(1).

IN RE O.P.M. LEASING SERVICES

United States Bankruptcy Court, Southern District of New York
21 B.R. 993 (1982)

BURTON R. LIFLAND, BANKRUPTCY JUDGE.

This matter is before the Court on the Motion of LaSalle National Bank ("LaSalle") for summary judgment pursuant to Bankruptcy Rule 756 and Rule 56 of the Federal Rules of Civil Procedure to dismiss the claim of the State of West Virginia, Department of Finance and Administration ("West Virginia"), and to recover judgment as to liability on LaSalle's counter-claim for accelerated rents.

I. STATEMENT OF FACTS

The instant adversary proceeding within this Chapter 11 case concerns a set of 22 leases of computer equipment (the "Equipment Schedules") by O.P.M. Leasing Services, Inc. ("OPM"), the debtor herein, to plaintiff West Virginia. Pursuant to three security agreements (the "Security Agreements") and three agreements captioned "Consent and Agreement," 19 of these leases are now pledged to defendant LaSalle as security for OPM's indebtedness under three notes held by LaSalle.

West Virginia commenced this adversary proceeding on August 19, 1981 against James P. Hassett as Reorganization Trustee of OPM ("the Trustee"), OPM, LaSalle, International Business Machines Corporation ("IBM") and Computer Equipment Services Corporation ("CES"). The complaint seeks a turnover of $107,252.36, plus accrued interest, from the OPM estate to IBM and CES ("the Maintenance Providers") for maintenance payments which OPM is alleged to have failed to provide, a declaration that the Equipment Schedules have been terminated and an order of the Bankruptcy Court enjoining the Maintenance Providers from terminating maintenance on the hardware pending resolution of the adversary proceeding.[1]

The basis which West Virginia has asserted for this relief is OPM's alleged breach of the Equipment Schedules in its failure to make monthly payments of maintenance fees directly to defendants IBM and CES on 20 of the 22 Equipment Schedules (the "Maintenance Providers"). According to West Virginia's pleadings, this breach by OPM terminates LaSalle's rights as assignee to receive lease payments. Alternatively, West Virginia asserts in its pleadings that LaSalle's purported knowledge of OPM's breach prevents it from claiming that the Equipment Schedules have not terminated.

LaSalle's answer denies all of the material allegations of the complaint and alleges as an affirmative defense that the terms of the Consent and Agreements executed by West Virginia bar West Virginia's claim. LaSalle also asserts in a counterclaim that beginning in March, 1981, West Virginia failed to make the full amount of lease payments under the Equipment Schedules assigned to LaSalle. LaSalle gave written notice of West Virginia's default and of its election to accelerate the balance of assigned lease payments pursuant to Section 12.2 of the Master Lease. Accordingly, LaSalle seeks judgment herein on its counterclaim in the amount of $2,115,388.30, although LaSalle's present motion seeks judgment on liability only.

The reply of West Virginia to LaSalle's counterclaim denies all its material allegations and asserts nine affirmative defenses. These defenses include sovereign immunity under the Tenth and Eleventh Amendments and under West Virginia law, waiver by LaSalle of its right to accelerate rent payments, full payment of all rentals due to LaSalle and that LaSalle is bound by its assignor's default in making maintenance payments.

The Trustee has also contemporaneously moved to reject the 19 leases which were assigned to LaSalle.[2] LaSalle opposes this motion to reject based on its concern that its security interest in the lease payments will not be adequately protected if West Virginia's absolute and unconditional promise to pay rents is not fully enforced.

The Agreements Governing the Transactions at Issue

The rights and duties of each of the three parties to the computer leases at issue herein are specified in the Master Lease as well as in the Equipment Schedules, the Security Agreements and the Consents and Agreements.

West Virginia, as lessee, and OPM, as lessor, are parties to the Master Lease dated March 28, 1980. Each Equipment Schedule incorporates all of the terms and conditions of the Master

---

[1] West Virginia and the Maintenance Providers entered into a stipulation in the adversary proceeding that the Maintenance Providers would continue to provide maintenance on the hardware pending resolution of the adversary proceeding in exchange for West Virginia's continued remittance of current maintenance payments. This stipulation was so ordered by the Bankruptcy Court on October 9, 1981.

[2] In the Trustee's motion to reject the 19 assigned leases, he also moved to assume the three unassigned leases. That portion of this motion relating to assumption only was the subject of a Stipulation of Settlement between West Virginia and the Trustee which was So Ordered by this Court on June 29, 1982.

Lease. The Master Lease and each Equipment Schedule are to be construed in accordance with New York law.

Section 5.3 of the Master Lease between OPM and West Virginia contains detailed provisions regarding assignments of Equipment Schedules by OPM. Section 5.3(ii) provides that OPM's "assignee shall not be obligated to perform any of the obligations of (OPM) under any Equipment Schedule other than [OPM's] obligation not to take any action to disturb Lessee's quiet and peaceful possession of the Equipment." In Section 5.3(iii) the parties agree that "(l)essee's obligation to pay directly to such assignee the amounts due from lessee under any Equipment Schedule . . . shall be *absolutely unconditional* and shall be payable whether or not any Equipment Schedule is terminated by operation of law, any act of the parties or otherwise." (emphasis added) ("the hell or high water clause"). In Section 5.3(iv), OPM and West Virginia is to pay all amounts due under any Equipment Schedule to OPM's assignee "notwithstanding any defense, offset or counterclaim whatever whether by reason of breach of such Equipment Schedule or otherwise which it may or might now or hereafter have as against Lessor (Lessee reserving its right to have recourse directly against Lessor on account of any such counterclaim or offset)" ("the waiver of defenses clause"). Section 14 of the Master Lease provides that the lessee's unconditional obligation to an assignee continues "until all amounts . . . shall have been paid in full."

Each Equipment Schedule obligates OPM to reimburse West Virginia for monthly maintenance charges actually paid by West Virginia under West Virginia's separate maintenance agreements with the Maintenance Providers for the leased equipment. However, Paragraph 4(a) of each Equipment Schedule provides that OPM's obligation to pay for maintenance of the equipment leased to lessee "shall in (no) manner diminish, impair or otherwise affect any of Lessee's obligations under this Equipment Schedule, including, without limitation, the payment of all monthly rental payments. . . ." Thus, by the terms of these Schedules, West Virginia specifically agreed that any breach of OPM's maintenance obligations shall not affect West Virginia's duty to make monthly lease payments.

The three Security Agreements, identical in form, assign as security to LaSalle OPM's interest in 19 of OPM's 22 Equipment Schedules.[3] Each Security Agreement provides for the assignment of all of West Virginia's monthly lease payments to LaSalle.[4] According to these Security Agreements, LaSalle may demand payment or delivery of and shall receive and collect all money under the assigned Equipment Schedules and apply the funds to OPM's indebtedness. Furthermore, according to Section 1.08 of these Security Agreements, upon a default by West Virginia under the Master Lease, LaSalle is entitled to exercise all of OPM's rights under the assigned Equipment Schedules, but is not thereby to assume any of OPM's obligations to West Virginia.

In each Consent and Agreement, West Virginia acknowledges and consents to OPM's assignment of Equipment Schedules to LaSalle. West Virginia also agrees therein to make all

[3] By these three Security Agreements, LaSalle originally held a security interest in 20 of the Equipment Schedules. However, a letter agreement dated August 29, 1980 released LaSalle's security interest in Equipment Schedule No. 1-02 and the computer equipment leased to West Virginia thereunder. LaSalle continues to hold a security interest in the remaining 19 Equipment Schedules.

[4] The 22 Equipment Schedules were classified as "Series A" (5 Schedules), "Series B" (4 Schedules), "Series C" (10 Schedules), and "Unclassified" (3 Schedules). LaSalle transferred funds to OPM in consideration of assignment of OPM's interest in these Schedules as follows:

Series A—June 10, 1980/Series C—August 28, 1980

Series B—August 28, 1980/Unclassified—Never Assigned

monthly lease payments to LaSalle "without abatement, reduction, counterclaim or offset . . . as a result of any breach of any obligation of OPM." *See* Affidavit of Ray H. Camp in support of LaSalle's Summary Judgment Motion ("Camp Affidavit"), Exhibits 9, 10 and 11 at 2.

In addition, opinions from the office of the highest legal officer of West Virginia as to the enforceability of the Equipment Schedules were provided on two occasions. The Deputy Attorney General wrote that the Equipment Schedules and Consents and Agreements each constituted "a legal, valid and binding instrument enforceable in accordance with its terms against (West Virginia)". He qualified this opinion only by asserting: "My opinion is qualified to the extent that the remedies available to enforce your rights under the Transactional Documents may be limited by bankruptcy, insolvency and other laws respecting creditors' rights and remedies generally." *See* Camp Affidavit, Exhibit 5, at 3, Exhibit 7 at 13.

West Virginia concedes having made no monthly lease payments during March, April, May and June 1981. Following these four successive months of default, on July 3, 1981, LaSalle gave West Virginia written notice of its default and of LaSalle's election to accelerate the balance of lease payments. It was not until after LaSalle's notice of acceleration in July 1981 that West Virginia made lease payments on the assigned Equipment Schedules totalling $160,125.00 for the months of March, April and May 1981. LaSalle contends that this amount was less than the properly corresponding amount of West Virginia's lease obligation.[5]

II. ISSUES PRESENTED

The issues presented by LaSalle's motion for summary judgment on its counterclaim and by West Virginia's cross-motion to dismiss LaSalle's counterclaim are:

(1) Whether West Virginia can validly assert that it is immune from LaSalle's counterclaim for accelerated rents because it chooses to invoke its sovereign immunity;

(2) Whether there remain any material issues of fact in dispute so as to preclude summary judgment in favor of LaSalle or whether LaSalle may be granted judgment as a matter of law on its counterclaim for accelerated rentals;

(3) Whether the clause in the Master Lease between OPM and West Virginia creating West Virginia's "absolutely unconditional" obligation to pay rents to OPM's assignee (LaSalle) shall be given full force and effect as a matter of law despite OPM's breach of its maintenance payments obligation.

For the reasons hereinafter stated we grant LaSalle summary judgment on its counterclaim for accelerated rentals and deny West Virginia's motion to dismiss this counterclaim.

III. DISCUSSION OF LAW

A. *Waiver of Sovereign Immunity*

West Virginia contends that LaSalle's counterclaim is not cognizable in this Court because it chooses to invoke its sovereign immunity to this counterclaim. For the reasons hereinafter

---

[5] West Virginia has failed to make any lease payments since the commencement of this adversary proceeding in August 1981. However, it has made "use and occupancy" payments into an escrow fund at the rate of $61,100 (exclusive of maintenance) per month retroactively and $86,060 (inclusive of maintenance) per month pursuant to an escrow order by this court dated December 11, 1981.

stated, this Court holds that West Virginia has irrevocably waived its sovereign immunity by initiating these proceedings.

[Extensive discussion omitted.]

B. *Merits of LaSalle's Counterclaim*

1. *Hell and High Water Clause*

LaSalle contends that it is entitled to summary judgment as to West Virginia's liability on LaSalle's counterclaim for accelerated rental payments[6] pursuant to Rule 56 of the Federal Rules of Civil Procedureas adopted in bankruptcy matters by Bankruptcy Rule 756. West Virginia contends that LaSalle is not entitled to judgment as a matter of law because there are material issues of fact in dispute as to whether LaSalle took its assignment of rents from OPM in good faith without notice of claims or defenses. For the reasons hereinafter detailed, we grant summary judgment to LaSalle on its counterclaim as to West Virginia's liability.

This holding is based on our view that under New York law, which applies pursuant to the terms of the Master Lease, the plain meaning of West Virginia's absolutely unconditional promise to make rental payments to OPM must be given full force and effect as a matter of law. *See, e.g., Breed v. Insurance Co. of North America*, 46 N.Y.2d 351, 385, N.E.2d 1280, 413 N.Y.S.2d 352 (1978); *Laba v. Carey*, 29 N.Y.2d 302, 277 N.E.2d 641, 327 N.Y.S.2d 613 (1971); *Luna Park Housing Corp. v. Besser*, 38 A.D.2d 713, 329 N.Y.S.2d 332 (2d Dep't 1972).

This "hell or high water" provision contained in Section 5.3 (iii) of the Master Lease provides:

(iii) (West Virginia's) obligation to pay directly to such assignee the amounts due from Lessee under any Equipment Schedule (whether as rent or otherwise) shall be *absolutely unconditional* and shall be payable whether or not *any* Equipment Schedule is terminated by operation of law, any act of the parties or otherwise . . . (emphasis added).[7]

In essence, this unequivocal provision mandates that regardless of any remedies West Virginia may invoke against OPM, including a defense or claim as to OPM's default in paying the Maintenance Providers, West Virginia may not terminate LaSalle's unconditional right to payment. West Virginia was well aware of this unconditional right to payment of rentals when it executed the Consent and Agreements to the assignments by OPM to LaSalle. *See* Camp Affidavit, exhibits 9, 10 and 11. In addition, the Attorney General of West Virginia gave his express written approval to the content of the Master Lease between OPM and LaSalle, including this hell and high water clause. *See* Camp Affidavit, Exhibit 5 at 3, and Exhibit 7 at 3.

To deny this clause its full force and effect would effectively reconstruct the contract contrary to the intent of the parties, which reconstructions would be impermissible. *See, e.g., Rodolitz*

---

[6] LaSalle is fully entitled to accelerate the rentals due it from West Virginia upon West Virginia's default pursuant to Section 12.2 of the Master Lease. In addition, it informed West Virginia in writing of its intention to accelerate although it was not obligated to give such notice pursuant to Section 12.2.

[7] In addition, Section 4(a) of the Equipment Schedules, the source of OPM's maintenance obligations to West Virginia, contains another express limitation on West Virginia's remedies for any failure by OPM to make maintenance payments. It provides:

(West Virginia) covenants and agrees that nothing contained in this Section 4(a) shall in any manner diminish, impair or otherwise affect any of (West Virginia's) obligations under this Equipment Schedule, including, without limitation, the payment of all monthly rental payments . . . (OPM) shall indemnify and hold (West Virginia) harmless in respect of any losses suffered by (West Virginia) by reason of a failure to pay (maintenance charges). . . .

v. Neptune Paper Products, Inc., 22 N.Y.2d 383, 386, 239 N.E.2d 628, 630, 292 N.Y.S.2d 878, 881 (1968).

Moreover, it is a well-settled principle that "parties to a contract are given broad latitude within which to fashion their own remedies for breach of contract . . . . It follows that contractual limitations upon remedies are generally to be enforced unless unconscionable".[8] *Wilson Trading Corp. v. David Ferguson, Ltd.*, 23 N.Y.2d 398, 404, 244 N.E.2d 685, 687, 297 N.Y.S.2d 108, 111-112 (1968).

More specifically, courts have uniformly given full force and effect to "hell and high water" clauses in the face of various kinds of defaults by the party seeking to enforce them. *National Equipment Rental v. J. & I. Carting*, Inc., 73 A.D.2d 666, 423 N.Y.S.2d 205 (2d Dep't 1979); *Dixie Groceries, Inc. v. Albany Business Machines*, 156 Ga.App. 36, 274 S.E.2d 81, 83 (1990). *See also First National Bank of Atlanta v. Harrison*, 408 F.Supp. 137, 140 (N.D. Ga. 1975), *aff'd*, 529 F.2d 1350 (5th Cir. 1976).[9]

The courts in all of the above-cited cases held that clauses containing unconditional promises are strictly enforceable as a matter of law. In so doing, they have found summary judgment in favor of the lessor or its assignee because no facts submitted or to be submitted by the lessee opposing summary judgment are in any way relevant to the lessee's unequivocal liability based on these hell and high water provisions.[10]

In *National Equipment Rental, supra*, the court, faced with a lessor's failure to file a criminal complaint against an alleged thief of the equipment at issue, held that the lessor's inaction did

---

[8] Even considering the law of the State of West Virginia (although West Virginia does not expressly dispute in its submissions to this Court that the rights and liabilities of the parties are governed by the law of the State of New York), the hell and high water clause herein is not illegal or unconscionable as West Virginia urges.

West Virginia has cited and this court has found no West Virginia Statute or other provision proscribing double payments by West Virginia. Also West Virginia has misconstrued the effect of a rejection of these leases would not terminate the Equipment Schedules and require the turnover of the equipment. Such a rejection merely constitutes a breach of the lease. *See* Code Section 365(g) Supp. IV 1980. Counsel for the Trustee and LaSalle, recognizing this point, expressly waiving rights, declared that they have absolutely no interest in retrieving the equipment while at the same time requiring West Virginia to pay rent for it. *See* Transcript of Oral Argument on the instant motions at pp. 40, 75-76.

Moreover, if West Virginia is required to make double maintenance payments, these payments are a foreseeable consequence flowing form the structure of the maintenance payments contracts. West Virginia and OPM structured the arrangement in such a way as to make West Virginia directly liable to the Maintenance Providers while making OPM liable to West Virginia for reimbursement of these payments. However, the Maintenance Providers were not made a party to OPM's agreement to reimburse West Virginia. By not making the Maintenance Providers a party to this agreement, West Virginia left itself vulnerable to the possibility of double payments.

Furthermore, the highest legal officer of the State of West Virginia expressly approved the content of these leases. The Attorney General's Office declared each of them "a legal, valid and binding instrument enforceable in accordance with its terms. . . ." Camp Affidavit, Ex 5 at 3, Ex 7 at 3.

[9] In addition, commentators have echoed the strict enforceability of these hell or high water clauses. *See, e.g.*, R. Contino, Legal and Financial Aspects of Equipment Leasing Transactions, 29, 87-88 (1979), where the author states:

Finance leases frequently contain a "hell or high water" rent commitment. Under this type of obligation, a lessee is required to *unconditionally* pay the full rent when due. He is not permitted to make any deduction even though he has a legitimate claim against the lessor for money owed. This is not as bad as it sounds for a lessee, since he can still bring a lawsuit against the lessor for any claims. *Id.* at 29.

[10] In addition, conspicuous disclaimers of warranty, like hell and high water clauses, have served as the basis for decisions enabling equipment lessors to collect lease paymentsnotwithstanding the merchantability of these products. *See, e.g., Glenn Dick Equipment Co. v. Galey Construction*, Inc., 97 Idaho 216, 541 P.2d 1184 (1975); *Bakal v. Burroughs Corp.*, 74 Misc.2d 202, 205, 343 N.Y.S.2d 541 (N.Y. Sup. Ct. 1972).

not constitute a defense as a matter of law to the lessee's obligation to pay rent unconditionally. Similarly, in *Dixie Groceries, supra*, the Georgia court held that such a clause in an equipment lease remains inviolate as a matter of law, even where facts submitted by the lessee show a failure by the lessor to repair or maintain the equipment.[11]

The essential practical consideration requiring liability as a matter of law in these situations is that these clauses are essential to the equipment leasing industry. To deny their effect as a matter of law would seriously chill business in this industry because it is by means of these clauses that a prospective financier-assignee of rental payments is guaranteed meaningful security for his outright loan to the lessor. Without giving full effect to such clauses, if the equipment were to malfunction, the only security for this assignee would be to repossess equipment with substantially diminished value. *See Contino, supra*, at 87; B. Fritch and A. Reitman, Equipment Leasing -Leveraged Leasing, 131-32 (1977).

Further justification for giving full force and effect to the hell and high water clause herein is found in the fact that OPM is a finance lessor, not a merchant lessor. Courts have distinguished between these two types of equipment lessors in determining whether a lessor's obligation to make payments is separate and apart from the maintenance and performance of the equipment. In the instant case, the lessor involved is a finance lessor whose only service is to provide funds and who is not merchant lessor. A merchant lessor is one who deals in goods and holds itself out as having specialized knowledge about the design, operation and repair of the chattel leased. *See Patriot General Life Insurance v. CFC Investment Co.*, —Mass. App.—, 420 N.E.2d 918 (1981). Since OPM only provided the financing for the lease to West Virginia and thus is a finance lessor, West Virginia had no independently justifiable reason to rely upon OPM for any technical judgment or to hold OPM responsible for the making of maintenance payments on its behalf. *See id.*

Accordingly, whether a bad faith assignment or an assignment on notice of default in maintenance payments took place is irrelevant in deciding this summary judgment motion because of the inclusion of a hell and high water clause in the Master Lease. Thus, under Rule 56(c), as applied in bankruptcy matters by Rule 756, West Virginia has failed to demonstrate a genuine issue of material fact and the case is ripe for summary judgment. *See Leasing Services Corporation v. Justice and Childers*, 673 F.2d 70 (2d Cir. 1982).

The argument advanced by West Virginia against summary judgment concerning facts to be raised by it imputing notice of lack of good faith to LaSalle is misplaced; such facts could only perhaps have relevance absent a hell and high water clause. West Virginia has apparently confused the hell and high water provision with the waiver of defenses clause which was also included in the Master Lease, Section 5.3(iv).[12] If only a waiver of defense clause were present, then, pursuant to Uniform Commercial Code Section 9-206,[13] this court would have to examine the

---

[11] In like fashion, the court in *Luna, supra*, found summary judgment based on the plain meaning of an unequivocal apartment lease provision. Furthermore, the court, in *First National Bank of Atlanta, supra*, held that the parol evidence rule barred the introduction of facts concerning an alleged oral contract in the face of an unconditional promissory note.

[12] This clause waiving defenses which West Virginia could have asserted against OPM absent an assignment to LaSalle is contained in Section 5.3(iv) of the Master Lease. It states:

Lessee shall pay all amounts due from Lessee under any Equipment Schedule (Whether as rent or otherwise) to such assignee, notwithstanding any defense, offset or counterclaim whatever, whether by reason of breach of such Equipment Schedule or otherwise which it may or might now or hereafter have as against Lessor. . . .

[13] Uniform Commercial Code Section 9-206 provides in relevant part:

sufficiency of the facts raised by West Virginia concerning LaSalle's purported lack of good faith and notice of default in taking the assignment. However, here, the hell and high water clause renders West Virginia liable as a matter of law irrespective of any inference raised as to notice or good faith.[14]

Accordingly, this court grants summary judgment on liability only in favor of LaSalle on its counterclaim for accelerated rentals.

2. *The Result Absent Hell and High Water*

Even absent this Court's granting full force and effect to the hell and high water clause in the Master Lease, West Virginia's merely conclusory allegation that LaSalle took the assignment in bad faith and with notice of default is insufficient to raise a triable issue of fact because West Virginia has failed to plead the facts constituting alleging fraud and notice with the specificity required by Rule 56(c). Thus, under Section 9-206 of the Uniform Commercial Code, West Virginia's contractual waiver of all defenses to LaSalle's counterclaim for rental payments, including the waiver of its defense of default in maintenance payments, is enforceable.

The thrust of West Virginia's Rule 3(g) statement[15] and other affidavits in opposition to summary judgment[16] is that at the time these assignments of rent were made, LaSalle either knew or should have known that OPM had defaulted on payments to the Maintenance Providers. Such knowledge, either actual or imputed, is alleged by West Virginia to constitute bad faith which, under U.C.C. § 9-206(1), permits West Virginia to assert a defense to LaSalle's counterclaim for accelerated rentals.

---

[1] [A]n agreement by a buyer or lessee that he will not assert against an assignee any claim or defense which he may have against the seller or lessor is enforceable by an assignee who takes his assignment for value, in good faith, and without notice of a claim or defense, except as to defenses of a type which may be asserted against a holder in due course of a negotiable instrument under the Article on Commercial Paper. U.C.C. § 9-206 (McKinney 1964).

[14] Our holding as to the full force and effect of the hell and high water clause as a matter of law is intended to be the law of the case on this issue. The only objection raised to the Trustee's motion to reject the 19 unassigned leases is raised by LaSalle and concerns the adequacy of protection of LaSalle's security interest in the rental payments absent full enforcement of the hell and high water clause. Accordingly, there appears to be no longer any impediment to the Trustee's motion to reject.

[15] Local Rule 3(g) provides:

(g) Upon motion for summary judgment to Rule 56 of the Federal Rules of Civil Procedure, there shall be annexed to the notice of motion a separate, short and concise statement of the material facts as to which the moving party contends there is no issue to be tried. Failure to submit such a statement constitutes grounds for denial of the motion. The papers opposing a motion for summary judgment shall include a separate, short and concise statement of the material facts as to which it is contended that there exists a genuine issue to be tried.

All material facts set forth in the statement required to be served by the moving party will be deemed to be admitted unless controverted by the statement required to be served by the opposing party. Local Rule 3(g), Rules for the Southern District of New York (1980).

[16] This Rule 56 motion was fully argued, briefed and marked "submitted" as ripe for determination by the Court on May 20, 1982. None of the parties requested leave of the court to submit post-submission papers or memoranda. Notwithstanding the consensual yield to this court's determination of a mature motion, West Virginia on June 30, 1982, more than one month after this court undertook deliberation, and six months after the original notice of motion, filed an additional affidavit with the court clerk with the apparent intention of raising belated issues of fact. The submission was without application to, or leave of, the court and is in violation of Rule 3(c)(3) of the Civil Rules of the District Court for the Southern District of New York. Accordingly, the affidavit is outside the scope of this Court's consideration.

Rule 56(e) of the Federal Rules of Civil Procedure provides in relevant part:

> When a motion for summary judgment is made and supported as provided in this rule, an adverse party may not rest upon the mere allegations or denials of his pleading, but his response, by affidavits or as otherwise provided in this rule, must set forth specific facts showing that there is genuine issue for trial. If he does not so respond, summary judgment, if appropriate, shall be entered against him.

Fed. R. Civ. P. 56(e).

LaSalle flatly denies having had any knowledge of OPM's default and any lack of good faith on its part. Rule 56(e) requires West Virginia to come forward with affirmative proof of specific facts to contradict this denial by LaSalle. As the court in *Applegate v. Top Associates, Inc.*, 425 F.2d 92 (2d Cir. 1970), stated: "To avoid summary judgment . . . a plaintiff must do more than whet the curiosity of the court; he must support vague accusations and surmise with concrete particulars." *Id.* at 96. *See also Maiorana v. MacDonald*, 596 F.2d 1072, 1080 (1st Cir. 1979); *Donnelly v. Guion*, 467 F.2d 290, 293 (2d Cir. 1972); *Radio City Music Hall Corp. v. United States*, 135 F.2d 715, 718 (2d Cir. 1943). West Virginia has failed completely in presenting such concrete particulars regarding its vague and illusory allegations of bad faith and notice.

West Virginia's affidavits are utterly devoid of any specific facts establishing LaSalle's actual knowledge of OPM's default in complying with the terms of the maintenance agreement.[17] The bare assertion that a dispute exists over the state of mind of a litigant is not *ipso factor* a reason to deny summary judgment. *See Feick v. Fleener*, 653 F.2d 69 (2d Cir. 1981); *Markowitz v. Republic National Bank of New York*, 651 F.2d 825, 828 (2d Cir. 1981); *S.E.C. v. Research Automation Corp.*, 585 F.2d 31, 33-34 (2d Cir. 1978). "Courts, refusing to exalt form over substance, cannot be awed by procedural specters and cannot be swayed by feigned issues." *Feick*, 653 F.2d at 77. *See also Quinn v. Syracuse Model Neighborhood Corp.*, 613 F.2d 438, 445 (2d Cir. 1980); *Applegate v. Top Associates, Inc.*, 425 F.2d at 96.

Similarly, a general innuendo alleging bad faith which points to no particular facts on which to ground the charge is no defense to a motion for summary judgment. *See* Fed. R. Civ. P. Rule 56(e); *Applegate v. Top Associates, Inc.*, 425 F.2d at 96; *In re Carnegie Industries, Inc.*, Bkrtcy. S.D.N.Y., 8 B.R. 983, 986-87, 24 C.B.C. 39; 6 Moore's Federal Practice 56.22(1) at 1324-25 (1982). West Virginia's vague assertion that LaSalle is somehow guilty of bad faith raises no genuine issue as to any material fact to preclude summary judgment. West Virginia's pointing to the general fact that OPM was involved in pyramid schemes without specific reference and without relating such fact to LaSalle is absolutely irrelevant here. *See id.*

Additionally, West Virginia argues that because LaSalle had the right to inspect OPM's books and records under the LaSalle-OPM agreements, knowledge of the default to the Maintenance

---

[17] With regard to constructive or imputed knowledge, that the Attorney General of West Virginia not only gave his approval to the content of the lease between West Virginia and OPM but also approved the assignment to LaSalle after the alleged default, militates against a finding of imputed knowledge and bad faith on the part of LaSalle. Such an imputing of knowledge cannot occur because the only circumstance which could impute bad faith is that LaSalle took the assignment two months after OPM first defaulted on its maintenance payments. This circumstance is greatly overshadowed by the Attorney General's approvals. The Court in *Credit Alliance Corp. v. David O. Crump Sand & Fill Co.*, 470 F. Supp. 489 (S.D.N.Y. 1979), similarly found summary judgment in favor of an equipment lessor although knowledge of default in maintenance could have been imputed from the circumstances. The Court in *Credit Alliance* found that given actual evidence that the lessee had unequivocally acknowledged in writing the complete and satisfactory delivery of the equipment, any knowledge of default that could have been imputed circumstantially was irrelevant. *Id.* at 492.

Providers should be imputed to LaSalle. . . . [T]his imputing of knowledge is greatly overshadowed by West Virginia's express approval of an assignment after the alleged default by OPM. In addition, this argument presupposes the existence of a duty to investigate upon the assignee who takes for value. In *Bankers Trust Co. v. Litton Systems, Inc.*, 599 F.2d 488 (2d Cir. 1979), a lessee of certain equipment similarly sought to impose upon the lessor's secured lender a duty to investigate into matters collateral to the assigned rental payments. In refusing to impose such a duty on the assignee, Second Circuit Judge Moore stated:

> [T]he holder in due course is protected not because of his praiseworthy character, but to the end that commercial transactions may be engaged in *without elaborate investigation of the process leading up to the contract or instrument* and in reliance on the contract rights of one who offers them for sale or to secure a loan. 599 F.2d at 494 (emphasis added). *See also* Gilmore, *The Commercial Doctrine of Good Faith Purchase*, 63 Yale L.J. 1057 (1954).

Although *Litton* involved a claim of bribery against the lessor rather than a default in a contract term as alleged herein, this rationale applies equally here.

Moreover, the opinion letter from the West Virginia Attorney General as to the validity of the rental payments to OPM coupled with West Virginia's execution of Consent and Agreements to the assignment to LaSalle satisfied whatever duty of inquiry LaSalle may have had insofar as OPM's obligations to West Virginia were concerned.

Since West Virginia has presented no specific facts demonstrating the alleged bad faith of LaSalle sufficient to defend against this motion for summary judgment under Rule 56(e), LaSalle is entitled to judgment on its claim for rent as a matter of law.[18]

Accordingly, LaSalle's motion for summary judgment as to West Virginia's liability for accelerated rental payments is granted.[19] West Virginia's cross motion to dismiss the counterclaim is denied.

In addition, in view of our holding affirming West Virginia's independent, absolutely unconditional liability to LaSalle, the rejection by the Trustee of the 19 leases assigned to LaSalle has no effect upon LaSalle's remedies against West Virginia in the event West Virginia defaults.

---

[18] West Virginia also attempts to raise two other kinds of factual issues in its Rule 3(g) statement and affidavits.

First, it states in conclusory terms that there is a factual issue as to whether or not LaSalle took an assignment of the net or gross rentals (including maintenance payments). However, West Virginia submits no facts to support its allegations that only net rentals were assigned to LaSalle. Indeed, the terms "gross" and "net rentals" are found in none of the agreements at issue herein. Moreover, in each Security Agreement, OPM assigns as security "all of its estate, right, title, interest, claim and demand in . . . *the rental payments and rental installments . . . damages and other moneys* (with certain exceptions not here pertinent) from time to time payable to or receivable by OPM under the Equipment Schedules. . . ." West Virginia not only received notice of these assignments, but expressly consented to them in each Consent and Agreement it executed. *See* Camp Affidavit, Exs 9, 10 and 11. Accordingly, this court finds from the Security Agreements that gross rentals were assigned to LaSalle.

Second, West Virginia attempts to raise an issue as to the possible waiver by LaSalle of its assignment from OPM by the means of collection of the rentals. However, all parties agreed in open court at the oral argument on this Motion that they were participants in a pass-through mechanism by which West Virginia would forward checks to OPM who would then endorse them directly over to LaSalle. Thus, there can be no issue as to the waiver of the assignment by the mode of rent collection. *See* Transcript of Argument at 22-23.

[19] The defense West Virginia has raised of lack of appropriations with which to pay a judgment against it is legally insufficient. LaSalle is entitled to a judgment on its counterclaim regardless of whether, as a practical matter, funds can be obtained to satisfy it.

Thus, LaSalle's security interest in the lease payment is fully protected. Therefore, the Trustee's motion to reject these 19 leases is granted.

Settle an order in conformity with this opinion.

NOTES AND QUESTIONS

(1) How would this case be decided assuming Article 2A is applicable? (Observe that the case is referenced in Comment 6 to § 2A-407.)

(2) *Consumer Finance Leases.* With regard to cutting off consumer defenses, King, *Major Problems With Article 2A: Unfairness, "Cutting Off" Consumer Defenses, Unfiled Interests, and Uneven Adoption*, 43 Mercer Law Rev. 869 at 878-80 (1992), observes:[20]

> One may understand why the drafters did not want to place positive liability for damages due to loss or injury from defective goods on the finance lessor; however, whether the financier remains subject to the buyer's defense that the goods are defective with regard to making payments is unclear. Can the buyer cease to make payments on the basis that the goods are defective? If the consumer must still make payments, then his or her defenses have been cut off just as effectively as they were under the old "holder in due course" doctrine. Under the former circumstances, the financier of the transaction purchases commercial paper, while in the lease situation, the financier holds a different piece of paper, a lease, over the head of the consumer. If adequate consumer protection is to exist, the results should be the same.
>
> . . . .

Why leave the matter to even the slightest doubt or to the courts' interpretation? An amendment is in order, and it might read:

Consumer Defenses Preserved

> No consumer shall be barred from raising any defense he or she has based on the quality or performance of the goods or based on the signing of legal documents against the finance lessor or any other party.

If a state has already adopted Article 2A or wants to cover this matter separately, it can pass a special consumer protection statute:

Consumer Protection Against Depriving Consumers Of Their Defenses by Finance Leasing

> No consumer shall be barred from raising against a finance lessor any defense to payment he or she might have concerning the goods or signing of legal documents. All rights preserved against holders in due course of commercial paper or contracts shall be applicable likewise to finance lessors.

The federal government could also enact a similar statute.

---

[20] Copyright © 1992 by Donald King. Reprinted with permission of the author.

CHAPTER 10

DOCUMENTARY TRANSACTIONS

§ 10.01 Documents of Title

[A] Introduction

Read: U.C.C. § 1-201(15), (6), (45); §§ 7-102(1)(d) and (e), 7-104.

Goods are often shipped or stored at certain stages of the contract for sale. Goods may be delivered to a carrier for shipment, or may be stored at a warehouse. In these situations, the carrier or warehouseman has the relationship of a bailee for the shipper or storer. The bailee-carrier will issue a bill of lading (bill). Likewise, the bailee-warehouseman will issue a warehouse receipt (receipt).

The bill or receipt serves two purposes: (1) the bill or receipt is a receipt for the goods received by the issuer (carrier or warehouseman); (2) the bill or receipt serves as evidence of the contract for shipment in the case of the carrier, or as evidence of the contract for storage in the case of the warehouseman. In addition, if the bill or receipt is negotiable, two additional aspects are manifested. Because of the negotiable quality, (1) the person in possession of the bill or receipt is entitled to receive, hold and dispose of the bill or receipt and the goods it covers (the concept of merger or "symbolism" whereby the possessor of the paper controls the right to that which the paper represents); (2) a good faith purchaser of the bill or receipt may acquire greater rights to the bill or receipt and the goods it covers than the purchaser's transferor.

Accordingly, U.C.C. Article 7, which deals with documents of title, involves an application of the law of bailments and the law of negotiable instruments.

Bailment. The three basic tenets of bailment are:

1. A bailment results when the bailee is in lawful possession of goods but the bailee does not have title to them. U.C.C. § 7-102(1)(a).

2. The bailee generally has a duty to exercise ordinary care toward the goods. U.C.C. §§ 7-204, 7-309.

3. Upon termination of the bailment, the bailee is under a duty to deliver the goods either to the bailor or otherwise in accordance with the bailor's instruction. Such delivery may be excused, for example, (a) if the bailed goods are delivered to a person with paramount rights to the goods, or (b) if the bailed goods are taken pursuant to legal process such as a levy or attachment, or (c) if the goods are damaged or destroyed notwithstanding bailee's exercising the proper degree of care.

U.C.C. § 7-403. Further, the bailee may be entitled to a possessory lien for storage or transportation charges. U.C.C. §§ 7-209, 7-307.

Document as negotiable instrument. A negotiable bill of lading or warehouse receipt is analogous to a promissory note under Article 3 Negotiable Instruments. Article 3 paper involves a promise to pay money "to order" or "to bearer." U.C.C. §§ 3-104(a), 3-109, 3-412. Article 7 paper involves a promise to deliver identified goods to "order" or "to bearer." U.C.C. §§ 7-104, 7-403. Appreciation of this similarity will be of assistance in studying both Articles 3 and 7. There is, however, one important distinction: Article 3 paper does not cover any particular money, but Article 7 paper purports to cover identified goods. U.C.C. § 1-201(15).

Also, a delivery order under Article 7 is analogous to a draft (*e.g.*, check) under Article 3. A draft is an order by a drawer to a drawee to pay money to a payee. A delivery order is an order by a bailor (*e.g.*, seller) to a bailee (*e.g.*, warehouse) to deliver goods to a deliveree (*e.g.*, buyer). U.C.C. §§ 3-103(a)(2) and (3), 3-104(e), 7-102(1)(b) and (d).

U.C.C. Article 7 has replaced the Uniform Bills of Lading Act, the Uniform Warehouse Receipts Act and the Uniform Sales Act. U.C.C. §§ 10-102(1), 10-104(1). Note, however, paramount federal law (§ 7-103), the Federal Bills of Lading Act (F.B.L.A.), 49 U.S.C. §§ 80101 et seq. (1994), which in § 80102 states the applicability of the Act:

This chapter applies to a bill of lading when the bill is issued by a common carrier for the transportation of goods —

(1) between a place in the District of Columbia and another place in the District of Columbia;

(2) between a place in a territory or possession of the United States and another place in the same territory or possession;

(3) between a place in a State and a place in another State;

(4) between a place in a State and a place in the same State through another State or a foreign country; or

(5) from a place in a State to a place in a foreign country.

Further, it should be borne in mind that federal legislation, such as the Interstate Commerce Act,[1] the Carriage of Goods by Sea Act,[2] the United States Warehouse Act,[3] etc., may also have an application to the shipment or storage of goods.

Peruse the forms on the following pages. Can you tell why they are negotiable or non-negotiable (aside from their being labeled as such)? Is the delivery order negotiable? Cf. U.C.C. §§ 3-104, 7-104.

---

[1] 49 U.S.C. § 11707.

[2] 46 U.S.C. § 1300 *et seq.*

[3] 7 U.S.C. § 241 *et seq.*

UNIFORM STRAIGHT BILL OF LADING
ORIGINAL—NOT NEGOTIABLE—DOMESTIC

Shipper's No._____

Agent's No._____

GATEWAY TRANSPORTATION CO., Inc.

RECEIVED, subject to the classifications and tariffs in effect on the date of the issue of this Bill of Lading.

From_____, Date_____, 196___

At_____Street,_____City,_____County,_____State

The property described below, in apparent good order, except as noted (contents and condition of contents of packages unknown), marked, consigned, and destined as shown below, which said company (the word company being understood throughout this contract as meaning any person or corporation in possession of the property under the contract) agrees to carry to its usual place of delivery at said destination, if on its own railroad, water line, highway route or routes, or within the territory of its highway operations, otherwise to deliver to another carrier on the route to said destination. It is mutually agreed, as to each carrier of all or any of said property over all or any portion of said route to destination, and as to each party at any time interested in all or any of said property, that every service to be performed hereunder shall be subject to all the conditions not prohibited by law, whether printed or written, herein contained, including the conditions on back hereof, which are hereby agreed to by the shipper and accepted for himself and his assigns.

Consigned to_____

Destination_____Street,_____City,

_____County,_____State

Routing_____

Delivering Carrier_____ Vehicle or Car Initial_____ No._____

Collect On Delivery $_____and remit to:_____

_____Street_____City_____State

No. Packages	DESCRIPTION OF ARTICLES, SPECIAL MARKS, AND EXCEPTIONS	*Weight (Subject to Cor.)	Class or Rate	Check Col.

C. O. D. charge to be paid by { Shipper □ Consignee □

Subject to Section 7 of conditions, if this shipment is to be delivered to the consignee without recourse on the consignor, the consignor shall sign the following statement:

The carrier shall not make delivery of this shipment without payment of freight and all other lawful charges.

_____ (Signature of Consignor)

If charges are to be prepaid write or stamp here, "To be Prepaid."

Received $_____ to apply in prepayment of the charges on the property described hereon.

_____ Agent or Cashier

Per_____ (The signature here acknowledges only the amount prepaid.)

Charges Advanced $_____

*If the shipment moves between two ports by a carrier by water, the law requires that the bill of lading shall state whether it is "carrier's or shipper's weight."

NOTE—Where the rate is dependent on value, shippers are required to state specifically in writing the agreed or declared value of the property.

The agreed or declared value of the property is hereby specifically stated by the shipper to be not exceeding_____ per_____

_____ Shipper_____ Agent

1 Per_____ Per_____

Permanent Address of Shipper:_____Street,_____City,_____State

Moore Business Forms, Inc., 9 Park Ridge, Ill. 40466-4

Form 10-1: Uniform Straight Bill of Lading

(Uniform Domestic Order Bill of Lading adopted by Carriers in Official, Southern, Western and Illinois Classification territories, March 15, 1922, as amended August 1, 1930, and June 15, 1941.)

UNIFORM ORDER BILL OF LADING
(ORIGINAL)

Shipper's No._____

Agent's No._____

RECEIVED, subject to the classifications and tariffs in effect on the date of the issue of this Bill of Lading,

at_____ 19___

from_____

the property described below, in apparent good order, except as noted (contents and condition of contents of packages unknown), marked, consigned, and destined, as indicated below, which said company (the word company being understood throughout this contract as meaning any person or corporation in possession of the property under the contract) agrees to carry to its usual place of delivery at said destination, if on its own road or its own water line, otherwise to deliver to another carrier on the route to said destination. It is mutually agreed, as to each carrier of all or any of said property over all or any portion of said route to destination, and as to each party at any time interested in all or any of said property, that every service to be performed hereunder shall be subject to all the conditions not prohibited by law, whether printed or written, herein contained, including the conditions on back hereof, which are hereby agreed to by the shipper and accepted for himself and his assigns.

The surrender of this Original ORDER Bill of Lading properly indorsed shall be required before the delivery of the property. Inspection of property covered by this bill of lading will not be permitted unless provided by law or unless permission is indorsed on this original bill of lading or given in writing by the shipper.

(Mail or street address of consignee—For purposes of notification and

Consigned to ORDER of_____

Destination_____ State of_____ County of_____

Notify_____

At_____ State of_____ County of_____

Route_____

Delivering Carrier_____ Car Initial_____ Car No._____

NO. PACKAGES	DESCRIPTION OF ARTICLES, SPECIAL MARKS AND EXCEPTIONS	*WEIGHT (Subject to Correction)	CLASS OR RATE	CHECK COLUMN	
					Subject to Section 7 of conditions, if this shipment is to be delivered to the consignee without recourse on the consignor, the consignor shall sign the following statement:
					The carrier shall not make delivery of this shipment without payment of freight and all other lawful charges.
					(Signature of Consignor.)
					If charges are to be prepaid, write or stamp here, "To be Prepaid."
					Received $_____ to apply in prepayment of the charges on the property described hereon.
					Agent or Cashier
					Per_____ (The signature here acknowledges only the amount prepaid.)
					Charges Advanced:
					$

* If the shipment moves between two ports by a carrier by water, the law requires that the bill of lading shall state whether it is "carrier's or shipper's weight."

NOTE—Where the rate is dependent on value, shippers are required to state specifically in writing the agreed or declared value of the property.

The agreed or declared value of the property is hereby specifically stated by the shipper to be not exceeding

_____ per _____

This is to certify that the above articles are properly described by name and are packed and marked and are in proper condition for transportation according to the regulations prescribed by the Interstate Commerce Commission.

The fibre boxes used for this shipment conform to the specifications set forth in the box maker's certificate thereon, and all other requirements of the Uniform Freight Classification.

_____Shipper   _____Agent

Per_____   Per_____

Permanent post-office address of shipper_____

6K 698 Rediform   (This Bill of Lading is to be signed by the shipper and agent of the carrier issuing same.)

Form 10-2: Uniform Straight Bill of Lading

Sec. 1. (a) The carrier or party in possession of any of the property herein described shall be liable as at common law for any loss thereof or damage thereto, except as hereinafter provided.

(b) No carrier or party in possession of all or any of the property herein described shall be liable for any loss thereof or damage thereto or delay caused by the act of God, the public enemy, the authority of law, or the act or default of the shipper or owner, or for natural shrinkage. The carrier's liability shall be that of warehouseman, only, for loss, damage, or delay caused by fire occurring after the expiration of the free time allowed by tariffs lawfully on file (such free time to be computed as therein provided) after notice of the arrival of the property at destination or at the port of export (if intended for export) has been duly sent or given, and after placement of the property for delivery at destination, or tender of delivery of the property to the party entitled to receive it, has been made. Except in case of negligence of the carrier or party in possession (and the burden to prove freedom from such negligence shall be on the carrier or party in possession), the carrier or party in possession shall not be liable for loss, damage, or delay occurring while the property is stopped and held in transit upon the request of the shipper, owner, or party entitled to make such request, or resulting from a defect or vice in the property, or for country damage to cotton, or from riots or strikes.

(c) In case of quarantine the property may be discharged at risk and expense of owner into quarantine depot or elsewhere, as required by quarantine regulations or authorities, or for the carrier's dispatch at nearest available point in carrier's judgment, and in any such case carrier's responsibility shall cease when property is so discharged, or property may be returned by carrier at owner's expense to shipping point, earning freight both ways. Quarantine expenses of whatever nature or kind upon or in respect to property shall be borne by the owners of the property or be a lien thereon. The carrier shall not be liable for loss or damage occasioned by fumigation or disinfection or other acts required or done by quarantine regulations or authorities even though the same may have been done by carrier's officers, agents, or employees, nor for detention, loss, or damage of any kind occasioned by quarantine or the enforcement thereof. No carrier shall be liable, except in case of negligence, for any mistake or inaccuracy in any information furnished by the carrier, its agents, or officers, as to quarantine laws or regulations. The shipper shall hold the carriers harmless from any expense they may incur, or damages they may be required to pay, by reason of the introduction of the property covered by this contract into any place against the quarantine laws or regulations in effect at such place.

Sec. 2. (a) No carrier is bound to transport said property by any particular train or vessel, or in time for any particular market or otherwise than with reasonable dispatch. Every carrier shall have the right in case of physical necessity to forward said property by any carrier or route between the point of shipment and the point of destination. In all cases not prohibited by law, where a lower value than actual value has been represented in writing by the shipper or has been agreed upon in writing as the released value of the property as determined by the classification or tariffs upon which the rate is based, such lower value plus freight charges if paid shall be the maximum amount to be recovered, whether or not such loss or damage occurs from negligence.

(b) As a condition precedent to recovery, claims must be filed in writing with the receiving or delivering carrier, or carrier issuing this bill of lading, or carrier on whose line the loss, damage, injury or delay occurred, within nine months after delivery of the property (or, in case of export traffic, within nine months after delivery at port of export) or, in case of failure to make delivery, then within nine months after a reasonable time for delivery has elapsed; and suits shall be instituted against any carrier only within two years and one day from the day when notice in writing is given by the carrier to the claimant that the carrier has disallowed the claim or any part or parts thereof specified in the notice. Where claims are not filed or suits are not instituted thereon in accordance with the foregoing provisions, no carrier hereunder shall be liable, and such claims will not be paid.

(c) Any carrier or party liable on account of loss of or damage to any of said property shall have the full benefit of any insurance that may have been effected upon or on account of said property, so far as this shall not avoid the policies or contracts of insurance: Provided, That the carrier reimburse the claimant for the premium paid thereon.

Sec. 3. Except where such service is required as the result of carrier's negligence, all property shall be subject to necessary cooperage and baling at owner's cost. Each carrier over whose route cotton or cotton linters is to be transported hereunder shall have the privilege, at its own cost and risk, of compressing the same for greater convenience in handling or forwarding, and shall not be held responsible for deviation or unavoidable delays in procuring such compression. Grain in bulk consigned to a point where there is a railroad, public or licensed elevator, may (unless otherwise expressly noted herein, and then if it is not promptly unloaded) be there delivered and placed with other grain of the same kind and grade without respect to ownership (and prompt notice thereof shall be given to the consignor), and if so delivered shall be subject to a lien for elevator charges in addition to all other charges hereunder.

Sec. 4. (a) Property not removed by the party entitled to receive it within the free time allowed by tariffs, lawfully on file (such free time to be computed as therein provided), after notice of the arrival of the property at destination or at the port of export (if intended for export) has been duly sent or given, and after placement of the property at destination has been made, may be kept in vessel, car, depot, warehouse or place of delivery of the carrier, subject to the tariff charge for storage and to carrier's responsibility as warehouseman, only, or at the option of the carrier, may be removed to and stored in a public or licensed warehouse at the place of delivery or other available place, at the cost of the owner, and there held without liability on the part of the carrier, and subject to a lien for all freight and other lawful charges, including a reasonable charge for storage.

(b) Where nonperishable property which has been transported hereunder to destination is refused by consignee or the party entitled to receive it, or said consignee or party entitled to receive it fails to receive it within 15 days after notice of arrival shall have been duly sent or given, the carrier may sell the same at public auction to the highest bidder, at such place as may be designated by the carrier: Provided, That the carrier shall have first mailed, sent, or given to the consignor notice that the property has been refused or remains unclaimed, as the case may be, and that it will be subject to sale under the terms of this bill of lading if disposition be not arranged for, and shall have published notice containing a description of the property, the name of the party to whom consigned, or, if shipped order notify, the name of the party to be notified, and the time and place of sale, once a week for two successive weeks, in a newspaper of general circulation at the place of sale or nearest place where such newspaper is published: Provided, That 30 days shall have elapsed before publication of notice of sale after said notice that the property was refused or remains unclaimed was mailed, sent, or given.

(c) Where perishable property which has been transported hereunder to destination is refused by consignee or party entitled to receive it, or said consignee or party entitled to receive it shall fail to receive it promptly, the carrier may, in its discretion, to prevent deterioration or further deterioration, sell the same to the best advantage at private or public sale: Provided, That if time serves for notification to the consignee or owner of the refusal of the property or the failure to receive it and request for disposition of the property, such notification shall be given, in such manner as the exercise of due diligence requires, before the property is sold.

(d) Where the procedure provided for in the two paragraphs last preceding is not possible, it is agreed that nothing contained in said paragraphs shall be construed to abridge the right of the carrier at its option to sell the property under such circumstances and in such manner as may be authorized by law.

(e) The proceeds of any sale made under this section shall be applied by the carrier to the payment of freight, demurrage, storage, and any other lawful charges and the expense of notice, advertisement, sale, and other necessary expense and of caring for and maintaining the property, if proper care of the same requires special expense, and should there be a balance it shall be paid to the owner of the property sold hereunder.

(f) Property destined to or taken from a station, wharf, or landing at which there is no regularly appointed freight agent shall be entirely at risk of owner after unloaded from cars or vessels or until loaded into cars or vessels, and, except in case of carrier's negligence, when received from or delivered to such stations, wharves, or landings shall be at owner's risk until the cars are attached to and after they are detached from locomotive or train or until loaded into and after unloaded from vessels.

Sec. 5. No carrier hereunder will carry or be liable in any way for any documents, specie, or for any articles of extraordinary value not specifically rated in the published classifications or tariffs unless a special agreement to do so and a stipulated value of the articles are indorsed hereon.

R47

Uniform Order Bill of Lading (Reverse)
(Sec. 1-5)

Sec. 6. Every party, whether principal or agent, shipping explosives or dangerous goods, without previous full written disclosure to the carrier of their nature, shall be liable for and indemnify the carrier against all loss or damage caused by such goods, and such goods may be warehoused at owner's risk and expense or destroyed without compensation.

Sec. 7. The owner or consignee shall pay the freight and average, if any, and all other lawful charges accruing on said property, but, except in those instances where it may lawfully be authorized to do so, no carrier by railroad shall deliver or relinquish possession at destination of the property covered by this bill of lading until all tariff rates and charges thereon have been paid. The consignor shall be liable for the freight and all other lawful charges, except that if the consignor stipulates, by signature, in the space provided for that purpose on the face of this bill of lading that the carrier shall not make delivery without requiring payment of such charges and the carrier, contrary to such stipulation, shall make delivery without requiring such payment, the consignor (except as hereinafter provided) shall not be liable for such charges. Provided, that, where the carrier has been instructed by the shipper or consignor to deliver said property to a consignee other than the shipper or consignor, such consignee shall not be legally liable for transportation charges in respect of the transportation of said property (beyond those billed against him at the time of delivery for which he is otherwise liable) which may be found to be due after the property has been delivered to him, if the consignee (a) is an agent only and has no beneficial title in said property, and (b) prior to delivery of said property has notified the delivering carrier in writing of the fact of such agency and absence of beneficial title, and, in the case of a shipment reconsigned or diverted to a point other than that specified in the original bill of lading, has also notified the delivering carrier in writing of the name and address of the beneficial owner of said property; and, in such cases the shipper or consignor, or, in the case of a shipment so reconsigned or diverted, the beneficial owner, shall be liable for such additional charges. If the consignee has given to the carrier erroneous information as to who the beneficial owner is, such consignee shall himself be liable for such additional charges. On shipments reconsigned or diverted by an agent who has furnished the carrier in the reconsignment or diversion order with a notice of agency and the proper name and address of the beneficial owner, and where such shipments are refused or abandoned at ultimate destination, the said beneficial owner shall be liable for all legally applicable charges in connection therewith. If the reconsignor or diverter has given to the carrier erroneous information as to who the beneficial owner is, such reconsignor or diverter shall himself be liable for all such charges.

If a shipper or consignor of a shipment of property (other than a prepaid shipment is also the consignee named in the bill of lading and, prior to the time of delivery, notifies, in writing, a delivering carrier by railroad (a) to deliver such property at destination to another party, (b) that such party is the beneficial owner of such property, and (c) that delivery is to be made by the carrier only upon payment of all transportation charges in respect of the transportation of such property, and delivery is made by the carrier to such party without such payment, such shipper or consignor shall not be liable (as shipper, consignor, consignee, or otherwise) for such transportation charges but the party to whom delivery is so made shall in any event be liable for transportation charges billed against the property at the time of such delivery, and also for any additional charges which may be found to be due after delivery of the property, except that if such party prior to such delivery has notified in writing the delivering carrier that he is not the beneficial owner of the property, and has given in writing to such delivering carrier the name and address of such beneficial owner, such party shall not be liable for any additional charges which may be found to be due after delivery of the property; but if the party to whom delivery is made has given to the carrier erroneous information as to the beneficial owner, such party shall nevertheless be liable for such additional charges. If the shipper or consignor has given to the delivering carrier erroneous information as to who the beneficial owner is, such shipper or consignor shall himself be liable for such transportation charges, notwithstanding the foregoing provisions of this paragraph and irrespective of any provisions to the contrary in the bill of lading or in the contract of transportation under which the shipment was made. The term "delivering carrier" means the line-haul carrier making ultimate delivery.

Nothing herein shall limit the right of the carrier to require at time of shipment the prepayment or guarantee of the charges. If upon inspection it is ascertained that the articles shipped are not those described in this bill of lading, the freight charges must be paid upon the articles actually shipped.

Where delivery is made by a common carrier by water the foregoing provisions of this section shall apply, except as may be inconsistent with Part III of the Interstate Commerce Act.

Sec. 8. If this bill of lading is issued on the order of the shipper, or his agent, in exchange or in substitution for another bill of lading, the shipper's signature to the prior bill of lading as to the statement of value or otherwise, or election of common law or bill of lading liability, in or in connection with such prior bill of lading, shall be considered a part of this bill of lading as fully as if the same were written or made in or in connection with this bill of lading.

Sec. 9. (a) If all or any part of said property is carried by water over any part of said route, and loss, damage or injury to said property occurs while the same is in the custody of a carrier by water the liability of such carrier shall be determined by the bill of lading of the carrier by water (this bill of lading being such bill of lading if the property is transported by such water carrier thereunder) and by and under the laws and regulations applicable to transportation by water. Such water carriage shall be performed subject to all the terms and provisions of, and all the exemptions from liability contained in the Act of the Congress of the United States, approved on February 13, 1893, and entitled "An act relating to the navigation of vessels, etc.," and of other statutes of the United States according carriers by water the protection of limited liability, as well as the following subdivisions of this section, and to the conditions contained in this bill of lading not inconsistent with this section, when this bill of lading becomes the bill of lading of the carrier by water.

(b) No such carrier by water shall be liable for any loss or damage resulting from any fire happening to or on board the vessel, or from explosion, bursting of boilers or breakage of shafts, unless caused by the design or neglect of such carrier.

(c) If the owner shall have exercised due diligence in making the vessel in all respects seaworthy and properly manned, equipped, and supplied, no such carrier by water shall be liable for any loss or damage resulting from the perils of the lakes, seas, or other waters, or from latent defects in hull, machinery, or appurtenances whether existing prior to, at the time of, or after sailing, or from collision, stranding, or other accidents of navigation, or from prolongation of the voyage. And, when for any reason it is necessary, any vessel carrying any or all of the property herein described shall be at liberty to call at any port or ports, in or out of the customary route, to tow and be towed, to transfer, trans-ship, or lighter, to load and discharge goods at any time, to assist vessels in distress, to deviate for the purpose of saving life or property, and for docking and repairs. Except in case of negligence such carrier shall not be responsible for any loss or damage to property if it be necessary or is usual to carry the same upon deck.

(d) General Average shall be payable according to the York-Antwerp Rules of 1924, Sections 1 to 15, inclusive, and Sections 17 to 22, inclusive, and as to matters not covered thereby according to the laws and usages of the Port of New York. If the owners shall have exercised due diligence to make the vessel in all respects seaworthy and properly manned, equipped and supplied, it is hereby agreed that in case of danger, damage or disaster resulting from faults or errors in navigation, or in the management of the vessel, or from any latent or other defects in the vessel, her machinery or appurtenances, or from unseaworthiness, whether existing at the time of shipment or at the beginning of the voyage (provided the latent or other defects or the unseaworthiness was not discoverable by the exercise of due diligence), the shippers, consignees and/or owners of the cargo shall nevertheless pay salvage and any special charges incurred in respect of the cargo, and shall contribute with the shipowner in general average to the payment of any sacrifices, losses or expenses of a general average nature that may be made or incurred for the common benefit or to relieve the adventure from any common peril.

(e) If the property is being carried under a tariff which provides that any carrier or carriers party thereto shall be liable for loss from perils of the sea, then as to such carrier or carriers the provisions of this section shall be modified in accordance with the tariff provisions, which shall be regarded as incorporated into the conditions of this bill of lading.

(f) The term "water carriage" in this section shall not be construed as including lighterage in or across rivers, harbors, or lakes, when performed by or on behalf of rail carriers.

Sec. 10. Any alteration, addition, or erasure in this bill of lading which shall be made without the special notation hereon of the agent of the carrier issuing this bill of lading, shall be without effect, and this bill of lading shall be enforceable according to its original tenor.

Uniform Order Bill of Lading (Reverse)
(Sec. 6-10)

NOT-NEGOTIABLE WAREHOUSE RECEIPT

NEW YORK TERMINAL WAREHOUSE CO.
INCORPORATED
MAIN OFFICE [address]

ISSUED AT

RECEIVED FROM

FOR ACCOUNT OF

IN WAREHOUSE AT

DEPOSITOR   WHSE. No. _____

RECEIPT HOLDER   RECEIPT No. _____

DATE _____

In apparent good order, except as noted, the following property. The Warehouseman, at his discretion, will treat property of a like kind or character as fungible. Property will be delivered to the above Receipt Holder or in accordance with the above Receipt Holder's instructions.

LOT No.	QUANTITY	UNIT	SAID TO BE OR TO CONTAIN	MARKS

NOT-NEGOTIABLE

UNIT:

The Warehouseman's liability shall not exceed the following value as declared by the Depositor

TOTAL VALUE:

Storage and other charges as per account with the Depositor, the provisions of which will be disclosed to the holder hereof upon request to the Warehouseman.

Location of goods is not given for inaccurate purposes and the Warehouseman disclaims all liability for error or insufficiency of the location shown.

Values shown hereon are declared by the Depositor and the Warehouseman disclaims all responsibility therefor.

The New York Terminal Warehouse Co., Incorporated, certifies its only relationship to the Depositor is that of a Warehouseman and it has no financial interest in the property covered by this receipt, except it claims a lien for all lawful charges for the storage, handling and preservation of the property.

NEW YORK TERMINAL WAREHOUSE CO.

By _____

CANCELLED

RECORD OF DELIVERIES AND BALANCES ON HAND

DATE	DELIVERY ORDER No.	QUANTITY DELIVERED	BALANCE	
		BALANCE F'WARD		

Form 10-3: Not-Negotiable Warehouse Receipt

Form 10-4: Negotiable Warehouse Receipt

DELIVERY ORDER

NEW YORK TERMINAL WAREHOUSE CO., Inc.   WHSE. No...

(Control Office)...   DATE.. 19 .....

WAREHOUSE ADDRESS...   No. (this form)...............................

You are hereby authorized to deliver to .... the following
described property, covered by warehouse receipts assigned to or held by us. You are hereby released from all liability for same.

SAID TO BE OR CONTAIN	UNIT	LOT NO.	QUANTITY	DEPOSITOR'S DECLARED VALUE	
				UNIT	EXTENSION
TOTAL QUANTITY				TOTAL DECLARED VALUE	

The values stated hereon are as declared by the depositor and the Warehouseman disclaims any responsibility therefor.

Date...............................19......   Yours truly,

Receipt of the above described property in good order is
hereby acknowledged.

....
                                                            Receipt Holder

....   By...Title.........................
                                                                 Authorized Signature

By..............................Title............................   Date signed:..

430/440 D

Form 10-5: Delivery Order

[B] Bailee's Delivery Obligation

Read: U.C.C. §§ 7-403, 1-201(20), 7-104.

Bailee-carrier or warehouseman must deliver the bailed goods to a "person entitled under the document." In the case of a non-negotiable document, this means:

1. The person to whom delivery is to be made by the terms of a non-negotiable document. Example: S delivers goods to C carrier who engages on the bill of lading to deliver the goods "to B." C fulfills its delivery obligation by delivering the goods to B.

2. The person to whom delivery is to be made pursuant to written instructions under a non-negotiable document. Example: S delivers goods to W warehouse who engages on the warehouse receipt to deliver the goods "to S." S issues a written order (delivery order) directed to W to deliver the goods "to B." W fulfills its delivery obligation by delivering the goods to B. See U.C.C. § 7-403(1), (4) and the Uniform Straight Bill of Lading, the Non-Negotiable Warehouse Receipt and the Delivery Order forms located in the introduction to this chapter above.

In the case of a negotiable document of title, the "holder" is the "person entitled under the document" to whom the bailee must deliver the goods. Upon delivery, the holder must surrender the negotiable document covering the goods. A "holder" is "the person in possession [of the negotiable document] if the goods are deliverable to bearer or to the order of the person in possession." U.C.C. § 1-201(5),(20). Example: S delivers goods to C carrier who engages on the bill of lading to deliver the goods "to the order of S." S indorses the bill (by signing S's name) and sends it to buyer through bank collection channels. C fulfills its delivery obligation by delivering the goods to holder B who must surrender the bill. See U.C.C. § 7-403(l), (3), (4) and the Uniform Order Bill of Lading form located in the introduction to this chapter above.

The requirement that the holder of the negotiable document must surrender it in order to obtain the goods is a manifestation of the "merger" or "symbolism" attribute of negotiability previously discussed. Accordingly, a bailee who has issued a negotiable document will never (or hardly ever) deliver the goods without surrender of the document. This conclusion is reflected on a negotiable bill which will state: "The surrender of this original order bill of lading properly indorsed shall be required before the delivery of property covered by the bill." Cf. U.C.C. §§ 7-403, 3-601, 3-602(a), 3-301, 3-501(b)(2); see § 7-601; cf. §§ 3-309, 8-405.

Several consequences occur when a document is utilized in a commercial transaction. This is particularly true if the document is negotiable. The following is a catalogue of the several provisions of U. C. C. Articles 2, 7 and 9 which deal with documents of title:

1. Passing of title — § 2-401(2), (3)(a).

2. Risk of loss — §§ 2-509(l)(a), (2)(a) and (c); 2-503(4)(b) and Comment 6; cf. § 3-414(f).

3. Seller's delivery obligation — §§ 2-503(2), 2-504(b); 2-503(3)-(5); cf. §§ 2-511(3). See § 2-319 et seq.

4. Buyer's obligation to accept and pay — §§ 2-310(a)-(c), 2-319(4), 2-320(4), 2-321(1) and (3), 2-505, 2-507(1), 2-511(1) and Comment 1.

5. Buyer's right to inspection of goods — §§ 2-513(1) and (3)(b); see § 2-310(a)-(c) and Comments 1 and 4, §§ 2-505, 2-320 Comments 1 and 12.

6. Buyer's right of rejection on improper delivery — §§ 2-601, 2-503.

7.   Stoppage of delivery in transit — § 2-705(2)(d); see §§ 2-705(3)(c) and (d), 7-501(1) and (2), 7-504(4).

8.   Seller's remedies in a cash sale transaction — §§ 2-507(2), 2-511(3).

9.   Buyer's right of replevin — § 2-716 and Comment 5, § 2-505.

10.   Diversion — § 7-303.

11.   Lost or missing documents — § 7-601; cf. §§ 3-309, 8-405.

12.   Attachment of goods covered by documents — § 7-602, cf. § 8-112; see §§ 2-503(4)(b), 7-504(2)(a).

13.   Secured transactions — §§ 9-105(1)(f), 9-305, 9-304(2) and 3.

An important use of this document of title is its utilization as a device to secure payment of the purchase price to seller. This is pointed out by the following excerpt:[4]

Secure payment of purchase price: exchange of goods or document for price. In instances Seller may be unwilling to deliver goods to Buyer without receiving payment. Likewise, Buyer may be unwilling to pay for goods before receiving them. Thus they can agree that at the time and place for delivery they will simultaneously exchange the goods for the purchase price. See §§ 2-310(a), 2-507(1), 2-511(1). If Seller and Buyer are at a great distance, an intermediary (*e.g.*, postman, truck driver) may deliver the goods in exchange for the price and remit the monies to Seller, *i.e.*, a C.O.D. transaction. Or, the terms of the sales agreement may provide for "sight draft against order bill of lading" or "payment against documents" or "shipment under reservation." See § 2-505(1)(a) re reservation of a security interest in the goods. This documentary sale is outlined thus:

(1) Seller delivers the goods to Carrier and Carrier issues to Seller a seller's [shipper's] order bill:

Consigned to ORDER OF *Seller*

Notify *Buyer*

(2) Seller draws a sight draft[5] on Buyer stating in part:

At Sight

Pay to the order of *Seller*

Five Thousand and no/100. . . . . . . .Dollars

To: Buyer

         (signed) Seller

Seller indorses the draft in blank or "Pay Seller City Bank, for collection"; Seller indorses the bill of lading in blank. See §§ 3-205, 1-201(20), 7-501(1). The draft and bill are then delivered to Seller City Bank for collection.

(3) Seller City Bank forwards the draft and bill to Buyer City Bank. See § 4-501 et seq. re collection of documentary drafts.

---

[4] Excerpt from B. Stone, Uniform Commercial Code In A Nutshell, pages 321-324; copyright © 1995 West Publishing Company, reprinted with permission.

[5] [Simply, the draft is an order made by seller addressed to buyer to pay the amount of the draft to the order of seller. It is a sight draft and, consequently, it is payable on demand. U.C.C. §§ 3-104(a) and (e), 3-108(a).—Ed.]

(4) Buyer City Bank notifies Buyer that the draft and bill have arrived. Buyer pays the draft and the draft and bill are delivered to Buyer.[6] See § 3-501(b)(2).

(5) Buyer is now the *holder* of the bill of lading since Buyer is in possession of a document issued to order and indorsed in blank. § 1-201(20). Buyer is the "person entitled under the document" to whom Carrier must deliver the goods. § 7-403(4). Thus Buyer surrenders the bill to Carrier and receives the goods. § 7-403(3). See §§ 2-310(b) and (c), 2-513(3)(b).

(6) Buyer City Bank transmits the proceeds (*e.g.*, by transfer(s) of bank credits) to Seller City Bank.

(7) Seller City Bank remits the proceeds to Seller (*e.g.*, by crediting Seller's account).

The above may be diagramed thus:

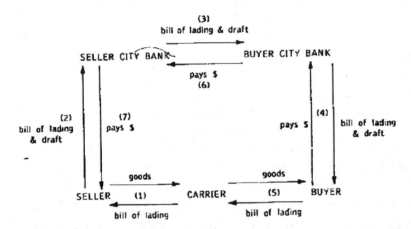

Use of "order bills" may be impeded by the fact that the goods may arrive at destination before the documents. Thus, the Code provides that bills may be issued at destination, thereby arriving before the goods. See § 7-305 and Comment re destination bills.

A non-negotiable document can reserve possession of goods as security thus: Suppose Carrier issued a non-negotiable bill "to Seller" (not "to the order of Seller"). Seller is the "person entitled under the document" to whom Carrier must deliver the goods. While the non-negotiable bill need not be surrendered, Carrier will not deliver to anyone (*e.g.*, Buyer) until it receives written instructions from Seller (a delivery order) to deliver to Buyer. Seller will not so instruct until Buyer has made satisfactory arrangements to pay for the goods. § 2-505(l)(b); see § 7-403(l), (3), (4).

---

[6] [In the event that Buyer will be given a period, *e.g.*, sixty days, in which to pay for the goods, the above procedure may be followed except that the draft, which may be referred to as a trade acceptance, will mature sixty days after delivery of the goods to Buyer rather than at sight. In this case Buyer will "accept" the draft (similar to a drawee-bank certifying a check) at Buyer City Bank instead of paying for the goods. Acceptance is Buyer's agreement to pay the draft upon maturity. See U.C.C. §§ 3-409(a), 3-413. Seller may then discount (sell) this draft to its bank. Thus Seller will receive the purchase price of the goods minus a modest discount—the difference reflecting the bank's charges—without having to wait for the draft to mature.—Ed.]

———

PROBLEM 10.1

Pillsbury (Seller) contracted to sell a quantity of corn to WJM Co. (Buyer), a supplier of chicken feed, for $51,207.80, F.O.B. Toledo, Ohio. Seller delivered the corn to Grand Trunk Eastern (Carrier) on October 28, 1994, and made a reasonable contract for its carriage to Buyer in Lewiston, Maine. Carrier issued to Seller a negotiable bill of lading wherein the corn was consigned "to the order of [Buyer]." (Seller retained possession of the bill of lading.) The corn arrived in Lewiston on November 7. Despite the fact that Buyer neither presented the bill of lading nor paid for the corn, Carrier released the corn to Buyer on November 12.

Did Carrier breach its obligation to Seller to deliver the corn to a person entitled under the bill of lading to receive the corn pursuant to the F.B.L.A.?; pursuant to the U.C.C. (assuming an intrastate shipment to Cincinnati)?

[Note: F.B.L.A. § 80110(a) and (b) (1994) provides:

(a) *General rules.* — Except to the extent a common carrier establishes an excuse provided by law, the carrier must deliver goods covered by a bill of lading on demand of the consignee named in a nonnegotiable bill or the holder of a negotiable bill for the goods when the consignee or holder —

(1) offers in good faith to satisfy the lien of the carrier on the goods;

(2) has possession of the bill and, if a negotiable bill, offers to indorse and give the bill to the carrier; and

(3) agrees to sign, on delivery of the goods, a receipt for delivery if requested by the carrier.

(b) *Persons to whom goods may be delivered.* — Subject to section 80111 of this title, a common carrier may deliver the goods covered by a bill of lading to —

(1) a person entitled to their possession;

(2) the consignee named in a nonnegotiable bill; or

(3) a person in possession of a negotiable bill if —

(A) the goods are delivered to the order of that person; or

(B) the bill has been indorsed to that person or in blank by the consignee or another indorsee.]

———

PROBLEM 10.2

The facts enumerated in Problem 10.1 continue: On November 12, Buyer presented carrier with an *order shipment bond* which purported to indemnify and hold Carrier harmless against all loss, damages, liability and costs by reason of Carrier delivering the corn to Buyer without surrender of proper documentation.

On November 24, Seller tendered the bill of lading and draft-invoices for collection to Lewiston Bank. After notice, Buyer failed to pay, and the bill of lading and draft-invoices were returned to Seller.

Seller next notified Carrier to ship the corn to another customer. In turn, Carrier, who had already delivered the corn to Buyer, demanded payment from Buyer as an alternative to proceeding upon the order shipment bond. Buyer paid Seller in full for the goods on February 6, 1995. Seller then sent the bill of lading to Carrier, who released its claims against the order shipment bond. On March 2, 1995, Buyer filed its petition under Chapter 11 of the Bankruptcy Code.

The Trustee in Bankruptcy alleges that the payment made to Seller on February 6 constituted a voidable preference under Section 547(b) of the Bankruptcy Code. This section provides that the Trustee may avoid a transfer of an interest of Buyer in property (Buyer's payment to Seller) if the transfer is: (1) for the benefit of Seller, (2) for or on account of an antecedent debt, (3) made while Buyer was insolvent, (4) made on or within 90 days before the date of the filing of the bankruptcy petition, and (5) one that enables Seller to receive more than Seller would receive in a Chapter 7 liquidation of the estate.

While bankruptcy is beyond the scope of our study, suffice it to say that the possibility is real that the Trustee may avoid the payment by Buyer to Seller. If this occurs, what recourse, if any, has Seller against Carrier or upon the order shipment bond? What is the counseling point for Seller the next time this situation arises? *See, In re Hillcrest Foods, Inc.*, 40 BR 360, 38 U.C.C. Rep. 1195 (1984).

———

NOTES AND QUESTIONS

Excuses to Bailee's Delivery Obligation. U.C.C. § 7-403(1)(a) through (g) enumerates excuses to the bailee's duty to deliver the goods to the "person entitled under the document." See also U.C.C. § 7-603. Subsection (l)(a) excuses delivery to a person entitled under the document where delivery of the goods is to a person whose receipt was rightful as against the claimant. Comment 2 illustrates:

> The principal case covered by subsection (1)(a) is delivery to a person whose title is paramount to the rights represented by the document. For example, if a thief deposits stolen goods in a warehouse and takes a negotiable receipt, the warehouseman is not liable on the receipt if he has surrendered the goods to the true owner, even though the receipt is held by a good faith purchaser. See Section 7-503(1). . . .

Under subsection (1)(b), damage to or delay, loss or destruction of the goods for which the bailee is not liable excuses delivery to a person entitled under the document. See U.C.C. §§ 7-204, 7-309. In *World Products, Inc. v. Central Freight Service, Inc.*, 222 F. Supp. 849 (N.J. 1963), Hurricane Donna struck the Metropolitan New York area. The tide waters of the Hudson River rose about four feet above the mean high water mark and flooded defendant's warehouse, ruining plaintiff's pipe fittings. The court held that the evidence established that the warehouseman was negligent in storing plaintiff's goods in its warehouse extending partly over the river without taking sufficient precautions to insure that the high tides caused by severe storm, such as the hurricane which resulted in damage to plaintiff's goods, would not cause flooding of the warehouse. Even though the hurricane qualified as act of God, defendant's negligence was a substantial factor in causing damage to the merchandise.

The court concluded:

On the question of damages, plaintiff has presented evidence that the replacement value of the damaged goods was $41,434.13. In addition, plaintiff adds freight and labor charges, and deducts salvage value, resulting in a total claim of $40,622.17. Defendant contends that its liability, if any, is limited under section 10(f) of the warehouse receipt, to $26,271.00, which is derived from the base storage rate of $.07 per cwt. and the weight of 75,060 lbs. listed on defendant's delivery order for the 1688 damaged cartons "returned for salvage" (500 x $.07 x 750.6).

Plaintiff argues that the limitation of liability in section 10(f) is not binding on it for the reason that said section was not specifically called to plaintiff's attention by defendant. See *Henningsen v. Bloomfleld Motors, Inc.*, 32 N.J. 358, 396-397, 161 A.2d 69, 75 A.L.R.2d 1(1960). However, *Henningsen* and the cases cited therein deal with situations where the seller has an unfair bargaining advantage over the buyer. Such cases have no application where both parties are business corporations, engaged in a commercial relationship with one another over an extended period of time, and where the contract fairly spells out the limitation of liability and contains a provision for extra charges if an excess value is declared. Such a reasonable contractual limitation of warehouseman's liability is not invalid under New Jersey law, in the absence of fraud or a violation of public policy. See *Henningsen v. Bloomfleld Motor, Inc.,* supra; Siliesh v. South Orange Storage Corp.*, 14 N.J. Super. 205, 81 A.2d 502 (1951); N.J.S.A. 12A:7-204(2), 12A:2-719(3). Therefore, the Court finds that defendant's liability in this case is limited to $26,271.00.

222 F. Supp. 852-53.

[C] Rights Acquired by "Due Negotiation"

Read: U.C.C. §§ 7-104, 7-501 through 7-504.

The classic case of *Weil Bros. v. Keenan*, 180 Miss. 697, 178 So. 90 (1938), illustrates rights acquired by "due negotiation." There Warehouse received from Chris Keenan 5 bales of cotton for storage and issued to him its standard negotiable receipt which stated that the cotton would be delivered to "Chris Keenan or bearer." On October 5, Keenan was induced by fraud to entrust the receipt to Spencer. Spencer had told Keenan that he, Spencer, had a buyer for the cotton. Further, he said that if Keenan would give him the receipt, he would sell the cotton and the receipt and would return with the money realized from the sale. Spencer never returned but rather on the same day sold the receipt, unindorsed, to Weil Bros., Inc. (Weil) who bought it in the usual ordinary course of business and who had no reason to be suspicious of Spencer.

When Spencer didn't return, Keenan began making investigations. He found out that he had been defrauded and that the receipt was in the hands of Weil. Both Keenan and Weil demand the cotton from Warehouse and Warehouse interpleads.

The court determined that Weil bought the cotton from Spencer in good faith and for value and that Weil was entitled to retain the warehouse receipt and the cotton.

PROBLEM 10.3

Resolve *Weil Bros. v. Keenan* under the U.C.C., assuming Weil took by "due negotiation." See U.C.C. §§ 7-104, 7-501 through 7-504.

———

Comment 1 to U.C.C. § 7-501 explains the rationale for the extraordinary rights acquired by the holder by "due negotiation":

> In general this section is intended to clarify the language of the old acts and to restate the effect of the better decisions thereunder. An important new concept is added, however, in the requirement of "regular course of business or financing" to effect the "due negotiation" which will transfer greater rights than those held by the person negotiating. The foundation of the mercantile doctrine of good faith purchase for value has always been, as shown by the case situations, the furtherance and protection of the regular course of trade. The reason for allowing a person, in bad faith or in error, to convey away rights which are not his own has from the beginning been to make possible the speedy handling of that great run of commercial transactions which are patently usual and normal.

In certain instances, however, the document of title to goods will be defeated even though "duly negotiated." Comment 1 to U.C.C. § 7-503 observes:

> In general it may be said that the title of a purchaser by due negotiation prevails over almost any interest in the goods which existed prior to the procurement of the document of title if the possession of the goods by the person obtaining the document derived from any action by the prior claimant which introduced the goods into the stream of commerce or carried them along that stream. A thief of the goods cannot indeed by shipping or storing them to his own order acquire power to transfer them to a good faith purchaser . . . .

Also, rights of a holder by "due negotiation" may be defeated: (1) where two or more documents are issued by different issuers which represent the same goods (U.C.C. § 7-503(2) and (3)), or where two or more documents are issued by the same issuer which represent the same goods (U.C.C. § 7-402). Title to fungible goods under a warehouse receipt may be defeated where the goods are sold to a buyer in ordinary course of business (U.C.C. § 7-205; cf. §§ 2-403(2), 9-307(1)).

Note that the rights of a holder by "due negotiation" are comparable to the rights of a "holder in due course" of negotiable instruments under U.C.C. Article 3. Also note that a "protected purchaser" of an investment security under Article 8 has rights comparable to a "holder in due course" under Article 3 and a holder by "due negotiation" under Article 7. See U.C.C. §§ 3-306, 8-303.

[D] Non-Receipt or Misdescription of Goods or Alteration of Document

Read: U.C.C. §§ 7-203, 7-301, see 7-502(1)(c); Read also: §§ 7-208, 7-306.

A warehouseman or carrier who issues a document of title when no goods have been received (or the goods are misdescribed) may have a liability to a purchaser who relies upon the description of the goods in the document. Such liability may be disclaimed by such language as "said to contain." U.C.C. §§ 7-203, 7-301; cf. § 3-305(b).

An altered document of title leaves the document enforceable according to its original tenor. In certain instances a purchaser may treat an insertion as authorized. U.C.C. §§ 7-208, 7-306; cf. §§ 3-407(c), 3-406, 3-115.

§ 10.02 Letters of Credit

In our discussion above concerning the documentary sale we saw that an important use of the document of title (*e.g.*, bill of lading) was its utilization as a device to secure payment of the purchase price to the seller. This was done by a correspondent bank in the buyer's city exchanging the negotiable bill to buyer for payment of the purchase price. Review this transaction at § 10.01[B] above.

While the documentary sale gives the seller assurance that the buyer in a distant city will not be able to obtain the goods without paying for them, there is still a significant risk for the seller. What if the buyer refuses to honor the draft drawn upon him by the seller? The seller, of course, will still control the goods, but the goods are now probably in the buyer's city. The seller may suffer heavy losses in seeking to sell the goods located there. The seller wants assurances *before* it ships that someone responsible has assumed the payment obligation. This is where the letter of credit is utilized.

Study 1995 Revised U.C.C. §§ 5-102(a)(10) and 5-103(a), then proceed to Chapter 11, entitled *"Letters of Credit."*

CHAPTER **11**

LETTERS OF CREDIT

§ 11.01 Background

[A] Introduction

Read: U.C.C. §§ 5-102, 5-103(1)(a); Revised §§ 5-102(a)(10), 5-103(a).

PROBLEM 11.1

Suppose a client asks you for advice on how to resolve the following problem. Your client, Clayton "Paris" Molinero, operates an exclusive gift shop in Duluth, Minnesota that deals in rare, often exotic gifts from around the world. Clayton has recently been contacted by Stephen Ryder, a large supplier of quality English goods, in particular split cane bamboo fly rods. Clayton is convinced he could sell a large quantity of these rods. He wishes to establish a working relationship with Stephen Ryder so that he may buy other luxury items from him in the future. Stephen Ryder, however, is apprehensive about sending several of the high priced rods across the Atlantic without any knowledge of Clayton's credit worthiness. Stephen also wishes to avoid the high cost and frustration of investigating the financial stability of an overseas businessperson. Stephen has indicated that he has dealt with Clayton's bank, Hayes' First International in St. Paul, Minnesota on several previous occasions.

Clayton, in return, has worries of his own. He is concerned that simply wiring the money to an account in London would be temerarious and put him in jeopardy if Stephen Ryder should ship shoddy merchandise, or worse, not ship anything at all. There is nothing to guarantee Stephen's performance, and the last thing a retailer from Duluth wants is to try and recoup lost payments in a foreign country. Clayton is curious if there is a payment mechanism that would allow Stephen Ryder the security he requires without forcing Clayton to send a check off with no guarantee that Stephen will send the fly-rods. Is there a possible solution that will appease both Clayton and Stephen?

——

A significant risk for the seller relates to whether the buyer will accept the goods and pay for them. What if the buyer refuses to honor the draft drawn upon him by the seller? The seller, of course, will still control the goods, but the goods are now probably in the buyer's city. The seller may suffer heavy losses in seeking to sell the goods located there. The seller wants assurances *before* it ships that someone responsible has assumed the payment obligation. This is where the letter of credit is utilized.

A "letter of credit" or "credit" is "an engagement by a bank or other person made at the request of a customer. . .that the issuer will honor drafts or other demands for payment upon compliance with the conditions specified in the credit." U.C.C. § 5-103(1)(a) [revised § 5-102(a)(10). In its usual form, a letter of credit is a written promise by a bank on behalf of its customer, who is a buyer of goods, to pay the beneficiary, the seller of the goods, in accordance with the terms and conditions of the promise. Such terms usually include presentation to the issuer of the seller's draft for the price, an order bill of lading properly indorsed, and an inspection certificate and insurance policy covering the goods. Credits of this type are denominated "documentary letters of credit."

The use of the letter of credit grows out of the mutual needs of sellers and buyers of goods who are at a distance from one another, and who are unwilling to rely upon the credit or the bare promises of the other. It enables the seller, before it ships goods to the buyer, to know that its draft for the price will be paid, and that a bank is lending its credit to the buyer to guarantee that payment is in fact made. On the buyer's side, through the condition of the letter of credit that the draft must be accompanied by an order bill of lading, insurance policy and inspection certificate relating to the goods, it assures the buyer that upon payment of the draft it will obtain control over the goods it has contracted for. Thus, the seller substantially diminishes the "credit risk" that the buyer will not pay for the goods, and the buyer reduces materially the "goods risk" that the seller will not deliver the goods the buyer has paid for, or that the goods will not conform to the contract, or that they will be damaged in transit after the risk of loss has passed to the buyer (although, as we shall see in this chapter, these risks are not entirely eliminated).[1]

As a starting point, study the following overview of the letter of credit transaction:[2]

The letter of credit transaction involves legal relations between (1) the customer (Buyer) and the beneficiary (Seller); (2) the issuer (Buyer City Bank) and the customer (Buyer); (3) the issuer (Buyer City Bank) and the beneficiary (Seller). § 5-103 Comment 3 [revised § 5-102 Comments]. These relationships arise per the following sequence:

1. *The underlying sales transaction.* Seller and Buyer enter into a contract for sale of goods with the following form of letter of credit term:

It is agreed that Buyer shall, within _____ days after the date of this agreement, establish with the Buyer City Bank an irrevocable letter of credit in the amount of the purchase price, naming Seller as beneficiary. The terms and conditions of the letter shall provide that Seller will present to the Buyer City Bank the following documents on or before _____ 19____:

---

[1] Letters of credit are not limited to sale of goods transactions. In addition to the documentary letter of credit, there is the "traveler's letter of credit," by which the issuing bank undertakes to pay drafts, up to a specified total, drawn when the letter of credit is presented to its correspondent banks. Such credits are drawn in so-called "circular form," whereby the correspondent bank paying the draft makes a notation upon the back of the letter as to the amount of each draft; drafts will be honored in this fashion until the amount of the credit is exhausted. The Code calls these "notation credits." § 5-108 (omitted as obsolete under 1995 Revised Article 5). Also, banks have found frequent use of letters of credit in many transactions other than the sale of goods; these are described as "clean" credits because they are not conditioned upon the presentation of documents such as bills of lading. See § 11.02 below for discussion of the "standby letter of credit" which represents an obligation to the beneficiary on the part of the issuer to make payment on account of any default by the customer in the performance of an obligation.

[2] Excerpt from B. Stone, Uniform Commercial Code In A Nutshell, pp. 516-521; copyright © 1995 West Publishing Company, reprinted with permission.

    a.   Commercial invoice

    b.   Ocean bill of lading adequately describing goods sold under this agreement.

    c.   Consular invoice

    d.   Inspection certificate issued by _____

    e.   Certificate or policy of insurance governing goods described in this agreement.

Any confirmation of the letter of credit shall be by the Seller City Bank.

U.C.C. § 2-325 applies to letter of credit terms and states that: A letter of credit is required to be irrevocable; delivery to seller of a proper letter of credit suspends buyer's obligation to pay; failure of buyer seasonably to furnish a letter of credit is a breach of the contract for sale. See U.C.C. § 5-103, Comment 1 [revised § 5-103 Comments].

Note that the underlying transaction above involved the sale of goods per Article 2. However, the underlying transaction may involve the sale of investment securities (per Article 8), the transfer of [negotiable instruments] (per Article 3), the transfer of documents of title (per Article 7), or be a transaction intended to create a security interest (per Article 9). § 5-103, Comment 3 [revised § 5-103 Comments].

2. *The Buyer (customer) [applicant] and Buyer City Bank (issuer) transaction.* Buyer applies to Buyer City Bank for a letter of credit and a letter of credit agreement is entered into. Per this agreement Buyer City Bank agrees to issue an irrevocable letter of credit to Seller; Buyer agrees to pay the bank a sum for this service and to reimburse immediately the bank for payment made under the credit. § 5-114(3) [revised § 5-108(i) Comments]. If the bank is to lend money to Buyer on a security basis (trust receipt financing, now Article 9 security agreement, see § 9-102(2)), Buyer will obtain the bill of lading without paying for the goods, but Buyer City Bank will obtain a purchase money security interest in the bill and the goods.

Note well: Buyer City Bank (issuer) must honor a draft which complies with the terms of the credit *regardless* of whether the goods or documents conform to the underlying contract for sale. § 5-114(1) [revised § 5-108(a) Comments]. Buyer City Bank's obligation to Buyer (customer) includes good faith and observance of any general banking usage but does not include liability or responsibility for performance of the underlying contract for sale between Buyer (customer) and Seller (beneficiary). § 5-109(1)(a) [revised § 5-108]. The basic obligation of Buyer City Bank is to examine the documents with care so as to ascertain that on their face they appear to comply with the terms of the credit. § 5-114(2) [revised § 5-109(a)].

Thus we see that a letter of credit is essentially a contract between the issuer (Buyer City Bank) and the beneficiary (Seller) and is recognized by Article 5 as independent of the underlying contract between the customer (Buyer) and the beneficiary (Seller). In view of this independent nature of the engagement, the issuer is under a duty to honor the drafts which in fact comply with the terms of the credit without reference to their compliance with the terms of the underlying contract. § 5-114, Comments 1 and 2 [revised § 5-108 Comments]. See UCP Arts. 3, 4.

The above rules rest on the following assumptions: Issuer (Buyer City Bank) has had no control over the making of the underlying contract or over the selection of the beneficiary (Seller); the issuer receives compensation for a payment service rather than for a guaranty of performance; the small charge for the issuance of a letter of credit ordinarily indicates that the issuer assumes minimum risks as against its customer; normally an issuer performs a banking and not a trade function. § 5-109, Comment 1 [revised § 5-108 Comments].

3. *The Buyer City Bank (issuer) and Seller (beneficiary) transaction.* Pursuant to the agreement with Buyer, Buyer City Bank issues an irrevocable letter of credit naming Seller as beneficiary. As we have observed, this is essentially a contract between Buyer City Bank and Seller and is independent of the underlying contract between Buyer and Seller. See §§ 5-102 through 5-106 [revised §§ 5-103 through 5-106]. The key language of the credit states:

> We hereby agree with the drawers, endorsers and bona fide holders of drafts drawn under and in compliance with the terms of this credit that such drafts will be duly honored on presentation to the drawee.

The credit is forwarded to Seller City Bank (the *advising* bank) which advises Seller that Buyer City Bank has issued the letter of credit in favor of Seller. The advising bank does not assume any obligation to honor drafts drawn under the credit. §§ 5-107(1), 5-103(1)(e) [revised §§ 5-107(a), 5-102(a)(4)]. If Seller City Bank is a *confirming* bank, the bank becomes directly obligated on the credit as though it were the issuer. §§ 5-107(2) and Comment 2, 5-103(1)(f). (Seller may not wish to rely on an engagement of a bank in distant Buyer City without an engagement from Seller's local bank.)

Seller now has assurance that Buyer City Bank will honor drafts upon compliance with the conditions specified in the credit, namely, the presenting of the following documents to the bank: the draft(s), commercial invoice, bill(s) of lading, consular invoice, inspection certificate, certificate of insurance. See §§ 2-320, 2-503, 2-504, 2-509, 3-106(a), 7-304.

4. *Performance.* Seller now performs Seller's obligations. Seller procures the appropriate inspection and insurance certificates; Seller delivers the goods to Carrier and receives appropriate bills of lading; Seller draws a draft on Buyer City Bank (or Buyer); Seller prepares and procures appropriate invoices. These documents are forwarded to Seller City Bank which sends the documents to Buyer City Bank. (Seller warrants to Buyer City Bank that the necessary conditions of the credit have been complied with an addition to warranties arising under Articles 3, 4, 7.) § 5-111 [revised § 5-110].

Buyer City Bank is thus called on to honor the draft drawn under the credit. Its duty is to examine the documents with care so as to ascertain that on their face they appear to comply with the terms of the credit. § 5-109(2) [revised § 5-108]. This may take time and § 5-112 [c.f. revised § 5-108(b)] gives the bank until close of the third banking day following receipt of the documents to make its decision. Cf. § 3-502(c). Thus Buyer City Bank must now determine whether the documents comply with the terms of the credit:

(1) If the documents do comply and Buyer City Bank (issuer) dishonors the draft, the bank is liable to Seller (beneficiary). §§ 5-114(1), 5-115 [revised §§ 5-108(a), 5-111].

(2) If the documents do not comply and Buyer City Bank (issuer) honors the draft, the bank is liable to Buyer (customer). § 5-109(1), (2) [revised § 5-108]. See § 5-114(2), (3) [revised §§ 5-108, 5-109].

The question of when the documents in fact and in law do or do not comply with the terms of the credit is not covered by Article 5 (which deals with some but not all of the rules and concepts of letters of credit). § 5-102(3) and Comment 2 [revised § 5-101 Comment] . . . [See § 11.01[D] below.]

Assuming that the documents comply with the terms of the credit and that Buyer City Bank honors the draft and obtains the documents, Buyer City Bank is entitled to reimbursement from

Buyer. § 5-114(3) [revised § 5-108(i)]. See § 2-707 and Comment. When Buyer reimburses the bank, Buyer obtains the bill of lading and presents the bill to Carrier and gets the goods.

––––––

Now study the diagram and explanation of the numbered steps:

Use of Documentary Letter of Credit in Sale of Goods

The following diagram illustrates the use of the documentary letter of credit in a transaction involving the sale of goods:

1. Contract for sale of goods from S to B, containing letter of credit term.

2. B applies to Issuing Bank for letter of credit, and B and Issuing Bank enter into letter of credit agreement—See Form 11-1.

3. Issuing Bank issues letter of credit and forwards it to Advising [or Confirming] Bank—See Forms 11-2, 11-3.

4. Advising [or Confirming] Bank issues Advice [or Confirmation] of Credit to S—See Forms 11-4, 11-5.

5. S secures insurance policy covering the goods while in transit.

6. S has goods inspected (by Inspection Agency designated in letter of credit) and secures inspection certificate — See Form 11-9.

7. S delivers goods to Carrier and receives negotiable bill of lading covering the goods.

8. Carrier transports goods to destination.

9. S draws draft upon Issuing Bank [or B] for purchase price, insurance and freight, and forwards draft and documents (bill of lading, insurance policy, and inspection certificate) to Advising [Confirming] Bank. (If Bank is Confirming Bank, S will receive payment at this point; if Advising Bank, S may receive immediate credit as the draft is forwarded to Issuing Bank for collection.)

10. Advising [Confirming] Bank sends draft and documents to Issuing Bank.

11. Issuing Bank examines draft and documents, and if in compliance with the letter of credit, remits payment to Advising [Confirming] Bank.

12. Advising Bank remits payment to S, deducting any credit already advanced to S upon the draft. (If Confirming Bank, S has already received payment under 9 above.)

13. B pays the amount of the draft to Issuing Bank and receives the documents (and the draft, if B is drawee).

14. B turns bill of lading over to Carrier and receives the goods.

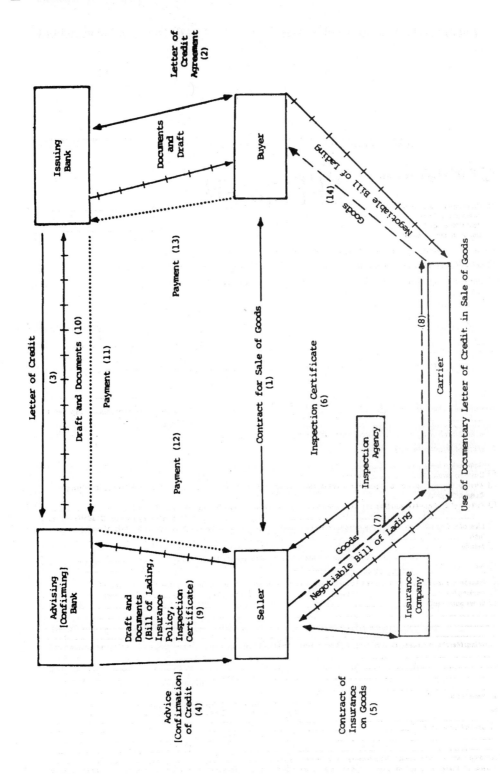

Use of Documentary Letter of Credit in Sale of Goods

Form 11-1: Commercial Letter of Credit Application and Agreement

Commercial Letter of Credit Application and Agreement

ComericA Bank-Detroit   SPECIMEN

To: Comerica Bank-Detroit
International Department
Post Office Box 858
Detroit, Michigan 48231

Number _____ (Bank use only)

Date _____

Please issue an irrevocable Letter of Credit (the "Credit") and either:

☐ notify through your correspondent by ☐ airmail, ☐ brief cable, full details by airmail or ☐ cable full details;

☐ airmail directly to beneficiary; or ☐ return to us for airmailing to beneficiary; as follows:

Advising Bank	For Account of (Applicant)
In Favor of (Beneficiary)	Amount —Drafts must be negotiated or presented to drawee on or before— (Expiration Date)

Available by drafts at sight or _____ drawn, at your opinion, on you or your correspondent for _____ % of the invoice value.

When accompanied by the following documents, as checked:

Check Documents Required

☐ Commerical Invoice in _____ copies
☐ Customs Invoice in _____ copies
☐ Airway Bill consigned to **Comerica Bank-Detroit** dated not later than _____ , bearing evidence that freight is **Collect/Prepaid.**
☐ Full set of **On Board Ocean Bills of Lading** issued to order of **Comerica Bank-Detroit, Michigan.** Marked _____ _____ **notify and marked freight: Collect/Prepaid.**
☐ Bills of lading must show that the merchandise has been loaded on board the vessel named in the bills of lading not later than _____
☐ Marine
☐ Air   Insurance Policy and/or Certificate in negotiable form covering: _____
(Specify war risks, S.R.C.C., etc)
☐ Insurance effected by ourselves. We agree to keep insurance coverage in force until this transaction is completed.
☐ packing list in _____ copies   ☐ weight list in _____ copies
☐ Other documents _____

Covering: Merchandise described in the invoice as: (Mention commodity only in generic terms omitting details as to grade, quality, etc.)

_____ Price Basis _____ (Specify F.O.B., C&F, FAS, etc.)

Shipment From:

To:

Partial Shipments ☐ Permitted ☐ Prohibited
Transshipments ☐ Permitted ☐ Prohibited

☐ Special Conditions: _____

Shipping documents for custom house entry are to be sent by you to _____

We warrant that no shipment involved in this Application is in violation of U.S. Treasury Foreign Assets Control or Cuban Assets Control **Regulations.**

In consideration of your opening at the request of the undersigned a Commercial Letter of Credit, in accordance with the foregoing application, the undersigned hereby agrees as follows:

F1314 (4-83)

1. As to drafts or acceptances under or purporting to be under the Credit, which are payable in United States Currency, we agree: (a) in the case of each sight draft, to reimburse you at your head office at **Detroit, Michigan,** on demand, in lawful money of the United States of America, the amount paid on such drafts, or, if so demanded by you, to pay you at your said office in advance in such money the amount required to pay such draft; and (b) in the case of each acceptance, to pay to you, at your said office, in lawful money of the United States of America, the amount thereof, on demand but in any event not later than one business day prior to maturity, or , in case the acceptance is not payable at your said office, then on demand but in any event in time to reach the place of payment in the course of the mails not later than one business day prior to maturity.

2. As to drafts or acceptances under or purporting to be under the Credit, which are payable in currency other than United States Currency, we agree: (a) in the case of each sight draft, to reimburse you, at your said office, the equivalent of the amount paid, in lawful money of the United States of America, at the rate of exchange then current in **Detroit** for cable transfers to the place of payment in the currency in which the draft is drawn; (b) in the case of each acceptance, to furnish you, at your said office, on demand, but in any event in time to reach the place of payment in the course of the mails not later than one business day prior to maturity with first class bankers' demand bills of exchange to be approved by you for the amount of acceptance, payable in the currency of the acceptance and bearing our endorsement, or, if you so request, to pay you, at your said office, on demand, the equivalent of the acceptance in lawful money of the United States of America, at the rate of exchange then current **Detroit** for cable transfers to the place of payment in the currency in which the acceptance is payable. Demand shall be considered made as of the time you leave same at, or send or telephone same to the respective addresses of mine or ours and a demand made on one of us shall fix the exchange rate as to all of us.

3. We also agree to pay you, on demand, a commission at the rate of

per cent (%),

on such part of the Credit as may be used, and, in any event, a minimum commission of and all charges and expenses paid or insured by you in connection therewith, and interest where chargeable.

4. We hereby recognize and admit your security interest in and an unqualified right to the possession and disposition of (a) all property shipped under or pursuant to or in conection with the Credit or in any way relative thereto or to the drafts drawn thereunder, whether or not released to any of us on trust or bailee receipt or otherwise; (b) all shipping documents, warehouse receipts, policies or certificates of insurance and other documents accompanying or relative to drafts drawn under the Credit; (c) the proceeds of each and all of the foregoing, until such time as all the obligations and liabilities of us or any of us to you at anytime existing under or with reference to the Credit or this agreement, or any other credit or any other obligation or liability to you, have been fully paid and discharged; (d) all deposits (general or special) and credits of ours with you and any claims by us against you at any time existing; an (e) any additional property in which we have granted a security interest to you, which we agree to convey on your demand; all as security for any such obligations and liabilities; and that all or any of such property and documents, and the proceeds of any thereof, coming into the possession of you or any of your correspondents, may be held and disposed of by you as herein provided; and the receipt by you, or any of your correspondents, at any time of other security, of whatsover nature, including cash, shall not be deemed a waiver of any of your rights or powers therein recognized.

5. We agree from time to time to execute in your favor security agreements in the nature of trust receipts in any form acceptable to you for any property released by you to any of us, to sign and deliver to you financing statements in any form acceptable to you and to pay related filing fees.

6. Except insofar as instructions have been heretofore given by us in writing expressly to the contrary, we agree that you and any of your correspondents may receive and accept as "Bills of Lading" under the Credit, any documents issued or purporting to be issued by or on behalf of any carrier which acknowledge receipt of property for transportation, whatever the specific provision of such documents, and that the date of each such document shall be deemed the date of shipment of the property mentioned therein; that you may receive and accept as documents of insurance either insurance policies or insurance certificates; and that any such bill of lading issued by or on behalf of an ocean carrier may be accepted by you as an "Ocean Bill of Lading" whether or not the entire transportation is by water.

7. Except insofar as instructions have been heretofore given by us in writing expressly to the contrary, we agree that partial shipments or shipments in excess of quantity called for in the Credit may be made under the Credit and you may honor the relative drafts; and that if the Credit specifies shipments in installments within stated periods, and the shipper fails to ship in any designated period, shipments of subsequent installments may nevertheless be made in their respective designated periods and you may honor the relative drafts.

8. We agree that in the event of any extension of the maturity or time for presentation of drafts, acceptances or documents,or any other modification of the terms of the Credit, at the request of any of us, with or without notification to the others, or in the event of any increase in the amount of the Credit at your request,this agreement shall be binding upon us with regard to the Credit so increased or otherwise modified, to drafts, documents and property covered thereby, and to any action taken by you or any of your correspondents in accordance with such extension, increase or other modification.

9. The users of the Credit shall be deemed our agents and we assume all risks of their acts or omissions. Neither you nor your correspondents shall be responsible: (a) for the existence, character, quality, quantity, condition, packing, value, or delivery of the property purporting to be represented by documents; (b) for any difference in character, quality, quantity, condition, or value of the property from that expressed in documents; (c) for the validity, sufficiency or genuineness of documents, even if such documents should in fact prove to be in any or all respects invalid, insufficient, fraudulent or forged; (d) for the time, place, manner or order in which shipment is made; (e) for partial or incomplete shipment, or failure or omission to ship any or all of the property referred to in the Credit; (f) for the character, adequacy, validity, or genuineness of any insurance; (g) for the solvency or responsibility of any insurer, or for any other risk connected with insurance; (h) for any deviation from instructions, delay,

default or fraud by the shipper or anyone else in connection with the property or the shipping thereof; (i) for the solvency, responsibility or relationship to the property of any party issuing any document in connection with the property; (j) for delay in arrival or failure to arrive of either the property or any of the documents relating thereto; (k) for delay in giving or failure to give notice of arrival or any other notice; (l) for any breach of contract between the shippers or vendors and ourselves or any of us; (m) for failure of any draft to bear any reference or adequate reference to the Credit, or failure of documents to accompany any draft at negotiation, or failure of any person to note the amount of any draft on the reverse of the Credit or to surrender or take up the Credit or to send forward documents apart from drafts as required by the terms of the Credit; each of which provisions, if contained in the Credit itself, it is agreed may be waived by you; (n) for any use which may be made of this Credit or for any acts or omissions of the beneficiary(ies) in connection herewith; or (o) for errors, omissions, interruptions or delays in transmission or delivery of any messages, by mail, cable, telegraph, wireless or otherwise, whether or not they be in cipher; nor shall you be responsible for any error, neglect, or default of any of your correspondents; nor shall you be responsible for errors in translation or for errors in interpretation of technical terms, nor shall you be responsible for any consequences arising from causes beyond your control; and none of the above shall affect, impair, or prevent the vesting of any of your rights or pwers hereunder. We shall protect you and any other drawee in paying any draft dated on or before the expiration of any time limit expressed in the Credit regardless of when drawn and when or whether negotiated. We are responsible to you for all obligations imposed upon you with respect to the Credit or the relative drafts, documents property. In furtherance and extension and not in limitation of the specific provisions hereinbefore set forth, we agree that any action taken by you or by any correspondent of yours under or in connection with the Credit or the relative drafts, documents or property, if taken in good faith, shall be binding on us and shall not put you or your correspondent under any resulting liability to us; and we make like agreement as to any inaction or omission, unless in breach of good faith.

You shall not any way be liable for any failure by you or anyone else to pay or accept any draft or acceptance under this Credit resulting from any censorship, law, control or restriction rightfully or wrongfully exercised by any de facto or de jure domestic or foreign   or agency or from any other cause beyond your control or the control of your correspondents, agents, or sub-agents or for any loss or damage to us or wnyone else resulting from any such failure to pay or accept all such risks being expressly assumed by us and we agree to indemnify and hold you harmless from any claim, loss, liability or expense arising by reason of any such failure to pay or accept.

10. We agree to procure promptly any necessary import, export or other licenses for the import, export or shipping of all property shipped under or pursuant to or in connection with the credit and to comply with all foreign and domestic governmental regulations in regard to the shipment of such property or the financing thereof, and to furnish such certificates in that respect as you may at any time require, and to keep the property adequately covered by insurance satisfactory to you, issued by companies satisfactory to you, and to assign such policies of insurance to you, or to make the loss or adjustment, if any, payable to you, at your option; and to furnish you if demanded with evidence of acceptance by the insurers of such assisngment.

11. Each of us agrees at any time and from time to time, on demand, to deliver, convey, transfer, or assign to you, as security for any and all of his and/or our liabilities hereunder, and also for any and all other liabilities, absolute or contingent, due or to become due, or held or to be held by you, whether created directly or acquired by assignment, tort, or otherwise, which are now or may at any time hereafter be owing by him or us or any of us (whether jointly, severally, jointly with any other or others, independently or otherwise) to you, additional property of a value and character satisfactory to you, or to make such payment as you may require. Each of us agrees that the balance with you existing from time to time of any deposit account (whether general or special or for any specific purpose) of him or us or in which he or we may have an interest and any claim of any of us against you existing from time to time and all property belonging to him or us, or in which he or we may have an interest, including power of hypothecation or disposition, now or hereafter in your possession or custody (all remittances and property to be deemed left with you as soon as put in transit to you by mail or carrier) for any purpose (including safekeeping or pledge for any liability of him or us) whether or not such property is in whole or in part released to any of us on security agreement in the nature of a trust or bailee receipt, are hereby made security and subject to a lien for any and all such liabilities of him or us or any of us. Any property so held as collateral may be transferred to and/or registered in the name of your nominee and to do so before or after the maturity of any of the obligations or liabilities hereunder without notice to us.

12. Each of us agrees that (a) upon his or our failure at all times to keep a margin of security with you satisfactory to you, or (b) upon the non-payment or non-fulfillment of any liabilities or obligations of any of us when they shall become due or be made due, or (c) upon his or our death, or (d) upon the insolvency of, or upon the application for the appointment or the appointment of a receiver of any of us or of any or all of the property of, or (e) upon an assignment for the benefit or creditors by any of us, or the filing by or against any of us of a voluntary or involuntary petition in bankruptcy or a voluntary or involuntary petition pursuant or purporting to be pursuant to any present or future acts or regulations of any jurisdiction on the subject of bankruptcies or relief of debtors or any amendments of any such acts or regulations, whether or not relating to bankruptcy, or (f) upon the issuance of any warrant of attachment or any attachment against the credits or property of him or us, or (g) upon the taking possession by any public official having regulatory powers over any of us of the property of any of us for the purpose of conserving his or our assets, or (h) upon the failure of the undersigned promptly to furnish satisfactory additional collateral then any and all such liabilities and/or obligations of any of us shall become and be immediately due and payable, without notice, presentment, demand of payment or protest, all such being hereby waived, and notwithstanding any credit or time allowed to any of us or any instrument evidencing such liabilities or otherwise. You are hereby authorized and empowered at your option at any time without notice to appropriate and apply to the payment of any such liabilities any and all moneys or other property or proceeds thereof, now or hereafter in your hands, on deposit or otherwise, for account of, to the credit of, or belonging to any of us (whether said deposit is general, or special or for any specific purpose including safekeeping or pledge for any liability of any of us) whether any of said liabilities and/or obligations are then due or not due. Each of us expressly authorizes you upon the nonpayment or non-fulfillment of any liabilities of any of us when they shall become due or be made due, to sell, without demand, advertisement or notice to us or any of us, all of which are hereby expressly waived, any or all property of every description securing any liabilities of any of us, arrived or to arrive, at private sale or at public auction or at brokers' board or exchange or otherwise, at your option, in such parcel or parcels, at such time or times, at such place or

places, either for cash or credit or future delivery and otherwise upon such terms and conditions as you may deem proper, and to apply the net proceeds of such sale or sales, together with any balance of deposits and any sums credited by or due from you to any of us in general account or otherwise, to the payment of any and all such liabilities. If any such sale be at brokers' board or exchange, or at public auction, you may yourself be a purchaser at such sale, free from any right of redemption, which we and each of us hereby expressly waive and release. Demands or calls for collateral on, or any notices to me or us respectively may be made or given by you by leaving same at the respective addresses given below or the last known address of mine or ours, provided you in writing, respectively or by sending or telephoning same to either such address, with the same effect as if delivered to me or us in person. In the event of the sale or other disposition of such property, you may apply the proceeds of any such sale or disposition first to the satisfaction of your reasonable attorney's fees, legal expenses and other costs and expenses incurred in connection with your retaking, holding, preparing for sale, and selling of the property. Each of us agrees that with or without notification to any of us, you may exchange, release, surrender, realize upon, release on trust receipt to any of us, or otherwise deal with any property by whomsoever pledged, mortgaged, or subjected to a security interest to secure directly or indirectly any of the obligations hereunder or for which any of the undersigned may be liable. Notice of acceptance of this agreement is waived.

We will bear and pay all expenses of every kind (including all charges for legal services) of the enforcement of any of your rights therein mentioned or of any claim or demand by you against us, or of any actual or attempted sale, exchange, enforcement, collection, maintenance, retention, insurance, compromise, settlement, release, delivery on security agreemnt in the nature of a trust receipt, or delivery of any such security, and of the receipt of proceeds thereof, and will repay to you any such expenses incurred by you.

13. You shall not be deemed to have waived any of your options, powers or rights (including those hereunder) unless you or your authorized agent shall have signed such waiver in writing. No such waiver, unless expressly as stated therein, shall be effective as to any transaction which occurs subsequent to the date of such waiver, nor as to any continuance of a breach after such waiver. No segregation or specific allocation by you of specified collateral against any liability shall waive or affect any lien of any sort against other securities or property or any of your options, powers or rights (including those hereunder).

14. The word "property" as used in this agreement includes goods, merchandise, securities, funds, choses in action, and any and all other forms of property, whether real, personal or mixed and any right or interest therein. Property in your possession shall include property in possession of any one for you in any manner whatsoever. Your options, powers and rights specified in this agreement are in addition to those otherwise created. 15. You may assign or transfer this agreement, or any instrument(s) evidencing all or any of the aforesaid obligations and/or liabilities, and may delivery all or any of the property then held as security therefor, to the transferee(s), who shall thereupon become vested with all the powers and rights in respect thereto and you shall thereafter be foreever relieved and fully discharged from any liability or responsibility with respect thereto. This agreement shall be binding upon the undersigned, there heirs, executors, administrators, successors and assigns of undersigned, and shall inure to the benefit of, and be enforceable by, you, your successors, transferees and assigns. If this agreement should be terminated or revoked by operation of law as to the undersigned, the undersigned will indemnify and save you harmless from any loss suffered by you in acting prior to receipt of notice in writing of such termination or revocation.

16. That, except as otherwise expressly provided in this agreement or as oyyou and the undersigned may otherwise expressly agree with regard to, or proir to your issuance of this credit, the "Uniform Customs and Practice for Documentary Credits (1974 Revision), International Chamber of Commerce Brochure 290" shall in all respects be deemed a part hereof as fully as if incorporated herein and shall apply to this credit. If this agreement is signed by one individual, the terms "we", "our", "us", shall be read throughout as "I", "my", "me", as the case may be. If this agreement is signed by two or more parties, it shall be the joint and several agreement of such parties. In addition, the laws of the State of Michigan shall govern all aspects of this agreement.

Firm Name

Address

Authorized Signature

Irrevocable Documentary Letter of Credit

IRREVOCABLE DOCUMENTARY
LETTER OF CREDIT NO. 1234   September 1, 1986

Overseas Export Co.

4321 Nathan Road

Kowloon, Hong Kong

Gentlemen

We hereby authorize you to draw on Comerica Bank, Detroit, Michigan 48264, for the account of Detroit Import Co., 1911 Smith St., Detroit Michigan 00000 up to the aggregate amount of U.S. $45,000.00 (Forty Five Thousand and 00/100 Dollars).

The credit amount is available to you by your drafts on us at sight for 100% of invoice cost bearing the clause: "Drawn under Comerica Bank Documentary Credit No. 1234", accompanied by:

Commercial invoice in triplicate covering: "10,000 Ceramic Ashtrays", CIF, New York.

Insurance certificate or policy covering all risks including war risks.

Full set clean onboard ocean bills of lading consigned to order of Comerica Bank marked "Notify Customs Brokers of Detroit, 321 W. Fifth Street, Detroit, Michigan and "Freight Prepaid" evidencing shipment from Hong Kong to any United States West Coast Port for final delivery to Detroit, Michigan.

Bills of lading must show that the merchandise was loaded on board the vessel named in the bills of lading not later than October 10, 1985.

Partial shipments are prohibited. Transhipment is permitted.

Advising bank's charges, if any, and negotiation charges are for your account. Negotiating bank is authorized to forward all documents in one airmail.

The amount of each draft negotiated must be endorsed on the original credit by the negotiating bank.

We hereby agree with drawers, endorsers and bonafide holders of drafts drawn under an in compliance with the terms of this credit that such drafts will be duly honored on due presentation to the drawees if negotiated on or before October 25, 1986.

Except so far as otherwise specified, this documentary credit is subject to the Uniform Customs and Practice for Documentary Credits (1983 Revision), International Chamber of Commerce Publication 400.

_____

(Authorized Signature)

Form 11-2: Irrevocable Straight Credit[3]

[Bank]

CABLE ADDRESS _____   *[Address]*
Irrevocable Straight Credit   *[Date]*

MAIL TO:

    [Beneficiary]   All drafts drawn must be marked:
    [Address]   [Bank] Ref. No.: 0000000
                                       Opener's Reference No:

Dear Sirs:

At the request of:

[Customer/Account Party]

and for the account of *[Customer/Account Party]* we hereby open in your favor our Irrevocable Credit, numbered as indicated above, for a sum or sums not exceeding a total of U.S. $ _____ available by your drafts [at SIGHT] on us subject to the following:

Expiration Date:

Trans shipment: [*not allowed*]

Partial shipment: [*not allowed*]

Ship from: [*Seller's Port*]

Ship to: [*Buyer, Country*]

and accompanied by the following documents:

1. [*Ocean bills of lading*].

2. [*Insurance certificates*].

3. [*Customs invoice combined with certificate of origin*].

4. [Etc.].

This letter is to accompany all draft(s) and documents. When presenting your draft(s) and documents or when communicating with us please make reference to our reference number shown above.

We hereby agree to honor each draft drawn under and in compliance with the terms of this credit, if duly presented (together with the documents specified) at this office on or before the expiration date.

The credit is subject to the Uniform Customs and Practice for Documentary Credits, 1993 revision, ICC Publication No. 500.

                    Yours very truly,
                    [Signature of Issuer]

---

[3] Excerpt from 15 *West's Legal Forms*, pages 392-393; copyright © 1985 West Publishing Company, reprinted with permission.

Form 11-3: Irrevocable Negotiation Credit[4]

[Bank]

CABLE ADDRESS _____   *[Address]*
Irrevocable Negotiation   *[Date]*
Credit

MAIL TO:

[Beneficiary]   All drafts drawn must be marked:
[Address]   [Bank] Ref. No.: 0000000
                             Opener's Reference No:

Dear Sirs:

At the request of:

[Customer/Account Party]

and for the account of *[Customer/Account Party]* we hereby open in your favor our Irrevocable Credit, numbered as indicated above, for a sum or sums not exceeding a total of U.S. $ _____ available by your drafts [at SIGHT] on us subject to the following:

Expiration Date:

Trans shipment: *[not allowed]*

Partial shipment: *[not allowed]*

Ship to: *[location]*

Latest shipping date:

and accompanied by the following Documents:

1. *[Ocean bills of lading]*.

2. *[Insurance policy or certificate]*.

3. *[Commercial invoice]* .

4. *[Etc.]*.

This letter is to accompany all draft(s) and documents. When presenting your draft(s) and documents or when communicating with us please make reference to our reference number shown above.

We hereby engage with the drawer, endorsers and bona fide holders that each draft drawn under, and in compliance with, the terms of the said credit, and accompanied by the above-specified documents will be duly honored if NEGOTIATED on or before the expiration date.

The credit is subject to the Uniform Customs and Practice for Documentary Credits, 1993 revision, ICC Publication No. 500.

Yours very truly,
[Signature of Issuer]

---

[4] Excerpt from 15 *West's Legal Forms*, pages 394-395; copyright © 1985 West Publishing Company, reprinted with permission.

Form 11-4: Uncomfirmed Cover Letter—Advise of Credit

Export - Unconfirmed Cover Letter

Comerica Bank
International Banking Department
Post Office Box 64858
Detroit, Michigan 48264

Date _____

Mail To

Our Advice Number _____

Correspondent's Number _____

We are informed by our correspondent that they have issued their Irrevocable Credit in your favor. Our correspondent's original credit is attached. A copy of it is being held by us.

This advice conveys no engagement or obligation on our part - however, our correspondent's credit is irrevocable on their part.

Documents must conform strictly with the terms of the enclosed credit. If you are unable to comply with its terms, please promptly communicate with us or your customer with a view to having the conditions changed.

Drafts when presented, must clearly specify the number of this advice, and be presented to us in the form prescribed on the attached original credit.

Please include one extra copy of your commercial invoice for our records.

This advice is subject to the Uniform Customs and Practice for Documentary Credits (1974 Revision) International Chamber of Commerce Publication 290.

F1932 (1-84)

Form 11-5: Confirmed Cover Letter—Confirmation of Credit

Export-Confirmed Cover Letter

ComericA Bank
Post Office Box 64858
Detroit, Michigan 48264

Mail To

Beneficiary

Date_____

Our Confirmed Advice No._____

Our Correspondent's No._____

We are informed by our correspondent that they have issued their Irrevocable Credit in your favor for $ expiring at our counters. Our correspondent's original credit is enclosed and a copy of it is being held by us.

Correspondent

Account

At the request of our correspondent, we confirm their Irrevocable Credit and engage with you that all drafts drawn under and in compliance with the terms of this credit will be duly honored.

Drafts when presented must clearly specify the number of this credit and be presented to us with the original credit and amendments, if any. Drafts are to be completed in the form prescribed.

Documents must conform strictly with the terms of this credit. If you are unable to comply with these terms, please communicate with us, or your customer, with a view to having the conditions changed.

This credit is subject to the Uniform Customs and Practice for Documentary Credits (1974 Revision) International Chamber of Commerce Publication 290.

Please include one extra copy of your Commercial Invoice for our records.

International Banking Department

_____
Authorized Signature

F1931 (11-82)

Form 11-6: Amendment to Documentary Credit

COMERICA Bank
International Banking Department
Post Office Box 64858
Detroit, Michigan 48264

Swift: DBTDUS33
Telex: 23-5393

[7]

Amendment to Documentary Credit No. _____ Dated _____

Advising Bank	
	Amendment Number _____
	Date _____
Beneficiary	☐ This refers to our cable of today through the Advising Bank
To ⟩	☐ This Amendment is forwarded to the Advising Bank by Air Mail
Applicant	This Amendment is to be considered part of the Letter of Credit described above and must be attached thereto.

Dear Sirs:
The above described Credit is amended as follows:

All Other Terms and Conditions remain unchanged.

The advising Bank is requested to inform the beneficiary of this amendment.	Advising Bank's Notification
Sincerely, Comerica Bank	
Issuing Bank's Authorized Signature	Place, Date, Name and Signature of Advising Bank

F-1585 01 (11-82)

Form 11-7: Commercial Invoice

[Name and Address of Seller]

CUSTOMER ORDER NO. NUMERO DE PEDIDO DEL CLIENTE	SELLER ORDER NO. NUMERO DE PEDIDO DE SELLER	SHPT. NO. DESPACHO
EXPORT SALES DEPT. CABLE ADDRESS	SELLER INVOICE DATE FECHA DE LA FACTURA	

SOLD TO
VENDIDO A

TERMS
PLAZOS

OF
DE

FAS/

IMPORT LICENSE
LICENCIA DE IMPORTACION

LETTER OF CREDIT
CARTA DE CREDITO

MARKS AND CASE NUMBERS MARCAS Y NUMEROS DE CAJA	QUANTITY SHIPPED CANTIDAD EMBARCADA	DESCRIPTION OF GOODS DESCRIPCION DEL MATERIAL	SELLING PRICE PRECIO DE VENTA	
			UNIT UNIDADES	TOTAL TOTAL

Form 11-8: Consular Service*

N?

República Dominicana

_____ 19___

FACTURA CONSULAR OFICIAL

FACTURA de mercancías embarcadas por _____ a bordo

del _____ nombrado __ su capitán __ dirigidas al puerto de __

    (Clase y Nacionalidad, del Buque)

a la consignación de _____ por cuenta y orden de _____

Marca	Número Marca	Número de Bultos	Clase de Bultos	CONTENIDO	Cantidad	Peso en Kilos		VALORES	Países de Origen de las Mercancías
						Bruto	Neto		

Juaramos y declaramos: Que las marcas, números de bultos, contenido de los mismos en lo que respecta a su peso, Vista y
registrada bajo el número_____cantidad y clase de mercancias y el valor de éstas aquí consignadas, son exactas.

           19   19

Lugar	Fecha	Firma	Lugar	Fecha	Cónsul

**·* Excerpt from 15 West's Legal Forms, page 418; copyright © West Publishing Company.
Reprinted with permission.**

Form 11-9: Inspection Certificate[5]

[*Letterhead*]

To [*name and address of buyer*]:

RE: Order No. 00000

Gentlemen:

We certify that we have examined [*describe goods*] comprising the above order and find them to be [*specify,quantity, quality, etc., of goods*] as specified in said order.

> Yours very truly,
> [*Signature of Inspection*
> *Certificate Issuer*]

[B]   Applicable Law: U.C.C. and Uniform Customs

U.C.C. Article 5 deals with letters of credit. It is the first substantial effort at codification of the law relating to letters of credit, but it should be noted that it expressly disclaims that it is all-encompassing: "This Article deals with some but not all of the rules and concepts of letters of credit as such rules or concepts have developed prior to this act or may hereafter develop." U.C.C. § 5-102(3) [revised § 5-101 Comment]

Prior to the promulgation of the Code, there was practically no legislation relating to letters of credit. For example, the only explicit provision in the United States Code relating to letters of credit is found in Section 615 of Title 12 of the United States Code, giving national banks the "power . . .to issue letters of credit."[6] The law was almost wholly case law, based originally upon common law principles and the custom of merchants, and traceable to an early date. However, with the great expansion of the use of letters of credit in the twentieth century, banking institutions in the various nations felt a need for a concise statement of the basic rules applicable to letters of credit. This culminated in 1933 in the adoption of the Seventh Congress of the International Chamber of Commerce of the "Uniform Customs and Practice for Commercial Documentary Credits." The Uniform Customs have been widely adopted by banks, and have been revised since 1933, most recently in 1993.

Because of the widespread use of the Uniform Customs by banks engaging in documentary letter of credit transactions, it was strongly argued that Article 5 of the Code was unnecessary. A major effort was made in New York to delete Article 5 entirely from the Code as adopted in that state; and while the opponents of Article 5 did not entirely succeed, they did accomplish a part of their goal through the addition of a new Subsection (4) to the New York version of Section 5-102:

> Unless otherwise agreed, this Article 5 does not apply to a letter of credit or a credit if by its terms or by agreement, course of dealing or usage of trade such letter of credit or credit is subject in whole or in part to the Uniform Customs and Practice for Commercial

---

[5] Excerpt from 15 West's Legal Forms, p. 419; copyright © 1985West Publishing Company. Reprinted with permission.

[6] For discussion of letters of credit and bank regulations, see J. Dolan, The Law of Letters of Credit, Ch. 12 (2d ed. 1991).

Documentary Credits fixed by the Thirteenth or by any subsequent Congress of the International Chamber of Commerce.[7]

Articles 1-4, 6, 9, 13, and 37c of the 1993 Uniform Customs for Documentary Credits (UCP) are summarized:

Article 1 applies to documentary credits (including standby letters of credit) where the UCP is incorporated into the text of the credit, viz., "The credit is subject to the Uniform Customs and Practice for Documentary Credits (1993 Revision), ICC Publication No. 500."

Article 2 defines a credit to mean any arrangement whereby an "issuing bank" acting on the instructions of an "applicant" (customer) is to make payment to the "beneficiary" against stipulated documents, provided that the terms and conditions of the credit are complied with.

Article 3 states that credits are separate transactions from the sales contracts on which they may be based and issuers are in no way concerned with or bound by these contracts.

Article 4 observes that issuers deal with documents and not with goods to which the documents relate.

Article 6 reverses the prior UCP by asserting that in the absence of an indication whether a credit is revocable or irrevocable, it is deemed to be irrevocable.

Article 9 states that an irrevocable credit constitutes a definite undertaking of the issuing bank, provided (1) the stipulated documents are presented to the issuing bank and (2) the terms and conditions of the credit are complied with.

Article 13 sets forth the standard for examination of documents: (1) Banks must examine all documents stipulated in the credit with reasonable care to ascertain whether or not they appear on their face to be in compliance with the terms and conditions of the credit. (2) Compliance shall be determined by international standard banking practice as reflected in the UCP. (3) Documents which appear on their face to be inconsistent with one another will be considered as not appearing on their face to be in compliance.

Article 37c provides that the description of the goods in the commercial invoice must correspond with the description in the credit. In all other documents, the goods may be described in general terms not inconsistent with the description in the credit. This article affirms *Laudisi v. American Exch. Nat. Bank*, 239 N.Y. 234, 146 N.E. 347 (1924) (The credit referred to Alicante Bouchez Grapes, the invoice specified Alicante Bouchez grapes, but the bill of lading said "grapes." The bank honored the draft; the court upheld the bank stating that taken together, the documents were adequate.)

The current version of the Uniform Customs and Practices for Documentary Credit, issued by the International Chamber of Commerce is entitled I.C.C. Publication No. 500 (1993). The U.C.P. becomes the governing law in any letter of credit that incorporates it as such. Because the U.C.P. is more detailed and is more familiar to international businessperson, many letters of credits opt for the U.C.P. over the U.C.C. The New York Article 5 provision states for a statutory preference of the U.C.P. as a default rule. See N.Y. Uniform Commercial Code § 5-102(4).

---

[7] See N.Y.— McKinney's Uniform Commercial Code § 5-102(4). See also, Code of Ala. 1975, § 7-5-102(4); Vernon's Ann.Mo.Stat. § 400.5-102(4).

See J. Dolan, The Law of Letters of Credit, ¶ 4.06, "The Code and the Uniform Customs" (2d ed. 1991).

The U.C.C. and the U.C.P. are similar in most regards, and Revised Article Five represents a conscious effort by the drafters to align the U.C.C. with its foreign cousin in areas of divergence. An important example of the new similarities, is Revised § 5-108(c) which provides that the issuer is precluded from asserting a discrepancy not stated in its timely notice. Under the prior U.C.C., there was no requirement that the issuer provide any explanation as to why the letter of credit demand had been denied. This new provision brings the Revised Article parallel to the U.C.P.

[C]   Requirements

Read: U.C.C. §§ 5-102 and 5-104; Revised §§ 5-103, 5-104.

TRANSPARENT PRODS. CORP. v. PAYSAVER CREDIT UNION

United States Court of Appeals
864 F.2d 60, 7 U.C.C. Rep. Serv. 2d 832 (7th Cir. 1988)

EASTERBROOK, CIRCUIT JUDGE.

Uncertain of the difference between a line of credit and a letter of credit, the president of Paysaver Credit Union signed this document on the Credit Union's letterhead:

Transparent Products Corporation
Bensenville, IL. 60101
RE: Thomas Wells

Gentlemen:

> We hereby establish our letter of credit at the request of Thomas Wells of 1003 South 23rd Avenue, Maywood and of Titan Tool of 1315 South 3rd Avenue, Maywood up to the aggregate amount of fifty-thousand dollars ($50,000).

At the time Paysaver signed this document, Titan Tool owed Transparent some $33,000 on open account credit for plastics. Titan wanted to buy another $61,000 worth, but Transparent had balked unless Titan's creditworthiness could be assured. Wells, an employee of Titan who had a $50,000 certificate of deposit with Paysaver, procured this document. Transparent apparently deemed it insufficient assurance of payment and did not sell additional goods to Titan. Some 13 months later Titan, then a debtor in bankruptcy, still had not paid the original $33,000. Transparent demanded that Paysaver make good the debt. Transparent believes that the document guarantees Titan's general debts; Paysaver believes that the document is a mishmash with no legal effect.

The district court concluded after a trial (at which the president of Paysaver allowed that he did not understand how letters of credit differed from lines of credit) that the document is a letter of credit. The court then held, in part on the basis of the intent underlying Paysaver's decision to send the document, that Transparent's delay in making a demand equitably estopped it from collecting. The injection of such considerations into the enforcement of letters of credit is unprecedented and would be most unfortunate. The district court did not find that Transparent deceived Paysaver or otherwise induced detrimental reliance on an unkept promise; it found only that Transparent tarried unduly. Letters of credit are designed to provide assurance of payment and could not serve that purpose if the beneficiary risked being denied payment for withholding a demand "for too long" while attempting to collect from the primary debtor. We need not consider, however, whether principles of estoppel are forever beyond the pale when dealing with letters of credit, for Paysaver defends its judgment on the ground that the document is not one.

Letters of credit facilitate commercial transactions by providing the assurance of a reliable party that a debt will be paid quickly and with no fuss. Letters often provide that the issuer will pay on presentation of shipping documents, relieving the seller of the risk of nonpayment (or delayed payment) while shifting to the buyer the risk that the goods will be defective and it will need to pursue the seller. Standby letters of credit do not contemplate immediate payment by the issuer but serve as assurance if the debtor does not pay. Guarantee letters of credit serve a role similar to more conventional guarantees of debt, but with the promise that the issuer will pay on demand rather than balk and precipitate litigation to determine whether the underlying debt was due (a common event when guarantees are issued by officers or shareholders of the debtor), and with the additional benefit of enabling banks to stand behind their customers' transactions when they are forbidden to issue straight guarantees. See generally Cassondra E. Joseph, *Letters of Credit: The Developing Concepts and Financing Functions,* 94 Banking L.J. 816 (1977). In any of these cases, the issuer specifies conditions under which payment will be made. The Uniform Commercial Code defines "credit" by reference to these conditions. The definition has two stages. Section 5-102, Ill. Rev. Stat. ch. 26 para. 5-102, establishes the scope of Article 5 (governing letters of credit), and § 5-103(1) defines "credit": 5-102. Scope. (1) This Article applies

(a) to a credit issued by a bank if the credit requires a documentary draft or a documentary demand for payment; and

(b) to a credit issued by a person other than a bank if the credit requires that the draft or demand for payment be accompanied by a document of title; and

(c) to a credit issued by a bank or other person if the credit is not within subparagraphs (a) or (b) but conspicuously states that it is a letter of credit or is conspicuously so entitled.

5-103. Definitions. (1) In this Article unless the context otherwise requires

(a) "Credit" or "letter of credit" means an engagement by a bank or other person made at the request of a customer and of a kind within the scope of this Article (Section 5-102) that the issuer will honor drafts or other demands for payment upon compliance with the conditions specified in the credit. A credit may be either revocable or irrevocable. The engagement may be either an agreement to honor or a statement that the bank or other person is authorized to honor.

Transparent relies on § 5-102(1)(c), observing that the document conspicuously calls itself a "letter of credit". (A statement is "conspicuous" if it is "so written that a reasonable person against whom it is to operate ought to have noticed it." U.C.C. § 1-201(10). Paysaver, which wrote this short letter, had to notice its own words.) But § 5-102(1)(c) applies only to "a credit", and under § 5-103(1)(a) a "credit" is an "engagement" to "honor drafts or other demands for payment upon compliance with the conditions" stated. The document Paysaver signed does not engage to do anything, under any conditions.

Sections 5-102 and 5-103, taken together with §§ 5-104 and 5-105 (saying that there are no formal requirements), show that a letter of credit need not be supported by consideration or contain any magic words or expiration date. They show with equal force that a letter of credit is an "engagement" to pay on the occurrence of specified events or the presentation of specified documents. A document engaging to do nothing and mentioning no events is simply a stray piece of paper. (A document labeled a "letter of credit" is a "guarantee" if its terms are the elements of guarantees and not letters of credit.)

The title controls only when the document contains the terms appropriate to the substance of such an instrument. The letter Paysaver signed is no different in principle from a pumpkin on which "$50,000" and "letter of credit" had been stenciled. Just as calling a sports car a "principal residence" will not permit the owner to take the deduction for interest under the tax laws, so calling a pumpkin a "letter of credit" will not make it one. This harmonizes our views with *Board of Inland Revenue v. Haddock*, in which String, J., concluded that a cow bearing the words "To the London and Literary Bank, Ltd.: Pay to the Collector of Taxes, who is no gentleman, or Order, the sum of fifty-seven pounds (and may he rot!). L 57/0/0", was a negotiable instrument.[8] The judge observed that the writing included all the terms necessary for negotiability, and that the cow could be endorsed over to any willing holder.

Insistence on having terms—a concrete "engagement"—is not mere pedantry. Letters of credit give assurance of payment; to promote the reliability of the device, courts do not look beneath the surface of the documents to discover side agreements, plumb the intent of the parties, and the like. Yet only such a detour could flesh out the document written by Paysaver. If this letter were viewed as an ordinary contract, it would be unenforceable on the ground that the undertaking is hopelessly indefinite. A document too vague to be enforced as a contract is an implausible candidate for an Article 5 letter of credit.

Consider what is missing. One item is the term most important to any letter of credit: specification of the circumstances requiring the issuer to pay. Transparent believes that the document commits Paysaver to make good Titan's existing debt. Yet letters of credit to guarantee payment of prior debts are rare. One could see the document alternatively as an undertaking to make good on any new transaction, such as the $61,000 sale under discussion. A letter with this meaning would not stand behind the $33,000 accrued debt. Only speculation or a detailed inquiry into oral negotiations—both anathema in letter of credit transactions—could supply the missing term. Contrast *Bank of North Carolina, N.A. v. Rock Island Bank*, 570 F.2d 202 (7th Cir. 1978) (holding an undertaking to be a letter of credit because it contained detailed terms on which payment would occur).

Another missing or confusing item is the customer. The document is captioned "RE: Thomas Wells". Wells was an employee of Titan and not indebted to Transparent. Counsel for Transparent conceded at oral argument that it had no claim against Wells personally. Only the recitation that the document was issued "at the request of" Titan in addition to that of Wells offers support for application to Titan's transactions. If we must choose between reading the document as standing behind Wells or standing behind Titan, where the former is what the caption says and the latter is a felony (given limitations on credit unions' activities, 12 U.S.C. § 1757), the choice is simple. Transparent balked (as well it should) when asked whether a document saying something like "at the request of Exxon Corp., we undertake to assume the obligations of Titan Tool" would allow Transparent to invoke the letter of credit to collect a debt due from Exxon. Transparent suggested that we dip beneath the surface of this document to see that the negotiations leading to its issuance grew out of commercial dealings between Transparent and Titan, but we

---

[8] This enlightening case does not appear in the official reports, perhaps because it is the invention of A.P. Herbert, Uncommon Law 201-06 (1935), but given what does appear in the official reports, *Board of Inland Revenue v. Haddock* has its attractions.

have explained already why courts do not consider parol evidence when evaluating letters of credit.

The document is silent or obscure on every significant question. Such writings do not promote certainty in commercial transactions. Why a credit union put the words "letter of credit" to a document is beyond us; perhaps the National Credit Union Administration ought to have a few words with the management at the Paysaver Credit Union. Whatever this document may be, it is not a "credit" under §§ 5-102 and 5-103 of the U.C.C.

AFFIRMED

NOTES

(1) The drafters of Revised Article Five have noted that nearly $250 billion of letter of credit financing occurs in the United States annually. It is thus surprising that the U.C.C. requires no formalities for creation of a letter of credit other than 1) a writing 2) that is signed by the issuer. A well drafted letter of credit will contain much more than the statutory minimum. As in all contracts, a skillfully crafted letter of credit will clearly express each parties intentions.

(2) *Letters of credit may be revocable or irrevocable.* See § 5-103 and 5-106 [revised §§ 5-102, 5-106 Comment]. A revocable letter of credit is similar to an illusory promise—issuer may revoke or modify the letter with out notice, or consent of either the customer or beneficiary. § 5-106(3) [revised § 5-106(b)]. Practitioner's query: Why would anyone ever accept a revocable letter of credit? An irrevocable letter of credit can be modified or revoked only with the consent of the customer; once the beneficiary receives the letter or the advice of letter, modification or revocation permitted only with beneficiary's consent. § 5-106(1) and (2) [revised § 5-106(a) and (b)]. Note that Article 6 of the U.C.P. provides that credits which do not explicitly state the status of a letter of credit clearly are deemed revocable. Can you hypothesize why a bank would find it advantageous to argue for a letter of credit being governed by the U.C.P. when all documents are silent to the governing law and the bank is aware that the customer is having financial difficulties? Why should the U.C.P. default rule favor that a letter of credit is "revocable?"

[D] Obligation of Issuer

Issuer's Responsibility for Performance of the Underlying Sale Contract. We have established from previous discussion that the issuer of a documentary letter of credit is generally in the banking business, and does not intend to become involved either as buyer or seller with reference to the goods transaction underlying the issuance of the credit. Performance of the sales contract is not the issuer's concern; it is only obligated under its agreement with its customer to honor the beneficiary's draft if the terms of the credit are met. Again, insofar as the documents accompanying the draft are concerned, the issuer must make a sufficient examination to ascertain that the documents are regular and appear to comply with the terms of the letter of credit, but does not become responsible for the genuineness of the documents themselves. All of this is made explicit in U.C.C. § 5-109(1), (2) [revised § 5-108]. Further, the issuer has no concern with the conformity of goods or documents to the underlying sale contract.[9] Several of the Articles of the Uniform Customs, 1993 revision, pertain to the issuer's duties in this regard. See Articles 2-4, 9 and 13.

---

[9] "An issuer must honor a draft or demand for payment which complies with the terms of the relevant credit regardless of whether the goods or documents conform to the underlying contract for sale. . ." U.C.C. § 5-114(1) [revised § 5-108(a)].

Compliance of Documents with the Terms of the Credit: Strict versus Substantial Compliance. Although the issuer generally need not be concerned with the goods but only with the documents, it nevertheless must determine whether the documents tendered by the seller comply with the terms of the credit. If the documents fail to comply, and the issuer pays the draft, it breaches its contract with the customer-buyer (U.C.C. § 5-109(1), (2); see § 5-114(3)) [revised §§ 5-108, 5-109]; on the other hand, if they in fact do comply but the issuer dishonors the draft, it is liable to the beneficiary-seller (U.C.C. §§ 5-114(1), 5-115) [revised § 5-108(a), 5-111].

One of the important areas *not* covered by Article 5 revolves around the question of "when documents in fact and in law do or do not comply with the terms of the credit." § 5-102(3) and Comment 2 [cf. § 5-108]. Therefore, we must look to case law and the Uniform Customs (UCP).[10]

Professor Kozolchyk remarks:[11]

One of the most often quoted and influential judicial statements in letter of credit law was made by Lord Sumner in the 1927 English case of *Equitable Trust Co. of New York v. Dawson Partners* [(1927, 27 Ll.L. Rep. 49, 52 (H.L.).]: "There is no room for documents which are almost the same or which will do just as well." In other words, the issuing bank's verification has to be governed by a strict standard which excludes deviations, however slight, from the customer's instructions and from the credit terms.

The major justification for this strict standard is that the successful utilization of commercial letters of credit depends on the trustworthiness of the promises made by the issuing banker to the customer and the beneficiary. Unless those promises are kept inviolate they are not likely to be relied upon by either party. A less apparent justification relates to the nature of the banking business. Banks are not normally interested in becoming involved in the underlying transactions as would be required if documents were to be checked for facts other than their apparent or formal regularity, or if their regularity had to be established by resorting to evidence extrinsic to the letter of credit transaction.

Nevertheless there is an economic if not a physical limit to the diligence required from a bank when checking formal or apparent regularity. As stated by an experienced banker, if an absolutely perfect tender were the required standard, very few tenders would qualify. . . .

One of the realities of "living" letters of credit law is that customers have a marked propensity to find deviations from strict compliance whenever there is a sharp drop in the market price of the goods purchased from the seller beneficiary. Such deviations are not too difficult to find given the large number of words and clauses normally involved in documentary credits.

Courts in major trading centers have become aware of this propensity and are, therefore, less insistent upon strict compliance. This attitude became apparent to this author . . .when comparing court decisions in different jurisdictions and legal systems on objections to strict compliance. Courts were inclined to take more seriously a banker's objection of noncompliance raised against a beneficiary's tender of documents than a customer's objection raised against the issuing bank's verification. . . . The second question posed in the introduction to this

---

[10] See, e.g., UCP Arts. 9, 13, 37c summarized at § 11.01[B] above.

[11] From Vol. IX, International Encyclopedia of Comparative Law, Chapter 5 by B. Kozolchyk at §§ 5-148 and 5-149, 5-155 and 5-156 (1978)." Compliance with the terms of a letter of credit is not like pitching horseshoes. No points are awarded for being close." *Fidelity Nat'l Bank v. Dade County*, 371 So. 2d 545, 546 (Fla.Dist.Ct.App. 1979).

subchapter can therefore be answered in the affirmative. There are differences in the application of the standard of strict compliance and they depend upon the parties involved in the controversy and the plaintiff's or defendant's relationship to the issuing bank. . . .

In *J.H. Rayner & Co. v. Hambro's Bank, Ltd.* [1943] 1 K.B. 37, B contracted to purchase Coromandel groundnuts from S, and secured a letter of credit requiring bills of lading covering "a shipment of about 1400 tons Coromandel groundnuts." S presented its draft with an invoice describing Coromandel groundnuts, but a bill of lading covering "machine-shelled groundnut kernels." It was understood in the trade that "Coromandel groundnuts" and "machine shelled groundnut kernels" were the same commodity. The issuing bank refused to pay the draft, claiming the bill of lading to be nonconforming to the terms of the credit. S brought suit against the bank, but the court upheld the bank's refusal.[12]

In *Courtaulds North America, Inc. v. North Carolina National Bank*, 528 F.2d 802, 806 (4th Cir. 1975), the bank denied liability chiefly on the assertion that the draft did not agree with the letter's conditions, viz., that the draft be accompanied by a "Commercial invoice in triplicate stating [inter alia] that it covers. . .100% acrylic yarn"; instead, the accompanying invoices stated that the goods were "Imported Acrylic Yarn." The court held for the bank and concluded:

Had Bank deviated from the stipulation of the letter and honored the draft, then at once it might have been confronted with the not improbable risk of [buyer Adastra] bankruptcy trustee's charge of liability for unwarrantably paying the draft moneys to the seller, Courtaulds, and refusal to reimburse Bank for the outlay. Contrarily, it might face a Courtaulds claim that since it had depended upon Bank's assurance of credit in shipping yarn to Adastra, Bank was responsible for the loss. In this situation Bank cannot be condemned for sticking to the letter of the letter.

BEYENE v. IRVING TRUST CO.

United States Court of Appeals
762 F.2d 4, 40 U.C.C. Rep. 1811 (2nd Cir. 1985)

KEARSE, CIRCUIT JUDGE.

Plaintiffs Dessaleng Beyene and Jean M. Hanson appeal from a final judgment of the United States District Court for the Southern District of New York, Morris E. Lasker, Judge, dismissing their complaint seeking damages for the alleged wrongful refusal of defendant Irving Trust Company ("Irving") to honor a letter of credit. The district court granted Irving's motion for summary judgment dismissing the complaint on the ground that, since the bill of lading presented to Irving misspelled the name of the person to whom notice was to be given of the arrival of

---

[12] Restatement, Second, Contracts § 221, Illustration 9 is based on this case. The section concludes: "Bank is not bound to honor drafts accompanied by bills of lading covering 'Machine-shelled groundnut kernels.' See Uniform Commercial Code § 5-109(1)(c)."

the goods and thereby failed to comply with the terms of the letter of credit, Irving was under no duty to honor the letter of credit. On appeal, plaintiffs contend, inter alia, that the mere misspelling of a name should not relieve a bank of its duty to honor a letter of credit. We agree with the district court that the misspelling in this case was a material discrepancy that relieved Irving of its duty to pay the letter of credit, and we affirm the judgment.

FACTS

The material undisputed facts may be stated briefly. In March 1978, Beyene agreed to sell to Mohammed Sofan, a resident of the Yemen Arab Republic ("YAR"), two prefabricated houses. Sofan attempted to finance the purchase through the use of a letter of credit issued by the Yemen Bank for Reconstruction and Development ("YBRD") in favor of Beyene. YBRD designated Irving as the confirming bank for the letter of credit and Irving subsequently notified Beyene of the letter's terms and conditions. Beyene designated the National Bank of Washington ("NBW") as his collecting bank.

In May 1979, NBW sent Irving all of the documents required under the terms of the letter of credit. Thereafter, Irving telephoned NBW to inform it of several discrepancies in the submitted documents, including the fact that the bill of lading listed the party to be notified by the shipping company as Mohammed Soran instead of Mohammed Sofan. The NBW official contacted testified at deposition that Irving never waived the misspelling discrepancy and continued to assert that it was a discrepancy, though it undertook to request authorization from YBRD to pay the letter of credit despite the discrepancy. Such authorization was not forthcoming, and Irving refused to pay.

Plaintiffs instituted the present suit seeking damages for Irving's failure to pay the letter of credit. Irving moved for summary judgment dismissing the complaint on a variety of grounds. The district court, in an opinion reported at 596 F Supp 438 (1984), granted the motion on the sole ground that the misspelling of Sofan's name in the bill of lading constituted a material discrepancy that gave Irving the right to dishonor the letter of credit. This appeal followed.

DISCUSSION

On appeal, plaintiffs contend principally that (1) the district court's ruling is unsound as a matter of precedent and of policy, and (2) Irving should be required to pay the letter of credit on grounds of waiver and estoppel. We find merit in none of plaintiffs' contentions. We need discuss only the first.

The nature and functions of commercial letters of credit have recently been explored by this court, see *Voest-Alpine International Corp. v. Chase Manhattan Bank*, N.A., 707 F2d 680, 682-83 (2d Cir 1983); *Marino Indus.tries Corp. v. Chase Manhattan Bank*, N.A., 686 F2d 112, 114-15 (2d Cir 1982), and will not be repeated in detail here. The terms of a letter of credit generally require the beneficiary of the letter to submit to the issuing bank documents such as an invoice and a bill of lading to provide "the accredited buyer [with] some assurance that he will receive the goods for which he bargained and arranged payment." H. Harfield, Bank Credits and Acceptances 57 (5th ed 1974). The issuing bank, or a bank that acts as confirming bank for the issuer, takes on an absolute duty to pay the amount of the credit to the beneficiary, so long as the beneficiary complies with the terms of the letter. In order to protect the issuing or confirming bank, this absolute duty does not arise unless the terms of the letter have been complied with strictly. Literal compliance is generally "essential so as not to impose an obligation upon the bank that it did not undertake and so as not to jeopardize the bank's right to indemnity from its customer." Voest-Alpine International Corp. v. Chase Manhattan Bank, 707 F2d at 683; see H. Haffield, Letters of Credit 57-59 (1979).

While some variations in a bill of lading might be so insignificant as not to relieve the issuing or confirming bank of its obligation to pay, see, *e.g.,* H. Harfield, Bank Credits and Acceptances 75-78, we agree with the district court that the misspelling in the bill of lading of Sofan's name as "Soran" was a material discrepancy that entitled Irving to refuse to honor the letter of credit. First, this is not a case where the name intended is unmistakably clear despite what is obviously a typographical error, as might be the case if, for example, "Smith" were misspelled "Smithh." Nor have appellants claimed that in the Middle East "Soran" would obviously be recognized as an inadvertent misspelling of the surname "Sofan." Second, "Sofan" was not a name that was inconsequential to the document, for Sofan was the person to whom the shipper was to give notice of the arrival of the goods, and the misspelling of his name could well have resulted in his nonreceipt of the goods and his justifiable refusal to reimburse Irving for the credit. (Indeed, the record includes a telex from Beyene, stating that Sofan had not been notified when the goods arrived in YAR and that as a result demurrage and other costs had been incurred.) In the circumstances, the district court was entirely correct in viewing the failure of Beyene and NBW to provide documents that strictly complied with the terms of the letter of credit as a failure that entitled Irving to refuse payment.

Plaintiffs do not contend that there was any issue to be tried as to the fact of the misspelling of Sofan's name. Their assertions that Irving waived the admitted discrepancy or was estopped from relying on it were not supported sufficiently to withstand a motion for summary judgment and were properly rejected by the district court for the reasons stated in its opinion, 596 F Supp at 439-41.

CONCLUSION

The judgment of the district court is affirmed.

———

NOTE

Letter of Credit Update 11-12 (August, 1985) comments on the *Beyene* case:[13]

Quoting from *Marino Industries v. Chase Manhattan Bank, N.A.,* 686 F. 2d 112 (2d Cir. 1982), the district court concluded that "a single discrepancy, including one involving the misspelling of a party's last name, is sufficient to excuse a confirming bank from paying the proceeds of a letter of credit." *Beyene,* 596 F. Supp. 438 at 441.

On appeal, the Second Circuit affirmed. "We agree with the district court that the misspelling in this case was a material discrepancy that entitled Irving to refuse to honor the letter of credit . . . . The district court was entirely correct in viewing the failure of Beyene and NBW to

---

[13] Copyright © 1985 by James E. Byrne. Reprinted by permission.

provide documents that strictly complied with the terms of the letter of credit as a failure that entitled Irving to refuse payment."

The Second Circuit's decision may muddy the waters of strict compliance even more. Despite its ruling that the district court was correct in granting summary judgment, the opinion is less clear as to the state of the doctrine of strict compliance.

The district court held that the discrepancy was sufficient to justify dishonor regardless of its materiality. According to its understanding of the law, "a confirming bank need not ascertain the magnitude of each discrepancy before its obligation to pay is relieved. Under the rule of 'strict compliance,' Irving did not have to scrutinize the underlying transaction between Beyene and Sofan, nor did it have to establish whether the misspelling of an Arab name was a meaningful mistake or find that it was a major error before it could claim that a discrepancy in the documents existed." *Beyene*, 596 F. Supp. 438 at 442.

The Second Circuit, however, clearly looked at whether the mistake was material and concluded that it was. Whatever one may think of its reasoning, the court drew upon the facts, as indicated in the quotation above, to justify its conclusion that materiality existed. Oddly enough, it perceived the position of the district court to be that there was a material discrepancy.

Whatever the courts may say, then, it would appear that not just any discrepancy will do, there must be some indication that it was material.

From the beneficiary's viewpoint, the entire scenario looks like a catch-22. According to Beyene's attorney, William L. Borden, the error was made by the Baltimore steamship company and noticed by the freight forwarder and collecting bank when the documents were assembled for presentation. At that time, Beyene contended, they determined that the discrepancy was too minor to bother correcting.

Sound like grounds for an action against the local bank? Beyene thought so and sued both the issuing bank and the collecting bank, figuring that one would be responsible. Because the action was brought in D.C., however, it was held that there was no jurisdiction over the issuing bank under the applicable long arm statute. Hence, the instant action in New York. The action against the collecting bank proceeded but Beyene was unable to produce Irving as a witness to prove that the bank's alleged error in judgment caused its loss because the D.C. rules in effect provided no means of process by which Irving could be compelled to testify.

"It is an example of how little people can get terribly hurt under this system," said attorney Borden in an interview. "As a result of a petty error of which he had no knowledge and as to which the two banks blame each other, both are exonerated and the small businessman is stuck with a crushing loss." Will Beyene utilize letters of credit again? "Not soon," exclaimed Borden.

AMERICAN COLEMAN CO. v. INTRAWEST BANK OF SOUTHGLENN, N.A.

United States Court of Appeals
887 F.2d 1382, 10 U.C.C.R. Serv. 2d 1361 (10th Cir. 1989)

BARRETT, SENIOR CIRCUIT JUDGE.

After examining the briefs and the appellate record, this panel has determined unanimously that oral argument would not materially assist the determination of this appeal. See Fed.R.App.P. 34(a); Tenth Cir. R. 34.1.9. The cause is therefore ordered submitted without oral argument.

In this diversity case, the American Coleman Company (American Coleman), plaintiff below, appeals from the district court's order granting summary judgment on behalf of the defendant below, Intrawest Bank of Southglenn, N.A., the predecessor to the United Bank of Southglenn, N.A. (Bank). The court dismissed, with prejudice, American Coleman's action for damages for an alleged wrongful dishonor of a request for payment pursuant to a letter of credit.

In 1984, American Coleman sold some real property located in Littleton, Colorado, to James E. Gammon (Gammon) and the South Santa Fe Partnership (the Partnership) and took a note secured by a first deed of trust on the property. The note and deed of trust were dated November 16, 1984, but not recorded until November 21, 1984. The terms of the repayment of the note required Gammon and the Partnership to post a letter of credit, of which American Coleman would be the beneficiary. The Bank, on behalf of its customer, Gammon and Associates, established a "Clean, Irrevocable Letter of Credit" in amount of $250,000 in favor of American Coleman. It was dated February 15, 1985, and was to expire on November 15, 1986. In consideration, the Bank received from Gammon a letter of credit fee and a second deed of trust on the Littleton property under a reimbursement contract whereby Gammon was to repay Bank for all payments made by Bank to American Coleman pursuant to the letter of credit. The letter of credit arrangement, once established, is often referred to as a statutory obligation on the part of the issuer (Bank) to honor drafts drawn by the beneficiary (American Coleman) that comply with the terms of the letter of credit. The transaction is separate and independent from the underlying business transaction between the beneficiary (American Coleman) and the Bank's customer (Gammon and Associates) which is contractual in nature. A letter of credit is not an evidence of indebtedness; it is merely a promise by a bank to lend money under certain circumstances.

The Bank was to make funds available to American Coleman pursuant to its sight drafts to be accompanied by the "original Letter of Credit and your signed written statement that Jim Gammon and Associates is in default on the Note and Security Agreement dated November 21, 1984, between American Coleman and Jim Gammon and Associates." (R., Vol. I, Tab 2, Exh. A). The above reference to a note and security agreement dated November 21, 1984, was an error, inasmuch as no such documents ever existed. The record does not resolve the dispute relative to the party responsible for the error. However, on November 16, 1984, Gammon and

Associates executed and delivered to American Coleman a note in the principal sum of $1,037,500 secured by a first deed of trust on the Littleton property sold which were recorded on November 21, 1984.

Thereafter, on December 31, 1985, and on May 16, 1986, American Coleman requested payments of $75,000, respectively, under the letter of credit. Both of these requests included the original letter of credit and the specific default language previously referred to, *i.e.,* "Jim Gammon and Associates is in default on the Note and Security Agreement dated November 21, 1984, between American Coleman and Jim Gammon and Associates." (R., Vol. I, Tab 5, Exhibits A and B). Thus, a balance of $100,000 remained available to be drawn on under the letter of credit when on November 13, 1986, American Coleman tendered to Bank a sight draft in amount of $100,000 with the following statement appended thereto:

> The American Coleman Company informs you that Jim Gammon and Associates is in default on the Note and Security Agreement dated November 21, 1984, and the Promissory Note dated November 16, 1984, between American Coleman and Jim Gammon and Associates.

(R., Vol. I, Tab 2, Exh. B).

Bank formally dishonored the draft on November 17, 1986, two days after the letter of credit expired because (1) the amount requested was in advance of any default, and (2) no default could occur until November 16, 1986. Bank did not give as a reason for dishonor the fact that the wording of American Coleman's request was not in strict compliance with the terms of the letter of credit.

In the district court, both parties moved for summary judgment, agreeing that there was no genuine dispute of material fact relative to Bank's liability for its dishonor of American Coleman's request of November 13, 1986, for the balance of funds under the letter of credit. Bank contended that the fact that the note was not then in default constituted a valid ground for dishonor and, further, that dishonor was proper because American Coleman's request was not in strict compliance with the terms of the letter of credit. American Coleman argued that Bank should be estopped from raising the defense of strict compliance because Bank had not asserted this defense at the time of dishonor. Further, should Bank not be estopped, American Coleman contended that its request for funds was in strict compliance with the terms of the letter of credit. In considering the cross-motions for summary judgment, the district court relied upon the pleadings, the briefs, affidavits and other documentation.

The district court found/concluded that Bank was not estopped from raising the defense of strict compliance and that American Coleman's request of November 13, 1986, was not in strict compliance with the terms of the letter of credit. The court did not reach the issue whether the original reason given by the Bank, i.e., that the note was not yet in default, was a valid ground for dishonor.

On appeal, American Coleman contends that the district court's decision was erroneous, contrary to law, and an abuse of discretion in the court's holdings that: (1) the note was not yet in default, (2) the demand was not in strict compliance, technically or literally, with the terms of the letter of credit, (3) the Bank was not estopped from raising lack of strict compliance as a reason for dishonor, and (4) the beneficiary (American Coleman) was not misled, and could not have cured the defect because Bank was allowed, pursuant to C.R.S. § 4-5-112(1)(a), to defer payment or dishonor for three banking days.

No contention is raised on appeal that substantial issues of material fact existed, precluding summary judgment under Rule 56(a) Fed R.Civ.P. Even so, it is our duty to examine the record on appeal to determine whether any genuine issue of material fact pertinent to the ruling remains and, if not, whether the district court properly applied the substantive law. And in making this evaluation, pleadings and documentary evidence must be construed liberally and in favor of the party opposing the motion. We are satisfied that no genuine issues of material fact remained when the district court granted summary judgment. Finally, in our de novo review, we have recognized different degrees of deference we must give to the interpretations and applications of state law by a resident federal judge sitting in a diversity action (some deference, great deference, clearly erroneous). We shall proceed under the "some deference" standard.

I.

American Coleman argues that the district court was clearly erroneous in finding/concluding that the Note of November 16, 1984, was not yet in default when the November 13, 1986, demand for payment was made by American Coleman upon Bank. The record shows, however, that the district court made no such finding.

It is true that after the draft of November 13, 1986 was submitted Bank did inform American Coleman that it would not fund the letter of credit because the Note was not in default and could not be in default until November 16, 1986. Because this was the only ground relied upon by Bank to dishonor the draft, American Coleman argued, unsuccessfully, that Bank should be estopped from raising the defense of strict compliance in the district court action because it failed to assert the issue of nonconformity at the time it dishonored the draft.

The district court plainly did not find/conclude that the Note of December 16, 1984, was in default. In the district court's Memorandum Opinion and Order of December 17, 1987, the court stated:

> Since I conclude that the bank is not estopped from raising the defense of strict compliance, and since I further find that American Coleman's request for funds was not in strict compliance with the terms and conditions of the letter of credit, I need not reach the issue of whether the original reason given by the bank (that the note was not yet in default) was a valid ground for dishonor.

(R., Vol. I, Tab 6, p. 5).

II.

American Coleman contends that the district court erred in holding that the doctrine of strict compliance required American Coleman, as beneficiary of the letter of credit from Bank, as issuer, to literally and technically adhere to the requirements of the letter of credit. The district court found/concluded:

> In the present case, it is clear that American Coleman's request for payment presented November 13, 1986 was not in technical or literal compliance with the terms of the letter of credit. American Coleman's reference to two different notes could easily have caused the bank's documents examiner some confusion. Accordingly, because I conclude that the rule of strict compliance, as it is applied in Colorado, requires literal compliance with the terms and requirements set forth in the letter of credit, and there was no such literal compliance in this case. . . .

(R., Vol. I, Tab 6, p. 13).

The district court recognized that many courts refuse to allow an issuing bank to dishonor a demand for payment when the nonconformity between the language contained in the draft or demand and the terms contained in the letter of credit is trivial or technical. *Id.* at 9. The court observed that the Colorado Supreme Court has not as yet ruled on the distinction between traditional strict compliance versus substantial compliance, and particularly so where the deviation is "as minor and technical as in this case." *Id.* at 13. Even so, based upon *Colorado National Bank v. Board of County Commissioners*, 634 P.2d 32, 40 (Colo. 1981) ("To maintain the commercial vitality of the letter of credit device, strict compliance with the terms of the letter of credit is required"); *Guilford Pattern Works, Inc. v. United Bank of Boulder*, 655 F. Supp. 378, 379-80 (D.Colo. 1987) ("Colorado courts have held that in order to maintain the commercial validity of the vehicle of letters of credit, strict compliance with the terms and conditions is necessary."), and other cases and authorities, the district court reasoned that the Colorado Supreme Court "would shun the non-standard of substantial compliance and would require literal and technical adherence to the requirements of the letter of credit." (R., Vol. I, Tab 6, p. 13). We agree.

C.S.R. § 4-5-114(1) provides:

> An issuer must honor a draft or demand for payment which complies with the terms of the relevant credit, regardless of whether the goods or documents conform to the underlying contract for sale or other contract between the customer and the beneficiary. The issuer is not excused from honor of such a draft or demand by reason of an additional general term that all documents must be satisfactory to the issuer, but an issuer may require that specified documents must be satisfactory to it.

In *Raiffeisen-Zentralkasse Tirol v. First National Bank*, 671 P.2d 1008 (Colo.App. 1983), the court held that the obligation of the issuer of a letter of credit to honor the letter is wholly separate from the beneficiary's compliance with the terms of the underlying contract and is dependent solely on the terms and conditions contained in the letter of credit. This separation is supportive of the rule laid down in *Colorado National Bank v. Board of County Commissioners*, *supra,* that strict compliance with the terms of a letter of credit is required to maintain the commercial vitality of the letter of credit device. Failure on the part of Bank to oversee careful compliance with the terms of the letter of credit would have prohibited Bank from collecting the funds paid to the beneficiary (American Coleman) from its customer, the Partnership (Jim Gammon and Associates). See *Philadelphia Gear Corp. v. Central Bank*, 717 F.2d 230 (5th Cir.), reh'g denied, 720 F.2d 1291 (5th Cir. 1983). The duty of the issuing Bank is ministerial in nature, confined to checking the presented documents carefully against what the letter of credit requires. Marino Industries *Corp. v. Chase Manhattan Bank, N.A.*, 686 F.2d 112 (2d Cir. 1982).

The district court found that the language in American Coleman's draft of November 13, 1986, referring to "The Note and Security Agreement dated November 21, 1984, and the Promissory Note dated November 16, 1984, between American Coleman and Jim Gammon and Associates" was not in strict compliance because of the extra language that was included. (R., Vol. I, Tab 6, pp. 5-6). We agree.

It has been observed that most courts apply the "strict compliance" standard which leaves "no room for documents which are almost the same or which will do just as well." A minority of the courts hold that a beneficiary's "reasonable" or "substantial" performance of the letter of credit's requirement will do. However, no matter how one reads the cases, strict compliance endures as the central test. White & Summers, Uniform Commercial Code, Third Edition (1988),

Vol. 2, § 19-5, p. 31. The authors state that cases applying the "reasonable" or "substantial" compliance standard "are so few and their notion so inherently fuzzy that they give little or no clue as to what might be 'reasonable' or 'substantial' compliance." *Id.*

While it is apparent from the cases that minute discrepancies which could not possibly mislead a document examiner are usually disregarded, this does not constitute a retreat from the strict compliance standard applicable in this case inasmuch as the district court found that "American Coleman's reference to two different notes could easily have caused the bank's documents examiner some confusion." (R., Vol. I, Tab 6, p. 13). We agree.

We hold that the district court did not err in applying the strict compliance standard. We reject American Coleman's argument that reference in the November 13, 1986, draft to the second note was mere "surplusage." The apparent existence of two promissory notes supports the district court's finding that Bank could have been misled by American Coleman's November 13, 1986, draft. American Coleman's contention that Bank could not have been misled by the draft because Bank drafted the letter of credit is without support in this record. The deposition testimony of American Coleman representative Joseph E. McElroy demonstrates that American Coleman's attorney assisted in drafting the letter of credit (R., Vol. I, Tab 4, Exh. F). There is no other evidence in the record on appeal relative thereto.

III.

American Coleman contends that the district court was clearly erroneous in holding that Bank was not estopped from raising the defense of lack of strict compliance as a reason for its dishonor of the November 13, 1986, draft.

The district court recognized that in Colorado the general rule is that "when an issuer of a letter of credit formally places its refusal to pay upon specified grounds, it is held to have waived all other grounds," quoting from *Colorado National Bank v. Board of County Commissioners*, 634 P.2d 32, 41 (Colo. 1981). However, the district court relied upon that same case for the proposition that the waiver-estoppel rule "is limited to situations where the statements have misled the beneficiary who would have cured the defect but relied on the stated grounds to its injury." *Id.* at 41.

The district court relied on *Colorado National Bank v. Board of County Commissioners*, supra, for its ruling that Bank was not estopped from raising a ground for dishonor in defense of suit brought by American Coleman even though it failed to state such ground at the time of dishonor.

In *Colorado National Bank v. Board of County Commissioners*, the letter of credit provided for a 15-day sight draft. However, the beneficiary submitted a demand draft on the day the letter of credit was to expire. Bank gave several reasons for dishonor, but did not rely upon the fact that the beneficiary had presented a demand draft in lieu of the required 15-day sight draft. Even so, the court held that the bank was not estopped from raising this ground in defense of the suit because the non-conforming demand draft was presented on the same day that the letter of credit expired. The court observed that under C.R.S. § 4-5-112(1)(a) a bank called upon to honor a draft or demand for payment under a letter of credit may defer payment or dishonor until the close of the third banking day following receipt of the documents. Thus, the court reasoned that the beneficiary could not have cured the defect since any subsequent presentment would have been untimely. Accordingly, the beneficiary could not have detrimentally relied on the bank's failure to state the discrepancy as a ground for dishonor.

We agree with the district court's conclusion that the facts of the instant case are quite similar to those in *Colorado National* and that American Coleman cannot be said to have detrimentally relied on Bank's failure to state the strict compliance discrepancy as one ground for dishonor, and that Bank is not estopped from raising the doctrine of strict compliance in its defense. November 13, 1986, was a Thursday. Three banking days thereafter would extend to November 18, 1986, just one day after Bank gave formal notice of dishonor. American Coleman could not have submitted another draft before the note expired. C.R.S. § 4-5-112(1) provides, in pertinent part:

A bank to which a documentary draft or demand for payment is presented under a credit may without dishonor of the draft, demand or credit (a) defer honor until the close of the third banking day following receipt of the documents. . . .

American Coleman insists that the letter of credit in this case is clearly denominated a "clean" letter of credit as distinguished from a "documentary" letter of credit and that, accordingly, the three-banking-day rule does not apply. We agree that this statute applies only to a documentary draft or demand for payment. We disagree with American Coleman's contention that simply because the letter of credit here was denominated "Clean Irrevocable Letter of Credit" (R., Vol. I, Tab 2, Exh. A), it was treated by the parties as such.

C.R.S. § 4-5-103(1)(b) defines a "documentary draft" or a "documentary demand for payment" as one honor of which is conditioned upon the presentation of a document or documents. "Document" is defined therein as any paper, including invoice, certificate, notice of default, and the like. In the case at bar, American Coleman was required under the terms of the letter of credit to present the original letter of credit (a document) and a notice of default (a document) with each draft. American Coleman's effort to restrict the definition of "documentary draft" to documents of title or shipping invoices must fail.

We Affirm.

NOTES

(1) Is the strict compliance doctrine required to ensure consistency and predictability in letters of credit, or is it a stubborn throwback to inflexible Blackstonian principles that ignore the realities of the business world? Is it fair for a bank to avoid paying an obligation it voluntarily assumed because of an innocent and insignificant error, such as the misspelling of a word in a bill of lading, or the improper invoice number? Or is the presentment of complying documents something so basic that an exacting standard should be a hurdle for payment? Some commentators have eloquently argued for the adoption of a "substantial performance" or "harmless error" standard to govern when a beneficiary attempts to draw on imperfect documents.

(2) The Revised U.C.C., although explicitly recognizing the strict compliance rule (Revised § 5-108), tempers the harsh results of a beneficiary's minor mistake by allowing a refusing bank only one shot to reject a substantially complying note. A diligent beneficiary will submit a request to honor a letter of credit several days in advance of any expiration date on the letter of credit. If the issuing bank refuses to honor the draft, however, it must do so within seven days and it must explain all defects at that time (except fraud), or be barred from asserting them later. See Revised § 5-108(c) (requiring a bank to provide timely notice of any discrepancies). Therefore, a beneficiary should be given enough time to clean up all actionable and objectionable blemishes of a presentment. Does the Revised U.C.C. strike an appropriate balance between predictability and equity?

PROBLEM 11.2

Assume the above structure of Revised Article 5 has been adopted in Minnesota. The letter of credit extended by the Hayes' First National Bank is set to expire on 12/01/97. Stephen Ryder has sent three dozen of the finest bamboo rods to Clayton Molinero. Stephen presents all necessary documents to the Hayes' Bank on 11/28/97, anticipating that the paperwork is in strict compliance. A keen-eyed bank clerk notices on 11/29/97 that the required bill of lading refers to the fly rods as "three dozen split cane rods." Hayes' Bank could refuse to honor the draft based on this discrepancy. Given that the line of credit is about to expire, is the Bank allowed to wait until 12/04/97 before providing Stephen notification of errors in the paper work (and thus avoiding all obligations under the letter of credit), or does the U.C.C. "within a reasonable time" standard require Hayes' Bank to provide Stephen with enough time to reasonably cure the documents?

BANK OF COCHIN LTD. v. MANUFACTURERS HANOVER TRUST CO.

Southern District of New York
612 F. Supp. 1533; 41 U.C.C. Rep. Serv. 920 (1985)

CANNELLA, D.J.:

FACTS

Bank of Cochin Limited ["Cochin"], an Indian corporation and the issuer of letter of credit BB/VN/41/80, commenced this diversity action against Manufacturers Hanover Trust Company ["MHT"], a New York corporation that acted as the confirming bank on the letter. Cochin seeks recovery of the amount paid by MHT, thereafter debited to Cochin's account at MHT, on drawings negotiated in New York between MHT and St. Lucia Enterprises, Ltd. ["St. Lucia"]. Codefendant St. Lucia, a purported New York corporation and the letter of credit beneficiary, has perpetrated a large fraud on both banks and nonparty customer Vishwa Niryat (Pvt.) Ltd. ["Vishwa"]. Unfortunately, St. Lucia has vanished and the Court must decide whose shoulders will bear the scam.

The parties agree on the salient events and have presented essentially identical and uncontroverted statements of fact pursuant to Rule 3(g) of the Civil Rules for the Southern District of New York. On February 8, 1980, in Bombay, India, Vishwa requested Cochin to issue an irrevocable letter of credit covering up to $798,000 for the benefit of St. Lucia. The letter was to have expired on April 15, 1980 and covered the anticipated shipment and purchase of 1,000 metric tons of aluminum melting scrap consisting of aluminum beverage cans.[14]

---

[14] Vishwa's application for documentary credit required that St. Lucia supply the following documents and shipment conditions as a prerequisite to payment:

Six copies of signed invoices;

One set of clean shipped on board bills of lading;

Notification of shipment to Vishwa;

A maritime insurance policy covering civil unrest, marine and war risks;

A certificate of United States origin in triplicate;

A certificate of analysis from "LLOYDS" [sic] [of London] ["Lloyd's"] confirming the quantity, quality and shipment of the aluminum scrap;

On February 14, 1980, Cochin requested MHT to supply financial information on St. Lucia. MHT responded by telex the following day that St. Lucia did not maintain an MHT account and that a thorough check of normal credit sources did not reveal any "pertinent" information. On February 22, Cochin conveyed the terms and conditions of the letter of credit to MHT by telex and requested MHT to advise "St Lucia Enterprises Ltd" of the establishment of the letter and to add MHT's confirmation.[15] The letter of credit was issued subject to the Uniform Customs and Practice for Documentary Credits (1974 Revision), Int'l Chamber of Commerce, Pub. No. 290 ["UCP"].[16]

On February 25, MHT mailed its written advice of the letter of credit establishment to St. Lucia and confirmed the amended letter on February 29.[17] Cochin amended certain terms of the letter on four occasions in March and April 1980. MHT mailed its advices of these amendments to St. Lucia from March to May and sent copies to Cochin, which were received without comment.[18] The final amended letter of credit contained the following relevant terms and conditions:

Shipment by conference or first class vessel;

Shipment by a non-Pakistani vessel.

[15] The documentary and other requirements for the letter of credit set forth in Cochin's telex included:

Sight drafts of the invoice value in duplicate;

Six copies of the signed invoices showing that the aluminum was covered under notice 44-ITC(PN) 79;

One set of clean shipped on board bills of lading to the order of Cochin;

A certificate of United States origin in triplicate;

A certificate of analysis of the aluminum from Lloyd's;

Shipment from a United States port to Bombay;

A marine insurance policy issued by a first class insurance company; A packing list in triplicate;

One set of nonnegotiable documents to be sent directly to Vishwa immediately after shipment documented by a "cable advise" to Vishwa;

Shipment by conference or first-class vessel.

[16] The UCP was revised effective October 1, 1984. UCP, Int'l Chamber of Commerce, Pub. No. 400 (1983). It is axiomatic that the Court must ordinarily apply the law in effect at the time it renders its decision. See *Thorpe v. Housing Authority of Durham*, 393 U.S. 268, 281, 21 L. Ed. 2d 474, 89 S. Ct. 518 (1969); *Byrne v. Buffalo Creek Railroad Co.*, 765 F.2d 364, slip op. at 4726 (2d Cir. 1985). The letter of credit was, however, governed by the 1974 UCP pursuant to its express terms. See *Marine Midland Grace Trust Co. v. Banco del Pais*, S.A., 261 F. Supp. 884, 886 n.1 (S.D.N.Y. 1966). Although the application of the 1983 UCP would favor MHT, see *infra*, it would not alter the Court's decision on the motions.

[17] MHT's February 25 form advice listed correctly all the letter of credit conditions. On February 26, MHT requested information from Cochin on the first class insurance company and an explanation as to what documentation was needed to ascertain compliance with shipment by conference or first class vessel. See UCP art. 14(b) (1974) (rejecting usage of "first class" to describe issuers of documents), art. 22(b) (1983) (same). Cochin responded on February 28 by amending the letter of credit insurance clause to require that St. Lucia send a cable to Oriental Fire and General Insurance Co. ["Oriental"] citing cover note 429711. Cochin also requested that the shipping company or Lloyd's certify that the shipment was made by first class or approved vessel. The cable and certificate were to be submitted with the other documents. MHT accurately relayed this information to St. Lucia in its February 29 confirming telex.

[18] Cochin sent telexes to MHT on March 3, March 15, March 27 and April 29 amending the letter to reflect that shipment should be made from a port in western Europe and extending the shipping date to May 31 and the letter of credit expiration date to June 15. The inspection clause was also changed to allow a certificate of analysis from Lloyd's or any international agency. Additionally, Cochin requested that St. Lucia produce a certificate that it had duly complied with all terms of the letter of credit.

MHT accurately conveyed these amendments to St. Lucia by written advices dated March 10, March 31, April 8 and May 2. The March 31 advice incorrectly identified the Oriental cover note as 4291, which MHT had properly

a. Sight drafts of the invoice values;

b. Six copies of the signed invoices;

c. One set of clean shipped on board bills of lading;

d. A west European certificate of origin;

e. A certificate of analysis of the aluminum scrap from Lloyd's of London ["Lloyd's"]or another international testings agency;

f. Shipment from a west European port to Bombay;

g. A maritime insurance policy, cover note 429711, to be confirmed by St. Lucia's cable to Oriental Fire and General Insurance Co. ["Oriental"];

h. A packing list in triplicate;

i. One set of nonnegotiable documents to be sent to Vishwa and a confirming cable to Vishwa;

j. A certification from Lloyd's or the shipping company that the ship was a first class or approved non-Pakistani vessel;

k. St. Lucia's certification that it had complied with all terms of the letter of credit;

l. Shipment by May 31, 1980; and

m. Letter of credit expiration on June 15, 1980.

The aluminum was allegedly shipped on May 29, 1980 from Bremen, West Germany to Bombay on the M/V Betelguese. On June 2, St. Lucia established an account at a Manhattan office of Citibank, N.A. ["Citibank"], the collecting bank, in the name of St. Lucia Enterprises, Ltd. On June 9, St. Lucia presented MHT with documents required by the letter of credit and ten sight drafts amounting to $796,603.50,[19] payable to St. Lucia Enterprises. The documents included five copies of the invoices, a clean shipped on board bill of lading, a St. Lucia certification that the aluminum was of west European origin, a certificate of analysis by an international Dutch materials testing agent, a telex confirmation of a telephone message to Oriental that the aluminum had been shipped to Bombay pursuant to cover note 4291, a packing list in triplicate, a St. Lucia certification that one set of nonnegotiable documents had been sent to Vishwa and that Vishwa had been advised by cable, certifications from the shipping company that the M/V Betelguese was an approved first class Panamanian vessel, and a St. Lucia cover letter specifying the documents submitted and requesting payment from MHT. The St. Lucia letter and certifications were on the letterhead of "St. Lucia Enterprises" and were signed by "D Agney".

MHT compared the documents against the requirements of the letter and determined that they complied with all the terms and conditions. On June 13, MHT negotiated the drafts and issued a check for $798,000 payable to St. Lucia Enterprises. The check was indorsed St. Lucia Enterprises Ltd. and was deposited in the Citibank account on June 17, 1980. Citibank collected the check from MHT through normal banking channels. MHT debited Cochin's account for

---

designated as 429711 in its February 29 confirming advice. Notwithstanding MHT's allegation that Cochin cited cover note 4291, Cochin accurately used cover note 429711 in its telex amendments of February 28 and March 27. Each form of advice sent to St. Lucia and Cochin contained a beneficiary box with the following address: St. Lucia Enterprises, 210 Fifth Avenue, Suite No. 1102, New York, N.Y. 10010.

[19] Invoice 36C was for $79,121.70; invoice 36D was for $79,321.20; invoice 36F was for $79,560.60 and invoices 36A, 36B, 36E, 36F, 36G, 36H, 36I and 36J were each for $79,800.

$798,000 on June 13. MHT sent a copy of its payment advice, the drafts and documents to Cochin by registered air mail on June 13. Unfortunately, Cochin apparently did not receive these documents until June 21. As it turned out, St. Lucia shipped nothing to Vishwa. The documentation submitted to MHT was fraudulent in every regard; indeed, the bills of lading, quality certification and vessel certification were issued by nonexistent corporations. St. Lucia received payment on the letter of credit and Cochin has been unable to locate any party connected with the fraudulent scheme.

Cochin sent a telex to MHT on June 18, inquiring whether St. Lucia had presented documents for negotiation. MHT responded by telex on June 20 that it had paid St. Lucia $798,000 on June 13 and had forwarded the documents to Cochin at that time. On June 21, Cochin sent the following telex to MHT:

We acknowledge receipt of the documents [sic] Stop We find certain discrepancies [sic] in the same Stop kindly do not [sic] make payment against the same until we telex you otherwise Stop.

On June 23, MHT replied to Cochin's telex as follows:

Reference your telex June 21 credit BB VN 4180 our 500748 Stop We note your telex fails to give reason for [sic] rejection documents as required UCP Article 8 Stop According our records documents fully complied credit terms and beneficiary already paid therefore we cannot accept your refusal of documents.

By telex dated June 27, Cochin informed MHT of alleged defects in the documents apparently uncovered by Vishwa: (1) St. Lucia's cable to Oriental showed the wrong insurance cover note number of 4291 instead of 429711; (2) St. Lucia did not submit "proof" that a set of nonnegotiable documents and confirming cable had been sent to Vishwa; (3) only one set of documents showed the original certificate of origin whereas the rest included only photocopies; and (4) the invoice packing list and certificate of origin were not duly authenticated. Cochin also noted (5) the overpayment of $1,396.50. MHT credited Cochin's account for $1,396.50 and notified Cochin by telex on June 30.

By telex dated July 3, Cochin asked MHT to recredit its account for $796,603.50 and advised MHT that it was returning the letter of credit documents. Cochin also cited an additional discrepancy that (6) MHT had negotiated documents for St. Lucia Enterprises but that the letter of credit was established for St. Lucia Enterprises Ltd. On July 4, Cochin informed MHT by telex that the documents negotiated by MHT contained the following additional defects: (7) only five signed copies of the commercial invoices, rather than six, were forwarded and (8) documents were signed by "D Agney" without specifying his capacity at St. Lucia.

MHT responded by telex of July 14 that Cochin had failed to timely and properly specify the alleged documentary variances as required by article 8 of the 1974 UCP. The telex also noted that Cochin had failed to promptly return the documents or advise MHT that Cochin was holding the documents at MHT's disposal as required by the UCP. MHT asserted in a telex dated July 16 that it still had not received certain documents from Cochin. The parties exchanged additional telexes confirming and denying that payment was proper. Cochin's Rule 3(g) statement adds the additional allegations that (9) St. Lucia failed to indicate the documents submitted in drawing against the letter of credit, and (10) the shipping company certificate fails to indicate the vessel registration number.

DISCUSSION

Letter of credit liability cases are particularly appropriate for judicial resolution without trial because they present solely legal issues. See *Dulien Steel Prod., Inc. v. Bankers Trust Co.,* 298 F.2d 836, 837 (2d Cir. 1962); *Transamerica Delaval Inc. v. Citibank, N.A.,* 545 F. Supp. 200, 203 (S.D.N.Y. 1982). The parties do not dispute the essential facts and agreed in pretrial conference to present joint summary judgment motions. This case raises novel and unsettled issues of letter of credit law concerning confirming bank liability to an issuing bank for wrongful honor of a letter of credit. The law, however, is sufficiently chartered to require summary judgment for MHT.

A letter of credit is a financing mechanism designed to allocate commercial credit risks whereby a bank or other issuer pays an amount of money to a beneficiary upon presentment of documents complying with specified conditions set forth in the letter. The beneficiary, typically the seller of goods to a buyer-customer, uses the letter to substitute the credit of the issuer for the credit of its customer. The customer applies for the letter of credit, specifies the terms of the letter and promises to reimburse the issuer upon honor of the beneficiary's draft. The letter of credit is thus an engagement by the issuer to the beneficiary to cover the customer's agreement to pay money under the customer-beneficiary contract. The reliability and fluidity of the letter of credit are maintained because the issuing bank is concerned exclusively with the documents, not the performance obligations created by the customer-beneficiary contract. Not a contract, the letter of credit has been best described as "a relationship with no perfect analogies but nevertheless a well defined set of rights and obligations." 1 A. Lowenfeld, International Private Trade § 5.53 at 103 (1977); see B. Kozolchyk, Letters of Credit, in 9 Int'l Encyclopedia of Comparative Law ch. 5 at 137-40 (1979) (negotiable instrument concept).

The central issue presented by this case is whether St. Lucia's demand for payment from MHT was in compliance with the conditions specified in the letter of credit. Cochin's action for wrongful honor is based upon its assertion that MHT's payment was improper because the documents submitted by St. Lucia did not comply with the letter. Neither the UCP nor the Uniform Commercial Code ["UCC"] specify whether a bank honoring a letter of credit should be guided by a standard of strict compliance or substantial compliance with the terms of the letter.

The great weight of authority in this jurisdiction, and elsewhere, holds that an issuing or confirming bank is usually obligated to honor the beneficiary's draft only when the documents are in strict compliance with the terms of the letter of credit. See H. Harfield, Bank Credits and Acceptances, 73-74 (5th ed. 1974) (a "basic principle" of letter of credit law is that "the beneficiary must strictly comply with the terms of the credit to compel performance by the bank. . . . 'There is no room for documents which are almost the same, or which will do just as well' ") (quoting *Equitable Trust Co. v. Dawson Partners,* [1927] 27 Lloyd's List 49, 52); G. McLaughlin, Commercial Law, N.Y.L.J., May 8, 1985 at 30 n.18 (strict compliance standard is "the prevailing view in the United States"). Thus, New York courts have traditionally held that letter of credit law requires a beneficiary to strictly comply with the conditions of the letter. Additionally, this Court has previously held that "[a] bank's obligation in a letter of credit transaction is defined by the contract between the bank and its customer. It is obliged to pay only if the documents submitted strictly comply with the essential requirements of the letter of credit." *Corporacion de Mercadeo Agricola v. Pan American Fruit & Produce Corp.,* Memorandum Decision at 4-5, 75 Civ. 1611 (JMC) (S.D.N.Y. Apr. 13, 1976), quoted in *Corporacion de Mercadeo Agricola v. Mellon Bank,* 608 F.2d 43, 48 n.1 (2d Cir. 1979). This principle of strict compliance has been recently reaffirmed by the Second Circuit and the New York Court of Appeals. See *Beyene v. Irving Trust Co.,* 762 F.2d 4, 6 (2d Cir. 1985) ("In order to protect the issuing or confirming bank, this absolute duty [of payment to the beneficiary] does not arise unless the terms of the letter have been complied with strictly."); *Voest-Alpine Int'l Corp. v. Chase Manhattan Bank, N.A.,* 707 F.2d 680, 682 (2d Cir. 1983) ("The doctrine of strict compliance with the terms of the letter of credit functions to protect the bank which carries the absolute obligation to pay the bank which carries the absolute obligation to pay the beneficiary."); *Marino Indus. v. Chase Manhattan Bank, N.A.,* 686 F.2d 112, 114 (2d Cir. 1982) (" The essential requirements of a letter of credit must be strictly complied with by the party entitled to draw against the letter of credit, which means that the papers, documents and shipping descriptions must be as stated in the letter. ") (quoting *Venizelos, S.A. v. Chase Manhattan Bank,* 425 F.2d 461, 465 (2d Cir. 1970)); *United Commodities-Greece v. Fidelity Int'l Bank,* 64 N.Y.2d 449, 455, 478 N.E.2d 172,, 489 N.Y.S.2d 31, 33 (1985) ("New York requires strict compliance with the terms of a letter of credit, rather than the more relaxed standard of substantial compliance.")

Courts and commentators have noted, however, that New York appears to maintain a bifurcated standard of compliance. This approach calls for a strict compliance standard when the bank is sued by the beneficiary for wrongful dishonor but allows for a substantial compliance test when the bank is sued by the customer for wrongful honor. The stated rationale for the bifurcated standard is that it accords the bank flexibility in reacting to "a cross-fire of pressures . . .especially in times of falling commodity prices," J. White & R. Summers, Handbook of the Law Under the Uniform Commercial Code, § 18-6, at 731-32 (quoting State of N.Y. Law Revision Comm'n, Study of Uniform Commercial Code: Article 5-Documentary Letters of Credit, at 66 (1955), by limiting the liability burden on the bank, which might otherwise be caught between the "rock of a customer insisting on dishonor for highly technical reasons, and the hard place of a beneficiary threatening to sue for wrongful dishonor." B. Clark, The Law of Bank Deposits, Collections and Credit Cards, para. 8.5[4], at 8-48 (1981).

MHT correctly asserts that Cochin was its "customer" in this transaction and therefore argues that a substantial compliance standard should be used to test its review of St. Lucia's documents. Although the ultimate customer, Vishwa, may be barred from a direct action against the confirming bank because of the absence of privity (confirming bank has "relation" with issuing bank, not customer),[20] it is undisputed that MHT owes a duty of care to Cochin, see UCP art. 7 (1974), art. 15 (1983). The question then is whether the bifurcated standard applies in a lawsuit by the issuing bank against the confirming bank.

The bifurcated standard is designed to permit the bank to retain flexibility in dealing with simultaneous customer pressure to reject and beneficiary pressure to accept. This discretion ostensibly preserves the bank's ministerial function of dealing solely with documents and the insulation of the letter of credit from performance problems. The difficulty with applying a

---

[20] The UCP suggests the better view, however, that there is a duty running from the confirming bank to the ultimate customer. See UCP art. 12(a) (1974), art 20(a) (1983) ("Banks utilizing the services of another bank for the purpose of giving effect to the instructions of the applicant for the credit do so for the account and at the risk of [such applicant]."); art. 12(c) (1974), art. 20(c) (1983) (customer indemnification of the confirming bank); see also *Pubali Bank v. City Nat'l Bank,* 676 F.2d 1326, 1329-30 & n.5 (9th Cir. 1982) (warranty and tort liability); *Instituto Nacional de Comercializacion Agricola (Indeca) v. Continental Ill. Nat'l Bank & Trust Co.,* 530 F. Supp. 279, 282-85 (N.D. Ill. 1982) (negligence and fraud); Dann, *Confirming Bank Liability in Letter of Credit Transactions: Whose Bank Is It Anyway?,* 51 Fordham L. Rev. 1219, 1238-53 (1983) (recommending creation of liability through extension of UCC and UCP provisions, negligent misrepresentation and warranty theory).

bifurcated substantial compliance standard to actions against a confirming bank is reflected in the realities of commercial transactions. An issuing bank's good faith discretion is most required when its customer seeks to avoid payment by objecting to inconsequential defects. Although the bank should theoretically take comfort from a substantial compliance test if it honors the beneficiary's drafts over its customer's protests, the bank would usually not want to exercise its discretion in favor of the beneficiary for fear that its right to indemnify would be jeopardized or that its customer would break off existing banking relationships. Accordingly, the looser test of compliance does not in practice completely remove the issuer from its position between a rock and a hard place, but has a built-in safety valve against issuer misuse if the documents strictly comply with the letter.

A confirming bank, by contrast, is usually in relatively close geographical proximity with the beneficiary and typically chosen by the beneficiary because of past dealings. Although the confirming bank should not want to injure purposely its relationship with the issuing bank, the confirming bank would usually be somewhat biased in favor of the beneficiary. Additionally, the confirming bank is not in privity with the ultimate customer, who would be most likely to become dissatisfied if a conflict is resolved by the confirming bank. A biased issuing bank that in bad faith uncovers "microscopic discrepancies", N.Y. U.C.C. Study at 66, would still be forced to honor the letter if the documents are in strict compliance. A biased confirming bank, however, can overlook certain larger variances in its discretion without concomitant liability. A safety mechanism against confirming bank misuse is therefore not present and it would be inequitable to let a confirming bank exercise such discretion under a protective umbrella of substantial compliance. Moreover, the facts of this case do not warrant the looser standard. MHT was not faced with a "cross-fire of pressures" or concern that a disgruntled "customer" would refuse reimbursement because Cochin had sufficient funds on deposit with MHT. The Court also notes that the bifurcated substantial compliance standard is only a suggested approach by courts and commentators and has not actually been followed by New York courts.[21] Finally, in *Voest-Alpine*

---

[21] In discussing New York's bifurcated standard, courts and commentators have mistakenly cited each other and the following cases as support for the proposition that New York courts use a bifurcated approach:

In *Bank of Montreal,* the New York Court of Appeals applied a strict compliance standard when it denied recovery in an action by the issuing bank for reimbursement from its customer who claimed that the bank wrongfully honored the letter of credit. The Court held that the draft advices describing shipments as "bales of hemp" were insufficient to comply with the letter of credit condition for invoices and bills of lading of "bales manilla hemp". In *Atterbury Bros.,* the plaintiff bank successfully sued its customer for reimbursement. The Court acknowledged that the bank took a "risk" by paying pursuant to shipping documents issued to "A. James Brown" when the letter of credit specified "Arthur James Brown". The parties, however, conceded that the intended person signed the documents. The "conclusive" point on the issue of "casein" versus "unground casein" was resolved by an "estoppel" against the customer because it had examined the documents prior to the bank's payment. The remaining objections, characterized as "afterthoughts", were dismissed on grounds of laches and because there was no possibility that a missing certificate could have misled the paying bank. See, *e.g., Beyene v. Irving Trust Co.,* 596 F. Supp. 438, 442 n.8 (S.D.N.Y. 1984), aff'd, 762 F.2d 4 (2d Cir. 1985). In *North American,* Judge Medina granted summary judgment to the bank against the beneficiary under a "strict compliance" standard. In *Chairmasters,* the court granted summary judgment to the defendant bank under the basic tenet that the bank's obligation to review documents for compliance is totally separate from the underlying transaction. In *Marine Midland,* Judge McLean ruled that letter of credit conditions must be "strictly complied" with by a beneficiary. In *Far Eastern,* the Ohio court used a strict compliance standard, but cited *Marine Midland* as the sole case law authority for its dictum discussion of the New York bifurcated standard, which was the initial judicial recognition of this approach. Similarly, in *Data General,* the Connecticut court cited only *Far Eastern* and *Marine Midland* for its dictum footnote comment on the development of "two different standards". Finally, in *Transamerica Delaval,* citing only *Far Eastern* as case law support, a New York court for the first time discussed the bifurcated standard. The court applied a substantial

Int'l Corp. v. Chase Manhattan Bank, N.A., supra, the Court implied that confirming bank actions should be judged under a strict standard in wrongful dishonor as well as wrongful honor actions. It ruled that if the confirming bank waived material discrepancies in the drafts, the confirming bank would not be entitled to reimbursement from the issuing bank, which timely discovered the mistakes, because "the issuing bank[] was entitled to strict compliance." 707 F.2d at 686. Accordingly, the Court finds that an issuing bank's action for wrongful honor against a confirming bank is governed by a strict compliance standard.

An analysis of the ten listed variances suggests that MHT failed to pick up two discrepancies not strictly complying with the letter of credit terms. The first alleged defect concerns St. Lucia's cable to Oriental using the wrong cover note number of 4291 instead of 429711. The insurance was procured by Vishwa and the cable was intended to give notice to Oriental of the shipment by quoting the proper cover note. The failure to provide the correct cover note was not inconsequential as the mistake could have resulted in Oriental's justifiable refusal to honor Vishwa's insurance policy. This mistake may appear immaterial on its face, but in *Beyene v. Irving Trust Co., supra,* 762 F.2d 4, slip op. at 3617-19, the Second Circuit affirmed the dishonor of a letter of credit on the sole ground that the misspelling of Mohammed Sofan as Mohammed Soran on the bill of lading constituted a material discrepancy.

The alleged noncompliance with conditions (2), (3), (4), (8), (9) and (10) is unsupported. These provisions were not explicitly required by the letter of credit. Nothing in the letter indicates that these requirements, some of which were essentially satisfied by the submitted documents, were implicit conditions for payment. If Vishwa or Cochin wanted additional protection, they could have requested it and so informed MHT.

The overpayment and overdebiting of $1,396.50, the fifth alleged error, is a mathematical mistake. Although this sum was reimbursed, it indicates that the documents were not carefully reviewed by MHT. It does not, however, affect whether or not the underlying documents were in compliance with the letter.

The sixth defect is that the payment was made on documents presented by St. Lucia Enterprises despite the fact that the letter of credit was established for St. Lucia Enterprises, Ltd. The result is similar to that caused by the deviation of the Oriental cover note. Although there does not appear to be any difference between the two entities, it is not clear that the "intended" party was paid. The difference in names could also possibly be an indicia of unreliability or forgery.

The seventh alleged defect is that only five copies of the documents, rather than six, were submitted to MHT. This deviation is similar to a hypothetical error not affecting strict compliance posited in *Beyene v. Irving Trust Co., supra,* 762 F.2d 4, at 6 ("Smith misspelled as Smithh"). These types of variances may be allowable "if there is no possibility that the documents could mislead the paying bank to its detriment." *Flagship Cruises, Ltd. v. New England Merchants Nat'l Bank,* 569 F.2d 699, 705 (1st Cir. 1978); see *Beyene v. Irving Trust Co.,* 596 F. Supp. 438, 442 n.8 (S.D.N.Y. 1984), aff'd, 762 F.2d 4 (2d Cir. 1985). The Court finds that the failure

---

compliance standard in a lawsuit by a customer against its issuing bank for wrongful honor. The customer used vague language as to what would constitute a proper demand for payment under the letter, necessitating the ruling that it would have been "unreasonable for [the customer] to insist upon strict compliance." This result is better viewed not as an adoption of the bifurcated approach, but as the use of a strict compliance test with the "corollary" that letter requirements must be "explicit" and that all ambiguities should be construed against the party formulating the language in the letter. See *Marino Indus. v. Chase Manhattan Bank, N.A., supra,* 686 F.2d at 115 (all ambiguities construed against the issuing bank in an action for wrongful dishonor by the beneficiary).

to provide a sixth set of identical documents could not have misled the bank and therefore, it does not violate the strict compliance standard.

In the final analysis, only the variances as to the Oriental cover note and the name St. Lucia Enterprises, Ltd., appear not to comply strictly with the letter of credit conditions. The inquiry is not ended at this point because courts in this Circuit have applied concepts of equitable waiver and estoppel in cases of issuer dishonor. Application of estoppel has been premised upon discoverable nonconformities that could have been cured by the beneficiary before the expiration of the letter, but were not raised by the issuing bank until its dishonor. The banks were estopped from asserting the variances because of previous assurances to the beneficiary of documentary compliance or because of silence coupled with the retention of nonconforming documents for an unreasonably long time after the beneficiary had submitted its drafts for payment.

Application of waiver has been predicated upon situations in which the issuer justifies dishonor on grounds later found to have been unjustified. In these instances, all other possible grounds for dishonor are deemed to have been waived. Waiver of nonconforming documents can also be found from statements by officials of the issuing bank or from customer authorization.

The quid pro quo for the application of a standard of strict compliance is that there be minimal obligations implicating waiver and estoppel defenses on the party benefiting from the literal compliance review. The UCP expressly provides that an issuer has the obligation to immediately notify the beneficiary by "expeditious means" of any reason for noncompliance and the physical disposition of the disputed documents. UCP art. 8(e) (1974), 16(d) (1983). The UCP also implicitly invites cure of any documentary deficiencies apparent before the letter of credit expiration by issuer notification to the beneficiary. See Thier, *Letters of Credit: A Solution to the Problem of Documentary Compliance,* 50 Fordham L. Rev. 848, 873-76 (1982) (advocating imposition of affirmative obligations on all parties to the letter). In the context of this case, "an equitable approach to a strict compliance standard demands that the issuer promptly communicate all documentary defects to the beneficiary [or confirming bank], when time exists under the letter to remedy the nonconformity." *Id.* at 873. The Court finds that Cochin is precluded from claiming wrongful honor because of its failure to comply with the explicit notice and affirmative obligation provisions of the UCP and its implicit duty to promptly cure discoverable defects in MHT's confirming advices to St. Lucia.

The issuing bank must give notice "without delay" that the documents received are (1) being "held at the disposal" of the remitting or confirming bank or (2) "are being returned" to the second bank. UCP art. 8(e) (1974), art. 16(d) (1983). An issuing bank that fails to return or hold the documents for the second bank is precluded from asserting that the negotiation and payment were not effected in accordance with the letter of credit requirements. UCP art. 8(f) (1974), 16(e) (1983); see *Manufacturer's [sic] Hanover Trust Co. v. Westport Bank & Trust Co.,* Ruling on Cross-Motion for Summary Judgment at 9-10, B-83-17 (TPS/TFGD) (D. Conn.) (issuing bank precluded from pursuing a strict compliance defense for wrongful dishonor because of its "crucial" failure to give "formal notice" that documents were being held for beneficiary despite a retrospective assertion that the documents were always available for inspection), endorsement approval, B-83-17 (TFGD) (D. Conn. 1983). The UCP also directs that an issuing bank intending to claim noncompliance shall have a "reasonable time" to examine the documents after presentment and to determine whether to make such a claim. UCP art. 8(d) (1974), art. 16(c) (1983). The revised UCP allows explicitly for the imposition of the 16(e) sanction for failure to comply with the "reasonable time" provision as well; however, this interpretation is not clear under the parties' explicit choice of law, the 1974 UCP.

Neither the 1983 UCP nor the 1974 UCP defines what constitutes a "reasonable time" to determine if the documents are defective or notice "without delay" that the documents are being held or returned. When the UCP is silent or ambiguous, analogous UCC provisions may be utilized if consistent with the UCP. The UCC provides for a period of three banking days for the issuer to honor or reject a documentary draft for payment. N.Y. U.C.C. § 5-112(1)(a)(McKinney's 1964) (issuer-beneficiary relationship). The letter of credit was issued subject to the 1974 UCP but it is silent as to what law governs its terms. Cochin cites to Indian statutes interpreting a "reasonable time" as a factual question depending on the nature of the negotiable instrument and the usual course of dealing. Under the circumstances of this case, however, it appears that under New York's comparative interest choice of law approach, New York UCC law would apply.

Cochin's failure to promptly notify MHT that it had returned the documents or that it was holding them at MHT's disposal thus violates the UCP. Cochin's telex of June 21 states that there are certain discrepancies in St. Lucia's documents, but Cochin did not advise MHT that it was returning the documents to MHT until the July 3 telex. The "reasonable time" three-day period should be the maximum time allowable for the notification "without delay" requirement. Because June 21, 1980 was a Saturday, Cochin should have complied with its notice obligations no later than June 26. The passage of an additional week before compliance precludes Cochin from asserting its wrongful honor claim. Moreover, it was not until June 27 that Cochin first specified any reason for its dishonor argument, and the St. Lucia Enterprises, Ltd. omission was not noted until July 4.

Cochin proposes that its failure to timely notify MHT was not violative of UCP or letter of credit policy because it caused no additional loss to MHT. Cochin argues that the defects were in any case incurable by the time Cochin received the documents, because St. Lucia had disappeared with the letter of credit proceeds. Although the UCP is not explicit, the Court finds that these provisions should be applied identically to an issuing bank's obligations to a confirming bank after the latter's honor of a demand for payment. Cochin's contention ignores the expectation in the international financial community that the parties will live up to their statutory obligations and is at odds with the basic letter of credit tenet that banks deal solely with documents, not in goods. Cochin's argument would defeat the letter of credit's function of being a swift, fluid and reliable financing device. Cf. *Voest-Alpine Int'l Corp. v. Chase Manhattan Bank, N.A., supra,* 707 F.2d at 684-85 (rejecting contention that a waiver analysis was inappropriate because the defects were "incurable").

Finally, the two documentary discrepancies could have been anticipated by Cochin and were curable before the demand for payment. Cochin received a copy of MHT's incorrect March 31 advice to St. Lucia, which mistakenly listed the insurance cover note as 4291. Similarly, Cochin received copies of all of MHT's advices to St. Lucia, which omitted the "Ltd." from the corporate name. Cochin had sufficient notice and time to correct MHT's confirming defects to St. Lucia and is therefore estopped from asserting them. Although MHT failed to strictly comply with the letter requirements, Cochin's failure to perform its affirmative obligations precludes an action for wrongful honor under the UCP and by letter of credit estoppel.

CONCLUSION

Accordingly, for the foregoing reasons, plaintiff's motion for summary judgment is denied, Fed. R. Civ. P. 56(a), and defendant's motion for summary judgment is granted, Fed. R. Civ. P. 56(b).

The Clerk of the Court is directed to dismiss the complaint and prepare and enter Judgment for defendant MHT.

PROBLEM 11.3

Under the Revised U.C.C., there is no longer an issue as to whether the issuing bank may accept documents that are not in complete compliance of the letter of credit requirements. Revised § 5-108 requires the bank to dishonor a presentation that does not strictly comply with the terms of the letter of credit. Is that a wise change?

NOTE

(1) Revised *U.C.C. § 5-108.* This section states that (1) an issuer shall *honor* a presentation that appears on its face *strictly* to comply with the terms and conditions of the letter of credit; (2) with two exceptions, an issuer shall *dishonor* a presentation that does not appear so to comply. Whether there has been a strict compliance is determined by the standard practice referred to in Section 5-108(e), viz., "[a]n issuer shall observe standard practice of financial institutions that regularly issue letters of credit." (Determination of the issuer's observance of that standard practice is a matter of interpretation for the court.)

The Reporter's Comments to an earlier version of this section state:

The section adopts the standard of strict compliance, but strict compliance does not mean slavish conformity to the terms of the letter of credit. By adopting reasonable commercial standards (the norm established by reasonable document checkers in commercial banks) as a way of measuring strict compliance, it indorses the conclusion of the court in *New Braunfels Nat. Bank v. Odiorne*, 780 S.W.2d 313 (Tex. Ct. App. 1989) (beneficiary could collect when draft requested payment on "Letter of Credit No. 86-122-5" and letter of credit specified "Letter of Credit No. 86-122-S" holding strict compliance does not demand oppressive perfectionism).

The section also indorses the result in *Tosco Corp. v. Federal Deposit Insurance Corp.,* 723 F.2d 1242 (6th Cir. 1983). The letter of credit in that case called for "drafts drawn under Bank of Clarksville Letter of Credit Number 105". The draft presented stated "Drawn under Bank of Clarksville, Clarksville, Tennessee letter of Credit No. 105." The court correctly found that despite the change of upper case "L" to a lower case "l" and the use of the word "No." instead of "Number," and despite the addition of the words "Clarksville, Tennessee," the presentment conformed.

By adopting the standard and endorsing the *New Braunfels* and *Tosco* cases, the section rejects the standard that commentators have called "substantial compliance."

Uniform Commercial Code, Revised Article 5, Letters of Credit, § 5-114 Comments (April 10, 1992 Draft) [see revised § 5-108 Comment 1].

New Braunfels at 316-17 states:

Most commentators agree that maintaining the integrity of the strict compliance rule is important to the continued usefulness of letters of credit as a commercial tool. *See, e.g.,* McLaughlin, *On the Periphery of Letter-of-Credit Law: Softening the Rigors of Strict Compliance*, 106 Banking L.J. 4 (1989); Dolan, *Strict Compliance with Letters of Credit: Striking a Fair Balance*, 102 Banking L.J. 18 (1985). That does not mean, however, that strict compliance demands an oppressive perfectionism. For example, one noted commentator has recognized a logical distinction between discrepancies that relate to the business of the underlying transaction and those that relate to the banker's own business:

> The strict-compliance rule rests on the judgment that issuers should not be forced into the position of determining whether a documentary discrepancy is significant. The rule assumes that issuers are not in a position to know whether discrepancies matter to the commercial parties. Nothing in that assumption requires courts to absolve issuers from knowing the significance of discrepancies for their own business; while it is consistent with the strict-compliance rule to say that an issuer should not be charged with knowledge of whether an air bill, rather than an ocean bill, covering computer components is a significant defect, it is not consistent with the rule to say that a bank issuer is absolved from knowing whether the abbreviation of the word "number" to "No." in the legend on a draft is a significant defect. Banks presumably know nothing about the shipment of computer components, but they know a great deal about legends on drafts—legends that credits require, usually because the banks insist on them.

J. Dolan, The Law of Letters of Credit ¶ 6.03, at S6-4 (Supp. 1989) (footnotes omitted).

Compare revised U.C.C. § 5-108 with Articles 13 and 37(c) of UCP 500.

[E]   Obligations of Advising or Confirming Bank

Read: U.C.C. § 5-107.

The issuing bank may send the letter of credit directly to the beneficiary. More commonly, however, it will forward the credit to a banking institution at the beneficiary's location, which will then act as an "advising" or "confirming" bank. If the second bank is to act as an advising bank, its duty is to advise the beneficiary of the issuance of the credit, and its terms. It will then act as a collecting bank to receive the beneficiary's draft and documents and forward them to the issuing bank for payment. Such advising bank acts solely as an agent, and does not itself become obligated upon the credit; it is responsible only for the accuracy of its statements to the beneficiary (U.C.C., § 5-107(1)) [revised § 5-107(a)].

The second bank may in addition lend its obligation to the credit by "confirming" it. The beneficiary may have insisted upon this, being unwilling to rely only upon the credit of the distant issuing bank, and desiring the commitment of a bank closer at hand. U.C.C. § 5-107(2) provides: "A confirming bank by confirming a credit becomes directly obligated on the credit to the extent of its confirmation as though it were its issuer and acquires the rights of an issuer." [See revised § 5-107(a).]

As to liability of advising and confirming banks under UCP 500, see Articles 7 and 9.

———

NOTES AND QUESTIONS

(1) *Confirming Bank. In Barclays Bank D.C.O. v. Mercantile National Bank*, 481 F.2d 1224, 1227-32 (5th Cir. 1973), Mercantile addressed the following letter to Barclays:

Mercantile National Bank
70 Broad Street, N.W.
Atlanta, Georgia 30303

June 1, 1970

Barclays Bank Limited D.C.O.
200 Park Avenue
New York, N.Y. 10017

Gentlemen:

We are enclosing an irrevocable letter of credit issued by Allied Mortgage Consultants, 127 Peachtree Street, N.E., Atlanta, Georgia dated June 1, 1970, in the amount of $400,000.00 in your favor for the account of Bay Holding Company Limited.

We can unconditionally confirm this is a valid letter of credit and that they have at all times sufficient funds to honor this commitment.

We hereby confirm the letter of credit and undertake to honor any drafts presented to us on or before expiration date of the letter of credit in accordance with the terms and conditions of said letter of credit.

Very truly yours
Carl M. Harris
/s/
Executive Vice President

CMH/ac

The court made a preliminary determination and said:

> With this preliminary determination aside, we are now in a position to confront the central legal issue—whether Mercantile can confirm this credit which was issued by a non-bank [Allied Mortgage Consultants]. This issue arises as a result of the definition of a confirming bank in § 5-103(1)(f).
>
> A "confirming bank" is a bank which engages either that it will itself honor a credit already issued by another bank or that such a credit will be honored by the issuer of a third bank.

. . . .

Having determined that the general purposes of the U.C.C. will be advanced by applying the Code to this case, we turn to the more precise question of whether the policies underlying Article 5 would be furthered by applying a rule which is not specifically articulated there, but which is nonetheless developed by analogy to specifically codified rules. Section 5-102(3) is the ready and definite answer to this question. This section reads:

> (3) This Article deals with some but not all of the rules and concepts of letters of credit as such rules or concepts have developed prior to this Act or may hereafter develop. The fact that this Article states a rule does not by itself require, imply or negate application of the same or a converse rule to a situation not provided for or to a person not specified by this Article.

Even considering the admonition in § 1-102(1) that the Code should be liberally construed in light of its general purposes and policies, the above-quoted section is somewhat unique in that it expressly contemplates court-managed expansion of the principles contained in Article 5. The drafters recognized that, although letters of credit have been used for a number of years, their use was "primarily as a financial adjunct to a contract for the sale of goods." The drafters believed that as innovative businessmen became more familiar with the credit device its use — particularly in domestic business circles — would in all likelihood increase. The rules codified in Article 5 are only the foundation from which courts must develop, by analogy, new concepts to meet novel and diverse uses of the letter of credit.

We have just this type of situation, a new and different use of a letter of credit, before us in the instant case. Rather than using some other financing tool the parties involved in the real estate venture here chose the letter of credit as a device for securing $350,000 in working capital for Bay Holding Company. Reasoning by analogy, we believe that if a bank becomes directly liable under § 5-107(2) by confirming a credit issued by another bank, then a bank which confirms a non-bank credit is also directly liable on that credit under the same section. We reach this conclusion notwithstanding that the operative facts here do not seem to fit within the literal definition of a confirming bank in § 5-103(1)(f). Mercantile has offered no other reason which militates against this conclusion. Moreover, no other provisions of Article 5 cast doubt on the propriety of holding that a bank may confirm a non-bank credit under the Uniform Commercial Code. This conclusion affords a liberal construction to the Code, and it will facilitate the continued and expanding use of the letter of credit as a financing tool in the hands of the business planner. Finally, it is expressly ordained by § 5-102(3) because "[t]he fact that this Article states a rule does not by itself require, imply or negate the application of the same . . . rule to a situation not provided for or to a person not specified by this Article."

Standby letters of credit are discussed at § 11.02 below.

(2) *Advising Bank. Sound of Market Street, Inc. v. Continental Bank International,* 623 F. Supp. 93 (E.D. Pa. 1985), rev'd, 819 F.2d 384 (3d Cir. 1987), involved an action by a beneficiary against an advising bank for failure to advise of the issuance of a letter of credit in a timely manner. (Held: For advising bank. There was no privity between advising bank and beneficiary. Beneficiary should recover its damages from the customer/applicant/account party not from advising bank.)

(3) *Indemnities for Particular Defects.* Illustration 10 to Restatement, Second, Contracts § 220 is based on *Dixon, Irmaos & Cia, Ltd a. v. Chase Nat'l Bank,* 144 F.2d 759 (2d Cir. 1944), *cert. denied,* 324 U.S. 850(1945). In the illustration a bank in New York City (Chase), issues to a seller (a Brazilian exporter) a letter of credit promising a payment on presentation of

documents including a "full set of bills of lading." By a general banking usage in New York City, banks accept less than a full set in such cases if there is a guaranty by a responsible New York bank (Guaranty Trust Company) in lieu of the missing part. The illustration states that unless otherwise agreed, the usage is part of the contract. The illustration then cites U.C.C. § 5-109. (See § 5-113 and Comment 4, § 2-323(2)(b) and Comment 2.) [Section 5-113 was omitted under revised Article 5. The rationalw is that indemnities are covered by other contract law.]

For a criticism of the *Dixon* case, see Backus and Harfield, *Custom and Letters of Credit: the Dixon, Irmaos Case,* 52 Colum. L. Rev. 589 (1952). In support of *Dixon,* see Honnold, *Letters of Credit, Custom, Missing Documents and the Dixon Case: A Reply to Backus and Harfield,* 53 Colum. L. Rev. 504 (1953). See also J. Dolan, The Law of Letters of Credit, ¶ 4.07, "Role of Custom and Usage" (2d ed. 1991).

[F]　Fraud in the Letter of Credit Transaction

Read: U.C.C. § 5-114(1), (2), (3); Revised § 5-109.

Throughout the chapter we have stressed the independence principle as an underlying foundation necessary to the stability and predictability of a letter of credit transaction. There is one limited exception to the above rule, an issuing bank has a discretionary privilege to dishonor a letter of credit where its customer has provided it with notice of fraud, forgery or other defects not apparent on the face of the documents. Note that the issuing bank may still pay on a draft that the customer has warned it about, so long as the payment was in good faith. But what is good faith if the issuing bank is fully cognizant of real fraud? The inclusion of the words, ". . . a court . . . may enjoin such an honor" at the tail end of § 5-114(3) has provided a doorway of judicial intervention that many customers have attempted to pass. When can a customer successfully block the payment of a letter of credit?

We know that an issuer of a letter of credit must honor a draft or demand for payment which complies with the terms of the credit regardless of whether the goods or documents conform to the underlying contract for sale.

———

UNITED BANK, LTD. v. CAMBRIDGE SPORTING GOODS CORP.

New York Court of Appeals
41 N.Y.2d 254, 392 N.Y.S.2d 265, 360 N.E.2d 943 (1976)

GABRIELLI, JUSTICE.

On this appeal, we must decide whether fraud on the part of a seller-beneficiary of an irrevocable letter of credit may be successfully asserted as a defense against holders of drafts drawn by the seller pursuant to the credit. If we conclude that this defense may be interposed by the buyer who procured the letter of credit, we must also determine whether the courts below improperly imposed upon appellant buyer the burden of proving that respondent banks to whom the drafts were made payable by the seller-beneficiary of the letter of credit, were not holders in due course. The issues presented raise important questions concerning the application of the law of letters of credit and the rules governing proof of holder in due course status set forth in article 3 of the Uniform Commercial Code. . . .

In April, 1971 appellant Cambridge Sporting Goods Corporation (Cambridge) entered into a contract for the manufacture and sale of boxing gloves with Duke Sports (Duke), a Pakistani corporation. Duke committed itself to the manufacturer of 27,936 pairs of boxing gloves at a sale price of $42,576.80; and arranged with its Pakistani bankers, United Bank Limited (United) and The Muslim Commercial Bank (Muslim), for the financing of the sale. Cambridge was requested by these banks to cover payment of the purchase price by opening an irrevocable letter of credit with its bank in New York, Manufacturers Hanover Trust Company (Manufacturers). Manufacturers issued an irrevocable letter of credit obligating it, upon the receipt of certain documents indicating shipment of the merchandise pursuant to the contract, to accept and pay, 90 days after acceptance, drafts drawn upon Manufacturers for the purchase price of the gloves.

Following confirmation of the opening of the letter of credit, Duke informed Cambridge that it would be impossible to manufacture and deliver the merchandise within the time period required by the contract, and sought an extension of time for performance until September 15, 1971 and a continuation of the letter of credit, which was due to expire on August 11. Cambridge replied on June 18 that it would not agree to a postponement of the manufacture and delivery of the gloves because of its resale commitments and, hence, it promptly advised Duke that the contract was canceled and the letter of credit should be returned. Cambridge simultaneously notified United of the contract cancellation.

Despite the cancellation of the contract, Cambridge was informed on July 17, 1971 that documents had been received at Manufacturers from United purporting to evidence a shipment of the boxing gloves under the terms of the canceled contract. The documents were accompanied by a draft, dated July 16,1971, drawn by Duke upon Manufacturers and made payable to United, for the amount of $21,288.40, one half of the contract price of the boxing gloves. A second set of documents was received by Manufacturers from Muslim, also accompanied by a draft, dated August 20, and drawn upon Manufacturers by Duke for the remaining amount of the contract price.

An inspection of the shipments upon their arrival revealed that Duke had shipped old, unpadded, ripped and mildewed gloves rather than the new gloves to be manufactured as agreed upon. Cambridge then commenced an action against Duke in Supreme Court, New York County, joining Manufacturers as a party, and obtained a preliminary injunction prohibiting the latter from paying drafts drawn under the letter of credit; subsequently, in November, 1971 Cambridge levied on the funds subject to the letter of credit and the draft, which were delivered by Manufacturers to the Sheriff in compliance therewith. Duke ultimately defaulted in the action and judgment against it was entered in the amount of the drafts, in March, 1972.

The present proceeding was instituted by the Pakistani banks to vacate the levy made by Cambridge and to obtain payment of the drafts on the letter of credit. The banks asserted that they were holders in due course of the drafts which had been made payable to them by Duke and, thus, were entitled to the proceeds thereof irrespective of any defenses which Cambridge had established against their transferor, Duke, in the prior action which had terminated in a default judgment. . . .

The trial court concluded that the burden of proving that the banks were not holders in due course lay with Cambridge, and directed a verdict in favor of the banks on the ground that Cambridge had not met that burden; the court stated that Cambridge failed to demonstrate that the banks themselves had participated in the seller's acts of fraud, proof of which was concededly present in the record. The Appellate Division affirmed, agreeing that while there was proof tending to establish the defenses against the seller, Cambridge had not shown that the seller's acts were "connected to the petitioners [banks] in any manner." . . .

We reverse and hold that it was improper to direct a verdict in favor of the petitioning Pakistani banks. We conclude that the defense of fraud in the transaction was established and in that circumstance the burden shifted to petitioners to prove that they were holders in due course and took the drafts for value, in good faith and without notice of any fraud on the part of Duke (Uniform Commercial Code, § 3-302).

This case does not come before us in the typical posture of a lawsuit between the bank issuing the letter of credit and presenters of drafts drawn under the credit seeking payment (see, generally, White and Summers, Uniform Commercial Code, § 18-6, pp. 619-628). Because Cambridge obtained an injunction against payment of the drafts and has levied against the proceeds of the drafts, it stands in the same position as the issuer, and, thus, the law of letters of credit governs the liability of Cambridge to the Pakistani banks.[22] Article 5 of the Uniform Commercial Code, dealing with letters of credit, and the Uniform Customs and Practice for Documentary Credits promulgated by the International Chamber of Commerce set forth the duties and obligations of the issuer of a letter of credit.[23] A letter of credit is a commitment on the part of the issuing bank that it will pay a draft presented to it under the terms of the credit, and if it is a documentary draft, upon presentation of the required documents of title (see Uniform Commercial Code, § 5-103). Banks issuing letters of credit deal in documents and not in goods and are not responsible

---

[22] Cambridge has no direct liability on the *drafts* because it is not a party to the drafts which were drawn on Manufacturers by Duke as drawer; its liability derives from the letter of credit which authorizes the drafts to be drawn on the issuing banks. Since Manufacturers has paid the proceeds of the drafts to the Sheriff pursuant to the levy obtained in the prior proceeding, it has discharged its obligation under the credit and is not involved in this proceeding.

[23] It should be noted that the Uniform Customs and Practice controls, in lieu of article 5 of the code, where, unless otherwise agreed by the parties, a letter of credit is made subject to the provisions of the Uniform Customs and Practice by its terms or by agreement, course of dealing or usage of trade (Uniform Commercial Code, § 5-102, subd.[4]). No proof was offered that there was an agreement that the Uniform Customs and Practice should apply, nor does the credit so state (cf. *Oriental Pacific* [U.S.A.] *v. Toro It to Dominion Bank*, 78 Misc.2d 819, 357 N.Y.S.2d 957). Neither do the parties otherwise contend that their rights should be resolved under the Uniform Customs and Practice. However, even if the Uniform Customs and Practice were deemed applicable to this case, it would not, in the absence of a conflict, abrogate the precode case law (now codified in Uniform Commercial Code, § 5-114) and that authority continues to govern even where article 5 is not controlling (see White and Summers, *op. cit.*, pp. 613-614, 624-625). Moreover, the Uniform Customs and Practice provisions are not in conflict nor do they treat with the subject matter of section 5-114 which is dispositive of the issues presented on this appeal (see *Banco Tornquist, S. A. v. American Bank & Trust Co.*, 71 Misc.2d 874, 875, 337 N.Y.S.2d 489; *Intraworld Ind. v. Girard Trust Bank*, 461 Pa. 343, 336 A.2d 316, 322; Harfield, Practice Commentary, McKinney's Cons & Laws of N. Y., Book 62 1/2, Uniform Commercial Code, § 5-114, p. 686). Thus, we are of the opinion that the Uniform Customs and Practice, where applicable, does not bar the relief provided for in section 5-114 of the code.

[New York § 5-102(4) reads:

(4) Unless otherwise agreed, this Article 5 does not apply to a letter of credit or a credit if by its terms or by agreement, course of dealing or usage of trade such letter of credit or credit is subject in whole or in part to the Uniform Customs and Practice for Commercial Documentary Credits fixed by the Thirteenth or by any subsequent Congress of the International Chamber of Commerce.]

for any breach of warranty or nonconformity of the goods involved in the underlying sales contract (see Uniform Commercial Code, § 5-114, subd. [1]; Uniform Customs and Practice, General Provisions and Definitions [c] and article 9. . . . Subdivision (2) of section 5-114, however indicates certain limited circumstances in which an issuer *may* properly refuse to honor a draft drawn under a letter of credit or a customer may enjoin an issuer from honoring such a draft.[24] Thus, where "fraud in the transaction" has been shown and the holder has not taken the draft in circumstances that would make it a holder in due course, the customer may apply to enjoin the issuer from paying drafts drawn under the letter of credit (see 1955 Report of N.Y. Law Rev., Comm., vol. 3, pp. 1654-1659). This rule represents a codification of precode case law most eminently articulated in the land mark case of *Sztejn v. Schroder Banking Corp.*, 177 Misc. 719, 31 N.Y.S.2d 631, Shientag, J., where it was held that the shipment of cowhair in place of bristles amounted to more than mere breach of warranty but fraud sufficient to constitute grounds for enjoining payment of drafts to one not a holder in due course. . . . Even prior to the *Sztejn* case, forged or fraudulently procured documents were proper grounds for avoidance of payment of drafts drawn under a letter of credit (Finkelstein, Legal Aspects of Commercial Letters of Credit, pp. 231-236-247); and cases decided after the enactment of the code have cited *Sztejn* with approval.

. . . .

. . .The evidentiary facts are not disputed and we hold upon the facts as established, that the shipment of old, unpadded, ripped and mildewed gloves rather than the new boxing gloves as ordered by Cambridge, constituted fraud in the transaction within the meaning of subdivision (2) of section 5-114. It should be noted that the drafters of section 5-114, in their attempt to codify the *Sztejn* case and in utilizing the term "fraud in the transaction," have eschewed a dogmatic approach and adopted a flexible standard to be applied as the circumstances of a particular situation mandate. It can be difficult to draw a precise line between cases involving breach of warranty (or a difference of opinion as to the quality of goods) and outright fraudulent practice on the part of the seller. To the extent, however, that Cambridge established that Duke was guilty of *fraud* in shipping, not merely nonconforming merchandise, but worthless fragments of boxing gloves, this case is similar to *Sztejn.*

If the petitioning banks are holders in due course they are entitled to recover the proceeds of the drafts but if such status cannot be demonstrated their petition must fail. . . .

In order to qualify as a holder in due course, a holder must have taken the instrument "without notice . . .of any defense against . . .it on the part of any person" (Uniform Commercial Code, § 3-302, subd. [1], par. [c]). Pursuant to subdivision (2) of section 5-114 fraud in the transaction is a valid defense to payment of drafts drawn under a letter of credit. Since the defense of fraud in the transaction was shown, the burden shifted to the banks by operation of subdivision (3) of section 3-307 [§ 3-308(b) (1990)] to prove that they were holders in due course and took the drafts without notice of Duke's alleged fraud. As indicated in the Official Comment to that subdivision, when it is shown that a defense exists, one seeking to cut off the defense by claiming the rights of a holder in due course "has the full burden of proof by a preponderance of the total evidence" on this issue. This burden must be sustained by "affirmative proof" of the requisites of holder in due course status (see Official Comment, McKinney's Cons. Laws of N. Y., Book 62 1/2, Uniform Commercial Code, § 3-307, p. 212). It was error for the trial court to direct a verdict in favor of the Pakistani banks because this determination rested upon a

---

[24] [Here the court cites § 5-114(2).]

misallocation of the burden of proof, and we conclude that the banks have not satisfied the burden of proving that they qualified in all respects as holders in due course, by any affirmative proof.

. . . .

Accordingly, the order of the Appellate Division should be reversed, with costs, and the petition dismissed.

———

NOTES

(1) *Injunctive Relief.* In *Enterprise International, Inc. v. Corporation Estatal Petrolera Ecuatoriana*, 762 F.2d 464, 471-74 (5th Cir. 1985), the court addressed the issue of injunctive relief in international letter of credit cases. The most relevant of the court's opinion is as follows [footnotes omitted]:

In order to secure a preliminary injunction, the movant has the burden of proving four elements: "(1) a substantial likelihood of success on the merits; (2) a substantial threat of irreparable injury if the injunction is not issued; (3) that the threatened injury to the movant outweighs any damage the injunction might cause to the opponent; and (4) that the injunction will not disserve the public interest."

. . . .

In considering whether to grant or deny preliminary injunctive relief, the district court "must remember that a preliminary injunction is an extraordinary and drastic remedy," and that "[t]he movant has a heavy burden of persuading the district court that all four elements are satisfied. Thus, if the movant does not succeed in carrying its burden on any one of the four prerequisites, a preliminary injunction may not issue and, if issued, will be vacated on appeal. When the movant fails to prove that, absent the injunction, irreparable injury will result, therefore, the preliminary injunction should be denied.

Federal courts have long recognized that, when "the threatened harm is more than de minimis, it is not so much the magnitude but the irreparability that counts for purposes of a preliminary injunction," In short, "[t]he key word . . .is *irreparable*," and an "injury is 'irreparable' only if it cannot be undone through monetary remedies." Thus, "[t]he possibility that adequate compensatory or other corrective relief will be available at a later date, in the ordinary course of litigation, weigh[]s heavily against a claim of irreparable harm." The absence of an available remedy by which the movant can later recover monetary damages, however, may also be sufficient to show irreparable injury.

Federal courts have consistently applied these principles to the issuance of preliminary injunctions in cases involving international letters of credit, and, consonant with them, have refused to enjoin the honoring of international letters of credit when, absent such injunctive relief the movants would have suffered only monetary loss, for which adequate remedies at law were available.

Most of the preliminary injunctions that have been issued in such cases were justified on the basis of the inadequacy of legal remedies in Iranian courts after that country's revolution in 1979 and the taking of the United States citizens as hostages, Thus, in *Itek Corp. v. First National Bank, Rockwell International Systems, Inc. v Citibank, NA., and Harris Corp. v. National Iranian Radio & Television*, for example, the First, Second, and Eleventh Circuits found that any resort to Iranian courts to recover the movant's monetary loss, should the preliminary injunction be denied, would be futile and that the existence of the Iran-United States Claims Tribunal did not "ameliorate the likelihood of irreparable injury."

In settings other than the Iranian crisis, however, when it has been shown that foreign courts provide a legal remedy or, at worst, that access to foreign courts is speculative, injunctive relief has been refused. Even in some cases related to and arising after the Iranian revolution, however, federal courts have refused to grant preliminary injunctive relief, finding that "[t]he 'unsettled situation in Iran' [was] simply insufficient to release any party from obligations under the letter of credit," that, even if resort to the Iranian courts was futile, an adequate remedy at law was available in federal court under the Foreign Sovereign Immunities Act, and that the political turmoil in Iran did not permit a federal court "to write into the letter of credit an excusing condition which the parties themselves did not adopt."

This reluctance to grant preliminary injunctive relief in international letter of credit cases is well founded in policy and business practice as well as in equity. The obligations created by a letter of credit are "completely separate from the underlying transaction, with absolutely no consequence given the underlying transaction unless the credit expressly incorporates its terms." This principle of independence provides the letter of credit with one of its "peculiar values," assurance of payment, and makes it "a unique device developed to meet the specific demands of the market place." Indeed, the "financial value of the letter of credit promise is predicated upon its degree of legal certainty."

These features of letters of credit are of particular importance in international transactions, in which sophisticated investors knowingly undertake such risks as political upheaval or contractual breach in return for the benefits to be reaped from international trade. As the First Circuit noted in *Itek Corp.*:

> The very object of a letter of credit is to provide a near foolproof method of placing money in its beneficiary's hands when he complies with the terms contained in the letter itself . . . . Parties to a contract may use a letter of credit in order to make certain that contractual disputes wend their way towards resolution with money in the beneficiary's pocket rather than in the pocket of the contracting party.

Thus, in this context, the requirements for preliminary injunctive relief, including the showing of a substantial threat of irreparable injury if the injunction is not issued, are to be strictly exacted so as to avoid shifting the contractual allocation both of the risk of loss and the burden of pursuing international litigation.

(2) *Revised U.C.C. § 5-109*. Recall that revised § 5-108 requires an issuer to honor a presentation that appears on its face strictly to comply with the terms and conditions of the letter of credit. But what if a required document is forged or materially fraudulent, or honor of the presentation would facilitate a material fraud by the beneficiary on the *issuer* or *applicant*? In these cases the issuer is required to honor the presentation *if* honor is demanded by four categories of innocent persons, e.g., holders in due course of drafts drawn under the credit taken after acceptance by the issuer, confirmers that have honored their confirmation in good faith. If the above conditions are not met, the issuer (acting in good faith) *may honor* or *dishonor* the presentation. Revised § 5-109(a). Assume, for example, it is the defrauder-seller-beneficiary that

is demanding honor of the draft by the issuer. If the applicant claims that honor of the presentation would facilitate a material fraud by the beneficiary on the issuer or applicant, a court may temporarily or permanently enjoin the issuer from honoring the presentation *only if* the court finds that:

(1) the relief is not prohibited under the law applicable to an accepted draft or deferred obligation incurred by the issuer;

(2) a beneficiary, issuer, or nominated person who may be adversely affected is adequately protected against loss that it may suffer because the relief is granted;

(3) all of the conditions to entitle one to the relief under the law of this State have been met; and

(4) on the basis of the information submitted to the court, the applicant is more likely than not to succeed under its claim of forgery or material fraud.

Revised § 5-109(b), cf. U.C.C. § 5-114(2) (1990).

INTRAWORLD INDUS. v. GIRARD TRUST BANK

Supreme Court of Pennsylvania
461 Pa. 343; 336 A.2d 316; 17 U.C.C. Rep. Serv. 191 (1974)

ROBERTS, J.

This appeal requires us to review the trial court's denial of a preliminary injunction to restrain honor of a draft under an international letter of credit. A precise statement of the facts, which are complex, is necessary for a proper understanding.

On February 11, 1972, a lease was executed by Intraworld Industries, Inc., a corporation[25] headquartered in Wilkes-Barre, Pennsylvania, and Paulette Cymbalista, a citizen of Switzerland and resident of Italy. Cymbalista agreed to lease to Intraworld the Hotel Carlton, a luxury hotel located in St. Moritz, Switzerland, for a term of 15 years at an annual rental of 800,000 Swiss francs, payable in semi-annual installments.[26] The lease provided that Intraworld was required to prepay the rent for the initial 18-month period. Intraworld was also obligated to procure, within the first 100 days of the term, a performance bond in the amount of $500,000.00 "to insure to lessor the payment of the rent."[27]

Intraworld entered into possession of the hotel on May 1, 1972. Shortly thereafter, Intraworld assigned its interest in the lease to its subsidiary, Vacanze In Paradiso Hotels, S.A., a Swiss corporation.[28]

---

[25] Intraworld is incorporated in either Pennsylvania or Delaware; the record is unclear on this point.

[26] The lease contained a formula for the adjustment of the annual rental with respect to changes in the value of the Swiss franc. At the time of the execution of the lease, the annual rental was approximately equivalent to $200,000.00.

[27] The record does not establish whether Intraworld performed its obligation to procure a performance bond.

The lease also provided: "This agreement shall be governed by the Swiss law. The competent forum shall be in Saint Moritz Court."

[28] For convenience we will refer to the lessee as Intraworld.

At a later time,[29] Intraworld and Cymbalista executed an addendum to the lease (to which the parties have referred by its German title "Nachtrag"). The Nachtrag cancelled Intraworld's obligation to procure a performance bond and substituted a duty to provide letters of credit issued by "the Girard Trust Company of Philadelphia" in order to guarantee rental payments one year in advance. Two letters of credit were specifically required, each in the amount of $100,000.00, maturing in November, 1973, and May, 1974, to secure the rent due at those times. After each rental payment, Intraworld was to provide a new letter of credit "in order that the lessor remains secured one years [sic] rent in advance." The Nachtrag also provided:

In the event the lessee should not fulfill its obligation to pay, so that the letter of credit must be used, . . .then the lessor can terminate the lease immediately without further notice. In this case, the lessor retains the rent paid or guaranteed for the following year as a stipulated penalty for non-performance of the contract from the lessee, in doing so the lessor retains the right to make a claim for additional damages not covered by the stipulated penalty.

On September 1, 1972, Intraworld and the Girard Trust Bank, Philadelphia, entered into an agreement to provide the letters of credit required by the Nachtrag. Girard agreed to "issue a letter of credit . . .in the amount of $100,000 under which the Lessor may draw a sight draft on [Girard] for payment of the sum due under said lease (a) on November 10, 1973 and (b) May 10, 1974. Under the terms of such letter of credit, payments will be made if the Lessor presents a draft as provided in such letter of credit. Each such letter of credit will expire . . .on the twentieth day after the payment under said lease is due."[30]

In accordance with the agreement, Girard issued two irrevocable letters of credit on September 5, 1972. Each authorized Cymbalista to draw a draft on Girard in the amount of $100,000.00 if Intraworld failed to pay the rent when due.[31]

---

[29] The record does not establish the exact date.

[30] The agreement also provided: "This agreement shall be construed in accordance with the law of the State of Pennsylvania and the Acts of Congress of the United States affecting transactions under the provisions hereof."

[31] "IRREVOCABLE LETTER OF CREDIT

NO. 35798

Date: September 5, 1972" Amount: $ 100,000.00.

"Beneficiary: Paulette Cymbalista
                                     c/o Carlton Hotel
                                         St. Moritz, Switzerland

"For account of: Intraworld Industries, Inc.
                                     116 South Main Street
                                     Wilkes Barre, PA 18701

"Madam:

"You are hereby authorized to draw on us at sight the sum of One Hundred Thousand and 00/100 Dollars United States Currency ($ 100,000.00) due on November 10, 1973 under a lease, a copy of which is attached to both Beneficiary's copy and Bank's copy of this letter of credit as Exhibit 1, available by your draft for said amount, accompanied by:

"1. Simple receipt for amount drawn.

"2. A signed statement of the drawer of the draft to the effect that the drawer is the lessor under said lease and that the lessee thereunder has not paid the installment of rent due under said lease on November 10, 1973 within 10 days after said installment was due and payable.

"This credit expires on November 30, 1973.

"Drafts under this credit must contain the clause 'drawn under Credit No. 35798 of Girard Trust Bank, dated September 5, 1972.'

In the summer of 1973, the relationship between Cymbalista and Intraworld began to go awry. Norbert Cymbalista, Paulette's husband, visited the hotel in August and, after discussions with the manager, became very concerned over the hotel's financial condition. He discovered that there were unpaid bills in excess of $100,000, that all telephone and Telex communications had been cut off for nonpayment of bills, and that the filing of mechanics liens against the hotel was imminent. After a trans-Atlantic telephone call, the Cymbalistas travelled to the United States within several days of Norbert's discoveries to attempt to resolve the hotel's difficulties with Intraworld. However, as Norbert testified, "I tried to reach [the president of Intraworld] innumerable times by telephone and each time his secretary answered that he would call me back and he never did. I stayed a whole month in the United States trying continually to reach him and it was never possible."

On August 20, 1973, apparently while the Cymbalistas were in the United States, their Swiss counsel sent a letter to Intraworld reciting the unpaid bills, erosion of the Carlton's reputation, and internal corporate difficulties (apparently of Intraworld's Swiss subsidiary). It concluded:

Based upon [Swiss law] and in reference to the provisions of the Lease Contract, we herewith extend to you a final time limit up to September 15, 1973 in order to:

(a) to pay all due debts,

(b) to supply the necessary means to safeguard proper management of the business,

(c) to complete the Board of Directors according to the law.

Within this time limit you must prove to the Hotel Owners that the aforementioned measures have been effectuated. Should you [fail to?] comply with this demand within the time-limit, the Lease Contract will be regarded as void.

Intraworld's Swiss counsel replied to the August 20 letter (but this reply is not in the record). Finding this reply unsatisfactory, Cymbalista's Swiss counsel answered on September 18, 1973:

As [Intraworld] did not comply with our demand within this time-limit, we regard the leasing contract as terminated effective from 15 September 1973.

. . . From now on, the proprietor will have direct and sole control over the hotel real estate respective to the hotel management.[32]

Further correspondence was exchanged by Swiss counsel, including, apparently, a demand on November 3 for the rent due in November. On November 7, 1973, Intraworld's Swiss counsel wrote to Cymbalista's counsel:

You state on behalf of the lessor that [Intraworld] has the obligation to pay . . .rent by November 1. My client [Intraworld], who is presently in close contact with their American Bank [Girard], however have [sic] informed me that the payment of the rent can be made up to November 10 . . . My client informed me further that accordingly these payments shall

---

"Girard Trust Bank hereby agrees with the drawers, endorsers and bona fide owners of the bills drawn strictly in compliance with the terms of this credit that the same will be duly honored upon presentation.

"Except so far as otherwise expressly stated, this credit is subject to the uniform customs and practices for documentary credits (1962 revision), International Chamber of Commerce Brochure No. 222."

Credit No. 35799 was identical to 35798, except that it applied to the rent due on May 10, 1974, and expired on May 30, 1974.

[32] Both letters were originally written in German. The translations which we have quoted were introduced by Intraworld in the trial court without objection by any party.

be legally undertaken by the "Girard Trust Bank" . . . [M]y client cannot agree with your position according to which the lease contract can be considered as terminated either because of [Swiss law] or because of the terms of the lease agreement. . .

That letter was followed on November 9, 1973, by another from Intraworld's counsel to Cymbalista's counsel in which he stated:

If the transfer of the rent from the United States should not be made in timely fashion, your client [Cymbalista] is at liberty to obtain payment by way of the guarantee contracts [*i. e.,* letters of credit]. In any event, there exist the two guarantee contracts, valid until November 30, 1973 and May 30, 1974, respectively, in order to preserve the rights of your client.[33]

The rent due on November 10, 1973, was not paid by Intraworld. Accordingly, on November 21, 1973, Cymbalista's American counsel presented to Girard a draft drawn on Girard for $100,000.00 under Credit No. 35798. The draft was accompanied, all parties agree, by documentation that conformed to the terms of the credit. In his letter to Girard, Cymbalista's counsel stated:

Your attention is directed to correspondence dated November 7 and November 9, 1973, copies of what are attached, in which Swiss counsel representing the Lessee invites the Lessor to draw upon the Letters of Credit; our client, as Lessor, takes the position that the lease . . .has terminated for various reasons, including the failure timely to pay the amount due pursuant to the "Nachtrag" . . . .

Girard informed Intraworld on November 21 that it intended to honor the draft. Intraworld immediately filed an action in equity in the Court of Common Pleas of Philadelphia seeking injunctive relief prohibiting Girard from honoring the draft. Cymbalista filed a petition to intervene, which was granted by the trial court.

The November action was terminated on December 6, 1973, by agreement of all parties. Pursuant to the agreement, Girard placed $100,000.00 in escrow with a Swiss bank, with entitlement to that fund to be determined by the courts of Switzerland.

The situation remained unchanged for about six months. The rent due on May 10, 1974, was not paid. On May 21, 1974, Cymbalista's American counsel presented to Girard a draft for $100,000.00 under Credit No. 35799, accompanied by conforming documentation. Girard immediately advised Intraworld that it intended to honor the draft.

On May 24, Intraworld filed this equity action in the Court of Common Pleas of Philadelphia. It sought preliminary and permanent injunctions restraining Girard from honoring Cymbalista's draft under the letter of credit. The court issued a preliminary restraining order and set a date

---

[33] Intraworld's Swiss counsel's letters were also in German. The record is confusing on the issue of translation. Apparently, Cymbalista offered two translations of each letter as exhibits in the trial court; exhibits 1(T) and 3(T) are translations of the November 7 letter, 2(T) and 4(T) of the November 9 letter. One set of translations was prepared by Girard, although it is unclear which one is Girard's. The other set seems to have been prepared by an associate of Cymbalista's American counsel. The confusion was compounded when an officer of Girard was cross-examined by Cymbalista's counsel. The witness was requested to read exhibit 4(T) into the record. What he actually read, as stenographically recorded in the notes of testimony, corresponds to the document in the record labelled 2(T). At the close of the trial, Intraworld's counsel objected to the admission of 2(T). However, Intraworld's counsel failed toobject when the officer of Girard read 2(T) into the notes of testimony. In any event, we find the differences between the translations to be immaterial. The translations we have quoted are exhibits 1(T) and 2(T).

for a hearing. Cymbalista again petitioned for leave to intervene, which the court granted on May 29.

After the filing of additional pleadings, including preliminary objections and an amended complaint, a hearing was held and testimony taken on May 30 and 31, 1974. On July 11, the trial court issued a memorandum and decree in which it denied a preliminary injunction. Intraworld has appealed to this Court.[34] We affirm.

At the outset we note the limited scope of our review:

In *Pa. P. U. C. v. Alleg. Co. Port Auth.,* 433 Pa. 495, 499, 252 A.2d 367 (1969), we stated that: "It has long been the rule in this Court that on an appeal from a decree, whether granting or denying a preliminary injunction, we will not inquire into the merits of the controversy, but will, instead, examine the record only to determine if there were any apparently reasonable grounds for the actions of the court below. [Citing cases.] Moreover, we will not 'pass upon the reasons for or against such action unless it is plain that no such grounds existed or that the rules of law relied on are palpably wrong or clearly not applicable . . . .'" *Credit Alliance Corp. v. Philadelphia Minit-Man Car Wash Corp.,* 450 Pa. 367, 370-71, 301 A.2d 816, 818 (1973).

Another preliminary matter is a determination of what law we are to apply. Each of the three parties before us has, by agreement, assumed obligations to the others, and each agreement has specified a different controlling law. The lease agreement between Intraworld and Cymbalista provided that it would be "governed" by the law of Switzerland. Cf. Restatement (Second) of Conflict of Laws § 187 (1971); see also *id.* § 189. Intraworld and Girard specified that their agreement would be "construed in accordance with" the law of Pennsylvania. In its letter of credit, Girard stated that its engagement was "subject to" the Uniform Customs and Practice for Documentary Credits (International Chamber of Commerce, 1962 revision).

It is clear that the law of Switzerland does not apply to the question whether the honor of a draft by Girard should be enjoined. While questions of the rights and obligations of the parties to the lease are involved, the action sought to be enjoined would not occur in Switzerland and the party sought to be bound is not located there. See Gewolb, *The Law Applicable to International Letters of Credit,* 11 Vill.L.Rev. 742, 753-54 (1966).

Girard's obligations to Cymbalista are "subject to" the Uniform Customs and Practice. However, the UCP "is by definition a recording of practice rather than a statement of legal rules," and therefore does not purport to offer rules which govern the issuance of an injunction against honor of a draft. Harfield, *Practice Commentary,* N.Y.U.C.C., § 5-114 (McKinney's Consol.Laws, c. 38, 1964).

All parties have briefed and argued the case on the assumption that the Pennsylvania Uniform Commercial Code[35] controls, and with this assumption we agree. See 12A P.S. § 1-105(1); Restatement (Second) of Conflict of Laws § 6(1) & comment a.; *Dynamics Corp. of America v. Citizens and Southern National Bank,* 356 F.Supp. 991, 997 (N.D.Ga.1973); Gewolb, *The Law Applicable to International Letters of Credit,* 11 Vill.L.Rev. 742, 753-54 (1966). In particular the applicable law is Article 5 of the Code. That article specifically states that it applies "to a credit issued by a bank if the credit requires a documentary draft or a documentary demand

---

[34] Appellate Court Jurisdiction Act of 1970, Act of July 31, 1970.

[35] Act of October 2, 1959, P.L. 1023, § 1-101 et seq., amending Act of April 6, 1953, P.L. 3, 12A P.S. § 1-101 et seq. (1970).

for payment . . . ." 12A P.S. § 5-102(1)(a). Since Cymbalista's draft on Girard was required by the letter of credit to be accompanied by a receipt and "signed statement that the drawer is the lessor under said lease and that the lessee thereunder has not paid the installment of rent due," the credit clearly "requires a documentary draft." See 12A P.S. §§ 5-102, comment 1; 5-103(1)(b). It is also clear that the credit was issued by a bank. Finally, the letter of credit that is the object of this controversy is a "credit" within 12A P.S. § 5-102(1)(a). The definition is found in 12A P.S. § 5-103(1)(a):

> "Credit" or "letter of credit" means an engagement by a bank . . .made at the request of a customer and of a kind within the scope of this Article (Section 5-102) that the issuer will honor drafts . . .upon compliance with the conditions specified in the credit. . . .The engagement may be either an agreement to honor or a statement that the bank or other person is authorized to honor.

The letter of credit here includes an agreement by Girard to honor drafts drawn in compliance with the credit. The credit was issued at the request of Intraworld as "customer," see 12A P.S. § 5-103(1)(g). Because it was issued by a bank and requires a documentary draft, it is "of a kind within" section 5-102. Thus, we conclude that Article 5 by its term governs the controversy before us.

Letters of credit have long served as a financial device in international sales of goods.[36] The primary purpose of a letter of credit is to provide assurance to the seller of goods, (*i.e.,* the "beneficiary," see 12A P.S. § 5-103(1)(d)) of prompt payment upon presentation of documents. A seller who would otherwise have only the solvency and good faith of his buyer as assurance of payment may, with a letter of credit, rely on the full responsibility of a bank. Promptness is assured by the engagement of the bank to honor drafts upon the presentation of documents.

The great utility of letters of credit flows from the independence of the issuer-bank's engagement from the underlying contract between beneficiary and customer. Long-standing case law has established that, unless otherwise agreed, the issuer deals only in documents. If the documents presented conform to the requirements of the credit, the issuer may and must honor demands for payment, regardless of whether the goods conform to the underlying contract between beneficiary and customer. Absent its agreement to the contrary, the issuer is, under the general rule, not required or even permitted to go behind the documents to determine if the beneficiary has performed in conformity with the underlying contract. Accord, Uniform Customs and Practice for Documentary Credits, General Provisions & Definitions c. (International Chamber of Commerce, 1962 revision).

This principle of the issuer's right and obligation to honor upon presentation of conforming documents has been codified in 12A P.S. § 5-114:

> (1) An issuer must honor a draft or demand for payment which complies with the terms of the relevant credit regardless of whether the goods or documents conform to the underlying contract for sale or other contract between the customer and the beneficiary. . . .

> (2) Unless otherwise agreed when documents appear on their face to comply with the terms of a credit but a required document . . .is forged or fraudulent or there is fraud in the transaction

---

[36] For an illustration of the operation of a letter of credit in an international sales transaction, see J. White & R. Summers, Handbook of the Law under the Uniform Commercial Code § 18-1(1972); and see *Kingdom of Sweden v. New York Trust Co.,* 197 Misc. 431, 441, 96 N.Y.S.2d 779, 788 (Sup.Ct.1949).

. . .

> (b) in all other cases as against its customer, an issuer acting in good faith may honor the draft or demand for payment despite notification from the customer of fraud, forgery or other defect not apparent on the face of the documents but a court of appropriate jurisdiction may enjoin such honor.

Intraworld seeks to enjoin honor under 12A P.S. § 5-114(2)(b)on the basis that there is "fraud . . .not apparent on the face of the documents." It points to what it believes are two respects in which Cymbalista's demand for payment and supporting documentation are false and fraudulent, although conceding that the documents on their face conform to the credit. First, it contends that Cymbalista's statement (as required by the credit) that "lessee . . .has not paid the installment of rent due under said lease on May 10, 1974," is false and fraudulent because, after Cymbalista purported to terminate the lease in September, 1973, Intraworld was not obligated to pay rent and because the statement failed to disclose the termination of the lease. Second, it argues that the demand is fraudulent because Cymbalista is not seeking rent at all (as, Intraworld contends, she represents in the documents) but rather the "stipulated penalty" pursuant to the Nachtrag.

In light of the basic rule of the independence of the issuer's engagement and the importance of this rule to the effectuation of the purposes of the letter of credit, we think that the circumstances which will justify an injunction against honor must be narrowly limited to situations of fraud in which the wrongdoing of the beneficiary has so vitiated the entire transaction that the legitimate purposes of the independence of the issuer's obligation would no longer be served. A court of equity has the limited duty of "guaranteeing that [the beneficiary] not be allowed to take unconscientious advantage of the situation and run off with plaintiff's money on a pro forma declaration which has absolutely no basis in fact." *Dynamics Corp. of America v. Citizens and Southern National Bank,* 356 F.Supp. 991, 999 (N.D.Ga.1973).

The leading case on the question of what conduct will justify an injunction against honor is *Sztejn v. J. Henry Schroder Banking Corp.,* 177 Misc. 719, 31 N.Y.S.2d 631 (Sup.Ct.1941). In that case as here, the customer sought an injunction against the issuer of a letter of credit restraining honor of a draft drawn by the beneficiary. The customer had contracted to purchase a quantity of bristles from the beneficiary and arranged to have the issuer issue a letter of credit in favor of the beneficiary. The credit required that the draft be accompanied by an invoice and bill of lading.

The beneficiary placed fifty cases of merchandise on a steamship and obtained a bill of lading describing the material as bristles. The beneficiary then drew a draft and presented it, along with the required documents, through a collecting bank. The customer's complaint alleged that the material shipped was not bristles as described in the documents, but rather "cowhair, other worthless material and rubbish [shipped] with intent to simulate genuine merchandise and defraud the plaintiff . . . ."

The collecting bank moved to dismiss the complaint for failure to state a cause of action. The court, assuming the pleaded facts to be true, denied the motion. The court recognized that the issuer's obligation was independent from the underlying contract between customer and beneficiary. That independence is predicated, however, on the genuineness of the documents. The court noted:

This is not a controversy between the buyer and seller concerning a mere breach of warranty regarding the quality of the merchandise; on the present motion, it must be assumed that the seller has intentionally failed to ship any goods ordered by the buyer.

177 Misc. at 721, 31 N.Y.S.2d at 634. When the beneficiary has intentionally shipped no goods at all, the court held, the documentation was not genuine and therefore the predicate of the independence of the issuer's engagement was removed.

We conclude that, if the documents presented by Cymbalista are genuine in the sense of having some basis in fact, an injunction must be refused. An injunction is proper only if Cymbalista, comparable to the beneficiary in *Sztejn,* has no bona fide claim to payment under the lease. *Dynamics Corp. of America v. Citizens and Southern National Bank*, 356 F.Supp. 991, 999 (N.D.Ga. 1973). Of course, neither the trial court nor this Court may attempt to determine Cymbalista's actual entitlement to payment under the lease. Such is not the proper standard for the grant or denial of an injunction against honor. Moreover, questions of rights and obligations under the lease are required by the lease to be determined under Swiss law in the court of Switzerland. See *Dynamics Corp. of America v. Citizens and Southern National Bank, supra.*

On this record, we are unable to conclude that Intraworld established that Cymbalista has no bona fide claim to payment or that the documents presented to Girard have absolutely no basis in fact. Intraworld's argument rests on the basic premise that the lease was terminated in September, 1973. From this premise Intraworld asserts the falsity of Cymbalista's representations that she is the lessor and that the rent was due and unpaid. However, Intraworld did not attempt to prove to the trial court that, under Swiss law, Cymbalista's attempted termination was effective. In fact, Intraworld's Swiss counsel informed Cymbalista's counsel on November 7, 1973, that Intraworld "cannot agree with your position according to which the lease contract can be considered as terminated . . . ." Counsel added that Cymbalista was "at liberty to obtain payment by way of" the letters of credit. Thus, Intraworld failed to prove that, under Swiss law, Cymbalista had no bona fide claim to rent under the lease despite Intraworld's repudiation of termination.

Intraworld's argument that Cymbalista fraudulently concealed the purported termination from Girard is unpersuasive. When presenting the draft and documents to Girard in November, 1973, Cymbalista's American counsel candidly admitted that "our client, as Lessor, takes the position that the lease has terminated . . . for various reasons . . . ." In addition, Girard was a party to the first equity action and its counsel joined the agreement which terminated that action. Cymbalista could reasonably have assumed in May, 1974, that Girard was fully aware of the positions of both Intraworld and Cymbalista.

Intraworld's further contention that Cymbalista's demand was fraudulent in that she was not seeking "rent" at all but the "stipulated penalty" pursuant to the Nachtrag is more substantial but, under scrutiny, also fails. It argues that payment under the credit was permitted only for "rent," and that Cymbalista (as she concedes) was in fact seeking the "stipulated penalty," which is not "rent." Intraworld concludes that Cymbalista was fraudulently attempting to draw under the credit for satisfaction of an obligation not secured by the credit. There are two flaws in this argument.

First, we are not persuaded that the credit was issued for payment of "rent," narrowly defined, only. The letter of credit authorized Cymbalista to draw "the sum . . . due . . . under [the] lease," without specifying that the "sum due" contemplated was only "rent." The letter required that a draft must be accompanied by Cymbalista's statement that "the lessee . . . has not paid the installment of rent due under said lease." This is not equivalent to a limitation on availability of the credit only for nonpayment of rent; in fact, such nonpayment of rent is precisely the condition which triggers Cymbalista's entitlement to the "stipulated penalty." In short, Intraworld has failed to persuade us that the letter of credit was not available to Cymbalista for satisfaction of the "stipulated penalty."

Second and more important, the Nachtrag does not, in our view, create the sharp distinction between "rent" and "stipulated penalty" that Intraworld hypothesizes. It provides that "[i]n the event the lessee should not fulfill its obligation to pay, so that the letter of credit must be used," then the lessor was entitled to terminate the lease and "retain the rent paid or guaranteed [by the letters of credit] for the following year as a stipulated penalty for non-performance of the contract . . . ." Because Intraworld did fail to pay the rent due on November 10, 1973, and May 10, 1974, Cymbalista could reasonably and in good faith have concluded that she had the right to draw on the credit for the "rent . . .guaranteed for the following year."

Whether Intraworld was in fact obligated to pay the rent nonpayment of which triggered Cymbalista's right to retain the "rent guaranteed" by the credit or whether Cymbalista is not entitled to the "stipulated penalty" for some other reason are questions to be decided under Swiss law in the courts of Switzerland. We hold only that Intraworld failed to establish that Cymbalista lacked a bona fide claim to the "rent . . .guaranteed . . .as a stipulated penalty" or that her demand under the credit lacked some basis in fact. Therefore, her documented demand was not shown to be fraudulent because she was seeking satisfaction of the "stipulated penalty."

In summary, we are unable to conclude on this record that Intraworld succeeded in proving that Cymbalista had no bona fide claim for payment under the lease and that her documented demand had absolutely no basis in fact. Accordingly, it is clear that there is an apparently reasonable ground for refusing an injunction.

In addition, Intraworld alleged in its complaint and contends in this Court that Girard's decision to honor Cymbalista's draft was not formed in good faith.[37] Intraworld asserts that Girard's bad faith constituted an additional ground justifying an injunction. It is clear that an issuer of a letter of credit must act in good faith, see 12A P.S. §§ 5-114(2)(b), 5-109(1). However, we are not persuaded that issuer bad faith is a circumstance justifying an injunction against honor; in most if not all instances of issuer bad faith, it would seem that a customer would have an adequate remedy at law in a claim against the issuer or a defense against the issuer's claim for reimbursement. In any event, in this case Intraworld has failed to prove the existence of bad faith on the part of Girard. It was proved no more than that Girard failed to resolve the dispute over the rights and obligations of the parties to the lease in Intraworld's favor. This Girard was not obligated to do. Its obligations included a careful scrutiny of the documents, but once it determined that the documents conformed to the requirements of the credit, it bore no responsibility for the performance of the lease obligations or the genuineness of the documents. 12A P.S. § 5-109(1)(a) & (2). It would, we think, place an issuer in an intolerable position if the law compelled it to serve at its peril as an arbitrator of contract disputes between customer and beneficiary.

The question between the customer and the bank which issues the letter of credit is whether the documents presented with the draft fulfill the specific requirements, and if they do . . ., the bank has the right to pay the draft no matter what may be the defects in the goods which have been shipped. The bank is not obliged to assume the burdens of a controversy between

---

[37] See 12A P.S. § 1-201(19); cf. 12A P.S. § 2-103(1)(b).

the beneficiary and customer and incur the responsibility of establishing as an excuse for not paying a draft that the customer's version is the correct one.

Laudisi v. American Exchange National Bank, 239 N.Y. 234, 243, 146 N.E. 347, 350 (1924).

Finally, Intraworld contends that the trial court erred in refusing to permit it to examine Norbert Cymbalista as on cross-examination as an adverse[38] or hostile witness. We need not decide whether the trial court erred, because it is clear that no prejudice whatsoever resulted. Intraworld claims that, if it had been permitted to cross-examine Norbert, his testimony would have established that Cymbalista's demand was for the stipulated penalty. Brief for Appellants at 15. Cymbalista conceded in the trial court and admits in this Court that her demand was for the "stipulated penalty." Therefore, we conclude that, because what Intraworld would have attempted to prove was admitted by Cymbalista, it was not prejudiced by the claimed error of the trial court.

Decree affirmed. Each party pay own costs.

FEDERAL DEPOSIT INSURANCE CORPORATION v. PLATO

United States Court of Appeals
981 F.2d 852 (5th Cir. 1993)

KING, J.

The Federal Deposit Insurance Corporation (FDIC) appeals from the district court's judgment against the FDIC as plaintiff and for Richard Plato and Henry Vanderkam (d/b/a the McMicken Group) as counter-plaintiffs. We reverse in all significant respects and remand to the district court.

I.

In 1985, Plato, Vanderkam, and Richard Fuqua[39] ("the buyers"), all attorneys, began negotiations with C.E. Vetco Services, Inc. (C.E. Vetco), to purchase an oil coating facility in Houston, Texas. On March 20, 1985, the parties entered into a tentative agreement to agree.[40] In an addendum to this preliminary agreement, the buyers agreed to post a $350,000 irrevocable standby letter of credit[41] in favor of C.E. Vetco as earnest money for the proposed purchase.

---

[38] See Act of May 23, 1887, P.L. 158, § 7, as amended by Act of March 30, 1911, P.L. 35, § 1, 28 P.S. § 381(1958).

[39] Fuqua was originally a party to this action, but has since filed bankruptcy and was dismissed.

[40] The letter agreement stated that "the parties agree to enter into an agreement to buy and sell the [herein] described assets . . . subject to mutual agreement" of the terms to be negotiated in the buy and sell agreement.

[41] A standby "letter of credit" is a common means of contingent financing. Such an arrangement involves a buyer contracting with a financial institution, whereby the institution will serve as a guarantor of a certain amount of money in a transaction between the buyer and a third-party seller. If the buyer breaches his agreement with the seller, the seller may seek payment from the institution. See generally *FDIC v. Philadelphia Gear Corp.,* 476 U.S. 426, 427-428, 106 S. Ct. 1931, 1932-1933, 90 L. Ed. 2d 428 (1986) (discussing standby letter of credit transaction); Arnold & Bransilver, *The Standby Letter of Credit,* 10 U.C.C.L.J. 272 (1978); Note, *FDIC v. Philadelphia Gear: A Standby Letter of Credit Backed By a Promissory Note is not a Deposit,* 41 U.Miami L.Rev. 357 (1986).

A letter of credit transaction actually consists of three distinct contracts: (i) the underlying purchase-and-sale agreement between buyer and seller; (ii) an application for the letter of credit filed with the financial institution by the buyer, *i.e.,* a contract between the bank and buyer; and (iii) the letter of credit itself, a contract between the bank

The buyers obtained financing for the letter of credit from Commonwealth Bank (Commonwealth), a Texas institution. The buyers completed and signed an application for the letter of credit in the amount of $350,000 on April 29, 1985. Commonwealth approved the application and C.E. Vetco was listed as the beneficiary of the letter of credit, which was to be in force through June 24, 1985. The letter of credit contained the following condition precedent: Commonwealth would pay C.E. Vetco $350,000 if C.E. Vetco presented the letter of credit and certified that the buyers had failed to comply with the terms of the March 24th agreement to agree. The buyers also signed a blank promissory note for $350,000, executed a related security agreement, and provided various assets as collateral. It was the mutual understanding of Commonwealth and the buyers that the bank was authorized to complete the blank promissory note in the event that C.E. Vetco properly presented the letter of credit for payment.

The next day, on April 30, 1985, the parties finalized their negotiations and entered into a purchase and sale agreement. The parties agreed to close the deal on or before June 24, 1985. Notably, Vetco, Inc., the parent corporation of C.E. Vetco, was substituted in place of its subsidiary as the named seller in the agreement.[42] Included in the final agreement was a provision similar to the one in the agreement to agree, which referred to a $350,000 letter of credit. This provision, however, referred to a letter of credit on behalf of Vetco, Inc., rather than C.E. Vetco, even though the latter was the only named beneficiary in the March 20th agreement to agree and the April 29th letter of credit.[43]

Sometime after April 30, 1985, Commonwealth—at the request of an official of Vetco, Inc., William Becker—altered certain terms of both the application and letter of credit itself. The beneficiary of the letter of credit was changed from C.E. Vetco Services, Inc., to Vetco, Inc. Commonwealth also changed the terms of the condition precedent in the application for the letter of credit: rather than requiring C.E. Vetco to present the letter of credit and certify that the buyers had breached the March 20th agreement to agree, the altered letter of credit required Vetco, Inc. to present the letter of credit and certify that the buyers were in breach of the April 30th purchase and sell agreement. These changes were in keeping with the substitution of Vetco, Inc. for C.E. Vetco as the named seller in the final purchase and sell agreement. Furthermore, the expiration date was changed from June 24, 1985, to June 28, 1985. A comparison of the original and altered versions of the two letters of credit indicates that Commonwealth simply whited out the altered portions of the original letter and typed over them.[44]

In the following months, the buyers failed to carry through with their obligations set forth in the purchase and sale agreement. On June 24, 1985, Vetco, Inc. responded by presenting the letter of credit to Commonwealth for payment. After Vetco, Inc. certified that the buyers had

and seller, whereby the bank will pay a certain amount of money to the seller in the event that the buyer fails to pay the seller in breach of the underlying contract between the buyer and seller. See *Bank of Cochin Ltd. v. Manufacturers's Hanover Trust Co.,* 612 F. Supp. 1533, 1537 (S.D.N.Y.1985), aff'd, 808 F.2d 209 (2d Cir.1986).

[42] In both the agreement to agree and the final purchase and sale agreement, the authorized representative and signatory for both parent and subsidiary was William Becker.

[43] The parties apparently considered the April 29th letter of credit to apply jointly to the parent and subsidiary. The purchase and sale agreement recited that a letter of credit "has been delivered to Seller," obviously referring to the letter executed the previous day.

[44] The parties are in dispute whether Commonwealth's alteration of the letter of credit was authorized by an agent of the buyers. The parties also are in dispute whether Commonwealth mailed copies of the altered letter of credit to the buyers. The buyers contend that they not only did not authorize the alteration, but also were entirely unaware that any alteration had occurred until many months after it took place.

breached the purchase and sale agreement, Commonwealth paid Vetco, Inc. $350,000 according to the terms of the altered letter of credit. Commonwealth then unilaterally completed the promissory note that the buyers had signed in blank. The buyers initially did not dispute the propriety of Commonwealth's payment of the letter of credit and consequent activation of the promissory note. Indeed, over the next few months, the buyers actually made numerous payments on the note. They also executed an extension of the loan in the form of a second promissory note.[45] However, by early 1986, the buyers fell behind in their payments and eventually defaulted on the note. At the time of the default, Vanderkam had paid the sum of $134,419, which included the liquidation of his collateral. Commonwealth also possessed Plato's collateral, 50,000 shares of preferred stock issued by Tejas Oil and Gas, Inc.

Commonwealth proceeded to file suit in Texas state court for the unpaid balance of the second promissory note. It was at this point that the buyers claim that they first discovered that Commonwealth had altered the original letter of credit. The buyers proceeded to file a counterclaim against Commonwealth for return of the payments made on the note and for return of all remaining collateral that had been pledged as security for the letter of credit. On April 29, 1989, Commonwealth was declared insolvent and the FDIC was appointed as receiver. All non-performing assets, including the buyers' $350,000 promissory note, were assigned to the FDIC in its corporate capacity. The FDIC was also substituted as plaintiff and counterdefendant in Commonwealth's pending state court suit against the buyers. The FDIC subsequently removed the action to federal court. In addition to its claim for the unpaid balance of the note, the FDIC also sought quantum meruit damages, claiming that the buyers had been unjustly enriched by Commonwealth's five-day extension of the expiration of the letter of credit.

After a two day bench trial, the district court entered judgment against the FDIC on its claims and for the buyers on their counterclaims. The district court found that Commonwealth, without authorization from the buyers, had materially altered the original application and letter of credit, which absolved the buyers of liability for their default on the promissory note. The district court also rejected the FDIC's contention that the buyers ratified the altered application and letter of credit by making payments on the promissory note; in this regard, the court specifically found that the buyers made the payment without any knowledge that any alteration had occurred. The court also held that the FDIC was not entitled to quantum meruit damages under well-established equity principles; the court imputed Commonwealth's "unclean hands" to the FDIC. Finally, the district court summarily rejected the FDIC's argument that it should prevail under either the holder-in-due-course or *D'Oench Duhme* doctrines. The court not only entered a "take nothing" judgment for the FDIC on its claim, but also ordered the FDIC to pay Vanderkam $134,419 and return Plato his 50,000 shares of stock. The court thereafter denied the FDIC's joint motion, pursuant to Federal Rules of Civil Procedure 59 and 60, for relief from judgment and a new trial.

II.

On appeal, the parties have raised myriad issues relating to liability and damages with respect to the FDIC's claims and the buyer's counterclaim. Because we believe that the district court committed error by summarily rejecting the FDIC's assertion of the *D'Oench Duhme* doctrine,[46]

---

[45] The renewal note was essentially identical to the first note, save the amount of payment and date of execution.

[46] See *D'Oench Duhme & Co. v. FDIC,* 315 U.S. 447, 62 S. Ct. 676, 86 L. Ed. 956 (1942). 12 U.S.C. § 1823(e) is the statutory analogue of the *D'Oench Duhme* doctrine. While related, the two are considered distinct. See *FDIC*

we need not address the bulk of issues on appeal, as our holding regarding *D'Oench* is dispositive of them.[47] Because we reverse the district court as a matter of law, we need not address any of the court's fact-findings that are challenged by the parties on appeal.

The district court rejected the FDIC's invocation of *D'Oench* with the following conclusory statement: "*D'Oench Duhme,* involving attempts by borrowers to avoid payment of promissory notes by asserting oral side agreements with the lender, is clearly inapplicable to the case at bar." The FDIC argues that the district court misunderstood *D'Oench.* The FDIC specifically contends not only that this case does in fact involve an "oral side agreement," but also that even if it did not *D'Oench* would still apply. We agree on both counts.

We have carefully examined the buyers' original and altered applications for the letter of credit filed with Commonwealth, as well as the two promissory notes (the first signed in blank by the buyers and later filled in by Commonwealth) and the security agreement governing the collateral provided to secure the promissory note. Nowhere in the applications is there any cross-reference to any promissory note. Indeed, the extensive boilerplate language appears to constitute a discrete bilateral contract between the applicant and the bank; no promissory note is contemplated by its terms. Furthermore, nowhere in the promissory notes or security agreement is there a cross-reference to either the applications for the letter or credit or the letter of credit itself. In particular, the promissory note simply states that it is "for value received"; it also contains standard boilerplate governing repayment and default. The security agreement likewise contains boilerplate and simply states that the $350,000 of indebtedness being secured with collateral was for the purpose of "personal indebtedness."

Thus, the promissory notes are facially distinct from the applications for the letter of credit. Cf. *FDIC v. Philadelphia Gear Corp.,* 476 U.S. 426, 428, 106 S. Ct. 1931, 1933, 90 L. Ed. 2d 428 (1986) ("Although the face of the note did not so indicate, both Orion and Penn Square understood that nothing would be considered due on the note, and no interest charged by Penn Square, unless Philadelphia Gear presented drafts on the standby letter of credit after nonpayment by Orion."). The only nexus between the promissory note and security agreement, on the one hand, and the application and letter of credit, on the other hand, is a parol agreement between Commonwealth Bank and the buyers entered into at the time that the application for the letter of credit was submitted in April 1985. While a strong case can be made that Commonwealth and the buyers mutually understood that the promissory note applied only to the letter of credit transaction, such a claim is simply not actionable under *D'Oench* and § 1823(e), which mandate that such collateral agreements must be in explicit written form.[48] As has been repeatedly

---

v. McClanahan, 795 F.2d 512, 514 n. 1 (5th Cir.1986). For purposes of this appeal, however, the two are interchangeable. The relevant portion of § 1823(e), that also finds expression in the common law doctrine, is as follows: "No agreement which tends to diminish or defeat the right, title, or interest of the [FDIC] in any asset acquired by it under this section . . . shall be valid against the corporation unless such agreement (1) shall be in writing. . . ."

[47] We note that *D'Oench* may serve not only as a sword but also as a shield for the FDIC: that is, the doctrine may be invoked by the FDIC not only in its capacity as a plaintiff suing to recover on a note or contract—the validity of which is disputed by the opposing party—but also in defeating a claim asserted against the FDIC. In the instant case, the FDIC invokes *D'Oench* both offensively and defensively.

[48] Similarly, we recognize that, if this were an action between Commonwealth and the buyers, principles of law specifically governing the relationship between a lending institution and an applicant for a letter of credit perhaps would dictate a different result. See, *e.g., Philadelphia Gear Corp. v. Central Bank,* 717 F.2d 230, 236 (5th Cir.1983) (discussing the doctrine of "strict compliance" in litigation concerning letters of credit, citing White & Summers, Uniform Commercial Code § 18.7at 742-43 (1972)). However, such principles have their origin in state commercial law, which is preempted by the federal doctrine embodied in *D'Oench, Duhme* and § 1823(e). See *D'Oench,* 315 U.S. at 473-74, 62 S. Ct. 676 at 686-87, 86 L. Ed. 956.

recognized, the common rationale of *D'Oench* and § 1823(e) is to facilitate to the maximum degree the FDIC's ability to assess the condition of an insolvent bank solely based on its written records. "The doctrine means that the government has no duty to compile oral histories of the bank's customers and . . . officers." See *Bowen v. FDIC,* 915 F.2d 1013, 1016 (5th Cir.1990). In this case, FDIC auditors found a promissory note that made no reference to any other agreement. Because the promissory note was facially unrelated to the letter of credit transaction, *D'Oench* forecloses any claim by the appellees that the promissory note is invalid.

Alternatively, even if we were to agree with the appellees that no unrecorded, oral agreement is at issue in the instant case, there is an alternative reason for reversing the district court on *D'Oench* grounds. As the FDIC correctly contends, the district court erred by limiting *D'Oench* to "oral side agreements." In its expansive evolution since 1942, the *D'Oench* doctrine and its statutory analogue have been applied to a wide variety of circumstances besides collateral oral agreements not evident in a failed bank's records. See *FDIC v. Hamilton,* 939 F.2d 1225, 1228 (5th Cir.1991); see generally, Note *Borrower Beware: D'Oench, Duhme and Section 1823 Overprotect the Insurer When the Bank Fails,* 62 S.Cal.L.Rev. 253 (1988). While most of that evolution has occurred in the lower courts, even the Supreme Court has applied *D'Oench* and § 1823(e) to tortious conduct committed by a failed financial institution. See *Langley v. FDIC,* 484 U.S. 86, 108 S. Ct. 396, 98 L. Ed. 2d 340 (1987) (failed bank's fraudulent misrepresentation and inducement trumped by *D'Oench*). In fact, the Supreme Court implied that only a species of tort actually rendering a contract void ab initio—*e.g.,* "fraud in the factum"—would prevent a court from applying *D'Oench. See id.* at 94. Plato and Vanderkam argue that "fraud in the factum" occurred in the present case.

We disagree.[49] Commonwealth's actions consisted of the alteration of the buyer's application and the letter of credit. While possibly a "material" alteration,[50] Commonwealth's unilateral changes hardly were injurious to the buyers. The substitution of Vetco, Inc. as the letter's beneficiary—merely substituting the parent corporation for its subsidiary—and the corresponding change in the condition precedent were simply nominal alterations contemplated by the express language of the purchase and sale agreement. Furthermore, the extension of the expiration date by five days in no way prejudiced the buyers.[51] It is not as if Commonwealth's alterations increased the amount or terms of repayment. Appellees appear to be clinging to a technicality in the hope of extinguishing their otherwise lawfully incurred debt.

Furthermore, even if Commonwealth's actions did constitute "material alteration" as that term is commonly understood, numerous courts, including this court, have addressed the question of whether *D'Oench* or § 1823(e) is operative when a failed financial institution materially altered, or wrongly augmented, the terms of a partially completed instrument or document. Such cases have relied on a well-recognized component of the larger *D'Oench* doctrine—that when a party

---

[49] We note that appellees did not make this argument below; therefore, they may not properly advance this claim for the first time on appeal. See *Lindsey v. FDIC,* 960 F.2d 567, 572 (5th Cir.1992) ("The Lindseys argue that even if title did pass to MBank upon foreclosure, . . . MBank committed real fraud, or fraud in the factum. The Lindseys did not raise this claim below. This Court will not address an issue raised below for the first time on appeal. . . ."). Thus, we reach the merits of this claim only in the alternative.

[50] See, *e.g.,* Tex.Bus. & Com.Code, § 3.407 (Vernon's 1992). Adopting the U.C.C. definition, the Texas statute defines "material" alteration as including a change in "the number or relation of the parties."

[51] Indeed, that extension is the basis of the FDIC's quantum meruit claim, which seeks to disgorge an unjust enrichment to the buyers. We also note that the alteration was in fact insignificant in that Vetco, Inc. presented the letter of credit on June 24, 1985, which was the last day it could have done so under the original agreement.

"lent himself" to a scheme that could mislead federal bank examiners, whether or not done unwittingly, he cannot circumvent *D'Oench* by arguing that the failed bank wrongly altered or augmented an incomplete instrument which he signed. See *D'Oench,* 315 U.S. at 460, 62 S. Ct. at 680; *Caporale,* 931 F.2d at 2 ("By signing blank notes, the Caporales 'lent themselves' to a scheme that could mislead bank examiners."); *McClanahan,* 795 F.2d at 515 (same). In the instant case, the buyers—all sophisticated attorneys—should have foreseen the consequences of signing a blank promissory note.[52]

III.

Accordingly, we REVERSE not only the district court's entry of a take-nothing judgment on the FDIC's claim, but also the court's order that the FDIC must return to Vanderkam the $134,419 that he had previously paid on the note and return to Plato his 50,000 shares of stock given as collateral. We AFFIRM the district court's judgment on the FDIC's claim only insofar as it refused to award quantum meruit damages. We REMAND for the entry of judgment (including, if and to the extent allowed under law, interest, costs, and attorneys fees). Costs of this appeal shall be borne by the appellees.

ROSE DEVELOPMENTS v. PEARSON PROPERTIES, INC.

Court of Appeals of Arkansas
38 Ark. App. 215, 832 S.W.2d 286, 19 U.C.C. Rep. Serv. 2d 55 (1992)

MAYFIELD, J.

Rose Developments appeals from the order of the circuit court which permanently enjoined the drawing on, or honor of, a letter of credit, pursuant to Ark. Code Ann. § 4-5-114(2)(b) (Repl. 1991), on the finding that appellant had committed fraud.

On December 6, 1988, appellee Pearson contracted with the appellant Rose to provide material and labor in connection with the construction of building "K" in a condominium project known as Solomons Landing Project. The amount of the contract was $458,200.00. In lieu of a performance bond, Pearson delivered an irrevocable letter of credit in the amount of $25,000.00 to secure its performance under the contract. The letter of credit authorized Rose to draw up to $25,000.00 available by "your drafts at sight" accompanied by an authorized statement that Pearson (d/b/a Homes, Inc.) had failed to perform its obligations as required under the terms

---

[52] We briefly note two other issues raised on appeal that are not disposed of by our application of the *D'Oench* doctrine in this case. First, FDIC argues that the district court erred in refusing to award the FDIC quantum meruit damages in addition to its contract claim on the promissory note. The FDIC specifically argues that the buyers were unjustly enriched on account of the five-day extension of the expiration date. We agree with the district court that restitutionary damages were not appropriate. The buyers did not request that extension and, according to the evidence at trial, the buyers were not even aware of the extension until well after the altered letter of credit had expired. Commonwealth's officious actions are not a proper basis for this type of equitable relief. Additionally, we note that it appears that there was no enrichment of any type based on the alteration of the expiration date from June 24, 1985, to June 29, 1985, as Vetco, Inc. presented the letter of credit on June 24th—the last valid day under the original letter of credit.

Another issue we must briefly address concerns Vanderkam and Plato's claim that the trial court failed to award them attorneys' fees under the Equal Access to Justice Act, 28 U.S.C. § 2412(d). Because the Act only applies to a "prevailing party," *id.* § 2412(d)(1)(A), our reversal renders this particular claim moot.

and conditions of its construction contract and the original of the letter of credit. Under the terms of the letter of credit, drafts had to be drawn and negotiated no later than July 15, 1989. Subsequently, buildings "E" and "L" were made addendum to the original contract. The only change was an increase in the price.

On July 5, 1989, S. Brooks Grady, Sr., Vice-President of Rose, stated in a letter to First National Bank (Bank) that "Homes, Inc. has been working on our job at Solomons Landing in Maryland since November 1988. We have been very satisfied with their work, and they are presently working on our third building." On July 15, 1989, the letter of credit was extended until January 12, 1990, for the purpose of working on buildings "E" and "L".

On December 4, 1989, the Bank was notified that Homes, Inc., had failed to perform its obligations as required under the terms and conditions of its construction contract and immediate payment of $25,000.00 was requested under the letter of credit.

On December 12, 1989, Pearson filed a petition for a temporary restraining order against Rose and the Bank alleging among other things that the draft was fraudulently presented upon misrepresentations by Rose, and alternatively that "Ark. Code Ann. Section 4-5-114 specifically grants the Court authority to enjoin the honor of a draft or demand based on 'fraud, forgery, or other defect not apparent on the face of the documents.'"

On December 13, 1989, the court granted the petition. Subsequently, the Bank filed an answer admitting its obligation to honor the draft drawn against the letter of credit unless enjoined by the court and tendered a cashier's check for $25,000.00 to the clerk of the court for safekeeping until further orders.

After a hearing, held May 31, 1990, the trial court found Rose had committed fraud which should prevent it from drawing on the letter of credit and permanently enjoined the Bank from honoring the draft and Rose from drawing on the letter of credit.

A letter of credit is a three-party arrangement involving two contracts and the letter of credit: 1) the underlying contract between the customer and the beneficiary, in this case between Pearson and Rose; 2) the reimbursement agreement between the issuer and the customer, in this case between First National Bank and Pearson; and 3) the letter of credit between the issuer and the beneficiary, in this case between First National Bank and Rose. The significant part of this arrangement is the "independence principle" which states that the bank's obligation to the beneficiary is independent of the beneficiary's performance on the underlying contract. 2 J. White & R. Summers, Uniform Commercial Code § 19-2 (3d ed. 1988). "Put another way, the issuer must pay on a proper demand from the beneficiary even though the beneficiary may have breached the underlying contract with the customer." *Id.* at 8. "It is not a contract of guarantee. . .even though the letter fulfills the function of a guarantee." *Id.* at 9.

The letter of credit involved in this case is a standby letter of credit which has been characterized as a "back-up" against customer default on obligations of all kinds. *Id.* § 19-1, at 4. Such letters function somewhat like guarantees because it is the customer's default on the underlying obligation that prompts the beneficiary's draw on the letter. *Id.* at 4. The risk to the issuer is somewhat greater than in a commercial letter of credit in that the commercial letter gives the issuer security in goods whereas the standby letter gives no ready security, and the banker behaves as a surety. *Id.* at 6. The standby letter of credit is somewhat akin to a performance bond in that:

In place of a performance bond from a true surety, builder (customer) gets his bank (issuer) to write owner (beneficiary) a standby letter of credit. In this letter, issuer engages to pay beneficiary-owner against presentment of two documents: 1) a written demand (typically a sight draft) which calls for payment of the letter's stipulated amount, plus 2) a written statement certifying that customer-builder has failed to perform the agreed construction work.

Id. at 4. One difference between the standby letter of credit and the surety contract is that the standby credit beneficiary has different expectations.

In the surety contract situation, there is no duty to indemnify the beneficiary until the beneficiary establishes the fact of the obligor's nonperformance. The beneficiary may have to establish that fact in litigation. During the litigation, the surety holds the money and the beneficiary bears most of the cost of delay in performance.

In the standby credit case, however, the beneficiary avoids that litigation burden and receives his money promptly upon presentation of the required documents. It may be that the account party has in fact performed and that the beneficiary's presentation of those documents is not rightful. In that case, the account party may sue the beneficiary in tort, in contract, or in breach of warranty; but during the litigation to determine whether the account party has in fact breached his obligation to perform, the beneficiary, not the account party, holds the money. J. Dolan, The Law of Letters of Credit, at 1-18, 1-19 (2d ed. 1991).

Letters of credit are governed by the "Uniform Commercial Code-Letters of Credit," Ark. Code Ann. § 4-5-101 through 117 (Repl. 1991). Section 4-5-114(1) provides that an issuer must honor a draft which complies with the terms of the relevant credit regardless of whether the goods or documents conform to the underlying contract between the customer and the beneficiary. However, the issuer does not have an absolute duty to honor a draft authorized by the letter of credit. An exception is provided by § 4-5-114(2) which provides that an issuer need not honor the draft if "a required document does not in fact conform to the warranties made on negotiation or transfer of a document of title (§ 4-8-306) or of a certificated security (§ 4-8-306) or is forged or fraudulent or there is fraud in the transaction." Section 4-5-114(2)(b) provides that in all other cases as against its customer an issuer may honor the draft despite notification from the customer of fraud, forgery, or other defect not apparent on the face of the documents but a court of appropriate jurisdiction may enjoin such honor.

On appeal, it is argued that the trial court erred in finding the appellant committed fraud which would prevent it from drawing on the letter of credit. Appellant admits that courts have allowed injunctions for "fraud in the transaction" but argues an injunction is proper only if there is no bona fide claim to payment, and the wrongdoing of the beneficiary has so vitiated the entire transaction that the legitimate purposes of the independence principle would no longer be served. See *Intraworld Industries, Inc. v. Girard Trust Bank,* 336 A.2d 316 (Pa. 1975); *Sztejn v. Henry Schroder Banking Corp.,* 31 N.Y.S.2d 631 (1941). Appellant contends that Pearson has established only that there may be a dispute as to some of the "back charges". (Back charges have to do with material and labor that needs or needed to be performed, that Pearson was supposed to be responsible for, but appellant had to take over.)

Appellees agree the only issue on appeal is whether appellant committed fraud which would justify the issuance of the injunction and argue the injunction was proper. Appellee Pearson contends that in December 1989 or January 1990 it received a number of back charges dating as far back as December 1988; that it had never previously received these charges; that appellant, while in possession of documents it claimed were back charges, wrote a letter to obtain an extension of the letter of credit stating it was "very satisfied with the work of Homes, Inc.";

and that appellant knowingly misrepresented the facts in order to obtain an extension of the letter of credit.

In support of its argument, appellee Pearson cites *W.O.A. Inc. v. City National Bank of Fort Smith, Ark.,* 640 F. Supp. 1157 (W.D. Ark. 1986), and *Shaffer v. Brooklyn Park Garden Apartments,* 250 N.W.2d 172 (Minn. 1977). Those cases, however, involved false certification accompanying drafts for payment and have no application here. In *City National Bank* the appellant intentionally misrepresented the state of affairs when, though it had been paid, it presented drafts for payment under a letter of credit. That case relied on *Roman Ceramics Corp. v. Peoples National Bank,* 714 F.2d 1207 (3d Cir. 1983), which held that a beneficiary who tenders a draft knowing that its certification of nonpayment by the buyers is false, is guilty of fraud in the transaction. Similarly, *Shaffer* involved a situation where letters of credit guaranteed payment of certain promissory notes. The issuer received documents which appeared to comply with the presentation requirements under the letters of credit; however, the certifications which stated the customers had defaulted on their loans were false.

In the instant case, the certification stated that "Homes, Inc., has failed to perform its obligations as required under the terms and conditions of their construction contract." At trial, Robert Pearson III, Vice-President of Homes, Inc., testified they did not allege that there were forgeries "or anything like that" involved in the demand for payment on the letter of credit. Pearson admitted the letter of credit was to protect appellant in the event Pearson did not pay for labor, materials and other supplies that might be incorporated into the structure; that there were outstanding materialmen's and laborers' liens against the project; and that some of those liens were for materials, labor, and supplies that were the responsibility of Pearson. Pearson testified his allegation of fraud was based on the contention that he had been billed for work outside his contract and that Rose had called upon the letter of credit based upon certain back charges. Pearson said the majority of the back charges were unacceptable, but acknowledged that 10% of the charges were legitimate.

Appellee Bank admits this case does not involve forgery or "other defect not apparent on the face of the documents". John Thornton, Executive Vice-President of the Bank, testified he would not have extended the original letter of credit without Rose's statement that the jobs were being done in a satisfactory manner. Appellee Bank argues that none of the back charges, that predated the extension of the letter of credit, were mentioned in appellant's letter which induced the Bank to extend the letter of credit. And the Bank contends that Rose's fraud can be categorized as both egregious and intentional and that the injunction was a proper statutory remedy.

The narrow question to be decided by this court is whether the evidence will support a finding that there was "fraud in the transaction." Our research has revealed no Arkansas cases containing a definition of "fraud in the transaction" as used in the section of the Uniform Commercial Code that is involved in this case. Some courts have held that fraud in the transaction must be of such an egregious nature as to vitiate the entire underlying transaction so that the legitimate purposes of the independence of the bank's obligation would no longer be served. Other cases and writers have suggested intentional fraud should be sufficient to obtain injunctive relief in letter of credit cases. Professor Symons concludes "a proper definition of fraud will necessarily encompass and be limited by the requirement of scienter: that there be an affirmative, knowing misrepresentation of fact or that the beneficiary state a fact not having any idea about its truth or falsity, and in reckless disregard of the truth." *Symons, supra* at 379. It has also been suggested that the lesson to be learned from this section of the Uniform Commercial Code (Ark. Code Ann. § 5-4-114(2)

(Repl. 1990), is that a court should seldom enjoin payment under a letter of credit on the theory that there is fraud in the documents or fraud in the underlying transaction. See 2 J. White & R. Summers, Uniform Commercial Code § 19-7(Supp. 1991).

From our consideration of the law and the evidence in this case, we think the trial court erred in enjoining payment under the letter of credit. In the first place, we do not believe appellant's general statement "we have been very satisfied with their work" is sufficient for a finding of fraud. At the time this statement was made, appellant had extended Pearson's contract for building "K" to include buildings "E" and "L", and it seems obvious that appellant's statement was truthful or appellant would not have extended the contract. Also, the testimony shows that the total amount of the contract for building "K" was $458,200.00 and that the back charges which pre-date the statement complained of totalled only approximately $1,944.81. We do not believe the existence of back charges in that small amount supports a finding that appellant committed fraud when it said "we have been very satisfied with their work."

As to the argument that appellant's fraud consisted of billing for work that was outside its contract and other disputed back charges, Robert Pearson III testified his allegation of fraud was that the letter of credit was being called upon because appellant said that based upon "these back charges" they were still owed money, but Pearson testified that as far as "these back charges" are concerned "the majority of them are unacceptable." Pearson testified appellant was claiming a total of $50,000.00 to $60,000.00 in back charges on a project which totaled over $1.2 million. This is simply a contract dispute relating to back charges which may have to be resolved in litigation. However, as explained in Dolan, supra, in the standby letter of credit case "the beneficiary avoids that litigation burden and receives his money promptly" and during the litigation "the beneficiary, not the account party, holds the money."

When we apply the law to the evidence in this case, we think it was clearly erroneous to find that appellant committed fraud that should prevent it from drawing on the letter of credit; therefore, it was error to grant permanent injunctive relief to appellee Pearson and prevent the Bank from honoring the draft drawn on the letter of credit.

Reversed and remanded for any necessary proceedings consistent with this opinion.

§ 11.02 Standby or Guaranty Letters of Credit

We have seen the commercial letter of credit used in connection with the purchase and sale of goods. This letter of credit gave assurances to a seller that it would receive payment for sale of its goods. A "standby letter of credit" can be utilized in a sale of goods transaction or other transactions. A standby letter of credit is basically a letter of credit which represents an obligation to the beneficiary on the part of the issuer to make payment on account of any *default* by the account party/customer in the performance of an obligation. See J. Dolan, The Law of Letters of Credit, ¶¶ 1.04, 1.05, 1.06 and 3.06 (2d ed. 1991).

A seller may use a standby arrangement to support sales. "Under this plan, the seller invoices the buyer directly and draws under the standby credit only if the buyer fails to honor the invoice. This invoice credit may be clean; that is, it may be payable against a draft alone, or it may require the beneficiary to submit the invoices and a certificate reciting that they are unpaid. Unless the buyer fails to pay the invoice, the seller-beneficiary will not draw on the credit." J. Dolan, The Law of Letters of Credit 1-30 (2d ed. 1991).

A standby credit can be used to give assurance to a buyer that seller will perform its obligation to transfer and deliver the goods to the buyer. See, e.g., *KMW Int'l v. Chase Manhattan Bank,*

27 U.C.C. Rep. 203 (2d Cir. 1979): Chase to pay Iran bank on behalf of Iran buyer of telephone poles from KMW seller upon receipt by Chase of Iran bank's

> authenticated cable certifying [that] the amount drawn is the amount you have been called upon to pay Khuzestan Water and Power Authority, P.O. Box 13, Ahwaz, Iran, under your guarantee issued at the request of KMW International due to nonperformance by KMW International under the terms of Khuzestan Water and Power Authority purchase order #4229 dated August 1, 1978. . . .

Other illustrations of standby (or guaranty) letters of credit are:

> 1. *Construction Contract.* Letter of credit issuer agrees to honor drafts drawn by Park District if the following document is furnished: "[Y]our signed statement dated January 5, 1974 and presented on that date that your drawing is in connection with failure by McCoy Enterprises, Inc. to construct two tennis courts in Westminster, Colorado on or before January 5,1974." (*Hyland Hills Metropolitan Park & Rec. Dist. v. McCoy Enterprises, Inc.*, 554 P.2d 708 (Colo. App. 1976).)

> 2. *Employment Contract.* Issuer will pay up to $ 70,000 in the event of default. "Drafts presented under this credit must be accompanied by a signed affidavit of [professional football player] stating that the Chicago Football Club, Inc. . . . has not paid [football player] for a scheduled football game by Tuesday of the following week." (*Beathard v. Chicago Football Club, Inc.*, 419 F.Supp. 1133 (N.D. Ill. 1976).) In *Beathard* the credit was revocable. Under UCP 500, Article 7, if a credit doesn't indicate whether it is revocable or irrevocable, it is deemed to be irrevocable. Also, revised U.C.C. § 5-106 states that a letter of credit is revocable only if it so provides.

> 3. *Lease.* Issuer authorized lessor to draw draft on issuer if draft accompanied by "signed statement of the drawer . . . to the effect that the drawer is the lessor under said lease and that the lessee thereunder has not paid the installment of rent due (*Intraworld Industries, Inc. v. Girard Trust Bank*, 336 A.2d 316 (Pa. 1975).)

> 4. *Loan Guaranty.* Issuer to honor drafts drawn by mortgagee-creditor upon presentation of affidavit that certain closing costs were not paid. (*Mid States Mtg. Corp. v. National Bank of Southfield*, 77 Mich. App. 651, 259 N.W.2d 175 (1977).) *See also, Brown v. United States National Bank*, 371 N.W.2d 692, 41 UCC Rep. 1765 (1985).

> 5. *Charter Air Service Contract.* Beneficiary (Westates) is to furnish airplanes and crews for customer/applicant's (Charter One's) charter air service; customer/applicant is to pay a monthly fee to beneficiary. The issuer's letter of credit read: "the credit is available to you [Westates] by your drafts on us at sight accompanied by: Dated notarized copy of the ten (10) day notice described in [Westates/Charter One contract]." (This is a default notice under the contract's special "default" provision.) *Ground Air Transfer, Inc. v. Westates Airlines, Inc.*, 899 F.2d 1269, 11 UCC Rep. 2d 177 (1st Cir. 1990).

See J. Dolan, The Law of Letters of Credit, ¶ 1.06, "Frequent Uses of Standby Credit" (2d ed. 1991).

Functionally, there is little difference between a standby and a regular letter of credit. The main distinction between the two types of letters is that parties to a transaction expect a standard letter of credit to be drawn on, where as a standby letter of credit there is a condition other than shipment of goods that must occur before payment on the letter is made to the beneficiary.

Because the standby letters of credit often serve as a guarantee, the independence principle becomes strained in many relationships. Customers frequently rely on their banks to deny honoring documents presented; imploring the financial institution to find any nonconformity in the documents. Equitable issues arise where a surreptitious party to a contract fraudulently draws on a standby letter of credit. Should an issuing bank have a duty to investigate the underlying transaction when it is serving as a guarantor of performance?

COLORADO NATIONAL BANK OF DENVER v. BOARD OF COUNTY COMMISSIONERS OF ROUTT COUNTY

Supreme Court of Colorado
634 P.2d 32; 31 U.C.C. Rep. Serv. (Callaghan) 1681 (1981)

CHIEF JUSTICE HODGES delivered the Opinion of the Court.

We granted certiorari to review the court of appeals' decision affirming a district court's judgment holding the petitioner, the Colorado National Bank of Denver (the Bank), liable for the face amounts of three letters of credit it issued to secure the completion of road improvements by its customer, the Woodmoor Corporation (Woodmoor). *Board of County Commissioners of Routt County v. Colorado National Bank of Denver,* 43 Colo. App. 186, 607 P.2d 1010 (1979). We reverse the judgment as to letters of credit No. 1156 and No. 1157, and affirm the judgment as to letter of credit No. 1168.

Woodmoor planned to develop a mountain recreation community in Routt County, Colorado (the County), to be known as Stagecoach. Early in 1973, Woodmoor obtained plat approval from the Routt County Board of County Commissioners (the Commissioners) for several Stagecoach subdivisions. Pursuant to section 30-28-137, C.R.S. 1973 (1977 Repl. Vol. 12), and county subdivision regulations, approval of three of these subdivision plats was conditioned upon Woodmoor's agreement to provide a bond or other undertaking to ensure the completion of roads in accordance with the subdivision design specifications. Accordingly, subdivision improvements agreements were executed between Woodmoor and the county.

At Woodmoor's request, the Bank issued three letters of credit to secure Woodmoor's obligations under the agreements. The first two letters of credit, No. 1156 and No. 1157, were issued January 23, 1973 in the respective amounts of $158,773 and $77,330 bearing expiry dates of December 31, 1975. The third letter of credit No. 1168 was issued March 7, 1973 in the amount of $113,732 bearing an expiry date of December 31, 1976. The face amounts of the letters of credit were identical to the estimated costs of the road and related improvements in the respective subdivision improvements agreements. The County was authorized by each letter of credit to draw directly on the Bank, for the account of Woodmoor, up to the face amount of each letter of credit. Each letter of credit required the County, in order to draw on the letters of credit, to submit fifteen-day sight drafts accompanied by:

A duly-signed statement by the Routt County Board of Commissioners that improvements have not been made in compliance with a Subdivision Improvements Agreement between Routt

County and the Woodmoor Corporation dated [either January 9, 1973 or March 7, 1973] and covering the [respective subdivisions] at Stagecoach and that payment is therefore demanded hereunder.

Woodmoor never commenced construction of the roads and related improvements. On December 31, 1975, the expiry date of letters of credit No. 1156 and No. 1157, the County presented two demand drafts to the Bank for the face amounts of $158,773 and $77,330. The demand drafts were accompanied by a resolution of the Commissioners stating that Woodmoor had failed to comply with the terms of the subdivision improvements agreements and demanded payment of the face amounts of the letters of credit. On January 5, 1976, within three banking days of the demand,[53] the Bank dishonored the drafts. The Bank did not specifically object to the County's presentation of demand drafts rather than fifteen-day sight drafts as required by the letters of credit.

On December 22, 1976, the County presented the Bank with a demand draft on letter of credit No. 1168 which was accompanied by the required resolution of the Commissioners. The Bank dishonored this draft because of the County's nonconforming demand, viz., that a demand draft was submitted rather than a fifteen-day sight draft. On December 29, 1976, the County presented a fifteen-day sight draft to the Bank. This draft was not accompanied by the resolution of the Commissioners. On December 31, 1976, the Bank dishonored this draft.

The County sued to recover the face amounts of the three letters of credit plus interest from the dates of the demands. The Bank answered the County's complaints alleging several affirmative defenses. The fundamental premise of the Bank's defenses was the assertion that the County would receive a windfall since it had not expended or committed to spend any funds to complete the road improvements specified in the subdivision improvements agreements.

The County filed a motion in limine seeking a determination by the trial court to exclude evidence concerning matters beyond the four corners of the letters of credit and the demands made on the letters of credit. The bank replied by filing a cross-motion in limine seeking a ruling that it would not be precluded at trial from offering evidence outside the four corners of the letters of credit. The trial court, after extensive briefing by the parties and a hearing, granted the County's motion to limit the admissibility of evidence to the letters of credit, documents and drafts presented thereunder, the demands on the letters of credit, and the Bank's refusals to honor the County's demands for payment.

The remaining issues were whether the County's demands conformed to the letters of credit or, if not, whether the Bank had waived nonconforming demands, and whether interest ought to be awarded. The parties agreed on a stipulated set of facts concerning these remaining issues. The Bank did, however, make an offer of proof as to the rejected affirmative defenses. The Bank would have attempted to prove that the subdivisions in question remained raw, undeveloped mountain property for which there was no viable market and that the County had neither constructed, made commitments to construct, nor planned to construct the roads or other improvements described in the subdivision improvements agreements secured by the letters of credit. These allegations were disputed by the County.

The trial court entered judgment against the Bank for the face amounts of the letters of credit plus accrued interest at the statutory rate from the date of the County's demands. Costs were

---

[53] Under section 4-5-112(1)(a), C.R.S. 1973, a bank called upon to honor drafts under a letter of credit may defer until the close of the third banking day following receipt of the documents.

awarded in favor of the County. The Bank's motion for new trial was denied, and the Bank appealed.

The court of appeals affirmed the judgment of the trial court ruling that standby letters of credit are governed by article 5 of the Uniform Commercial Code, section 4-5-101 et seq., C.R.S. 1973, and that an issuer must honor a draft or demand for payment which complies with the terms of the relevant credit regardless of whether the goods or documents conform to the underlying contract. The court of appeals affirmed the trial court's refusal to consider any evidence regarding the County's alleged windfall. The court of appeals also held that any defects in the form of the county's demands were waived by the Bank.

I.

We first address the question whether the trial court properly limited the evidence to be presented at trial to the letters of credit, the demands by the County, and the Bank's replies to the demands. The Bank has continually asserted during each stage of this action that it ought to be permitted to show that the County will receive a windfall if the County is permitted to recover against the letters of credit. The Bank requested an opportunity to prove that the County will utilize the funds it would receive in a manner other than that specified in the road improvements agreements. Fundamentally, the Bank seeks to litigate the question of the completion of the purpose of the underlying performance agreements between Woodmoor and the County. This the Bank cannot do.

An overview of the history and law concerning letters of credit is useful in the consideration of this issue. The letter of credit arose to facilitate international commercial transactions involving the sale of goods. Today the commercial utility of the letter of credit in both international and domestic sale of goods transactions is unquestioned and closely guarded. In recent years, the use of the letter of credit has expanded to include guaranteeing or securing a bank's customer's promised performance to a third party in a variety of situations. See *First Empire Bank—New York v. Federal Deposit Insurance Corp.,* 572 F.2d 1361 (9th Cir.), cert. denied 439 U.S. 919, 99 S. Ct. 293, 58 L. Ed. 2d 265 (1978). This use is referred to as a standby letter of credit. Article five of the Uniform Commercial Code governs both traditional commercial letters of credit and standby letters of credit. *East Bank of Colorado Springs v. Dovenmuehle,* 196 Colo. 422, 589 P.2d 1361 (1978).

Three contractual relationships exist in a letter of credit transaction. Underlying the letter of credit transaction is the contract between the bank's customer and the beneficiary of the letter of credit, which consists of the business agreement between these parties. Then there is the contractual arrangement between the bank and its customer whereby the bank agrees to issue the letter of credit, and the customer agrees to repay the bank for the amounts paid under the letter of credit. See also section 4-5-114(3), C.R.S. 1973. Finally, there is the contractual relationship between the bank and the beneficiary of the letter of credit created by the letter of credit itself. The bank agrees to honor the beneficiary's drafts or demands for payment which conform to the terms of the letter of credit. See generally sections 4-5-103(1)(a) and 4-5-114(1), C.R.S. 1973; White and Summers, Uniform Commercial Code § 18-6(2d ed. 1980).

It is fundamental that the letter of credit is separate and independent from the underlying business transaction between the bank's customer and the beneficiary of the letter of credit. "The letter of credit is essentially a contract between the issuer and the beneficiary and is recognized by [article 5 of the Uniform Commercial Code] as independent of the underlying contract between the customer and the beneficiary . . . . In view of this independent nature of the letter of credit engagement the issuer is under a duty to honor the drafts for payment which in fact conform with the terms of the credit without reference to their compliance with the terms of the underlying contract." Section 4-5-114, Official Comment 1, C.R.S. 1973.

The independence of the letter of credit from the underlying contract has been called the key to the commercial vitality of the letter of credit. The bank must honor drafts or demands for payment under the letter of credit when the documents required by the letter of credit appear on their face to comply with the terms of the credit. Section 4-5-114(2), C.R.S. 1973. An exception to the bank's obligation to honor an apparently conforming draft or demand for payment, see *Foreign Venture Ltd. Partnership v. Chemical Bank,* 59 App. Div. 2d 352, 399 N.Y.S. 2d 114 (1977), is when a required document is, inter alia, forged or fraudulent, or there is fraud in the transaction. Section 4-5-114(2). The application of this narrow exception is discussed in detail later in this opinion.

As mentioned above, letters of credit have recently come to be used to secure a bank's customer's performance to a third party. When a letter of credit is used to secure a bank's customer's promised performance to a third party, in whatever capacity that might be, the letter of credit is referred to as a "guaranty letter of credit," see *East Bank of Colorado Springs v. Dovenmuehle, supra*; Verkuil, *Bank Solvency and Guaranty Letters of Credit, supra,* or a "standby letter of credit," Arnold & Bransilver, *The Standby Letter of Credit—The Controversy Continues, supra,* 12 C.F.R. § 7.1160(1980). Standby letters of credit are closely akin to a suretyship or guaranty contract. The bank promises to pay when there is a default on an obligation by the bank's customer. "If for any reason performance is not made, or is made defectively, the bank is liable without regard to the underlying rights of the contracting parties." Verkuil, *Bank Solvency and Guaranty Letters of Credit, supra* at 723.

While banks cannot, as a general rule, act as a surety or guarantor of another party's agreed performance, see generally Lord, *The No-Guaranty Rule and the Standby Letter of Credit Controversy,* 96 Banking L. J. 46 (1979), the legality of standby letters of credit has been uniformly recognized. *E.g., United Bank of Denver v. Quadrangle, Ltd.,* 42 Colo. App. 486, 596 P.2d 408 (1979). What distinguishes a standby letter of credit from a suretyship or guaranty contract is that the bank's liability rests upon the letter of credit contract rather than upon the underlying performance contract between the bank customer and the beneficiary of the letter of credit.

The utilization by banks of standby letters of credit is now wide-spread, although some commentators suggest that bankers may not appreciate the legal obligations imposed by the standby letter of credit. Where the bank issues a standby letter of credit, the bank naturally expects that the credit will not be drawn on in the normal course of events, *i.e.,* if the customer of the bank fulfills its agreed-upon performance, then the credit will not be drawn upon. This expectation of the bank must be compared to the bank's expectation with respect to a traditional letter of credit issued as a means of financing a sale of goods. In the latter situation, the bank expects that the credit will always be drawn upon. See Arnold & Bransilver, *The Standby Letter of Credit—The Controversy Continues, supra*; Note, *Letters of Credit: Injunction As A Remedy For Fraud In U.C.C. Section 5-114, supra.* It has been suggested that bankers may be lax in considering the credit of a customer with respect to issuing a standby letter of credit to secure the integrity of its customer to complete an agreed-upon performance, since it could be easily assumed by the bank that demand for payment would never be made. See Harfield, *The Increasing*

Domestic Use of the Letter of Credit, supra at 258-59. See also, Note, *Guaranty Letters of Credit: Problems and Possibilities,* 16 Ariz. L. Rev. 823, 832 (1974). One solution suggested by many commentators is that the issuing bank treat a standby letter of credit like an unsecured loan. Harfield, *Increasing Domestic Use of the Letter of Credit, supra*; Verkuil, *Bank Solvency and Guaranty Letters of Credit, supra*; Note: *Guaranty Letter of Credit: Problems and Possibilities, supra.* National Banks issuing standby letters of credit are subject to the lending limits of 12 U.S.C. § 84 (1976).[54]

We now turn to a discussion of the present case, and why the Bank cannot introduce evidence beyond that directly relating to its contract with the County. As discussed above, the letters of credit, and the Bank's obligations thereunder, are separate and independent from the underlying subdivision improvements agreements between Woodmoor and the County. The fact that the letters of credit issued by the Bank are standby letters of credit does not alter this general rule. The Bank is bound by its own contracts with the County.

Each of the letters of credit prepared and issued by the Bank in this case sets forth specifically the condition for payment, *i.e.,* that Woodmoor failed to make the improvements in conformance with the respective subdivision improvements agreements. Had the Bank desired additional conditions for payment, such as the actual completion of the road improvements prior to payment under the letters of credit, it could have incorporated such a condition in the letters of credit. To demand payment under the letters of credit, the County was only required to submit a "duly-signed statement by the [Commissioners] that improvements have not been made in compliance with [the] Subdivision Improvements Agreement[s]. . . ."

The Bank cannot litigate the performance of the underlying performance contracts. "Performance of the underlying contract is irrelevant to the Bank's obligations under the letter of credit." *West Virginia Housing Development Fund v. Sroka, supra* at 1114 (W.D. Pa. 1976). Likewise, the question of whether the beneficiary of the letter of credit has suffered any damage by the failure of the bank's customer to perform as agreed is of no concern.

The Bank argues that it is entitled to dishonor the County's drafts under section 4-5-114(2), C.R.S. 1973. This section provides:

Unless otherwise agreed, when documents appear on their face to comply with the terms of a credit but a required document . . . . is forged or fraudulent or there is fraud in the transaction:

> (a) The issuer must honor the draft or demand for payment if honor is demanded by a negotiating bank or other holder of the draft or demand which has taken the draft or demand under the credit and under circumstances which would make it a holder in due course . . . . and in an appropriate case would make it a person to whom a document of title has been duly negotiated . . . . or a bona fide purchaser of a security . . . .; and

> (b) In all other cases, as against its customer, an issuer acting in good faith may honor the draft or demand for payment despite notification from the customer of fraud, forgery, or other defect not apparent on the face of the documents; but a court of appropriate jurisdiction may enjoin such honor.

---

[54] 12 U.S.C. § 84 (1976) provides that a national bank may not lend more than ten percent of its capital funds to any one customer. Traditionally, standby letters of credit did not fall within the aegis of this statute as they were considered contingent liabilities, and thus not reflected in a bank's balance sheet; however, the modern view, as codified in 12 C.F.R. § 7.1160 (1981), is that letters of credit are actual liabilities of a bank which must be included when calculating the marginal reserve required under this statutory provision. See Verkuil, *Bank Solvency and Guaranty Letters of Credit, supra.*

Under this section, the issuer of a letter of credit may in good faith honor a draft or demand for payment notwithstanding notice from its customer that documents are forged or fraudulent, or there is fraud in the transaction. The issuer may, however, be enjoined from honoring such drafts or demands for payment. Impliedly, the issuer may also refuse to honor such drafts or demands for payment when it has been notified by its customer of these defects. Section 4-5-114, Official Comment 2, C.R.S. 1973; *Siderius, Inc. v. Wallace, supra.*

In this case, the Bank has not argued, nor can it reasonably assert, that the documents presented by the County are forged or fraudulent. The Bank has not challenged the authenticity of the drafts and demands for payment by the County or the truthfulness of the statements that the requirements of the underlying subdivision improvements agreements have not been fulfilled. The Bank does assert, however, that there has been fraud in the transaction on the basis that the funds the County would receive would be utilized by the County other than to pay for the completion of the road improvements.

Fundamentally, "fraud in the transaction," as referred to in section 4-5-114(2), must stem from conduct by the beneficiary of the letter of credit as against the customer of the bank. See generally White and Summers, Uniform Commercial Code § 18-16 (2d ed. 1980). It must be of such an egregious nature as to vitiate the entire underlying transaction so that the legitimate purposes of the independence of the bank's obligation would no longer be served. "It is generally thought to include an element of intentional misrepresentation in order to profit from another . . . ." *West Virginia Housing Development Fund v. Sroka, supra.* This fraud is manifested in the documents themselves, and the statements therein, presented under the letter of credit. *Dynamics Corporation of America v. Citizens & Southern National Bank, supra; Shaffer v. Brooklyn Park Garden Apartments,* 311 Minn. 452, 250 N.W. 2d 172 (1977). One court has gone so far as to say that only some defect in these documents would justify a bank's dishonor. *O'Grady v. First Union National Bank of North Carolina,* 296 N.C. 212, 250 S.E. 2d 587 (1978).

In this case, the Bank has not asserted that there is fraud in the transaction between Woodmoor and the County, nor can it reasonably make such an argument. No facts have been pled to establish fraud which vitiated the entire agreement between the County and Woodmoor. No fraud has been asserted by the Bank's offer of proof which would entitle it to dishonor the County's drafts and demands for payment. See *West Virginia Housing Development Fund v. Sroka, supra; Mid-States Mortgage v. National Bank of Southfield, supra.* Thus, the trial court properly granted the County's motion in limine excluding all evidence beyond the four corners of the letters of credit, the demands thereunder, and the Bank's replies.

II.

We next consider whether the drafts and demands for payment by the County complied with the terms of the letters of credit, or if not, whether the Bank waived any nonconforming demands.

The Bank was obligated to examine the documents "with care so as to ascertain that on their face they appear[ed] to comply with the terms of the credit . . . ." Section 4-5-109(2), C.R.S. 1973. To maintain the commercial vitality of the letter of credit device, strict compliance with the terms of the letter of credit is required. If the drafts or demands for payment on their face complied with the terms of the letters of credit, the Bank was obligated to honor the drafts. Section 4-5-114(1), C.R.S. 1973. See also, *e.g.,* Annot., 35 A.L.R. 3d 1404 (1971).

In this case, the Bank promised to pay the County, for the account of Woodmoor, upon the County's presentation of fifteen-day sight drafts accompanied by a "duly-signed statement by the Routt County Board of Commissioners that improvements have not been made in compliance with [the respective Subdivision Improvements Agreements.]" In order to determine whether the County's drafts and demands for payment complied with the terms of the letters of credit, we must analyze the drafts on the first two letters of credit numbers 1156 and 1157 separately from the drafts on the third letter of credit number 1168.

Letters of credit No. 1156 and 1157 bore expiry dates of December 31, 1975. On that date, the County presented two demand drafts to the Bank in the full face amounts of the respective letters of credit. The drafts were accompanied by, as required by the letters of credit, a resolution of the Commissioners stating that Woodmoor failed to comply with the terms of the underlying subdivision improvements agreements and demanded payment under the terms of the respective letters of credit. On January 5, 1976, within three banking days of the demand, the Bank dishonored the drafts. The Bank did not object to the County's presentation of demand drafts as opposed to fifteen-day sight drafts.

A demand draft is not the same as a fifteen-day sight draft. A fifteen-day sight draft provides the issuer an additional period of time not conferred by a demand instrument to examine the draft and determine whether the conditions of payment, if any, have been fulfilled. Thus, the County's demand did not strictly conform to the terms of the letters of credit. Accord, *Bounty Trading Corp. v. S.E.K. Sportswear, Ltd., supra*.

The Bank did not, however, object to the form of the demands by the County. As a general rule, when an issuer of a letter of credit formally places its refusal to pay upon specified grounds, it is held to have waived all other grounds for dishonor. *Barclays Bank D.C.O. v. Mercantile National Bank, supra; East Bank of Colorado Springs v. Dovenmuehle, supra; Siderius, Inc. v. Wallace Co., supra*. "However, the application of the rule confining an issuer to its stated grounds for dishonor is limited to situations where the statements have misled the beneficiary who could have cured the defect but relied on the stated grounds to its injury . . . ." *Siderius, Inc. v. Wallace Co., supra* at 862.

In this case, the County did not present its drafts and demands for payment on the letters of credit until the final day of their vitality. The Bank then had three banking days before it was required to honor or dishonor the drafts and demands for payment. Within this period the Bank dishonored the drafts. The County could not have cured the defect since the presentment would have then been untimely. Consequently, the County did not detrimentally rely on the Bank's failure to state as one ground for its dishonor of the drafts that the County presented demand instruments rather than fifteen-day sight drafts. Accordingly, since the County could not have cured its nonconforming demand, we therefore hold that the Bank did not waive its objections to the County's nonconforming demands on letter of credit numbers 1156 and 1157.[55] Therefore, the Bank is not liable on these letters of credit.

---

[55] The County also asserts that long before the expiry dates of the letters of credit the Bank notified the County that the Bank would only honor drafts for amounts the County had actually expended on improvements before the expiry dates of the letters of credit. The County argues that the Bank anticipatorily repudiated its obligations under the letters of credit and consequently waived subsequent nonconforming demands by the County.

The sole substantiation in the record before us for this allegation of fact is contained in the Defendant's [Bank's] response to Plaintiff's [County's] request for production of documents and interrogatories, signed by one vice president of the Bank:

Interrogatory # 3. Please state in what way you believe that the plaintiff has waived any rights it may have to assert any claim against you under letters of credit numbered 1156 and/or 1157.

Letter of credit number 1168 bore an expiry date of December 31, 1976. On December 22, 1976, the County presented the Bank with a demand draft on this letter of credit accompanied by a resolution by the Commissioners that Woodmoor had not fulfilled its obligations on the underlying subdivision improvements agreement. The Bank timely dishonored this draft on the basis, inter alia, that the County submitted a demand draft rather than a fifteen-day sight draft. The County cured this defect by presenting a fifteen-day sight draft to the Bank on December 29, 1976. This fifteen-day sight draft was not accompanied by the required resolution of the Commissioners. On December 31, 1976, the Bank sent the County a letter notifying the County that this draft had also been dishonored.

The same rules of strict compliance discussed above must be applied to determine whether the County's drafts and demands for payment complied with the terms of letter of credit number 1168. The County's first draft on letter of credit number 1168 was nonconforming since it was submitted as a demand instrument rather than a fifteen-day sight draft. On December 29, 1976, the County presented a fifteen-day sight draft which cured this defect. While the County failed to attach the required statement and demand for payment by the Commissioners with the fifteen-day sight draft, it was not required to do so. The County was merely curing a prior nonconforming demand. The two demands, taken together, consequently strictly complied with the terms of the letter of credit. The Bank therefore wrongfully dishonored this draft and demand for payment.

We reverse the judgment as to letters of credit No. 1156 and No. 1157, and affirm the judgment as to letter of credit No. 1168. This case is returned to the court of appeals for remand to the trial court for the entry of judgment in consonance with the views expressed in this opinion.

Justice Lohr concurring in part and dissenting in part.

I concur in part I of the majority opinion and in that portion of part II which treats letter of credit number 1168 and affirms the court of appeals' opinion upholding the district court's judgment against the Colorado National Bank of Denver (Bank) on that letter of credit. I dissent to that portion of Part II which reverses the judgment against the Bank on letters of credit numbers 1156 and 1157. I would affirm the decision of the court of appeals in its entirety.

The majority finds that the Bank justifiably dishonored letters of credit numbers 1156 and 1157 because the draft presented by Routt County (County) did not strictly comply with the terms of the credit. See section 4-5-114(1), C.R.S. 1973. Because I conclude that this was an improper application of the rule of strict compliance to a non-material term of the letters of credit, I respectfully dissent.

As the majority indicates, the prevailing rule requires strict compliance with the terms of a letter of credit. But the rule of strict compliance is not dictated by the language of the controlling

Answer: . . . . The Bank notified the Board well in advance of the expiry dates of the letters of credit of the Bank's position that it should make payments under the letters of credit only prior to their expiry date and only as the Board incurred or committed to incur expenses for the particular improvements called for in the Subdivision Improvements Agreements . . . .

No other portion of the record substantiates or clarifies this statement. Nor do the parties' stipulated facts refer to this question of fact. We cannot conclude from this answer to the County's interrogatories that the Bank anticipatorily repudiated its obligation to honor drafts under letter of credit numbers 1156 and 1157. The Bank merely indicated that it should not be required to honor drafts unless the County had incurred or committed to incur expenses to complete the road improvements not that it would not honor the County's drafts unless this condition had been met. "Anticipatory repudiation centers upon an overt communication of intention or an action which renders performance impossible or demonstrates a clear determination not to continue with performance." Section 4-2-610, Comment 1, C.R.S. 1973.

statute, Uniform Commercial Code -Letters of Credit, sections 4-5-101 to 117, C.R.S. 1973 (1980 Supp.). Section 4-5-114(1), C.R.S. 1973, merely requires that the issuer honor a draft or demand for payment "which complies with the terms of the relevant [letter of] credit . . . ." Specifically, the code does not state whether strict compliance is necessary or "substantial performance" is sufficient. It was apparently a conscious decision of the drafters of the uniform act which is the source of our statute to leave this question unresolved. See J. White and R. Summers, Uniform Commercial Code, section 18-6at 729 (1980).

The prevailing view stated by the majority not only lacks statutory mandate but also has not been uniformly accepted. A minority position has been adopted by a number of courts, rejecting a formalistic application of the rule of strict compliance where this would not be consistent with the policies underlying the use of letters of credit. As stated by Judge Coffin in *Banco Espanol de Credito v. State Street Bank and Trust Co.,* 385 F.2d 230 (1st Cir. 1967), cert. denied 390 U.S. 1013, 88 S. Ct. 1263, 20 L. Ed. 2d 163 (1968):

> But we note some leaven in the loaf of strict construction. Not only does haec verba not control absolutely [citation omitted], but some courts now cast their eyes on a wider scene than a single document. We are mindful, also, of the admonition of several legal scholars that the integrity of international transactions (*i.e.,* rigid adherence to material matters) must somehow strike a balance with the requirement of their fluidity (*i.e.,* a reasonable flexibility as to ancillary matters) if the objective of increased dealings to the mutual satisfaction to all interested parties is to be enhanced. See *e.g.,* Mentschicoff, *How to Handle Letters of Credit,* 19 Bus. Lawyer 107, 111 (1963). *Banco Espanol de Credito v. State Street Bank and Trust Co., supra,* at 234.

Other cases have also recognized that non-material variations from the terms of a letter of credit do not justify the issuer in dishonoring a draft or demand for payment.

In the instant case, the majority found that the County's submission of a demand draft rather than the fifteen-day sight draft required by the letters of credit rendered the presentment defective.[56] In my opinion this is the sort of non-material, technical condition which should properly be treated under a standard of substantial rather than strict compliance.[57]

There is no danger that the Bank would be misled by the use of the demand draft, nor did the use of that draft place the Bank at risk by providing a basis for its customer Woodmoor to refuse reimbursement. In this context, the Bank's contention is no more than a technical defense which frustrates equity without furthering the policies and purposes underlying the use of letters of credit.

I am not unmindful of the need for certainty in letter of credit transactions, where a bank's function is designed to be primarily ministerial, see, *e.g., Far Eastern Textile, Ltd. v. City National Bank and Trust,* 430 F. Supp. 193, 196, 197 (E.D. Ohio 1977). However, I believe that upholding the County's claim in this case would require only a limited but beneficial exception to the general rule of strict compliance. The alleged nonconformance did not relate to the underlying transaction. Rather, the nonconformity concerned only a provision designed to assure the Bank adequate time to review and consider the adequacy of the demand for payment. Thus, I would hold only that

---

[56] Although I conclude that substitution of a demand draft for the fifteen-day sight draft required by the letters of credit does not excuse the Bank from all liability, this is not to suggest that the County could demand immediate payment. As noted *infra,* the Bank had a right to insist upon the fifteen-day review period, and the County could not unilaterally impair that right.

[57] It is of interest on the issue of materiality that the Bank made no mention of the fact that the drafts were demand drafts in its letter of January 5, 1976, dishonoring the drafts and stating its reasons.

non-material defects, independent of any requirements relating to the underlying transaction, do not excuse the duty to honor a letter of credit.[58] This would avoid placing the issuer in the undesirable position of choosing between a suit by the beneficiary of a letter of credit and the risk of refusal of reimbursement by the customer who obtained that letter, while simultaneously avoiding the assertion of a technical defense to defeat payment where that payment would not place the issuer at risk.

Of course, the Bank was free in this case to inform the County that the demand draft was improper and that payment would be made as if a fifteen-day sight draft had been submitted. The County could not unilaterally deprive the Bank of the fifteen-day period for payment prescribed by the letter of credit. But the Bank should not be able to elevate a minor nonconformance into a total exoneration from liability. Neither existing law nor sound policy requires this result.

I would affirm the decision of the court of appeals.

Justice Rovira joins in this opinion.

FDIC v. PHILADELPHIA GEAR CORP.

Supreme Court of the United States
476 U.S. 426, 106 S. Ct. 1931, 90 L. Ed. 2d 428 (1986)

JUSTICE O'CONNOR delivered the opinion of the Court.

We granted certiorari to consider whether a standby letter of credit backed by a contingent promissory note is insured as a "deposit" under the federal deposit insurance program. We hold that, in light of the longstanding interpretation of petitioner Federal Deposit Insurance Corporation (FDIC) that such a letter does not create a deposit and, in light of the fact that such a letter does not entrust any noncontingent assets to the bank, a standby letter of credit backed by a contingent promissory note does not give rise to an insured deposit.

I

Orion Manufacturing Corporation (Orion) was, at the time of the relevant transactions, a customer of respondent Philadelphia Gear Corporation (Philadelphia Gear). On Orion's application, the Penn Square Bank, N.A. (Penn Square) issued a letter of credit for the benefit of Philadelphia Gear in the amount of $145,200. The letter of credit provided that a draft drawn

---

[58] That holding would not be inconsistent with those cases requiring strict compliance with letter of credit requirements necessary to ensure that a substantive condition precedent to payment has been met. See, *e.g., Courtaulds North America, Inc. v. North Carolina Nat. Bank, supra* (packing lists which were attached to invoices accompanying draft by beneficiary and which stated that the shipment was 100% acrylic yarn did not satisfy requirement that invoices specify shipment was 100% acrylic yarn); *Far Eastern Textile, Ltd. v. City National Bank and Trust, supra* (requirement that principal sign purchase orders evidencing underlying transaction not satisfied by the signature of an agent on those orders). When the disputed condition relates to the underlying transaction, a standard of strict compliance may well be preferable. Thus, if the nonconformance had related to the requirement that the County certify Woodmoor's failure to construct the agreed-upon improvements a different question would be presented. In this respect, it is not necessary to apply the rule of substantial compliance as broadly as some courts have. See, *e.g., U.S. Industries, Inc. v. Second New Haven Bank, supra* (failure to certify expressly that payment for goods had been demanded as required by letter of credit excused where other documents satisfied the purpose of this requirement).

upon the letter of credit would be honored by Penn Square only if accompanied by Philadelphia Gear's "signed statement that [it had] invoiced Orion Manufacturing Corporation and that said invoices have remained unpaid for at least fifteen (15) days." App. 25. Because the letter of credit was intended to provide payment to the seller only if the buyer of the invoiced goods failed to make payment, the letter of credit was what is commonly referred to as a "standby" or "guaranty" letter of credit. See, *e. g.,* 12 CFR § 337.2(a), and n. 1 (1985) (defining standby letters of credit and mentioning that they may " 'guaranty' payment of a money obligation"). A conventional "commercial" letter of credit, in contrast, is one in which the seller obtains payment from the issuing bank without looking to the buyer for payment even in the first instance. See *ibid.* (distinguishing standby letters of credit from commercial letters of credit). See also Verkuil, *Bank Solvency and Guaranty Letters of Credit,* 25 Stan. L. Rev. 716, 717-724 (1973); Arnold & Bransilver, *The Standby Letter of Credit — The Controversy Continues,* 10 U. C. C. L. J. 272, 277-279 (Spring 1978).

On the same day that Penn Square issued the standby letter of credit, Orion executed an unsecured promissory note for $145,200 in favor of Penn Square. App. 27. The purpose of the note was listed as "Back up Letter of Credit." *Ibid.* Although the face of the note did not so indicate, both Orion and Penn Square understood that nothing would be considered due on the note, and no interest charged by Penn Square, unless Philadelphia Gear presented drafts on the standby letter of credit after nonpayment by Orion. 751 F.2d 1131, 1134 (CA10 1984). See also Tr. of Oral Arg. 32.

On July 5, 1982, Penn Square was declared insolvent. Petitioner FDIC was appointed its receiver. Shortly thereafter, Philadelphia Gear presented drafts on the standby letter of credit for payment of over $700,000 for goods delivered before Penn Square's insolvency. The FDIC returned the drafts unpaid. 751 F.2d., at 1133-1134.

Philadelphia Gear sued the FDIC in the Western District of Oklahoma. Philadelphia Gear alleged that the standby letter of credit was an insured deposit under the definition of "deposit" set forth at 12 U. S. C. § 1813(l)(1), and that Philadelphia Gear was therefore entitled to $100,000 in deposit insurance from the FDIC. See 12 U. S. C. § 1821(a)(1) (setting forth $100,000 as the maximum amount generally insured by the FDIC for any single depositor at a given bank). In apparent hopes of obtaining additional funds from the FDIC in the latter's capacity as receiver rather than as insurer, respondent also alleged that terms of the standby letter of credit allowing repeated reinstatements of the credit made the letter's total value more than $145,200.

The District Court held that the total value of the standby letter of credit was $145,200, App. B to Pet. for Cert. 20a, 28a-30a; that the letter was an insured deposit on which the FDIC was liable for $100,000 in deposit insurance, *id.,* at 37a-43a; and that Philadelphia Gear was entitled to prejudgment interest on that $100,000, *id.,* at 43a. The FDIC appealed from the District Court's ruling that the standby letter of credit backed by a contingent promissory note constituted a "deposit" for purposes of 12 U. S. C. § 1813(l)(1) and its ruling that Philadelphia Gear was entitled to an award of prejudgment interest. Philadelphia Gear cross-appealed from the District Court's ruling on the total value of the letter of credit.

The Court of Appeals for the Tenth Circuit reversed the District Court's award of prejudgment interest, 751 F.2d, at 1138-1139, but otherwise affirmed the District Court's decision. As to the definition of "deposit," the Court of Appeals held that a standby letter of credit backed by a promissory note fell within the terms of 12 U. S. C. § 1813(l)(1)'s definition of "deposit," and was therefore insured. Id., at 1134-1138. We granted the FDIC's petition for certiorari on this aspect of the Court of Appeals' ruling. 474 U.S. 918 (1985). We now reverse.

II

Title 12 U. S. C. § 1813(l)(1) provides:

The term "deposit" means —

(1) the unpaid balance of money or its equivalent received or held by a bank in the usual course of business and for which it has given or is obligated to give credit, either conditionally or unconditionally, to a commercial . . .account, or which is evidenced by . . .a letter of credit or a traveler's check on which the bank is primarily liable: Provided, That, without limiting the generality of the term "money or its equivalent," any such account or instrument must be regarded as evidencing the receipt of the equivalent of money when credited or issued in exchange for checks or drafts or for a promissory note upon which the person obtaining any such credit or instrument is primarily or secondarily liable . . . .

Philadelphia Gear successfully argued before the Court of Appeals that the standby letter of credit backed by a contingent promissory note constituted a "deposit" under 12 U. S. C. § 1813(l)(1) because that letter was one on which the bank was primarily liable, and evidenced the receipt by the bank of "money or its equivalent" in the form of a promissory note upon which the person obtaining the credit was primarily or secondarily liable. The FDIC does not here dispute that the bank was primarily liable on the letter of credit. Brief for Petitioner 7, n. 7. Nor does the FDIC contest the fact that the backup note executed by Orion is, at least in some sense, a "promissory note." See Tr. of Oral Arg. 7 (remarks of Mr. Rothfeld, representing the FDIC) ("It was labeled a note. It can be termed a note"). The FDIC argues rather that it has consistently interpreted § 1813(l)(1) not to include standby letters of credit backed only by a contingent promissory note because such a note represents no hard assets and thus does not constitute "money or its equivalent." Because the alleged "deposit" consists only of a contingent liability, asserts the FDIC, a standby letter of credit backed by a contingent promissory note does not give rise to a "deposit" that Congress intended the FDIC to insure. Under this theory, while the note here may have been labeled a promissory note on its face and may have been a promissory note under state law, it was not a promissory note for purposes of the federal law set forth in 12 U. S. C. § 1813(l)(1).

The Court of Appeals quite properly looked first to the language of the statute. Finding the language of the proviso in § 1813(l)(1) sufficiently plain, the Court of Appeals looked no further. But as the FDIC points out, the terms "letter of credit" and "promissory note" as used in the statute have a federal definition, and the FDIC has developed and interpreted those definitions for many years within the framework of the complex statutory scheme that the FDIC administers. The FDIC's interpretation of whether a standby letter of credit backed by a contingent promissory note constitutes a "deposit" is consistent with Congress' desire to protect the hard earnings of individuals by providing for federal deposit insurance. Since the creation of the FDIC, Congress has expressed no dissatisfaction with the FDIC's interpretation of "deposit"; indeed, Congress in 1960 adopted the FDIC's regulatory definition as the statutory language. When we weigh all these factors together, we are constrained to conclude that the term "deposit" does not include a standby letter of credit backed by a contingent promissory note.

A

Justice Holmes stated that, as to discerning the constitutionality of a federal estate tax, "a page of history is worth a volume of logic." *New York Trust Co. v. Eisner,* 256 U.S. 345, 349 (1921). Although the genesis of the Federal Deposit Insurance Act may not be quite so powerful a substitute for legal analysis, that history is worthy of at least a page of recounting for the light it sheds on Congress' purpose in passing the Act. Cf. *Watt v. Alaska,* 451 U.S. 259, 266 (1981) ("The circumstances of the enactment of particular legislation may persuade a court that Congress did not intend words of common meaning to have their literal effect").

When Congress created the FDIC, the Nation was in the throes of an extraordinary financial crisis. See generally F. Allen, Since Yesterday: The Nineteen-Thirties in America 98-121 (1940); A. Schlesinger, The Crisis of the Old Order 474-482 (1957). More than one-third of the banks in the United States open in 1929 had shut their doors just four years later. Bureau of the Census, Historical Statistics of the United States: Colonial Times to 1970, pt. 2, pp. 1019, 1038 (1976). In response to this financial crisis, President Roosevelt declared a national banking holiday effective the first business day after he took office. 48 Stat. 1689. Congress in turn responded with extensive legislation on banking, including the laws that gave the FDIC its existence.

Congress' purpose in creating the FDIC was clear. Faced with virtual panic, Congress attempted to safeguard the hard earnings of individuals against the possibility that bank failures would deprive them of their savings. Congress passed the 1933 provisions "[in] order to provide against a repetition of the present painful experience in which a vast sum of assets and purchasing power is 'tied up.' " S. Rep. No. 77, 73d Cong., 1st Sess., 12 (1933). The focus of Congress was therefore upon ensuring that a deposit of "hard earnings" entrusted by individuals to a bank would not lead to a tangible loss in the event of a bank failure. As the chairman of the relevant Committee in the House of Representatives explained on the floor:

[The purpose of this legislation is to protect the people of the United States in the right to have banks in which their deposits will be safe. They have a right to expect of Congress the establishment and maintenance of a system of banks in the United States where citizens may place their hard earnings with reasonable expectation of being able to get them out again upon demand. . . .

. . . .

[The purpose of the bill is to ensure that] the community is saved from the shock of a bank failure, and every citizen has been given an opportunity to withdraw his deposits. . . .

. . . .

The public . . .demand of you and me that we provide a banking system worthy of this great Nation and banks in which citizens may place the fruits of their toil and know that a deposit slip in return for their hard earnings will be as safe as a Government bond.

77 Cong. Rec. 3837, 3838, 3840 (1933) (remarks of Rep. Steagall). See also *id.,* at 3913 (remarks of Rep. Keller) ("[We must make] it absolutely certain that . . .any and every man, woman, or child who puts a dollar in any bank can absolutely know that he will under no circumstances lose a single penny of it"); *id.,* at 3924 (remarks of Rep. Green) ("It is time that we pass a law so secure that when a man puts his money in a bank he will know for sure that when he comes back it will be there"). To prevent bank failure that resulted in the tangible loss of hard assets was therefore the focus of Congress' effort in creating deposit insurance.

Despite the fact Congress revisited the deposit insurance statute in 1935, 1950, and 1960, these comments remain the best indication of Congress' underlying purpose in creating deposit insurance. The Reports on the 1935 amendments presented the definition of "deposit" without any specific comment. The floor debates centered around changes in the Federal Reserve System made in the same bill, not on deposit insurance. Indeed, in light of the fact that instruments denominated "promissory notes" seem at the time to have been considered exclusively uncontingent, see, *e. g.,* 16 Fed. Res. Bull. 520 (1930) (Regulation A) (defining promissory note as an "unconditional promise to pay [a sum certain in dollars] at a fixed or determinable future time"); *Gilman v. Commissioner,* 53 F.2d 47, 50 (CA8 1931) ("The form of these [contingent] instruments referred to as 'promissory notes' is very unusual"), it is unlikely that Congress would have had occasion to refer expressly to contingent notes such as the one before us here even if Congress had turned its attention to the definition of "deposit" when it first enacted the provision treating "money or its equivalent."

The legislative history of the 1950 amendments is similarly unhelpful, as one would expect given that the relevant provisions were reenacted but unchanged. The Committee Reports on the 1960 amendments likewise give no indication that the amendments' phrasing was meant to effect any fundamental changes in the definition of deposit; those Reports state only that the changes are intended to bring into harmony the definitions of "deposit" used for purposes of deposit insurance with those used in reports of condition, and that the FDIC's rules and regulations are to be incorporated into the new definition.

Congress' focus in providing for a system of deposit insurance — a system that has been continued to the present without modification to the basic definition of deposits that are "money or its equivalent" — was clearly a focus upon safeguarding the assets and "hard earnings" that businesses and individuals have entrusted to banks. Congress wanted to ensure that someone who put tangible assets into a bank could always get those assets back. The purpose behind the insurance of deposits in general, and especially in the section defining deposits as "money or its equivalent," therefore, is the protection of assets and hard earnings entrusted to a bank.

This purpose is not furthered by extending deposit insurance to cover a standby letter of credit backed by a contingent promissory note, which involves no such surrender of assets or hard earnings to the custody of the bank. Philadelphia Gear, which now seeks to collect deposit insurance, surrendered absolutely nothing to the bank. The letter of credit is for Philadelphia Gear's benefit, but the bank relied upon Orion to meet the obligations of the letter of credit and made no demands upon Philadelphia Gear. Nor, more importantly, did Orion surrender any assets unconditionally to the bank. The bank did not credit any account of Orion's in exchange for the promissory note, and did not treat its own assets as increased by its acceptance of the note. The bank could not have collected on the note from Orion unless Philadelphia Gear presented the unpaid invoices and a draft on the letter of credit. In the absence of a presentation by Philadelphia Gear of the unpaid invoices, the promissory note was a wholly contingent promise, and when Penn Square went into receivership, neither Orion nor Philadelphia Gear had lost anything except the ability to use Penn Square to reduce Philadelphia Gear's risk that Philadelphia Gear would go unpaid for a delivery of goods to Orion.

B

Congress' actions with respect to the particular definition of "deposit" that it has chosen in order to effect its general purpose likewise lead us to believe that a standby letter of credit backed by a contingent promissory note is not an insurable "deposit." In 1933, Congress amended the Federal Reserve Act to authorize the creation of the FDIC and charged it "to insure . . .the deposits of all banks which are entitled to the benefits of [FDIC] insurance." § 8, Banking Act of 1933, ch. 89, 48Stat. 168. Congress did not define the term "deposit," however, until the Banking Act of 1935, in which it stated:

> "The term 'deposit' means the unpaid balance of money or its equivalent received by a bank in the usual course of business and for which it has given or is obligated to give credit to a commercial, checking, savings, time or thrift account, or which is evidenced by its certificate of deposit, and trust funds held by such bank whether retained or deposited in any department of such bank or deposited in another bank, together with such other obligations of a bank as the board of directors [of the FDIC] shall find and shall prescribe by its regulations to be deposit liabilities by general usage . . . ." § 101, Banking Act of 1935, ch. 614, 49 Stat. 684, 685-686.

Less than two months after this statute was enacted, the FDIC promulgated a definition of "deposit," which provided in part that "letters of credit must be regarded as issued for the equivalent of money when issued in exchange for . . .promissory notes upon which the person procuring [such] instruments is primarily or secondarily liable." See 12 CFR § 301.1(d) (1939) (codifying Regulation I, rule 1, Oct. 1, 1935), revoked after incorporation into statutory law, 12 CFR 234 (Supp. 1962).

In 1950, Congress revisited the provisions specifically governing the FDIC in order to remove them from the Federal Reserve Act and place them into a separate Act. See Act of Sept. 21, 1950, ch. 967, 64 Stat. 874. The new provisions did not modify the definition of "deposit." In 1960, Congress expanded the statutory definition of "deposit" in several categories, and also incorporated the regulatory definition that the FDIC had employed since 1935 into the statute that remains in force today. See *supra*, at 430 (quoting current version of statute).

At no point did Congress disown its initial, clear desire to protect the hard assets of depositors. See *supra*, at 432-435. At no point did Congress criticize the FDIC's longstanding interpretation, see *infra*, at 438, that a standby letter of credit backed by a contingent promissory note is not a "deposit." In fact, Congress had reenacted the 1935 provisions in 1950 without changing the definition of "deposit" at all. Compare 49 Stat. 685-686 with 64 Stat. 874-875. When the statute giving rise to the longstanding interpretation has been reenacted without pertinent change, the "congressional failure to revise or repeal the agency's interpretation is persuasive evidence that the interpretation is the one intended by Congress." *NLRB v. Bell Aerospace,* 416 U.S. 267, 275 (1974). Indeed, the current statutory definition of "deposit," added by Congress in 1960, was expressly designed to incorporate the FDIC's rules and regulations on "deposits." As Committees of both Houses of Congress explained the amendments: "The amended definition would include the present statutory definition of deposits, and the definition of deposits in the rules and regulations of the Federal Deposit Insurance Corporation, [along] with . . .changes [in sections other than what is now § 1813(l)(1)]." H. R. Rep. No. 1827, 86th Cong., 2d Sess., 5 (1960); S. Rep. No. 1821, 86th Cong., 2d Sess., 10 (1960) (same). Congress, therefore, has expressly incorporated into the statutory scheme the regulations that the FDIC devised to assist it in determining what constitutes a "deposit" within the statutory scheme. Under these circumstances, we must obviously give a great deal of deference to the FDIC's interpretation of what these regulations do and do not include within their definition of "deposit."

C

Although the FDIC does not argue that it has an express regulation excluding a standby letter of credit backed by a contingent promissory note from the definition of "deposit" in 12 U. S. C. § 1813(l)(1), that exclusion by the FDIC is nonetheless longstanding and consistent. At a meeting of FDIC and bank officials shortly after the FDIC's creation, a bank official asked whether a letter of credit issued by a charge against a customer's account was a deposit. The FDIC official replied:

> " 'If your letter of credit is issued by a charge against a depositor's account or for cash and the letter of credit is reflected on your books as a liability, you do have a deposit liability. If, on the other hand, you merely extend a line of credit to your customer, you will only show a contingent liability on your books. In that event no deposit liability has been created.' " Transcript as quoted in *FDIC v. Irving Trust Co.*, 137 F.Supp. 145, 161 (SDNY 1955).

Because Penn Square apparently never reflected the letter of credit here as a noncontingent liability, and because the interwoven financial instruments at issue here can be viewed most accurately as the extension of a line of credit by Penn Square to Orion, this transcript lends support to the FDIC's contention that its longstanding policy has been to exclude standby letters of credit backed by contingent promissory notes from 12 U. S. C. § 1813(l)(1)'s definition of "deposit."

The FDIC's contemporaneous understanding that standby letters of credit backed by contingent promissory notes do not generate a "deposit" for purposes of 12 U. S. C. § 1813(l)(1) has been fortified by its behavior over the following decades. The FDIC has asserted repeatedly that it has never charged deposit insurance premiums on standby letters of credit backed by contingent promissory notes, and Philadelphia Gear does not contest that assertion. See Tr. of Oral Arg. 42. Congress requires the FDIC to assess contributions to its insurance fund at a fixed percentage of a bank's "deposits" under 12 U. S. C. § 1813(l)(1). See 12 U. S. C. §§ 1817(a)(4), (b)(1), (b)(4)(A). By the time that this suit — the first challenge to the FDIC's treatment of standby letters of credit backed by contingent promissory notes — was brought, almost $100 billion in standby letters of credit was outstanding. See Board of Governors of the Federal Reserve System, Annual Statistical Digest 71 (1983); FDIC, 1983 Statistics on Banking (Table 110F). The FDIC's failure to levy premiums on standby letters of credit backed by contingent promissory notes therefore clearly demonstrates that the FDIC has never considered such letters to reflect deposits.

Although the FDIC's interpretation of the relevant statute has not been reduced to a specific regulation, we conclude nevertheless that the FDIC's practice and belief that a standby letter of credit backed by a contingent promissory note does not create a "deposit" within the meaning of 12 U.S.C. § 1813(l)(1) are entitled in the circumstances of this case to the "considerable weight [that] should be accorded to an executive department's construction of a statutory scheme it is entrusted to administer." *Chevron U.S.A. Inc. v. Natural Resources Defense Council, Inc.*, 467 U.S. 837, 844 (1984). As we have stated above, the FDIC's interpretation here of a statutory definition adopted wholesale from the FDIC's own regulation is consistent with congressional purpose, and may certainly stand.

III

Philadelphia Gear essentially seeks to have the FDIC guarantee the contingent credit extended to Orion, not assets entrusted to the bank by Philadelphia Gear or by Orion on Philadelphia Gear's behalf. With a standard "commercial" letter of credit, Orion would typically have unconditionally entrusted Penn Square with funds before Penn Square would have written the letter of credit, and thus Orion would have lost something if Penn Square became unable to honor its obligations. As the FDIC concedes, deposit insurance extends to such a letter of credit backed by an uncontingent promissory note. See Tr. of Oral Arg. 8 (statement of Mr. Rothfeld, representing the FDIC) ("If this note were a fully uncontingent negotiable note that were not limited by any side agreements, it would be a note backing a letter of credit within the meaning of the statute"). See also *id.,* at 17-18. But here, with a standby letter of credit backed by a contingent promissory note, Penn Square was not in possession of any of Orion's or Philadelphia Gear's assets when it went into receivership. Nothing was ventured, and therefore no insurable deposit was lost. We believe that, whatever the relevant State's definition of "letter of credit" or "promissory note," Congress did not by using those phrases in 12 U. S. C. § 1813(l)(1) intend to protect with deposit insurance a standby letter of credit backed only by a contingent promissory note. We thus hold that such an arrangement does not give rise to a "deposit" under 12 U. S. C. § 1813(l)(1).

Accordingly, the judgment of the court below is reversed, and the case is remanded for further proceedings consistent with this opinion.

Reversed and remanded.

JUSTICE MARSHALL, with whom JUSTICE BLACKMUN and JUSTICE REHNQUIST join, dissenting.

There is considerable common sense backing the Court's opinion. The standby letter of credit in this case differs considerably from the savings and checking accounts that come most readily to mind when one speaks of an insured deposit. Nevertheless, to reach this common-sense result, the Court must read qualifications into the statute that do not appear there. We recently recognized that even when the ingenuity of businessmen creates transactions and corporate forms that were perhaps not contemplated by Congress, the courts must enforce the statutes that Congress has enacted. See *Board of Governors, FRS v. Dimension Financial Corp.,* 474 U.S. 361, 373-375 (1986). Congress unmistakably provided that letters of credit backed by promissory notes constitute "deposits" for purposes of the federal deposit insurance program, and the Court's attempt to draw distinctions between different types of letters of credit transactions forces it to ignore both the statute and some settled principles of commercial law. Here, as in *Dimension,* the inflexibility of the statute as applied to modern financial transactions is a matter for Congress, not the FDIC or this Court, to remedy.

It cannot be doubted that the standby letter of credit in this case meets the literal definition of a "deposit" contained in 12 U. S. C. § 1813(l)(1). It is "a letter of credit . . .on which the bank is primarily liable . . .issued in exchange for . . .a promissory note upon which [Orion] is primarily or secondarily liable." The Court, however, holds that the note in this case, whether or not it is a promissory note under the Uniform Commercial Code (UCC) and Oklahoma law, is not a promissory note for purposes of the Federal Deposit Insurance Act. We should assume, absent convincing evidence to the contrary, that Congress intended for the term "promissory note" to derive its meaning from the ordinary sources of commercial law. I believe that there is no such evidence in this case.

The Court justifies its restrictive reading of the term "promissory note" in large part by arguing that Congress would not have wanted to include in that term any obligation that was not the present equivalent of money. The keystone of the FDIC's arguments, and of the Court's decision, is that Orion did not entrust "money or its equivalent" to the bank. The note in this case, however, was the equivalent of money, and the Court's reading of Congress' intent is therefore largely irrelevant.

FDIC concedes, as it must, that Congress has determined that a promissory note generally constitutes money or its equivalent. Moreover, that statutory definition comports with economic reality. Promissory notes typically are negotiable instruments and therefore readily convertible into cash. The FDIC argues, and the Court holds, that the promissory note in this case is "contingent" and therefore not the equivalent of money. However, while the FDIC argues strenuously that Orion's note is not a promissory note in the usual sense of the word, one could more plausibly state that it is not a "contingent" obligation in the usual sense of that word. On its face the note is an unconditional obligation of Orion to pay the holder $145,200 plus accrued interest on August 1, 1982. It sets out no conditions that would affect the negotiability of the note, and therefore is fully negotiable for purposes of the UCC, U.C.C.§ 3-104(1)(1977); Okla. Stat., Tit. 12A, § 3-104(1)(1981).

The Court therefore misses the point when it states that at the time of the original banking Acts, the term "promissory note" was not understood to include a contingent obligation. Ante, at 434. The note at issue in this case is an unconditional promise to pay, and satisfies all the requisites of a negotiable promissory note, either under the UCC or the common law as it existed in the 1930's. The only contingencies attached to Orion's obligation arise out of a separate contract. As to such contingencies, the law was well settled long before 1930:

> "[In] order to make a note invalid as a promissory note, the contingency to avoid it must be apparent, either upon the face of the note, or upon some contemporaneous written memorandum on the same paper; for, if the memorandum is not contemporaneous, or if it be merely verbal in each case, whatever may be its effect as a matter of defence between the original parties, it is not deemed to be a part of the instrument, and does not affect, much less invalidate, its original character." J. Thorndike, Story on Promissory Notes 34 (7th ed. 1878) (footnotes omitted). [59]

It is far from a matter of semantics to state that while Orion and the bank may have an oral understanding concerning the bank's treatment of Orion's note, that note itself is unconditional and equivalent to money. The Court correctly observes that the bank would have breached its oral contract had it attempted to sue on the note; nevertheless, Orion would have had separately to plead and prove a breach of contract in that case, because parol evidence that the contract between the parties differed from the written instrument would have been inadmissible in the bank's action to collect the debt. See *American Perforating Co. v. Oklahoma State Bank*, 463 P. 2d 958, 962-963 (Okla. 1970). Similarly, should the note have found its way into the hands of a third party, Orion would have had no choice but to honor it, again being left with only the right to sue the bank for breach of the oral contract. Orion's entrustment of the note to the bank was not, therefore, completely risk free.

The risk taken on by Orion may not differ substantially from the risk assumed by one who hands over money to the bank to guarantee repayment of funds paid out on a letter of credit. The bank typically undertakes to put such cash collateral into a special account, where it never enters into the general assets of the bank. See U. C. C. § 5-117, comment (1977). Should the bank cease operations, the customer will enjoy a preference in bankruptcy, entitling it to receive

---

[59] We would have a very different case if the conditions put upon Orion's obligation to the bank were reflected on the face of the note, as they were in *Allen v. FDIC*, 599 F. Supp. 104 (E.D. Tenn. 1984), appeal pending, No. 85-5003 (CA6), a case raising the same issue as the present one. Because such a note is not negotiable, it is much more plausible to argue that Congress would not have considered it "money or its equivalent." The note in this case, however, is in no sense a contingent note.

its money back before general unsecured creditors of the bank are paid. U. C. C. § 5-117; Okla. Stat., Tit. 12A, § 5-117(1981). Like Orion, then, that hypothetical customer has little to fear absent misconduct by the bank or a third party. If the federal deposit insurance program should not protect Philadelphia Gear, therefore, it probably should not protect any holder of a letter of credit, whether commercial, standby, funded, or unfunded.[60] That, however, is clearly a matter for Congress to determine.

While the Court purports to examine what Congress meant when it said "promissory note," in fact the Court's opinion does not rest on any special attributes of Orion's note. Rather, the Court rules that when an individual entrusts a negotiable instrument to a bank, that instrument is not "money or its equivalent" for purposes of § 1813(l)(1) so long as the bank promises not to negotiate it or collect on it until certain conditions are met. That is a proviso that Congress might have been well advised to include in the Act, but did not. I therefore dissent.

NOTES

(1) Note that a standby letter of credit often is simply a performance bond. Why would a party demand a standby letter of credit in lieu of a performance bond?

(2) Does the introduction of a standby letter of credit influence your approval/rejection of the complete compliance doctrine?

PROBLEM 11.4

An excited Clayton Molinero calls you on the phone with yet another financing problem. Because business has been booming (in part, due to the cane rods) Clayton plans to expand his retail floor space and has contracted with Spellman & Wu Construction, Inc. to have the work done. Spellman & Wu are known for its low prices, and unfortunately, sometimes, low quality workmanship. Clayton would like to structure a payment framework allowing Spellman and Wu to be paid at three stages of the construction process, provided that at each stage the work completed meets an inspection by an independent third party. What do you suggest to Clayton? Is possible solution a standby letter of credit?

─────

§ 11.03   "Trust Receipt" Secured Financing of Buyer

Review the diagram above at page 11.01[A]. Note step 13 where "B pays the amount of the draft to Issuing Bank and receives the documents (and the draft, if B is drawee)." But what happens if B doesn't wish to pay for the goods at this point? In that situation, "trust receipt" financing can be arranged. Issuing Bank will deliver the documents to B in exchange for B signing trust receipts whereby Issuing Bank is given a security interest in the bill of lading and the goods

─────────────────

[60] It seems odd that Philadelphia Gear's status as an insured depositor should depend on the terms of the repayment agreement between Orion and the bank. Ordinarily, Philadelphia Gear would be indifferent to the agreement between Orion and the bank, and might not even be aware of the terms of that agreement. The Court, therefore, is not necessarily bringing greater rationality to this area of the law by creating distinctions between types of letters of credit for purposes of federal deposit insurance coverage.

represented thereby. If B defaults, Issuing Bank as a secured party can "foreclose" on the collateral. This "trust receipt" financing is now governed by Article 9 Secured Transactions. See U.C.C. § 9-102(1)(a) and (2). An example of this transaction is found in Comment 2 to § 9-303.

A bank which has issued a letter of credit honors drafts drawn under the credit and receives possession of the negotiable bill of lading covering the goods shipped. Under Sections 9-304(2) and 9-305 the bank now has a perfected security interest in the document and the goods. The bank releases the bill of lading to the debtor for the purpose of procuring the goods from the carrier and selling them. Under Section 9-304(5) the bank continues to have a perfected security interest in the document and goods for 21 days. The bank files before the expiration of the 21 day period. Its security interest now continues perfected for as long as the filing is good. The goods are sold by the debtor. The bank continues to have a security interest in the proceeds of the sale to the extent stated in Section 9-306.

If the successive stages of the bank's security interest succeed each other without an intervening gap, the security interest is "continuously perfected" and the date of perfection is when the interest first became perfected (i.e., in the example given, when the bank received possession of the bill of lading against honor of the drafts). If however, there is a gap between stages—for example, if the bank does not file until after the expiration of the 21 day period specified in Section 9-304(5), the collateral still being in the debtor's possession — then, the chain being broken, the perfection is no longer continuous. The date of perfection would now be the date of filing (after expiration of the 21 day period); the bank's interest might now become subject to attack under Section 60 of the Federal Bankruptcy Act [now Bankruptcy Code § 547] and would be subject to any interests arising during the gap period which under Section 9-301 take priority over an unperfected security interest.

-----

§ 11.04　Secured Financing of Seller: Transfer and Assignment

Read: U.C.C. § 5-116 and Revised §§ 5-112, 5-114; cf. §§ 2-210, 9-318.

We have seen the letter of credit used to assure seller that it will receive *payment* for the sold goods. The letter of credit can also be used as a device to assist the *financing* of seller. For example, suppose seller wishes to purchase from its supplier goods which it has agreed to sell to buyer. The problem is that supplier may not sell to seller on unsecured credit. Seller, as beneficiary of the letter of credit, can use the letter to obtain the necessary financing:

1. The seller-beneficiary might transfer its rights and duties under the letter of credit to its supplier. U.C.C. § 5-116(1) [revised § 5-112], see § 2-210.

2. The seller-beneficiary might transfer its prospective right to the proceeds of the letter of credit to a financier as security for a loan. U.C.C. § 5-116(2) [revised § 5-114].

3. The seller-beneficiary might use the letter of credit to procure the issuance of a second letter of credit in favor of its lender or supplier ("back-to-back" letters of credit).

For discussion of these matters, see J. White and R. Summers, Handbook of the Law Under the Uniform Commercial Code § 26-12(4th Practitioner's Ed., 1995). See also, J, Dolan, The Law of Letters of Credit, Ch. 10 (Transfer and Assignment) (2d ed. 1991).

The corresponding provisions of the Uniform Customs, 1993 Revision, are Articles 48 and 49. See Reviseed U.C.C. §§ 5-112, 5-113, 5-114.

§ 11.05 Letters of Credit in Bankruptcy

IN RE COMPTON CORP.

United States Court of Appeals
831 F.2d 586 (5th Cir. 1987)

JERRE S. WILLIAMS, CIRCUIT JUDGE

This is a bankruptcy preference case in which a bankruptcy trustee seeks to recover a transfer made via a letter of credit for the benefit of one of the debtor's unsecured creditors on the eve of bankruptcy. The bankruptcy court and the district court found there to be no voidable preference. We reverse.

I. Factual Background

In March 1982, Blue Quail Energy, Inc., delivered a shipment of oil to debtor Compton Corporation. Payment of $585,443.85 for this shipment of oil was due on or about April 20, 1982. Compton failed to make timely payment. Compton induced Abilene National Bank (now MBank-Abilene) to issue an irrevocable standby letter of credit in Blue Quail's favor on May 6, 1982. Under the terms of the letter of credit, payment of up to $585,443.85 was due Blue Quail if Compton failed to pay Blue Quail this amount by June 22, 1982. Compton paid MBank $1,463.61 to issue the letter of credit. MBank also received a promissory note payable on demand for $585,443.85. MBank did not need a security agreement to cover the letter of credit transaction because a prior 1980 security agreement between the bank and Compton had a future advances provision.[61] This 1980 security agreement had been perfected as to a variety of Compton's assets through the filing of several financing statements. The most recent financing statement had been filed a year before, May 7, 1981. The letter of credit on its face noted that it was for an antecedent debt due Blue Quail.

On May 7, 1982, the day after MBank issued the letter of credit in Blue Quail's favor, several of Compton's creditors filed an involuntary bankruptcy petition against Compton. On June 22, 1982, MBank paid Blue Quail $569,932.03 on the letter of credit after Compton failed to pay Blue Quail.

In the ensuing bankruptcy proceeding, MBank's aggregate secured claims against Compton, including the letter of credit payment to Blue Quail, were paid in full from the liquidation of Compton's assets which served as the bank's collateral. Walter Kellogg, bankruptcy trustee for Compton, did not contest the validity of MBank's secured claim against Compton's assets for the amount drawn under the letter of credit by Blue Quail. Instead, on June 14, 1983, trustee Kellogg filed a complaint in the bankruptcy court against Blue Quail asserting that Blue Quail had received a preferential transfer under 11 U.S.C. § 547 through the letter of credit transaction. The trustee sought to recover $585,443.85 from Blue Quail pursuant to 11 U.S.C. § 550.

Blue Quail answered and filed a third party complaint against MBank. On June 16, 1986, Blue Quail filed a motion for summary judgment asserting that the trustee could not recover any

---

[61] A future advances clause in a security agreement subjects the specified collateral to any future loan made by the creditor in addition to the current loans.

preference from Blue Quail because Blue Quail had been paid from MBank's funds under the letter of credit and therefore had not received any of Compton's property. On August 27, 1986, the bankruptcy court granted Blue Quail's motion, agreeing that the payment under the letter of credit did not constitute a transfer of debtor Compton's property but rather was a transfer of the bank's property. The bankruptcy court entered judgment on the motion on September 10, 1986. Trustee Kellogg appealed this decision to the district court. On December 11, 1986, the district court affirmed the bankruptcy court ruling, holding that the trustee did not establish two necessary elements of a voidable transfer under 11 U.S.C. § 547. The district court agreed with Blue Quail and the bankruptcy court that the trustee could not establish that the funds transferred to Blue Quail were ever property of Compton. Furthermore, the district court held that the transfer of the increased security interest to MBank was a transfer of the debtor's property for the sole benefit of the bank and in no way benefitted Blue Quail. The district court therefore found no voidable preference as to Blue Quail. The trustee is appealing the decision to this Court.

II. The Letter of Credit

It is well established that a letter of credit and the proceeds therefrom are not property of the debtor's estate under 11 U.S.C. § 541. When the issuer honors a proper draft under a letter of credit, it does so from its own assets and not from the assets of its customer who caused the letter of credit to be issued. *In re W.L. Mead*; I*n re M.J. Sales.* As a result, a bankruptcy trustee is not entitled to enjoin a post petition payment of funds under a letter of credit from the issuer to the beneficiary, because such a payment is not a transfer of debtor's property (a threshold requirement under 11 U.S.C. § 547(b)). A case apparently holding otherwise, *In re Twist Cap., Inc.,* 1 Bankr. 284 (Bankr. Fla. 1979), has been roundly criticized and otherwise ignored by courts and commentators alike.

Recognizing these characteristics of a letter of credit in a bankruptcy case is necessary in order to maintain the independence principle, the cornerstone of letter of credit law. Under the independence principle, an issuer's obligation to the letter of credit's beneficiary is independent from any obligation between the beneficiary and the issuer's customer. All a beneficiary has to do to receive payment under a letter of credit is to show that it has performed all the duties required by the letter of credit. Any disputes between the beneficiary and the customer do not affect the issuer's obligation to the beneficiary to pay under the letter of credit.

Letters of credit are most commonly arranged by a party who benefits from the provision of goods or services. The party will request a bank to issue a letter of credit which names the provider of the goods or services as the beneficiary. Under a standby letter of credit, the bank becomes primarily liable to the beneficiary upon the default of the bank's customer to pay for the goods or services. The bank charges a fee to issue a letter of credit and to undertake this liability. The shifting of liability to the bank rather than to the services or goods provider is the main purpose of the letter of credit. After all, the bank is in a much better position to assess the risk of its customer's insolvency than is the service or goods provider. It should be noted, however, that it is the risk of the debtor's insolvency and not the risk of a preference attack that a bank assumes under a letter of credit transaction. Overall, the independence principle is necessary to insure "the certainty of payments for services or goods rendered regardless of any intervening misfortune which may befall the other contracting party." *In re North Shore*, 30 B.R. at 378.

The trustee in this case accepts this analysis and does not ask us to upset it. The trustee is not attempting to set aside the post petition payments by MBank to Blue Quail under the letter of credit as a preference; nor does the trustee claim the letter of credit itself constitutes debtor's property. The trustee is instead challenging the earlier transfer in which Compton granted MBank an increased security interest in its assets to obtain the letter of credit for the benefit of Blue Quail. Collateral which has been pledged by a debtor as security for a letter of credit is property of the debtor's estate. *In re W.L. Mead*, 42 B.R. at 59. The trustee claims that the direct transfer to MBank of the increased security interest on May 6, 1982, also constituted an indirect transfer to Blue Quail which occurred one day prior to the filing of the involuntary bankruptcy petition and is voidable as a preference under 11 U.S.C. § 547. This assertion of a preferential transfer is evaluated in Parts III and IV of this opinion.

It is important to note that the irrevocable standby letter of credit in the case at bar was not arranged in connection with Blue Quail's initial decision to sell oil to Compton on credit. Compton arranged for the letter of credit after Blue Quail had shipped the oil and after Compton had defaulted in payment. The letter of credit in this case did not serve its usual function of backing up a contemporaneous credit decision,[62] but instead served as a back up payment guarantee on an extension of credit already in jeopardy. The letter of credit was issued to pay off an antecedent unsecured debt. This fact was clearly noted on the face of the letter of credit.[63] Blue Quail, the beneficiary of the letter of credit, did not give new value for the issuance of the letter of credit by MBank on May 6, 1982, or for the resulting increased security interest held by MBank. MBank, however, did give new value for the increased security interest it obtained in Compton's collateral: the bank issued the letter of credit.

When a debtor pledges its assets to secure a letter of credit, a transfer of debtor's property has occurred under the provisions of 11 U.S.C. § 547. By subjecting its assets to MBank's reimbursement claim in the event MBank had to pay on the letter of credit, Compton made a transfer of its property. The broad definition of "transfer" under 11 U.S.C. § 101(50) is clearly designed to cover such a transfer. Overall, the letter of credit itself and the payments thereunder may not be property of debtor, but the collateral pledged as a security interest for the letter of credit is.

Furthermore, in a secured letter of credit transaction, the transfer of debtor's property takes place at the time the letter of credit is issued (when the security interest is granted) and received by the beneficiary, not at the time the issuer pays on the letter of credit. *In re Briggs Transportation Co.*, 37 Bankr. 76, 79 (Bankr. Minn. 1984). *In re M.J. Sales, supra* (transfer of pledged collateral occurs not when bank forecloses on it, but when it is pledged.)

The transfer to MBank of the increased security interest was a direct transfer which occurred on May 6, 1982, when the bank issued the letter of credit. Under 11 U.S.C. § 547(e)(2)(A), however, such a transfer is deemed to have taken place for purposes of 11 U.S.C. § 547 at the time such transfer "takes effect" between the transferor and transferee if such transfer is perfected within 10 days. The phrase "takes effect" is undefined in the Bankruptcy Code, but under Uniform Commercial Code Article 9 law, a transfer of a security interest "takes effect" when the security interest attaches. Because of the future advances clause in MBank's 1980 security agreement with Compton, the attachment of the MBank's security interest relates back to May 9, 1980, the date the security agreement went into effect. The bottom line is that the direct transfer of

---

[62] As was the case in In re W.L. Mead, Inc., In re Leisure Dynamics, In re North Shore & Central Illinois Freight Co., and In re M.J. Sales, all *supra*.

[63] The letter of credit was dated May 6, 1982, and noted that it covered delivery of Oklahoma Sweet crude oil during March 1982.

the increased security interest to MBank is artificially deemed to have occurred at least by May 7, 1981, the date MBank filed its final financing statement, for purposes of a preference attack against the bank.[64] This date is well before the 90 day window of 11 U.S.C. § 547(b)(4)(A). This would protect the bank from a preference attack by the trustee even if the bank had not given new value at the time it received the increased security interest. MBank is therefore protected from a preference attack by the trustee for the increased security interest transfer under either of two theories: under 11 U.S.C. § 547(c)(1) because it gave new value and under the operation of the relation back provision of 11 U.S.C. § 547(e)(2)(A). The bank is also protected from any claims of reimbursement by Blue Quail because the bank received no voidable preference.

The relation back provision of 11 U.S.C. § 547(e)(2)(A), however, applies only to the direct transfer of the increased security interest to MBank. The indirect transfer to Blue Quail that allegedly resulted from the direct transfer to MBank occurred on May 6, 1982, the date of issuance of the letter of credit. The relation back principle of 11 U.S.C. § 547(e)(2)(A) does not apply to this indirect transfer to Blue Quail. Blue Quail was not a party to the security agreement between MBank and Compton. So it will not be able to utilize the relation back provision if it is deemed to have received an indirect transfer resulting from the direct transfer of the increased security interest to MBank. Blue Quail, therefore, cannot assert either of the two defenses to a preference attack which MBank can claim. Blue Quail did not give new value under § 547(c)(1), and it received a transfer within 90 days of the filing of Compton's bankruptcy petition.[65]

III. Direct/Indirect Transfer Doctrine

The federal courts have long recognized that "to constitute a preference, it is not necessary that the transfer be made directly to the creditor." *National Bank of Newport v. National Herkimer County Bank,* 225 U.S. 178, 184, 32 S. Ct. 633, 635, 56 L. Ed. 1042 (1912). "If the bankrupt has made a transfer of his property, the effect of which is to enable one of his creditors to obtain a greater percentage of his debt than another creditor of the same class, circuity of arrangement will not avail to save it." *Id.* To combat such circuity, the courts have broken down certain transfers into two transfers, one direct and one indirect. The direct transfer to the third party may be valid and not subject to a preference attack. The indirect transfer, arising from the same action by the debtor, however, may constitute a voidable preference as to the creditor who indirectly benefitted from the direct transfer to the third party.

This is the situation presented in the case before us. The term "transfer" as used in the various bankruptcy statutes through the years has always been broad enough to cover such indirect transfers and to catch various circuitous arrangements. *Katz v. First National Bank of Glen Head,* 568 F.2d 964, 969 n. 4, (2d Cir.), cert. denied, 434 U.S. 1069, 98 S. Ct. 1250, 55 L. Ed. 2d 771 (1978). The new Bankruptcy Code implicitly adopts this doctrine through its broad definition of "transfer."[66] Examining the case law that has developed since the *National Bank of Newport*

---

[64] Tex. Bus. & Com. Code Ann. § 9.312(g) specifies that for purposes of priority among competing secured parties, the security interest for a future advance has the same priority as the security interest for the first advance. Conflicting security interests rank according to priority in time of filing or perfection. Tex. Bus. & Com. Code Ann. § 9.312(e)(1).

[65] Nor does Blue Quail have the protection of the 11 U.S.C. § 547(c)(2) "ordinary course of business" preference exception. Getting a standby letter of credit issued to cover a debt several weeks past due does not constitute ordinary course of business.

[66] "Transfer" means every mode, direct or indirect, absolute or conditional, voluntary or involuntary, of disposing of or parting with property or with an interest in property, including retention of title as a security interest and foreclosure

case yields an understanding of what types of transfers the direct/indirect doctrine is meant to cover.

In *Palmer v. Radio Corporation of America,* 453 F.2d 1133 (5th Cir. 1971), a third party purchased from the debtor a television station for $40,000 cash and the assumption of certain liabilities of the debtor, including unsecured claims by creditor RCA. This Court found the direct transfer from the debtor to the third party purchaser constituted an indirect preferential transfer to creditor RCA. We found that the assumption by the third party purchaser of the debt owed by the debtor to RCA and the subsequent payments made there-under constituted a voidable transfer as to RCA. The court noted that such indirect transfers as this had long been held to constitute voidable preferences under bankruptcy laws. 453 F.2d at 1136.

Although the *Palmer* court did not elaborate its reasoning behind this holding, such reasoning is self evident. A secured creditor was essentially substituted for an unsecured creditor through the transfer of the television station to the third party purchaser and the assumption of the unsecured debt by the purchaser. The third party purchaser was in effect secured because it had the television station. Creditor RCA would receive payments directly from the solvent third party without having to worry about its original debtor's financial condition. The original debtor's other unsecured creditors were harmed because a valuable asset of the debtor, the television station, was removed from the debtor's estate. The end result of the *Palmer* case was that the third party's payments on the RCA debt were to be made to the debtor's estate instead of to RCA. RCA would then recover the same percentage of its unsecured claim from the estate as the other unsecured creditors.

In *In re Conrad Corp.,* 806 F.2d 610 (5th Cir. 1986), we found a voidable indirect transfer on facts similar to those of *Palmer v. Radio Corporation of America.* In the *Conrad* case, the debtors bought several restaurants from the Burtons in exchange for an unsecured promissory note. A third party in turn purchased the restaurants from the debtors and assumed the payments to the Burtons on the promissory note. Relying on the analysis of the *Palmer* case, we held that the transfer of the restaurants by the debtors in exchange for a simultaneous assumption of the Burton debt by the third party benefitted the Burtons and constituted a voidable indirect transfer as to the Burtons.

We observed that as a result of executing the assumption of debt agreement, the debtors transferred to the Burtons the debtors' right to receive from the third party so much of the sales price for the restaurants as was needed to reimburse the Burtons on their unsecured note. Once again a secured creditor, in effect, was substituted for an unsecured creditor by the transfer, and a depletion of the debtor's estate occurred. We held that the trustee of the debtor could recover from the Burtons the payments made by the third party to the Burtons and that the Burtons would recover only their proportionate share of the value of the unencumbered assets of the debtor along with the other unsecured creditors.

There are a number of federal cases in the other circuits supporting the holdings and reasoning in our direct/indirect doctrine cases. In *Aulick v. Largent,* 295 F.2d 41 (4th Cir. 1961), a third party endorsed the debtor's antecedent obligation to one of the debtor's unsecured creditors in exchange for the transfer of some stock within the preference time period. The creditor eventually received payment from the third party who in turn retained the pledged stock. The Fourth Circuit

---

of the debtor's equity of redemption. 11 U.S.C. § 101 (50). See also the Notes of the Committee on the Judiciary under 11 U.S.C. 101 ("The definition of transfer is as broad as possible.")

held that while the direct transfer of the stock to the third party to secure the contingent liability of the endorsement was not voidable because it was a transfer for consideration presently furnished, the indirect transfer to the unsecured creditor via the third party endorser was a voidable preference. The creditor in *Aulick* made the same argument that Blue Quail makes in the case at bar. The creditor claimed that the payment to it by the third party endorser came from the endorser's personal funds and thus the payment did not deplete the debtor's estate. Therefore one of the essential elements of a voidable preference was lacking.

The court rejected this argument relying on *National Bank of Newport*. The *Aulick* court found there to be two transfers arising from the pledge of stock to the third party, one direct and one indirect, and then collapsed them, in effect, into a single one for a preference attack against the indirect transferee creditor. The court noted that if the debtor had delivered the shares of stock directly to the unsecured creditor as security for the antecedent debt, the creditor would have clearly received a voidable preference. The court held that such a result could not be avoided by indirect arrangement.[67] "Preferences obtained by indirect or circuitous arrangements are to be struck down just as quickly as those obtained by direct arrangements." 295 F.2d at 52.

In *Virginia National Bank v. Woodson,* 329 F.2d 836 (4th Cir. 1964), the debtor had several overdrawn accounts with his bank.[68] The debtor talked his sister into paying off $8,000 of the overdrafts in exchange for an $8,000 promissory note and an assignment of some collateral as security. The debtor's sister made the $8,000 payment directly to the bank. The $8,000 technically was never part of the debtor's estate. The court, however, held that the payment of the $8,000 by the sister to the bank was a preference as to the bank to the extent of the value of the collateral held by the sister. The court noted that the measure of the value of a voidable preference is diminution of the debtor's estate and not the value of the transfer to the creditor.

In the *Woodson* case the sister was secured only to the extent the pledged collateral had value; the remainder of her loan to her brother was unsecured. Swapping one unsecured creditor for another unsecured creditor does not create any kind of preference. The court held that a preference in such a transaction arises only when a secured creditor is swapped for an unsecured creditor. Only then is the pool of assets available for distribution to the general unsecured creditors depleted because the secured creditor has priority over the unsecured creditors. Furthermore, the court held that the bank and not the sister had received the voidable preference and had to pay back to the trustee an amount equal to the value of the collateral.

A slightly different indirect transfer was involved in *In re Mercon Industries, Inc.,* 37 Bankr. 549 (Bank. E.D. Penn. 1984). In that case a debtor paid off a non-insider unsecured creditor within one year of the filing of the bankruptcy petition on a debt guaranteed by insiders of the debtor. The payment to the creditor had the effect of releasing the insider guarantors from contingent liability on the debt, thereby benefitting the insiders. The court held that releasing an insider guarantor from contingent liability is a beneficial transfer to the guarantor for purposes of 11 U.S.C. § 547.

---

[67] Apparently the bottom line in the *Aulick* case was that the creditor and not the third party endorser was ultimately liable for the preferential transfer. This is the way the preference provisions are supposed to work; it was the creditor, after all, and not the endorser who was preferred. It should also be noted that there would have been no preference attack against the creditor had not the endorser received the assignment of stock from the debtor to secure its contingent liability on the endorsement. It is the substitution of a secured creditor for a general unsecured creditor that constitutes the voidable transfer as to the unsecured creditor. This is a common theme underlying the direct/indirect cases and applies with equal force to the case at bar.

[68] Unsecured antecedent debts.

The court in *Mercon* viewed the payment to the non-insider creditor as effecting two transfers under the Bankruptcy Code because of the secondary liability of the guarantors on the debt. The court held that while the direct transfer from the debtor to the non-insider creditor in satisfaction of the primary debt may not be a voidable preference (if it was made over 90 days of filing), the court found that the indirect transfer to the insider guarantors extinguishing their contingent liability (and their contingent unsecured claim for reimbursement) was a separate voidable transfer under 11 U.S.C. § 547. Such an indirect transfer is voidable if it occurred within one year of filing pursuant to § 547(b)(4)(B). Furthermore, the court held that because the Bankruptcy Code "dictates that there are two transfers rather than one, liability of the guarantors under § 547(b) need not be predicated on a finding of an avoidable transfer to [the non-insider creditor], since a finding of liability on one transfer is independent of the other, rather than derivative." 37 B.R. at 552. The court held that the insider guarantors, and not the non-insider creditor, were ultimately liable for this preference.[69]

IV. The Direct/Indirect Doctrine in the Context of a Letter of Credit Transaction

The case at bar differs from the cases discussed in Part III *supra* only by the presence of the letter of credit as the mechanism for paying off the unsecured creditor. Blue Quail's attempt to otherwise distinguish the case from the direct/indirect transfer cases does not withstand scrutiny.

In the letter of credit cases discussed in Part II *supra*, the letters of credit were issued contemporaneously with the initial extension of credit by the beneficiaries of the letters. In those cases the letters of credit effectively served as security devices for the benefit of the creditor beneficiaries and took the place of formal security interests. The courts in those cases properly found there had been no voidable transfers, direct or indirect, in the letter of credit transactions involved. New value was given contemporaneously with the issuance of the letters of credit in the form of the extensions of credit in the form of the extensions of credit by the beneficiaries of the letters. As a result, the 11 U.S.C. § 547(c)(1) preference exception was applicable.

The case at bar differs from these other letter of credit cases by one very important fact: the letter of credit in this case was issued to secure an antecedent unsecured debt due the beneficiary of the letter of credit. The unsecured creditor beneficiary gave no new value upon the issuance of the letter of credit. When the issuer paid off the letter of credit and foreclosed on the collateral securing the letter of credit, a preferential transfer had occurred. An unsecured creditor was paid in full and a secured creditor was substituted in its place.

The district court upheld the bankruptcy court in maintaining the validity of the letter of credit issued to cover the antecedent debt. The district court held that MBank, the issuer of the letter of credit, could pay off the letter of credit and foreclose on the collateral securing it. We are in full agreement.

But we also look to the impact of the transaction as it affects the situation of Blue Quail in the bankrupt estate. We hold that the bankruptcy trustee can recover from Blue Quail, the beneficiary of the letter of credit, because Blue Quail received an indirect preference. This result preserves the sanctity of letter of credit and carries out the purposes of the Bankruptcy Code

---

[69] See also *In re Deprizio Construction Co.*, 58 Bankr. 478 (N.D. Ill. E.D. 1986) (case with similar facts and a similar holding). This case also described the bankruptcy courts' equitable powers under 11 U.S.C. § 550 to preclude a trustee from recovering from innocent creditors who were the initial direct transferees of a voidable indirect preference.

by avoiding a preferential transfer. MBank, the issuer of the letter of credit, being just the intermediary through which the preferential transfer was accomplished, completely falls out of the picture and is not involved in this particular legal proceeding.

MBank did not receive any preferential transfer–it gave new value for the security interest. Furthermore, because the direct and indirect transfers are separate and independent, the trustee does not even need to challenge the direct transfer of the increased security interest to MBank, or seek any relief at all from MBank, in order to attack the indirect transfer and recover under 11 U.S.C. § 550 from the indirect transferee Blue Quail.

We hold that a creditor cannot secure payment of an unsecured antecedent debt through a letter of credit transaction when it could not do so through any other type of transaction. The purpose of the letter of credit transaction in this case was to secure payment of an unsecured antecedent debt for the benefit of an unsecured creditor. This is the only proper way to look at such letters of credit in the bankruptcy context. The promised transfer of pledged collateral induced the bank to issue the letter of credit in favor of the creditor. The increased security interest held by the bank clearly benefitted the creditor because the bank would not have issued the letter of credit without this security. A secured creditor was substituted for an unsecured creditor to the detriment of the other unsecured creditors.

We also hold, therefore, that the trustee can recover under 11 U.S.C. § 550(a)(1)the value of the transferred property from "the entity for whose benefit such transfer was made." In the case at bar, this entity was the creditor beneficiary, not the issuer, of the letter of credit even though the issuer received the direct transfer from the debtor. The entire purpose of the direct/ indirect doctrine is to look through the form of a transaction and determine which entity actually benefitted from the transfer.[70]

The fact that there was a prior security agreement between the issuing bank and the debtor containing the future advances clause does not alter this conclusion. As we pointed out in Part II *supra*, this prior security agreement gave MBank an additional shield from preferential attack because of the relation back mechanism of 11 U.S.C. § 547(e)(2)(A). 11 U.S.C. § 547(e)(2)(A), however, does not avail Blue Quail to shield it from a preferential attack for the indirect transfer. The indirect transfer to Blue Quail occurred on May 6, 1982, when the letter of credit was issued and the increased security interest was pledged. This was the day before the involuntary bankruptcy petition was filed. For purposes of 11 U.S.C. § 547, a transfer of Compton's property for the benefit of Blue Quail did occur within 90 days of the bankruptcy filing. The bankruptcy and district courts erred in failing to analyze properly the transfer of debtor's property that occurred when Compton pledged its assets to obtain the letter of credit. This transfer consisted of two aspects: the direct transfer to MBank which is not a voidable preference for various reasons and the indirect transfer to Blue Quail which is a voidable preference.

All of the requirements of 11 U.S.C. § 547(b) have been satisfied in the trustee's preferential attack against Blue Quail. There was (1) a transfer of Compton's property for the benefit of Blue Quail (2) for an antecedent debt owed by Compton (3) made while Compton was insolvent[71]

---

[70] We have found only one prior case that has fully addressed the application of the direct/indirect doctrine in the context of a letter of credit transaction. *In re Air Conditioning, Inc. of Stuart,* 55 Bankr. 157 (Bankr. S.D. Fla. 1985), affirmed in part, reversed in part 72 Bankr. 657 (S.D. Fla. 1987) (currently on appeal to the Eleventh Circuit). In a carefully and thoroughly reasoned opinion, the court reached the same conclusion we reach in this case.

[71] There is a presumption that a debtor is insolvent at least 90 days prior to its bankruptcy filing. 11 U.S.C. § 547(f).

(4) within 90 days before the date of the filing of the petition (5) that enabled Blue Quail to receive more than it would receive under a Chapter 7 liquidation.[72] The net effect of the indirect transfer to Blue Quail was to remove $585,443.85 from the pool of assets available to Compton's unsecured creditors and substitute in its place a secured claim for the same amount.

The precise holding in this case needs to be emphasized. We do not hold that payment under a letter of credit, or even a letter of credit itself, constitute preferential transfers under 11 U.S.C. § 547(b) or property of a debtor under 11 U.S.C. § 541. The holding of this case fully allows the letter of credit to function. We preserve its sanctity and the underlying independence doctrine. We do not, however, allow an unsecured creditor to avoid a preference attack by utilizing a letter of credit to secure payment of an antecedent debt. Otherwise the unsecured creditor would receive an indirect preferential transfer from the granting of the security for the letter of credit to the extent of the value of that security. Our holding does not affect the strength of or the proper use of letters of credit. When a letter of credit is issued contemporaneously with a new extension of credit, the creditor beneficiary will not be subject to a preferential attack under the direct/ indirect doctrine elaborated in this case because the creditor will have given new value in exchange for the indirect benefit of the secured letter of credit. Only when a creditor receives a secured letter of credit to cover an unsecured antecedent debt will it be subject to a preferential attack under 11 U.S.C. § 547(b).

V. Liability of MBank for the Preferential Transfer

Blue Quail has no valid claim against MBank for reimbursement for any amounts Blue Quail has to pay the trustee under the trustee's preference claim, just as the trustee has no preference challenge against MBank. Blue Quail received the preferential transfer, not MBank. MBank gave new value in exchange for the increased security interest in its favor. Thus, it is insulated from any assertion of a voidable preference. The bank in no way assumed the risk of a preference attack by issuing the letter of credit. For these reasons, we affirm the district court's dismissal of Blue Quail's request to proceed against MBank for reimbursement.[73]

In addition, the trustee may not set aside the $1,463.61 fee Compton paid MBank to issue the letter of credit. This payment is not a preferential transfer. MBank has fully performed its duties under the terms of the letter of credit and has earned this fee. The services MBank rendered in issuing and executing the letter of credit constitute new value under the 11 U.S.C. § 547(c)(1) preference exception.

VI. Conclusion

Blue Quail Energy received an indirect preferential transfer from Compton Corporation on May 6, 1982, one day prior to the filing of Compton's bankruptcy petition. We reverse the district court and render judgment in favor of Trustee Kellogg against Blue Quail Energy, Inc. in the amount of $585,443.85 plus interest to be fixed by the district court pursuant to 11 U.S.C. §§ 547, 550. The district court's dismissal of Blue Quail's claim against MBank for reimbursement is affirmed.

---

[72] There was undisputed evidence below that the other unsecured creditors of Compton would receive less than fifty cents on the dollar for their unsecured claims.

[73] The liability of MBank to Blue Quail in the event of this Court's finding a preferential transfer to Blue Quail is interrelated with the Trustee's preference challenge against Blue Quail. The briefs of Blue Quail and Trustee Kellogg both addressed this issue.

Reversed in Part, Affirmed in Part, and Remanded.

NOTE

The *Compton* court refused to allow a creditor to secure payment of an unsecured antecedent debt by utilizing a letter of credit. Always alert of the independence principle, the court wrote, "The holding of this case fully allows the letter of credit to function. We preserve its sanctity and the underlying independence doctrine . . . Our holding does not affect the strength or proper use of letters of credit. When a letter of credit is issued contemporaneously with the extension of credit, the creditor beneficiary will not be subject to a preferential attack under the direct/indirect doctrine elaborated in this case because the creditor will have given new value in exchange for the indirect benefit of the secured letter of credit." Do you agree that this case does not infringe on the independence doctrine? How is an issuing bank suppose to evaluate whether a transaction will violate the direct/indirect doctrine presented in this case?

TABLE OF CASES

[Principal cases appear in solid capitals. Cases cited or discussed by the authors in lower case type. References are to sections.]

[Principal cases appear in solid capitals. Cases cited or discussed by the authors in lower case type. References are to sections.]

[Principal cases appear in solid capitals. Cases cited or discussed by the authors in lower case type. References are to sections.]

[Principal cases appear in solid capitals. Cases cited or discussed by the authors in lower case type. References are to sections.]

TABLE OF UNIFORM COMMERCIAL CODE

[References are to sections.]

[References are to sections.]

[References are to sections.]

[References are to sections.]

INDEX

[References are to sections.]

A

B

C

[References are to sections.]

D

[References are to sections.]

[References are to sections.]

[References are to sections.]

[References are to sections.]